Egypt
Handbook

with eastern Libya

Anne & Keith McLachlan

Footprint Handbooks

*The arch is broken and the splendor fled
Where every aspect once was brave and fair,
This Palace none inhabits save the dead
Whose ivory bones the desert breezes stir.
The Hall of Audience desecrated lies -
Though Princes came to make obeisance here -
And from the ruined tower an owlet cries:
"The glory is departed - where? where? where?"*

by Omar Khayyam

2

Footprint Handbooks

®

6 Riverside Court, Lower Bristol Road
Bath BA2 3DZ England
T 01225 469141   F 01225 469461
E mail handbooks@footprint.cix.co.uk

ISBN 1 900949 20 2   ISSN 1363-7983
CIP DATA: A catalogue record for this book is
available from the British Library

In North America, published by

PASSPORT BOOKS
NTC/Contemporary Publishing Group

4255 West Touhy Avenue, Lincolnwood
(Chicago), Illinois 60646-1975, USA
T 847 679 5500   F 847 679 24941
E mail NTCPUB2@AOL.COM

ISBN 0-8442-4894-0
Library of Congress Catalog Card
Number: 98-65734
Passport Books and colophon are registered
trademarks of NTC/Contemporary Publishing
group, Inc.

Every effort has been made to ensure that
the facts in this Handbook are accurate.
However travellers should still obtain
advice from consulates, airlines etc about
current travel and visa requirements and
conditions before travelling. The authors
and publishers cannot accept responsibility
for any loss, injury or inconvenience,
however caused.

Maps - the black and white text maps are
not intended to have any political
significance.

Cover design by Newell and Sorrell; cover
photography by Trip, Images and Pictor

Production: Design by Mytton Williams;
Typesetting and mapping by Jo Morgan, Alex
Nott, Ann Griffiths, Richard Ponsford and
Kevin Feeney; Original maps by Sebastian
Ballard; Charts and mapping by Angus
Dawson; Proofread by Rod Grey, Jim Kelsey
and Tim Heybyrne.

Printed and bound in Italy by
L.E.G.O. SpA, Vicenza

Contents

4

4
Information for travellers

5
Excursion into Eastern Libya

Benghazi, the Jabal Al-Akhdar, Al-Khalij and the Oases of the South 448-499

6
Rounding up

6

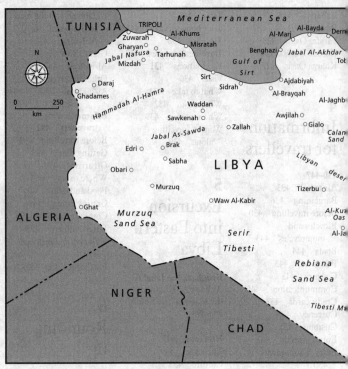

Map of Libya showing major cities and geographic features:

TUNISIA • TRIPOLI • Mediterranean Sea • Al-Khums • Al-Mari • Al-Bayda • Dern • Zuwarah • Misratah • Benghazi • Jabal Al-Akhdar • Tob • Gharyan • Tarhunah • Jabal Nafusa • Mizdah • Gulf of Sirt • Daraj • Sirt • Sidrah • Ajdabiyah • Ghadames • Hammadah Al-Hamra • Al-Brayqah • Al-Jaghb • Waddan • Awjilah • Sawkenah • Zallah • Gialo • Calan Sand • Jabal As-Sawda • Edri • Brak • LIBYA • Libyan desert • Sabha • Obari • Tizerbu • Murzuq • Al-Ku Oas • Waw Al-Kabir • Al-Ja • ALGERIA • Murzuq Sand Sea • Serir Tibesti • Ghat • Rebiana Sand Sea • NIGER • Tibesti M • CHAD

N

0   250
km

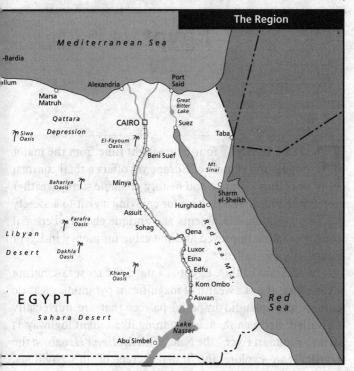

Egypt

E GYPT IS ONLY four hours flight time from the major population centres of Europe yet offers a total contrast in culture, climate and history. Reliable sunny weather provides the ideal atmosphere for enjoying a visit to a society rich in present entertainments and antique charms. Personal security is much improved and the value for money in Egypt is currently unrivalled.

In addition to this, Egypt is among the most fascinating of countries. It has a wealth of magnificent pyramids, gigantic temples and splendid imperial palaces that are universally unrivalled. Between them all, running like a giant highway, is Africa's proudest river – the Nile. With the *Egypt Handbook* the traveller can explore the inner secrets of the pavilions, playgrounds and tombs of the pharaohs. The imperial palaces of Luxor and Karnak have a splendour of scale which is unparalleled, with their soaring columns and obelisks and more than life-like wayside ramheaded sphinxes. At Luxor there is access to the famous Valley of the Kings where Ramses the Great set up his wonderful memorial temple and where lies the recently opened tomb of King Tutankhamen. Nearby the perfectly decorated Tomb of Queen Nefertari is now open to the visitor and the wall paintings of the Tombs of the Nobles can be viewed in colours as fresh as if they had been finished only yesterday. From Luxor the temptations of the peace and grandeur of Aswan with its mix of ancient wonders and modern dam building can be reached by river boat, train, bus or camel. South of, but easily accessible from, Aswan lies Abu Simbel, saved from drowning in Lake Nasser by the United Nations, and a true marvel of the skills of ancient Egypt.

The pyramids improve with age! Their massive and dominating presence has to be seen at Giza, near to Cairo, to be enjoyed to the full. The puzzle of their construction 4,000 years ago still entrances modern engineers and to travel deep into their bowels below the earth is an event as inspiring now as when the pharaohs built them as space capsules to eternity. A new beard is being grafted on to the Sphinx, bringing a new look to the famous monuments at Giza. This handbook will show the way round these and others of the many pyramids of the kings and queens of ancient Egypt.

Modern Egypt is a throbbing society with roots going back beyond the pharaohs. It is a land of rich variety, part based in the narrow ribbon of the Nile Valley, part on the thick fertile silt plain of the Nile Delta and part pure desert. The fellahs, their ample wives and many children, who work the fields and who crowd the busy markets of the Nile lands are buzzing with life and good humour. Their villages and small towns are ideal for human surprises and unusual bargain commodities.

So different the big cities! Cairo – largest city in Africa and living off the River Nile which slices its thronging streets in two. Here are some of the most inspiring mosques in the world, wealthy bazaars and, of course, the unmatched Egyptian Museum where even the museum-allergic can find solace in the arms of the treasures of Tutankhamen and a host of other delights. Cairo has a wide range of hotels, both cheap and luxurious. Whatever your budget take tea on the terrace of the *Shepheard's Hotel* on the Nile Corniche to complete the social circuit of Cairo. Alexandria is another world from the capital – quiet, provincial and cultured. Its seaside location joins it to the Mediterranean world and makes it the gateway to the coast fought over by WW2 armies.

Yet another Egypt lies beyond the green belt of the Nile lands – the desert. On the west is a wasteland for the explorer with seemingly limitless space, just sand, rock and the rare oasis. The oases of Siwa where the 20-year-old Alexander the Great planned his design of Asian conquest, El-Fayoum the favourite hideaway of the 20th century Egyptian kings and the little visited oases of Dakhla, Kharga and Bahariya in the western valleys. To the east lies the Sinai and Red Sea where both the desert traveller and the scuba diver can find their respective paradises in unlimited expanses of unspoiled surroundings.

Egypt is a dazzling country which offers a cornucopia of exotic sights, smells and noises. It is currently lightly populated with tourists which makes the major sites easy and cheap to visit. Go to Egypt now before the crowds return! There have never been such travel bargains to be had as in today's Egypt.

Eastern and southern Libya are now being opened for the traveller, giving access to Cyrene, Apollonia and the Green Mountains as well as to the deserts of Calanscio and Serir in the south. These areas contain magnificent Greek and Roman cities with more recent Islamic and vernacular Arab architecture.

The authors

Anne McLachlan

Anne McLachlan visits Egypt, North Africa and the Middle East each year, building on her experiences as a life-long traveller and resident of the region. Her high regard for Egypt makes her an ideal and practical guide to this engaging country. For this present volume, her field work has been concentrated on Upper Egypt to enhance coverage of the monuments and facilities at Luxor and the West Bank tomb areas, where the Egyptian authorities have done so much in recent years to improve both the quality of the monuments and access to them. This volume also benefits from intensive studies on site of the Aswan region, where the author finds some of her favourite places in a most tranquil atmosphere.

Anne McLachlan has also given her time to exploring the excellent floating hotels that ply the fascinating waters of the River Nile and Lake Nasser. She uses this new edition of *Footprint Egypt Handbook* to give hints on how to get best value from cruising in Egypt and suggests that there are few experiences that can beat the sight of a floodlit Abu Simbel seen in the early evening from aboard ship at anchor on Lake Nasser or the midday scenes of villagers farming the valley terraces observed from the deck of a Nile cruise boat!

Keith McLachlan

Keith McLachlan is a professional traveller and analyst in Egypt and the wider Middle East. He made his first trans-Saharan voyage in 1958 in Libya and has kept in close touch with Egypt and Libya since that time through regular annual travel. To provide information for this *Egypt Handbook*, journeys were made to Cairo and the Nile Delta, the Red Sea resorts, Qena, Sharm el-Sheikh, Luxor and Aswan with special reference to the wonderfully decorated and engaging Tombs of the Nobles at the latter two sites.

Keith McLachlan is emeritus professor of the School of Oriental & African Studies and a well-known scholar on regional economy and society as well as a consultant on Middle Eastern affairs. He has a long-acquaintance with the quirks of travel in Egypt and Libya as researcher, explorer and guide. Among his recent publications are (with R T Tapper, eds) *Material Cultures of the Middle East & Central Asia*, London, Cass, 1998 and a series of client studies on political and economic conditions in Libya, Egypt and the Eastern Mediterranean.

Travelling in Islamic Countries

THE COUNTRIES adjacent to the River Nile are principally Islamic. Islam is similar to Judaism and Christianity in its philosophical content and Muslims recognize that these three revealed religions (religions of the book *Ahl Al-Kitab*) have a common basis. Even so, there are considerable differences in ritual, public observance of religious customs and the role of religion in daily life. When travelling through Islamic countries it is necessary to be aware that this is the case. The Islamic revivalist movement has in recent years become strongly represented in North African countries, particularly in Egypt, though it is important elsewhere too.

Travel, tourism and foreign workers are common throughout the region so that the sight of outsiders is not unusual. Tourists attract particular hostility, however. They are seen as voyeuristic, short-term and unblushingly alien. Tourists have become associated with the evils of modern life – loose morals, provocative dress, mindless materialism and degenerate/Western cultural standards. In many cases these perceptions are entirely justified and bring a sense of infringed Islamic values among many local people, most of whom are conservative in bent. Feelings are made worse by apparent differences in wealth between local peoples whose per head income ranges from US$6,500 in Libya to US$710 in Egypt and foreign tourists living on an average of US$32,000 per head in the industrialized states. Tourists, whose way of life for a few weeks a year is dedicated to conspicuous consumption, attract dislike and envy. Muslims might wonder why a way of life in Islam, seen as superior to all other forms of faith, gives poor material rewards vis-à-vis the hordes of infidels who come as tourists.

The areas where sensitivity can best be shown are:

THE DRESS CODE

Daily dress for most North Africans is governed by considerations of climate and weather. Other than labourers in the open, the universal reaction is to cover up against heat or cold. The classic case is Libya, where the traditional dress, the *barakan*, is a successor of the Roman toga made up of five or more metres length by

The inner sanctum – realities of the harem

Hollywood and the popular image have vested the 'harem' with a fanciful aura that fails entirely to approximate to reality. Perhaps the fact that women in urban great houses and the courts of rulers in North Africa and the Middle East were contained within a protected zone, forbidden to all males but the patron and his eunuch managers, gave the harem a certain mystique to inquisitive Europeans. Architecturally, too, the marvellous apartments with their geometrically decorated *mashrabiyya*, spacious rooms and wonderful plaster arches have an alluring atmosphere of quiet and peace. In the same way the gardens set out for the ladies of the harem to take exercise remain fine monuments to the use of sheltered space.

The romantic side of the harem and those – generally young men of good but undisclosed royal antecedents – who sought to find their loved ones locked within its fortresses is possibly a legacy of the tales of *A Thousand and One Nights*, which early found their way into western literature in romanticized and bowdlerized forms.

In the 19th century a number of European artists such as Delacroix, Roberts and Gleyre were attracted to North Africa by the exotic images of a different and colourful culture. Paul Lenoir, who travelled with Gérôme in the 1860s, indicated that the harem it was that took prime attention, "... during the 19th century, the harem, the bath and the guard to the seraglio remained amongst the most popular manifestations of Orientalism in painting and literature".

Inevitably it was images of the Ottoman seraglio and the Islamic harem that were widely painted by Europeans in North Africa. Paintings of women in the bath house such as the *Harem in the Kiosk* and the *Moorish Bath* by Gérome did much to give graphic pictures of the subject. In Great Britain, there was also a flurry of orientalist painting, poetry and other literature, with J F Lewis (1805-75) particularly concentrating on the subject of the harem. He travelled in Morocco and Spain and later lived in Egypt for many years. His watercolours have a particular attraction and were widely acclaimed in their day. In addition to *The Hareem* of 1854, pictures like *The Intercepted Correspondence* with its portrayal of richly elaborated backgrounds in the oriental house and images of Islamic domestic action in the harem, set the tone of interest in the West. The works of the European orientalist artists and their romantic preoccupation with women of the seraglio has been roundly attacked by feminists but, for better or worse, remains the dominant influence on mental pictures of the harem.

The harem in Islamic society was and is an urban rich man's way of interpreting the words of the Koran "good women are obedient, guarding the unseen because God has guarded them". In the harem women are kept totally unseen and unable to defile themselves. In all Muslim houses, rich and poor, the women's part of the establishment is forbidden to outsiders, although in many cases in the houses of the ordinary people the harem is no more than a section of the house separated only by an imaginary line or *hoddud* across the floor space. Women themselves, who might circulate throughout the house, withdraw to their quarters when a stranger is about. Even in contemporary Egypt and North Africa there are women's movements that propagate the notion that the greater the seclusion and veiling of

2m width of woven wool material which wraps round the head and body. For males, therefore, other than the lowest of manual workers, full dress is normal. Men breaching this code will either be young and regarded as of low social status or very rich and Westernized. When visiting mosques (where this is allowed), *medressa*

women, the more their purity and religious/social standing. Segregation of men and women in public places is a growing feature of Islamic society: the harem is merely a reflection of that same feature in the rich and conservative. In the geography of the family the male has sole access to the world beyond the door of the house and women must stay within according to the teachings of recent Islamic theologians such as al-Mawdudi.

Of course, the containment of women in a harem also had an important function in a community where purity of ancestry permeated traditional tribal and extended family groups. The worst slur on a man's origins could be eliminated where all the women of the family were kept permanently separated from male company of any kind but that authorized by the senior male. The limitations on female mixing outside her own house were once defined as "a woman should leave her house only on three occasions – when she is taken to the house of her husband, when her parents die and when she is carried to her own grave".

The harem was populated by the ladies of the house, usually the wives of an extended family. Given that families were large and that any one man could marry four wives, the harem in a noble house would be very large. Additionally, unlimited numbers of concubines could be brought into the harem without benefit of matrimony. The religious sanction for concubinage has always been disputed but it was practised widely regardless of this. The number of women in a harem of a major ruler could be as high as 300. In effect, a large house and its harem even in rural areas had a great variety of people within it and women could socialize freely within that group. Similarly, visiting groups of women would be met and entertained by the women of the house.

A vicarious pleasure in the larger houses and palaces was watching events through a *mashrabiyya* or wooden grill protecting the women's quarters. By a paradox, it was often the wives of the richest men of traditional social inclination who saw least of the world and who literally saw few visitors, went visiting little themselves and whose only outings were to the *hammam*.

The harem on the model of the Ottoman seraglio is no more. But segregation of the sexes in the home is common unless families are thoroughly westernized. A significant number of women are cloistered in their homes and veiled outside it. Women's rights in law are gradually increasing but in traditional households change is very slow, impeded as much by a rising tide of Islamism as by neglect by the authorities.

Meanwhile, the architecture of the traditional family house continues to reflect the need for exclusive areas for women. Naguib Mahfouz in his book (in English translation) *Midaq Alley* shows how 20th century realities in a tightly packed urban community play tricks with the seclusion and the frustration of the women trapped within the home. For an insight into the magnificent provision for the women of the harem in the past visit the **Palace of Amir Bashtak** (see page 104) or the **Beit al-Sihaymi** (see page 105) both in Cairo, where the vestiges of harems can be seen.

or other shrines/ tombs/religious libraries, men wear full and normally magnificently washed and ironed traditional formal wear. In the office, men will be traditionally dressed or in Western suits/shirt sleeves. The higher the grade of office, the more likely the Western suit. At home people relax in loose *jallabah*. Arab males will be less constrained on the beach where Bermuda shorts and swimming trunks are the norm.

For women the dress code is more important than for men. Quite apart from dress being tell-tale of social status among the ladies of Cairo or Alexandria or of tribal/regional origin, decorum and religious sentiment dictates full covering of body, arms and legs. The

The practice of Islam: living by the Prophet

Islam is an Arabic word meaning 'submission to God'. As Muslims often point out, it is not just a religion but a total way of life. The main Islamic scripture is the Koran or Quran, the name being taken from the Arabic *al-qur'an* or 'the recitation'. The Koran is divided into 114 *sura*, or 'units'. Most scholars are agreed that the Koran was partially written by the Prophet Mohammed. In addition to the Koran there are the *hadiths*, from the Arabic word *hadith* meaning 'story', which tell of the Prophet's life and works. These represent the second most important body of scriptures.

The practice of Islam is based upon five central tenets, known as the Pillars of Islam: Shahada (profession of faith), Salat (worship), Zakat (charity), *saum* (fasting) and Haj (pilgrimage). The mosque is the centre of religious activity. The two most important mosque officials are the *imam* (leader) and the *khatib* (preacher) who delivers the Friday sermon.

The **Shahada** is the confession, and lies at the core of any Muslim's faith. It involves reciting, sincerely, two statements: 'There is no god, but God', and 'Mohammed is the Messenger [Prophet] of God'. A Muslim will do this at every **Salat**. This is the prayer ritual which is performed five times a day, including sunrise, midday and sunset. There is also the important Friday noon worship. The Salat is performed by a Muslim bowing and then prostrating himself in the direction of Mecca (Arabic *qibla*). In hotel rooms throughout the Muslim world there is nearly always a little arrow, painted on the ceiling – or sometimes inside a wardrobe – indicating the direction of Mecca and labelled *qibla*. The faithful are called to worship by a mosque official. Beforehand, a worshipper must wash to ensure ritual purity. The Friday midday service is performed in the mosque and includes a sermon given by the *khatib*.

A third essential element of Islam is **Zakat** – charity or alms-giving. A Muslim is supposed to give up his 'surplus' (according to the Koran); through time this took on the form of a tax levied according to the wealth of the family. Good Muslims are expected to contribute a tithe to the Muslim community.

The fourth pillar of Islam is **saum** or fasting. The daytime month-long fast of Ramadan is a time of contemplation, worship and piety – the Islamic equivalent of Lent. Muslims are expected to read one-thirtieth of the Koran each night. Muslims who are ill or on a journey have dispensation from fasting, but otherwise they are only permitted to eat during the night until "so much of the dawn appears that a white thread can be distinguished from a black one".

The **Haj** or Pilgrimmage to the holy city of Mecca in Saudi Arabia is required of all Muslims once in their lifetime if they can afford to make the journey and are physically able to do so. It is restricted to a certain time of the year, beginning on the 8th day of the Muslim month of Dhu-l-Hijja. Men who have been on the Haj are given the title *Haji*, and women *Hajjah*.

The Koran also advises on a number of other practices and customs, in particular the prohibitions on usury, the eating of pork, the taking of alcohol, and gambling.

The application of the Islamic dress code varies. It is least used in the larger towns and more closely followed in the rural areas.

veil is increasingly common for women moving in public as a reflection of growing Islamic revivalist views. There are many women who do not conform, including those with modern attitudes towards female emancipation, professional women trained abroad and, remarkably, many Berber women or women with genuinely nomadic or semi-nomadic lives. The religious minorities – Copts in Egypt and Jews in Libya, for example – do not wear the veil. Jewellery (see page 39) is another major symbol in women's dress especially heavy gold necklaces.

The role of dress within Islamic and social codes is clearly a crucial matter. While some latitude in dress is given to foreigners, good guests are expected to conform to the broad lines of the practice of the house. Thus, except on the beach or 'at home' in the hotel (assuming it is a tourist rather than local establishment), modesty in dress pays off. This means jeans or slacks for men rather than shorts together with a shirt or tee-shirt. In Islamic places such as mosques or *medressa*, hire *jallabah* at the door. For women, modesty is slightly more demanding. In public wear comfortable clothes that at least cover the greater part of the legs and arms. If the opportunity arises to visit a mosque or *medersa* open to tourists, *jallabah* and slippers are available for hire at the doors. Elsewhere full covering of arms and legs and a head scarf is necessary. Offend against the dress code – and most Western tourists in this area do to a greater or lesser extent – and risk antagonism and alienation from the local people who are increasingly fundamentalist in their Islamic beliefs and observances.

Female circumcision

It is small comfort to know that despite pressure from Islamic extremists the Egyptian authorities say they will ignore a court recommendation to lift the ban on female circumcision in state hospitals. The Mufti has issued a *fatwa* decreeing that it should be allowed.

FORBIDDEN PLACES

Do not enter mosques during a service. In other places dedicated to religious purposes behave with decorum – refrain from shouting, unseemly laughter and take photographs only when permitted. Outsiders have spent much time and ingenuity in penetrating Islam's holiest shrines. This is not worth the effort here since the most interesting sites are open to visitors in any case. People who are clearly non-Muslim will be turned away by door keepers from places where they are not wanted. Those who try to slip past the guardians should be sure they can talk their way out of trouble!

GOOD MANNERS

Islam has its codes of other practices and taboos but few will affect the visitor unless he or she gains entry to local families or organisations at a social level. A few rules are worth observing in any case by all non-Muslims when in company with Muslim friends. (i) Do not use your left hand for eating since it is ritually unclean. If knives and forks are provided, then both hands can be used. (ii) Do not accept or ask for alcohol unless your host clearly intends to imbibe. (iii) If eating in traditional style from a common dish, use your right hand only and keep your feet tucked under your body away from the food. (iv) Never offer pork or its derivatives to a Muslim visitor. Buy *hallal* meat killed in accordance with Muslim ritual and/or provide a non-meat dish. Do not provide alcoholic drink.

RELIGIOUS FESTIVALS AND HOLIDAYS

The Islamic year (Hejra/Hijra/Hegira) is based on 12 lunar months which are 29 or 30 days long depending on the sighting of the new moon. The lengths of the months vary therefore from year to year and from country to country depending on its position and the time at sunset. Each year is also 10 or 11 days shorter than the Gregorian calendar. The Islamic holidays are based on this Hejarian calendar and determining their position is possible only to within a few days.

Ramadan is a month of fasting (see below). The important festivals which are public holidays (with many variations in spelling) are *Ras al Am*, the Islamic New Year; *Eïd al-Fitr* (also called Aïd es Seghir), the celebration at the end of Ramadan; Eïd al-Adha (also called Aïd el Kebir), the celebration of Abraham's willingness to sacrifice his son and coinciding with the culmination of the Haj in Mecca; *Mouloud*, the birthday of the Prophet Mohammad.

The day of rest for Muslims is Friday. Observance of Friday as a religious day is general in the public sector though privately owned shops may open for limited hours. The main exception is tourism where all systems remain operative other than in Libya. Holy days and feast days are taken seriously throughout the North African region.

Approximate dates for 1998/99:

20 Dec	Beginning of Ramadan
21 Jan	End of Ramadan
31 Mar	Feast of Sacrifice
17 Apr	Islamic New Year 1420
1 Jul	Prophet's Birthday
9 Dec	Beginning of Ramadan

Ramadan, the 9th month of the Muslim calendar, is a month of fasting for Muslims. The faithful abstain from eating between dawn and sunset for the period until an official end is declared to the fast and the start of the festival of the Eïd al-Fitr. During the fast, especially if the weather is difficult or there are political problems affecting the Arab world, people can be depressed or irritable. The pace of activity in official offices slows down markedly. Travellers have to manage in these conditions by leaving even more time to achieve their aims and being even more patient than usual. If you have a choice, stay out of the area during Ramadan and the Eïd al-Fitr. Travel, services and the atmosphere are all better at other times of year. Travel facilities immediately before and

immediately after Ramadan are often very congested since families like to be together especially for the Eïd al-Fitr.

BUREAUCRACY AND THE POLICE

This region is mainly Islamic in religion, oriental in civilization and despotic in political tradition.

Avoid trouble The main areas of difficulty affect relations with the bureaucrats, police and other officials. To avoid trouble bear in mind:

Documents: do not lose your passport and ensure that all travel documents are in order. Passports are lost but they are also traded for cash/drugs and officials can be very unsympathetic. Long and often expensive delays can occur while documents are replaced, especially in Libya where there is no diplomatic help for US, British, Venezuelan and several other nationals. Keep all forms such as landing cards and currency documents together with bank receipts for foreign exchange transactions.

Prices: understand what prices are being asked for taxis, meals and hotels. Do not accept 'favours', like 'free lunches' they do not exist. Shop owners will attempt to give you gifts. At best these are used as a lever to get you to buy other items expensively or can lead to disputes over alleged non-payment for goods. It is also a matter of discretion how you handle friendly relations with locals who invite you home for a meal/visit. In Libya, only hospitality will be involved and the same will largely be true in Egypt.

Drugs: do not get involved in buying and selling drugs. It is an offence in the countries in this *Handbook* to handle drugs. Penalties can be severe including jail sentences in dismal prison conditions.

Politics: keep clear of all political activities. Nothing is so sensitive as opposition to the régimes. By all means keep an interest in local politics but do not become embroiled as a partisan. The *mokharbarat* (secret services) are singularly unforgiving and unbridled in taking action against political dissent.

Black Market: make use of black market currency only when it is private and safe. Most countries have tight laws against currency smuggling and illegal dealing.

Driving: keep to driving regulations and have an appropriate international licence. Bear in mind that the incidence of traffic accidents is high and that personal rescue in the event of an accident can be protracted and not necessarily expert.

Antiquities: trading in antiquities is everywhere illegal. Most items for sale are fakes. Real artifacts are expensive and trading in them can lead to confiscation and/or imprisonment.

Keep cool Remain patient and calm whatever the provocation. Redress against officials is next to impossible. Keep the matter from becoming serious by giving no grounds for offence to officials. Be genial and low key. Aggression and raised voices do little to help. Where you feel you are right, be smilingly persistent but not to the point of a break down in relations.

Get help Getting help can often be cheap or free. Start off with agencies used to foreigners, namely travel agents, airline offices and hotels. They will have met your problem before and might offer an instant or at least painless solution on the basis of past experience. They will know the local system and how it works. They act as free translators. Friends who are either locals or who live locally can act as translators and helpers. They will often have networks of family and acquaintances to break through the bureaucratic logjams. Last, and only last, turn to your embassy or consulate. Embassies are there principally to serve the needs of the home country and the host government, not the demands of travellers, though they have ultimate responsibility for official travel documents and, at their own discretion, for repatriation in cases of distress. Treat embassy and consular officials calmly and fairly. They have different priorities and do not necessarily feel themselves to be servants for travellers in trouble.

INTERNAL SECURITY

Risks are not necessarily higher in this region than in other parts of the 'developing world' but they do exist. Any traveller who intends to be travelling for a protracted period should check with his/her national authorities on the advisability of visiting the area. In the UK, the relevant Foreign and Commonwealth Office T 0171 2333000 desk will give you the latest assessment from their embassies overseas. If you are deeply concerned, where possible phone your national embassy direct and ask for the press/information officer. Otherwise, take an interest in trends in the countries you intend to visit before leaving home. Some newspapers can be very helpful in this area notably the *Financial Times*, *Le Monde*, and the *International Herald Tribune*.

EGYPT

The large and complex organizations of state and society in Egypt make generalizations difficult. It is currently clear that the government faces great political problems. The opposition, principally a long established Islamic revivalist group known as *Ikhwan Al-Musalmin* (Muslim Brotherhood), is large and well organized. In addition to the assassination of President Sadat in 1981, it is claimed that Islamic fundamentalists have murdered a number of leading individuals within the régime and there have been attacks on tourists. The government has held elections of sorts and has a political mandate on that basis, but the régime is unpopular at a variety of levels. The economy is not performing well and the expulsion of Egyptians from employment in the Gulf states, particularly Iraq, is still widely felt. There is no sense among Egyptians that the economic struggle against rising population numbers is being won, while external threats to reduced flows of Nile water adds to tensions. The close association of the régime with the USA and the history of links with Israel since the Camp David accords, distances the government from mass opinion. Yet the régime has its supporters through the co-option of the military and many senior Egyptian families. A deeply conservative streak runs through the population and a feeling that Egypt should look, as the régime does, first to Egyptian interests rather than 'Islamic' or 'Arab' ideals.

The support for the régime from the USA has a strong positive side. Aid and food supply are guaranteed within limits so that the population can be fed and the state kept on an economic even keel. Care for foreign visitors by the régime is vital to keep the tourist industry alive and the opposition has in the past deliberately targeted tourist facilities to make a political point. Egypt is a large country and 'troubles' tend on most occasions to be regional rather than national. A day's rioting in Giza will leave the Upper Nile and Sinai untouched. Similarly, some towns are far more fundamentalist inclined than others with Assiut and Qena being noted for their Islamic revivalist sentiment.

Although Egypt has a troubled history of foreign relations in the 1950s-1970s, it is now comparatively stable. Travellers should check with their national authorities before departure for Egypt.

LIBYA

Libya is a political oddity. In a general sense there are few domestic risks to the stability of the régime. There is negligible organized political opposition. Colonel Ghadhafi has a certain populist appeal which should not be underestimated. The security services and Colonel Ghadhafi's bodyguard battalions are relatively very powerful. The main risks in Libya are that Colonel Ghadhafi, who is the undisputed and sole centre of power, is removed by natural or other means or that there is a palace coup d'état. The Libyan state is so bound with personalities and so weak in national institutions that change could bring comparative anarchy for a period.

The main risks for foreigners are from capricious alterations in Libyan government policies on visas, internal movements and taxation on foreigners. Decisions are taken overnight by the ruling personalities and implemented without due notification to the public. A second area of risk is the actions of foreign governments against Libya. Libya is believed in some Western countries to be involved in state terrorism. The Lockerbie incident is currently at the centre of attention but other issues of a similar kind also exist. The bombing of Tripoli by the USA in 1986 was not notified in advance while the cessation of international air traffic in 1992 was. Measures of this latter kind are more of an inconvenience to travellers than an absolute block. But the tensions that go with failures in diplomatic relations mean that foreign visitors should be highly sensitive to personal risks. Care in taking photographs and asking questions needs to be doubled in Libya. Some European governments and the US administration advise their nationals to take care when visiting Libya but the realities on the ground suggest that travellers are suffering no problems other than those arising through the UN embargo on air transport to/from Libya.

What to do if unrest occurs

It is wise in circumstances of political uncertainty for a foreigner to be very discreet:

1. Stay in your hostel or hotel.
2. If the telephones are working, get in touch with your embassy or consulate so that your location is known.
3. Conserve any rations you might have.
4. Do not join in any action by locals. Your motives could be misunderstood.
5. Make contact in your hostel or hotel with other foreigners so that you can form a mutual-assistance group.
6. Listen carefully to the advice given by local hostel or hotel officials.

History

THE SAHARA began to dessicate some 10,000 years ago and divided the Caucasoid populations of North Africa from the Negroid populations of West and Equatorial Africa. The original agricultural mode of production which had been the basis of settlement there was gradually replaced by nomadic pastoralism which, by around 4000 BC, had become the preserve of two groups, the Libyan-Berbers in the east part and the ancestors of the modern Touareg in the west. North African populations, all classified as part of the Hamito-Semitic group which stretched east into Arabia, soon became sub-divided into the Berbers in the west, the Egyptians in the east and the Nilo-Saharians and Kushites to the south in what today is Sudan.

The key to the development of a complex civilization lay in the water and soils of the Nile valley. By 3000 BC, the Nile was supporting a dense sedentary agricultural society which produced a surplus and increasingly allowed socio-economic specialisation. This evolved into a system of absolute divine monarchy when the original two kingdoms were amalgamated by the victory of King Menes of Upper Egypt who then became the first Pharaoh. Pharaonic Egypt was limited by an inadequate resource base, being especially deficient in timber. Although it was forced to trade, particularly with the Levant (Eastern Mediterrean), it never became a major seafaring nation. Equally, the growing desertification of Libya meant that its influence never extended west. Instead, the Egyptian Empire sought control up the Nile valley, towards Kush (or Nubia) which it conquered as far south as the Fourth Cataract by 1500 BC. It also expanded east into the Levant, until it was restrained by the expanding civilisations of the Fertile Crescent after 2300 BC.

By 1000 BC, Pharaonic Egypt was being pressured from all sides. The Hyksos threatened the Delta from the Mediterranean, whilst the Lebu from Libya began to settle there too. They eventually created the 21st (Sheshonnaq) dynasty of the New Kingdom in 912 BC which, for a short time, extended its power east as far as Jerusalem. In the 7th century BC, however, Egypt was conquered by its Kushitic imitators to the south in the Nubian kingdom under King Piankhy who founded the 25th Pharaonic Dynasty.

The Nubians were expelled some years later by the Assyrians, but their conquest marked the end of the greatness of Pharaonic Egypt. Thereafter, Egypt was to be a dependency of more powerful states in the Middle East or the Mediterranean. The rulers of Nubian Kush in their turn, having been expelled from Egypt, looked south from

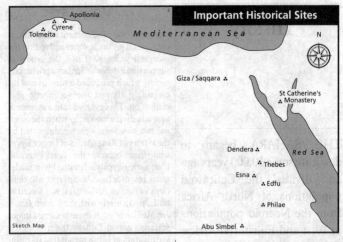

Important Historical Sites

Apollonia

Cyrene

Tolmeita

Mediterranean Sea

N

Giza / Saqqara

St Catherine's Monastery

Dendera

Red Sea

Thebes

Esna

Edfu

Philae

Sketch Map

Abu Simbel

their new capital at Meroe – to which they had moved as a result of the subsequent Persian conquest of Egypt in 525 BC and later Persian attempts to conquer Kush. Kush became, instead, the vehicle of transmission of iron-working technology and of Egyptian concepts of divine political organisation southwards as well.

GREEKS AND PHOENICIANS

In North Africa, Egypt's failure to expand westward permitted other developments to occur. The coastal area became the arena for competition between those Mediterranean civilizations which had acquired a naval capacity – the Greeks and the Phoenicians. Indeed, this became the future pattern and resulted in the history of the region being described in the terms of its conquerers.

We do know, however, that the Greek and Phoenician settlements on the coast provoked a response from the nomadic communities of the desert such as the Garamantes around the Fezzan in Libya. These communities appear to have specialized in warfare based on charioteering and they began to raid the new coastal settlements. At the same time, they also controlled trans-Saharan commerce – one of the major reasons why the Phoenicians, at least, were so interested in North Africa. As a result, they also engaged in trade with the new coastal communities, particularly those created by the Phoenicians. Other invasions also took place, this time of Northeast Africa from Southern Arabia, bringing Arab tribes into Africa. The new Arab invaders spread rapidly into modern Ethiopia and Eritrea.

The Greeks had begun to colonize the Egyptian and eastern Libyan coastline as part of their attempt to control Egyptian maritime trade. Cyrene, the first of five Greek colonies in Cyrenaica in Libya, was founded about 625 BC and, a little earlier, three Phoenician colonies were created in Western Libya, on the coast of what is today Tripolitania – hence the name – in order to exploit new commercial opportunities, for the Phoenicians were first-and-foremost traders.

Greeks and Phoenicians competed for control of the coastal areas in Libya and eventually created an uneasy division of the region between themselves. The Greeks took over Egypt after the creation of the Ptolemaic Kingdom on the death of Alexander the Great in 323 BC and incorporated Cyrenaica into the new kingdom. The Phoenicians, by now being harried in their original Lebanese home base of Tyre by the Assyrians and Persians, created a new and powerful maritime commercial empire based on Carthage, with outlying colonies to the west, right round to the Atlantic coast at Lixus (Larache).

THE ROMAN EMPIRE

Control of Egypt and North Africa passed on once again, this time to the rapidly expanding city-state of Rome. Control of the Ptolemaic Kingdom of Egypt passed to Rome because of Roman interest in its agricultural produce and Egypt became a province of Rome in 30 BC. Cyrenaica had become a Roman province in 74 BC.

The difficult problem of border security for Roman administrators was solved by creating the limes, a border region along the desert edge which was settled with former legionaries as a militarized agriculturalist population. Thus, although the border region was permeable to trade, resistance to tribal incursion could be rapidly mobilized from the resident population, while regular forces were brought to the scene. The limes spread west from Egypt as far as the Moroccan Atlantic coast.

CHRISTIANITY

Egyptian Christianity became the major focus of the development of Christian doctrine. The Coptic Church became the major proponent of Monophysitism after the Council of Chalcedon in 451 AD; Donatism dominated Numidia. At the same time, official Christianity in Egypt – the Melkite Church – combined with the Coptic Church to convert areas to the south of Egypt to Christianity.

THE ISLAMIC PERIOD

In 642 AD, 10 years after the death of the Prophet Mohammed, Arab armies, acting as the vanguard of Islam, conquered Egypt. To secure his conquest, the Arab commander, Amr bin al-As, immediately decided to move west into Cyrenaica where the local Berber population submitted to the new invaders. Despite a constant pattern of disturbance, the Arab conquerers of Egypt and their successors did not ignore the potential of the region to the south. Nubia was invaded in 641-42 AD and again 10 years later. Arab merchants and, later, bedouin tribes from Arabia were able to move freely throughout the south. However, until 665 AD, no real attempt was actually made to complete the conquest, largely because of internal problems within the new world of Islam.

THE GREAT DYNASTIES AND THEIR SUCCESSORS

(1) The Fatimids The first of the great dynasties that was to determine the future of North Africa did not, however, originate inside the region. Instead it used North Africa as a stepping stone towards its ambitions of taking over the Muslim world and imposing its own variant of Shi'a Islam. North Africa, because of its radical and egalitarian Islamic traditions, appears to have been the ideal starting point. The group concerned were the Isma'ilis who split off from the main body of Shi'a Muslims in 765 AD.

The Fatimids took control over what had been Aghlabid Ifriquiya, founding a new capital at Mahdia in 912 AD. Fatimid attention was concentrated on Egypt and, in 913-14 AD, a Fatimid army temporarily occupied Alexandria. The Fatimids also developed a naval force and their conquest of Sicily in the mid-10th century provided them with a very useful base for attacks on Egypt.

After suppressing a Kharejite-Sunni rebellion in Ifriquiya between 943 AD and 947 AD, the Fatimids were ready to plan the final conquest of Egypt. This took place in 969 AD when the Fatimid general, Jawhar, finally subdued the country. The Fatimids moved their capital to Egypt, where they founded a new

Coptic Monasteries in Egypt

Cairo
Convent of St George, page 85.
Convent of (Abu Seifein) St Mercurius 87.
Saqqara – remains of the Monastery of St Jeremias, page 155.
Giza – Monastery of (Abu Seifein) St Mercurius, page 87.

El-Fayoum
Deir al-Adhra (Monastery of the Virgin), page 174.
Deir Malak Ghobrial (Monastery of the Angel Gabriel), page 174.
Deir Anba Samwail (Monastery of St Samuel), page 174.
Deir Mari Girgis (Monastery of St George), page 174.
Deir Hammam, page 174.

Northern Egypt
Abu Mina near Mobarak – Deir Mari Mina (St Menas), page 347.
Wadi el-Natrun – Deir el-Baramous (of the Romans), page 325.
Deir el-Suriani (of the Syrians), page 324.
Deir Anba Bishoi (St Bishoi), page 324.
Deir Abu Maqar (St Makarios), page 323.
El-Mansura – Deir Sitt Damyanah (St Damyanah), page 317.

Red Sea
Monastery of St Anthony, page 405.
Monastery of St Paul, page 406.

Middle and Upper Egypt
Dirunka near Assuit – Deir Dirunka (Convent of St Mary the Virgin), page 185.
El-Qusiya – Deir el-Muharraq (St Mary) (Burnt Monastery), page 185.
Sohag – Deir al-Abyad White Monastery (St Shenuda), page 187.
Sohag – Deir al-Ahmar Red Monastery (St Bishoi), page 187.
Akhmim – Deir al Adra (Convent of the Holy Virgin), page 188.
Akhmim – Deir al Shuhada (Monastery of the Martyrs), page 188.
Nag Hammadi – Monastery of St Palomen, page 192.
Luxor – St Theodore, page 263.
Esna – Convent of St George, page 85.
Esna – Convent of the Holy Martyrs, page 266.
Esna – Deir al Shuhuda (Monastery of the Martyrs), page 188.
Edfu – Anba Bakhum al Shayib Monastery of St Pachom, page 272.
Edfu – St Pachom, page 272.
Aswan – St Simeon, page 287.

Kharga
Necropolis of el-Baqawat, page 427.

urban centre, al-Qahira (from which the modern name, Cairo, is derived) next to the old Roman fortress of Babylon and the original Arab settlement of Fustat.

The Fatimids' main concern was to take control of the Middle East. This meant that Fatimid interest in North Africa would wane and leave an autonomous Emirate there which continued to recognize the authority of the Fatimids, although it abandoned support for Shi'a Islamic doctrine.

(2) The Hillalian invasions Despite Fatimid concerns in the Middle East, the caliph in Cairo decided to return North Africa to Fatimid control. Lacking the means to do this himself, he used instead two tribes recently displaced from Syria and at that time residing in the Nile Delta – the Banu Sulaim and the Banu Hillal – as his troops. The invasions took place slowly over a period of around 50 years, starting in 1050 or 1051 AD, and probably involved no more than 50,000 individuals.

The Banu Sulaim settled in Cyrenaica, although, two centuries later, factions of the tribe also moved westwards towards Tripolitania and Tunisia. The Banu Hillal continued westwards, defeating and destroying the Zirids in a major battle close to Gabés in 1052.

The Hillalian invasions were a major and cataclysmic event in North Africa's history. They destroyed organized political power in the region and ensured the break up of the political link between Muslim North Africa and the Middle East. They also damaged the trading economy of the region. There was a major cultural development too for the Hillalian invasions, more than any other event, ensured that Arabic eventually became the majority language of the region.

(3) **Egypt after the Fatimids** Fatimid power in Egypt did not endure for long. They were forced to rely on a slave army recruited from the Turks of Central Asia and from the Sudanese. They found it increasingly difficult to control these forces and, eventually, became their victims. In 1073 AD, the commander of the Fatimid army in Syria, which had been recalled to restore order in Egypt, took power and the Fatimid caliph was left only with the prestige of his office.

What remained of the Fatimid Empire was now left virtually defenceless towards the east and the Seljuk Turks, who were already moving west, soon took advantage of this weakness. They were spurred on by the growth of Crusader power in the Levant and, after this threat had been contained, Egypt soon fell under their sway. Control of Egypt passed to Salah

ad-Din ibn Ayyubi in 1169 AD and, for the next 80 years, the Ayyubids ruled in Cairo until, they in their turn, were displaced by their Mamluk slaves.

The first Mamluk Dynasty, the Bahri Mamluks, were excellent administrators and soldiers. They expanded their control of the Levant and the Hijaz and extended their influence into Nubia. They cleared the Crusaders out of the Levant and checked the Mongol advance into the Middle East in the 1250s. They also improved Egypt's economy and developed its trading links with Europe and Asia. Indeed, the fact that the Mamluks were able to control and profit from the growing European trade with the Far East via Egypt was a major factor in their economic success.

In 1382 AD, the Bahri Mamluks were displaced from power by the Burgi Mamluks. Their control of Egypt was a period of instability and decline. The Ottoman Turks, in a swift campaign in 1516-17, eliminated them and turned Egypt into a province of the Ottoman Empire.

THE OTTOMANS IN NORTH AFRICA

The arrival of the Ottomans in North Africa was the last invasion of the region before the colonial period began in the 19th century.

THE OTTOMAN OCCUPATION

The Ottomans emerged with some strength from the Northwest heartlands of Anatolia in the 15th century. By 1453 they controlled the lands of the former Byzantine Empire and 65 years later took over Syria and Egypt before expanding deep into Europe, Africa and the Arab Middle East. The Syrian and Egyptian districts became economically and strategically important parts of the empire with their large populations, fertile arable lands and trade links.

Administratively, Palestine west of the Jordan Rift Valley was split into the *wilayat* (province) of Beirut along the

The *souq* mentality

🦶 An enduring characteristic of all *souqs* is their use of pricing through bargaining for every transaction, however large or small. This bargaining, so unfamiliar to the European, has brought rather differing responses. On the one hand bargaining is seen as a sign of the efficiency of the *souq*. Each separate business transaction is done with the finest of margins so that prices are very sensitive and really reflect the value. Contrary opinions strongly maintain that, far from being efficient, bazaar transactions only maximize profits for the seller for each article sold rather than getting the best potential profit flow. *Souqs* or bazaars thus actually act as a brake on the expansion of commerce as a whole. They also rely on the ability of the seller to exploit the absence of quality controls, trade mark conventions and other types of consumer protection. In these situations, the seller treats each transaction as an opportunity to cheat the customer. *Souqs* are, in this view, places where the buyer must be doubly wary since short measure, adulteration of goods and falsification of origin of goods for the benefit of the seller is normal. By definition this system can operate only in countries like Egypt with minimal regulatory régimes and where consumer information is unorganized.

When shopping in Egypt the best advice is to be fully aware that the system is designed to work to the seller's advantage.

northern coastal strip and the Sanjak (district) of Jerusalem in the south reaching down towards the Gulf of Aqaba. The east bank of the Jordan River fell within the *wilayat* of Syria and included Aqaba. Egypt was also a valued part of the Ottoman Empire, ownership of which provided the Porte with control over the Nile Valley, the east Mediterranean and North Africa. Power was exercised through governors appointed from Constantinople but over the centuries an Egyptian, mainly Mamluke (Caucasian-origin) elite imposed themselves as the principal political force within the country and detached the area from the direct control of the Ottomans. In most areas of the empire, the ability of the sultan to influence events diminished with distance from the main garrison towns and a great deal of independence of action was open to local rulers and tribal chiefs outside the larger towns.

The great benefit of the Ottoman Empire was its operation as an open economic community with freedom of movement for citizens and goods. Traders exploited the Ottoman monopoly of land routes from the Mediterranean to Asia to handle the spice, gold and silk from the East, manufactures from Europe and the slave and gold traffic from Africa. Ottoman tolerance of Christian and Jewish populations led in Palestine/Syria to the growth of large settlements of non-Muslim. Arabic continued as the local language and Islamic culture was much reinforced. Outside the larger towns, however, pastoralism, farming and parochial affairs remained the major occupation of the people and cultural and other changes were slow to occur.

Until the late 18th century the Ottoman Empire was wealthy, its armies and fleets dominant throughout the region but after that date a marked decline set in. European powers began to play a role in politics and trade at the expense of the sultan. The empire began to disintegrate. During the 19th century Egypt under the Khedives, the famous Mohammad Ali and his successor Ismael, were only nominally under the sultan's control. Egypt adopted Western ideas and technology from Europe and achieved some improvements in agricultural productivity. The cost was ultimate financial and political dominance of the French and British in this part of the empire. In Palestine, too, colonial interventions by the French in Syria and Lebanon reduced Ottoman control so that by the time of WW1 the collapse of the Ottoman Empire was complete and the former provinces emerged as modern states, often under a European colonial umbrella.

The Ottoman occupation of North Africa was a by-product of Ottoman-Venetian competition for control of the Mediterranean, itself part of the boundless expansionism of the Ottomans once they had conquered Constantinople in 1453. The Ottoman attack was two-pronged, involving their newly acquired maritime power to establish a foothold and then backing it up with the janissary, land based forces that formed the empire's troops. The decrepit Mamluk Dynasty in Egypt fell to the Ottomans in 1517 and a new, centralized Ottoman administration was established there.

Ottoman interests were soon attracted westward and a maritime campaign was launched on the North African coastline. It was carried out mainly by privateers, attracted both by the religious confrontation between Christian powers in Southern Europe and Islam in North Africa and by the growing practice of corsairing.

The Ottoman moves on North Africa were precipitated by the privateering activities of the Barbarossa brothers, Uruj and Khayr al-Din. The Ottomans eventually occupied Tunis permanently in 1574. Before this, however, they had gained a hold over Libya. Khayr al-Din Barbarossa occupied Tajura, on the coast close to Tripoli, in 1531 and was consequently able to threaten the precarious hold of the Knights of the Order of St John of Jerusalem on Tripoli itself. They had just occupied Tripoli and Malta at the request of Charles V of Spain, but were forced out of Tripoli altogether by the Ottomans in 1551. For 270 years North Africa, except for Morocco, was an Ottoman preserve.

THE BARBARY REGENCIES

Direct control from Istanbul did not last long. The North African coastline was divided into a series of administrative units, with power divided among the *bashas*, sent from Istanbul, the *deys* who were in charge of the permanent janissary garrisons and, in Algiers at least, the *taifa*, the captains of the corsairing privateers that continued to operate.

Tripoli

At the beginning of the 18th century, the final formal links with Istanbul were broken. In 1711 a dynasty was founded in Tripoli by Ahmad Karamanli, who seized power in the temporary absence of the Ottoman governor and then massacred the leaders of the janissaries. The new autonomous government eventually controlled Tripolitania and the coastal regions of Cyrenaica. After a tussle for influence in Tripoli between Britain and France, the Ottoman Empire re-occupied the Regency of Tripoli and ejected the Karamanlis in 1835.

Egypt and Sudan

In Egypt, the newly centralized Ottoman administration soon found itself struggling against the unreconstructed remnants of Mamluk society, with the province frequently splitting into two units, each controlled by a different section of the Mamluk Dynasty. By 1786, the Ottomans had destroyed the Mamluk factions and restored central control. In 1798, Napoleon's army conquered Egypt, delivering a profound cultural shock to the Muslim world by demonstrating, in the most graphic manner, the technological superiority of Europe. In 1805 Mohammed Ali was appointed governor and lost no time in breaking away from the Ottoman Empire to found a new dynasty, the *khedivate*, which remained in power until a revolution in 1952.

Mohammed Ali sought to modernize Egypt and to expand its power. He brought in European military advisers, destroyed the remnants of the old political elite in

Egypt and instituted wide-ranging economic reforms. In the Sudan, Mohammed Ali's Egypt was more successful; after the initial invasion in 1820, some 40 years were spent consolidating Egyptian rule, although, in 1881, the experiment failed (see box, page 62).

By that time, Egypt itself had succumbed to the financial pressures of its modernisation programme. Borrowings from Europe began, with the inevitable consequence of unrepayable debt. In addition, Britain realized the potential importance of Egypt for access to its Indian Empire, particularly after the Suez Canal was opened in 1869. A debt administration was instituted in 1875, under joint British and French control. In 1881 AD, a nationalist officers' rebellion against what they saw as excessive European influence in the *khedivate*, provoked a British take-over which lasted until 1922. Following General Gordon's death in Khartoum and the consequent British campaign against the Mahdist state in the Sudan, which culminated in the Battle of Omdurman in 1898, Britain instituted an Anglo-Egyptian condominium over Sudan.

COLONIALISM

The British occupation of Egypt introduced a régime which, as the well known historian Ira Lapidus said 'managed the Egyptian economy efficiently but in the imperial interest'. Railways were built and widespread irrigation was introduced; the population virtually doubled inside 35 years; private property was increasingly concentrated in the hands of a new elite; and the foreign debt was repaid. Industrialisation was, however, neglected and Egypt became ever more dependent on cotton exports for revenue.

Social and political relations were not so smooth. The British occupation of Egypt coincided with a wave of Islamic revivalism. At the same time, a secular nationalist tradition was developing in Egypt which crystallized into a political movement at the end of the 19th century

and was stimulated by Egyptian resentment at British demands on Egypt during WW1.

After 3 years of agitation Britain granted limited independence in 1922. It retained control of foreign affairs, foreigners in Egypt, the Sudan and the Egyptian army although some of these controls were abandoned in 1936. By the end of WW2, this complex political system had outlived its usefulness. In 1950, Egypt unilaterally abrogated the Canal Zone Treaty. After 2 years of guerrilla warfare and a military coup in Cairo which ended the *khedivate*, Britain finally agreed to abandon its position in the Canal Zone and its remaining hold over Egypt in 1952.

THE COLONIAL PERIOD IN LIBYA

The re-imposition of Ottoman rule in Libya in 1835 marked an end to the corsairing economy of the Regency of Tripoli. Ottoman control was never fully applied throughout the country.

The Sanusi Order, which was named after its Algerian founder, Sayyid Muhammad bin Ali al-Sanusi was an Islamic revivalist movement. It chose the Sahara for its arena and settled amongst the Cyrenaican tribes, where it was welcomed for its piousness and for its ability to arbitrate tribal disputes. Later on, the Order also coordinated tribal resistance throughout the Sahara to French colonial penetration. The Order also began to control the eastern trade routes across the Sahara and, as a result, effectively became, an autonomous government of the central Saharan region. In Cyrenaica its power was so great that, outside the major urban settlements such as Benghazi, the Ottomans accepted it as the de facto government and a Turkish-Sanusi condominium developed.

The Ottoman administration in Tripoli had to cope with continuing European pressure, particularly from Italy and Malta. British and French influence led to the end of the slave trade towards the end of the 19th century, while the economy of Tripoli became increasingly integrated into the global economy of the Mediterranean region. By the start of the 20th century Italy's intention to colonize Tripolitania, Cyrenaica and the Fezzan became clear.

Fighting broke out between tribes backed by dissident Ottoman officers and the Italian army. The outbreak of WW1 allowed the Ottoman Empire to provide military aid to the resistance and eventually a peace agreement was signed between Italy and the Sanusi at Akrama in April 1917. In 1922, with the Fascists in power, Italy again decided to occupy Libya. The second Italo-Sanusi war was between the Italians and the bedouin of Cyrenaica, for resistance in Tripolitania and the Fezzan was quickly broken. The ferocious struggle continued to 1930 when the last remnants of resistance were wiped out and Italy finally occupied the vast Libyan desert hinterland.

The Fascist victory was short-lived, for the Italian army was forced out of Libya during WW2 and British military administrations took over in Cyrenaica and Tripolitania with the French in Fezzan. Under the Italians, Libya had acquired the basic elements of a communications infrastructure and some modernisation of the economy. It had also acquired a 50,000 strong Italian settler population, a substantial portion of whom remained until they were expelled by the Ghadhafi régime in 1970.

The situation of Libya posed problems. By the end of WW2 it had acquired strategic significance for Britain and, after the Cold War began, for the USA as well. Britain had promised Cyrenaica that Italian control would never be restored. A series of proposals were made including Soviet Union trusteeship over Libya and the Bevin-Sforza Plan, whereby Britain would take a mandate for Cyrenaica, Italy for Tripolitania and France for the Fezzan for a period of 10 years, after which the country would be granted Independence. These were clearly unacceptable to the Libyans themselves, and the whole issue was dropped in the lap of the newly created United Nations in 1949.

The United Nations' special commissioner was able to convince all the Libyan factions that the only solution was a federal monarchy, bringing the provinces of Cyrenaica, Tripolitania and the Fezzan together under the Sanusi monarchy of Sayyid Idris. In December 1951, the independent kingdom of Libya came into being.

Wildlife

occasional flourishing oasis. The Red Sea provides a colourful and unusual selection of sea creatures.

THE AREA covered by this *Handbook* is predominantly desert yet there are many sub-regions providing a wide variety of habitats. The northern coast of Egypt is influenced by the Mediterranean but the scrub vegetation soon gives way to semi desert; the Nile Delta area includes coastal wetlands and salt marsh; inland lakes and reservoirs provide saltwater and freshwater sites for migrating and resident birds. The limited areas of arable agriculture along the narrow Nile valley and in the extensive delta contrast with the vast expanses of scrub. The mountain ranges of Sinai provide their own climate, delaying flowering and shortening the growing season. Even the desert areas which cover so much of this region provide contrasts, the sands (*erg*), gravels (*reg*) and rock (*hammada*) being interspersed with the

Many of the habitats mentioned above are under threat, either from pollution, urbanisation, desertification or advanced farming techniques. Fortunately the conservation movement is gaining pace and many National Parks and Nature Reserves have been created and programmes of environmental education set up. However, regrettably, wildlife is still regarded as a resource to be exploited, either for food or sport.

In desert regions, wildlife faces the problem of adapting to drought and the accompanying heat. The periods without rain may vary from 4 months on the shores of the Mediterranean to several years in some parts of the Sahara. Plants and animals have, therefore, evolved numerous methods of coping with drought and water loss. Some plants have extensive root systems; others have hard, shiny leaves or an oily surface to reduce water loss through transpiration. Plants such as the broom have small, sparse leaves, relying on stems and thorns to attract sunlight and produce food. Animals such as the addax and gazelle obtain all their moisture requirements from vegetation and never need to drink, while the ostrich can survive on saline water. Where rain is a rare occurence, plants and animals have developed a short life cycle combined with years of dormancy. When rain does arrive, the desert can burst into life, with plants seeding, flowering and dispersing within a few weeks or even days. Rain will also stimulate the hatching of eggs which have lain dormant for years. Many animals in the desert areas are nocturnal, taking advantage of the cooler night temperatures, their tracks and footprints being revealed in the morning. Another adaption is provided by the sandfish, which is a type of skink (lizard) which 'swims' through the sand in the cooler depths during the day. Perhaps the most remarkable example of adaption is shown by the camel (see box, page 419). Apart from its spreading feet which enable it to walk on sand, the camel is able to adjust its body temperature to prevent sweating, reduce urination fluid loss and store body fat to provide food for up to 6 months.

MAMMALS

Mammals have a difficult existence throughout the area, due to human disturbance and the fact that the species is not well adapted to drought. Many have, therefore, become nocturnal and their presence may only be indicated by droppings and tracks. Mammals represented here include the Red fox which is common in the Delta, the Sand fox, a lighter coloured hare, the shrew and two species of hedgehog, the Long-eared and the Desert. The appealing large-eyed and large-eared Desert fox or Fennec is less common and is often illegally trapped for sale. Despite widespread hunting wild boar survive. Hyenas and jackals still thrive particularly in Sinai while wild cats are found in Sinai and the Delta. The leopard, formerly common in North Africa, is now extremely rare, but is occasionally seen in some isolated regions in Sinai, to the panic of the local people.

There are three species of gazelle, all well adapted to desert conditions; the Dorcas gazelle preferring the Western Desert, the Mountain gazelle inhabiting locations above 2,000m in Sinai and the Desert gazelle locating in the *reg* of the northern Sahara. The latter is often hunted by horse or vehicle, its only defence being its speed. There are over 30 species of bat in the area, all but one – the Egyptian Fruit bat – being insectivorous. Recent ringing has shown that bats will migrate according to the season and to exploit changing food sources. Many species of bat have declined disastrously in recent years due to the increased use of insecticides and disturbance of roosting sites.

Rodents are well represented. They include the common House rat and the Large-eyed Sand rat, the gerbil and the Long-tailed jerboa which leaps like a tiny kangaroo. Many gerbils and jerboas, sadly, are found for sale in pet shops in Europe.

Weasels are common in the Delta region, even in urban areas such as Cairo, where they keep down the numbers of rats and mice. The snake eating Egyptian mongoose with a distinctive tuft on the end of its tail is frequently sighted but sightings of porcupines are rare and then only in the far south. The ibex too is only found in the south.

REPTILES AND AMPHIBIANS

The crocodile, treated as a sacred animal by the Egyptians (see El-Fayoum) who kept them in tanks by their temples, is no longer found north of the Aswan Dam. A few remain in Sudan. Tortoises are widespread. Terrapins are less common. Both tortoises and terrapins are taken in large numbers for the pet trade. There are over 30 species of lizard in the area, the most common being the Wall lizard, which often lives close to houses. Sand racers are frequently seen on dunes, while Sand fish and Sand swimmers take advantage of deep sand to avoid predators and find cooler temperatures in the desert *reg*. Spiny lizards have distinctive enlarged spiked scales round their tails. The waran (or Egyptian Monitor) can grow to over a metre in length. Geckoes are plump, soft-skinned, nocturnal lizards with adhesive pads on their toes and are frequently noted running up the walls in houses. The chameleon is a reptile with a prehensile tail and a long sticky tongue for catching insects. Although basically green, it can change colour to match its surroundings.

Snakes are essentially legless lizards. There are some 30 species in Egypt but only the viperine types are dangerous.

These can be identified by their triangular heads, short plump bodies and zig-zag markings. The Horned sand-viper lies just below the surface of sand, with its horns projecting, waiting for prey. The Carpet viper is twice the size but don't stay to measure, it is considered the most dangerous snake in Egypt. The cobra, up to 2m long, was the symbol of Lower Egypt. It too is deadly. Sand boas stay underground most of the time. Most snakes will instinctively avoid contact with human beings and will only strike if disturbed or threatened. For what to do if you are bitten by a snake, see page 510.

RIVER, LAKE AND MARINE LIFE

There are over 190 varieties of fish in the River Nile, the most common being the Nile bolti with coarse scales and spiny fins and the Nile perch, frequently well over 150 cm in length. Bolti are also found in Lake Nasser. Other fish include the inedible puffer fish, lungfish which can survive in the mud when the waters recede, grey mullet and catfish which are a popular catch for domestic consumption but some species can give off strong electric shocks. Decline in fish numbers is blamed on pollution, over-fishing and change of environment due to the construction of the Aswan Dam. Marine fish such as sole and mullet have been introduced into Lake Qaroun which is becoming increasingly saline.

The Mediterranean Sea has insufficient nutrients to support large numbers of fish. The numerous small fishing boats with their small mesh nets seriously over-exploit the existing stock. The catch is similar to the North Atlantic – hake, sole, red mullet, turbot, whiting. Sardines occur off the Nile Delta but in much reduced quantities due to pollution. Tuna, more common to the west, are caught off Libya too. Grey mullet is fished in and off the Nile Delta while sponges, lobsters and shellfish harvested.

The fish of the Mediterranean pale into insignificance against 800 species of colourful tropical fish in the Red Sea.

Tiger and Hammerhead sharks, Moray eels, Slender barracudas and Manta rays, all thriller material, occur. Here, while sport and commercial fishermen chase after tuna, bonita and dolphin, scuba divers pay to explore the fringing coral reefs and view the paint box selection of Angel, Butterfly and Parrot fish and carefully avoid the ugly Scorpion fish and the even more repulsive Stone fish.

INSECTS

There are a number of insects that travellers might not wish to encounter – bedbugs, lice, fleas, cockroaches, sand flies, house flies, mosquitoes, wasps and ants. By contrast there are large beautiful dragonflies which hover over the river, the destructive locusts fortunately rarely in swarms, and the fascinating Black dung beetles, the sacred Scarab of the Egyptians, which roll and bury balls of animal dung as food for their larvae (see box, page 154).

Scorpions, not insects, are all too common in Egypt and Libya. Check the details in the box, page 475.

BIRDS

The bird life in the region is increased in number and interest by birds of passage. Four categories of birds may be noted. Firstly, there are 150 species of **resident** birds, such as the Crested lark and the Sardinian warbler. Resident birds are found mainly in the fertile strip of the Nile Valley and in the Nile Delta. There are surprisingly few in the oases. Secondly, there are the **summer visitors**, such as the swift and swallow, which spend the winter months south of the Equator. **Winter visitors**, on the other hand, breed in Northern Europe but come south to escape the worst of the winter and include many varieties of owl, wader and wildfowl. **Passage migrants** fly through the area northwards in spring and then return southwards in increased numbers after breeding in the autumn. Small birds tend to migrate on a broad front, often crossing the desert and the Mediterranean Sea without stopping. Such migrants include the Whitethroat, plus less common species such as the Nightjar and Wryneck. Larger birds, including eagles, storks and vultures, must adopt a different strategy, as they depend on soaring, rather than sustained flight. As they rely on thermals created over land, they must opt for short sea crossings following the Nile Valley, Turkey and the Bosphorus.

There are a number of typical habitats with their own assemblage of birds. The Mediterranean itself has a poor selection of sea birds, although the rare Audouins gull always excites 'twitchers'. Oceanic birds such as gannets and shearwaters, however, over-winter here. The Red Sea coast hosts the indigenous White-eyed Gull and White-cheeked Tern, migrant pelicans, gregarious flamingos and, near Hurghada, Brown boobies. Ospreys breed on the nearby Isle of Tiran.

Wetland areas attract numerous varieties of the heron family such as the Night heron and Squacco heron, while spoonbill, ibis and both Little and Cattle egrets are common. Waders such as the avocet and Black-winged stilt are also typical wetland birds. The species are augmented in winter by a vast collection of wildfowl. Resident ducks, however, are confined to specialities such as the White-headed duck, Marbled teal and Ferruginous duck. On roadsides, the Crested lark is frequently seen, while overhead wires often contain Corn buntings, with their jangling song, and the Blue-cheeked and Green Bee-eaters. Mountain areas are ideal for searching out raptors. There are numerous varieties of eagle, including Bonelli's, Booted, Short toed and Golden. Of the vultures, the griffon is the most widely encountered. The Black kite is more catholic in its choice of habitat, but the Montagu's harrier prefers open farmland.

The desert and steppe areas have their own specialist resident birds which have developed survival strategies. Raptors include the Long-legged buzzard and the lanner, which prefer mountain areas. The Arabian rock pigeon of Sinai is a protected species. Among the ground-habitat birds are the Houbura bustard and the Cream coloured courser. Duponts lark is also reluctant to fly, except during its spectacular courtship display. The Trumpeter finch is frequently seen at oases, while the insectivorous Desert wheatear is a typical bird of the *erg* and *reg* regions.

Special mention must be made of the **Nile Valley** (see page 197). Essentially a linear oasis stretching for hundreds of kilometres, it provides outstanding bird watching, particularly from the slow-moving cruise boats, which are literally 'floating hides'. Apart from the wide range of herons and egrets, specialities include the African skimmer, Egyptian geese, Pied kingfisher and White pelican. Even the tombs and monuments are rewarding for the ornithologist, yielding Sakar falcons, Levant sparrowhawks and the Black shouldered kite.

Lake Nasser provides a good habitat for over 100 species of birds (see box, page 312).

Travel and survival in the desert

TRAVELLERS AND THE NATURE OF DESERTS

For those travellers staying in well regulated accommodation in good hotels, the realities of the desert can be disguised for as long as electricity and pure water supplies are sustained. Much of the information in the following section can thus be ignored, though not with total impunity. Trips into the desert even by the most careful of tour operators carry some of the hazards and a knowledge of good practice might be as helpful on the beach or tourist bus as for the full-blooded desert voyager.

There is a contemporary belief that the problems of living and travelling in deserts have been solved. Much improved technology in transport together with apparent ease of access to desert areas has encouraged these comfortable ideas. The very simplicity of the problems of deserts, lack of water and high temperatures, make them easy to underestimate. In reality, deserts have not changed and problems still arise when travelling in them, albeit with less regularity than twenty or so years ago. One aspect of the desert remains unchanged – mistakes and misfortune can too easily be fatal.

Desert topography is varied. Excellent books such as Allan JA & Warren A (1993) *Deserts: a conservation atlas*, Mitchell Beazley, show the origins and constant development of desert scenery. In the region covered by this *Handbook*, desert and semi-desert is the largest single surface area and so has an importance for travellers rarely met with elsewhere. Its principal features and their effects on transport are best understood before they are met on the ground. The great *ergs* or sandseas comprise mobile dunes and shifting surface sands over vast areas. Small mobile *barkhans*, which are crescent shaped, can often be driven round on firm terrain but the larger transverse and longitudinal dunes can form large surfaces with thick ridges of soft sand. They constantly change their shape as the wind works across them. While not impassible, they can be crossed only slowly and with difficulty. The major sand seas such as those at Calanscio, Murzuq, and Brak should be treated as no-go areas for all but fully equipped and locally supported expeditions. Similar conclusions apply to the extensive outcrops of rocky desert as exemplified by the Jabal As-Sawda in Libya. The *wadi* beds which penetrate much of the Sahara, *serirs* and gravel plains provide good access for all-terrain vehicles.

The main characteristic of the desert is its **aridity**. Aridity is calculable and those navigating deserts are advised to understand the term so that the element of risk can be appraised and managed with safety. CW Thornthwaite's aridity index shows water deficiency relative to water need for a given area. There is a gradient from north to south throughout the region, of rising temperatures, diminishing rainfall and worsening aridity. Aridity of the desert is thus very variable, ranging from the Mediterranean sub-tropical fringe to a semi-arid belt to the south and a fully arid desert interior. In basic terms, the further south you are the more dangerous the environment. Do not assume that conditions on the coast properly prepare you for the deep south. The Sahara is also very varied in its topography, climate and natural difficulties posed for the traveller. Rapid transition from rough stone terrain to sand sea to salt flat has to be expected and catered for.

For practical purposes, aridity here means lack of moisture and **very high temperatures**. The world's highest temperatures are experienced in the Sahara, over 55°C. Averages in the southern desert run in summer at more than 50°C in the shade at midday. In full sun very much higher figures are reached. High temperatures are not the only difficulty. Each day has a large range of temperature, often of more than 20°C, with nights being intensely cold, sometimes below freezing. In winter, air temperatures can be very low despite the heat of the sun and temperatures drop very rapidly either when the sun goes down or when there is movement from sunlight to shade, say in a deep gorge or a cave.

Increasing aridity means greater **difficulty in water availability**. Scientists define the problem in terms of water deficits. The region as a whole and the deep Sahara in particular are very serious water deficit areas. Surface waters are lacking almost everywhere except in the case of the River Nile in Egypt. Underground water is scarce and often available only at great depths. Occasional natural seepages of water give rise to oases and/or palmeries. They are, however, rare. Since water is the key to sustaining life in deserts, travellers have always to assume that they must be self-sufficient or navigate from one known water source to another.

Isolation is another feature of the Sahara. Travellers' tales tend to make light of the matter, hinting that bedouin Arabs will emerge from the dunes even in the most obscure corner of the desert. This is probably true of the semi-desert and some inland *wadi* basins but not a correct assumption on which to build a journey in the greater part of the Sahara. Population numbers in the desert are very low, only one person per 20 km sq in Al-Kufrah in Southeast Libya, for example, and most of these are concentrated in small oasis centres. Black top road systems are gradually being extended into and through the Sahara but they represent a few straggling lines across areas for the most part without fixed and maintained highways. The very fact that oil exploration has been so intense in the Sahara has meant that the surface of the desert is criss-crossed with innumerable tracks, making identification of all routes other than black top roads extremely difficult. Once off the main roads, travellers can part from their escorts and find no fixed topography to get them back on course. Vanishing individuals and vehicles in the Sahara are too frequent to be a joke. To offset this problem read on.

The most acute difficulty with off-road emergencies is finding the means of raising assistance because of isolation. Normal preventative action is to ensure that your travel programme is known in advance by some individual or an institution to whom regular check-in is made from points on the route. Failure to contact should automatically raise the alarm. Two vehicles are essential and often obviate the worst problems of break-down and the matter of isolation. Radio communication from your vehicle is an expensive but useful aid if things go wrong.

Bear in mind the enormous distances involved in bringing help even where the location of an incident in the desert is known. Heavy rescue equipment and/or paramedical assistance will probably be 500 km or more distant. Specialist transport for the rescuers is often not instantly available, assuming that local telecommunications systems work and local administrators see fit to help.

LIVING WITH THE CLIMATE

Living with desert environments is not difficult but it does take discipline and adherence to sensible routines at all times. It is an observed fact that health problems in hot and isolated locations take on a greater seriousness for those involved than they would in temperate climates. It is still common practice with Western oil companies and other commercial organisations regularly engaged

Sand on the move

Egypt has some 97% of its surface area under deserts and is therefore rich in sand dunes. The main areas of dunes occur in the west of the country with the most accessible large sand seas in the Western Desert.

Dunes form under various wind conditions. Barchan or crescent dunes tend to be found where a steady wind blows from one direction and where the volume of loose quartz sand is limited. The sand in the horns of the crescent is blown ahead of the main mass of the dune as it migrates across the usually flat landscape. Ridge dunes occur at right angles to the direction of the wind, though other theories for their form are proposed by the experts and are known as linear or in Arabic *saif* dunes. They are well developed in the Egyptian desert lands and can be several kilometres in length and rise to 170m high. Typical of some of the greatest sand masses in the Sahara and the sand seas such as the Western Desert, particularly south of Siwa oasis, adjacent to the Libyan border, where sand sheets and dune formations are both found covering large surface areas. In Egypt there are star dunes, in which wind prevails from different directions or is erratic in direction, giving what appear to be multiple crescent shaped dunes in the configuration of a star when seen from above. The star dunes can become centres of massive sand accumulation as with altitudes of 300m and a length of 1 km.

The mobility of dunes varies. The largest move perhaps no more than a metre each year. Barchans can, especially if of low altitude, travel far more quickly, at up to 50m per year. Mobile dunes create a hazard for transport since roads can be covered quickly in high wind conditions, as is frequently the case on roads linking settlements in the New Valley. Elsewhere, cultivated lands can slowly be inundated with sand.

Stabilizing sand dunes is a difficult matter. The large dune systems are unstoppable and man's attempts to halt their advance have rarely succeeded for long. Smaller dunes can be stabilized by planting them with a close graticule of drought resistant grass or other plants, which once established can be inter-planted with desert bushes and shrubs. This process is slow and expensive though generally very effective even in very dry conditions. More cheap and dramatic is to build sand fences to catch moving sand, tar-spraying dunes or layering dunes with a plastic net. The results are less aesthetically pleasing than using the traditional vegetation cover system and are less long-lasting unless combined with planting, though in the driest areas of the Sahara these are the only possible methods of fixing mobile dunes.

at desert sites to fly ill or injured persons home as a first measure in the knowledge that most will recover more rapidly without the psychological and environmental pressures of a desert site. Most health risks in the desert are avoidable. The rules, evolved over many years, are simple and easy to follow:

1. Allow time to acclimatize to full desert conditions. Conserve your energy at first rather than acting as if you were still in a temperate climatic régime. Most people take a week or more to adjust to heat conditions in the deep Sahara.

2. Stay out of direct sunlight whenever possible, especially once the sun is high. Whenever you can, do what the locals do, move from shade to shade.

3. Wear clothes to protect your skin from the sun, particularly your head and neck. Use a high Sun Protection Factor (SPF) cream, preferably as high as SPF15 (94%) to minimize the effects of Ultraviolet-B. Footwear is a matter of choice though many of those from the temperate parts of the world will find strong, light but well ventilated boots ideal for keeping sand, sun, venomous livestock and thorns off the

Dunes in the desert

Star Dunes

Barchans

Saif Dunes

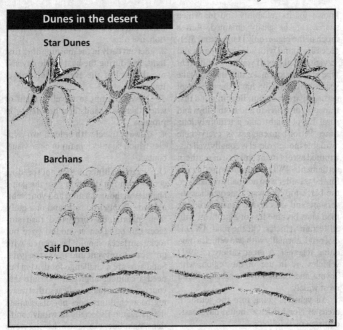

feet. Slip on boots are best of all since they are convenient if visiting Arab encampments/housing/religious sites, where shoes are not worn.

4. Drink good quality water regularly and fully. It is estimated that 15 litres per day are needed by a healthy person to avoid water deficiency in desert conditions, even if there is no actual feeling of thirst. The majority of ailments arising in the desert relate to water deficiency and so it is worth the small effort of regular drinking of water. Too much alcoholic drink has the opposite effect in most cases and is not, unfortunately, a substitute for water!

5. Be prepared for cold nights by having some warm clothes to hand.

6. Stay in your quarters or vehicle if there is a **sand storm**.

7. Refrain from eating dubious foods. Deserts and stomach upsets have a habit of going hand in hand. Choose hot cooked meals in preference to cold meats and tired salads. Peel all fruit and uncooked fresh vegetables. Do not eat 'native' milk-based items or drink untreated water unless you are absolutely sure of its good quality.

8. Sleep off the ground if you can. There are very few natural dangers in the desert but scorpions (see box, page 475), spiders and snakes are found (but are rarely fatal) and are best avoided.

TRANSPORT AND COMMON SENSE IN THE DESERT

The key to safe travel in desert regions is reliable and well equipped transport. Most travellers will simply use local bus and taxi services. For the motorist, motorcyclist or pedal cyclist there are ground rules which, if followed, will help to reduce risks. In normal circumstances travellers will remain on black top roads and for this need only a well prepared 2WD vehicle. Choose a machine which is known for its reliability and for which spares can be easily obtained. Across much of the region only Peugeot and Mercedes are found with adequate spares and servicing facilities. If you have a different type of car/truck, make sure that you take spares with you or have the means of getting spares sent out. Bear in mind that transport of spares to and from Libya and rural Egypt might take a tediously long time. Petrol/benzene/gas is everywhere available though diesel is equally well distributed except in the smallest of southern settlements. 4WD transport is useful even for the traveller who normally remains on the black top highway. Emergencies, diversions and unscheduled visits to off the road sites become less of a problem with all-terrain vehicles. Off the road, 4WD is essential, normally with two vehicles travelling together. A great variety of 4WD vehicles are in use in the region, with Toyota and Land Rover probably found most widely.

All vehicles going into the southern areas of North Africa should have basic equipment as follows:

1. Full tool kit, vehicle maintenance handbook and supplementary tools such as clamps, files, wire, spare parts kit supplied by car manufacturer, jump leads.

2. Spare tyre/s, battery driven tyre pump, tyre levers, tyre repair kit, hydraulic jack, jack handle extension, base plate for jack.

3. Spare fuel can/s, spare water container/s, cool bags.

For those going off the black top roads other items to include are:

4. Foot tyre pump, heavy duty hydraulic or air jack, power winch, sand channels, safety rockets, comprehensive first aid kit, radio-telephone where permitted.

5. Emergency rations kit/s, matches, Benghazi burner (see page 39).

6. Maps, compasses, latest road information, long term weather forecast, guides to navigation by sun and stars.

Driving in the desert is an acquired skill. Basic rules are simple but crucial.

1. If you can get a local guide who perhaps wants a lift to your precise destination, use him.

2. Set out early in the morning after first light, rest during the heat of the day and use the cool of the evening for further travel.

3. Never attempt to travel at night or when there is a sandstorm brewing or in progress.

4. Always travel with at least two vehicles which should remain in close visual contact.

Other general hints include not speeding across open flat desert in case the going changes without warning and your vehicle beds deeply into soft sand or a gully. Well maintained corrugated road surfaces can be taken at modest pace but rocky surfaces should be treated with great care to prevent undue wear on tyres. Sand seas are a challenge for drivers but need a cautious approach – ensure that your navigation lines are clear so that weaving between dunes does not disorientate the navigator. Especially in windy conditions, sight lines can vanish, leaving crews with little knowledge of where they are. Cresting dunes from dip slope to scarp needs care that the vehicle does not either bog down or overturn. Keep off salt flats after rain and floods especially in the winter and spring when water tables can rise and make the going hazardous in soft mud. Even when on marked and maintained tracks beware of approaching traffic.

In the desert border areas of Egypt and the Western Desert of Libya unexploded mines are a hidden danger. Maps of mined areas are unreliable, some were never marked. Always obey the precautionary signs. Floods can move mines considerable distances from the original site. Be warned, people do die.

EMERGENCIES

The desert tends to expose the slightest flaw in personnel and vehicles. Emergency situations are therefore to be expected and planned for. There is no better security than making the schedule of your journey known in advance to friends or embassy/consulate officials who will actively check on your arrival at stated points. Breakdowns and multiple punctures are the most frequent problem. On the highway the likelihood is always that a passing motorist will give assistance, or a lift to the nearest control post or village. In these situations it is best simply remain with your vehicle until help arrives making sure that your are clear of the road and that you are protected from other traffic by a warning triangle and/or rocks on the road to rear and front.

Off the road, breakdowns, punctures and bogging down in soft sand are the main difficulties. If you have left your travel programme at your last stop you will already have a fall back position in case of severe problems. If you cannot make a repair or extricate yourself, remain with your vehicle in all circumstances. Unless you can clearly see a settlement (not a mirage) stay where you are with water, food and shelter. The second vehicle can be used to search for help but only after defining the precise location of the incident. In the case of getting lost, halt, conserve fuel while you attempt to get a bearing on either the topography or the planets/stars and work out a traverse to bring you back to a known line such as a highway, mountain ridge or coastline. If that fails, take up as prominent a position as possible for being spotted from the air. Build a fire to use if and when y ou hear air activity in your vicinity. Attempt to find a local source of water by digging in the nearest *wadi* bed, collecting dew from the air at night. If you have fuel to spare it can be used with great care both as a means of attracting attention and a way of boiling untreated water. A *Benghazi burner*, two crude metal cones welded together to give a water jacket and space for a fire in the centre can achieve this latter purpose. As ever in this region, be patient and conserve your energy.

Jewellery and dress

JEWELLERY

The dynamic history of the region has produced imaginative traditionial designs mixed with foreign elements leading to a range of decoration few regions in the world can rival. Influences from the Phoenicians, Greeks and Romans, Arabs and Andalusians have each contributed subtly to the immense range of jewellery found in this part of the world.

Although some urban dwellers have adopted Western attitudes to dress and decoration, at times of festivals and especially for marriage ceremonies, traditional dress and elaborate jewellery that has changed little since the Middle Ages is still worn. The increase of tourism, while in some cases destroying traditional values, is in fact promoting and preserving crafts, especially jewellery making, by providing an eager and lucrative market for ornaments that was rapidly declining. Unfortunately, with the changes of cultural values, changes in fashion and style also occur and unfortunately large quantities of old, exquisite silver jewellery have been destroyed to provide raw materials for new pieces.

There is a division of tastes and wealth between towns where gold is favoured and the countryside where silver predominates. Basically, traditional styles continue to be popular and jewellery tends to become more traditional the further south one goes. A general shift can be discerned away from silver towards gold, especially in Egypt, where it is now believed to be a better investment.

Despite a whole field of inspiration being forbidden to Muslim jewellers, that of the human form, they developed the art of decorating jewellery in ways that eventually merged to become a distinctive 'Islamic' style. Using floral (arabesque), animal, geometric and calligraphic motifs fashioned on gold and silver with precious and semi-precious gems, coral and pearls they worked their magic.

According to Islamic law, silver is the only pure metal recommended by the Prophet Mohammad. For the majority of Muslims this sanction is felt to apply only to men who do not, as a rule, wear any jewellery other than a silver wedding ring or seal ring.

Every town has its own jewellery *souq* with larger centres providing a greater

Ankh (Cross of Life)

Nefertiti's head

Bracelet from Egypt

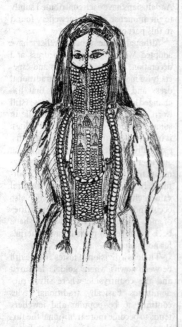

A Bedouin woman from the Nile

One of the many styles of Khamsa
or Hand of Fatima

Siwan earring

range of jewellery. There is almost always a distinction between the goldsmiths and the silversmiths and there are also shops, designated in Egypt by a brass camel over the door, which produce jewellery in brass or gold plate on brass for the cheap end of the market.

The tourist industry keeps whole secions of the jewellery business in work, especially in Egypt where designs which have a historical base – the Scarab, the Ankh (the symbol of eternal life), the Eye of Horus, Nefertiti's head and heiroglyphic cartouches – predominate. The jewellery spans the entire range of taste and quality from the very cheap mass-produced pendants to finely crafted very expensive pieces. Jewellers also sell a great number of silver items at the cheaper end of the tourist market which is very popular as 'ethnic' jewellery. Gold and silver jewellery is usually sold by weight and, although there might be an additional charge for more intricate craftmanship, this means the buyer must judge quality very carefully.

The **earring** is by far the most popular and convenient ornament. It appears in an infinite variety of styles with the crescent moon shape being the most common. The earring from Siwa is a particularly fine example. This is closely followed by the **bracelet** or **bangle** which is also very much part of a woman's everyday wardrobe.

North African anklets or *Khul-Khal* (always worn in pairs)

Most of the jewellery is worn both as an **adornment** and as an indication of social status or rank. It generally has some symbolic meaning or acts as a charm. Jewellery is usually steeped in tradition and is often received in rites of passage like puberty, betrothal and marriage. Women receive most of their jewellery upon marriage. This is usually regarded as their sole property and is security against personal disaster.

Many of the **symbols** recurrent in jewellery have meanings or qualities which are thought to be imparted to the wearer. Most of the discs appearing in the jewellery represent the moon which is considered to be the embodiment of perfect beauty and femininity. The greatest compliment is to liken a woman to the full moon. Both the moon and the fish are considered as fertility symbols. The cresent is the symbol of Islam but its use actually predates Islam. It is the most common symbol throughout the region and acquires greater Islamic significance with the additon of a star inside. Other symbols frequently seen are the palm and the moving lizard both of which signify life and the snake which signifies respect.

Amulets are thought to give the wearer protection from the unknown, calamities and threats. They are also reckoned to be curative and to have power over human concerns such as longevity, health, wealth, sex and luck. Women and childen wear amulets more frequently as their resisitance to evil is considered to be weaker than that of a man.

The most popular amulets are the *Hirz*, the Eye and the *Khamsa* or hand. The *Hirz* is a silver box containing verses of the Koran. Egypt in particular has a preoccupation with the Eye as an amulet to ward off the 'evil eye', usually modelled on the Eye of Horus which, as with most symbols in Ancient Egyptian jewellery, has always had mystical connotations. The *Khamsa* is by far the most widespread of the amulets. It comes in a multitude of sizes and designs of a stylized hand and is one of the most common components of jewellery in the region. This hand represents the 'Hand of Fatima', Mohammed's favourite daughter. Koranic inscriptions also form a large section of favoured pendants and are usually executed in gold and also heavily encrusted with diamonds and other precious stones.

Coins or *mahboub* form the basis of most of the traditional jewellery, from the veils of the bedouins of the Nile Delta to the bodices of the women from the Egyptian oases. Spectacular ensembles are worn at festivals and wedding ceremonies. Each area, village or tribe has its own unique and extraordinary dress of which jewellery, be it huge amber beads as in Sudan or hundreds of coins, forms a fundamental part.

Among the more interesting items are **anklets** called *khul khal*, worn in pairs and found in a great variety of styles. In Egypt they are mostly of solid silver fringed with tiny bells. Fine examples are expensive due to their weight. They are losing popularity among the younger generation as

Silver pendant -
Lizard, a talisman against the evil
eye on a Hand of Fatima

they are cumbersome to wear with shoes and because of their undertones of subservience and slavery. It is still possible to see them being worn by married women in the remoter villages of Egypt.

Characteristic **Libyan** jewellery is gold plated silver though both silver and gold are common. The predominant motif, a tiny version of the 'Hand of Fatima', appears on every piece.

Today the main jewellery bazaars are Khan el-Khalili in Cairo (see page 147) and Souq al-Mushir in Tripoli. Jewellers in all main cities will sell you modern versions of traditional jewellery.

Marie-Claire Baker contributed the text and some illustrations for this section. Other illustrations were produced by Geoff Moss.

DRESS

First time visitors will be fascinated by the variety and colour of the garments worn as 'everyday' wear. This section sketches in the background and attempts an explanation of what is being worn and why.

The dress traditions are striking and colourful evidence of a rich cultural heritage. Here, as in all societies, dress is a powerful form of cultural expression, a visual symbol which reveals a wealth of information about the wearer. Dress also reflects historical evolution and the cumulative effects of religious, ethnic and geographical factors on a society.

It is hardly surprising that the many influences which have shaped Middle Eastern history have produced an equally diverse dress culture in which elements from antiquity, the Islamic world and Europe are found. The heritage from earlier times is a rich blending of decorative motifs and drapery. Carthaginian material culture drew upon local tradtions of colourful geometric ornament, which is still seen in Berber clothing and textiles, and luxury goods from Egypt. Greek and Roman fashions have survived in the striking dress of the inhabitants of the deserts and mountains. The *barakan* in Libya is based on the

Roman toga. The Arabs introduced a different dress tradition, influenced by the styles of Egypt and Syria. Here the main features were loose flowing robes and cloaks, wrapped turbans and headcovering which combined a graceful line, comfort and modest concealment. The establishment of Islamic cities encouraged a diverse range of professions and occupations – civil and religious authorities, merchants, craftsmen – all with their distinctive dress. Within cities such as Cairo specialist trades in textiles, leather and jewellery supported dress production. Widening political and commercial relations stimulated new elements in dress.

The Ottoman Turks introduced another feature into city dress, in the form of jackets, trousers and robes of flamboyant cut and lavishly embroidered decoration. Finally European fashion, with emphasis on tailored suits and dresses entered the scene. The intricate pattern of mixed dress styles reflects an adjustment to economic and social change.

The widest range is seen in urban environments where European styles mingle with interpretations of local dress and the clothing of regional migrants. Men have adopted European dress in varying degrees. The wardrobes of civil servants, professional and business men include well-cut sober coloured European suits, which are worn with toning shirts, ties and smart shoes. Seasonal variations include fabrics of lighter weight and colour and short-sleeved shirts and 'safari' jackets. Casual versions of this dress code, including open-necked shirts, are seen in more modest levels of urban society. Blue jeans, blouson jackets, T shirts and trainers may be worn equally by manual workers and students.

Men's city dress alternates between European and local garments according to taste and situation. Traditional dress is based on a flexible combination of loose flowing garments and wraps which gives considerable scope for individuality. One

Barakan

Jallabah

of the most versatile garments is the *jallabah*, an ankle length robe with long straight sleeves and a neat pointed hood, made in fabrics ranging from fine wool and cotton in dark and light colours to rough plain and striped homespun yarn. Elegant versions in white may be beautifully cut and sewn and edged with plaited silk braid. A modern casual version has short sleeves and a V-shaped neck and is made of poly-cotton fabric in a range of plain colours. Professional men may change from a suit into a *jallabah* at home, while working class men may wear a plain or striped *jallabah* in the street over European shirt and trousers.

The more traditional interpretation of dress can be seen in the medinas. Here the *jallabah* is worn with the hood folded at the the back or pulled up and draped over the head. In the past a fez or turban was worn under the hood and a white cotton high-necked shirt with long sleeves and loose white trousers gathered just below the knee were worn under the *jallabah*.

A handsome and dignified garment worn by high ranking state and religious officials is the *caftan*, another long robe with very wide sleeves and a round neck. The cut and detail, such as the use of very fine braid around the neck and sleeves and along the seams, are more formal than those of the *jallabah*. The modern *caftan* has narrower sleeves and is worn in public by men of an older and more conservative generation. Traditional dress may be completed with the addition of drapery. Examples include the selham or

Turban

Kiffiyeh and igal

burnous, a wide semicircular cloak with a pointed hood and the ksa, a length of heavy white woollen cloth which is skilfully folded and wrapped around the head and body in a style resembling that of the classical Roman toga.

Headcoverings are a revealing indication of status and personal choice. A close fitting red wool felt pillbox cap, a *fez*, *tarboosh* or *chechia*, with a black tassle can be seen more often on older men both in traditional and European dress. The distinctive, often checked, headsquare (*kiffiyeh*) of the Bedouin is secured by a heavy double coil (*igal*) of black wool. The ends of the cloth may hang loose or be wrapped around the face and neck for protection against heat or cold. The more traditional loose turban of a length of usually white, less commonly brown, cotton is widespread in Egypt, worn by a wide selection of the working men.

Women's town dress is also a mixture of traditional and modern European forms and depends on wealth, status and personal taste. In the larger cities where women are employed in business and professions, European clothes are worn, cleverly accessorized with scarves and jewellery. Longer skirts and long-sleeved blouses are worn, being a more modest form of European dress.

Traditional dress is remarkably enduring among women of all classes. The most important garments are the *caftan* and *jallabah* of the same basic cut and shape as those for men. The *caftan*, as worn in the past by wealthy women, was a sumptuous garment of exaggerated proportions made of rich velvet or brocaded silk embroidered with intricate designs in gold thread. The modern *caftan* is usually made of brightly coloured and patterned light-weight fabric and edged with plaited braid. The shape is simple and unstructured with a deep slit at each side from waist to hem. Variations can be found in texture and colour of fabric, changes in proportions of sleeves and length of side slits. The *caftan* in its many variations is always worn as indoor dress and can suit all occasions. Traditionally it is worn as an everyday garment belted over a long underskirt. A light shawl may be draped around the neck and the hair tied up with a patterned scarf. Women who normally wear European dress to work often change into a *caftan* at home. Very chic versions of the *caftan*, combined with modern hairstyles and accessories, are worn as evening wear at private and official functions.

Jennifer Scarce, Curator of Eastern Cultures, National Museums of Scotland contributed the text. Illustrations by Geoff Moss.

Horizons

Official name

Jumhuriyah Misr al-Arabiyah (Arab Republic of Egypt)

National flag

Equal horizontal bands of red, white and black with a central emblem of Salah al-Din's golden eagle clutching a panel bearing the country's name in its claws.

Official language

Arabic

Official religion

Islam

Egypt statistics

Population: 62.1 million (official estimate 1997). *Urban population*: 43%. *Religion*: Muslim (mainly Sunni) 90%, Christian 10%. *Birth rate*: 28 per 1,000. *Death rate*: 9 per 1,000. *Life expectancy*: 65/69. *GNP per capita*: US$790.

The Land

EGYPT IS among the most influential of Arab states, lying at the crossroads of Africa and the Middle East as well as extensive borders on the Mediterranean and Red Sea. This ancient country with a continuous history of over 6,000 years holds a tantalizing attraction for travellers. The Pyramids, the Sphinx, the tomb of young Tutankhamen intrigue and enchant while the narrow green ribbon of the Nile cuts its way from south to north through the seemingly endless desert. This is however, only a small part of Egypt: and travellers are recommended to explore the small palm-sheltered settlements in the oases of the Sahara Desert or the empty expanses of Sinai. There is an additional 2,000 km of Red Sea where the coasts are fringed with teeming coral reefs and Mediterranean Sea coast, the former being promoted as an alternative or supplement to a Nile visit.

GEOGRAPHY

The overall area of the country is 1,002,000 sq km, which is over twice the size of Morocco.

Egypt's location in Northeast Africa gives it great strategic importance because it is at the junction of the land routes joining Africa to the Near and Middle East and the sea routes from the Atlantic/ Mediterranean and the Indian Ocean/Red Sea. Its borders abut in the north on to the Mediterranean coast and for much of the east on to the Red Sea. These two coastal reaches are separated by the isthmus of Suez, a 150 km land bridge linking the eastern outliers of the Nile Delta with Sinai. The international frontier with Israel runs northwest across the Sinai peninsula from the Taba strip at the head of the Gulf of Aqaba, to the coastal plain of the Negev with a deviation to take account of the Gaza strip.

Travellers coming into Taba from **Israel** intending to stay in northern Sinai and people going to Israel from Taba only need border permits. Travellers crossing from Israel into Egypt or vice-versa can expect two frontier checks one at either end of the Taba strip. People intending to visit most Arab countries should avoid passport stamps at either Egyptian or Israeli border posts here. The border area is clearly marked and the area is monitored by UN forces. Off-shore in the Gulf

of Aqaba care is needed not to stray across undemarcated 'frontiers' because the Israelis are particularly sensitive about the possibility of terrorists crossing by sea from the three neighbouring Arab countries just across the water.

Egypt's 1,000 km southern border is with **Sudan**. There is a dispute over ownership of land and economic rights in the Halaib area immediately adjacent to the Red Sea which travellers should avoid. Egypt's 1,300 km long border with **Libya** (see page 346) on the west is one where there have always been periodic tensions. Nomads often smuggle goods across the border in the area between Siwa/Al-Jaghbub and the coastline in the territory of Ulad Ali tribe. The only easy and official crossing point is in the north on the coast road near Sollum. There is some dispute in the Egyptian-Libyan offshore zone about the alignment of the boundary but this does not currently affect either land or sea transport.

MAIN REGIONS

Egypt is correctly said to be "the gift of the Nile" and Egypt's two most important regions – the Delta and the Nile Valley – are both clustered close to its water supplies. The Delta lies north of Cairo and is a vast, low, flat triangle of land through which the tributaries of the Nile pass to the sea. South of Cairo the Nile is contained within a rich and fertile but narrow 2-3 km incised valley which eventually reaches Lake Nasser which is a 425 km ribbon of water extending up to and beyond the border with Sudan. The Delta and the Nile Valley contain almost 99% of the country's cultivated land and approximately the same proportion of the population. East of the Nile Valley is the Eastern Desert and the narrow Red Sea coastline. To the east of the Delta lies the formerly isolated Sinai peninsula which now has international airports and harbours and is traversed by major roads. West of the River Nile is the Libyan Desert which is often referred to as the Egypt's Western Desert. It is broken up by the occurrence of the Al-Uwenat Heights in the southwest which extend in an elongated plateau towards the lowlands of Dakhla Oasis, which has larger parallel formations in the north as the Qattara and Siwa depressions which, together with Dakhla, form the eastern edge of the Sitican embayment. The long coastal plain between Alexandria and Marsa Matruh gets narrower towards the west as it approaches the Libyan frontier in the Gulf of Sollum.

Egypt is a country of lowlands and low-lying plateaux of which 60% is less than 400m above sea-level. The few areas of high relief are the Al-Uwenat Heights in the southwest and in the Eastern Desert adjacent to the Red Sea coast where mountains rise to over 1,000m. The highest mountain in the country is Jebel Katrinah next to St Catherine's Monastery (see page 391) which reaches 2,228m at its summit.

Egypt has the **River Nile** as its only but vital river. The total annual flow down the Nile, from the **Blue Nile** and **River Atbara** which both start in the Ethiopian highlands and the **White Nile** which begins in East Africa's Lake Victoria, is normally 55 cubic km. Under the 1959 Nile Waters Agreement, Egypt is entitled to take 37 cubic km but, because Sudan so far does not use its full allocation, has been able to take more. There is now growing pressure in all the upstream states for more water and another water crisis is looming.

Egypt has undertaken extensive engineering projects on the River Nile over the centuries which reached a peak with work by the British authorities in the 19th and early 20th centuries. In the modern period the Aswan High Dam, (see page 289) which was designed to give Egypt both water storage facilities and hydro-electric power for its new industries, was built with Russian assistance in the 1960s. In fact the low level of the River Nile in the late 1980s led to a major crisis and precipitated a crash programme to build power stations dependent on locally produced natural gas. If flows continue to remain low, there may not be enough water to drive the dam's turbines.

The construction of the Aswan High Dam also reduced the deposition of silt on Egyptian farmlands in the Nile Valley and the Delta. This has necessitated the use of large quantities of fertilizer and led to a decline in the offshore fishing production. Despite some initial success in the search for sub-surface water reservoirs under the deserts the River Nile remains the very lifeblood of Egypt. There are no other perennial streams, although *wadis* run elsewhere after heavy rain as brief but dangerous spates.

THE NILE AND MAN

The River Nile runs for 6,435 km and drains one fifth of the entire African continent. It rises as the White Nile in Lake Victoria close to Jinja in Uganda and flows as the Victoria Nile through the tropics to Lake Albert. The Nile then begins its course through The Sudan as the Bahr el-Jebel eventually reaching the central plains of Sudan and becoming sluggish and ponding up during the annual flood in the marshy papyrus swamps of the Sudd (Arabic for 'dam'). Tributaries such as the Bahr el Ghazal and the Sobat enter the Nile and north from that point the river for its next 800 km is called the White Nile. The Sobat, which takes its source in the Ethiopian Highlands, is an important water supply for the White Nile system. It joins the Blue Nile at Khartoum. The Blue Nile drains an area deep in the Ethiopian Highlands and, like the Atbara which also joins from the east bank, provides run-off from the Northeast African monsoon. Between Khartoum and Aswan the river passes over six cataracts. The cataracts are wide rapids which make navigation impossible,

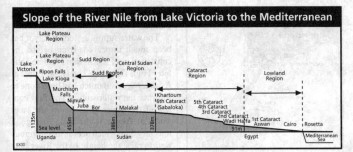

Slope of the River Nile from Lake Victoria to the Mediterranean

the steepest of the cataracts, the sixth, is at Sababka 80 km north of Khartoum.

The River Nile in Egypt is entrenched in a narrow valley below the surrounding land and has only one cataract at Aswan. In its last 325 km before entering its Delta the River Nile tends to keep to the east bank with the main cultivated zone of the valley on the west bank. Most irrigation requires water to be lifted from the river by traditional means such as the *saqiya*, *shadoof* or by mechanical pumps (see page 53).

The Nile Delta is the heartland of Egypt. It covers a great silt plain built up by the river over centuries. The Delta stretches 160 km from the vicinity of Cairo north to the Mediterranean coast and 250 km across the Mediterranean end of the wedge. The main distributaries in the delta are the Western Rosetta and Eastern Damietta 'mouths', which are the axes of intensive irrigation networks.

The flow of the River Nile has been influenced by fluctuations in rainfall in the countries where the river has its sources. It is possible that long term climatic change is involved, indicating that the flow in the river might never recover to the average of 84 cu km in the period 1900-59 from the 1984-87 level of less than 52 cu km. The water flow during floods has always varied, as we know from inscriptions in pharaonic times, but recent trends are worrying for the states that rely on the river.

Division of Nile waters is governed by the international agreements of 1929 and 1959, which ultimately gave 48 cu km to Egypt and 4 cu km to Sudan but the arrangement involved only Egypt and Sudan and excluded Ethiopia and the East African states. Argument over allocation of Nile waters continues, with Egypt's rights as the downstream state most at risk. Egyptian governments have felt so strongly on the issue of maintaining their share of Nile waters that they have threatened to go to war if the traditional division was changed against Egyptian interests. A master plan for the future use of Nile waters seems in the 1990s to be a distant prospect.

FINDING THE SOURCE OF THE RIVER NILE

The ancient Egyptians believed that the waters of the River Nile came from a mystical paradise of plenty. Early exploration by the Greeks and Romans established that the River Nile ran at least from the site of modern day Khartoum. In the 17th century there began a steady stream of European explorers and adventurers seeking the source of the River Nile. Most notable was James Bruce, a Scotsman who in 1769 began a trip which led him to the head waters of the Blue Nile. He was followed by the Englishmen Richard Burton, John Speke and James Grant, who traced the River Nile back to the Lake Victoria connection and, finally, Sir S W Baker, who went further south to Lake Albert. Full mapping of the Nile Basin as a whole went on until the 1960s.

River Nile Barrages

TRADITIONAL IRRIGATION IN EGYPT

In Egypt a basic problem for farmers was lifting water from the River Nile up the river banks which enclosed it. Simple systems of lifting water included windlasses and pulleys were used initially to enable humans or animals pull up leather bags full of river water (see Delu Well, page 483). Some mechanization followed in which flow-turned wheels were used. These were driven by the current of the river and had pots or wooden containers to carry the water to be deposited at a higher level as at El-Fayoum (see page 168). In much of the country where irrigation canals have little or no flow an animal powered wheel is exploited. Perhaps the classic and oldest water lifting device in Egypt is the *shadoof*, a weighted beam which is swung into the water by its operator and swung up and on to land with the help of a counter balance on the other end of the beam. In recent times water has

been led to the fields by diesel and electric pumps.

The water supply system of Egypt has been much improved. Even before the construction of the Aswan Dam and the later High Dam (see The Great Dams at Aswan, page 289) much had been done to improve the water storage and flow control of the River Nile. Below the river works at Aswan is the Esna barrage, a masonry dam which acts as an enormous weir to raise the height of the River Nile so that water can be led off in side channels to serve the lands lying under the canal. Downstream at Assiut a diversion dam was constructed to send water throughout the year into the existing Ismail Pasha Canal. A second diversion dam was built at Nag Hammadi between Assiut and Esna. In the delta, the replacement Mohammed Ali barrage was erected on the Rosetta branch. Other dams exist at Edfina and at Sennar in Egypt and Jebel Awlia in Sudan.

The use of the River Nile for navigation has been limited by the narrow, gorge-like nature of some stretches of the upper valley, by the Sudd of Sudan and the existence of the six cataracts in the river bed downstream of Khartoum. In Egypt the River Nile unites the country and local and long-distance craft ply the waterway on a scheduled basis. A large fleet of passenger vessels transport tourists on the River Nile particularly from Luxor to Aswan to serve the great monuments of ancient Egypt (see Nile Cruisers, page 274).

One of the most splendid sights on the river is the local *feluccas* under sail. The *felucca* is a lanteen rigged sailing vessel for inshore or river work. It has very shallow draught so that it can safely cross shoals and can be easily rowed if the wind is absent or unfavourable. Most *feluccas*, once for transporting produce up and down the Nile, are now available for hire by tourists by the hour or the day for a suitably bargained price which will depend on the season and other factors.

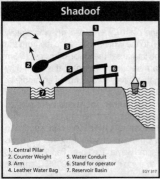

Shadoof

1. Central Pillar
2. Counter Weight
3. Arm
4. Leather Water Bag
5. Water Conduit
6. Stand for operator
7. Reservoir Basin

EGY 317

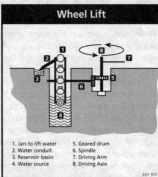

Wheel Lift

1. Jars to lift water
2. Water conduit
3. Reservoir basin
4. Water source
5. Geared drum
6. Spindle
7. Driving Arm
8. Driving Axle

EGY 317

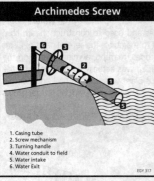

Archimedes Screw

1. Casing tube
2. Screw mechanism
3. Turning handle
4. Water conduit to field
5. Water intake
6. Water Exit

EGY 317

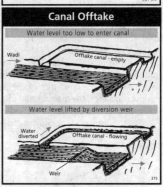

Canal Offtake

Water level too low to enter canal

Wadi

Offtake canal - empty

Water level lifted by diversion weir

Water diverted

Offtake canal - flowing

Weir

375

The *felucca* is much smaller and less magnificent than the Nile boats of the ancient Egyptians. These ancient craft developed from bundles of papyrus reeds, woven or bound together to make a buoyant crescent-shaped hull for carrying light loads. Later in the Old Kingdom wood was the principal raw material for constructing larger vessels whose shape followed that of the papyrus craft. Most wood was imported to make a keelless craft with a sail and steering gear made up paddles at the stern. By the Middle Kingdom boats took on a more crescent-shaped silhouette, while a cabin was added to the deck immediately before the stern deck. In the New Kingdom boats on the River Nile were longer and more sophisticated, with deckhouses sited round the mast and ceremonial daises both stern and aft. The sail on the New Kingdom vessels was rigged between top and bottom spars and was much wider than earlier types of sail. An example of an Old Kingdom (4th Dynasty) boat was found at the Great Pyramid at Giza. It was 433.6m long and 5.9m beam and when found was still unbuilt kit. The ship was made to be constructed with boards bound to ribs and to carry a small deckhouse and a single steering paddle. It is lodged in a store near the Cheops pyramid.

CLIMATE

Egypt is a desert country. Even its frontage to the Mediterranean offers only a modest tempering of Saharan conditions

Papyrus

🌿 This word was the name given to the plant *Cyperus papyrus* which grew alongside the River Nile. Later it was also given to the writing material made from the plant. Papyrus is a straight, tall, reed-like plant. Its leafless triangular stems rise to 5m above the water being as 'thick as a man's arm' at their lower part. It is topped by drooping spikelets of insipid flowers and long thin leaves like soft ribs of an umbrella.

To produce writing paper the pith from the stem was cut into narrow strips and arranged in alternate layers at right angles to each other. The sheets were pressed together and dried in the sun, the natural juice of the plant making the pieces stick together. The sheets were pasted together to form rolls which varied in length. An example in the British Museum is 30m long. On the inner side of the roll the fibres went across and the writing usually went the same way as the fibres. Paper made this way was cheap. The Egyptians are recorded as using it soon after 3000 BC and the Greeks around 500 BC.

The more slender stalks were woven into baskets (Miriam made a basket for Moses out of papyrus before she hid him in the same plants by the water's edge) and the thicker ones were tied into bundles and used to construct cheap, light boats, the earliest craft on the Nile. Isis went to search for the several parts of Osiris in a papyrus boat. The fibre used to make ropes, matting, awnings, sails and the pith, in addition to its important use for paper, was actually used as food by the less fortunate. The dried root of the papyrus plant was used as fuel and being a harder substance, the manufacture of utensils. The papyrus plant no longer grows in Egypt but can be found in the Sudan.

See the displays at the papyrus museums by the Nile at Cairo, Luxor and Aswan.

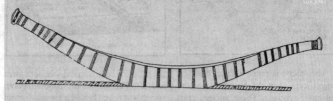

Papyrus Boat

in the vicinity of the coast in the Alexandria region. Here rainfall is at a maximum with an average of 188 mm per year with summer maximum temperatures averaging 30°C and diurnal ranges rarely more than 10°C. Moving inland brings a rapid decline in rainfall. Cairo, some 150 km from the sea, has an annual average rainfall of 25 mm, a maximum temperature of 35°C and average diurnal ranges of temperature of up to 15°C. Progression southwards brings even greater extremes. At Aswan rainfall drops away to 1 mm per year and average maximum temperatures rise to 37°C with a diurnal range of as much as 18°C. The profound aridity of Egypt outside the Nile Valley makes it absolute desert for the most part, relieved only where water occurs such as the Kharga, Dakhla and Siwa oases (see pages 427, 424 and 355).

The **best time for travelling** everywhere except possibly the Alexandria region is the period October-April but best of all November-February. Travellers in Egypt in April-May should be prepared for the *khamseen* wind – the wind of 50 days – which blows sand and heat to the discomfort of those caught in the open. Relative humidity can be high (over 70%) on the coast and the Delta. Inland, humidity is not a problem with Aswan, for example, having averages of less than 50% for the whole year and a mere 30% in the summer months. At the height of the summer humidity falls in many places to less than 20%. Climate figures are given in regional sections.

FLORA AND FAUNA

In the desert environment, annual plants have a very short life span, growing, blooming and seeding in a few short days, covering the ground, when moisture content permits, with a patchy carpet of low-lying blooms. Desert perennials are sparse, tough and spiny with deep root systems. Desert animals are rarely seen, being generally nocturnal and/or underground dwellers to avoid the heat. With water from the River Nile, an oasis or precipitation in the south, the plants are tropical and subtropical and the wildlife becomes more obvious in the form of small and medium size mammals like rats and the Egyptian mongoose. Bird life proliferates by the water, with roosting egrets, herons, kingfishers and hoopoes all very common. The birds of prey range in size from kestrels to black kites and Egyptian vultures. The number of Nile fish is decreasing but the coasts continue to teem with fish.

AGRICULTURE

Agriculture is the basis of the Egyptian economy accounting for 16% of total national output and 35% of employment. Despite very rapid urbanization, farming and the rural community remains at the cultural heart of the country. Current land patterns show the vital importance of the Nile Valley and Delta because the rest of the country is little better than waste land. Unfortunately even this very limited arable area is being reduced by the encroachment of Cairo and other urban areas.

Land use	(%)
Arable and orchards	2.1
Forests	0.0
Meadows and pastures	0.6
Desert, waste and other	97.3
Total	100.0

Source: FAO

LAND TENURE

Until the 1952 land reforms, 1% of Egypt's land owners possessed 90% of the farming land. The reform stripped the former royal house of its lands and the state took the estates of the great families who had controlled rural Egypt. In their place the revolutionary authorities established centrally controlled co-operatives which substituted civil servants for the former landlords, a move which did little to alter the agricultural system or indeed benefit the peasants. At the present time the peasantry is either landless or has tiny fragments of land which are mainly uneconomic. The average availability of land per cultivator is put at 0.35 ha. Attempts to reclaim land in the desert regions using underground water and high technology irrigation systems have, at best, been of marginal use in resolving Egypt's shortage of agricultural land. Many Egyptian farmers now emigrate to adjacent countries and travellers in North Africa will come across large numbers of Egyptian *fellahin* (peasants) working the land and undertaking manual labour in Libya.

POTENTIAL

Egypt's potential is hindered by its paucity of natural resources which, besides oil and natural gas produced in large enough quantities to meet domestic demand and some exports, are limited to iron, phosphate and a few other non-hydrocarbon minerals. The principal difficulty for Egypt, however, is its meagre area of fertile land and its reliance on the waters of the Nile. The growth of irrigation and hydro-electric schemes in the Upper Nile countries is putting Egypt's water supply at risk and there is no available substitute. Industrialization has some scope for expansion but the past record here is not encouraging.

Ultimately it seems that Egypt will have to continue to rely on its current principal sources of foreign exchange – oil, tourism, Suez Canal fees, and expatriate remittances – for its economic salvation. Unfortunately all four are dependent on stable political conditions in Egypt and the rest of the Middle East

The final problem for Egypt is that economic growth has to exceed its 1.9% annual population increase which implies no mean rate of development simply to stand still. For some years Egypt has relied, and will have to continue to rely, on predominantly US and European foreign aid for the 50% of food supplies needed annually from abroad to enable it to feed itself.

Jewish communities in Egypt (Pre-World War 2)

Culture

PEOPLE

The Arab Republic of Egypt had a population of 62.1 million in mid-1997. The growth rate of Egypt's population remains a sensitive matter given the difficulties of the government in providing jobs and feeding the people. It had seemed in the 1970s that the annual rate of increase was tailing off at 2.1% per year but there was a spurt again in the mid-1980s to 2.9% per year, which decreased the time in which the population will double to only 29 years. There are currently indications that the rate of increase has fallen back slightly to 1.9% in 1997. In the recent past there were high levels of emigration to the oil-exporting states of the Persian Gulf but this diminished during the Gulf War but has since recovered. Meanwhile, the crude death rate has fallen over the last 25 years and life expectancy at birth has gone up to male 65 and female 69, thus adding to the growth of the population size.

RACIAL ORIGINS

Egyptians living in the Nile Valley between Aswan and the sea have ancient origins. It is speculated that the people of the Nile Valley were of Berber origin with some Arab and Negroid admixtures. The people of the Delta had a slightly different early history and thus had distinct racial origins in which Armedoid and Arab elements were fused with the other peoples of the Nile Valley. Other racial additions were made from invasions from Libya, then from the desert lands of Arabia and Persia in the east, and finally the

Mediterranean connections which are most graphically illustrated by the Alexandrine conquest and the Roman establishment in northern Egypt. Present day Egyptians see themselves as having common racial and cultural origins which increasingly are not identified absolutely with the Arabs and Arab nationalism as a whole.

DISTRIBUTION/DENSITY

The Egyptian population is concentrated in the Nile Valley and Delta where 98% of people are found. Average densities are put at 62 people per sq km but in Cairo and the irrigated lands densities of many thousands per sq km are recorded.

AGE GROUPS

The population is youthful with 37% under the age of 15, 58% in the working age group 15-59, and 5.8% over 60. Literacy is high at 51%, with males at 64% being better placed than women at 39% literate.

INCOME PER HEAD

Egyptian income is put at US$790 per head of population. UN sources suggests that there was a sprightly level of growth of 3.6% per year in real personal incomes in the 1980s, stimulated by inflows of earnings from workers abroad. But since then growth has been dismal, labour productivity has stagnated and labour market conditions have deteriorated dramatically. By 1993 the World Bank considered that 75-80% of the population had an average monthly family income at or below US$50.

History

"There is no country which possesses so many wonders."– Herodotus, 450 BC.

For tens of thousands of years the focal point of Egyptian life has been the River Nile. The availability of this vast supply of water permitted the creation of a society which produced the wonders of ancient Egypt. Today modern Egypt depends on the river to support its huge population. The River Nile continues to be 'the lifeblood of Egypt'.

About 3100 BC, **King Menes** succeeded in uniting Upper and Lower Egypt into a single kingdom. His new capital at **Memphis**, about 15 km to the south of modern-day Cairo, was deliberately located on the border of Upper and Lower Egypt. Despite this the rivalry between the two parts of Egypt continued until the end of the Early Dynastic Period (3100-2686 BC).

The **Old Kingdom** (2686-2181 BC) began with the 3rd Dynasty and ushered in a major period of achievement. A series of strong and able rulers established a highly centralized government. The 'Great House' per-aha, from which the word pharaoh is derived, controlled all trade routes and markets. The calendar was introduced and the sun-god **Re** was

Symbol of Sun-god Re

The Jews in Egypt

Jewish involvement in Egyptian affairs has long historical roots. Twelve tribes of Israel were forced by famine to migrate to Egypt where they remained as an underprivileged minority until led out by Moses 13th century BC, eventually to move to Canaan in today's Palestine. During the period of dominance of Egypt by Greek and Roman cultures, the Jews became scattered around the major lands of the respective empires in the *Diaspora*. At that time Egypt was a major destination for the Jews in exile. It is estimated that as many as 1 million Jews lived in Egypt, with important centres of Jewish activity in Alexandria (see page 336), Leontopolis (north of Cairo in the eastern delta) and even in Lower Egypt as far south as Elephantine Island.

The Jewish population in Egypt declined with the passing of the Hellenistic tradition and the imposition of a less tolerant Roman government. During the Islamic era, the Jews, though subject to some social constraints and dealt with separately for tax purposes, thrived as traders and bankers in addition to their role as skilled craftsmen in the **souqs**. Occasional violence occurred against the Jews, who tended to be associated in the Egyptian popular mind with the foreign community and thus attacked at times of anti-British or anti-French riots in the major cities, as for example in 1882, 1919, 1921 and 1924. In general, however, it was true that Jews in Egypt fared far better and were more tolerated than Jews in some countries of Europe.

This all changed dramatically with the rise of Zionism in the period from 1890 and the return of Jews to Palestine. Even before WW2 the scale of Jewish migration to Palestine provoked fears in the Egyptian body politic and there were serious riots against the Jews in eight cities, most importantly in Alexandria and Cairo in 1938-39. Foundation of the State of Israel in 1948 brought an inevitable outbreak of rioting in which the Jews were a principal target. The Arab-Israeli wars of 1948, 1957, 1968 and 1973 added to the problem. Some 29,500 Jews left Egypt for Israel alone in the years 1949-72, in the latter years in official expulsions. Under pressure from both the flight to Israel and migration elsewhere, the Jewish population in Egypt fell from approximately 75,000 in 1948 to a few families by 1998.

A return of diplomatic relations between Egypt and Israel after President Anwar Sadat's visit to Jerusalem in 1977 improved official links and economic contacts between the two sides (albeit put in jeopardy by Israel's break of faith with the peace process in 1997), but the Jews have never returned as a community to Egypt.

---

the most revered deity. Until then it was common practice for leaders to be buried in underground mausoleums (*mastabas*). In the 27th century BC **King Zoser** and his chief architect **Imohotep** constructed the first **step pyramid** in Saqqara, the huge necropolis across the river from Memphis, and pyramids became the principal method of royal burial for the Pharaohs during the next millennium. The scale of organization required to mobilize the resources and manpower to build these phenomenal pyramids is testimony to the level of sophistication of this period. The three 4th Dynasty (2613-2494 BC) giant pyramids of Cheops, Chephren and Mycerinus erected on the Giza plateau still awe the world.

By the end of the Old Kingdom, the absolute power of the Pharaohs declined. Local leaders ruled their own *nomes* (provinces) and a second capital emerged at Heracleopolis. Few great monuments were built in this very unstable **First Intermediate Period** (2181-2050 BC).

During the 11th Dynasty **Menutuhotep II** reunited the country and created a new capital at **Thebes** (Luxor).

The Three Crowns of Egypt

🐾 The king was a reincarnation of a god – Re, Aten, Amun or Horus. He was addressed by the god as "my living image upon earth".

A king was recognized on illustrations by his garments and paraphernalia. The most important of these was his crown. The earliest kings wore the white bulbous crown of Upper Egypt. The red crown of Lower Egypt was even more distinctive with a high back and forward thrusting coil. A king wearing the double crown was thought to symbolize his control over all Egypt.

The ultimate sign of kingship however was the uraeus on his forehead, a rearing cobra with an inflated hood – generally in gold.

Other items of importance associated with kingship included the hand held crook and flail and the false plaited beard.

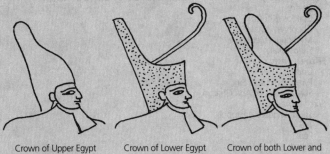

Crown of Upper Egypt
known as the white
crown or *Hedjet*

Crown of Lower Egypt
known as the red crown
or *Deshert*

Crown of both Lower and
Upper Egypt of Sekhemti

Remains from this era, the **Middle Kingdom** (2050-1786 BC), demonstrate its prosperity.

During the five dynasties of the **Second Intermediate Period** (1786-1567 BC), central authority again disintegrated and Egypt was controlled briefly by Asiatic kings known as the **Hyksos** (foreign princes) rulers who introduced horses and chariots to Egypt.

The **New Kingdom** (1567-1085 BC), spanning the 18th-20th Dynasties and based at Thebes, ushered in a period of unparalleled wealth and power. During these 400 years the kingdom prospered and expeditions led to the creation of a huge empire. Military campaigns in Western Asia by Tuthmosis III, now known as the Napoleon of Ancient Egypt, brought Palestine, Syna and Nubia into the empire and their wealth and cheap labour poured into Thebes. The temple complex of **Karnak** and the Valley of the Kings are but two of the astounding remains of the era. During this period (1379-62 BC), Akhenaten renounced the traditional gods in favour of a monotheistic religion based on the sun-god Re but his boy-king successor **Tutankhamen** immediately reverted to the former religion and its principal god Amun. In 1922 archaeologists discovered Tutankhamen's undisturbed tomb and its treasures are displayed at the museum in Cairo. After the military dictatorship of Horemheb, a general who seized the throne, royal power was restored by Ramses I. Ramses II, a most prestigious builder, reigned for 67 years. Following

Dynasties in Egypt up to 30 BC

(with rulers as mentioned in text)
Dates of dynasties and individual reigns are as precise as possible.

Early Dynastic Period (3100-2686 BC)

Ruler	Date
First Dynasty	*3100-2890 BC (Memphis established)*
Menes	
Second Dynasty	*2890-2686 BC*

The Old Kingdom (2686-2181 BC)

Third Dynasty	*2686-2613 BC*
King Zoser	2667-2648 (Step Pyramid in Saqqara)
Huni	
Fourth Dynasty	*2613-2494 BC (Pyramids of Giza)*
Snefru	
Cheops (Khufu)	
Chephren (Khafre)	
Mycerinus (Menkaure)	
Shepseskaf	
Fifth Dynasty	*2494-2345 BC*
Unas	
Pyramids of Abu Sir	
Sun Temples of Abu Gharub	
Sixth Dynasty	*2345-2181 BC*
South Saqqara necropolis	
Teti	
Pepi I	
Pepi II	

First Intermediate Period (2181-2050 BC)

Seventh Dynasty	*2181-2173 BC*

Middle Kingdom (2050-1786 BC)

Eleventh Dynasty	*2050-1991 BC*
King Menutuhotep II	Creation of Thebes (Luxor)
Twelfth Dynasty	*1991-1786 BC*
Amenemhat I	1991-1961
Senusert I	1971-1928
Senusert II	1897-1878
Amenemhat III	1842-1797
Queen Sobek-Nefru	1789-1786

Second Intermediate Period (1786-1567 BC)

Fifteenth Dynasty	*1674-1567 BC (capital Avaris)*

New Kingdom (1567-1085 BC) based on Thebes

Eighteenth Dynasty	*1567-1320 BC (Temples of Luxor & Karnak)*
Amenhotep I	1546-1526
Tuthmosis I	1525-1512

Tuthmosis II	1512-1504
Hatshepsut	1503-1482
Tuthmosis III	1504-1450
Amenhotep II	1450-1425
Tuthmosis IV	1425-1417
Amenhotep III	1417-1379
Amenhotep IV (Akhenaten)	1379-1362
Tutankhamen	1361-1352
Ay	1352-1348
Horemheb	1348-1320
Nineteenth Dynasty	*1320-1200 BC*
Ramses I	1320-1318
Seti I	1318-1304
Ramses II	1304-1237
Seti II	1216-1210
Twentieth Dynasty	*1200-1085 BC*
Sethnakht	1200-1198
Ramses III	1198-1166
Ramses IV	1166-1160
Ramses V	1160-1156
Ramses VI	1156-1148
Ramses VII	1148-1141
Ramses IX	1140-1123
Ramses XI	1114-1085

Late Dynastic Period (1085-332 BC)

Twenty-second Dynasty	*945-715 BC*
Twenty-fifth Dynasty	*747-656 BC*
Shabaka	716-702
Twenty-sixth Dynasty	*664-525 BC*
Necho II	610-596
Twenty-seventh Dynasty	*525-404 BC (Persian occupation)*
Cambyses	525-522
Darius I	521-486
Thirtieth Dynasty	*380-343 BC*
Nectanebo I	380-362
Nectanebo II	360-343

Late Period (332-30 BC) (Macedonian Kings, capital Alexandria)

Alexander III (The Great)	332-323
Philip Arrhidaeus	323-317
Ptolemaic Era	*323-30 BC*
Ptolemy I	Soter 323-282
Ptolemy II	282-246
Ptolemy III	246-222 (Edfu Temple)
Ptolemy IV	222-205
Ptolemy V	205-180 (Kom-Ombo Temple)
Ptolemy VII	180-145
Ptolemy VIII	170-145
Ptolemy IX	170-116
Ptolemy XIII	88-51
Cleopatra VII	51-30

Mohammed Ali and his successors

Mohammed Ali, the founder of the Khedival Dynasty, was born in Macedonia in 1769, came to Egypt in 1800 as an officer in the Turkish army, and was made governor under the nominal control of the Ottoman Sultan in 1805. He remained in post as a vigorous and development oriented ruler until 1848. Mohammed Ali died in 1849 having begun the modernization of Egypt and the creation of an Egyptian national identity. He is buried in the eponymous mosque in the Citadel in Cairo.

Ibrahim Pasha, eldest son of Mohammed Ali, was trained as a political leader as well as a soldier. He acted very successfully as his father's right hand man but in his own right ruled for just 4 months in 1848. See his imposing statue erected in Midan Opera by his son.

Abbas Pasha (1848-54) was the son of Mohammed Ali's third son, Tusun. He organized the laying of a railway from Cairo to Alexandria with British support and encouragement. In other respects he was reactionary, closing schools of advanced studies and slowing down the modernization process.

Sa'id Pasha (1854-63), second son of Mohammed Ali, served as an admiral in the Egyptian fleet and gave permission for the Suez Canal to be constructed. Sadly a large foreign debt was left as a legacy to his successor.

Khedive Ismail (1863-79), son of Ibrahim Pasha, was considered one of the builders of modern Egypt, being responsible for the building of the Suez Canal, the Opera House, Ras el-Tin Palace and Abdin Palace. He was a man of great energy and vision. He expanded Egyptian influence in the south and east but eventually led the country deeper into debt and into subservience to French and British power.

Khedive Tawfik (1879-92) was the son of Ismail, during whose reign Egypt's financial problems led to foreign take over of her affairs and, finally, the beginning of the British occupation in 1882. Manial Palace, his dwelling in Cairo, houses an important museum (see page 137).

Khedive Abbas Hilmi II (1892-1914), son of Tawfik, was noted for his interest in preservation and conservation of the country's ancient monuments. His attempts to develop a nationalist political movement came to nothing. He was deposed by the British in 1914.

Sultan Hussain Kamal (1914-17) was the second son of the Khedive Ismail. He owed his throne to the British and, despite the hardships of the war period 1914-18, he ruled without challenging British power in Egypt.

King Fuad (1917-36) was another son of the Khedive Ismail, though much more an Egyptian nationalist than his brother Hussain Kamal. Egypt became more politically active and was given a form of independence in 1922 as a constitutional monarchy. However, Fuad was unable to create an acceptable political role for himself and was caught up in the political battles between the British and the nationalist politicians.

King Farouk (1936-52) was Fuad's son and the penultimate Khedival ruler of Egypt. He became, like his father, unable to manage an increasingly radical nationalist community in Egypt and the British occupiers distracted by the demands of WW2 and its legacies of change. Farouk had few political friends and he was forced to abdicate in 1952 in the face of the revolution by the Young Officers led by Gemal Abdel Nasser. Farouk's infant son, **Fuad II**, was nominally successor to the throne but lost all rights in the new constitution of 1953.

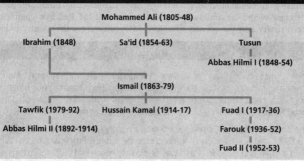

Mohammed Ali and his successors as rulers of Egypt

Mohammed Ali (1805-48)

Ibrahim (1848)   Sa'id (1854-63)   Tusun

Abbas Hilmi I (1848-54)

Ismail (1863-79)

Tawfik (1979-92)   Hussain Kamal (1914-17)   Fuad I (1917-36)

Abbas Hilmi II (1892-1914)

Farouk (1936-52)

Fuad II (1952-53)

the death of Ramses III, the last great pharaoh, effective power moved increasingly into the hands of the Amun priests and the empire declined.

During the **Late Dynastic Period** (1085-332 BC), the succession of dynasties, some ruled by Nubians and Persians, became so weak that **Alexander the Great** had little difficulty in seizing the country. Although he did not spend long in Egypt his new capital city of Alexandria where he is believed to be buried, still flourishes. His empire was divided among his generals and **Ptolemy** established the Ptolemaic Dynasty (332-30 BC) which ended with the reign of **Cleopatra VII** (51-30 BC), the last of the Ptolemies, before Egypt became a province of the **Roman Empire**.

The division of power between Rome and Constantinople resulted in the virtual abandonment of Egypt. Egypt's autonomy led to the development of the **Coptic church** which was independent from both the Byzantines and the Romans, and whose calendar dates from 284 AD when thousands were massacred by the Roman emperor Diocletian.

MUSLIM AND OTTOMANS

The **Muslim** seizure of Egypt in 642 AD was, despite the introduction of Islam, broadly welcomed by the Copts in preference to remaining under the Byzantine yoke. Islam slowly prevailed as did the introduction of Arabic as the official language although there remained a significant Coptic minority. Cairo became the seat of government and emerged as a new Islamic city. Whilst the seeds of Islam itself strengthened and blossomed there were centuries of political instability which led to the creation of countless dynasties, mainly ruled by foreign Muslim empires. The new faith was only fleetingly threatened when the **Christian Crusader** armies attacked Cairo and were repelled by **Salah al-Din** (1171-93 AD).

The **Ottomans** absorbed Egypt into their empire in 1517 and met with little resistance. The **Mamlukes**, a class of Turkic slave-soldiers, had already governed Egypt between 1250-1517 AD so Ottoman rule changed little. A significant proportion of tax revenues were remitted to Constantinople but day to day power remained in Mamluke hands. In the first centuries of Ottoman suzerainty of Egypt the nation flourished. Elaborate mosques were added to the already diverse cultural heritage. Later, as Britain and France sought to extend their empires, Egypt became subject to their designs. Napoleon invaded in 1798 but by 1801 the French had surrendered to British and Ottoman forces.

After a vicious power struggle, **Mohammed Ali** (1805-48) became **Pasha**. He sought to implement dramatic reforms which would drag Egypt from the

Middle Ages into the modern world. Unfortunately economic mismanagement by his successors and the continuing Anglo-French rivalry over the country actually brought Egypt to her knees. The French-inspired Suez Canal linking the Mediterranean and the Red Sea, completed in 1869, bankrupted the country and led to

Myths

Myths have always played a very important part in the religion of ancient Egypt and it is not possible to separate the myths from the religious rituals. The story of Isis and Osiris, one of the chief Egyptian myths was written on papyrus some 5,000-6,000 years ago. That certainly makes it ancient.

The story of Isis and Osiris According to the story Osiris was the son of Geb, the earth-god and was therefore descended from the sun-god Re. He was known to have been a great and good king and was particularly concerned with agricultural techniques, growing crops to provide the essentials, bread, beer and wine. He ruled wisely and when he travelled abroad Isis, his sister and wife, most competently took charge.

Now enters the bad guy. His bother Seth was filled with jealously and hatred for his brother Osiris and was determined to be rid of him. This he did with the help of the Queen of Ethiopia and another 72 conspirators. Seth had constructed a most magnificent chest which exactly fitted the measurements of Osiris. At the feast all the guests tried the chest for size and when Osiris took his turn the conspirators (surprise, surprise) nailed down the lid and sealed it with boiling lead. Well Isis had warned about the dangers of going to that particular party.

The sealed chest was carried to the river bank and thrown into the Nile where it floated out to the sea and came to land at Byblos in Syria. There a tamarisk tree grew up immediately and enclosed the chest. The size of this magnificent new tree caught the eye of the king of Byblos, his name was Melcarthus, and he had it cut down to make a pillar to support the roof of his palace.

Isis, distressed by the disappearance of her husband's body and aware that without funeral rites he could never rest in eternity, went out to search. It took some time to trace the route to Byblos, find the chest still encased in the trunk of the tree but now supporting a main room in the king's palace and even longer to persuade them to part with that pillar and the chest.

She made her way back to Egypt with the body of Osiris still in the chest. Here she was a little careless for leaving the chest hidden but unguarded, she went off to be reunited with her young son. By some mischance Seth, hunting by the light of the moon, stumbled on the chest. He immediately recognized the container and in his rage cut the body into 14 separate pieces.

Seth, determined to rid himself of his brother once and for all took the pieces and scattered them through all the tribes of Egypt. Undaunted Isis set out again, this time in a papyrus boat, to retrieve the separate pieces which she did with the help of her sister Nephthys, the gods Thoth and Anubis and some magic. At every place where she found a part of her husband she set up a shrine. The severed parts where brought together and Osiris was restored to eternal life.

Horus, the son of Isis and Osiris, was brought up in secret to protect him from harm (no doubt his uncle Seth). When he reached manhood he swore to avenge the wrong done to his father and mother. The myth describes his victory over Seth after one or two setbacks and how he was declared by the tribunal of gods to be Osiris's rightful heir.

The Talisman

The use of amulets and other charms was well developed in ancient Egypt when magic charms were worn like jewellery or put into the wrappings round a mummy – to ward off evil. Among the most sought after charms was the Eye of Horus illustrated here or the *ankh* (see page 427), the cross of life. Protective necklaces were particularly treasured and among the beads would be small carvings of animals representing gods – a hawk for Horus, or a baboon for Thoth. In the same way stelae (marker stones) or house charms stood at the door begging the gods to protect the family from danger.

The 'evil eye' is a powerful force in the contemporary local societies of Egypt and North Africa. It is believed that certain people have the power to damage their victims, sometimes inadvertently. Women are thought to be among the most malignant of possessors of the 'evil eye', a factor associated with the 'impurities' of the menstrual cycle. Even a camera can be considered as an alien agent carrying an 'evil eye' – so only take photographs of country people where they are comfortable with the idea and be exceptionally careful in showing a camera at weddings and above all funerals. Envy too is a component of the 'evil eye' and most conversations where any praise of a person or object is concerned will include a *mashallah* or 'what god wills' as protection against the evil spirits that surround human kind.

Major victims of the 'evil eye' are the young, females and the weak. Vulnerability is seen to be worst in marriage, pregnancy and childbirth, so that women in particular must shelter themselves from the 'evil eye'. Uttering the name of Allah is a good defence against the 'evil eye'. Alternatively amulets are used, this practice originating from the wearing of quotations from the Koran written on to strips of cloth which

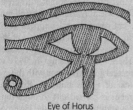

Eye of Horus

were bound into a leather case which was then strapped to the arm. The amulet developed as a form in its own right, made of beads, pearls, horn or stone brought back from a pilgrimage. Amulets also have the power to heal as well as to protect against the occult.

In contemporary Egypt and North Africa, medicine, superstition and ornament combine to give a wonderful array of amulets worn for both everyday and specific use.

---

its subsequent temporary control by Britain in 1882.

At the beginning of **WW1**, the potential vulnerability of the Suez Canal and the strategic implications of the Turkish-German alliance led **Britain** to increase its control over Egypt by declaring it a Protectorate. This led to the emergence, over the following 20 years, of both Arab and Egyptian nationalist movements which eventually procured nominal independence for Egypt in 1936, although Britain reserved the right to protect the Suez Canal and defend Egypt.

In 1952 the constraints of the **British Mandates** and the frustration following the defeat in the 1948 Arab-Israeli war led to the emergence of a new class of young army officers who staged a bloodless coup overthrowing **King Farouk** and ousting the remaining British troops. The new leader, **Colonel Gamal Abdel Nasser**, inherited a politically fragmented and economically weak state burdened with an ever-increasing demographic problem.

When the World Bank, at the behest of the USA, refused to help finance the construction of the new Aswan High Dam in 1956 Nasser nationalized the Suez Canal in order to raise the necessary revenues. This led to shock waves throughout the world and to the **Suez crisis** in which an Anglo-French force invaded and occupied temporarily the Canal zone. Nasser's dreams of development were hampered by Egyptian/Israeli tensions including the shattering Egyptian defeat in the 1967 war. He died in 1970 and was succeeded by **Anwar Sadat**. Sadat was aware that Egypt could not sustain the economic burdens of continual conflict with Israel so, despite the partially successful October 1973 war which restored Egyptian military pride, sought peace with his neighbour. In 1977 he made a historic trip to Jerusalem and laid the foundations for the 1979 **Camp David Peace Accords** which enabled Egypt to concentrate on her own economic development and firmly allied Egypt with the USA. While he was applauded abroad he was considered a traitor in the eyes of the Arab world and Egypt was diplomatically isolated. His assassination by Islamic fundamentalists in October 1981 brought vice-president **Hosni Mubarak** to power.

Modern Egypt

GOVERNMENT

Egypt became a republic in 1952 with a presidential system of government. The current president is Hosni Mubarak who has effective control of the armed forces and the cabinet and can convene or dissolve the single tier People's Assembly virtually at will. President Mubarak is also head of the ruling National Democratic Party (NDP). There have been efforts to introduce an element of democracy into government with general elections for the People's Assembly. The cabinet is led by Atef Sedki but the principal influence on the membership of the cabinet is the president. The Assembly has worked well but, until recently, was seen as a puppet organization for the régime. The speaker of the Assembly was assassinated in October 1990. There was an attempt in 1991 to improve local administration with the appointment of a new minister. Regional government is carried out through four groups of administrations – the governorates for the Desert, Lower Egypt, Upper Egypt and the urban areas. Sub-districts operate from regional capitals and separately for the cities of Port Said, Alexandria, Cairo and Suez. The administration is very bureaucratic and slow. There have been generally fruitless attempts to reform the civil service but, with 22% of the work force in public administration and defence, progress has been slow. Travellers should not have high expectations of officials and official agencies, though there are some institutions, mainly military, which function well. Personal influence is a key element in making the system work.

The government is only partially representative of the people and there are major dissident groups whose activities could affect the traveller. The **Muslim Brotherhood** – a form of fundamentalist Islamic organization – has flourished in Egypt for many years. While the Muslim Brotherhood is now the leading opposition group and is generally tolerated by the government the more extreme splinter groups, which have resorted to terrorism, are pursued by state agencies (see page 19). In addition to attacking members of the government, often successfully, the extremists are opposed to corrupt foreign influences, of which the excesses of the tourist industry, including the country's 20,000 belly dancers, are seen as a key part. Opposition groups are suppressed by severe laws such as the detention regulations and by an ever-present security service, the **mokhabarat**.

WARNING Travellers should bear in mind this aspect of security during their stay in Egypt and not act in ways that exacerbate local Muslim sensitivities.

HERITAGE

Egypt's natural assets in the form of her skills and her fabric are at risk. There is now a clear need for the advanced industrialized countries to understand the basis of Islamic science and technology. Certainly this would help to bridge the growing cultural divide between themselves and their more numerous neighbours to the east. In particular, appreciation of the way in which Islamic culture has matured over the long-term is required so that the valuable skills and technologies of Egypt are not wastefully discarded for short-term gains. The rapid pace of 20th century modernizations might all too quickly sweep away the remains and the folk memories associated with traditional culture.

There is also a risk that rapid technological change forced on a developing Egypt by the industrialized nations could lead to the indigenous technology being unnecessarily discarded instead of being used and, in the future, being deployed with advantage. The urgency of the problem of conservation or rescue of traditional Islamic technologies is acute. War and strife are depleting physical assets such as buildings and other works. Quite apart from man-made disasters, the processes of weathering on mud brick, from which many Islamic traditional constructions are made, is considerable. The comparatively recent abandonment of traditional villages, old mosques and underground water cisterns in Egypt has exposed traditional technology/material culture to destruction by natural erosion.

There is a real threat that the existing stock of examples of traditional Egyptian and Islamic technology of this kind could vanish with little trace in less than a generation.

ECONOMY

TRADITIONAL AGRICULTURE

The great mass of Egyptian farmland is under traditional forms of agriculture and worked by the *fellahin*, the Egyptian peasantry. Farming is based on use of the waters of the River Nile for irrigation which are now available, theoretically, throughout the year from Lake Nasser. In fact, approximately 65% of Egypt's agricultural land is under perennial cultivation and the remainder carries only one crop each year and/or is under a cultivation/fallow rotation. There has been a gradual increase in production of commercial crops but self-sufficiency is an important aim of small farmers. Wheat, rice, vegetables and fodder are the main crops, the latter to support the considerable number of draught (3.47 million buffalo, transport (2 million asses and 200,000 camels) and other animals (3.23 million cattle, 3 million goats, 3.71 million sheep and 38 million chickens) kept mainly on farms. It is estimated that 6 million people are engaged directly in the traditional farming sector.

MODERN AGRICULTURE

Modern farming is principally a matter of the operations of the centrally managed co-operatives on 'reformed' land and the activities of the mixed farms on recently reclaimed land in the rimlands of the delta and the newlands in the desert interiors. The co-operatives are still managed with a large participation by the government, who control the crops within the central rotation and handle credit and technical matters. These farms have been turned over to commercial crops for the most part – cotton, sugar cane, maize and rice, some destined for export. The newland farms specialize in exploiting the opportunities for early cropping for the supply of fruit and vegetables to the European market. The new farms stand out in the landscape with their contemporary buildings and rectangular field patterns.

Agricultural Output 1997

	(tonnes)
Sugar Cane	14,105,000
Maize	5,180,000
Wheat	5,600,000
Tomatoes	5,038,000
Rice	4,900,000
Sorghum	650,000
Oranges	1,608,000
Cotton	890,000

Source: FAO

ENERGY/PETROLEUM

Egypt has made major strides in the petroleum industry in recent decades without, however, joining the league of principal oil-exporters. Reserves of crude oil are put by the Egyptian authorities at a modest 3.3 billion barrels, with Egypt expected to become a net energy importer by the turn of the century. Production of crude oil ran at 900,000 barrels per day in 1996. Crude sales abroad are important, accounting in 1994 for 50% of all exports. Natural gas resources are more significant than oil with reserves of 20.4 trillion cubic feet and output at 10.4 million tonnes of oil equivalent in 1996. The oilfield areas are widely distributed among the Suez/Sinai zone to the east and the more recently discovered Western Desert fields. Western oil companies play a key role in oil development in Egypt. The Aswan High Dam now supplies only around 10% of the country's total electricity of 47 billion kwh per year.

ECONOMIC PLANS

Egypt was an early devotee of development planning, reinforced by the desire for a socialist centrally controlled economy under Gamal Abdel Nasser, the first president after the 1952 revolution. The plans were taken seriously and great efforts were made to use national resources to beat the twin difficulties of shortages of domestic natural resources and a burgeoning population. Some successes were won but the constant involvement of the country at the forefront of the Arab-Israeli wars diverted attention, funds and materials away from the economy. Under President Sadat the dedication to centralized control was gradually watered down and the plans became little more than indicative long-term budgets. Strategies were set at the top – development of the Suez Customs Free Zone under Sadat and privatization under Mubarak. The latest development plan for the period 1990/95, continued emphasis on growth of the private sector including the transfer to it of some state assets. The government has limited means at its disposal to promote economic expansion given the high costs of debt repayment at US$4.72bn and defence US$1.70bn, together representing 30% of the budget for 1995/96 fiscal year.

INDUSTRY

Since the time of the 1952 revolution, there has been a growing tendency to turn to industrialization as a means of achieving faster economic growth and providing for the needs of an expanding population. Most industries were then state-owned, carried very large workforces and were inefficient. The country did nonetheless lay the basis for iron and steel, automobile

Why do *souqs* survive?

The survival of the *souq*/bazaar system calls for an explanation. Why do the *souqs* in Egypt flourish while in other countries this is not the case? Part of the explanation is straightforward. Governments in Egypt, with few exceptions, have left the merchants of the *souq* to undertake most of their traditional trading functions unhindered. This seems to indicate a first principle for the survival of the bazaar, that it be left to operate a generally unrestricted trading network. The converse is also true, that the bazaar system will not survive the socialization/nationalization of trade as the example of Egypt's neighbour Libya so recently proved with the total demise of the Tripoli *souq* in the 1970s.

Also immature economies are much more favourable to the bazaar than modernized economic systems. The bazaar must stay at the apex of the commercial hierarchy, unchallenged by modern high-tech businesses. In traditional society, the bazaar is an important source of informal lending to both rural and urban enterprises or to individuals. Non-Muslim bazaar merchants were not of course impeded by the taboo within Islam on taking interest on loans made to third parties. In Egypt the Christian and Jewish merchants of the *souq* undertook this important task of funding investment and providing short term credits.

It might be suggested that bazaar economies thrive best where there are, as in Egypt, generally low average incomes, say, of US$1,500 per year or less. In such societies the structure of demand is oriented towards survival, with foodstuffs, traditional clothing and textiles and locally manufactured material objects in demand rather than modern consumer durables. Where there is least heavy direct government involvement in trade and nationalization of trade has been avoided, *souqs* show the strongest continuity.

Closely collating with the matter of the structure of supply and demand, bazaars survive best when they have long-standing local manufacturing industries based within them. The more individual and highly prized the goods manufactured, the more competitive the individual or national bazaars will be. Egypt illustrates the situation rather well with hand crafted gold, silver and settings of precious stones.

It might also be concluded that, economic factors aside, those societies which still have a vibrant bazaar culture, with all its human colour, noise and bustle are far richer than those who have, in the process of 'modernization', lost their traditional central markets.

and petrochemical sectors. Industry was concentrated around Cairo and its outliers such as Helwan. In recent years Egypt has industrialized steadily through a growth of small, private and/or foreign funded plants producing consumer goods, textiles, arms and processed foodstuffs. These factories are often highly efficient. Egypt has still however to diversify effectively into industry. In 1995/96 oil, mining and manufacturing together accounted for 26.9% of the value of national output and employed 13% of the work force. The country was a long way from achieving its

ideal of being the manufacturing centre for the Arab world.

Industrial output 1995/96

	(tonnes)
Cement	17,200,000
Fertilizers	7,354,000
Iron ore	2,430,000
Salt	1,900,000
Phosphates	1,225,000*
Sugar	1,131,000
Soap	370,000*
Cotton yarn	275,000

Source: Central Bank of Egypt
Note: * 1992/93

TRENDS IN THE ECONOMY

Economic growth has been erratic, but mainly too low to enable the economy to reach a level of self-sustaining development. The most significant change in fortunes came in 1991 when its US$5.8bn military debt to the USA was written off and a separate debt of US$7bn owed to the Arab oil-exporters was also liquidated in acknowledgement of Egypt's positive role in the Gulf War, thereby removing at a stroke part of the heavy foreign debt burden – US$46bn – on the economy. Egypt continues to borrow overseas and the trend towards external dependence has not been fully reversed.

Economic structure 1995/96

	(%)
Trade, Finance, Insurance	24.4
Industry, Mining	26.9
Agriculture	16.0
Electricity etc	2.1
Transport, Communications	10.5
Construction	5.1
Total incl others	100.0

Source: Central Bank of Egypt

Recent policies, enforced by the IMF, are designed to rid the state of its ownership of economic assets, to expand the private sector and remove distortions in the economy arising from subsidies and restrictive practices. Domestic food production has steadily risen in response to the gradual removal of heavy state control on crops. Agricultural production grew by 2.5% in 1994 despite unusual weather patterns affecting harvests. Tourism recovered after the Gulf War to a record US$2.8bn in 1995 (3.2 million visitors) but the activities of militant Islamist groups have discouraged many visitors. The use of the Suez Canal continued to increase with revenues standing at US$1.9bn in 1994. Moderately good flows of water in the upper Nile catchment area improved the reserves in Lake Nasser and offer some certainty for agricultural output.

THE NEW INTERNATIONAL CONTEXT FOR EGYPT

The political economy of Egypt and that of the Middle East as a whole is in course of rapid adjustment to the effects of the implementation of the Middle East Peace Process and the realities of the situation following the demise of the USSR. The two elements are, of course, closely related. A third influence is at work for Egypt in particular – the new inclination of the country towards the Mediterranean Basin and the EU.

The removal of many barriers between the Arab states and Israel, signified in the renewal of diplomatic relations and the Jordan-Israel peace agreement indicates that, whereas some frictions will remain, the over-riding trend in the area is towards reconciliation and the beginning of a new era. The openings for Egypt in the new market zone of the Eastern Mediterranean comprising Jordan, Israel, Lebanon and (eventually Syria) are considerable, although there will be competition. But for Egypt to be a principal neighbour of an expanding new economic region will represent a welcome change in the country's situation.

In this historic change, all the factors at work contain far more positive than negative components and Egypt finds itself for the first time since WW2 with clear opportunities for both internal and regional economic expansion. Indeed, Egypt, which suffered for its early and far-sighted agreements with Israel at Camp David, has now begun to reap some rewards from its pioneering role in the Sadat era. Egypt is also helped in the political arena by hard-won acceptance as a long-term and valued ally of the USA and the EU.

The outlook towards the Mediterranean is very recent but in truth the outcome of a well established and steady trend of Egypt to look as much westwards as to the Arab heartlands to the east. In North Africa Egypt's aim is to support political stability among its neighbours.

The Bazaar and bargaining

An enduring characteristic of bazaars is their use of pricing through bargaining for every transaction, however large or small. Economists certainly have rather divided views on bargaining. On the one hand it is seen as a function of the efficiency of the bazaar with each business transaction being done with the finest of margins so that prices are very sensitive. Other contrary opinions maintain that, far from being efficient, bazaar transactions maximize profits for the seller per article sold rather than maximizing potential total profit flows. Bazaars thus act as a brake on the expansion of commerce as a whole. They also rely on the ability of the seller to exploit the absence of quality controls, trade mark conventions and other types of consumer protection. In these situations, the seller treats each transaction as an opportunity to cheat the customer. Bazaars are, in this view, places where the buyer must be doubly wary since short measure, counterfeit and adulterated goods are traded for the benefit of the seller is normal. By definition this system can operate only in countries with minimal regulatory régimes and where consumer information is unorganized, mainly therefore, in the third world.

More importantly, the Egyptian government sees that the continuing emergence of the EU as a major market on its immediate doorstep offers great possibilities for trade and development.

On grounds, therefore, of a slightly erratic but certain advance of the Middle East Peace Process, an end to great power (cold war) rivalry in the region, and the construction of an economic axis into Europe and the Mediterranean, the international and regional strategic structures within which Egypt has newly begun to operate are politically helpful and economically well timed.

THE REGIONAL BASE – THE EASTERN MEDITERRANEAN

Egypt's regional partners currently involved in the bi-lateral and multilateral peace talks are Jordan, Israel, Syria and, implicitly, any notional Palestine entity. In economic terms and in other dimensions, too, Egypt is in a very strong competitive position vis-à-vis the East Mediterranean area. Egypt, as with other Arab states has, however, a great distance to go to catch up Israel.

To Egypt's advantage, the Eastern Mediterranean area is now showing a markedly improving performance after an extended period of poor economic growth. Jordan's specific difficulties as a result of the outcome of the Iraqi invasion of Kuwait have begun to evaporate and the economic dividend of peace with Israel is already being felt. Lebanon is undergoing a positive rebirth from the ashes of the civil war, while even Syria is experiencing a more rapid rate of economic change than formerly. Most importantly, Israel meanwhile is growing expansively in the high income group affiliated to OECD. It attracts considerable foreign investment and offers a local source of financial expertise. The hope is that the now unrestrained economic multiplier effect will spread from Israel to the other local states, including Egypt, to give some prospect for raising themselves from the ranks of the Third World. Overall, therefore, the economic prospects for Egypt and its neighbours affected by the Peace Process are looking bright.

THE REGIONAL BASE – NORTH AFRICA

Egypt was a notable participant at the Casablanca Peace Summit in October 1994, encouraged by the incentive of the establishment of a US$10bn regional development bank. The summit examined the ways in which economic gains could be made from the Middle East Peace Process. Of the Arab states the only notable absentees were Syria and its client Lebanon. A bonus for Egypt was the proposal emerging from Casablanca that Egypt should affiliate itself to the existing United Maghreb Association (UMA), which includes Morocco, Tunisia, Algeria and Libya (aggregate GDP worth US$108bn). Egypt's aims here are mainly political and designed to contain the problem of the extreme Islamist parties in the region. There are economic benefits even here for Egypt as a transit state between North Africa and the Eastern Mediterranean as transport/communications systems are reopened. In so far as Morocco is in the vanguard of North African-EU special economic relationship, Egypt might in the long run benefit from an association with Moroccan successes in respect to its links to the EU.

POLITICAL CONSTRAINTS

The dramatic improvement in Egypt's Middle East regional and international opportunities are only partially strengthened by consideration of the domestic scene. Politically, the government has not found a way successfully either to repress or co-opt the extreme Islamist movements which have been responsible for the murder of and injury to foreign tourists and Egyptians over recent years. At the same time, legitimate opposition groups have found it difficult to operate in the political atmosphere of tension and extremism.

This lack of a working arrangement between the government and the opposition gives Egypt's political system an unneeded air of fragility. President Mobarak has responded as a soldier – with violence against violence – to armed political attacks on his régime. The attack on the state by the Islamists is serious and likely to be protracted unless terminated by a political solution – unlikely at the present. Despite the damage done by the extreme Islamic fundamentalist groups, not least to the important tourist sector, the country carries a comparatively modest risk factor. This is in acknowledgement that although as assassination of individuals within the government is always possible, and the president himself is a prime target of dissidents, the régime as a whole is very solidly based. The army, the security services, most of the bureaucracy, the private sector and a large proportion of the population firmly support the political status quo. While these props remain to support the régime, its troubles will be well advertised abroad but its domestic stability undamaged.

ECONOMIC DEVELOPMENT – STEADY PROGRESS IS ENVISAGED

Egypt is at the beginning of a second stage of a far-reaching reform of its economy, urged on by the USA. The main planks for the new phase of change are:

• Deregulation of the business environment.
• Privatization of government industrial and commercial holdings.
• Improved efficiency of public institutions.
• Streamlined judicial practices affecting business.
• Provision of more credits to businesses.
• Reform of the educational system to provide appropriate supply of trained labour.
• Establishment of confidence in the long-term business climate.

Other important elements underpinning the economic reform programme are the acquisition of improved technology. The September 1994 US-Egypt partnership for growth agreement was an important step in this process. Egypt's priorities lie in the industrial field, which offers the only realistic area for absorbing available labour and for lifting living standards. The long-term limitation of water supply gives little hope that agriculture can do the same job. Underwriting of the stability of the Egyptian pound is important. The country survived a devaluation crisis in mid-1994 and the Central Bank will be eager to keep the pound steady. There is a need to support an expanded export promotion programme through preferential interest rates and for the development of commercial linkages to the Eastern Mediterranean and European markets for the Egyptian private sector. Some encouragement is wanting to get more foreign investment in Egyptian industry. Vigilance will be required in protecting Egyptian rights to Nile waters and managing the reallocation of water in Egypt from agriculture to industrial and municipal sectors.

Egypt's performance in economic change has been good. Foreign debt has continued to decline and most other key indicators of economic welfare remain unexciting. Optimism on this score is moderated only by the obstruction of reform by vested interests, especially in the bureaucracy, where change comes very slowly. There is political opposition against and apathy/passive resistance to the régime. Non-participation by the population at large is dimming popular enthusiasm for and acceptance of economic reform.

THE OUTLOOK

It is apparent that the Egyptian economy is poised for steady growth in the near future. Rapid growth of GDP at more than 3% per year is feasible but will depend heavily on the effective implementation of the reform programme. This in turn will require Egypt to co-operate with the IMF and the World Bank to ensure that structural changes to the economy are consistent and internationally acceptable by scale and pace affecting:

- Trade liberalization through the elimination of protective tariffs notably the customs' 'users fee'.
- Harmonization of energy prices through removal of subsidies.
- Privatization, which has gone too slowly over too limited a field for the taste of the World Bank.

In the meantime, key indicators of future economic activity rates mainly look encouraging. Egypt's foreign debt is falling and will come down further by approximately £4 billion when an arrangement is finalized under the debt relief plan through the Paris Club. An improved debt position would make Egypt more credit-worthy and relieve strains on the balance of payments where charges of US$1.5bn/year are currently incurred on interest payments alone.

The Government will continue to do a good job in holding down the budget deficit. There is a continuing trend to remove subsidies on products but only slowly and the trend does not necessarily go hand in hand with liberalizing prices for manufacturers, as the pharmaceutical sector found to its cost in 1994. Tax reforms will be pursued, with an emphasis on higher indirect taxation. Inflation is being curbed and should stabilize at some 7% annually.

The government's strong pound policy (£E3.4=US$1) seems likely to persist. In effect, the currency has been successfully 'de-dollarized'. Reserves at the Central Bank will stay high, probably over US$18bn, but these could be rapidly eroded if the pound has to be defended. The Central Bank will remain firmly committed to a comparatively uncontrolled exchange mechanism following the liberalization of controls in the recent past.

Privatization will be continued but not rapidly in the teeth of ministerial lack of conviction and professional obstruction at all levels of the civil service. It is probable that the contentious system of private bidding will increasingly be replaced by public auction of stock. It still has to be proved that privatization can be applied to the many and often languishing state-owned industries nationalized by President Nasser in the 1950s.

Trade liberalization will slowly make progress but will be constrained in scope by the need to protect the large scale and inefficient state industries which cannot survive even slight external competition.

The matter of intellectual property rights will be sensitive for Egypt. The balance of trade in intellectual property rights favours the highly developed states rather than countries like Egypt. Deals affecting high tech ventures, especially in sectors such as pharmaceuticals, are seen as adverse for Egypt where patent fees and royalties have to be paid. However Egypt cannot afford to be excluded from the import of key technology given the strategic emphasis on industrialization within the programme for economic development. In 1994 the Egyptian parliament passed an amendment to the copyright law to give protection to computer software to international (mainly US standards). So far the government has stopped short of introducing a patents law to match or better GATT standards as they are urged by the USA. It is likely that some attempt will be made at least for pharmaceuticals to improve on the 5-year pause/5-year implementation period before application of full protection for foreign patentees.

In the realm of deregulation of the business environment, optimism for rapid future change must be limited. Little has so far been achieved by the government as a result of passive resistance and obstruction throughout the bureaucracy. There are, however, opportunities in the immediate future for a more flexible labour law, which would greatly assist all – local and foreign – businesses.

The outlook for investment is set fair. Although there is a pervasive air of wariness and uncertainty concerning the progress of economic reform and the political stability of the régime, there is enough confidence to give a steady if unspectacular flow of funds. Growth of fixed investment in the next year is expected to grow.

At the heart of the modern economy is the petroleum sector. Despite the levelling off of the oil industry, natural gas production and export seem set for an expansion as new fields come on stream in the Mediterranean coast, Red Sea and Eastern desert zones. Egypt's strength in gas is shown, for example, by the planned export of natural gas to Israel by 1997. Egypt will also continue to gain enormous benefits from employment of its nationals in the Middle Eastern oil industry, worth US$6bn in 1995/96. The country's income from Suez Canal dues, valued at US$1.9bn, will come principally from oil tanker movements.

The overall picture of the economy thus contains a growing range of positive factors, although problems are not wanting:

• The declining natural resource base in hydrocarbons in which Egypt could in the near future become marginally import-dependent for oil.

• The need for higher expenditures on job creation and on the military.

• Defending the currency will mean higher interest rates than the 11%, which might deter new borrowing and investment in productive enterprise. IMF will also not be pleased with a high exchange rate for the Egyptian pound.

• Tourism will remain depressed as a result of the publicity given to terrorism against tourist targets. With one job in ten dependent on tourism this situation will inevitably slow the economy.

• Long-term economic problems will cure only slowly – ie unemployment at 17.5% of workforce and low productivity of employed labour.

• Manufacturers in Egypt will face a greater governmental policy emphasis on environmental protection. A new law is expected and there will be a need for all new projects to undergo environmental impact assessments.

Despite this list of caveats, there is a useful and growing economy to be found in an economically buoyant Egypt. Disposable incomes are at last beginning to rise appreciably in what after all is a large and youthful country. Egypt looks in the year ahead to be more favourably placed for economic growth than several of the larger Middle Eastern oil-exporting economies because of its diversified base.

The opportunities for Egypt to make negotiated inroads into the EU market through attachment to a Mediterranean oriented policy are very considerable and will grow exponentially over time. It is early days yet but it is clear that the EU needs to coopt Egypt if it is to succeed in the political stabilization of its southern flank in the face of the threat of extreme Islamism. The EU too officially now sees North Africa as a natural prolongation of its interests in the Mediterranean.

Beyond the EU, Egypt has another powerful political and economic patron – the USA. Favourable treatment of Egypt by the USA in defence, technology and investment does no harm to Egypt's economic prospects and has the bonus of guaranteeing a steady commitment to reform within the country which might otherwise be very much neglected.

The question of political stability of the State as a context for economic growth has obvious thorny aspects. But they are generally overstated by the media. The régime has its brittle aspects and is less legitimate in a democratic sense than most Egyptian intellectuals would like. Reliance on a single charismatic leader with powers concentrated in his hands is to an extent outdated in a global though not in a Middle Eastern context. But beyond individuals in power, the Egyptian ruling elite and the régime that represents it has as deep a stability now as at any time since 1970. Thus the prospects for steady growth should not be undermined by significant political upheavals in the immediate future.

EGYPT FIGHTS TO DEVELOP A NEW STRUCTURE

Egypt is classified by the International Bank as a poor third world country, in 1997 rating 48th in the bank's league table. Intriguingly, Egypt fails by only a short margin to rank as a 'middle income economy' and leaping this gap is critically important to the Egyptian government as it seeks to accelerate the economy into sustained growth. For this to happen the International Monetary Fund (IMF) estimates that every year the Egyptian economy must grow by 7% in order to outstrip the rate of increase in population numbers and provide the financial sinews for new investment.

In recent years Egypt has lifted its growth rate to some 5% per year, which is a major achievement given the domestic problems of the massacre of tourists at Luxor in November 1997 and the turn down in the Middle Eastern and Asian economies. But, whatever the difficulties, more economic miracles are now needed including:

- greater efficiency within the country's rigid and slow-moving bureaucracy,
- modernization of traditional industry and agriculture which have scarcely been touched by the revolution in management that has affected urban services,
- higher investment by Egyptians and foreigners,
- create 500,000 new jobs every year, and privatize the inefficient state industries.

Additionally, there is a need to mobilize general support for economic change which will only come when political reform is introduced and the deadening hand of the security services is mitigated. And progress in this sphere is imperceptible. Indeed, the dilemma of keeping the country on an even political keel yet releasing the energies of the people into pursuing economic growth has not begun to be solved.

If the country fails in the current effort to prosper, the IMF foresees that Egypt will relapse back to a moribund third world status where another opportunity to break the shackles of mass poverty might be a long time in coming.

Cairo

C AIRO TODAY is the result of many different cities which have been built on top of one another over the centuries and a cosmopolitan population with connections far beyond the Arab world. It is a teeming mega-city with an estimated 13 million people living in a fabric designed for 2 million. Standing at the crossroads of Africa and the Middle East it has dominated the region for centuries.

BASICS (*Pop* 13 million; *Alt* 75m)

HISTORY

Since the Arab conquest in 641 AD most Egyptians have called both the city and the whole country **Misr** (pronounced Masr), which was the ancient Semitic name for Egypt and was also mentioned in the Koran. Having rejected Alexandria as the capital of his Egyptian province, because it was considered a Christian stronghold, the Arabs chose **Fustat** (encampment) in the middle of modern-day Cairo as their administrative and military capital. Consequently Cairo rapidly grew in size and importance and it is thought that the name Misr was used in order to distinguish the new city from the many other towns called Fustat in the Arab world. **Al-Qahira** (the Conqueror), which is the city's official but less commonly used name, is derived from Al-Qahir (Mars) because the planet was in ascendance when the Fatimids started the construction of their new city in 971 AD. **Cairo** was the Latin version of the name which was given to the city in mediaeval times.

Although the city of Cairo is younger than Alexandria the surrounding region has a very ancient and impressive past. **Memphis**, which lies 15 km south of Cairo across the River Nile, was established as the capital in 3100 BC because of its geographical and symbolic position

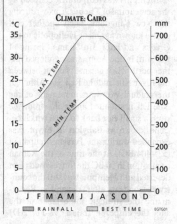

CLIMATE: CAIRO

EGTG01

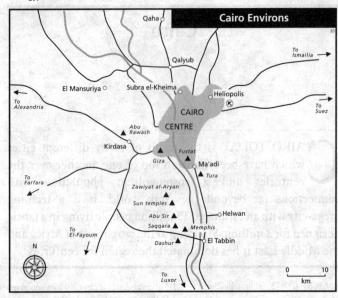

Cairo Environs

Qaha

Qalyub

To Ismailia

El Mansuriya

Subra el-Kheima

Heliopolis

To Alexandria

CAIRO CENTRE

To Suez

Abu Rawash

Kirdasa

Fustat

Ma'adi

Giza

Tura

To Farfara

Zawiyat al-Aryan

Sun temples

Abu Sir

Helwan

Saqqara

Memphis

To El-Fayoum

Dashur

El Tabbin

To Luxor

N

0   10
km

in controlling both Upper and Lower Egypt. It was during this period that the huge necropolis was developed across the river on the west bank first at **Saqqara** and then at the site of modern-day Giza where the largest pyramids were built (see Pyramids, page 160).

Memphis was temporarily eclipsed by the new capital of **Thebes** (Luxor) during the New Kingdom. Then another cult centre known as On, or **Heliopolis** to the Greeks and later Aïn Shams (Spring of the Sun) by the Arabs, was developed further north when a canal was cut between the River Nile and the Red Sea. Although the gradual westward movement of the Nile left it stranded and miles from the river, a small east bank fortress which became known as **Babylon in Egypt**, was expanded during the Persian occupation (525-404 BC). At the time of the Roman occupation in 30 BC the fortress had been deserted and Memphis was still the country's second city after Alexandria. Recognizing the strategic importance of the site, the emperor Trajan (98-117 AD)

rebuilt and reinforced Babylon and a thriving town soon sprung up around its walls. During the subsequent Christian era Memphis was completely abandoned and never rose again, while Babylon became the seat of the bishopric and the west bank village of **Giza** grew into a large town.

When the **Arabs** conquered Egypt in 641 AD, they were given specific instructions by Khalifa Omar in Damascus to establish their administrative capital in Babylon rather than at the larger Alexandria. His general Amr Ibn Al-As built his encampment (or Fustat) in the middle of a deserted triangular plain on the east bank which was bounded by Babylon in the south, Aïn Shams (ancient Heliopolis) to the northeast and Al-Maks (the Customs Point), which was the Arab name for Heliopolis' former port of Tendunyas and is now the site of Ramses Station, to the northwest. The Amr mosque was the first of a number of new and permanent buildings which were erected as the plain was developed and the foundations of modern Cairo were laid.

Under successive Muslim dynasties additions were made to the area as new mini-cities, each to the northeast of the previous one, were built. By the time the Fatimid heretical Shi'a invaders arrived from North Africa in 969 AD, under the military command of Gohar, only the south of the plain had been developed. He therefore chose to build a new walled city (which included the Al-Azhar mosque, palaces pavilions and gardens for the sole use of the Khalifa, his family and retainers), about 1½ km north of the Fustat complex and called it Al-Qahira. Two centuries later in 1168 AD calamity struck the Fustat area when, fearing occupation by the invading Crusaders, the Egyptian wazir Shawar set fire to the city. Over 54 days the fire almost totally destroyed Fustat whose inhabitants fled to Al-Qahira and constructed temporary housing. Three years later the last Fatimid khalifa died and his wazir, the Kurdish-born **Salah al-Din**, assumed

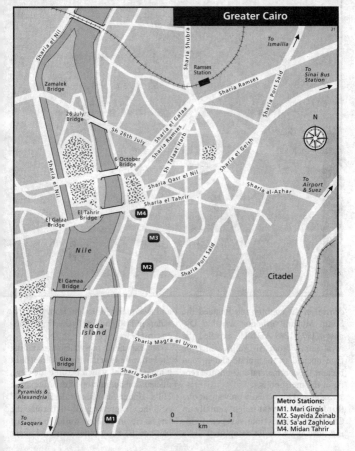

Greater Cairo

Metro Stations:
M1. Mari Girgis
M2. Sayeida Zeinab
M3. Sa'ad Zaghloul
M4. Midan Tahrir

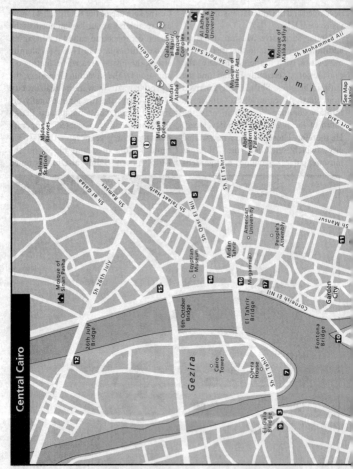

Central Cairo

control of the country and founded the Sunni Muslim orthodox Ayyubid Dynasty (1171-1249 AD). He expelled the royal family from Al-Qahira which he then opened to the public and it soon became the commercial and cultural centre of the metropolis.

Salah al-Din actually only spent one third of his 24-year reign actually in Cairo. Much of his time was spent fighting abroad where he recaptured Syria

and eventually Jerusalem from the Crusaders in 1187 and finally died in Damascus in 1193.

He expanded the walls surrounding the Fatimid city and in the southeast built a huge **Citadel**, which became the city's nucleus, on an outcrop of the Muqattam Hills. Under Mamluke rule (1250-1517 AD) the city grew rapidly to become the largest city in the Arab world. As the east bank of the River Nile continued to silt

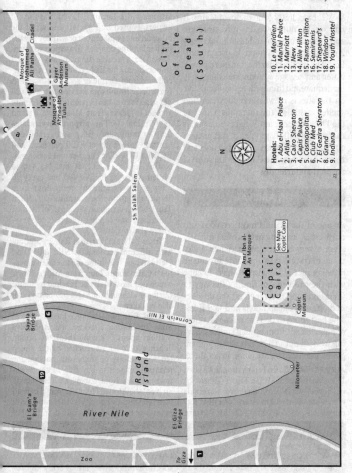

Hotels:
1. *Abu el-Haal Palace*
2. *Atlas*
3. *New Sheraton*
4. *Capis Palace*
5. *Cosmopolitan*
6. *Club Med*
7. *El Gezira Sheraton*
8. *Grand*
9. *Indiana*
10. *Le Meridien*
11. *Manial Palace*
12. *Marriott*
13. *Mena*
14. *Nile Hilton*
15. *Ramses Hilton*
16. *Semiramis*
17. *Shepeard's*
18. *Windsor*
19. *Youth Hostel*

up, the newly elevated areas provided additional space which were developed to house the expanding population.

Under the **Ottomans** (1517-1798 AD) both Cairo and Alexandria were relegated to the position of mere provincial cities with little in the way of public building undertaken in the whole of the 17th and 18th centuries. This changed, however, with the combination of the arrival of the French in 1798 and the coming to power

in 1805 of the Albanian-born Ottoman officer Mohamed Ali. As part of his ambitious plan to drag Egypt into the modern world by introducing the best that Europe had to offer, he embarked on a project which included a huge public building programme in Cairo and turned it into a large modern capital city.

The combination of very rapid population growth and extensive rural-urban migration to the city, particularly since

WW2, has totally overwhelmed Cairo. It has totally outgrown its infrastructure and today a city, intended to house only 2 million people, is home to over 13 million. The result is that the transport, power, water and sewage systems are completely inadequate and hundreds of thousands live on the streets or wherever they can find shelter including the infamous 'Cities of the Dead' cemeteries. What is amazing is that, despite all its problems, this ancient city actually functions as well as it does and that in adversity the Cairenes are so good natured and friendly.

ON ARRIVAL

As one of the world's most crowded and noisy cities, arriving in Cairo can initially seem a very daunting experience. Independent travellers, without the advantage of being met at the airport, have to cope with the problems of finding the way to their hotel and must fend off the unsolicited offers of cheap hotels and taxi rides. The best thing to do is to refuse all offers of help, except from official sources, having worked out in advance where you are going and how you are going to get there.

ACCESS **Air** Cairo International Airport, 15 km northeast of Midan Tahrir (Tahrir Sq) in downtown Cairo, has two terminals which are about 3 km apart. The new Terminal 2 is used by most of the Western airlines while Terminal 1, which is the old airport, is used by Egyptair and all of the other airlines who cannot or will not pay the higher landing charges. **Transport to town**: Taxis are available immediately on exit from customs for E£40 (check current official fare from airline or airport official). A fixed price **limousine service** taxi at E£20 per head for a max of 4 people (check before you get in) leaves from Misr Travel's stand at Terminal 1. The **airport service bus** drops a minimum of 5 passengers at any central Cairo hotel for E£20 per head and E£25 for Giza. The cheaper and easier way, costing less than E£1, is bus No 410 to Midan Ataba or the No 400 bus every 30 mins or No 27 minibus every hour from Terminal 1 to the bus terminal at Midan Tahrir which is right in the centre of the city. From here one can get transport to everywhere else in Cairo.

Train All trains arrive at Ramses Station, with different sections for Nile Valley and Delta tracks. It is at the north end of downtown Cairo about 2 km from Midan Tahrir which can most easily be reached by metro (2 stops) although bus (No 95) or taxi can also be taken.

Road **Bus**: long-distance buses arrive at Sinai Bus Station, also known as Abbassiya Station, about 5 km northeast of Midan Tahrir which can be reached by the cheap No 32 minibus or taxi from outside the terminal (expect to pay E£5 to get downtown). Buses from Luxor and Hurghada arrive at the Ahmed Helmi Terminal behind Ramses Station. The city's other two arrival points are the Koulali Terminal, in front of

Gentle persuasion

🐾 Some of the owners of horses do not have perhaps as much consideration for their animals as European visitors might expect. Some animals are 'a sorry sight'. Something can be done to improve their lot. See first the Box Brooke Hospital for Animals, page 220. As a guest it is not permissible to intrude but gentle persuasion can be used.

Before accepting a ride in a horse-drawn carriage cast your eye over the horse. You don't need to be a vet to recognize an underfed animal, a limp or an untreated open sore. Refuse to use the carriage and quietly explain your reason to your guide or the driver. Free treatment is available. Does the driver know? As tourism pays the driver's wages the opinion of a tourist may have some sway. If tourists only rode in carriages pulled by healthy horses, the message would be loud and clear.

If you want to take this further the driver's licence number is displayed at the back of the carriage. This can be given to the Brooke Hospital and they can try to get treatment for the animal.

the Ramses Station, for buses from the Suez Canal Zone and the Delta while the Al-Azhar Terminal for those from the Western Desert, is about 450m east of Midan Ataba which is only one stop from both Midan Tahrir and Ramses Station.

PLACES OF INTEREST

It certainly makes sense, if time permits, to visit the major sights of this area in chronological order. Therefore, rather than rushing to the large and exhausting Egyptian Museum, start outside the city at the pyramids and trace their development from the earliest in Saqqara to the splendours of Giza (see separate section **The Pyramids**, page 160). In Cairo city there are few remains from the pre-Christian era other than in the Egyptian Museum, so the logical sequence of visits would be – **Coptic Cairo** in the ancient fortress of Babylon-in-Egypt; the mosques, cemeteries and *souqs* of **Islamic Cairo**; and the modern sites and museums of **Contemporary Cairo**.

Sample prices of organized tours:
Half day tour to Egyptian Museum US$45
Half day tour to Pyramids and Sphinx US$53
Half day tour to Memphis and Saqqara US$58
Half day tour to Citadel an, Mosques and Bazaar US$60
Half day tour to Pharonic Village US$52
Half day tour to Islamic Museum and Gayer-Anderson Museum US$41
Sound and Light performance at Pyramids US$35

COPTIC CAIRO

This settlement was constructed by the Persians in about 500 BC to guard the junction of the River Nile and the canal linking it to the Red Sea. During the Christian period the fortified settlement of Babylon in Egypt grew into a large town. It was perhaps named by the fort's homesick building workers from modern-day Iraq or from the name for Gate of Heliopolis (Bab-il-On). Later the Arabs called it Qasr al-Sham'ah (Fortress of the Beacon).

Whatever its origins it is now known, not entirely accurately, as Coptic Cairo.

Copts – The native Christians of Egypt

The Copts take their name from a corruption of the Greek word *aigupioi* for Egyptian. The Copts were concentrated in the region from Girga to Assiut and had a community in old Cairo until recently. Now many have moved to the metropolitan area of Cairo and its suburbs. The number of Christians of all kinds in contemporary Egypt is put officially at 3.5 million but is thought to be much larger (6 million) of which the majority (4.4 million) are of the Coptic Church. There are also some 90,000 members of the Alexandrian rite, affiliated to Rome and quite separate from the Coptic Church proper.

The Coptic language is no longer spoken. It originated from the language spoken in Egypt in the early Christian era, at that time written in Greek characters. Although there were regional variations in the Coptic language, by the 5th century AD they had merged into a form universal throughout Egypt. The language has been in disuse since the 16th century as a working language though it survived in use in religious rituals. Arabic is the language of the Coptic church services. The Coptic Church is very old – for it is believed that St Mark who wrote the gospel preached in Egypt during the time of Emperor Nero and founded a church in Alexandria. He is considered the first

Months in the Coptic Calendar	
All the months have 30 days except Ayam el Nasite which has 5 or 6.	
Kiyahk	Abib
Tuba	Misra
Amshir	Ayam el Nasite
Baramhat	Tut
Baramoda	Baba
Beshens	Hatur
Bauna	

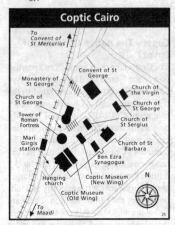

Coptic Cairo

To Convent of St Mercurius

Monastery of St George

Convent of St George

Church of the Virgin

Church of St George

Church of St George

Tower of Roman Fortress

Church of St Sergius

Mari Girgis station

Church of St Barbara

Ben Ezra Synagogue

Hanging church

Coptic Museum (New Wing)

Coptic Museum (Old Wing)

N

To Maadi

25

patriarch. The Coptic Church is close in belief and form to the Armenian, Ethiopian and Syrian Orthodox rites and differs from Rome which believe in the dual nature of Christ and God while the Copts believe in the unity of the two. The Arab invasion of Egypt in the 7th century put the Coptic Church under siege and made it a minority religion in the country. It survived, however, despite some persecution.

The Coptic Church is led by the patriarch of Alexandria and all Egypt from Cairo with 12 bishops. The Church runs a series of Coptic Churches and monasteries throughout the country and has a foundation in Jerusalem. The Copts are heirs to a rich Christian literature going back to the 3rd century AD. Egyptian governments have normally recognized the historical and religious importance of the Coptic community by giving cabinet posts to at least one of its members. The appointment of Boutros Boutros Ghali as Secretary General of the United Nations in January 1992 did much to highlight the strength of the Coptic role in Egypt.

Religious practices in the Coptic church

Baptism of infants takes place when the child is about 6 weeks old, with three immersions in consecrated water in the plunge bath. Confirmation takes place at the same time. Men and women are segregated during church services (to left and right) and while men must remove their shoes before moving through the screen from the nave to the altar women are forbidden to enter that part of the church.

The most important celebration in the church's calendar is Holy Week, culminating with the Resurrection on Easter Day. This is preceded by a fasting time of 55 days during which no animal products may be eaten, nor wine or coffee drunk. Like the Muslims no food or drink is permitted between sunrise and sunset (without special dispensation). Holy Week is a time of special prayers beginning with a mass on Palm Sunday, after which family graves are visited and decorated with palm fronds and flowers, as are house doors and rooms where visitors are entertained. These very cleverly crafted decorations of palm fronds are offered for sale in Coptic Cairo. On Good Friday altars are draped with black and many candle-light processions take place at dawn – commemorating the entry of Jesus into Jerusalem. Easter Sunday is a day of celebration, a time for special food, new clothes, visiting relations but also of giving to the less fortunate. As in other Christian communities coloured hardboiled eggs and chocolate eggs are consumed.

Christmas is preceded by 43 days of fasting (see above), ending on 6 January (Christmas Eve) with a midnight service and a celebratory meal. Christmas Day, after church, is a time for visiting relations and friends. Other times of fasting occur during the year.

ACCESS   Coptic Cairo is located on the east bank of the River Nile about 5 km south of Midan Tahrir opposite the southern tip of Roda Island to which it was connected by a pontoon bridge. From Midan Tahrir there are taxis and buses (Nos 134 and 814) and the metro (a better option) to **Mari Girgis** (St George), four stops in the Helwan direction. The churches are open 0900-1800, 1200-1800 on Sunday. Some charge may be made to visitors.

Leaving the station, one is confronted by two circular Roman towers which comprised the west gate of the fortress built on what was at that time the east bank of the Nile and on foundations now smothered beneath 10m of Nile silt and rubble. Much of the original fortress was demolished as part of extensive alterations and today only its towers and gates have survived. The new **Church of St George**, built in 1904 and the only circular church in Egypt, is actually on top of the north tower and is part of the **Monastery of St George**, which is the seat of the Greek Orthodox Patriarchate of Alexandria, with the **Convent of St George**, the **Church of the Virgin** and the remains of the original fire-damaged **Church of St George** to the northeast.

To the south of the Roman towers is the Church of the Virgin (Coptic masses held on Friday 0800-1100 and Sunday 0700-1000), better known as the **Hanging Church** (Al-Mu'allaqah or 'The Suspended') because it stands on top of the three stone piers of the semi-flooded Roman **Water Gate** from where the Melkite bishop Cyrus, the last Byzantine viceroy, fled by boat as the Muslim army arrived. The gate below the church is reached via a stairway behind the piers, by buying a ticket at the Coptic Museum.

The original church built in the 4th century was demolished in 840 AD by Ali Ibn Yahya who was the Armenian Governor. It was rebuilt in 977 AD and modified several times, most recently in 1775. The church is approached though a wonderful narrow courtyard from which steps lead, via a 19th century vestibule, to the church's entrance. In the vestibule is a more modern approach – the sale of videotapes and religious artefacts. It is divided into a wide nave and two narrow side aisles by two rows of columns with Corinthian capitals. Look out for the odd black basalt capital. The vaulted roof is of timber. There are three supporting columns in the centre of the nave and a marble pulpit supported by 12 delicate

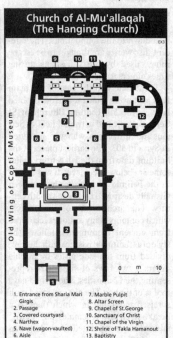

Church of Al-Mu'allaqah (The Hanging Church)

EX3

1. Entrance from Sharia Mari Girgis
2. Passage
3. Covered courtyard
4. Narthex
5. Nave (wagon-vaulted)
6. Aisle
7. Marble Pulpit
8. Altar Screen
9. Chapel of St.George
10. Sanctuary of Christ
11. Chapel of the Virgin
12. Shrine of Takla Hamanout
13. Baptistry

columns – each representing an apostle. On examination each pair of columns is identical but no two pairs are the same. A very fine piece of work. The 13th century *iconostasis* (wooden screen supporting icons), which separates the congregation from the three *haikals* (altar areas) behind the marble pulpit is an incredible feat of fine woodwork and appears virtually transparent. The central icon depicts Christ on the throne, with the Virgin Mary, Archangel Gabriel and St Peter to the right and John the Baptist, Archangel Michael and St Paul to the left. To the right of the altar is a room which overlooks one of the towers. It contains the shrine of Takla Hamanout, an Ethiopian saint, and a small room with a font. The screen dividing this room from the main church is a very delicate woodwork – the mother of pearl inlay is enhanced by holding a candle or torch behind. To its left and right, two secret passageways lead down to the foundations. These recent discoveries are thought to be escape routes used by the Christians during times of persecution.

Immediately to the east of the main Roman towers, down a narrow cobbled lane, is the 5th century **Church of St Sergius**, dedicated to two soldiers, St Sergius and St Bacchus, who were martyred in Syria in 303. The earliest pieces of the building date from the 5th century. It lies some 3m below street level. It was rebuilt in the Fatimid period after having been virtually destroyed by fire in the 8th century. The architecture of the church, which contains many antiques recovered from ancient monuments, follows the style of a traditional basilica with the nave divided from the side aisles by marble pillars – two rows of six pillars representing the 12 apostles. The arched nave roof is of timber. The altar is edged with a raised moulding in which there is a break. It closely resembles an offering table. This is separated from the main part of the church by a 13th century wooden sanctuary screen which has fine encrustations and beautiful ornamentation. The marble pulpit is supported by ten columns. Pieces of an earlier pulpit, rosewood with inlays of ivory and ebony, is on show in the nearby museum. The crosses in the upper section are ivory. The icons depict the twelve apostles. The partially flooded crypt, to the left of the sanctuary, is the only remaining vestige of the original church, is intriguing because it is claimed that the Holy Family sought refuge there during their flight to Egypt and the places where they sat are still visible. A special mass is held annually on 1 June to commemorate the Flight into Egypt of the Holy Family. There are two smaller chapels, one on either side of the altar.

Just behind the church of St Sergius is the very similar 11th century **Church of St Barbara** standing on the site of an older church dedicated to St Cyrus and St John

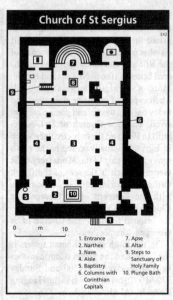

Church of St Sergius

EX2

0   m   10

1. Entrance
2. Narthex
3. Nave
4. Aisle
5. Baptistry
6. Columns with Corinthian Capitals
7. Apse
8. Altar
9. Steps to Sanctuary of Holy Family
10. Plunge Bath

in 684 AD which was destroyed during an Arab assault. It is told that when some Christians from Damanhur, including Cyrus and John confessed to their faith they were shot with arrows, burned in a furnace, tied to a horse's tail and dragged through the streets and survived – to be beheaded. The remains of these two martyrs are in the side chapel approached from the left of the altar. The 3rd century's St Barbara's relics were brought to the church and are now contained in a lovely little chapel to the left of the altar. The 13th century iconostasis (screen) is another fine example of encrustation work with some very fine inlaid carved ivory. The original screen is in the nearby museum and the wooden panel linking the columns is an equally characteristic example of delicate Coptic architecture. The domed apse behind the main altar has seven steps which are decorated with bands of marble – red, black and white. The baptistry in the chapel dedicated to Cyrus and John has a polygonal font. This church is now dedicated to St Barbara, a young woman from Nicomedia in Asia Minor. In version one she tried to convert her father to Christianity and he killed her. In version two she was denounced by her family when she decided to become a nun – then tortured and killed by the Romans.

Just to the south of the Church of St Barbara is the **Ben Ezra Synagogue** in the former 6th century Church of St Michael the Archangel, which itself had been built on the site of a synagogue destroyed by the Romans. Hence, this is the oldest surviving synagogue in Egypt. In the 12th century it was sold back to the Jews by the Copts in order to raise funds to pay taxes being raised to finance the Ibn Tulun mosque. The synagogue is built in the basilica style with three naves and an altar hidden by doors, which are wonderfully worked and encrusted with ivory. When the synagogue was extensively repaired in the 19th century, medieval Hebrew manuscripts, known collectively as the **Geniza documents** and providing details of the history of the 11th-16th centuries, were discovered. Women sit outside the **Church of the Virgin** selling bunches of the herb basil as this church is also known as 'the container of basil'.

Church of St Barbara

1. Entrance	7. Chapels of	10. Domed Apse
2. Narthex	St Cyrus &	11. Baptistry
3. Nave	St John	
4. Pulpit	8. Aisle	
5. Altar Screen	9. Shrine to	
6. Altar	St Barbara	

The Convent of St George St George was a Roman soldier and one of the many Christians who fell foul of Diocletian. His body was brought to Egypt in the 12th century. One remarkable feature of the central room is the wooden doors which lead to the shrine. They are 6m high. The convent is closed to visitors except for the chaplet which has some interesting icons. The custodians here are very keen to display a chain which, it is claimed, was used to secure early martyrs.

The **Convent dedicated to St Mercurius** is situated just north of this central Coptic area. After a vision in which he was presented with a luminous sword (hence his Arabic name Abu Seifein – Mr Two Swords), with which he was to fight for the cause of Christianity, he was persecuted and killed for his faith. Relics are said to be here in the convent and also in the adjacent church. The convent has its origins in the 6th century but has gone through many stages of rebuilding especially in the 10th century. The **Church of St Mercurius** is actually a church and four large chapels, that on the ground floor dedicated to St Jacob (containing the font used for adult baptism) and those upstairs dedicated to St George, John the Baptist and the Children killed by Herod.

The church contains a plunge bath in the narthex, many recycled marble columns in the nave, some/all of which once decorated with religious illustrations and a very attractive dome-shaped wooden canopy dating back to the 10th century over the altar. One side chapel is dedicated to Angel Raphael and contains a baptistry with a shallow font, the other is dedicated to the Virgin Mary. A flight of stairs near the north aisle leads up to a small unlit crypt, the abode of St Barsum (known as Barsum the Naked) for 20 years of his life.

In the **Church of St Shenuda**, adjacent to the church of St Mercurius, a central nave is divided from the side aisles by two rows of marble columns, 10 in each row. The screen dividing the altar from the main body of the church is a lovely red

Coptic Museum, Cairo

Stairs to upper floor

Garden — Entrance — To Old Wing

Steps down to museum entrance

Administration offices

New Wing - Ground Floor Rooms
1. Sculptures
2. Burial ground reliefs
3. Masonry monuments
4. Carved masonry
5. Stone reliefs and capitals
6. Monastery objects
7. Graeco-Egyptian sculptures
   from Saqqara (Graeco-Coptic)
8. Reliefs and figures of Biblical scenes
9. Christian and traditional Egyptian paintings

Stairs down

Administration offices

New Wing - First Floor Rooms
10. Mummy case and Graeco-Byzantine tapestries. Manuscripts.
11. Textiles
12. Religious textiles
13. Female ornaments
and toiletries. Icons
14. Metalwork, crucifixes
15. Eagle statue. Roman metalwork
16. Keys, door furniture, surgical instruments
17. Church wall paintings

Library

Route to stairs to upper floor

Entrance at ground floor

Old Wing
1-5. Church wall paintings
6. Funeral objects
7. Wooden panel carvings
8. Carved panels. Portraits
9. Objects fom Saqqara
10. 7th-17th century woodwork objects
11. Patriarchal furniture
12. Monastery doors
13. Pottery/ceramics
14. Pottery
15. Glass objects

cedarwood. There are seven icons in the screen, the central one shows the Virgin Mary and the others each have pictures of two apostles. Shenuda is associated with the Red and White monasteries (see page 187).

Beside the Hanging Church is the **Coptic Museum**, the other main tourist attraction in Coptic Cairo. It is closed on Sunday but open Saturday-Thursday 0900-1700, Friday 0900-1100 and 1300-1600, but the old wing when it can be visited closes 30 mins earlier. Entry for all the Coptic sites here is E£16 (students E£8), cameras E£10 and E£100 for video cameras. The museum is regarded as among Egypt's principal display of antiquities and houses a fine collection of mainly Coptic treasures. It was founded by a rich and influential Copt, Morcos Simaika, with the support of the royal court. The collection began in 1908 as a means of preserving Coptic artefacts and Egypt's Christian heritage against the acquisitive activities of local and foreign collectors. From 1931 the museum has been managed by the Egyptian Government. There was an expansion programme in 1947 which enabled the collection to include a number of small but very valuable private holdings of objects and items from Coptic churches throughout Egypt and much of the Coptic collection of the Cairo Museum was transferred here too. The enclosed garden is neatly laid out with benches for a well earned rest. Here many large pieces of old stonework have been incorporated into the garden design. There is also a small café.

The Coptic Museum gives an excellent insight into the evolution of Christian and to some extent secular art and architecture in Egypt in the period 300-1800 AD and shows some of the interchange of ideas and forms with the larger Islamic community. The displays are arranged thematically, with the Old Wing of the museum holding glass, ceramics and masonry and the New Wing showing manuscripts, metalwork and textiles. Begin in the ground floor of the New Wing. Leave the museum from the ground floor of the New Wing through the garden via the steps that lead down to the Water Gate.

The most convenient way of getting the best from the displays is to circulate round each main room in a clockwise direction. Key items to look out for on the ground floor of the New Wing are: **Room 2** some early Christian reliefs which give strength to the suggestion that the Christian cross developed from the Pharaoic *ankh*; **Room 3** the main semi-dome of the 6th century Bawit Monastery south of Dairut which shows a wonderful painting of Christ enthroned with four mythological creatures of the Apocalypse; **Room 4** the classical depiction of the sacred eagle with wings spread out and the figure of a saint above and two cuddly children, naked, with lovely curly hair carrying a cross encircled with a garland; **Room 6** in which all the artefacts come from the 5th century monastery of St Jeremias in Saqqara. Huge columns march the length of the hall with lotus leaves, vines, palm fronds and acanthus leaves as decoration. A 6th century stone pulpit (the earliest recorded), and a perfectly preserved and fresh painted niche of Christ floating above a sitting Virgin Mary holding an infant; **Room 8** dominated by biblical themes in which all the figures face forwards and have somewhat enlarged heads; **Room 9** the 11th century Fayoumi painting of Adam and Eve in the Garden of Eden is well executed and a good Coptic example of biblical stories told in pictures. Upstairs in **Room 10** is a cabinet displaying what is claimed to be the oldest surviving book in the world – 1,600 years old. It is a small wooden covered book containing 500 handwritten pages of the Psalms of David and here also there is a fine mummy case, painted in full colour of a robed inmate, who was not necessarily a Christian.

Upstairs in **Room 11** there are some exquisite Coptic funeral robes carrying traditional symbols such as the sign of the fish; **Room 12** look for the copes and other priests' garments, mainly 18th century, with clever silk embroidery; **Room 13** displays a feast of delicate toiletry objects, including illustrations of women dressed for high days; **Room 14** has ecclesiastic paraphernalia, some, like the marvellous set of crucifixes, not to be missed; **Room 15** contains a figure of a Roman eagle from the Babylon site; **Room 16** some heavy bolts and keys off monastery doors, musical instruments and at one side a fascinating collection of surgical instruments specifically for childbirth; also a fine collection of early Christian wall paintings from Nubia – the faces being rounder and the eyes larger than in the Egyptian illustrations.

In the Old Building, currently closed for renovation, there are rewarding sights. The ceiling carving throughout this section are from Coptic houses in Old Cairo and have been incorporated into the building along with panels and tiles. They make a magnificent background to the exhibits. Also look for the very varied and ornate woodwork, heavy work being executed in acacia and palm and finer work in imported cedar, pine and walnut. Ebony too was very popular. **Room 1** has the original Fatimid pine altar dome from the Church of St Sergius (see page 86) while **Room 5** has the sanctuary screen from the Church of St Barbara (see page 86). The wood used is sycamore and the panels are carved with scenes from the bible. **Room 8** has painted biblical scenes too, panels with apostles and saints as well as a very wide range of animals and birds. The pottery in **Room 13** is arranged according to decoration and size. There is a very interesting range of decorative symbols in this pottery. Small pots were for make-up. Flat flasks were carried by pilgrims and larger more finely decorated storage pots came from monasteries.

There are more than 100 Coptic Orthodox churches in Cairo but the special pride is the new (1965) Coptic Orthodox

Find your way around the Mosque

✍ The mosque serves as a centre for congregational worship in Islam. The word *mosque* implies a place of prostration and this is borne out in the plan of every mosque. The architecture of mosques, like that of traditional Christian churches, was designed to induce quiet and contemplation, above the noise and bustle of everyday life – to induce a subjection of the individual to God *Allah*.

Most important is prayer and the *mihrab* is the niche in the mosque wall (known as the *qibla* wall) which indicates the direction of Mecca and hence the direction in which to pray. The main prayer hall is called the *sahn*. The *sahn* can

Medersa of Sultan Barquq (Simplified plan)

be a simple square, though more often it has (usually four) arcaded porticoes the longest and most decorated of which is the sanctuary or *liwan*. In the main Friday mosques the porticoes can be elaborate and reminiscent of transepts in a church. A pulpit, *minbar*, is sited to the right of the *mihrab* and opposite the lectern from which readings are made from the Koran. In larger mosques there can be a screen, *mashrabiyya*, normally made as a wooden grill, in the sanctuary to separate the officiating *imam* from the congregation.

An outer courtyard or *ziyada* is generally found or a recess with flowing water or water jugs where people gather and perform their ritual ablutions before prayer. In the teaching mosques the *liwan* or specially created cloisters or side rooms served as classrooms or hospital sick-rooms.

Thus, while all mosques vary in detail of lay-out and decoration, the basic floor plan remains more or less uniform.

Muslims pay particular attention to the solemn sanctity of the mosque. Behaviour is muted and decorous at all times, particularly during services, of which the main ones are Friday Prayers. Women are not forbidden from taking part in public services at the mosque but very rarely do so.

Egyptian mosques show great variety of decoration and some differences in ground plan. Even to the untutored eye, five principal styles of mosque can be seen in most Egyptian cities – Fatimid (967-1171), Ayyubid (1171-1250), Mamluk (1250-1516), Ottoman (1516-1905) and modern (1905-present).

The Fatimids left as their monument the great Mosque of Al-Azhar in Cairo (see page 95), square in plan with a roofed and cloistered sanctuary borne on twin pillared colonnades. There were two side *liwans*.

After the overthrow of the Fatimids by Salah al-Din a new mosque style grew up in Egypt, reflecting the mosque as a major public building by scale and ornamentation. A good example of this style is the Medersa of Sultan al-Salih Ayyub (see page 98). Unlike all previous mosques, it provided separate teaching rooms for the four great schools of Orthodox Islam in a pair of mosques, each with a double *liwan*. Look out for the windows at ground level and for the discordance between the alignment of the adjacent street and the *liwans*, resulting from the need to set the *liwans* facing Mecca.

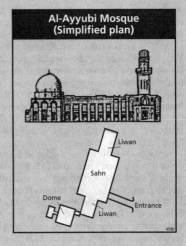

The legacy of the Mamluks includes the Mosque of Sultan Hassan (see page 115), built in 1356-60. It is an Islamic building on a giant scale with the tallest minaret in Cairo. Architecturally, it is also distinct for its simplicity and for the separate *liwans*, entrances to which are all offset from the magnificent *sahn*.

The Ottomans ruled Egypt for several centuries during which time it experienced a flood of new architectural ideas such as the use of light as a motif, and the deployment of slender pillars, arches and minarets of Turkish origin. The Mosque of Suleyman Pasha dated to 1528 was the first Ottoman mosque to be built in Cairo (see page 119) exhibiting these features, that of Mohammed Ali Pasha (see page 119), with its tall octagonal minaret and fine Ottoman dome being one of the last.

The modern period is represented by the Al-Rifai mosque (see page 116), completed in 1911, which blends Mamluk with contemporary architecture and by the standard village mosque, small, block built, neat but uninspired.

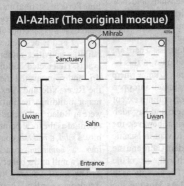

No peace for the holy either

In the grim, barren desolation of the Moqattam hills to the south of Cairo were a number of abandoned windmills. These had been used by the British army during WW1 to produce flour supplies and were no longer required.

In 1936 a monk called Mina obtained one to use as a place of retreat and prayer. With the door replaced and the roof made safe he constructed a small living area downstairs and an even smaller chapel above. His intention to devote himself to peaceful contemplation proved impossible. The monk in the windmill was good news to those needing a release from their mental and physical problems. The number of visitors increased and set times were allocated for services each day.

The area was declared unsafe during WW2 and Mina moved, with some reluctance, to the neighbouring churches of Archangel Michael and St Mary in Old Cairo just 3 km distance.

After the hostilities Mina purchased the land adjacent to the former windmill site and built a church dedicated to St Mina the martyr. To this was added a large monastic complex complete with accommodation where he stayed until he was elected patriarch in 1971 and became Pope Shenuda III.

Whereas the monasteries in Egypt had suffered from serious decline the influence of a Pope who had spent so many years in retreat caused a revival of interest in monasticism among the Coptic community. Buildings have been restored, visitors welcomed and the number of monks has increased.

Cathedral dedicated to St Mark. This is just off Sharia Ramses. This can seat 5,000 worshippers, houses the patriachal library and accommodates the patriarch Pope Shenuda III.

ISLAMIC CAIRO

As already noted in the history of Cairo (see page 79), the city was initially developed as a series of extensions and new walled mini-cities which radiated in a northeast direction from the original encampment of Fustat outside the walls of the Babylon in Egypt fortress. There are literally hundreds of mosques in this Islamic city and it is difficult to know where to begin. All the mosques in Cairo are open to the public outside prayer times except those of Sayyidah Hussein and Sayyidah Nafisah. Broadly speaking, however, the most important places to visit in Islamic Cairo are away from modern Cairo and the River Nile in a broad belt to the east of the main Sharia Port Said. The exceptions to this are the **Amr Ibn al-As Mosque**, the oldest mosque in the country which is just

near Babylon in Egypt (visit this while seeing Coptic Cairo) and the **Mosque of Sinan Pasha** nearer the River Nile and further north. The rest of Islamic Cairo can be visited by following a series of routes most beginning from the **Al-Azhar Mosque**.

The **Mosque of Sinan Pasha (1571)** is located in Bulaq (see map, page 80).

The Albanian-born Sinan Pasha was recruited for service as a boy at the Sublime Porte in Istanbul and rose to become Sulayman the Magnificent's chief cupbearer. He was governor of Cairo between 1571-72 and is best remembered for his building activities rather than political events. He erected buildings in Alexandria and re-excavated the canal between the River Nile and Alexandria but the major buildings he initiated in Egypt were at Bulaq and included the mosque, essential as the focal point of the community, a *sabil*, a *maktab*, commercial buildings, a *hammam*, residential houses, shops, a mill and a bakery.

The small, square Ottoman mosque stands in a garden. There are entrances into three sides of the mosque into the large central domed chamber which is surrounded on three sides by a colonnade with shallow brick domes. The decorative S-shaped curved windows – 16 in the dome and eight in the outer area – provide, together with the distinctive marble *mihrab*, the only colour. The *dikka* is above the northwest entrance, a gallery running round the brick interior of the dome is reached from the entrance passage while the minaret and ablution area are to the south.

While most of the Sinan Pasha complex has long since disappeared the adjacent public bath, men only, is still in operation.

The original **Mosque of Amr Ibn al-As (Gama Amr)**, 500m north of Mari Girgis metro station, was built in 642 AD by Amr Ibn el-As, commander of the Arab army which captured Egypt in that year. Built near both Babylon in Egypt and the Arabs' encampment (Fustat) it is the oldest mosque in Egypt and one of the oldest in the entire Islamic world. Because of the continual enlargements, which began in

673 AD only 10 years after Amr's death aged 93 and included major restoration work in the 15th and 18th centuries and the most recent work in the 1970s, nothing of the original mud-brick 30m by 17m thatched-roof mosque exists. Recently repainted and cleaned, its aspect today is virtually modern. As is often the case in the older mosques the interior includes many pillars taken from the ancient Egyptian monuments. As a result the whole mosque is a hybrid with parts of the fabric dating from before the conquest of Egypt until the 19th century alterations. In the north corner under the dome and surrounded by a bronze screen, on the site of Amr's house in Fustat, is the tomb of his son Abdullah who was born when Amr was only 13, became a Muslim before him and was a close companion of the Prophet.

SUGGESTED ROUTES (see map, page 94).

1. North via the concentration of buildings in the **Qalaoun/Al-Nasir/Barquq** complex, to the **Al-Hakim Mosque** at the north gates of the old city.

2a. South to the **Al-Muayyad Mosque** which stands at the **Bab el-Zoueila** gate at

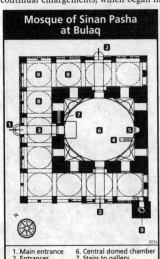

Mosque of Sinan Pasha at Bulaq

1. Main entrance	6. Central domed chamber
2. Entrances	7. Stairs to gallery
3. Passage	8. Shallow domes over
4. Minbar	arcade
5. Marble Mihrab	9. Minaret

EX3a

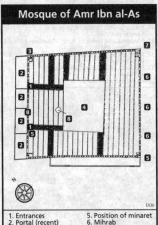

Mosque of Amr Ibn al-As

1. Entrances	5. Position of minaret
2. Portal (recent)	6. Mihrab
3. Tomb of Abdullah	7. Tomb
(son of Amr Ibn al-As)	8. Fountain
4. Sahn	

EX3b

Islamic Cairo

1. Al-Azhar Mosque & University
2. Khan el-Khalili
3. Sayyidah Hussein Mosque
4. Medersa of Sultan al-Ashraf Barsbay
5. Medersa & Mausoleum of Sultan al-Salih Ayyub
6. Medersa of Sultan Al-Mansur Qalaoun al-Alfi
7. Medersa of Sultan Al-Nasir Mohamed
8. Medersa & Tomb of Sultan Barquq
9. House of Uthman Kathuda
10. Palace of Amir Bashtak
11. Sabil-Kuttab of Abd al-Rahman Kutkhuda
12. Mosque of al-Aqmar
13. Beit al-Sihaymi
14. Mosque & Sabil-Kuttab of Suleyman Agha al-Silahdar
15. Mosque of Al-Hakim
16. North Wall
17. Bab al-Nasr
18. Bab al-Futrah
19. Wikala of Sultan al-Ashraf Qansuh II al-Ghawri
20. Ghuriyya
21. Fakahani Mosque
22. House of Gamal al-Din al-Dhahabi
23. Sabil-Kuttab of Tusan Pasha
24. Hammam as-Sukariyah
25. Bab el-Zouela
26. Mosque of Sultan al-Muayyad Sheikh
27. Hammam of Al-Muayyad
28. Zawiya & Sabil of Sultan al-Nasir Farag
29. Mosque of Vizir al-Salih Tala'i
30. Mosque Gani-bak al-Ashrafi
31. Mosque Qajamas al-Ishaqi
32. Mosque & Tomb of Amir Aslam al-Silahdar
33. Mosque & Tomb of Ahmed al-Mihmandar
34. Mosque of Altunbugha al-Maridani
35. Medersa of Sultan al-Ashraf Sha'ban II
36. Mosque of Amir Aqsunqur
37. Mosque of Sultan Hassan
38. Al-Rifai Mosque
39. Bab al-'Azab
40. Bab al-Gadid
41. Sabil-Kuttab of Sultan Qaitbai
42. Mosque of Qanibai al-Muhammadi
43. Mosque of Amir Shaykhu
44. Khanqah of Amir Shaykhu
45. Sabil-Kuttab of Um Abbas
46. Mosque of Amir Taghri Bardi
47. Mosque of Ahmed Ibn Tulun
48. Beit al-Kridliyah
49. Medersa and Tombs of Salar and Sangar al-Gawli
50. Medersa and Tomb of Amir Khayrbak
51. Mosque of Malika Safiya
52. Medersa and Tomb of Tartar al-Higaziya
53. Medersa of Amir Sayf al-Din Ilgay al-Yusufi
54. Musafirkhana Palace

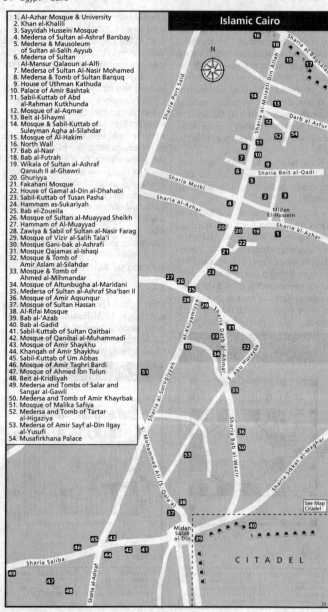

the south edge of the old city and the buildings on Sharia Darb al-Ahmar to the **Sultan Hassan Mosque** and the modern **Al-Rifai Mosque**.

2b. Continuing to the mosques and museums in the imposing **Citadel** and the huge ancient **Ahmed Ibn Tulun Mosque**.

3. To the mosques and tombs in the **City of the Dead** which lies in the 'Northern Cemetery' to the east of Islamic Cairo.

The ancient **Al-Azhar Mosque (1)** and the nearby *souqs* in the **Khan el-Khalili (2)** district are at the centre of modern-day Islamic Cairo. They are located SE of Midan Ataba (reached by taxi or No 66 bus from Midan Tahrir). You can either walk east from Midan Ataba beneath the flyover along Sharia al-Azhar or, better still, along the congested but fascinating Sharia Muski which, once across the tramlines of busy Sharia Port Said, becomes more attractive as you approach Khan el-Khalili.

Although it also refers to a specific street, the **Khan el-Khalili** (open daily except Sunday) is the general name given to this district of Cairo which has a large number of individual *souqs*. The Arab/Islamic system of urban planning has traditionally divided the *souqs* by professions or guilds. While the system is less rigid than formerly there is still a concentration of one particular trade in a particular area. The Khan el-Khalili includes streets which almost exclusively sell gold, silver, copper, perfume, spices, cloth or any one of a number of particular products. Many of the products are manufactured within the *souq*, often in small workshops behind or on top of the shops.

The **Khan el-Khalili** has been the main *souq* in Cairo since 1382 when it was first created around a caravanserai by Amir Jarkas al-Khalil who was the Master of Horse to the first of the Burji Mamluke Sultans, Al-Zahir Barquq (1382-89). The caravanserai attracted many foreign and local traders and expanded rapidly, to become a base for the city's subversive groups and was consequently frequently raided. Much of the area was rebuilt by Sultan Al-Ashraf Qansuh al-Ghawri (1501-17) but it still maintained its role as Cairo's main area for traders and craftsmen. Today the main area of the *souq* is occupied by tourist shops but a few of the streets to the west are more authentic and much more interesting. Here you will find souvenirs including gold, silver, copperware, leather goods, perfume oils, alabaster, boxes, herbs and spices. Many of the shops are closed on both Friday and

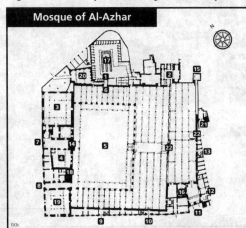

Mosque of Al-Azhar

N

1. Entrance
2. Gawhar Medersa
3. Aqbugha Medersa
4. Taybars Medersa
5. Sahn
6. Bab Qaitbai (Barber's Gate)
7. Bab al-Muzayyinin
8. Bab al-Abbas
9. Bab al-Maghariba
10. Bab al-Shawam
11. Bab al-Saayidal
12. Bab al-Haramayn
13. Bab al-Shurbah
14. Bab and minaret of Qaitbai
15. Tomb of Sitt Nafisa
16. Tomb of Abdel al-Rahman Karkhuda
17. Toilets
18. Minaret of Qahnsuh al-Ghawri
19. Riwaq of Abbas II
20. Riwaq Al-Hanafiyyah
21. Qibla
22. Mihrab

EX3c

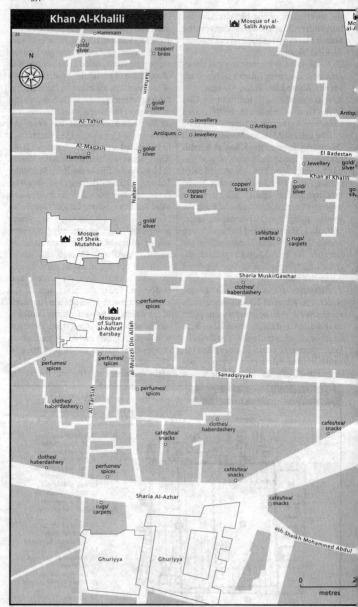

Khan Al-Khalili

N

Hammam

gold/
silver

copper/
brass

Mosque of al-
Salih Ayyub

Mo
al-A

Nahasin

gold/
silver

Jewellery   Antiques

Antiq

Al-Tahus

Antiques   Jewellery

Al-Maqasis

gold/
silver

El Badestan

Hammam

Jewellery   gold/
silver

Khan el Khalili

Nahasin

copper/
brass

copper/
brass   gold/
silver

go
sil

Mosque
of Sheik
Mutahhar

gold/
silver

cafés/tea/
snacks   rugs/
carpets

Sharia Muski/Gawhar

clothes/
haberdashery

Mosque
of Sultan
al-Ashraf
Barsbay

perfumes/
spices

al-Muizzli Din Allah

perfumes/
spices

perfumes/
spices

Sanadqiyyah

perfumes/
spices

cafés/tea/
snacks

Al-Tarbiah

clothes/
haberdashery

clothes/
haberdashery

cafés/tea/
snacks

clothes/
haberdashery

perfumes/
spices

cafés/tea/
snacks

cafés/tea/
snacks

Sharia Al-Azhar

rugs/
carpets

cafés/tea/
snacks

ash-Sheikh Mohammed Abdul

Ghuriyya   Ghuriyya

0   2

metres

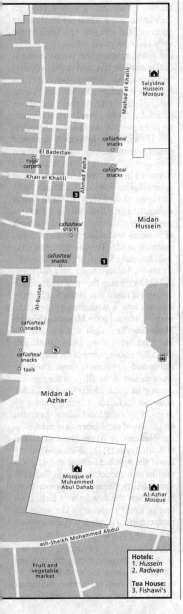

Sunday. **NB** It is essential to bargain because the traders will always start at about double the price they actually expect. It is traditional to respond by offering them about one third of what they originally quoted. This is not so for precious metals which are sold by weight, prices for gold and silver being given daily in the paper. On a bracelet for example a small percentage is added for workmanship, and this is the only thing that is negotiable. Antique jewellery is of course more expensive.

Both Khan el-Khalili's Sharia Muski which is virtually a pedestrian precinct and the more congested Sharia al-Azhar lead east into Midan El-Hussein.

On the southwest of the Midan El-Hussein, an underpass below the busy Sharia al-Azhar leads to the famous and very influential **Al-Azhar Mosque & University (1)** whose leader, known as the Sheikh al-Azhar, is appointed for life and is Egypt's supreme theological authority. It is open Saturday-Thursday 0900-1500, Friday 0900-1100 and 1300-1500, E£12 entry fee plus tip for any guides, no bare legs allowed, shawls provided for women. At present this mosque is undergoing renovation and entry is restricted.

The mosque was built in 970 AD and established as a university in 988 AD which, despite a counter-claim by Fes' Qarawiyin Mosque in Morocco, may make it the world's oldest university. With the exception of the main east *liwan*, however, little remains of the original building because additions and modifications were made by successive rulers, including modern buildings to the north, designed to house the university's administration block.

Initially during the Shi'a Fatimid era (969-1171), the university was used as a means to propagate the Shi'a faith in a predominantly Sunni city, but it fell into disrepair under Salah al-Din and his successor Ayyubids (1171-1250) Sunni Muslim rulers before being reopened by the Bahri Mamlukes (1250-1382) and eventually became a bastion of Sunni orthodoxy.

Later during the rise in Arab nationalism in the late 19th and early 20th centuries, Al-Azhar became a stronghold for independent thinkers. It is no coincidence that in 1956 Nasser made his speech against the Suez invasion in the university.

The entrance to the mosque is through the Barber's Gate (where students traditionally had their hair shaved), which was built in the second half of the 15th century by Qaitbai (1468-96). This opens out on to the 10th century Fatimid *sahn* (courtyard) which is 48m by 38m and is overlooked by three minarets. With the exception of the Mamluke *medressa* (theological schools) surrounding the *sahn*, most of the buildings date back to the Fatimid period. The carpeted east *liwan* is particularly impressive with a great number of ancient alabaster columns. The *mihrab* is strangely placed in the middle of the *liwan*, with no *qibla* wall behind it. An extension of the *liwan* by Sultan Abd el-Rahman in 1751 left the *mihrab* in this unusual position. Take the opportunity to climb one of the five minarets for an excellent view over the surrounding area.

Immediately to the south of Al-Azhar is an area known as **Butneya** once notorious as the base for Cairo's underworld where drugs were openly traded by powerful and locally popular gangsters. After a major crack-down in 1988 most of them left but the area is still home to minor local gangs who tend to prey on shops, restaurants and middle-class Egyptians rather than on tourists who should be perfectly safe.

Route 1: North from Al-Azhar

The area with the greatest concentration of historic buildings in Islamic Cairo lies north from the Al-Azhar complex and the Khan el-Khalili to the north gates of the old city. On the north side of Midan El-Hussein is the **Sayyidah Hussein Mosque (3)**, Cairo's official mosque where President Mubarak and other dignitaries worship on important occasions. This is closed to non-Muslims. This mosque is named after and contains the head of the Prophet Mohamed's grandson Hussein. He was killed at Karbala in 680 AD at the climax of the struggle which led to the early and continuing schism in the Muslim world between the orthodox Sunni (followers of the way) and the Shi'a (party) followers of Ali. Hussein, because of his marriage to Mohamed's daughter Fatima, was the father of the Prophet's only direct descendants, who revere Hussein as a martyr and a popular saint like his sister Zeinab. His mosque is the focus of his annual *moulid*, one of the city's most important festivals which is held over a fortnight climaxing in September, and a number of other religious festivals. Walk back 200m northwest along Sharia Muski to Sharia al-Muizzli Din Allah. **NB** On the southwest corner of the crossroads the **Medersa of Sultan al-Ashraf Barsbay (4)** (1422-37), entrance fee E£6. This liberal and enlightened Mamluke Sultan, originally from the Caucasus, financed his capture of Cyprus in 1426 by turning the spice trade, which in Cairo is based just to the south of the *medersa*, into a state monopoly. At the northwest corner is the **Mosque of Sheikh Mutahhar**. Turn right at the crossroads and head north along Sharia al-Muizzli Din Allah passing some of the many goldsmiths and coppersmith shops. These are concentrated in the alleys to the right including the actual Sharia Khan el-Khalili. Although its façade is largely hidden by shops, at the right hand side of the street, on the site of the former slave market, is the **Medersa & Mausoleum of Sultan al-Salih Ayyub (5)** (1240-49) who was the last of the Ayyubid Sultans and who was the first to introduce the foreign Mamluke slave-soldiers. The *medersa* was special because it was the first built to include all four of Egypt's schools of law while the tomb is the first example where it is placed next to the *medersa* of its founder.

Opposite, with a wonderful unbroken 185m long façade, stands an amazing complex of three *medressa* founded by three of the most influential mediaeval sultans, Qalaoun, Al-Nasir and Barquq.

Herbs and spices

A visit to the spice market (Souq al-Attarin) is highly recommended both for the visual impact and the tremendous aromas. Anything that could possibly be wanted in the way of herbs, spices, henna, dried and crushed flowers and incense are on display, piled high on the ancient pavements in massive burlap bags or secreted away in tin boxes in various drawers inside. Ask if what you want does not appear to be in stock but do not be fobbed off with old merchandise, fresh spices are always available. Prices are extremely low by western standards and shopkeepers are prepared to sell small amounts, weighing out the purchase into a little paper cornet. Saffron is the best buy, far cheaper than at home, but sometimes only the local rather than higher quality Iranian saffron is available. The main street of the spice market runs parallel to Sharia al-Muizzli Din Allah beginning at the Ghuriyya. Here, many of the shops have been in the same family for over 200 years. Some of the owners are also herbalists *etara*, practising traditional medicine and offering cures for everything from bad breath to rheumatism. Cairo's most famous herbalist, however, is Abdul Latif Mahmoud Harraz, 39 Sh Ahmed Maher, T 923754, near Bab el-Khalq. Founded in 1885, the shop attracts a devoted following throughout the Middle East.

The Arabic names for the more common herbs and spices are:

Allspice	*kebab es-seeny*	Ginger	*ginzabeel*
Arabic gum	*mystica*	Horseradish	*figl baladi*
Bay leaf	*warra randa*	Mace	*bisbassa*
Basil	*rihan*	Marjoram	*bardakosh*
Cardamon	*habbahan*	Mint	*naanaa*
Cayenne	*shatta*	Oregano	*zaatar*
Celery salt	*boudra caraffs*	Paprika	*filfil ahmar roumi*
Chervil leaves	*kozbarra*	Peppercorns	*filfil eswed*
Chilli	*filfil ahmar*	Rosemary	*hassa liban*
Cinnamon	*erfa*	Saffron	*zaa'faran*
Cloves	*orumfil*	Sage	*maryameya*
Coriander	*kosbara*	Savory	*stoorya*
Cumin	*kamoon*	Sesame	*semsem*
Dill	*shabat*	Tarragon	*tarkhoun*
Fennel	*shamar*	Tumeric	*korkom*

This section of the street is known as Bayn al-Qasrayn (between two palaces) because of the Fatimid period's magnificent Great Western Palace and Eastern Palace which stood on either side.

The earliest and most impressive *medersa* is the **Qalaoun (6)** complex built by Sultan Al-Mansur Qalaoun al-Alfi (1280-90), entrance fee E£6. Like so many other Mamlukes ('possessed') slave-soldiers he was a Kipchak Turk who used the name Al-Alfi because he was originally bought for the high price of 1,000 (or alf) dinars.

He subsequently diluted the influence of his own Kipchaks amongst the Mamlukes by importing Circassians whom he billeted in the Citadel. These Burgis Mamlukes (*burg* = tower) were rivals to the Bahri Mamlukes (1250-1382) stationed on Roda Island and eventually created their own dynasty (1382-1517). Qalaoun was constantly fighting the Crusaders and eventually died of a fever in 1290 aged 79, on an expedition to recapture Acre.

The complex was built in just over a year in 1284/85 on the site of the Fatimid's

Islamic Monuments – A chronological list

814	Nilometer
827	Mosque of Amr Ibn al-As
876-9	Mosque of Ahmed Ibn Tulun

Fatimid Monuments

970-2	Mosque of Al-Azhar
990-1013	Mosque of Al-Hakim
1087	Bab al-Nasr
1087	Bab al-Futrah
1090	Bab el-Zoueila
1125	Mosque of al-Aqmar
1154	Mosque of Sayyidah Hussein
1160	Mosque of Visir al-Salih Tala'i

Ayyubid Monuments

1176 etc	Citadel
1211	Mausoleum of the Imam al-Shafi'i
1240-49	Medersa and Mausoleum of Sultan al-Salih Ayyub

Mamluk Monuments

1295-6	Medersa and Mausoleum of Sultan al-Nasr Mohamed
1298	Medersa and Mausoleum of Zayn al-Din Yusef
1303	Medersa and Tombs of Sakar and Sangar al-Gawli
1318-35	Mosque of Sultan al-Nasr Mohamed (Citadel)
1324	Mosque and Tomb of Ahmed al-Mihmander
1334-9	Palace of Amir Bashtak
1339-40	Mosque of Altunbugha al-Maridani
1344-5	Mosque and Tomb of Amir Aslam al-Silahdar
1346-7	Mosque of Amir Aqsunqur
1349	Mosque of Amir Shaykhu
1350	House of Uthman Kathuda
1355	Khanqah of Amir Shaykhu
1356-63	Mosque of Sultan Hassan
1360	Mausoleum of Tatar al-Higaziya
1368-9	Mosque of Sultan al-Ashraf Sha'ban II
1373	Medersa and Mosque of Amir Sayf al-Din Ilgay al-Yusufi
1384-6	Medersa of Sultan al-Zahir al-Barquq

Western Palace and includes a *medersa* and mausoleum to the left and right, respectively, of the entrance with a *maristan* down a now closed 10m high corridor to the rear of the two linked buildings.

The 20.5m by 17m *sahn* of the *medersa* has only two *liwans* while the northeast wall has 3 storeys of tunnel-vaulted alcoves which were used as student rooms. Of particular interest is the *qibla liwan* and the *mihrab* arranged into three aisles with a glass mosaic around the *mihrab*.

On the north side of the corridor is the beautiful mausoleum (open 0900-1700) which is a 21m by 23m rectangular room with four pillars and four piers arranged in an octagon below an 11.5m diameter 30m high dome built in 1903 to replace the original wooden dome which was demolished in the 18th century. The rose granite pillars have Corinthian capitals and the ceilings are finely carved. The walls are decorated with beautiful marble and mosaics topped by a frieze. The 7m

1384-9	Medersa and Tomb of Sultan al-Zahir Barquq
1409	Zawiya and Sabil of Sultan al-Nasir Farag
1413	Mosque of Qanibai al-Muhammadi
1415-21	Mosque of Sultan al-Muayyad Sheikh
1420	Hammam al-Muayyad
1423-37	Medersa of Sultan al-Ashraf Barsbay
1426	Mosque of Amir Gani-bak al-Ashrafi
1432	Mausoleum of Sultan al-Ashraf Barsbay
1440	Mosque of Amir Taghri Bardi
1444-53	Mosque of Yehia Zein al- Din
1456	Mausoleum of Barsbay
1472-77	Medersa, Mausoleum and Sabil-Kuttab of Sultan al-Qaibai
1480-1	Mosque of Qajamas al-Ishaqi
1502	Medersa and Mausoleum of Amir Khayrbak
1503-4	Wikala and Mosque of Sultan al-Ashraf Qansuh II al-Ghawri
1501-16	Gates of Khan Khalili
1501-17	Ghuriyya Complex of Sultan al-Ashraf Qansuh II al-Ghawri

Ottoman Monuments

| 1528 | Mosque of Suleyman Pasha |

Ottoman Monuments

1567	Mosque of Sinan Pasha
1610	Mosque of Malika Safiya
1631	Beit al-Kridliyah
1637	House of Gamal al-Din al-Dhahabi
1648	Beit al Sihaymi
1697	Mosque of Ahmed Katkhuda al-Azab
1735	Fakahami Mosque
1744	Sabil-Kuttab of Abd al-Rahman Katkhunda
1820	Sabil-Kuttab of Tusan Pasha
1824	Qasr al-Gawharah
1824-57	Mosque of Mohammed Ali Pasha
1837-39	Mosque and Sabil-Kuttab of Suleyman Agha al-Silahdar
1867	Sabil-Kuttab of Umm Abbas
1869-1911	Mosque of Al-Rifa'i

high horse-shoe shaped *mihrab* is particularly outstanding with columns on either side and covered with rich mosaics and marble. The tomb of Qalaoun and his son Al-Nasir Mohamed is in the middle of the room surrounded by a beautifully sculpted wooden rail.

The *maristan* is now reached via an alley along the southwest wall of the *medersa*, but little remains of the original hospital except for one of the *liwans* and the remnants of a marble fountain.

Since 1910 it has been the site of a modern eye clinic.

To the north is the **Sultan Al-Nasir Mohamed (7)** complex which was started by Sultan Kitbugha in 1295 and finished by Al-Nasir during his second reign in 1304 which is commemorated by over 30 mosques and other public buildings throughout the city. Qalaoun's eldest son Khalil (1290-94), was assassinated in 1294 and his 9-year-old brother Mohamed (1294-95) was elected Sultan. He

Medersa – Education for Islam

The *medersa* in North Africa is a college of higher education in which Islamic teachings lead the syllabus. It was an institution which originated in Persia and developed in the west in the 13th century. The construction of places of advanced learning was a response by orthodox Sunni Islam to the growth of Shi'ite colleges but they soon became important centres in their own right as bastions of orthodox Islamic beliefs. Subjects other than theology were taught at the *medersa* but only in a limited form and in ways that made them adjuncts to Sunni teachings and acceptable to a very conservative religious hierarchy. Unfortunately, therefore, the *medersa* became associated with a rather uninspired and traditional academic routine in which enquiry and new concepts were often excluded. Knowledge and its transmission sadly fell into the hands of the least academic members of the theological establishment. The poor standards of science, politics, arts and ethics associated with the Arab world in the period since the 13th century is put down to the lack of innovation and experiment in the *medersa*, a situation which has only very recently begun to break down in Sunni Islam. It can, however, be argued that formal Islam needed firm basic teachings in the face of rapidly expanding popular Islam and its extravagant sufi beliefs.

The short comings of the *medersa* in creative teaching terms was in part compensated for by the development of the college buildings themselves. The Egyptian style before the beginning of the 10th century were based on norms borrowed from Syria and Iraq but after that time were mainly modelled on a more Mediterranean tradition with use of a high domed roof as in the mosque of al-Guyushi in Cairo, east of Qasr al-Gawhara. The small courtyard is separated from the *sahn* by a vaulted transect. The ancient al-Azhar mosque complex in old Cairo (see page 95) began life as a principal congregational mosque but become a great teaching university for Islam, much added to and altered and thus at the apex of the *medersa* form.

The *medersa* was until quite recently widely used for student accommodation and teaching. Entry is restricted to specific times but visitors are allowed fairly free access to the building. Other fine architectural works can be seen at the Sultan Barquq Medersa in Cairo (see page 103) with its marbled entrance and wonderful four-*liwan* courtyard and the Medersa of Tatar al-Higaziya with its ribbed stone dome (see page 104).

The rise in awareness of Islam among the young signalled by the high tide of Islamism in Egypt has given the *medersa* an added political interest and social vitality in recent years.

was deposed the following year by the Mongol regent Kitbugha (1295-97) who in turn was soon forced into exile. Kitbugha was replaced by Lajin (1297-99) but he was assassinated after a short reign while playing chess. Following this chapter of 'accidents', Mohamed was restored to the throne, but was kept in terrible conditions by his regent until he escaped to Jordan 10 years later. He eventually returned with a large army the following year, executed his enemies, and ruled happily for another 30 years until his death in 1341.

The complex (open 0900-1600) consists of a mosque, *medersa* and tomb. Although restoration work is still in progress it is worth trying to get in to see the *qibla* wall which still has its original decoration and Kufic inscriptions. The *mihrab*, although incomplete, is also interesting because it is one of the last stucco *mihrabs*. Little remains of the mausoleum and parts of the walls have been removed to the Museum of Islamic Art. It was originally built for Al-Nasir but he was buried next door in his father's mausoleum and the two tombs here belong to his mother Bint Suqbay and Anuq, his favourite eldest son who died the year before his own death. The 3-storey minaret is very beautiful with a richly ornamented Andalusian style first storey and the other 2 storeys surmounted with delicate stalactite cornices. The main door is Gothic and was brought back from the Church of St George in Acre during a campaign against the Crusaders.

This is followed to the north by the *medersa* and tomb which make up the **Sultan Barquq (8)**, entrance fee E£6, complex which was built in 1384-86. The marble entrance and the silver-encrusted bronze-plated door are very impressive and lead into a corridor to the *sahn* which has four *liwans* arranged in a cruciform shape. The *qibla liwan*, to the east, is divided into three aisles by four ancient columns which support beautifully carved and painted ceilings. Upstairs

there are cells for the Sufi monks who once inhabited the building. To the north of the *medersa* a door leads to the mausoleum where Sultan Barquq was originally buried before being transferred to the mausoleum specially built by his son Al-Nasir Farag (1399-1405 and 1405-12) in the city's northern cemetery (see below).

Sultan Al-Zahir Barquq (1382-89 and 1390-99) reigned twice and was the founder of the dynasty of Circassian slave-soldiers who became the Burgis Mamlukes rulers of Egypt. He was reportedly an enlightened Sultan, who admired piety and intelligence and surrounded himself with learned scholars, before dying of pneumonia aged 60 in 1399.

Besides the Qalaoun/Al-Nasir/Barquq complex which is on the west side of Sharia al-Muizzli Din Allah there is a number of other interesting, if less important buildings on and near the east side of the street on the route north to the Al-Hakim mosque. This area, which is heart of Islamic Cairo, is definitely worth exploring for a full day.

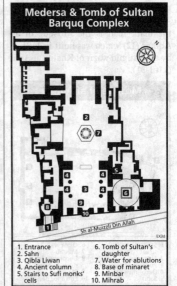

Medersa & Tomb of Sultan Barquq Complex

1. Entrance
2. Sahn
3. Qibla Liwan
4. Ancient column
5. Stairs to Sufi monks' cells
6. Tomb of Sultan's daughter
7. Water for ablutions
8. Base of minaret
9. Minbar
10. Mihrab

Sh al-Muizzli Din Allah

EX3d

Directly opposite the Qalaoun complex is Sharia Beit al-Qadi and 40m down on the left hand side is the modern looking house No 19 which is marked with a green plaque where visitors should knock to be shown around in return for a little *baksheesh*. This is the remains of a palace built in 1350 but better known as the **House of Uthman Kathuda (9)** who restored it during the 18th century.

Further north opposite Barquq's complex are the beautiful if neglected remains of the 5-storey **Palace of Amir Bashtak (10)** (Al-Nasir's son-in-law) built in 1334-39, entrance fee E£6. The warden is usually to be found at the nearby **Sabil-Kuttab of Abd al-Rahman Kutkhunda (11)**. There used to be many of the these Ottoman-influenced *sabil-kuttab*, which combine a water supply for the public at street level and a Koranic school in the building above, throughout Cairo. This example, built in 1744 by a powerful amir seeking absolution for his former sins, stands on a triangular piece of land where two roads meet.

About 75m further north on the right up the main road is the **Mosque of al-Aqmar (12)** which was built in 1121-25 by the Fatimid wazir of Khalifa al-Amir (1101-31).

Mosque of al-Aqmar

N

EX3e

1. Stairs down from street
2. Entrance
3. Position of minaret
4. Decorative recess
5. Sahn
6. Qibla wall
7. Mihrab
8. Decorative light stone façade
9. Stair case
10. Entrance passage

It was originally at the northeast corner of the great eastern Fatimid palace. It is particularly important because: it was the first Cairo mosque with a façade following the alignment of the street, rather than the *qibla* wall, so that its ground plan was adjusted to fit into an existing urban environment; it was the first to have a decorated stone façade, the colour giving it its name which means moonlight; it introduced the shell motif and the stalactite into architectural styles which subsequently became favourites in Cairo.

The mosque has been restored over the centuries. Amir Yalbugha al-Salami restored the *minbar*, *mihrab* and ablution area in 1393 and added the minaret in 1397. The minaret was apparently removed in 1412 because it had started leaning, but the current structure includes the original first storey which is made of brick covered with very uncommon carved stucco decorated with chevron patterns. Because the street level has risen since the mosque was built there are steps down to the entrance which is offset from the main part of the mosque. Despite its importance and unique features the original interior of the mosque is unspectacular. Around the base of the almost square *sahn* the arches bear Koranic verses in the early angular and unpointed Kufic script on an arabesque background.

The **Medersa-Mausoleum of Tartar al-Higaziya (52)** is located in a small street which connects Sharia al-Gamaylia with Midan Bayt al-Qadi. It was built in two phases with the mausoleum, which was connected to the princess's palace, being built in 1347 for her recently murdered husband and the palace itself being converted into a *medersa* in 1360 which explains its irregular shape.

Tartar was the daughter of Sultan al-Nasr Mohamed, the sister of Sultan Hassan and the wife of the Amir Baktimur al-Higazi. The mosque was built on the site of the residence of Amir Qawsun who had married one of Tartar's sisters in

Medersa-Mausoleum of Tatar al-Higaziya

1. Entrance
2. Domed mausoleum
3. Sahn
4. Sarcophagus of Tatar
5. Mihrab
6. Octagonal minaret
7. Porch (lovely ceiling)
8. Ablutions liwan
9. Qibla liwan
10. Princess's liwan
11. External courtyard

1347. Little else is known about Tartar except that she died of the plague in 1360.

Entrance to the building is via a corridor which leads via a porch with a lovely ceiling into the *sahn* which has a *qibla liwan* to the southeast, the ablution *liwan* to the northwest and the princess's much larger liwan to the southwest which contains a large and most attractive *mihrab* with marble pillars. The *liwans* are united by a beautiful inscription, bands of Koranic script on a blue background which surround them. The triple arcade is supported by reused Byzantine columns. A series of stucco niches are set in the upper section of the *sahn* and the semi-domes of the two *mihrabs*. The high quality craftsmanship is matched by three carved and painted wooden ceilings. The octagonal minaret to the southwest of the *sahn* has been missing its top for over a century. Access to the minaret, the ablution area and storage areas are all via doors off the *liwans*. The ribbed stone dome, one of the earliest in Cairo, over the mausoleum is in the north end of the complex on the corner of two streets and passers-by can solicit a blessing or invoke a prayer via the open windows.

The restoration work carried out in the 1980 was done with care and consideration. Further east stands **Musafirkhana Palace** (House of Guests), a rather fine rambling building constructed between 1779 and 1788 and noted as the birth place of Khedive Ismail in 1830. The public are welcome to enter and examine the products of the resident artists and sculptors and see the intricate *mashrabiyya* in the harem on the second storey. Note the two wind catchers which provide cool air. Return to the main thoroughfare.

Take the next right hand turn for a brief detour to No 19 Darb al-Asfur which is 50m along the left hand side of the street. This is the **Beit al-Sihaymi (13)** (open 0900-1600), actually two houses, built in 1648 and 1796 and inhabited until 1961, and probably one of the finest examples of a luxurious Mamluke mansion in the whole of the city. It has a lovely courtyard and a *haramlik (harem)* for the women including a domed bathroom.

Returning to the main street and continuing north, one reaches the **Mosque and Sabil-Kuttab of Suleyman Agha al-Silahdar (14)**, built in 1837-39 by one of Mohamed Ali's ministers who also built many other *sabils* throughout the city. The style of the building is very much influenced by the contemporary style in Istanbul including the minaret with an Ottoman-style cylindrical shaft and conical top.

Continuing to the north end of the street is the giant **Mosque of Al-Hakim (15)** (open 0900-1600, E£6 plus a tip for both your guide and minder in the mosque), which abuts the **North Wall (16)** of the old city of Fustat/Cairo between the **Bab al-Nasr (17)** and **Bab al-Futrah (18)** gates and commemorates its most notorious ruler (see box, page 106). Entrance fee E£6 gives access to both gates. It was begun in 990 by the Shi'a Muslim Fatimid Khalifa Al-Aziz (975-996) and was eventually finished some 23 years later by his son who took the name **Al-Hakim bi-Amr**

Allah (Ruler by God's Command) and ruled between 996-1021.

Possibly having a Christian wife was the reason why his reportedly tolerant and humane father Al-Aziz had been more forbearant towards Christians and Jews than towards the indigenous Sunni Muslim population. In contrast his son was very intolerant to everyone. With such a colourful history, the large 122m by 115m mosque itself is actually rather plain. It is organized around a large central *sahn* and built of bricks with a large porch in the traditional Fatimid style. It

has been restored many times throughout the centuries, notably after the major earthquake in 1302 and by Sultan al-Hassan in 1359. After the 14th century it was converted to house Crusader prisoners-of-war, then as a stable by Salah al-Din, during the French occupation as a fortified warehouse, and in the mid-19th century to store items destined for the **Museum of Islamic Art** which opened in 1896. Since 1980 the mosque has been restored by the Indian based Bohra sect of Ismaili Muslims who claim direct spiritual descent from the Fatimid imams

Al-Hakim – The Vanishing Despot

In 996 AD at the age of 11 Al-Hakim succeeded his father as the second Egyptian Fatimid Khalifa and began a despotic reign. At the age of 15 he had his tutor assassinated and started his extremely cruel and relentless persecution of Christians, Jews, Sunni Muslims, women and dogs. He prohibited any Christian celebrations and had the Church of the Holy Sepulchre in Jerusalem demolished. He also prohibited Sunni ceremonies and tried to established Shi'a Islam as the only form of Islam. Women were forbidden to leave their homes and, in order to enforce this, cobblers were not permitted to make or sell women's shoes. At one time all of Cairo's dogs were exterminated because their barking annoyed him. Merchants who were found to have cheated their customers were summarily sodomized by his favourite Nubian slave whilst Al-Hakim stood on their head. Wine, singing, dancing and chess were also prohibited and the punishments for disobeying this laws were very severe and usually resulted in a gruesome death.

His erratic rule, with laws often changing overnight, led to tensions within Fustat/Cairo, particularly between the various religious communities. In 1020, the news that Al-Hakim was about to proclaim that he was a manifestation of Allah provoked serious riots to which he responded by sending in his Sudanese troops to burn down the city where they clashed not only with the civilians, but also the Turkish and Berber soldiers. An alternative story is that one particular quarter of Fustat was torched because he thought that was where his favourite sister Sitt al-Mulk (Lady of Power) took her lovers, but when she was proved to be a virgin by the midwives he examined the ruins and asked "who ordered this?". Whatever the truth, he then sent his chief theologian Al-Darazi to Syria for safety where he is believed to have originated the theology of the Druze who consider Al-Hakim to be divine.

Despite his ruthless public acts Al-Hakim's personal life was very abstemious and he was a very generous alms-giver. He took to riding around the city and surrounding countryside on a donkey with only a couple of servants but disappeared in February 1021. Following the discovery of his knife-slashed robe, it is believed he was murdered, possibly on the instructions of his Sitt al-Mulk with whom he apparently argued because of her refusal to begin an incestuous marriage with him. The fact that his body was never discovered led the Druze to believe that he had retreated from the world to return at a later date, whilst the Copts believe that he had a vision of Jesus, repented and became a monk.

who they worship. Its twin minarets have been reinforced by stone carvings and from these and from the roof there is a wonderful view over Cairo.

Route 2a: South from Al-Azhar

The route south from Al-Azhar mosque has a number of very interesting buildings including the **Mosque of Sultan Al-Muayyad Sheikh** at the medieval **Bab el-Zoueila**. Further to the south of Fustat is the **Sultan Hassan Mosque** and the much more modern **Al-Rifai Mosque** which stand side-by-side below the mighty **Citadel** (see page 117) and its various mosques. One can then head west to the huge and very old **Mosque of Ahmed Ibn Tulun** and the nearby **Gayer-Anderson Museum** before returning to the river. Allow a minimum of half a day to take in all of the sites on this tour of the south part of Islamic Cairo.

Immediately to the south of the Al-Azhar complex are a few of the 20 remaining *wikalas*, hostels for merchants which were usually above a bonded warehouse for their goods, which numbered over 200 in the 1830s. The wonderfully preserved **Wikala of Sultan al-Ashraf Qansuh II al-Ghawri (19)**, which was originally built in 1504, is just off the southwest corner of Al-Azhar: it now houses a permanent exhibition of desert life and is also used as workshops for artisans. Traditional handicrafts for sale. Open daily (except Friday) 0900-1700 or 0900-1100 and 1400-1600 during Ramadan, entry E£6.

50m to the northwest back on Sharia al-Azhar just near the footbridge, is the **Ghuriyya (20)**, the magnificent complex of **Sultan al-Ashraf Qansuh II al-Ghawri** (1501-17), which is bisected by a continuation of Sharia al-Muizzli Din Allah. The complex, made up of his domed mausoleum to the east of the street and his mosque and *medersa* to the west, was built in 1504-05 and was the last great Mamluke public building before the Ottoman conquest. He died of a stroke in 1516, aged about 76, during a battle near Aleppo against the Turks who then immediately invaded and captured Egypt and began their long rule which lasted from 1517 to 1805. Because Al-Ghawri's body was never found, he was not buried in this magnificent and hugely expensive tomb. The west side of the complex is closed for renovation until the end of 1998. The north side is open and on Wednesday and Saturday evenings at 2000 holds a short exhibition of Dervish dancing, good entertainment, no charge.

Sharia al-Muizzli Din Allah between the two buildings, originally roofed, was the site of the exotic silk market. Today mainly household goods are sold in the shops. Each section of this main thoroughfare, Islamic Cairo's main street, was named after the merchandise sold in that particular stretch. For example the fruit-sellers had their own mosque, the **Fakahani Mosque (21)** (built in 1735), about 200m down the street on the left hand side. Make a detour by walking left from its northwest corner and then left again where, 70m to the east at No 6, is the **House of Gamal al-Din al-Dhahabi (22)**, Cairo's richest gold merchant in 1637 when this beautiful house was built. It is used as a documentation centre and is

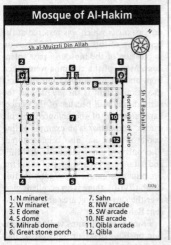

Mosque of Al-Hakim

Sh al-Muizzli Din Allah

North wall of Cairo

Sh al Baghalah

EX3g

1. N minaret	7. Sahn
2. W minaret	8. NW arcade
3. E dome	9. SW arcade
4. S dome	10. NE arcade
5. Mihrab dome	11. Qibla arcade
6. Great stone porch	12. Qibla

open to visitors (daily 0900-1400 except Friday). Back to the south of the mosque, is the ornate **Sabil-Kuttab of Tusan Pasha (23)**, built in his name by his father Mohamed Ali Pasha in 1820. From here the south gates of the ancient city are just ahead. Before going through the gates turn left or east at the *sabil-kuttab*. About 75m along the side street is an old 18th century men's bath-house known as **Hammam as-Sukariyah (24)** which was originally owned by a rich woman who also owned the nearby *wikala* and *sabil* of Nafisah Bayda. Although like the other remaining bath-houses in the city it is no longer a den of vice, it is still an interesting place to visit and relax. Today it helps the local community by allowing its fire for heating the water to be used to cook *ful mudammas* (beans) for the locals' breakfast.

Bab el-Zoueila (25), built by Badr al-Gamali in 1092 when Fatimid fortifications were being reinforced, was one of the three main gates in the city walls. It is named after mercenaries from the Al-Zoueila tribe of Berbers who were stationed in the nearby barracks. The gate was soon inside the city following the successive expansions and Salah al-Din's construction of larger walls further out from the centre. Cairo was in effect divided into two with the inner walls still in existence and both sets of gates locked at night.

Bab el-Zoueila also has a more popular history linked to the caravans departing both to Mecca and the south. It was not only the location of street performers including snake-charmers, story tellers and dancers, but after the 15th century it also became the site of public executions. Common criminals were beheaded, garrotted or impaled, while cheating merchants were hanged from hooks or rope. Defeated Mamluke Sultans, including the last one in 1517, were hanged and sometimes nailed to the doors. Even today the 20m high Bab el-Zoueila, which comprises a 4.8m wide multi-storey arch between two solid stone towers, is still an

impressive sight particularly from the south.

Immediately to the west of the gate is the **Mosque of Sultan al-Muayyad Sheikh (26)** (1412-21) built on the site of the old Kazanat al-Shamaii prison. Entrance fee E£6. Al-Muayyad had been incarcerated here on a number of occasions because of his love of alcohol when he was a Mamluke slave-soldier. On being released after one particularly long and unpleasant stretch, he vowed to replace the prison with a mosque which he began in 1415 after becoming Sultan.

The mosque, which is sometimes known as the Red Mosque because of the colour of its external walls, was one of the last to be built in the ancient large enclosure style before the Turkish style was adopted as the norm. The superb bronze-plated wooden entrance doors leading to the mosque were originally intended for the Sultan Hassan Mosque but were purchased by Al-Muayyad for his own mosque. The entrance leads into a vestibule with an ornate stalactite ceiling. From the vestibule, the door on the left leads to the Al-Muayyad's mausoleum and marble tomb with Kufic inscription, while nearby is the tomb of his son, Ibrahim, who died in 1420.

From the mausoleum a door leads to the east *liwan* which was restored at the beginning of this century and gives an impression of the mosque's past splendour. Many of the columns were taken from ancient monuments but the most exceptional sight is the *mihrab* and the surrounding wall because of the perfect harmonization of the coloured marble stucco. The *minbar* is an example of fine woodwork, but has also been restored. The courtyard is now planted with shrubs and palm trees. From the top of one of the two minarets (expect to pay extra for this climb (E£10)), there is an excellent view over the surrounding area and the adjacent Bab el-Zoueila.

From here a 20 mins walk or 5 mins ride on bus No 75 to the west of Bab

The Hammam

A visit to the *hammam* or Turkish bath is still part of the way of life for many Egyptians. Many Egyptian families have no bathing facilities at home and rely on the public *hammam*. A ritual purification of the body is essential before Muslims can perform prayers, and even for the well-off classes in the days before bathrooms, the 'major ablutions' were generally done at the *hammam*. Segregation of the sexes is of course the rule at the *hammam*: some establishments are open only for women, others only for men, while others have a shift system (mornings and evenings for the men, all afternoon for women). In the old days, the *hammam*, along with the local *zaouia* or saint's shrine, was an important place for women to gather and socialize, and even pick out a potential wife for a son.

In the older parts of the cities, the *hammam* is easily recognizable by the characteristic colours of its door. A passage leads into a large changing room cum post-bath rest area, equipped with masonry benches for lounging on and (sometimes) small wooden lockers. Here one undresses under a towel. *Hammam* gear today is football or beach shorts for men and knickers for women. A token must be purchased at the cash desk for a massage/scrub down, where shampoo can also be bought.

This is the procedure. Next first into the hot room. 5-10 mins with your feet in a bucket of hot water will see you sweating nicely, and you can then move back to the raised area where the masseurs are at work. After the expert removal of large quantities of dead skin, you go into one of the small cabins or *mathara* to finish washing. (Before doing this, catch the person bringing in dry towels, so that they can bring yours to you when you're in the *mathara*.) For women, in addition to a scrub and a wash, there may be the pleasures of an epilation with *sokar*, an interesting mix of caramelized sugar and lemon. Men can undergo a *taksira*, which although it involves much pulling and stretching of the limbs, ultimately leaves you feeling pretty good. And remember, allow plenty of time to cool down reclining in the changing area before you dress and leave the *hammam*.

el-Zoueila along Sharia Ahmed Maher brings you to the **Museum of Islamic Art** (see page 135).

En route immediately next to the mosque is a large and elegant building which looks like a small palace but is in fact the **Hammam al-Muayyad (27)** bath-house, built 1420. This has fallen into disrepair and is now often flooded. The area between the two is known as the Bab el-Khalq after a mediaeval gate which has long since vanished.

From the south of Bab el-Zoueila there are two routes you can take to reach the **Sultan Hassan** and **Al-Rifai mosques** which stand north of the Citadel. One is to continue southwest along what is officially known as Sharia al-Muizzli Din Allah but which, like so many other long roads, changes its name in different

sections and at this point is also known as Sharia al-Khiyamiyya (Tentmakers) because of its bazaar. After about 1 km you reach a major crossroads where you should turn left or southeast along Sharia al Qala'a which leads to the rear of the two mosques. A much more interesting route includes a few nearby sites on Sharia al-Khiyamiyya before heading east along Sharia Darb al-Ahmar, after which the whole area is named, towards the Citadel.

Immediately south of the gates are two buildings which are bisected by Sharia al-Khiyamiyya. To the west is the *zawiya* (Sufi monastery) and *sabil* (public fountain) of **Sultan al-Nasir Farag (28)** (1405-12) who was Barquq's son and successor. To the east is the much more magnificent **Mosque of Visir al-Salih Tala'i (29)**

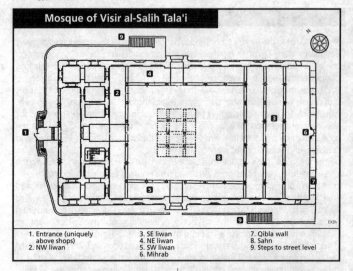

Mosque of Visir al-Salih Tala'i

1. Entrance (uniquely above shops)	5. SW liwan
2. NW liwan	6. Mihrab
3. SE liwan	7. Qibla wall
4. NE liwan	8. Sahn
	9. Steps to street level

EX3h

which was both the last Fatimid mosque and, when it was built in 1160, was the country's first suspended mosque resting on top of a series of small vaulted shops which, with the rise in the street level, are now in the basement. Tala'i reportedly died regretting the construction of the mosque because, being located directly outside the walls of the city, it could be used as a fortress by an enemy.

In 1160 the enfeebled Fatimid Dynasty was about to fall as one child khalifa succeeded another, ruling in name only, whilst a powerful vizir really wielded royal authority. When the Armenian-born Tala'i ibn Ruzzik came to power he called himself al-Salih hence the mosque's name.

The mosque, about 60m by 20m in size, was originally intended as a mausoleum for the remains of the martyr Hussein which were brought to Cairo from Ashkalon when the latter was under threat from the Franks. The great earthquake of 1303 severely damaged the mosque and destroyed the minaret which was restored together with the rest of the mosque by Amir Baktimur al-Gukandar (Polo-Master) and

subsequently in 1440, 1477 and lastly and very badly in the 1920s after the minaret had collapsed yet again.

It was only in about 1920 that it was discovered that the street level had risen so much and that the mosque was suspended on shops below. The shops – seven at the front, 12 on either side but none below the *qibla* wall – were part of the *waqf* and whose rents supported the upkeep of the mosque. The northwest entrance porch, with its large portico and an arcade of keel-arches raised on ancient columns with Corinthian capitals, is unique in Cairo. The decoration around the entrance is, however, similar in style to the earlier al-Aqmar mosque. The porch's *mashrabiyya* dates from the first restoration and the bronze facings on the exterior door are also from 1303 while the carvings on the inside of the door are a copy of the original which is now in the Islamic museum.

From the entrance a tunnel-vaulted passage leads into the *sahn* surrounded on four sides by *liwan* but the northwest *liwan* is not original. In the northeast *qibla* *liwan* the tie-beams, which are inscribed

Adhan – The Call to Prayer

This is know as the *adhan* and is performed by the *muezzin* who calls the faithful to prayer, originally by the strength of his own voice from near the top of the minaret but today, taking advantage of technological advances, it is probably a recording timed to operate at a particular hour. Listening to the first call to prayer just before the sun begins to rise is an unforgettable memory of Egypt.

There is no fixed tune, perhaps tune is too definite a description, but in Egypt there is one particular rhythm used all over the country for the *adhan*. The traditional Sunni *adhan* consists of seven phrases, with two additional ones for the morning prayer. There are some variations which the well-tuned ear will pick up.

1. *Allahu Akbar* (Allah is most great) is intoned four times. This phrase is called *al takbir*.
2. *Ashhadu anna la ilah ill'-Allah* (I testify that there is no god besides Allah) is intoned twice.
3. *Ashhadu anna Muhammadan rasul Allah* (I testify that Mohammed is the apostle of Allah) is intoned twice. This and the preceeding phrase are called the *shihada*, a confession of faith.
4. *Hayya 'ala 'l-salah* (come to prayer) is intoned twice.
5. *Hayya 'ala'l-falah* (come to salvation) is intoned twice. This and the preceeding phrase are called *tathwib*.
6. *Allahu Akbar* is intoned twice.
7. *La ilah ill'Allah* (there is no god besides Allah) is intoned once.

The two additions to the morning prayer are: *Al-salatu khayr min al-nawm* (Prayer is better than sleep) which intoned twice between the fifth and sixth phrases, and *Al-salatu wa'l-salam 'alayka ya rasul Allah* (Benediction and peace upon you, Oh Apostle of Allah) intoned after the seventh phrase.

with Koranic inscriptions in what is known as floriated Kufic script, are original but the ceiling is modern.

The highlight of the interior is the exquisite *minbar*, the fourth oldest in Egypt and a very fine example of Mamluk wood carving, which was donated to the mosque in 1300 by Amir Baktimur al-Gukandar. Above is the first appearance in a Cairo mosque of a *malqaf* (wind vent) which was an ingenious early Islamic form of air conditioning.

Further south down the street is what is probably the city's best preserved example of a **roofed market** which, because of the multitude of coloured printed fabrics sold here, is known as the **tentmakers bazaar**. Situated slightly further along the street is the **Medersa-Mosque of Amir Gani-Bak al-Ashrafi (30)** which was built in 1426 and is named after a

favourite of Sultan al-Ashraf Barsbay (1422-37). Although the mosque has similarities with a number of other Mamluk mosques of the same period and despite the loss of both a coloured marble lintel over the portal door and the windows, its decoration even now is more ornate than other examples.

One enters the mosque from the south and passing through a serpentine corridor arrives in the central domed cruciform area with the usual *qibla* wall, *mihrab* and *minbar*. There is a 2-storey minaret, to the right of the entrance, which is very plain and utilitarian.

The Amir Gani-Bak al-Ashrafi had been brought up by Sultan al-Ashraf Barsbay and his meteoric rise to amir in 1422 naturally created many enemies. He was poisoned and died aged 25. He was such a favourite that the Sultan had his body transferred to a tomb in the Sultan's own Eastern Cemetery complex.

Nearby is what little remains of the **Souq al-Surugiyyah** (saddle-makers market).

The **Mosque of Malika Safiya (51)**, built in 1610, lies to the west in a small street off Sharia Mohamed Ali (see map, page 80). It is one of the few mosques in Cairo which bears a woman's name although Queen Safiya acquired it deviously rather than constructed it herself.

Safiya, who was from the noble Venetian family of Baffo, was captured by pirates along with a large party of other women in 1575 on their way to Corfu where her father was governor. Because of her beauty she was presented to the Sublime Porte where she became chief consort of Sultan Murad III. He made her his *Sultana Khasski* (favourite) which gave her considerable power and influence which was increased further when she produced Murad's first-born son who succeeded his father in 1595. At her son's death Safiya was exiled to Seraglio where she lived in obscurity until she died in 1618.

This Turkish style mosque, which was originally set in gardens, is entered on the southwest side via some very high steps which lead to a square courtyard. The cloister which runs all round the forecourt has three arches above columns on each side, and is vaulted by a series of small supported Byzantine style domes of a type unknown in Egypt before the Turkish conquest. The roof in the centre of each side is oblong in plan.

One small Mamluk-style dome, entirely distinct from the others, covers a small room in the northeast corner of the sanctuary. This room was probably intended for women because a *mashrabiyya* separated it from the sanctuary.

A fine stalactite doorway leads into the sanctuary over which lies the great brick dome, resting on six pointed arches, and surrounded by smaller arches. The *mihrab*, which except for the blue Iznik tiles is in the earlier Mamluk style of coloured marble panels, stands at the back of a square domed annex. The beautiful *minbar* is characteristically Turkish, being entirely carved in white marble with a pointed conical top.

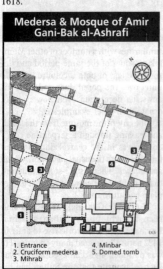

Medersa & Mosque of Amir Gani-Bak al-Ashrafi

1. Entrance
2. Cruciform medersa
3. Mihrab
4. Minbar
5. Domed tomb

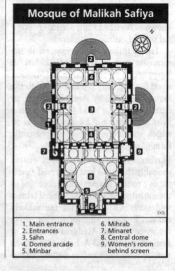

Mosque of Malikah Safiya

1. Main entrance
2. Entrances
3. Sahn
4. Domed arcade
5. Minbar
6. Mihrab
7. Minaret
8. Central dome
9. Women's room behind screen

Returning to Bab el-Zoueila and turning right (east) into Sharia Darb al-Ahmar (Red Rd) there is an interesting 1¼ km walk to the Citadel. The street gets its name from the incident in May 1805 when the Mamlukes were tricked into going to discuss their grievances with Mohamed Ali Pasha (1805-48). He had them slaughtered as they travelled 'Between the Two Palaces' and their heads sent to Istanbul as a demonstration of his power and independence. In March 1811 he did a similar thing again on the same street when 470 Mamlukes and their retainers were persuaded into going to a banquet at the Citadel to celebrate his son's imminent departure to fight the Wahabis in modern day Saudi Arabia. They were slaughtered on their return near Bab el-Zoueila.

About 150m after the Mosque of Wazir al-Salih Tala'i the road bends towards the south and on the corner of the fork in the road is the beautiful late-Mamluke era **Mosque of Qajamas al-Ishaq I (31)** who was Sultan Qaitbai's Viceroy of Damascus where he died and was buried in 1487. Although the mosque was built in 1480-81, it is now known locally as the **Mosque of Abu Hurayba** after the 19th century sheikh who occupies the tomb.

At this point you can could make a detour off the main road east up Sharia Abu Hurayba where the left hand fork leads 250m to the **Mosque & Tomb of Amir Aslam al-Silahdar (32)** built in 1344-45 and then follow the road around southwest and back to the main Sharia Darb al-Ahmar.

Alternatively you can forget about the detour and just continue south from the Mosque of Qajamas al-Ishaqi along Sharia Darb al-Ahmar. About 50m on the right is the **Mosque & Tomb of Ahmed al-Mihmandar (33)**, built in 1324 but restored in 1732, but much more interesting is the beautiful, relaxing and very peaceful **Mosque of Altunbugha al-Maridani (34)** (1339-40) which is 100m further along the street. This is amongst

the most impressive 14th century buildings in Cairo. Altunbugha (Golden Bull), who was originally from the Turkish town of Mardin, rose through the ranks to become amir and then married one of Sultan al-Nasir Mohamed's daughters and became his cupbearer (*saqi*). After the sultan died in 1340 his successors imprisoned Altunbugha until 1342 when he was made governor of Aleppo in modern-day Syria. He died there the following year at the age of 25.

Altunbugha's courtyard mosque, which was extensively restored in 1895-1903, is one of the oldest remaining buildings in this area. The minaret was the first in Cairo with an entirely octagonal shaft. It was built by Mu'allim al-Suyufi, who was the royal chief architect, who also built the minaret of Aqbugha at al-Azhar. The shafts of both are decorated by 2-coloured inlaid stone work. Fortunately the restoration work followed the original plans so that the bulb crowned canopy supported on stone pillars, the earliest existing example, was retained.

The main entrance in the northeast wall is composed of a high-pointed vaulted recess which is decorated by a

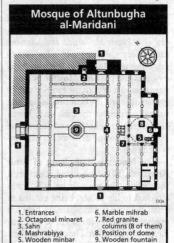

Mosque of Altunbugha al-Maridani

1. Entrances
2. Octagonal minaret
3. Sahn
4. Mashrabiyya
5. Wooden minbar
6. Marble mihrab
7. Red granite columns (8 of them)
8. Position of dome
9. Wooden fountain

stalactite frieze and inlaid black and white marble. Inside the mosque the large *sahn* with a later Ottoman octagonal wooden fountain canopy, is surrounded by four *riwaq* but the *qibla riwaq* is separated from the rest of the mosque by a beautifully carved part-original, part-restored *mashrabiyya*. There is a 3-bay by 3-bay domed area, supported by eight red granite pharaonic columns, in front of the marble mosaic and mother-of-pearl *mihrab* and the wooden carved and inlaid *minbar*. There is a stone *dikka* on raised pillars where the Koran is recited. The painted and gilded ceiling above has been partially restored which reveals the glorious original colour but also shows the need for further renovation.

Another 200m further south past a small Turkish mosque, by which time the road is now called Sharia Bab al-Wazir in memory of the Gate of the Wazir which once stood there, is the large **Medersa of Sultan al-Ashraf Sha'ban II (35)** (1363-78). It was built in 1368 when he was only 10, for his mother, who was one of al-Nasir Mohamed's (1310-40) concubines, which is why it is known locally as *Umm Sultan Sha'ban* ('mother of Sultan Sha'ban') but he died before her and is buried there.

On the road south is the **Mosque of Amir Aqsunqur (36)** who was the son-in-law of al-Nasir Mohamed and later became Viceroy of Egypt. It is sometimes known as the **Mosque of Ibrahim Agha** by locals and the **Blue Mosque** by Europeans because of both the exterior's blue-grey marble and the beautiful indigo and turquoise tiling of the *qibla* wall. In the 1650s Ibrahim Agha usurped the mosque started in 1346 and decorated it with imported tiles.

The **Medersa-Mausoleum of Amir Khayrbak (50)** was built in stages with the earliest, the mausoleum, which was attached to his palace, being erected in 1502. Because it was squeezed between existing buildings the shape of the complex is very irregular. The complex is best viewed from the Citadel end to the south

from where one can see that the minaret, undated, which has the upper storey missing and the intricately carved dome of the tomb raised above arched windows.

Unlike most Mamluk *medressa* it was initially not a Friday mosque although this was subsequently introduced in 1531 when the *minbar* was added. Documents show that the *medersa* staff included one imam, six *muezzins*, two *qari* (Koran readers) at the *medersa*, nine *qari* to recite the Koran at the windows, a sufi shaykh, 10 *qari* to perform daily in two shifts, and two *qari* at the mausoleum.

The entrance is through a corridor to the left of which is the *sabil-kuttab* and to the right of which is the portal entrance to the mosque which one enters by stepping over a piece of pharaonic stone. Three cross vaults cover the mosque's

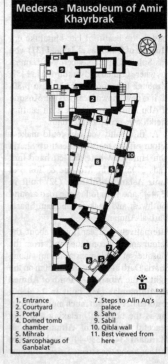

Medersa - Mausoleum of Amir Khayrbrak

1. Entrance	7. Steps to Alin Aq's
2. Courtyard	palace
3. Portal	8. Sahn
4. Domed tomb	9. Sabil
chamber	10. Qibla wall
5. Mihrab	11. Best viewed from
6. Sarcophagus of	here
Ganbalat	

interior but it is noticeable that the arches strangely obscure the windows on the *qibla* wall suggesting a change in plan during construction. The stonework is red and yellow and the *qibla* wall of coloured marble. To the left of the *mihrab* with its pointed arch is a door which leads down stairs direct to the adjacent Alin Aq palace which Khayrbek had requisitioned. Past the wooden *minbar* is the entrance to the rather plain but extraordinarily tall tomb containing the sarcophagus of Ganbalat, Khayrbak's brother. From the windows of the tomb one has a good view of the Alin Aq palace and Salah al-Din's city walls.

For the record, as you admire this building, Khayrbak who was the Mamluk governor of Aleppo, betrayed his master Sultan al-Ghuri at the Battle of Marj Dabiq in 1516 when the Turks routed the Mamluks which led to the Ottoman occupation of Egypt. He was rewarded for his treachery by being appointed as the first Ottoman governor of Egypt where he was reportedly known for his cruelty and greed.

From here the road slopes up to the left to meet the approach road to the Citadel but we continue right to the two imposing mosques.

Directly below the Citadel are two adjacent mosques. The **Sultan Hassan Mosque (37)** (entry E£12) was started in 1356 and finished 6 years later during the second reign of Sultan Hassan (1354-61). The building is a masterpiece of Islamic art and is of incomparable simplicity and beauty. The main entrance is through a large, impressive doorway decorated with stalactites and finely sculpted ornaments. This leads into an antechamber connected to the main courtyard. The magnificent cruciform courtyard has an ablutions fountain at the centre covered by a large dome which was originally painted blue. Each of the vaulted *liwans* served as a place for the teachings of one of the four doctrines of Sunni Islam. The *liwan* containing the *mihrab* has richly

decorated marble lined walls and a Koranic frieze in Kufic writing. Its height is accentuated by hanging lamp-chains.

From here an ornate bronze door with gold and silver motifs leads to Sultan Hassan's tomb. The room is dominated by a large 21m diameter dome which was actually built later during the Turkish period. The 3-section 86m minaret by the mausoleum is the highest in Cairo, with each new section richly decorated at its base with numerous stalactites. Another much smaller 55m minaret on the east side of the mosque was built in 1659 to replace the existing one which was decaying. The building also contains four *medressa* with one for each of the four – Malaki, Hanafi, Hanabali and Shafi'i – Islamic schools of law. Each *medersa* forms a virtually autonomous part of the

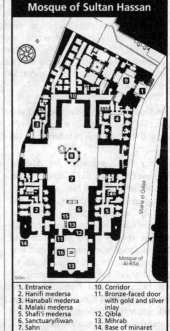

Mosque of Sultan Hassan

1. Entrance	10. Corridor
2. Hanifi medersa	11. Bronze-faced door
3. Hanabali medersa	with gold and silver
4. Malaki medersa	inlay
5. Shafi'i medersa	12. Qibla
6. Sanctuary/liwan	13. Mihrab
7. Sahn	14. Base of minaret
8. Water for ablutions	15. Minbar
9. Antechamber	16. Tomb chamber/
(domed)	mausoleum

The Marabout

The landscape in western Egypt and the settled areas of eastern Libya is dotted with white painted monuments scattered about the hillsides, hilltops and cemeteries. These are the burial places of the holy men or *marabouts* (*marabit* in Arabic) though the practice of adopting seers and ascetics is thought to have preceded the coming of Islam. The *marabout* was a religious teacher who gained credibility by gathering disciples around him and getting acknowledgement as a man of piety and good works. *Marabouts* were in many cases migrant preachers travelling to and from Mecca or were organizers of sufi schools. Place names of *marabout* sites are mainly after the names of the holy man interred there usually prefixed by the word 'sidi'. Some sites are very modest, comprising a small raised tomb surrounded by a low wall, all whitewashed. Other *marabouts* have a higher tomb several metres square topped by a dome (*koubba*). In some instances, the tombs of saints, especially in Egypt, are large house-like structures acting as mausoleums and shrines. Most tombs in rural areas can carry stakes bearing flags in green cloth as symbols of the piety of their donors and as a token of the continuing protection provided by the *marabout*.

Annual processions or pilgrimages are made to the *marabout* shrines for good luck, fertility and protection against the evil spirits. This is particularly the case where the area around is occupied by a tribe claiming descent from the holy man in question.

building. The ground floor is used as a place for teaching, meditation and praying and the first floor as lodgings for the students.

Despite its appearance, the **Al-Rifai Mosque (38)** (entry E£12), directly to the east of Sultan Hassan Mosque, was only started in the late 19th century and was actually finished in 1912. However the mosque, which is named after Sheikh Ali al-Rifai who was the founder of the Sufi Muslim *tariqa* bearing his name and who was originally buried there, blends remarkably well into the surroundings. It was built over and expanded by the Dowager Princess Khushyar, the mother of Khedive Ismail who died in 1885 before it was finished, and was intended to contain the tombs of her descendants. Besides Al-Rifai and herself it contains the tombs of Khedive Ismail (1863-79), his sons Sultan Hussein Kamil (1914-17) and King Ahmed Fouad I (1917-36) but not King Farouk who died in exile and is buried in the southern cemetery. It is also the last resting place of the last Shah of Iran (Mohamed Reza Pahlavi), who died in exile in 1980 and, on President Sadat's instructions, was buried with great ceremony in a tomb made of green marble imported from Pakistan.

The **Medersa of Amir Sayf al-Din Ilgay al-Yusfi (53)** built 1373, is located on Sharia Souq al-Salih to the north of Bab Mangak al-Silahdar (1346-47).

Sayf al-Din Ilgay rose through the ranks to become an Amir of the Sword and eventually commander-in-chief of the army. He married Khwand Baraka, who was the mother of Sultan Shaban

(1363-77), and he found himself one of the powers behind the throne. After his wife died, however, he quarrelled with the Sultan over her property and lost his influence. He had to flee the court and was drowned in uncertain circumstances while trying to cross the River Nile on horseback. His body was recovered and he was buried in the *medersa* that he had built a few years earlier in 1373. His tomb lies beneath the dome at the western corner of the mosque.

It is a late Mamluk complex with an unusual curved and fluted dome which is quite unique. The ribs twist across the dome at an angle of 45° to the right and then swing back to the left before fusing together at the apex. The minaret has an octagonal base and the usual further two storeys above, the galleries of the first of which are supported by attractive corbels of stalactite form. The upper storey of the minaret is a later reconstruction with a pillared pavilion.

The main façade is made up of an ornate formal entrance on the extreme north corner with the remaining façade being divided into two recesses headed with stalactite cornices and crennellated hoods separated by two narrower full-height ornamental arches headed with decorated fluted stone. The recesses and arches carry 36 windows in three courses; the second and third courses are elegant windows with tracery masonry lights.

The entrance to the traditional Mamluk cruciform mosque is via the northwest steps near the street corner which lead via a winding corridor into the central *sahn* which is surrounded by four *liwan* each of which have a frontal arch and above which is gilded decoration, now somewhat deteriorated in quality. The *qibla liwan* has been depleted of its former marble dado and the *minbar* has lost its top but still has fine carving and inlay. The entrance to the Ilgay's tomb is between the northwest and southwest *liwans*. To the right of the *minbar* on the southwest wall is an exit to the small outside courtyard.

Route 2b: The Citadel

The magnificent **Citadel** reached direct from Midan Tahrir by taking a No 82 bus, is also known as Al-Qala'a al-Gabal (Citadel of the Mountain) or Al-Burg, is open daily 0800-1700 in winter and 0800-1800 in summer (except 1130-1300 on Friday), entry E£20 for the mosque of Mohammed Ali Pasha and E£20 for the second section of the complex containing the mosque of Suleyman Pasha, the Carriage museum and the Seized museum. 50% discount available for students. Camera tickets for the area are E£10 and E£100 for video cameras. Tips should be reserved for guides in the museums but not the Police or Military museums. Entrance into the museums ends at 1530. Enter via **Bab al-Gabal (5)**.

It was built by Salah al-Din (1171-1193) as part of a very ambitious general fortification plan which included enclosing the whole city with a new wall which could be controlled from the Citadel. The original fortress and remaining fortifica-

Medersa of Amir Sayf al-Din Ilgay al-Yusfi

1. Entrance	5. Qibla wall
2. Sahn	6. Minaret
3. Mihrab	7. Dombed tomb
4. Minbar	

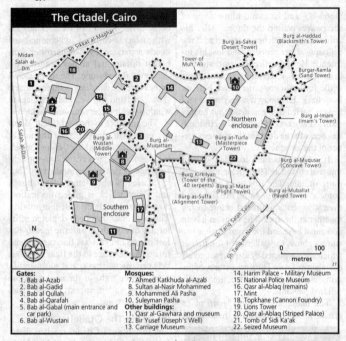

The Citadel, Cairo

Gates:
1. Bab al-Azab
2. Bab al-Gadid
3. Bab al Qullah
4. Bab al-Qarafah
5. Bab al-Gabal (main entrance and car park)
6. Bab al-Wustani

Mosques:
7. Ahmed Katkhuda al-Azab
8. Sultan al-Nasir Mohammed
9. Mohammed Ali Pasha
10. Suleyman Pasha

Other buildings:
11. Qasr al-Gawhara and museum
12. Bir Yusef (Joseph's Well)
13. Carriage Museum

14. Harim Palace - Military Museum
15. National Police Museum
16. Qasr al-Ablaq (remains)
17. Mint
18. Topkhane (Cannon Foundry)
19. Lions Tower
20. Qasr al-Ablaq (Striped Palace)
21. Tomb of Sidi Ka'ak
22. Seized Museum

tions were strongly influenced by the architecture of castles built in Palestine and Syria by the Crusaders. It was built in two walled enclosures, linked by their shortest walls, with the military area to the northeast and the residential quarters in the southwest. Every 100m or so along the walls there is a tower and there are numerous gates. The whole complex is still under military control and there are large areas which are closed to the public.

Later the Citadel was abandoned until the Mamlukes' arrival, when it became the Sultan's residence and the *Burji Mamlukes* (1382-1517) took their name from their base in the Citadel. In the 14th century Sultan al-Nasir Mohammed (1310-40) added a number of buildings including a mosque and later, because of the development of warfare and the use of canons, the Turks undertook major reinforcements. The most recent modification to the Citadel was by Mohamed Ali Pasha (1805-40) who built an impressive mosque on the site of the original palaces. Today the most interesting features of the Citadel are the **Mosque of Mohamed Ali Pasha**, which provides an amazing view west over Cairo and the restored **Sultan al-Nasir Mohamed Mosque**.

Walls, Towers and Gates The Ayyubid walls and towers (1176-83) around part of the Northern enclosure are from the time of Salah al-Din. The walls are 10m high and 3m thick interspersed with half-round towers. Some of the larger/later towers (1207) such as Burg at-Turfa which enclose parts of the wall were built by al-Kamir (nephew of Salah al-Din and the first Ayyubid sultan to live in the Citadel). **Bab al-Azab** enclosed by a pair of round headed towers stands on the west side of the Citadel. It was the original entrance to the Southern enclosure and is no longer open to the public. The brass bound wooden doors date from 1754. **Bab al-Qullah** (16th century) connects the two separate parts of the Citadel. The original Mamluk gate was replaced after the Ottoman conquest and was widened in 1826 to allow Mohamed Ali's carriage to pass through. **Bab al-Gadid** (New Gate) was built in 1828 and is in reality a large tunnel with a vaulted ceiling. There are guard rooms on either side.

Burg as-Siba (Lion's Tower) was built in 1207 by the Mamluk Sultan Baybars. The frieze of stone lions, the sultans' heraldic symbol, gives it its name. **Burg al-Muqattam** (16th century) is the largest tower in the citadel, being over 25m high and 24m in diameter. The 7m thick walls were built to withstand artillery attack.

The **Mosque of Mohammed Ali Pasha** (Entry E£10, E£5 students) was started in 1824 but only finished 8 years after his death in 1857. The architecture was strongly influenced by the Turkish mosques of Istanbul with the characteristic high, slender, octagonal minarets and an imposing dome which had to be rebuilt in the 1930s. The marble floored courtyard is very finely proportioned, with a beautiful central ablutions fountain. To the

Mosque of Mohammed Ali Pasha

1. Main entrance	8. Sahn
2. Entrance from courtyard	9. Ablutions fountain
3. Domed turret	10. Clock tower
4. Octagonal minaret	11. Tomb of Mohammed Ali
5. NE arcade	12. Subsidiary mihrab
6. SW arcade	13. Minbar
7. Mihrab	

northwest is a small square tower for a clock which was a gift from King Louis-Philippe of France in 1846 in exchange for the obelisk now sited in Paris' Place de la Concorde, but the clock has never worked. The mosque is covered by a large dome with four half domes on each side. Once inside, it takes some time to become accustomed to the dim lighting. The white marbled tomb of Mohamed Ali is on the right of the entrance, behind a bronze grille.

The **Sultan al-Nasir Mohammed Mosque** was built between 1318 and 1335. It is certainly the best preserved Mamluk building in the Citadel and is claimed to be one of the finest arcade-style mosques in Cairo, the arches being supported by pharaonic and classical columns plundered from elsewhere. The two distinctive minarets covered in the upper part with ceramic tiles are attributed to Persian craftsmanship. The magnificent marble which covered the floors and lined the walls to a height of 5m was unfortunately removed on instructions of the Ottoman ruler Selim I. The *mihrab* is still in good condition.

The **Mosque of Suleyman Pasha** (1528), in the northern enclosure of the Citadel, was the first to be built in Cairo during the Ottoman period and is believed to be dedicated to the janissary corp of soldiers of which Sulayman Pasha was earlier governor. It may have been designed by one of the architects sent to Cairo to repair the damage caused to the Citadel and the city walls by the Ahmed Pasha revolt.

The main entrance to the mosque is to the left of the minaret. Its stalactite portal leads not directly into the paved courtyard like most Ottoman mosques but into the prayer hall on its southwest side. This is due to its cramped position by the Citadel's walls. The minaret is typical of the style common in Istanbul, a tall slender cylinder with a conical top, but like the Mamluk minarets it has two galleries. Like the domes of the surrounding mosque and prayer hall the minaret's

Mosque of Suleyman Pasha, Citadel

N

1. Entrance
2. Domed central area
3. Sahn
4. Roofed arcade
5. Marble minbar
6. Mihrab
7. Mausoleum of Suleyman
8. Maq'Ad
9. Minaret

pointed cap is covered with green tiles which are similar to a number of Cairo's mosques of the period.

The mosque interior comprises a richly painted domed central area flanked on three sides by three supported semi-domes. The *sahn* is surrounded by a shallow-dome roofed arcade and in the northwest corner is the slightly larger dome of the mausoleum containing tombs of a number of janissaries.

The frescoes on the walls were restored in the 19th century and it is uncertain how faithful they are to the original Ottoman decoration. The conical top of the marble *minbar*, is decorated with a Mamluk inspired geometric pattern based on the stars and polygon forms, similar to the Ottoman minarets.

The **Mosque of Ahmed Katkhuda al-Azab** was built in 1697, Ottoman style.

Museums The **Carriage Museum (13)** is in the dining hall used by British officers who were stationed in the Citadel and on display are eight carriages once used by the Egyptian royal family and some painted wooden horses. The **Military Museum (14)** is situated in the **Harim Palace** built in 1827 as the private residence of Mohamed Ali. There are three extensive wings with many halls and side rooms all decorated in lavish style. King Farouk ordered its conversion into a museum which traces the history of the Egyptian army from pharaonic times to the present day. There are military uniforms, rifles and cannons on display. Tanks captured in the October 1973 conflict are in the courtyard. Open 0900-1400 except Monday. The **National Police Museum (15)** has some strange and interesting exhibits of policing problems ranging from assassination attempts to protection of Egyptian antiquities. It is constructed on top of Burg as-Siba. **Seized Museum (22)**, entry E£40, provides a very interesting hour. In two small rooms the exhibits, confiscated from dealers in the antiquities black-market, span the history of Egypt. The first room is set aside for Pharonic items including a painted wooden sarcophagus and funerary beads in excellent condition. The second room is cramped with an assortment of treasures, including a collection of Byzantine, Islamic and European gold coins, a small group of beautiful books in the Arabic script, seven stunning Coptic icons and a set of official seals from the reign of the Mohammed Ali.

Qasr al-Gawhara (Palace of Jewels) stands on the site of the palace of the Circassian Mamluk sultans. It was built in 1814 as the first of two palaces with French-style salons that Mohamed Ali built in the Citadel. It contains an impressive audience hall and guest rooms. Having been the residence of Egypt's rulers since the 12th century he predicted that his descendants would rule Egypt as long as they lived in the Citadel: sure enough, Ismail's move to the Abdin Palace foreshadowed the decline in their fortunes.

Today it is a museum with displays of portraits, costumes, furniture and ornaments which belonged to King Farouk. The **Archaeological Garden Museum** in the Northern Enclosure contains an interesting collection of bits and pieces –

monuments and statues – as well as welcome benches.

Joseph's Well named after Salah al-Din built in 1183 is also known as the well of the snail as there is a spiral staircase which leads down some 87m through solid rock to the water level of the River Nile. There are two platforms where pumps operated by oxen raised the water which was then carried to the surface by donkeys. It is possible to go down, but take great care. It was built by Crusader prisoners and provided a secure supply of drinking water for all of the Citadel. It is covered by a tower and stands just south of the Mosque of Sultan al-Nasir Mohammed.

Qasr al-Ablaq (Striped Palace) was built in 1315 by al-Nasr Mohamed for official receptions. Mohamed Ali Pasha had the building torn down but a remaining portion of outer wall shows it was constructed in alternating bands of black and yellow marble, hence the name.

West from the Citadel

From Midan Salah al-Din to the west of the Citadel and in front of the Sultan Hassan Mosque make your way west along Sharia Saliba. On the left is the highly decorated **Sabil-Kuttab of Sultan Qaitbai** (1477) **(41)**. This is another *sabil* and *medersa* but has, unusually, no connection to a larger religious foundation. Continue west past the small **Mosque of Qanibai al-Muhammadi (42)** to the imposing architectural buildings with matching minarets which face each other across the Sharia Saliba. On the right, north, is the **Mosque of Amir Shaykhu** (1349) **(43)** and on the left, south, the **Khanqah of Amir Shaykhu** (1355) **(44)**. Amir Shaykhu was the Commander in Chief of the Mamluk army during the reign of Sultan Hassan. The *khanqah* had small cells for up to 70 sufis around the inner courtyard and in the northeast corner of the arcaded prayer hall is Amir Shaykhu's tomb. There is an option to turn left here and travel south down Shari al Ashraf. After 500m one reaches Midan Sayyidah Nafisah on the corner of which is the Gate of Ali Pasha Hakim. Turn left through here to the modern **Mosque of Sayyidah Nafisah**, one of the very few mosques closed to non-muslims. Sayyidah Nafisah was a direct descendant of the Prophet Mohammed. She was born in Mecca and came to Egypt with Imam Shafi where she settled in Cairo and lived on the site where this mosque now stands. She was known for her piety, her complete knowledge of the Quran and the more dubious fact that she dug her own grave. Large crowds gathered to receive her blessing and perhaps healing. She died in 824 and the first shrine over the tomb was constructed soon afterwards. The

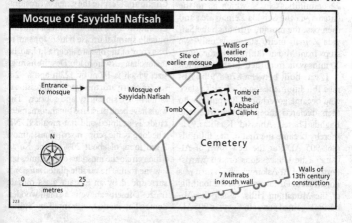

Mosque of Sayyidah Nafisah

Site of earlier mosque

Walls of earlier mosque

Entrance to mosque

Mosque of Sayyidah Nafisah

Tomb

Tomb of the Abbasid Caliphs

N

Cemetery

0   25
metres

7 Mihrabs in south wall

Walls of 13th century construction

223

shrine has been rebuilt and enlarged many times, the present construction, the last of a series of tombs, which dates from 1893-7 was erected following a destructive fire.

Continue beyond the mosque entrance, turn right at the end of the covered passage and right again into the courtyard into the cemetery. Among the many tombs the one of note is the domed mausoleum in the centre, the mid 13th century square tomb of the Abbasid Caliphs.

The next turning left going south down Sharia al Ashraf is Sharia al Sayyidah Nafisah which leads to the Southern Cemetery (see page 126). Return to the main route turning west (right) at the cross roads, with the **Sabil-Kuttab of Um Abbas (45)** on the corner, passing the small but impressive **Mosque of Amir Taghri Bardi** (1440) **(46)** with a carved stone dome. While the external structure of this building follows the east-west line of Sharia Saliba the interior is aligned southeast to Mecca.

The largest mosque in Cairo and the oldest one which retains its original features is the **Mosque of Ahmed Ibn Tulun (47)** (open daily 0900-1600), entrance fee E£6, which is located about 15 mins walk west of the Citadel along Sharia Saliba on the way towards the river. Alternatively it can be reached from Midan Tahrir by bus No 72 or minibus No 54 which go to the Citadel via the Saiyida Zeinab area and then past the mosque. Although the Saiyida Zeinab metro station is only two stops from Midan Tahrir it is probably a 30 mins walk from there to the mosque.

It was built between 876-879 by Ahmed Ibn Tulun, the son of a Turkish slave who became governor of Egypt but who then declared independence from the Baghdad-based Abbasid Khalifas. He thereby became the first of the Tulunids (868-905 AD), at the new town of Al-Qata'i (the Concessions or the Wards) northeast of Al-Askar which, in turn was northeast of Fustat, and near the foothills of the Muqattam Hills. When the Abbasids regained power in Egypt in 905 AD

Mosque of Ahmed Ibn Tulun

1. Minaret	8. To Gayer Anderson
2. 13th century	Museum
fountain	9. NW arcade
3. Sahn	10. SW arcade
4. Sanctuary arcade	11. NE arcade
5. Mihrab	12. Sabil of Sultan
6. Minbar	Qaitbai
7. Qibla	

they destroyed much of the town except for the mosque which fell into decay until it was restored in 1296 by Sultan Langin who had hidden there after he was implicated in an assassination attempt against his predecessor.

The mosque was originally built in 876 by a Syrian Jacobite Christian architect which probably explains the presence of many designs and motifs inspired by Coptic art. Despite the extensive restoration work by Sultan Lagin, but apart from the addition of a minaret with an unusual outside spiral staircase which appears to be a copy of the one at Samarra in Iraq, no major changes were made. Despite its huge size, which is 140m by 122m and a 92m square courtyard, the overall impression is of harmony, simplicity and sobriety. The walls have been plastered but the ornamentation is sculpted and not moulded. **NB** The long Kufic script inscriptions, almost 2 km long, of about 20% of the Koran which circle the mosque several times below the roof. The marble plated *mihrab* is surrounded by an elegant glass mosaic frieze. Directly above is a small wooden dome. The *minbar*, presented by Sultan

Mosque of Ahmed Ibn Tulun

Lagin in 1296, is a fine work of art. The view from the top over the surrounding area is excellent and worth the climb.

The **Gayer-Anderson Museum** T 364 7827, entrance E£16 (E£8 for students) plus E£10 for cameras using the same ticket as for the Islamic museum (open 0800-1700, Friday 0900-1100 and 1330-1530), which is also called **Beit al-Kridliyah (48)** (House of the Cretan Woman), abuts the southeast corner of Ahmed Ibn Tulun's mosque and has its own entrance into the mosque precinct. It is contained in two houses, the one on the west dating back to 1540 and the one to the east to 1631, on either side of a small alley called Atfat al-Gami which originally belonged to the Al-Kiridhi family. Originally one house was for men's accommodation *salamlik* and the other for women *haramlik*. The roof area was solely for the women who crossed from one building to the other by a small bridge on the second floor. A screened balcony *mashrabiyyah* which overlooks the large 2-storey sitting room *qa'ah* with its marble floor and ornately tiled fountain permitted the women to see the male visitors and the entertainments without being seen themselves.

The houses were sold to the government which in 1934 gave them to Major Robert Gayer-Anderson (1881-1945), a retired doctor and member of the Egyptian Civil Service, when he expressed a desire in restoring them and refurnishing them with Ottoman furniture and fittings. A tour of the houses give a good insight into the decoration and organization of a house during the Ottoman rule. Each of the main rooms has a different theme, Damascus room, Persian room, Turkish room and Byzantine room. Other rooms include a library, a writing room and a display room for the Major's collection of pharaonic antiquities.

The Medersa and Tombs of Amirs Salar and Sangar al-Gawli (49) This was once a much larger set of buildings, even so the remaining tombs and the *medersa* indicate the original grandeur. The domes over the tombs are of different sizes, that to the east being the largest. The slender minaret immediately to the right of the entrance stands about 45m high. The first storey is square, the second is octagonal

Medersa and Tomb of Amirs Salar and Sangar al-Gawli

1. Entrance
2. Domed tomb of Salar
3. Domed tomb of Sangar
4. Tomb of unknown amir
5. Porch
6. Stairs up to roof
7. Corridor to tombs
8. Mihrab
9. Liwan
10. Rooms for students
11. Small cemetery

Minarets

👣 The minaret (*ma'dhana*) evolved to provide a high point from which the prayer leader (*muezzin* or *mu'adhdhin*) could make the call (*adhan*) to the faithful to their devotions five times each day. Construction of minarets to give a vantage point for the *muezzin* began in Damascus at the end of the 7th century AD. The earliest minaret that has survived is the one at the Great Mosque in Kairouan, Tunisia, built in the 8th-9th centuries. The minaret of the Ibn Tulun Mosque in Cairo with its external spiral staircase (see page 103) is dated 876-879. There is some belief by scholars that the three-part form of the Egyptian minaret was taken from the 135m Lighthouse of Pharos at Alexandria (see page 331), of which the extant Abu Sir lighthouse 43 km west of Alexandria (see page 347) is a small scale copy.

The minarets of the Egyptian mosque are quite distinct despite reflecting influences from elsewhere in the Islamic world. There is great variety in the shape and architectural effects of Egyptian minarets as may be seen from the illustration of three fine minarets in Cairo, the minaret of the Ibn Tulun Mosque has an external stairway and octagonal third section while the minaret of Sangar al-Gawli Medersa (see page 123) carries an extended square base with short and delicate second and third sections. In contrast, the splendid early 15th century minaret of the Sultan al-Zahir Barquq mausoleum (see page 128) displays great variety as it changes from square to modified cruciform to circular to octagonal. Yet there is an underlying general tendency for the Egyptian minaret to have three separate levels including a base of square section, overlain by a multifaced column usually octagonal in shape surmounted by a circular tower, itself terminating in an elaborate miniature pavilion. The finial is provided by a small gilded spire carrying a crescent.

The original brick-built minarets in Egypt used finely worked panelling and line work as on the Ottoman minaret of Sultan Hassan Mosque (1356-62) near the Cairo citadel (see page 115). The passage of time saw the expensive kiln brick medium dropped in favour of stone and finally rough random stone laying covered with a plaster rendering. These painted towers have been augmented in the recent past both in Egypt and other Muslim countries by what has become a standard modern equivalent, reproduced in new urban and country settlements alike. It is plain and repetitive – scarcely a description of the more traditional and characterful minarets – but serves its purpose (see box, The Call to Prayer, page 111), and remains a principal topographic marker in the Egyptian landscape.

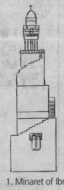

1. Minaret of Ibn Tulun Mosque, Cairo

2. Minaret of Medersa Sangar Al-Gawli, Cairo

3. Minaret of Sultan Al-Zahir Barquq Mosque, Cairo

and the third is cylindrical, culminating in a cornice of stalactites capped with a ribbed dome. The entrance is up the steps through a stalactite arch into a porch. Further steps lead to the vaulted corridor and to the tombs. The Tomb of Amir Salar, 7m sq, is encircled by a wooden frieze and has a fine marble mihrab. Note the design of the windows in the dome. The adjacent Tomb of Amir Sangar is smaller at 6.5m sq and is less ornate than its neighbour. Still further west is a third tomb called the Tomb of the Unknown Amir. Even smaller, at only 4.5m sq, the unnamed occupant died in 1348. Turning east from the stairs leads to the mosque. The larger courtyard had small rooms for students (the grills over the doors need some explanation) and a smaller courtyard off which is the *mihrab*.

The area to the west of the giant mosque is known as **Sayyidah Zeinab** after the Prophet Mohammed's granddaughter Zeinab (628-680 AD) who settled in Fustat/Cairo in 679 with her five children and the son of her brother Hussein who was murdered at Karbala in the Sunni-Shi'a conflict. Because of her position as closest kinswoman to the martyred Ali and Hussein the area has become a site of pilgrimage for foreign Shi'a Muslims. This is focused on the mosque built and continuously rebuilt over her tomb which is located off Sharia Bur Said but is closed to non-Muslims. Her moulid (saint's day) between 13-27 Ragab (December 1994) attracts up to half a million revellers who come to watch the wild Sufi parades and evening festivities.

Route 3: The Cities of the Dead

The **Cities of the Dead** is the name given by Europeans to Cairo's two main cemeteries which spread from the Citadel. The **Southern cemetery** is older and spreads to the southeast but there are few monuments to see. The **Northern cemetery**, which is known locally as Qarafat al-Sharqiyyah (the Eastern Cemetery) because it was east of the old city, is much more interesting and has been the burial place of the sultans since the 14th century. It contains a number of interesting mausoleums including those of Barquq and Qaitbai.

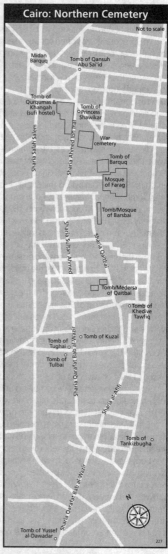

Cairo: Northern Cemetery

Not to scale

Midan Barquq

Tomb of Qansuh Abu Sai'id

Tomb of Qurqumas & Khangah (sufi hostel)

Tomb of Princess Shawikar

Sharia Salah Salem

Sharia Ahmed Ibn Tini

War cemetery

Tomb of Barquq

Mosque of Farag

Tomb/Mosque of Barsbai

Sharia Sultan Ahmed

Sharia Qaitbai

Tomb/Medersa of Qaitbai

Tomb of Khedive Tawfiq

Tomb of Kuzal

Sharia Qarafat Bab al-Wazir

Tomb of Tughai

Tomb of Tulbai

Sharia al-Afifi

Tomb of Tankizbugha

N

Sharia Qarafat Bab al-Wazir

Tomb of Yussef al-Dawadar

227

Muslim cemeteries

One of the lasting monuments in Islam is the *qarafah* or graveyard. All are different, ranging from undefined rocky areas near villages, where unnamed head and foot stones are barely distinguishable from the deserts surrounding them, to the elaborate necropoli of Cairo, where veritable cities of the dead are established. In all cemeteries bodies are interred with head towards the *qibla* – Mecca.

In Egypt graveyards often contain a series of simple whitewashed mud brick tombs of holy men or *marabouts* (see box page 64), around which his disciples and their descendants are laid. More grandly in Cairo at the *City of the Dead* is the Eastern Cemetery known as the *Tombs of the Mamlukes* (see page 125) a set of Muslim grave yards, developed particularly from the 15th century. It contains large numbers of notable tombs, most important of which is the Tomb of Sultan al-Zahir Barquq (see page 128). A second and even more elaborate cemetery is Cairo's Southern Cemetery, situated close to the Citadel. This ancient graveyard includes a number of the earliest examples of Muslim funerary architecture in Egypt and is home to the Tomb of the Imam Shafa'i, the most significant mausoleum in Cairo. The Imam Shafa'i was born in Palestine in 767 and was the originator of the Shafi'ite School of Islamic jurisprudence, one of the four great Sunni Schools of Law. The Imam ash-Shafa'i spent his last years (until his death in 820) in Fustat in Cairo. Salah al-Din set up the Shafa'i Mosque in 1180, which included the Imam's new tomb. Although subject to numerous subsequent reconstructions, of which the last was under the Khedive Tawfiq in 1891, the tomb is in an adequate state of repair to justify a visit. The large Shafa'i complex takes in a mosque, a ceremonial gateway and the mausoleum itself. The tomb is simple but decorated at various times with silver and paintings. The mausoleum has some fine beams and a wooden cupola together with much of the original inscriptions and ornamentation undertaken by Salah al-Din's builders. Shafa'i's tomb lies to the north of the building. Its religious focus is a delicate 20th century sandalwood screen or *maqsurah* and a marble stele. These are kissed by visiting Muslims as a sign of faith. Also entombed at the site are Mohammed abd al-Hakim and Princess Adiliyyah, the mother of Sultan al-Kamel, while the Sultan Kamel Ayyub himself (interred elsewhere) is commemorated by an uninscribed tomb in the south of the chamber. A walk along Sharia Sidi Uqbah and Sharia Imam Shafa'i will take the visitor past a wide variety of funerary constructions, many in a sad state of decay. Also visit the al-Basha *Housh* (house) which backs on to the Shafa'i tomb on a parallel road (Shariyah Imam al-Lais) to the west. This is the family mauasoleum of the family of Mohammed Ali Pasha in a set of pavilions of 19th century origin.

Muslim graveyards have no flowers unless they grow wild and by chance. Instead of buying flowers to decorate family graves on their routine weekly visit, relatives will often give a simple dish to the poor to provide a meal for their children.

Death and funerals are times for noisy outbreaks of wailing and crying. In traditional families, the approach of a person's death is signified by wailing, increased on actual death by the addition of the mourning neighbours and relatives. Occasionally in villages the body is laid in a large room where funeral dances are performed by wailing women, singing the praises of the deceased. Corpses are washed and wrapped in a simple shroud for interment. Mourners follow the cortege to the cemetery often in large crowds since every person who walks 40 paces in the procession has one sin remitted. At the grave side a *shedda* or declaration of Islamic faith is recited. Urban funerals are more ornate than those in the country districts and the passing of public figures is often accompanied by some pomp.

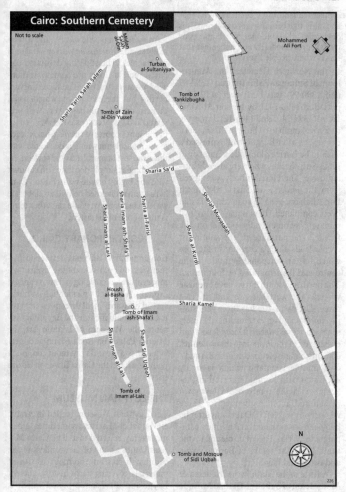

Cairo: Southern Cemetery

Not to scale

Mohammed Ali Fort

Midan Salah al-Din

Turban al-Sultaniyyah

Sharia Tariq Salah Salem

Tomb of Tankizbugha

Tomb of Zain al-Din Yussef

Sharia Sa'd

Sharia Imam ash-Shafa'i

Sharia al-Farisi

Sharia al-Kurdi

Shariah Muwasalah

Housh al-Basha

Sharia Kamel

Tomb of Imam ash-Shafa'i

Sharia Imam al-Lais

Sharia Sidi Uqbah

Tomb of Imam al-Lais

N

Tomb and Mosque of Sidi Uqbah

226

ACCESS The easiest way to the Southern san and Ibn Tulun mosques, and head south along Sharia el-Khalifa for about 1 km. The easiest way to the Northern cemetery is either by taking a taxi direct to Qarafat al-Sharqiyyah or by walking east along Sharia al-Azhar from the Al-Azhar mosque for about 15 mins until you reach the round-about junction with the north-south dual carriageway of Sharia Salah Salem and then

north for 250m. Then cut into the cemetery and head for the dome and minaret which are clearly visible.

WARNING This area is densely populated by Cairenes who live in or near the tombs. In Egypt there has long been a tradition of living close to the dead but the very large numbers are a relatively recent trend caused by an acute scarcity of housing. Con-sequently the people who live in the cemeteries tend to be comparatively poor and, although certainly not dangerous, it is obviously advisable not to flaunt your wealth, dress modestly and remember that this is where people live.

In the Northern Cemetery the **Mausoleum of Sultan al-Zahir Barquq** (1382-89 and 1390-99) was built over a 12 year period in 1398-1411 by his son Al-Nasir Farag (1399-1405 and 1405-12). It was the first royal tomb to be built in this modern necropolis after Barquq had expressed a wish to be buried alongside a number of pious Sufi sheikhs who were already buried there. Therefore his body was moved from the *medersa* on Sharia al-Muizzli Din Allah once the 75 sq m complex had been completed. It is square with two minarets symmetrically placed on the façade. The entrance in the southwest corner leads along a corridor to the *sahn* which has an octagonal fountain in the centre and is surrounded by four *liwans*. The north and south *liwans* have one aisle whereas the west has two and the east three. The east *liwan* has three very simple *mihrabs* and an extraordinarily finely sculpted stone *minbar*. Doors lead from either side of the *liwan* into mausoleums. The north mausoleum contains Barquq's own marble cenotaph which is richly decorated with Koranic inscriptions, together with the tombs of an unknown person and another intended for Farag whose body was left in Damascus after he had been assassinated on a military campaign in Syria. The mausoleum to the south holds the tombs of Barquq's wife and two granddaughters.

A little to the south is the **Medersa & Mausoleum of Sultan al-Qaitbai Mosque** (1468-96), built in 1472-74, which is a magnificent example of 15th century Arab art and possibly one of Egypt's most remarkable monuments from the Arab era. From the outside the building has very harmonious proportions with the dome finely decorated with polygonal motifs. The minaret is also remarkable because it has a square base, octagonal middle section and a cylindrical top tier. The mosque is reached by climbing 17 steps to the entrance which leads into the southeast *liwan*. The cruciform *medersa* has side *liwans*, and a relatively small covered *sahn* with an octagonal roof lantern. The superbly decorated coloured marble floors are somewhat damaged but still attractive. The *liwans* are very narrow but the east *liwan*, which has a modern ceiling, still has a very well preserved and finely encrusted *minbar*. A door in the south corner of the *qibla liwan* leads to the mausoleum which is decorated with the same sort of marbles as the *medersa*. Its high dome is simply decorated, in contrast with the highly ornate walls. Sultan Qaitbai's tomb is enclosed behind an elaborate wooden *mashrabiyya* while the other tomb is that of one of his sisters.

CONTEMPORARY CAIRO

Contemporary Cairo has developed further west on both sides of the river into a modern and increasingly Europeanized capital. Although residential suburbs spread outwards in all directions any visit to Cairo should include the **Egyptian Museum**, the **Museum of Islamic Art**, the **Manial Palace** on Roda Island and, provided it is a clear day without too much pollution haze, the **Cairo Tower** on Gezira Island.

THE EGYPTIAN MUSEUM

The Egyptian Museum (called in Arabic el-Mathaf el-Misri and sometimes, albeit mistakenly, referred to as The Cairo Museum) rates as one of the wonders of the country. It has an enormous wealth of materials covering early history, ancient Egypt and the Islamic period which is unrivalled even in the grand museums of Berlin, London, New York and Paris. For tourists and scholars alike, the museum is a must if only for a few hours.

The museum is situated in the centre of Cairo taking up the north side of Midan el-Tahrir. Entry is from the sculpture garden fronting the building. The museum is worth visiting either early in the day or during the late afternoon since at other

Egyptian antiquities in Paris

Every serious student of Egyptology undertakes a course of study, before travel, from libraries or at museums. Most visitors from Europe have the benefit of proximity to a wide range of high calibre artefacts in their homeland. The most recent collection to come to the eyes of the public is in the Louvre which until now has had insufficient room to display its very numerous high quality possessions. Egyptian antiquities are the centre piece of the newly opened extension there where an amazing 30 rooms and galleries on three floors display over 6,000 objects ranging from minute scarabs to monumental sphinxes. This is just over 10% of the full collection. When, if ever, will the rest be displayed? The curators have done a fine job of balancing the needs of the casual viewer with that of the serious specialist with both thematic galleries and dynastic chronological displays, as best suit the materials and hopefully the visitor. If the opportunity arises for a visit here or to the British Museum in London or the Egyptian Museum in Turin – take it.

times it is taken over by coach parties. The Tutankhamen exhibit is particularly in demand and it might be necessary to queue for entry. The museum is open daily 0900-1645 (Friday 0900-1115, 1330-1600, Ramadan closes at 1500). From time to time rooms are closed for repair, decoration and for setting up new exhibitions. Similarly there are changes in the lay-out of exhibits. Tickets cost E£20 or E£10 for students. Cameras E£10, E£100 amateur videos, no flash photography. There is an additional fee of E£40 (students E£20), for the Royal Mummy Room, reopened in March 1991. Not recommended except for specialists. It is worth buying a detailed guide to the rooms (E£5), where the layout of displays can change from time to time (but also see plan of Egyptian Museum in this *Handbook*). There is a souvenir shop outside of the Museum on the right of the entrance and an official sales area on the left inside the main building. Café and restaurant facilities are available on the first floor.

The new museum was set up and opened in 1902, the brainchild of Francois Auguste Ferdinand Mariette (1821-81), a Frenchman who was a distant relation of Champollion, the decipherer of Egyptian hieroglyphic writing. He was a great scholar of Egyptology who excavated widely in Egypt throughout the second half of the 19th century. He won the confidence of the crown prince Sa'id Pasha proposing greater preservation of monuments and artefacts and more controls on the export of antiquities. Mariette was appointed to oversee all excavations in Egypt through the Egyptian Antiquities Service and also took responsibility for the setting up of the museum of antiquities. His reign was not without its upsets since he quarrelled violently both with Egyptian officialdom and with rival archaeologists but he was successful in creating the present museum which was specially designed to house the Egyptian national collection. It remains well planned for its age and a great treasure house of objects. There are hopes of a new purpose-built museum to be established, possibly at Giza to overcome the complaint that the present rooms are inadequate to handle exhibits in a satisfactory way and that too many major objects are never seen by the public.

A visit to the museum begins in the sculpture garden, where there is a statue and tomb of Auguste Mariette, a number of sphinx-headed statues and a sarcophagus. The main museum building has two floors, both with 51 principal exhibition rooms. Circulate from the entrance in a clockwise direction. The exhibits are distributed in a generally chronological order beginning in the hallway (Room 48-GF). **NB** GF = Ground Floor; UF =

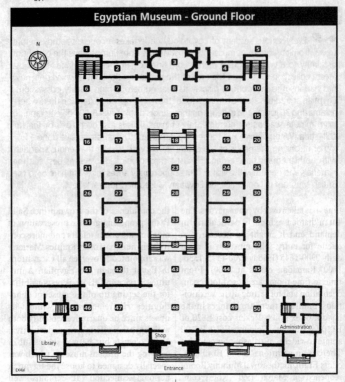

Egyptian Museum - Ground Floor

Upper Floor rooms. Rooms and galleries are both included as 'Rooms'.

The museum is fairly large and for a full initial viewing of both floors and all rooms needs some 4 hrs. A shortened tour is recommended for those with only 2 hrs to spend in the museum, with a circuit of the ground floor followed by a visit to the Tutankhamen Gallery in rooms on the upper floor. If there is scope for a 1-hr visit then the entrance hall (Room 43-GF) and the Tutankhamen galleries, though bear in mind that there can be queues/congestion in this area, especially in Room 3-UF where the principal treasures are stored.

Touring the Museum

The museum also has many other individual objects of great distinction on display.

The guide that follows is no more than a check list of items than those in the collections above in this museum's rich holding of objects. In the entrance room (48-GF, display unnumbered) is a cast of the Rosetta Stone, from which Champollion (see his biography, page 320) decoded the hieroglyphic writing of ancient Egypt. The original is in the British Museum. In the same room are recent additions to the museum's collection out of chronological sequence. Room 43-GF holds a number of Early Dynastic period statues. Old Kingdom (2613-2181 BC) objects take up GF Rooms 47, 46, 41, 42, 36, 31 and 32. In Room 42-GF there is a notable standing wooden statue of the priest Ka-aper and a statue of King Chephren, one of the builders of the Giza pyramids. There is also a painted

Egyptian Museum - First Floor

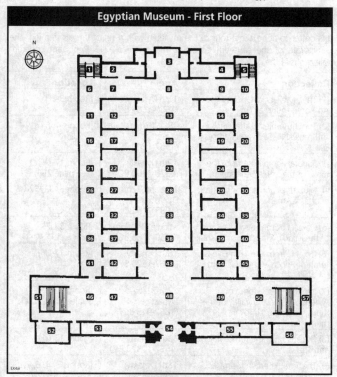

N

EX4ar

stone statue of a 5th Dynasty scribe, cross-legged on a plinth. In Room 32-GF, display 39, is a painted effigy of Seneb the dwarf and his family. He was a keeper of the royal wardrobe in the 5th Dynasty. A well sculptured painted statue of Ti, a noble of the same period and other figures such as Prince Ra-hoptep and his wife Nofert are also to be found in Rooms 32 and 31-GF (display 27).

The Middle Kingdom period (2050-1786 BC) is represented in Rooms 26, 21, 22 and 16-GF. The painted statue of King Menutuhotep is in Room 26-GF (display 67). It was found at Bahr el-Bahari and is 11th Dynasty. Room 26-GF also houses a series of sarcophagi of painted limestone from this period. In particular see the Sarcophagus of Dagi (display 71), a tomb

beautifully illustrating objects in everyday use such as sandals and linen items together with hieroglyphs of magic spells and offerings. King Senusert I (Sesostris) is depicted in 10 limestone statues in Room 22-GF though these are outshone for visual impact by the 56 cm wooden statuette of Senusert I (display 88) carrying sceptres in both hands to denote his royal authority. A granite statue of Amenemhat III is occasionally on show in the same room (display 105) and there are a double statue of that king as the Nile god (display 104) and several sphinxes of the same provenance in Room 16-GF (display 102). The four sphinxes are in grey granite and come from the find by Auguste Mariette at Tanis.

The New Kingdom ran from 2567-1085

Key Targets in the Museum

It is better to approach a tour of the museum with a set of targets in mind. The Directorate of the Museum considers that there are 13 important coherent collections in the galleries.

Collection	Age	Location
(1) The jewellery of Queen Ah-hotep found at Thebes.	17th Dynasty (1650-1567 BC)	[Room 3-EF]
(2) The mummies of the Kings Tuthmosis I-III, Seti I and Ramses II & III.	18-19th Dynasties (1567-1200 BC)	[Rooms 46, 47, 52-UF]
(3) Funeral equipment from the tomb of the noble Sennedjem.	19th Dynasty (1320-1200 BC)	[Room 17-UF] (See page 256)
(4) Mummies and coffins of the priests of Amen.	21st and 22nd Dynasties (1085-715 BC)	[Room 3, 32, 57-UF]
(5) Objects from the royal tombs of the Middle Kingdom at Dashur.	Middle Kingdom (2050-1786 BC)	[Room 3-UF]
(6) Objects from the 18th Dynasty tomb of Prince Maherperi from the Valley of the Kings.	18th Dynasty (1567-1320 BC)	[Room 17-UF]
(7) Items from the tomb of Amenophis II in the Valley of the Kings, including 14 royal mummies.	17th-21st Dynasties (1650-945 BC)	[Room 52-UF – Subject to closure]
(8) Objects from the tomb of Yuya and Thuya.	18th Dynasty (1567-11320 BC)	[Room 13-UF]
(9) The Tutankhamen rooms and galleries with 1,700 objects exhibited.	18th Dynasty (1361-1352)	[Rooms 3, 4, 6, 7, 8, 9, 10, 15, 20, 25, 30, 35, 40 and 45]
(10) Objects from the tomb of Hetep-heres.	4th Dynasty (2613-2181 BC)	[Room 2-UF]
(11) Funeral items of the rule of Akhenaten.	18th Dynasty (1379-1362 BC)	[Room 3-GF]
(12) Monuments from the tomb of Hemaka.	1st Dynasty (3100-2890 BC)	[Room 42-UF]
(13) Artifacts from the Tanis tombs.	21st and 22nd Dynasties (1085-715 BC)	[Room 2-UF]

BC. The exhibits in the set of galleries 11, 12, 6 and 7 are mainly from the 18th Dynasty, with more complex garments and headgear than in previous eras. Room 12-GF is well endowed with notable objects, mainly statues in granite. Most important are the statues of Senen-mut, steward of Queen Hatshepsut and tutor to her daughter. He was responsible for designing the temple of Hatshepsut at Deir el-Bahari. The examples here in Room 12-GF include his block statue (display 132) with his pupil, Princess Nefure, peering below his chin. The plaque carries inscriptions of his titles and merits. Queen Hatshepsut is seen in a variety of statues (Room 12-GF, display 952) and in the remnants of her red sandstone sarcophagus (Room 28-GF, display 131), while there is a variety of statues of Tuthmosis III and Isis, his mother. Hatshepsut is represented in a large restored statue in Room 7-GF.

Room 3-GF is given over to objects from the reign of Akhenaten (Amenhotep IV), who set up his capital at Tell el-Amarna (North of Assiut) and altered the mode of public art and architecture in Egypt to one of realism. There are sandstone statues of Amenhotep IV, of which the presentation of an offering tablet (display 160) is perhaps the most interesting, and a gilded coffin lid of Amenhotep's brother, Smenkhkara. Several heads of women are on display in Room 3-GF, with the unfinished head of Nefertiti (display 161) being the most famous, and the head of a princess (display 163) most exquisitely portrayed. Representations of the 'royal family' in the form of what seems to be a shrine (display 167) are also on show.

The central hall of the museum (Rooms 13, 18, 23, 28, 33 and 38-GF) is used to exhibit giant statues of a mixture of periods. As an example, it is worth while to look at the 7m statue of Amenhotep III and his wife Tyi (display 610).

Objects of the 19th and 20th Dynasties are displayed in Rooms 9, 10, 15, 14 and 20-GF. Room 9-GF contains the Tablet of Saqqara (display 660), which lists the kings of Egypt to Ramses II. The crystalline limestone head of General Nakhtmin (display 195) is in Room 15-GF and shows fine workmanship. The painted bust of Meritamoun, daughter of Ramses II and queen in succession to Nefertari, when available, is also in Room 15-GF.

Best of the Late Period (1085-332 BC) is concentrated in Rooms 25, 24 and 30-GF. Key items include the Psametik group of statues in greenstone of which those of the Psametik, a head jeweller, with Hathor (display 857) and of Isis, wife of Osiris (display 856), are particularly well executed. A statue of Princess Amenartais in alabaster (display 930 in Room 30-GF) is a beautiful example of 25th Dynasty sculpture.

The pride of the museum is contained in the Tutankhamen collection of the 18th Dynasty (years 1361-52) in rooms 3, 4, 6, 7, 8, 9, 10, 15, 20, 25, 30, 35, 40 and 45-UF with 1,700 objects on exhibition. This remarkable treasure was found intact by the Englishman Howard Carter in 1922 in the Valley of the Kings. Tutankhamen ruled for only 9 years between the ages of 9-18. His tomb was saved from heavy destruction grave robbers by its position low in the valley and by the construction of workmens' huts across its entrance. Unlike most other archaeological finds before 1922, the Tutankhamen treasure was retained in Egypt and its full glory can be seen in the Egyptian Museum. All the exhibits have their own value both decorative and academic. Visitors are recommended to look at the entire set of Tutankhamen displays. If time is very short at least look at the following items: (1) **Colossal statue of Tutankhamen** (Room 9-UF, display 173). This is executed in painted quartzite which shows Tutankhamen as a youth and complete with ceremonial beard and hieroglyphs of Horemheb who stole the statue for his own tomb; (2) **The gold mask of Tutankhamen** (Room 4-UF, display 174). The mask is made of gold garnished with carnelian, coloured glass, lapis lazuli, obsidian, quartz, and turquoise. The 54 cm high figure came from the head of the mummy. The blue stripes are in lapis lazuli, there is a ceremonial beard and a head-dress knotted at the back of the neck. There is a gold uraeus and vulture head above the brow; (3) **The gold coffin of Tutankhamen** (Room 4-UF, display 175). This is rendered in gold and semi-precious stones with coloured glass. It is the inner of three coffins, the outer two made in wood. Some 187.5 cm long and weighing 110.4 kg, the coffin is in the form of a mummy in the shape of Osiris with the crossed arms carrying divine emblems. The body is covered by carved feathers and the representations of Upper and Lower Egypt – the vulture and cobra; (4) **Lid of canopic jar** (Room 8/9-UF, display 92), **The goddess Selket** with **The golden shrine** (Room 8/9-UF, display 177). This group of objects includes a wooden shrine gilded with gold and with silver which was in the antechamber of the king's tomb. It is ornately decorated with family and hunting scenes. The jar lid, containing the remains of the king's entrails, is of alabaster, carrying the king's image and lightly painted. There were four Canopic jars as miniature sarcophagi in the tomb. The golden shrine was protected by four goddesses, of which Seket, the water goddess, is displayed in gilded and painted wood about 90 cm high; (5) **Wooden funerary bed** (Room 9/10-UF, display 183). Made of stuccoed wood, these three funerary beds gilded and painted. The most remarkable is the couch with the image of the primordial cow with cow's heads and lyre-like horns set about sun disks; (6) **The Throne of Tutankhamen** (Room 25-UF, display 179). The throne is 102 cm high and 54 cm wide, made of gilded wood and ornamented with semi-precious stones. In addition to the winged serpent arms of the throne, the seat back carries a gilded and painted scene in which Tutankhamen's wife anoints him with oil; (7) **Ceremonial chair** (Room 25-UF, display 181). The finely inlaid ebony and ivory chair of Tutankhamen is regarded as among the best examples of Egyptian cabinet-making ever found. It is decorated with uraeus snakes and divinities; (8) **Funerary statues 'shawabti'** (Room 35-UF, display 182). The tomb of Tutankhamen contained 413 small, approximately 50 cm high, figures of the king as workers, foremen and overseers, giving one workman per day of the year. They are made of wood, which is painted and gilded; (9) **Tutankhamen with a harpoon** (Room

35-UF, display 182). Among the seven royal statuettes found in the tomb of Tutankhamen, the two gilded wooden statues of Tutankhamen hunting in gallery 35 are most pleasing. One shows the king on a papyrus board hunting in the marshes, harpoon in hand. A second is of the king wearing the crown of Upper Egypt riding the back of a panther. (10) **Painted chest** (Room 40-UF, display 186). This is a 44 cm tall/61 cm wide wooden chest, stuccoed with paintwork above. It is in a good state of preservation and carries pictures of battle against Asians and Africans and a set of hunting scenes; (11) **Anubis chest** (Room 45-UF, display 185). A carrying chest made in stuccoed wood and ornamented with black resin, gold, silver and varnish. The chest itself contained jewellery, cups and amulets. Anubis as a jackal sits on the chest ready to act as a guide for Tutankhamen in the after-world; (12) **Ka statue of Tutankhamen** (Room 45-UF, display 180). This large (192 cm tall) statue is one of two guardians of the tomb. It is made in wood and painted in bitumen. The king holds a mace in his right hand and a staff in his left. He is wearing a *khat* head-dress and has a gilded kilt.

On leaving the Tutankhamen galleries there is much still to see in the museum, including jewellery and monuments. Important objects include the wonderful 25-piece collection of **Meketra's models**, in fact models found in the tomb of Meketra, a noble of the Middle Kingdom (2000 BC), at a site south of Deir el-Bahari.

The miniatures show the form, dress, crops, vessels and crafts of the period. The best known is the offerings bearer (display 74), 123 cm high and made of painted wood. It shows a servant, carrying a basket of vases on her head and a duck in her right hand. There are also models of fishermen, cattle, weavers and carpenters in displays 75, 76, 77 and 78, respectively. In Room 32 (display 117) is a **Ka statue of King Auib-re Hor** in wood now bereft of its stucco coating. The head-dress of up-raised arms symbolizes *ka*, the vital force of the king.

Worth looking out for if you have time are the **Fayoum portraits** in Room 141-UF for the most part encaustic (wax) painted in wooden bases and painted by Greek artists in the 2nd century AD to leave a likeness of the deceased for his family. (See page 173.)

THE MUSEUM OF ISLAMIC ART

Open Saturday-Thursday 0900-1600, Friday 0900-1100 and 1330-1600, Entry E£16, students E£8, ticket is also valid for Gayer-Anderson House – see above, is ideally located on the junction of Sharia Port Said and Sharia Qalaa about equidistant between Midan Ataba and the Bab el-Zoueila.

It was originally established in the courtyard of the Al-Hakim Mosque (see above) in 1880 but it was moved to the present building, containing over 75,000 exhibits from various Islamic periods, in 1903. The dates indicated in the museum's exhibits are AH (After the Hegira), which is the starting point of the Islamic Calendar in 622 AD when Mohamed is thought to have fled from Mecca. The rooms follow a chronological order through from the Umayyads to the Abbasids, Fatimids, Ayyubids, Mamlukes and Ottomans. Of particular interest are **Room 1** which contains recent discoveries like the very long papyrus over in the right hand corner; **Room 2** is the beginning of the Umayyad collection, considered the first true Islamic period with the first pieces of Islamic coinage in bronze and gold; **The Fatimid panels** in **Room 4** which depict animals and birds because, unlike the Sunni Muslims, the Fatimid Shi'a have no objection to portraying living things; the doors to **Room 6** which were originally from the Al-Azhar Mosque; the reconstruction of

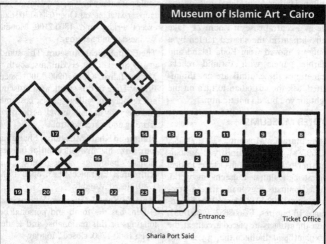

Museum of Islamic Art - Cairo

Entrance

Ticket Office

Sharia Port Said

1. Mainly recent acquisitions
2. Ommayyad (7-8th century) - mainly from Fustat
3. Abbasid (8-10th century) - stucco pannels
4. Fatimid (10-12th century) - panels depicting living things
5. Mamluk (13-16th century) - woodwork and ceramics
6-10. Woodworking in chronological order
11. Chandeliers and other metalwork
12. Armour and weapons
13. A mixture - a room not to miss
14-16. Pottery
17. Upstairs from garden - textiles and carpets
18. Outdoors - Turkish headstones/tombs/sundial
19. Books and manuscripts - a changing exhibition
20. Turkish art - wall hangings, china and jewellery
21. Glass - lamps from mosques arranged in chronological order
22. Persian exhibition - mainly pottery
23. Temporary exhibitions

EX4b

Never smile at a crocodile

Here in the Ancient Egyptian Agricultural Museum the 5m-long crocodile complete with wicked grin is fortunately very dead as are the many other animals here on display. A dog lies on its side, prostrate, seemingly sleeping in the sun and a baboon sits back resting on its haunches, huge hands hanging over its knees.

Collected here are the animals worshipped, pampered, hunted and husbanded by the Ancient Egyptians: fat cats, even fatter Apis bulls, domesticated sheep and horses; birds ranging is size from the falcon and duck to the ostrich and fleet of foot gazelles and the venerated ibis. The animals depicted in hunting scenes on countless reliefs and tomb paintings have not, fortunately, come to life, but their skeletal and mummified remains are on display.

an 18th century Ottoman patio in **Room 10**; the Mamluke astrolabe used by Muslim navigators in **Room 11**; just before leaving **Room 13** on the right the 10th century 'Fayoumi' plate in Chinese style; **Room 20** Persian carpets; the glassware in **Room 21** and the Persian art in **Room 22**. The oil lamps from the mosque of Sultan Hathor, considered one of the most beautiful exhibits in the museum, are in a central case in **Room 21**. Take refreshment in the shaded garden by a fountain moved from Roda Island and marble panels with Fatimid reliefs. Sometimes the exhibits are not illuminated, ask the custodian to turn on the light for you but do not tip him.

OTHER MUSEUMS

Agricultural Museum, T 3608682, F 3607881, adjacent Ministry of Agriculture in Dokki at end of 6th October Bridge. Oldest agricultural museum in world, stuffed animals, Egyptian farming practices, open 0900-1330, closed Monday, entrance 10 piastres, T 3608682, F 3607881. Here the artifacts are placed in context, the flax plant beside the linen, the papyrus plant beside the rope and paper. The many animals that were worshipped, hunted or eaten – cats, ostrich, Apis bulls and falcons are there as mummies or skeletons. Unfortunately the labels, in a variety of languages, give little information and often there are no labels at all.

Cotton Museum, next to Agricultural Museum, survey of cotton growing in Egypt, open 0900-1400, closed Monday and Friday afternoon, entrance free.

The **Entomological Museum** is situated at 14 Sharia Ramses near the railway station. It houses an old (it was founded by King Fuad) but interesting collection of Egyptian birds and insects and is very useful if you could not name what you saw, what ate your crops or what bit you. Open 0900-1300 daily except Friday and 1800-2100 Monday, Wednesday and Saturday.

The **Ethnological Museum** This stands at 109 Sharia Qasr el Aini, just south of Midan Tahrir. Open 0900-1300 except Friday. Here in this small, neat museum are displays of village crafts, costumes and everyday utensils as well as details of farming and water control.

Mahmoud Khalil Museum, 1 Sharia Kafour, Giza has his collection of impressionist paintings and some fine sculptures. Entrance E£25, open 1000-1730, closed Monday.

Mustafa Kamel Museum, Midan Salah el-Din, has the tomb and personal belongings of this nationalist and leader. Open 1000-1700, closed Monday.

Post Office Museum, Midan El-Ataba, second floor in main post office building. Here there are displays of memorial stamps and illustrations of the ways in which the post was transported. Open 0900-1300 except Friday. No charge.

Railway Museum, next to Ramses station, automated display, coaches for

Khediv Ismail's private train, open 0830-1300, closed Monday, entrance E£1.50, Friday E£3.

The **Manial Palace** on Roda Island in the middle of the Nile is an oasis of tranquillity in noisy Cairo and are well worth visiting. Entry is E£5 for foreigners and E£2.50 for students. There is also a fee for normal cameras (E£10), video cameras (E£100). Open daily 0900-1600.

The palace, which was built in 1903 and is now a museum, was the home of King Farouk's uncle Prince Mohamed Ali and comprises a number of buildings in various styles including Moorish, Ottoman, Persian, Rococo and Syrian. The first is the Reception Palace at the gate which is beautifully decorated with polychrome tiles and stained glass. Upstairs are a number of luxurious rooms, of which the Syrian Room is the finest, and a mother-of-pearl scale model of Sultan Qaitbai's mausoleum. To the right is a mosque with a tall mock Moroccan minaret and then a revolting Trophies Museum with tatty and poorly stuffed animals including a hermaphrodite goat and a table made of elephant's ears. Much more interesting is the royal residence in the middle of the garden which is a mixture of Turkish, Moroccan, Egyptian and Syrian architectures and contains a number of rooms, nearly all of which are decorated with blue earthenware tiles. The Throne Hall behind the residence is of little interest but the Private Museum, which includes a very varied collection of Korans, manuscripts, carpets, plates and glassware, is fascinating.

Having been satiated with mosques, mausoleums and museums it is probably worth visiting the top of **Cairo Tower** to get a bird's eye view of the city before treating yourself to a relaxing mini-cruise along the Nile and away from the noisy traffic. The 87m tower (open daily 0900-2400, E£14), is located on Gezira Island and its lotus-shaped top is one of the city's most visible landmarks. It was built with Soviet help in 1957-62. Although the restaurant and cafeteria are OK it is the viewing platform that is most important. Providing the pollution is not too bad, which it often is, you can look east across the modern city centre to the minarets and mosques of Islamic Cairo and the Muqattam Hills beyond; west beyond the residential areas to the Pyramids and the edge of the desert; north towards Zamalek and beyond; or south upstream to Roda Island and the original pre-Coptic settlement of Babylon in Egypt where this teeming mega-city first began almost 2,000 years ago.

Other places to visit

Dr Ragab's Papyrus Institute, boat moored alongside Cornich el-Nil opposite *Cairo Sheraton*. The museum displays the processes involved in the making of papyrus. It is possible to purchase copies of illustrations and writing on papyrus found in tombs. Open 0900-2100, entrance E£4.

Rare Books and Special Collections Library, 22 Sharia Sheikh Rihan. Definitely for the specialist. Open 0800-1700. Closed Friday and Saturday and all August.

Dr Ragab's Pharaonic Village open 0900-1700 in winter and until 2100 in summer, entrance E£35 is more fun than culture, a great place, especially for those with children. It is located on Jacob Island 3 km south of the city centre. Numerous actors perform the daily activities of the ancient Egyptians. It gives background to the main sites and as the pace is set by the boat tour through the village on the bullrush-fringed Nile allow at least 2 hrs. Avoid February when the boat does not run as the river is too low and the journey then is on foot.

October War Display, junction of Sharia Oruba and Ismail el-Fangari, Heliopolis.

Take a breather

Hold your breath. According to UN figures lead pollution in the atmosphere in Cairo is equivalent to 1 tonne per car per year, and Cairo has over 1 million cars.

This illustrates the October 1973 War with the crossing of the Suez Canal and the attack on the Bar-Lev line, the air battle led by the Egyptian Air Force and an almost life-size painted scene of the battle to take Qantara. The commentary is in Arabic. Shows at 0930, 1000, 1230, 1800 and 1930. Closed Tuesday. Entrance E£10.

GARDENS

There are several spacious gardens for the visitor to find some tranquillity away from the city bustle. These include the **Zoological Gardens** in Giza, The **Fish Gardens** in Zamalek, The **Japanese Gardens** in Helwan, The **Meryland Gardens** in Heliopolis, The **International Garden** in Nasr City and the **Kanater al-Khaireya Gardens** (the Good Barrage) about 25 km from the capital. Unfortunately at present there are a number of open spaces which need more attention and others which have been closed down (**Andalusian Garden** closed since 1987) as they are being worn away by too much public use! Perhaps a charge will have to be made for entry to pay towards upkeep. The **River Nile Promenade**, constructed at huge expense and opened in 1996, has also been closed to protect it from the wear and tear.

Manial Palace Garden. After years of neglect the rare botanical garden annexed to Mohammed Ali Palace on Roda Island is to be renovated. The garden is 5,500 sq m and contains a rare collection of trees brought back to Egypt by Mohammed Ali. Once returned to its original splendour it will be opened to the public who will now have to pay to enter.

Zoo

Giza zoo has many claims to fame. In particular it is the biggest exhibitor in Africa, having on display the largest number of endangered species. Its situation near the west bank of the River Nile at Giza makes it easily accessible over El Gamea Bridge. The zoo is organized into five huge grottos, one holding statues of rare Egyptian mammals. There are over 6,000 animals and birds on display from around 40 species. Features include the Reptile House and the Lion House. The zoo is proud of its record in breeding and returning to the wild Barbary Sheep, Nubian Ibex, Dorcas Gazelle and Sacred Ibis. Visitors used to western zoos may find a visit here very distressing and hence not a recommended stop. Entrance 10 piasters. Open 0800-1800 in summer, 0900-1700 in winter.

● **Accommodation**

Price guide:			
AL	US$150+	**D**	US$25-50
A	US$100-150	**E**	US$10-25
B	US$75-100	**F**	under US$10
C	US$50-75		

As the largest city in Africa and the Middle East and one of the world's great tourist destinations it is not surprising that Cairo has hundreds of hotels ranging from deluxe accommodation, often run if not owned by the major international chains, to some really unpleasant places. The listing below, which has sought to avoid the worst, provides a wide range to suit every budget. The expensive and medium price hotels have been grouped by region for convenience.

City Centre: AL *Cairo Marriott Hotel*, Sharia Saray el-Gezira, Zamalek, T 3408888, F 3401108, 1,250 rm, built around a lavish 19th century Gezira Palace built to commemorate the opening of the Suez Canal and still retains some of its real spendour. 12 restaurants, bars, night club and Egypt's largest casino, located in the heart of the city, has own sporting facilities – tennis court, health club, etc, beautiful gardens, simply palatial, a good place to unwind from the bustle of Cairo; **AL** *Cairo Ramses Hilton*, 1114 Corniche el-Nil, Maspero, T 5754999, F 5757152, 850 rm, in heart of Cairo, overlooking the River Nile nr Midan Tahrir, within walking distance Egyptian museum. Tower block of 28 flrs, do your birdwatching from the balcony, pool, healthclub, plus a variety of restaurants, bars, lounges and boutiques, first class business centre; **AL** *Cairo Sheraton*, Midan Gala', Dokki, Giza, T 3488600, F 3489051, 660 rm, located just south of the Gala bridge, views of River Nile, Sheraton high quality service, visible as twin

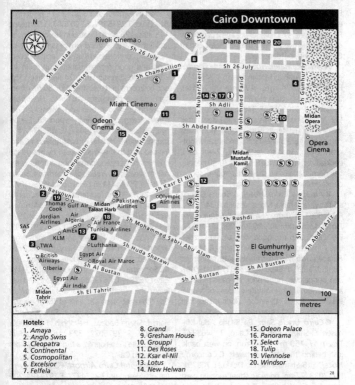

Cairo Downtown

Hotels:

1. Amaya
2. Anglo Swiss
3. Cleopatra
4. Continental
5. Cosmopolitan
6. Excelsior
7. Felfela
8. Grand
9. Gresham House
10. Grouppi
11. Des Roses
12. Ksar el-Nil
13. Lotus
14. New Helwan
15. Odeon Palace
16. Panorama
17. Select
18. Tulip
19. Viennoise
20. Windsor

towers on west bank of River Nile, views of the pyramids from the restaurant, circular pool; **AL** *El-Gezira Sheraton*, Gezira Island, PO Box 264, Orman, Giza, T 3411333, F 3405056, opp the *Cairo Sheraton*, circular tower, 27 flrs, on the south tip of Gezira Island is one of the Cairo's most distinctive landmarks, business provision is excellent, *El-Samar*, riverfront restaurant/nightclub and *Regine's* discotheque; **AL** *Helnan Shepheard*, Corniche el-Nil, Garden City, T 3553900, F 3557284, 281 rm, all with good views, south end of Gezira Island, varied cuisine, pool, business centre. A modern structure named after the original hotel which burnt down in 1952, good Nile view, glory is fading; **AL** *Le Méridien Le Caire*, Corniche el-Nil, Garden City, T 3621717, F 3621927, 275 rm, very well-managed French hotel, located by the River Nile on north tip of Roda Island, with excellent service for businessmen and tourists, and popular French restaurant; **AL** *Nile Hilton*

Hotel, Corniche el-Nil, Midan Tahrir, T 5780444, F 5780666, 434 large rm, located on the River Nile, adjacent to Egyptian Museum, recently modernized but showing its age as it was opened in 1959 by President Nasser. Like many international Hiltons, is the place for the jet set of the capital. The Ibis Club is the meeting place for coffee, Jacky's one of the best nightclubs in the city – swinging until the early hours, for the more active the pool is rec. Business centre for those who must keep in touch; **AL** *Safir Cairo Hotel*, Midan El-Misaha, PO Box 138 Orman, Dokki, T 3482424, F 3608453, 280 rm, located relatively close to but without view of the Nile, offers good group discounts; **AL** *Safir Zamalek Hotel*, 21 Sharia Mohamed Mazar, Zamalek, T 3420055, F 3421202, 104 rm, expensive but pleasant hotel with a good view of the Nile from the northwest end of Gezira Island; **AL** *Semiramis Inter-Continental*, Corniche el-Nil, Garden City, T 3557171,

F 3653020, 840 rm, an ugly building and very expensive, is possibly the best hotel in Egypt with French cuisine, excellent service and a good view of River Nile overlooking the southeast end of Gezira Island, outdoor pool.

A *Atlas Zamalek Hotel*, 20 Sharia Gamaet el Dowal al Arabia, Mohandiseen, T 3465782, F 3476958, 74 rm; **A** *Flamenco Hotel*, 2 Sharia el-Gezira el-Wasta, Abu al-Feda, Zamalek, T 3400815, F 3400819, 132 a/c rm (33 singles and 77 twins and suites), new hotel, located on quieter but less scenic northwest corner of Gezira Island, high standard and spotlessly clean, Spanish restaurant, 24-hr café, cocktail bar, conference room for 30-40 people, ballroom, takeaway shop, tea room, shops, bank, business centre.

B *Alnabila Cairo Hotel*, 4 Sharia Gamiat ad-Duwal al-Arabia, Mohandsseen, T 3461131, F 3475661, 170 rm, 364 beds; **B** *Belair Cairo Hotel*, Mokattam Hill, PO Box 996, T 916177, F 922816, 276 rm, good view of the Citadel, badly located for downtown Cairo; **B** *Manial Palace (Club Mediterranee)*, Kasr Mohamed Ali, El-Manial, T 846014, F 3631737, 190 rm and bungalows, huge pool, an oasis of peace and tranquillity in exquisite gardens of Manial Palace on the north end of Roda Island, half board only, discotheque open from 2300-dawn.

C *Cairo Uncle Sam*, 54 Sharia Abul Mahasen El-Shazli, Agouza, Cairo, T 3465377, Tx 20147, 150 rm, family-run, on west bank, just behind the *Atlas Zamalek*; **C** *Concorde Hotel*, 146 Sharia el-Tahrir, Dokki, T 708751, F 717033, 72 rm, on main street running west from the Gala' bridge; **C** *Marwa Palace*, 11 Sharia el-Khatib, Dokki, T 3433380, Tx 23000, 28 rm, very noisy but clean; **C** *Pharaoh Egypt Hotel*, 11 Sharia Ahmed Orabi, Mohandsseen, T 3471619, F 3474196, 138 rm, on west bank; **C** *Pharaohs*, 12 Sharia Lutfi Hassuna, Dokki, T 712314, Tx 93383, 96 rm, friendly, very clean, family-run hotel with good service but a poor breakfast, located in a street parallel to the River Nile and northnorthwest between the Gala' and 6th October bridges; **C** *President Hotel*, 22 Sharia Dr Taha Hussein, Zamalek, T 3400718, Tx 93655, F 3413195, 119 comfortable clean rm, very good well-run hotel, provides good value for money, quiet and convenient location in the middle of the north end of Zamalek, restaurant with good food and excellent service, try downstairs for snacks and atmosphere, business facilities, slow and inadequate lift.

Airport: **AL** *Baron Hotel Heliopolis*, 8 Sharia Ma'ahad el-Sahara, off Sharia el-Uraba (also known as Airport Rd), PO Box 2531, El-Horriya, Heliopolis, T 2915757, F 2907007, 126 rm and 14 suites, 226 beds, located in Heliopolis overlooking palace, a good businessman's hotel, clean and comfortable, if unspectacular, decent food and good service, banqueting room for 700 people, 2 restaurants, 24-hr coffee shop, bar, ballrooms and discotheque, 150 rm extension almost complete; **AL** *Cairo Heliopolis Movenpick* (also known as *Movenpick Concorde*), Cairo International Airport Rd, El-Horriya, Heliopolis, T 2470077, F 667374, 412 soundproofed rm, one of best hotels in Cairo, located next to the airport, used by transit and business passengers, good food and really excellent service; **AL** *Heliopolis Sheraton*, Sharia el-Uraba, PO Box 11361, Heliopolis, T 2902027, F 2904061, 90 rm, located nr airport, currently only the front building is in use; **AL** *Le Méridien Heliopolis*, 51 Sharia el-Uraba, PO Box 2928 El-Horriya, Heliopolis, T 2905055, F 2918591, pool, good hotel located only 10 mins from airport, French restaurant very popular, well equipped health club, business centre rec; **AL** *Sonesta Hotel*, 4 Sharia el-Tayaran, Nasr City, T 2628111, F 619980, 210 rm, located half way to the airport just off Sharia el-Uraba in Nasr City (Medinet Nasr) just east of the main stadium; **AL** *Swissotel Cairo el-Salam*, Abdel Hamid, Sharia Badawi, Heliopolis, T 2974000/ 2976000, F 2976037, 323 rm, located in wooded site in Heliopolis, a taxi ride away from downtown Cairo.

A *Novotel Cairo Airport*, PO Box 8, Cairo Airport, Heliopolis, T 2474772, F 2914794, 209 rm, 415 beds, an unspectacular airport version of the Novotel 4-star chain, almost all the guests are transit and business passengers.

C *Beirut Hotel*, 56 Sharia Beirut, Heliopolis, T 662347, Tx 22115, 91 rm; **C** *Egyptel*, 93 Sharia el-Merghani, Heliopolis, T 2907444, Tx 93987, 78 rm, nr the *Baron Hotel*; **C** *Horriya Hotel*, 14 Sharia el-Horriya, Heliopolis, T 2903472, Tx 94332, 57 rm, budget hotel nr *Baron Hotel*.

Pyramids: **AL** *Cairo Jolie Ville Movenpick*, Desert Rd, PO Box 1, Giza, T 3852555, F 3835006, 240 rm, located nr the Pyramids, lovely gardens and excellent food; **AL** *Forte Grand Pyramids*, Desert Rd, T 3830383, F 3831730, 523 rm, a/c, some with balcony, recently renovated, rooms with view of pyramids cost more, direct dial phone and sat TV, 4 restaurants, 5 bars, large heated pool, fitness centre, business facilities, shops, bank, hairdresser, beauty salon. Small charge made for shuttle bus to town centre which takes minimum of 35 mins. A really grand hotel, able to cope with businessmen and honeymooners; **AL** *Mena House Oberoi*, Pyramids Rd, El-Ahram, T 3833222, F 3837777, 520 rm, very attractive old style hotel built in 1869, excellent view of Pyramids, set in 16 ha of gardens, superb nightclubs and restaurants, discotheque, casino, largest outdoor pool in Cairo, tennis, a nearby 18 hole golf course, horse and camel riding with experienced instructors, take a room in the renovated older part for preference; **AL** *Pyramids Park Sofitel*, Desert Rd, T 3838666, F 3839000, 481 double rm incl 31 duplex suites, good service, located 2.5 km outside Cairo nr the Pyramids, facilities incl 4 restaurants, nightclub with oriental floorshow, banqueting and conference centre for up to 400 delegates, pool, health club, gym, sauna, tennis, and nearby golf course and horse-riding clubs.

A *Europa Cairo*, 300 Pyramids Rd, T 621100, F 2907077, 250 rm, 450 beds; **A** *Siag Pyramids Penta Hotel*, 59 Mariuteya, Saqqara Rd, PO Box 107, Ahram, T 3856022, F 3840874, 352 rm, large hotel located nr, and with a good view of the Saqqara pyramids, good room service reportedly better than eating in the restaurant.

B *Green Pyramids*, 13 Sharia Helmiat, El-Ahram, T 537619, F 537232, 84 rm, on the main road to the Pyramids; **B** *Holiday Sphinx*, Cairo/Alex, Desert Rd, T 854930, 182 rm, out of town; **B** *Kaoud Delta Pyramids*, end of King Faisal Rd, El-Ahram, T 3833000, F 3830957, 140 rm, pool, a room with view of Pyramids, also suffers from traffic noise; **B** *Oasis Hotel*, Cairo/Alex Desert Rd, PO Box 44, Pyramids, T 3831777, F 3830916, 260 rm, good motel style hotel nr Pyramids, large clean pool and a 24-hr restaurant.

C *Chateau des Pyramides Hotel*, 10 Sharia Sadat, PO Box 167, Cairo-Alexandria Desert Rd, T 3871342, F 3838545, 75 rm, very good; **C** *Pyramids Hotel*, 198 Sharia el-Ahram, El-Ahram, T 3875100, F 3874974, 84 rm, located on the main road to the Pyramids, caters for budget groups; **C** *Saqqara Country Club & Hotel*, Saqqara Rd, Abu el-Nomros, T 852282, 20 rm, located outside the city nr the Saqqara pyramids, very highly rec, well run with good food and excellent horse-riding facilities, temporary club membership available.

Maadi: **AL** *Sofitel Maadi Towers*, 29 Corniche el-Nil, PO Box 217, Ma'adi, Cairo, T 3506092, F 3518449, 176 excellent rm, good view of the Nile, excellent service, located at south end of Corniche and a long way from downtown Cairo.

A *Ma'adi Hotel*, 55 Sharia Misr Helwan, PO Box 196, Ma'adi, T 3505050, F 3518710, 145 rm, 219 beds, a long way from downtown Cairo in the south suburb of Ma'adi.

B *Residence*, 11th Rd 18, PO Box 418, Ma'adi, T 3507189, 28 rm.

C *Atlas*, Sharia Mohamed Roushdi, Midan Opera, T 3918311, Tx 92564, 110 rm, a decent downtown hotel but is noisy because it is next to a large mosque.

D *Abu el-Hoal Palace*, 161 Sharia el-Ahram, El-Ahram, T 856043, 20 rm, located on way to the Pyramids; **D** *Arabia*, 31 Sharia Abdel Aziz al-Saud, El-Manial, T 841444, 16 rm, 40 beds, family run hotel on Manial Island which specializes in budget groups; **D** *Cairo Crillon*, 19 Sharia el-Montaser, Agouza, T 3477570, 38 rm, very good hotel in the west bank area of Agouza; **D** *Cairo Inn*, Sharia 26 Syria, Mohandsseen, T 3490661, 25 rm, off Midan an-Nasr; **D** *Caesar's Palace Hotel*, 45 Sharia Abdel Aziz Fahmi, Heliopolis, Cairo, T 2457241, F 2457240, 60 rm, family-run hotel nr the main Heliopolis Hospital; **D** *Carlton*, 21 Sharia July 26th, Azbakia, T 755323, Tx 20734, 60 rm, family-run, located on a noisy downtown street; **D** *Cosmopolitan*, 1 Sharia Ibn Tahlab, Kasr el-Nil, T 3923845, F 3933531, 84 a/c rm incl 6 suites, recently refurbished, located in centre of downtown Cairo in a relatively quiet side-street in an elegant building, restaurant which serves reasonable food, bars, café, nightclub, excellent laundry service; **D** *El-Kanater Chalets*, El-Kanater Gardens, Kalioubeya, T 958328, 24 rm, good location but a long way from downtown Cairo; **D** *El-Manar*, 19 Sharia Abdel Hamid, off Sharia Lutfi, Mohandsseen, T 709299, Tx 94004, 85 rm, caters for budget groups; **D** *El-Nil Hotel*, 12 Sharia Ahmed Raghab, Garden City, T 3542800, Tx 93284, F 3552878, 272 rm, rather dark and dreary; **D** *El-Nil Zamalek*, 21 Sharia Maahad, Sharia el-Swisri, Zamalek, T 3401846, 38 rm, 60 beds; **D** *Fontana*, Midan Ramses, T 922145, 93 rm, cheap hotel with pool, located nr the very noisy and crowded Ramses station; **D** *Heliopark*, 100 Sharia el-Hegaz, Heliopolis, T 2451346, F 2459789, 96 rm; **D** *Horus House Hotel*, 21 Sharia Ismail Mohamed, Zamalek, T 3403977, F 3403182, 35 rm, friendly, clean , cheaper tariff for extended visits; **D** *Indiana*, 16 Sharia el-Saray, Dokki, T 714422, F 3493774, 115 rm; **D** *Jasmin Hotel*, 29 Sharia Geziret el-Arab, Mohandsseen, Cairo, T 3472278, F 3421907,

65 rm, off Midan an-Nasr; **D** *Kanzy*, 9 Sharia Abu Bakr el-Siddik, Mohandsseen, T 709461, 57 rm; **D** *Kemet Hotel*, Midan Abbasiya, PO Box 46, Abbasiya, T 824018, Tx 93256, 96 rm, poor location halfway between Heliopolis and downtown Cairo but good hotel; **D** *King Hotel*, 20 Sharia Abdel Rahim Sabri, Dokki, T 710939, Tx 22393, 90 rm, family-run hotel; **D** *Longchamps*, 21 Sharia Ismail Mohamed, Zamalek, T 3409644, 30 rm, decent well located hotel run by a very helpful and friendly family; **D** *New Star*, 34 Sharia Yiyha Ibrahim, Zamalek, T 3401865, Tx 23000, 28 rm; **D** *Odeon Palace Hotel*, 6 Sharia Abdel Hamid Said, Kasr el-Nil, T 776637, Tx 21708, 30 rm, modern hotel with a roof garden in a noisy but central location; **D** *Salma Hotel*, 12 Sharia Mohamed Kamel Morsi, Mohandsseen, T 700901, F 701482, 54 rm, good view of Cairo from the rooftop bar and on a clear day you can see pyramids, good and friendly service, an English pub, bar, restaurant with good food and cheap drinks; **D** *Saqqara Palm Club*, Saqqara Rd, Badrashin, T 200791, Tx 23646, 21 rm, clean, excellent pool, set in beautiful gardens, excellent hotel but located right outside Cairo; **D** *Sheherazade*, 182 Sharia el-Nil, Agouza, T 3461326, F 3460634, 160 rm, budget hotel with a good view of the Nile overlooking the Gezira Island; **D** *Sweet Hotel*, 39 Rd 13, Ma'adi, T 3504561, 6 rm, in the south suburbs; **D** *Tonsi Hotel*, 143 Sharia el-Tahrir, Dokki, T 3484600, 37 rm; **D** *Vendome*, 287 Sharia el-Ahram, El-Ahram, T 538904, F 854138, 60 rm, clean and comfortable family-run hotel on the way to the Pyramids; **D** *Victoria*, 66 Sharia el-Gumhorriya, Midan Ramses, T 918766, 105 rm, located in noisy, crowded area nr Ramses station, has large a/c rooms, restaurant, bar; **D** *Windsor*, 19 Sharia Alfi Bey, T 915277, F 921621, 55 rm, rec as best 3-star hotel in downtown Cairo, clean, well run, one of the nicest bars in the city, Michael Palin stayed here while going round the world in 80 days – not very reliable plumbing!

E *Amun*, Midan Sphinx, Agouza, T 3461434, 40 rm, noisy hotel a the busy west end of the 26th July bridge; **E** *Cairo Commodore*, 10 Sharia Fawzi Ramah, Mohandsseen, T 3460592, 25 rm; **E** *Caroline Crillon*, 49 Sharia Syria, Mohandsseen, T 3465101, Tx 23158, 38 rm; **E** *Gabali Hotel*, 221 Sharia el-Higazt, Heliopolis, T 2455224, Tx 23568, 68 rm; **E** *Grand Hotel*, 17 Sharia July 26th, Azbakia, T 757700, F 757593, 99 rm, 180 beds, located in a crowded downtown area, has much of its original Art Deco

fixtures and furniture; **E** *Green Valley*, 33 Sharia Abdel Khalek Sarwat, Kasr el-Nil, T 3936317, 28 rm, a decent budget hotel nr the noisy Opera Square; **E** *Kinow*, 382 Sharia el-Ahram, El-Ahram, T 859260, 36 rm, located on way towards the Pyramids; **E** *Lotus Hotel*, 12 Sharia Talaat Harb, T 750627, F 921621, 50 rm some have bath and a/c, clean, comfortable and friendly budget hotel in very central location, reception is on the 7th flr and is reached via the Malev Airlines arcade; **E** *New Hotel*, 21 Sharia Adli, T 3927033, F 3929555, 65 rm; **E** *Oasis Hotel*, 15 Sharia Abdel-Wahab el-Kadi, Kolleyet el-Banat, Heliopolis, T 2917312, F 2907912, 60 rm; **E** *Omayad Hotel*, 22 Sharia July 26th, T 755044, 72 rm, noisy downtown location; **E** *Rose*, 6 Sharia Iran, Midan Dokki, T 707059, 40 rm, located just off Dokki's Sharia el-Tahrir; **E** *Sphinx*, 8 Sharia Magles el-Sha'b, Abdin, T 3557439, 80 rm, located in a tower block on the south side of the Peoples' National Assembly (parliament); **E** *Tiab House Hotel*, 24 Sharia Mohamed Khalaf, Dokki, T 709812, 33 rm, 60 beds; **E** *Zayed*, 42 Abul Mahasen el-Shazli, Agouza, T 3463318, 40 rm, nr Midan Sphinx and the west end of the 26th July bridge to Zamalek.

F *Anglo-Swiss*, 14 Sharia Champollion, T 751479, 1930s style, decaying charm, downtown *pensión* with fairly clean shared bathrooms, drinks but no food except breakfast; **F** *Aviation Hotel*, PO Box 2688, S Fatima, Heliopolis, T 2450393, 29 rm, 46 beds, used almost exclusively by foreign air crews; **F** *Big Ben*, 33 Sharia Emad el-Din, T 908881, 37 rm, 82 beds, nr Ramses Station, reception is on the 8th flr; **F** *Blue Nile*, 4 Sharia el-Hokama, off Manshiet el-Bakri, T 291078, 27 rm, located between downtown Cairo and Heliopolis; **F** *Cairo Palace*, Sharia el-Gumhorriya, Midan Ramses, T 906327, 24 clean rm, located in the very noisy area outside Ramses Station, rooftop restaurant and a friendly staff; **F** *Capsis Palace*, 117 Sharia Ramses, Midan Ramses, T 754219, 72 rm, clean and comfortable, located in crowded and noisy area; **F** *Garden City*, 23 Sharia Kamel el-Din Salah, Garden City, T 3544969, 38 rm, 1930s style *pensión* hotel located behind *Semiramis*, some rooms have Nile view; **F** *Gresham House Hotel*, 20 Sharia Talaat Harb, T 759043, F 762298, 45 rm, centrally located downtown; **F** *Happy Town*, 10 Sharia Ali el-Kassar, Emad el-Din, T 928600, 66 rm, 113 beds; **F** *Helio Cairo*, 95 Sharia Abdel Hamid Badawi, Heliopolis, T 2450682, Tx 20327, 41 rm; **F** *Hotel Des Roses*, 33 Sharia

Talaat Harb, Cairo, T 758022, 32 rm, 51 beds, clean and comfortable, centrally located, make sure you get one of the refurbished rooms; **F** *Kasr el-Nil*, 33 Sharia Kasr el-Nil, T 754523, 62 rm, central location, noisy disco; **F** *Lido Hotel*, 465 Sharia el-Ahram, El-Ahram, T 727373, Tx 93661, 90 rm, on road to the Pyramids; **F** *New Helwan*, 29 Sharia Sherif, Helwan Hamamat, T 784508, 31 rm, on main industrial area; **F** *New Riche*, 47 Sharia Abdel-Aziz, Midan Ataba, T 3900145, 37 rm, cheap hotel located equidistant between the downtown area and the Islamic section with a sympathetic female proprietor; **F** *Radwan*, 83 Sharia Gawhar el-Kaaid, Midan Azhar, T 901311, 45 rm, noisy, not advisable for single women; **F** *Safa Inn Hotel*, Sharia Abbas el-Aqqad, Medinet Nasr, Cairo, T 2619022, F 2619022, 50 rm, 85 beds, located far from centre; **F** *Select*, 8th Flr, Sharia Adli, highly rec downtown budget hotel located on 8th flr, breakfast incl; **F** *Tourist Palace Hotel*, 12 Sharia el-Baidak, El-Muski, T 915126, 51 rm, nr noisy and crowded Midan Ataba; **F** *Tulip*, 3 Midan Talaat Harb, T 766884, 22 rm, good location on 3rd flr and above an office block in the heart of downtown Cairo, clean and comfortable; **F** *Viennoise*, 11 Sharia Mahmoud Bassyouni, Kasr el-Nil, T 751949, Tx 94285, 26 rm, atmospheric downtown hotel which retains its turn of the century character.

Camping Because there are so many hotels there is little demand for camping. One of the very few is called *Salma Camping* which can be reached by turning off from Harraniya village on the road between the Pyramids and Saqqara. It offers both cabins, a camping ground, hot showers, a buffet and a bar.

Youth hostel 2 km south of city centre, 135 Sharia Abdel-Aziz al-Saud, El-Manial, nr University Bridge, T 2 840729, 204 beds, kitchen, meals available, family rooms, laundry, overnight fee E£5, station 3 km. Book 1 month in advance. **Egyptian Youth Hostel Association (EYHA)**, 7 Sharia Dr Abdel Hamid Said, Marouf, Cairo, T 2 758099.

● **Places to eat**

Price guide:
♦♦♦Expensive; ♦♦average; ♦cheap.

The numerous high quality hotels can be relied upon to serve good, anxiety-free meals and usually have a range of expensive and average meals. Cheap meals are available in the many *fuul* restaurants (see **Information for travellers**, page 440).

♦♦♦: *Al-Adin*, in *Cairo Sheraton*, Lebanese and Middle Eastern specialities open 1300-1600 and 2000-2400. A very sophisticated setting, very expensive. Live entertainment of exceptional quality.; *Al-Saraya*, in *Heliopolis Movenpick*, seafood specialities and gourmet menu, open 1800-2400; *Amici*, 20 Sharia El-Haram, T 3830088. Spanish/Italian food spiced with a view of the Pyramids. Best choice is the seafood, choose your own fish. Open 1000-0100. Limited takeaway menu. Price reflects the location so stay and eat; *Arabesque*, 6 Kasr el-Nil downtown, T 5747898, open 1230-1530 and 1930-0030, the surroundings are exceedingly elegant, service is excellent and the food, whatever the choice, is first class. Expensive, but a meal to remember; *Chin Chin*, at The Four Corners, 4 Sharia Hassan Sabri, Zamalek, T 3412961. Open 1930-2400. High quality Chinese food, beautifully presented, home delivery also available but why miss the ambience? *Justine's*, 4 Sharia Hassan Sabri, Zamalek, at The Four Corners, T 3412961, excellent service, noted for high quality French food, the place for a special meal; *La Mamma*, open 1000-0100, in *Cairo Sheraton* cheerful atmosphere, serves Italian food with live entertainment which makes conversation difficult; *La Piazza*, Four Corners, 4 Sharia Hassan Sabri, Zamalek, T 3412961, open 1230-0030, very welcoming and friendly service. Desserts are a weight-watcher's nightmare; *Le Chalet*, Swissair Restaurant, El Nasr Building, Nile St, Giza, T 3485321, Swiss and French specialities, good service, open 1200-2400; *Moghul Room*, Mena House Oberoi, T 3833222, open 1230-1445 and 1930-2345, authentic Indian food, soothing atmosphere, live Indian entertainment every evening; *Movenpick*, Cairo International Airport, Swiss and Far Eastern specialities; *Starlight*, in Baron Hotel, 8 Sharia Maahad El-Sahari open 1930-0030, international food, panoramic views; *Tokyo*, 4 Sharia el-Maahad el-Swissry, Zamalek, T 816610, excellent service, interesting Japanese food, if this is what you came to Egypt for!

♦♦: *Ali Hassan el-Hati*, 8 Sharia July, T 918829, open 1100-2200, fish and kebab both rec; *Cellar*, at The President Hotel, Western/Egyptian food in a convivial bar setting, popular socially with young affluent Egyptians, open 1200-0200; *Christo's*, 10 Sharia El-Haram, another restaurant with a view of the Pyramids. Here the speciality is fish – choose your own as you enter. Open 1100-0300. Sometimes busy at lunch times with tour groups; *El-Dar*, Saqqara Rd, T 852289, Western/Egyptian food; *Felfela*, 15 Sharia Talaat Harb, T 3922822, open 0700-0000, one of downtown Cairo's most famous and popular tourist restaurants, serves good decent food and beer but its fame has allowed it to rest on its laurels and put up its prices, now very over-rated and too much plastic; *Le Rendezvous*, in shopping arcade of *Hotel Ramses* for quick service, open 1000-2200; *The Marina* opp *Cairo Marriott Hotel*, open 1800-2400, fish specialities; *Mr Maxim*, Sharia El Shaheed Abdel Moneim Riyadh, Mohandessen, T 3606121, restaurant, lunch and dinner, French, Lebanese, Moroccan and Greek food, sea food speciality, open 1200-0200; *Roy's*, in *Marriott Hotel*, serves Mexican food from 1200-2400; *Silver Fish*, 39 Mohy El Din, Sharia Abu El Ezz, Dokki, T 3492272, good seafood in a relaxed setting.

♦ : *Andreya*, 59 Mariuteya Canal, T 851133, specialities are chicken/pigeon, eat out of doors; *El Omda*, 6 Sharia El Gazzor, Mohandiseen, next to *Atlas Zamalek Hotel*, famous for Egyptian specialities, especially *koshari*; *La Rose*, 58 Sharia Mariuteya Canal, T 855712, clean surroundings, tasty food; *Zamalek Restaurant*, 118 Sharia 26th July, for *fuul* and *tameya*; Best fast food at *Al-Dente* for pasta, 26 Sharia Bahgat Ali, Zamalek T 3409117; *El-Shabrawi* for ful and tameya, 7 Sharia Ibrahim, Heliopolis, T 4178191; *Lan Yuan* for Chinese food, 84 Road 9, Ma'adi, T 3782702; *Maroush*, Lebanese cuisine, 64 Midan Lebanon, Mohandiseen, T 3450972; *Kenny Rogers Roasters*, roast chicken, 21 Sharia Nadi el-Seid, Dokki, T 3366344; *Smiley's Grill*, 75 Sharia Abu Bakr el-Sedik, Midan Safir, Heliopolis, T 2406258, open 1000-0200, except Sunday. For international fast food ask the taxi driver for Pizza Hut, McDonalds or KF Chicken – they are all in the same street.

Floating restaurants: *Nile President*, good efficient service, clean, well maintained, excellent and varied food; *The Nile Maxim*, T 3408888, two nightly cruises at 2000 and 2300 and weekend lunch at 1430, wide choice of menu, fish specialities, live entertainment and show, moored opp entrance to *Cairo Marriott Hotel*; *Le Steak* on *Le Pacha 1901*, Sharia Saray el-Gezirah, T 3406730, an elegant Nile River boat, steaks plain or with all the trimmings. Book to get a river view seat, open 1200-0200.

If you want something that stays open a bit later try the following; *Cairo Cellar* under *President Hotel*, cosy, often bordering on crowded; *Deals*,

cheap, cheerful and very noisy at 2 Sharia el-Maahad el-Swissri; *Harry's Pub* in *Cairo Marriott Hotel*; *Johnny's Pub* on *Le Pacha 1901* (see above) rather pricey; *Piano-Piano*, in World Trade Centre, open until 0300 serving Chinese and French cuisine.

● **Airline offices**
Air France, 2 Midan Talaat Harb, T 743300; **Air India**, 1 Midan Talaat Harb, T 3922529 (Airport T 966756); **Alitalia**, *Nile Hilton Hotel*, T 743488 (Airport T 655143); **British Airways**, 1 Sharia Abdel Salam Aref, T 762914 (Airport 963456); **Egyptair**, 9 Sharia Talaat Harb, T 3932836, or *Nile Hilton* (Airport 697022); **Iberia**, 15 Midan Tahrir, T 749955; **KLM**, 11 Kasr el-Nil, Cairo, T 5740999; **Lufthansa**, 6 El-Sheikh el-Marsafi, Zamalek, Cairo, T 3420471; **Quantas**, 1 Sharia Kasr el-Nil, T 749900; **Royal Air Maroc**, 9 Sharia Talaat Harb, T 740378; **Swissair**, 22 Sharia Kasr el-Nil, T 741522 (Airport 669537); **Tunis Air**, 14 Talaat Harb, Cairo, T 769726.

● **Banks & money changers**
American Express, 4 Sharia Syria, Mohandiseen, T 3605256; **Bank of Alexandria**, T 3913822-3, and **Egyptian Central Bank**, in Sharia Ksar el-Nil, T 3926211; **Barclays International Bank**, 1 Sharia Latin America, Garden City, T 3540431, 3542195; **British-Egyptian Bank**, 3 Sharia Abu El Feda, Zamalek, T 3409186; **Chemical Bank**, 3 Sharia Ahmed Nessim, Giza, T 3610393; **Citibank**, 4 Sharia Ahmed Pasha, Garden City; **National Bank of Egypt**, 24 Sharia Sherif, T 3924022, F 3924177. Western Union Money Transfers are now available from branches of International Business Associates throughout the city, T 3571300.

● **Cultural Centres**
American, US Embassy, 5 Sharia Latin America T 3549601, closed Friday and Saturday; **Austrian**, Austrian Embassy, Sharia El-Nil T 5702975; **British** in British Council, 192 Sharia El-Nil, Agouza. T 3031514, closed Sunday; **Canadian**, Canadian Embassy, Garden City, T 3543110, only Tuesday and Wednesday; **Dutch**, 1 Sharia Dr Mahmoud Azmi, Zamalek, T 3400076; **German**, Goethe Institute, 5 Sharia Abd El-Salam Arif, T 5759877; **Israeli**, Israeli Embassy, 92 Sharia El-Nil, T 3488995; **Italian**, 3 Sharia Sheikh el-Marsafi, behind *Marriott Hotel*, Zamalek T 3408791, closed Friday and Saturday; **Swiss**, Swiss Embassy, 10 Sharia Abd el-Khalek Tharwat, T 5758284, closed Friday and Saturday.

Mummy Come Home

✈ An elegant new tomb has been constructed, its pillars supporting a deep blue ceiling studded with gold stars. This is an attempt by the Egyptian Museum in Cairo to recreate the ambience of Thebes in around 1300BC and provide a final resting place for some of its most famous pharoahs.

The mummies have suffered many indignities. Take Merneptah, grandson of Seti I. Having survived a spectacular first burial with all the pomp and splendour due to Egyptian royalty, tomb robbers flung his mummy aside and 21st Dynasty priests rewrapped him and placed him with eight other displaced persons in a side chamber in the Tomb of Amenhotep II. Rediscovery in 1898 was followed by transport to Cairo where he was put on view. Queen Nedjemet, another resident was slashed by the knives of those who unwrapped her. The great Ramses II unwrapped in public in 1886 in an unseemly 15 mins strip has also found a decent home here. In 1946 public display of mummies was banned as improper. But in March 1994 the special tomb tastefully displays these bodies neatly wrapped once again, complete with dimmed lighting and dehumidifiers to protect the desiccated remains. Among the eleven who have found, hopefully, a final resting place here beside Queen Nedjemet, Merneptah and Ramses II are Merytamum his queen and his father Seti I.

● **Embassies & consulates**

Embassies in Cairo: Algeria, 14 Sharia Brazil, Zamalek, T 3418527; **Canada**, Sharia Mohamed Fahmi el-Sayed, Garden City, T 3543110/9; **France**, 29 Sharia el-Nil, Giza, T 3415694/7; **Germany**, 8A Sharia Hassan Sabri, Zamalek, T 3418153; **Libya**, Sharia el-Saiobh, Zamalek; **Morocco**, 10 Sharia El Din Ayoub, Zamalek, T 3409677; **Spain**, 25 Sharia Gamal el-Din Abu al-Mahasen, Garden City, T 3547069; **Sudan**, 3 Sharia El Ibrahimi, Garden City, T 3549661/3545043, letter of recommendation required; **UK**, 7 Sharia Ahmed Raghab, Garden City, T 3540852/9; **USA**, 5 Sharia Latin America, Garden City, T 3557371.

● **Entertainment**

Casinos: found in the following hotels: *Cairo Heliopolis Movenpick, Cairo Marriot, Cairo Sheraton, El Giza Sheraton, Mena House Oberoi, Nile Hilton, Ramses Hotel, Semiramis Intercontinental, Shepheard Hotel.*

Cinemas: Current information on cinema performances is given in the Egyptian Gazette and Egyptian Mail as well as the monthly Egypt Today publication. Commercial cinemas change their programmes every Monday so check the programme. Arabic films rarely have subtitles. The World Trade Centre offers two venues, Upstairs and Katcho's.

Cinema in English: Al Tahrir, 122 Sharia al Tahrir, Dokki, T 3354726, daily at 1000, 1300, 1500, 1800, 2100; **Cosmos 1 and Cosmos 2**, 12 Sharia Emad el Dine, T 5742177, shows at 1030, 1300, 1530, 1830 and 2130; **El Haram**, 147 Sharia El Haram, T 5742177, shows at 1230, 1530, 1830, and 2130, midnight shows Thursday, Friday and Saturday; **El Salam**, 65 Sharia Abdel-Hamid Badawi, Heliopolis, T 2931072, daily at 1530, 1830, 2130 and midnight; **Karim I/Karim II**, 15 Sharia Emad el Dine, T 5924830, shows at 1000, 1300, 1500, 1800 and 2100; **Metro** in *Swissotel el-Salam*; **MGM**, 4th Floor Maadi Grand Mall, T 3523066. Shows at 1230, 1530, 1830 and 2130 with midnight shows Thursday and Friday; **New Odeon**, *Cairo Sheraton*, Sharia El-Galaa, Giza, T 3606081 (50% discount for students), daily 1000, 1300, 1500, 1800, 2100 and 0000; *Ramses Hilton Cinema*, 7th flr of the hotel's shopping annex. See also map, page 139.

Galleries: *Ewart Gallery*, Main Campus, American University in Cairo, Sharia El-Sheikh Rihan, open daily except Friday and Saturday 0900-2100; *French Cultural Centre*, 27 Sharia Sabri Abu Alam, Midan Ismailia, open daily except Friday and Saturday 1000-1400 and 1700-2000; *Khan el-Maghraby Gallery*, 18 Sharia El-Mansour Mohamed, Zamalek, daily except Sunday, 1030-2100; *Mashrabiya Gallery*, 8 Sharia Champollion, Downtown, daily except Friday 1100-2100; *Salama Gallery*, 36a Sharia Ahmed Orabi, Mohandessin open daily, 1000-1400 and 1700-2100.

Nightclubs/discos: all with live entertainment and most with belly dancer: *Abu Nawas*, in *Mena House Oberoi Hotel*, open 2000-0300, T 3833444; *Aladin*, open air, and *Alhambra*, in *Cairo Sheraton Hotel*, summer only, closed Monday, T 336970; *Belvedere*, in *Nile Hilton*, open 2000-0230, closed Tuesday, T 767444; *El-Samar*, in *El-Gezira Sheraton Hotel*, T 3411555; *El-Torero*, in *Hotel Sofitel*, T 3506092; *Empress*, in *Cairo Marriott*, T 3408888, is very popular; *Haroun el-Rachid*, in *Semiramis Intercontinental Hotel*, closed Monday, T 3557171; *La Belle Epoque* in *Le Méridien Cairo Hotel*, T 3621717; *Tent*, in *Heliopolis Sheraton Hotel*, closed Monday, T 2455155; *Ya Salam*, in *El-Salam Hotel*, closed Monday, T 2974000, ext 7003.

Most popular discos with young and affluent Egyptians and expatriates: *Atlantis* at *Shepheard Hotel*, open 2300-0400, entrance E£50; *Borsalino's*, 15 Sharia Rustum Basha, Garden City, open 2300-0300, entrance E£20, for a more basic club playing African influenced pop and reggae; *Saddle* at the *Mena House Oberoi*, open 2200-0400, closed Sunday, entrance, E£40; *Tamango* in *Atlas Zamalek Hotel*, T 3466567, open 2200-0300, entrance E£40.

Sound & light: 3 performances daily at the Sphinx and Pyramids, Giza: at 1830, 1930 and 2030 in Winter, 2030, 2130, 2230 in Summer. Entrance: E£33. Information: T 3852880. Bring a sweater as it gets quite chilly in the evening and use insect repellent as the mosquitoes become active at dusk.

Monday	English/French/German
Tuesday	English/French/Italian
Wednesday	English/French
Thursday	Arabic/English/Japanese
Friday	English/French
Saturday	English/Spanish
Sunday	French/German/Japanese

Theatres: current information for theatre performances is given in the *Egyptian Gazette* and *Egyptian Mail* as well as the monthly *Egypt Today* publication.

The 7-storey *Opera House*, T 3420598, in the Gezira Exhibition Grounds has a main hall with 1,200 seats for opera, ballet and classical music performances, a second hall with 500 seats for films and conferences and an open air theatre. Advance booking is rec. Men must wear jacket and tie. *Al-Gumhorriya*, in Sharia Gumhorriya, T 919956; *Balloon*, Sharia el-Nil nr al-Zamalek Bridge, T 3477457; *Mohamed Farid*, in Sharia Mohamed Farid, T 741204; *Puppet Theatre*, Azbakiah, T 910954; *The National*, in Azbakiah, T 917783. Apart from the *Opera House*, all performances are likely to be in Arabic; Whirling dervishes – Egyptian members of the Sufi sect – perform at the Ghuriyya Cultural Centre housed in the Mausoleum of al-Ghawri, Sharia al-Azhar on Wednesday and Saturday evenings, starting about 2000, T 909146.

● **Hospitals & medical services**
Chemists: 24-hr service: *Ataba Pharmacy*, Midan Ataba, T 920831; *Helwan Pharmacy*, 17 Sharia Ahmed Anas, T 38018; *Isa'f Pharmacy*, Sharia Ramses, T 743369; *Magsoud*, 29 Sharia Mahmoud Shahk, Heliopolis, T 2453918; *New Cairo airport*, T 2446032; *Old Cairo airport*, T 2903964; *Zamalek Pharmacy*, 3 Shagaret El Dor, Zamalek, T 3402406.
Dentists: Maadi Dental Centre, Digla, Maadi, T 3534311.

Hospitals: *Anglo-American Hospital*, behind Cairo Tower, T 3406162; *Coptic Hospital*, Sharia Ramses, T 904435; *Damascus Hospital*, 1 Sharia Damascus, Mohandiseen, T 3470194; *El-Salam International*, Maadi, T 3507592; *Shaalan Surgical Centre*, 10 Abdel Hamid Loth, Mohandiseen, T 3605180.

● **Places of worship**
Anglican/Episcopalian, *All Saints' Cathedral*, 5 Sharia Michel Lutfalla, Zamalek, T 3418391, services in English Sunday at 0800, 1030 and 1930, Holy Communion Saturday at 0830, for weekday services please enquire; *St John the Baptist*, Sharia Port Said, Maadi, services Saturday at 1730; **St Michael's**, 10 Sharia Seti, off Sharia Baghdad, Heliopolis, Eucharist Saturday at 1830, Sunday at 1030 and 1930 in Arabic and 1800 in English; **Christian Science Society**, 3 Midan Mustafa Kamel, T 3929032, Sunday at 1830 and Wednesday at 1930, reading room available; **Coptic/Orthodox**, Church of St Anthony and Girgis, Heliopolis, T 821274, mass in English third Sunday in month at 0800; **German Evangelical/Lutheran Church**, 6 Sharia Gaber Ben Hayyan, Dokki, T 3614398, Sunday at 1730; **Quaker**, alternate Sunday at 1900, T 3576969; **Roman Catholic**, *Holy Family Church*, Maadi, T 3502004, daily Mass Monday-Thursday at 0615, Friday at 0900, service in English Saturday 1730 and Sunday 1800, French Saturday at 0630, Spanish Saturday at 1700; *St Joseph's Church*, T 3408902, 2 Sharia Bank Misr, Downtown, Mass in French daily at 0730 and 1830, also Sunday in French 0730, 0830 and 1830, in Arabic at 1000, Italian at 1200 and English at 1630; *St Joseph's Church*, 4 Sharia Ahmed Sabri, Zamalek, Mass (English) Sunday 1800.

● **Post & telecommunications**

Area code: 02.

Post Office: Cairo's main post office is on Midan Ataba. Major hotels can possibly provide the same services without the crowds.

Telecommunications: there are International telephone, telex and fax services at all major hotels.

● **Shopping**

Egypt's low labour costs mean that a number of western clothing chains manufacture high quality cotton goods in-country incl Benetton, Naf Naf, Mexx. Prices are considerably lower than in the West. Visit Cairo's trendiest shopping mall, *The World Trade Centre*, 1191 Corniche el-Nil, Maspero, for the full selection. Moiré silk handmade shoes available from *Atlas* nr *Nagib Mahfouz Café* in Khan El Khalili, T 5906139, or in *Semiramis Intercontinental Hotel*. Among the most attractive areas to shop is the *Khan el-Khalili Bazaar* and *Sagh* comprising an array of shops dating from the 14th century. Renowned for craftsmanship in silver and gold, embroidered cloth, copper ware, leather and ivory inlaid goods. (Remember that the import of ivory is forbidden into most Western countries.) The Kerdassa village, east of Giza, is noted for its embroidered cotton and silk dresses, *galbeyas*, and other handmade goods while Haraneya, west of Giza, is the main centre for quality carpets.

Bookshops: those selling books and periodicals in European languages. *Academic Bookshop*, 121 Sharia el-Tahrir, Dokki, open 1000-1500 and 1700-2000, closed Thursday pm and all Friday; *Al-Ahram*, 165 Sharia Mohamed Farid, downtown in *Nile Hilton*, open 0830-2200; *Al-Arab Bookshop*, 28 Sharia Faggala, T 908025, open 0900-1400, 1700-2000, closed Sunday; *Alexandria Bookshop*, 134 Sharia Omar Ibn el-Khatab; *American University in Cairo Bookstore*, on main campus, closed Friday and all August; *Anglo-Egyptian Bookshop*, 165 Sharia Mohamed Farid, Downtown, open 0900-1330 and 1630-1930, closed Sunday; *Baron Books*, *Méridien Heliopolis Hotel* 0830-2330; *Dar ek Shark*, Sharia Brazil, Zamalek, open 1000-1400 and 1700-2000, closed Friday; *Everyman's Bookshop*, 12 Sharia Baghdad, Heliopolis, open 0930-1430 and 1700-2130 except Sunday; *Lehnert & Landrock*, 44 Sharia Sherif, books in German and English, open 0930-1330 and 1530-1930, closed Saturday afternoon and Sunday; *Livres de France*, 36 Sharia Kasr el-Nil, T 3935512. Open 1000-1900, morning only on Saturday and closed Sunday; *L'Orientaliste*, 15 Sharia Kasr el-Nil, nr Midan Tahrir, T 5753418, for oriental and rare books – old maps, lithographs and post cards, open daily 1000-1930 except Sunday, has been in the hands of the same French family for generations.*Reader's Corner*, 33 Sharia Abd el-Khalek Tharwat, open 1000-2200, closes at 1500 on Saturday and all day Sunday.

● **Sports**

Bowling: *MISR Bowling Centre*, 9th flr, Al Bustan Centre, Bab Ellouk, T 392229.

Cycling: T 3526310 for meeting each Friday at 0700 by Cairo American College.

Diving: Meeting 1900 first Monday each month at *Helnan Shepheard Hotel*.

Golf: there is a public golf course at the foot of the pyramids. Also at *Mina House Oberoi* and *Pyramid Park Sofite*. *Katameya Heights Golf Course* is located just 23 km south east of Cairo. Here the annual membership is E£5,000 with a restriction of 600 players. Currently it has 18 holes with another 9 being constructed.

Gym: at *Nile Hilton*.

Horse riding: Guezira, T 3405690. But much more pleasant to ride in the desert by the pyramids, particularly for sunrise or sunset. Avoid the haggard looking horses lined up for tourists by the pyramid's gate and head for the stables in Kafr el-Gabal (straight on past the entrance to the Sound and Light). *AA Stables* (T 3850531) and *MG Stables* (T 3583832) are the most highly rec, have regular Western clients, and offer a variety of excursions from the standard hour-long ride around the pyramids (E£15), riding lessons (E£20/hr) to a trip to Saqqara (E£60). More elaborate excursions and night rides need to be booked in advance.

Rugby: Club meets for training at 1830 each Monday and Wednesday at the Victory College fields, T 3750840 for details.

Running: Cairo Hash House Harriers, meet each Friday approximately 2 hrs before sunset. For differing venues contact T 3476663.

Shooting: *Shooting Club*, Dokki, T 3498479.

Swimming: use the pools at the hotels. Those in the 5-star establishments cost more. Heliopolis, Giza and Gezira sporting clubs have pools; daily and weekly membership available. Public pools are to be avoided.

Sub Aqua Club: at British embassy each Tuesday. Monthly dive trips and training schedule, T 3654567.

Egyptian handmade carpets

🦶 The variety and high quality of Egyptian handmade carpets is still not fully known outside the country. Yet they are every bit as valuable and decorative as most Persian and Turkish products. Nothing can be better as a memento of Egypt than a locally made carpet or rug and a better choice will be made with a little knowledge and by taking your time in making your selection. If you do buy, make sure that you pick a rug that you like and can live with. Acquiring carpets as an investment is only for the experts.

In Egypt there are two main types of handmade carpet, the flat woven *kilims* and knotted carpets usually of wool on a cotton base.

Kilims are flat woven rugs and include tapestries with woven scenes. They have the great virtue of being cheap, light in weight and easily packed. Very decorative are the thin Bedouin rugs in bright reds and golds, while there are also coarse rag rugs made from scraps of material common in Egypt. Most valuable are the *kilims* made entirely of wool and dyed in natural colours or mixed fibres, some in very bright hues.

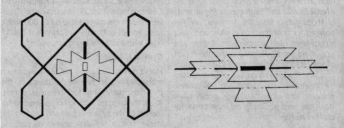

Typical Kilim designs from Assiut

Handknotted carpets and rugs are more expensive than *kilims*. The number of knots per square centimetre determines the quality of a handknotted carpet, as does the materials of which it is constructed. The backing (the warp) may be of cotton, wool or silk and the knots of wool or silk. Coarse woollen material is used when knot densities are low, on average about 25 per cm, while the fine wools and silks require higher densities of up to 69 knots per cm, take longer to make and therefore cost more.

Designs for the handknotted carpets are very varied, though the best usually take their patterns from tile designs from the walls of the famous mosques. Often however designs are adapted from traditional patterns made popular elsewhere in the Middle East – Persian, Turkish and Caucasian being most widespread. Pleasing designs on small rugs follow the classical patterns of the tree of life, formal hunting scenes, the Persian garden, bird carpets and central medallions. Most small rugs were, and to an extent, are still produced as prayer mats and incorporate a triangular top portion to act as the indicator of the direction to Mecca copied from the *mihrab* in the wall of the mosque.

The Egyptian carpet industry is relatively recent in origin, though there is evidence in ancient Egyptian monuments such as the Tomb of Kheti at Beni Hassan, that mat weaving existed from at least 2000 BC. In Egypt today carpets are woven by the Bedouin, household weavers and by workers in small workshops. Most weaving is done on a horizontal loom with the weaver sitting on the ground. More recently the vertical loom has been used for manufacturing high quality and ornate Egyptian hand-knotted carpets and tapestries. Hand-looms are all different and little credit is given in the traditional weaving areas to mathematical accuracy. Expect, therefore, that even best quality carpets and rugs will be slightly misshapen.

Most wool for carpet making is imported though some Bedouin still use wool from their own or neighbours' flocks. Camel hair and cotton are also important parts of rug-making, camel hair giving a natural colour for traditional rugs and cotton providing the long warps through which the wool is woven.

Designs vary greatly from the simple provincial mosque wall derived patterns of Assiut to the ornate medallions of the Senna and Persian types. Colours are most subtly used in the complicated designs of the hand-knotted carpets of the small workshops but the brightly-coloured narrow strips of the Bedouin weavers have their own charm.

Machine-made carpets, normally to be avoided, can be distinguished by the fringe which will often have been sewn on later, or by the sides which are much neater and flatter than handmade rugs, and by the back which does not show the pattern very clearly and is quite smooth. Fold back the carpet for a close examination of the knots and pattern on the rear of the carpet to check the mathematical precision of weaving which gives away the fact that it is factory made.

Purchase Each carpet will need to be bargained for with patience and humour. The following points might help during this process. (1) Before entering the bargaining process make sure that you know what you are looking for – rug, tapestry or carpet – and what size of carpet your rooms can accommodate (and you can comfortably carry with you out of Egypt). (2) If possible take an independent Egyptian friend with you to the shop who understands carpets and rugs. He will help to overcome language and bargaining hurdles. (3) Take your time by shopping around and calling more than once at a shop before purchase. There is no need to be rushed whatever the inducement. (4) Remember that you must pay for your purchase in Egyptian pounds – exchanging currency through a shop keeper can be very expensive – and that posting a carpet home from Egypt is technically difficult and best avoided.

The most famous carpet shop in Egypt are to be found in Cairo, first in the Khan el-Khalili where the best and most expensive wares are on sale. The Cairo city centre and main streets of Zamalek also have their specialist carpet dealing shops, while Alexandria and its adjacent villages such as Hammam have both a carpet school and commercial carpet shops.

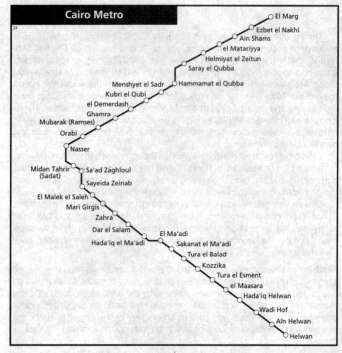

Cairo Metro

El Marg
Ezbet el Nakhl
Ain Shams
el Matariyya
Helmiyat el Zeitun
Saray el Qubba
Menshyet el Sadr — Hammamat el Qubba
Kubri el Qubi
el Demerdash
Ghamra
Mubarak (Ramses)
Orabi
Nasser
Midan Tahrir
(Sadat) — Sa'ad Zaghloul
Sayeida Zeinab
El Malek el Saleh
Mari Girgis
Zahra
Dar el Salam — El Ma'adi
Hada'iq el Ma'adi — Sakanat el Ma'adi
Tura el Balad
Kozzika
Tura el Esment
el Maasara
Hada'iq Helwan
Wadi Hof
Aïn Helwan
Helwan

Tennis: tennis courts can be booked at the *Marriott Hotel*. *Katameya Tennis Resort* has 10 clay courts and 2 of grass.

Yachting: *Yacht Club*, Maadi, T 3505169.

● **Sport (spectator)**

Football: at the stadium in Heliopolis, weekends at 1500.

Horse racing: weekends from 1300 in winter at the Guezira race-course and weekends mid October to end of May at Heliopolis race-course.

Rowing: races each Friday on the River Nile.

● **Tour companies & travel agents**

Abercrombie and Kent, 5 Sharia Bustan, Tahrir, T 761324; *Academy Tours*, 95 Sharia el-Herghani, Heliopolis, T 345050; *American Express*, 21 Sharia Giza, Nile Tower Building, T 3703411; *Astra Travel*, 15 Sharia Demashk, Mohandsseen, T 3446445; *Egyptian Express*, 8 Sharia Kasr el-Nil, T 750620; *Etam Tours*, Egyptian Tourism and Medical Services, 3 Sharia Kasr el-Nil, T 754721, F 5741491, ask for Dr Bishara, along established firm offering specialized handling of handi-

capped visitors; *Gaz Tours*, 7 Sharia Bustan, T 752782; *Hermes Travel*, 1 Montaser Bldg, Sharia Sudan, Sahafeyeen, T 3451474; *Isis Travel*, 48 Sharia Giza, Orman Bldg, T 3494326; *Karnak Travel and Touristic Services*, 12 Sharia Kasr el-Nil, T 750600; *Mena Tours*, El-Nasr Bldg, Sharia el-Nil, Giza, T 3482217 and 14 Sharia Talaat Harb, T 740955; *Misr Travel*, 1 Sharia Talaat Harb, T 3930010, ask for Mr Mohamed Halawa; *Seti First Travel Co*, 16 Sharia Ismail Mohamed, Zamalek, T 3419820, F 3400855; *Thomas Cook Overseas*, 12 Midan El-Sheikh Youssef, Garden City, T 3564650.

● **Useful telephone numbers**

Accident: T 123; **Cairo Airport**: T 2472548/2914255; **Cairo Railway Station**: T 5764214; **Fire**: T 125; **International collect call**: T 146; **Police**: T 122; **Pyramids Office**: T 850259; **Tourist Police**: T 126 or T 926028; **Tourist Police Head Office**: T 3906027.

● **Useful addresses**

Major police offices: at Railway Station, Cairo

Airport, Midan Tahrir, Sharia 26th July/Mansour Mohamed.

● **Transport**

Local Bus: buses in Cairo are only for the strong and the brave. They are very crowded. They tend to slow down rather than stop which requires some agility. One enters at the rear and leaves by the front which means pushing the length of the bus. The main bus station is in Sari al Gala behind the Egyptian Museum. Bus No 997 goes to the pyramids and Nos 356 and 400 (hourly) to the airport. **Calèche**: for a tourist ride. This is expensive but an experience. **Car hire**: Avis, 16 Sharia Ma'amal el-Soukkar, Garden City, T 3547081, also at *Hotel Méridien, Nile Hilton Hotel, Hotel Jolie Ville* and *Sheraton Hotel*; **Bita**, 15 Sharia Mahmoud Bassyouni, T 746169; **Budget**, 1 Sharia Mohamed Ebeid, Heliopolis, T 666027, also at *Marriott Hotel*; **Hertz**, 195 Sharia July 26, Agouza, T 3474172, also at *Ramses Hotel, Sonesta Hotel, Maadi Hotel* and *President Hotel*. **Metro**: in addition to the Heliopolis Metro connecting Midan Ramses to Heliopolis, Nasr City and Mattareya, there is the Helwan Metro from Helwan, stopping at 14 stations incl Old Cairo and Maadi, operates daily every 6 mins from 0530-2400 (summer 0530-0100). (See page 150 for map.) Tickets E£0.50. Don't lose your ticket as you will need it at the exit and don't smoke. There are separate 'women-only' carriages on all trains, generally the first one. Many stations are only named in Arabic. **Taxis**: ramshackle but the best way of getting around. Check current prices with locals or at your hotel. Best not to ask the price first or to bargain but just pay the current price at the destination and don't ask for change.

Train Sleeping cars: T 753555/3484633. To **Alexandria**: 17 daily; **Aswan**: 0730, 1545, 1900, 1915, 1930, 2000, 2030, 2100; to **Beni Suef and Assiut**: 0700, 1000, 1240, 1410, 1600; to **Luxor**: 0100, 1200, 1400; to **Port Said and Ismailia**: 0620, 0845, 1240, 1425, 1830.

Road Bus: for destinations outside Cairo: *East Delta Bus Co*, from Midan Abbassiya, T 824753; *Middle Delta Bus Co*, T 946286; *West Delta Bus Co*, T 759701. The Cairo-Fayoum City bus leaves every 30 mins from Midan Ahmad Helmi just behind Ramses Railway Station.

Cairo Environs: The Pyramids & El-Fayoum

EVER SINCE the Greek and Roman era, if not earlier, the Pyramids at Giza just to the west of Cairo have been one of the world's great tourist attractions. Although there are other pyramids in Egypt, the ones at Giza are almost certainly the largest, most imposing and best preserved ancient monuments in the world. In order to see the development from the simple underground tomb to the audacious concept and awesome majestic splendour of the Pyramid of Cheops it is undoubtedly worth visiting Saqqara before going on to Giza.

MEMPHIS

The oldest known imperial city on earth, was founded in the 1st Dynasty (3100-2890 BC) at the start of the Early Dynastic Period (3100-2686 BC), and lies 15 km south of Cairo. It was established sometime around 3100 BC by Menes who may have actually been several successive kings rather than a single person. It was the Pharaohs' capital city throughout the Old Kingdom (2686-2181 BC) and was inhabited for 4 millennia, until it was eventually abandoned by the Moors, and returned to the Nile silt from which it was originally constructed. Sadly all that remains today is a limestone Colossus of Ramses II (1304-1237 BC) and a giant alabaster sphinx weighing 80 tonnes, both of which may have stood outside the huge Temple of Ptah, and the remains of the Embalming House, where there are several alabaster tables, weighing up to 50 tonnes, which were used to embalm the sacred Apis bulls before burial at Saqqara. Beyond these its former glories can only be imagined. Entrance fee E£14, students E£7, camera E£10 and video camera E£100.

SAQQARA

ACCESS To reach **Saqqara** (open daily 0900-1600, entry fee E£20 or E£10 for students with cards, camera fee E£10 or E£100 for video cameras) by public transport take the No 121 bus from Giza Pyramids to Badrashin (E£0.35) and then Badrashin to Saqqara village (E£0.40) after which it is a 3 km walk. Giza to Saqqara by camel costs E£150 per person and takes 4-5 hrs or E£160 and 2 hrs by horse. People who really want to ride a camel around the pyramids could get a 10 mins ride for E£15. Horses can be hired to ride from Giza to Saqqara. Avoid the Sphinx stable where the horses are reported to be tired and in poor condition. There are better stables such as AA or MG at the right of the main entrance. Because of the hassle of public transport and the fascinating information an informed tour guide can provide about the area it is probably best to spend E£50-E£60 to go with a reputable tour group. All guides will expect *baksheesh* of a few E£ at the end of the tour but only give it if you genuinely feel that they have been good. On the journey between Saqqara and Giza most tour coaches will stop at some of the numerous carpet schools. Avoid Fridays, Saturdays and public holidays when Egyptians turn out for picnics, games of football and general merriment in such numbers that it is hard to get through the crowds. You would do well to avoid the expensive cafeteria too and take some sandwiches.

Saqqara, which faces Memphis across the River Nile from the west bank, was the enormous necropolis for the first pharaohs. It extends for over 7 sq km. With many tombs believed to be still undiscovered it is currently Egypt's largest archaeological site. From its inception it expanded west into the desert until the 4th Dynasty (2613-2494 BC) when the Giza plateau superseded it. At the end of the 5th Dynasty (2494-2345 BC) a more systematic construction of pyramids and *mastabas* began which resulted in many splendid monuments around Saqqara. In 1883 a Middle Kingdom (2050-1786 BC) necropolis was found to the east but it was not until the New Kingdom (1567-1085 BC) that Saqqara is thought to have regained its importance as a burial ground.

ZOSER'S FUNERARY COMPLEX

This complex, the largest in Saqqara, is an example of some of the world's most ancient architecture. The whole complex, including but not confined to the **Step Pyramid**, was designed and built by Zoser (2667-48 BC), the second king in the 3rd Dynasty, under the control of his chief architect Imhotep who some regard as the world's first architect. At its heart is the Step Pyramid, the first of its kind, which can be seen as a prototype for the Giza Pyramids. This marked the evolution of burial tombs from *mastabas* with deep shafts for the sarcophagus to imposing elevated mausoleums. It was constructed in steps building up from the traditional *mastaba*. The original tomb was initially expanded to a 4-step and then to a 6-step

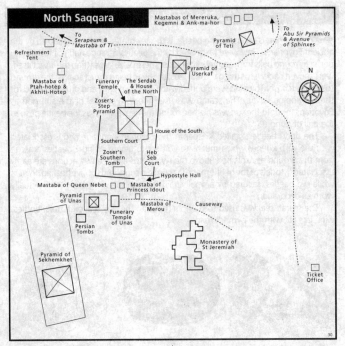

North Saqqara

Refreshment Tent

To Serapeum & Mastaba of Ti

Mastabas of Mereruka, Kegemni & Ank-ma-hor

To Abu Sir Pyramids & Avenue of Sphinxes

Pyramid of Teti

Mastaba of Ptah-hotep & Akhiti-Hotep

N

Pyramid of Userkaf

Funerary Temple

The Serdab & House of the North

Zoser's Step Pyramid

House of the South

Southern Court

Zoser's Southern Tomb

Heb Seb Court

Hypostyle Hall

Mastaba of Queen Nebet

Mastaba of Princess Idout

Pyramid of Unas

Mastaba of Merou

Causeway

Persian Tombs

Funerary Temple of Unas

Monastery of St Jeremiah

Pyramid of Sekhemkhet

Ticket Office

30

pyramid. Although the external white limestone casing has disappeared over time this step structure is still clearly visible. The pyramid eventually reached a height of 62m which, although small by comparison with those at Giza, is still an amazing feat because of the primitive building techniques. The advances represented by Zoser's Pyramid were not in the building techniques or materials, which were already established, but the concept, design and calculations involved which made such a monument possible.

In accordance with the traditional *mastaba* technique, the Royal Tomb lies 28m underground at the bottom of a vertical shaft. The shaft was then sealed with a 3 tonne granite block but this did still not prevent the tomb from being looted. Another 11 shafts were found, 32m deep, under the east side of the Pyramid, which lead to the tombs of the queens and royal children. Unfortunately these are no longer open to the public.

The whole funerary complex was completely surrounded by buttressed walls which were over 544m long, 277m wide and 10.4m (20 cubits) high. Although 14 fake doors were built, only the one in the southeast corner, which leads into the colonnade **Hypostyle Hall** actually gives access to the site. It is thought that the area was walled in order to deter intruders and thieves, and to provide space for the Pharaoh's *Ka* (spirit) to live in the after-life. Before entering the Colonnade, observe the fake door complete with hinges and sockets in the Vestibule on the right. The Colonnade leads through to the **Southern Court**, on the south side of which there is a frieze of cobras. This represents the fire-spitting goddess of destruction Edjo who was adopted as the Uraeus, the emblem of

The Sacred Scarab

Scarabaeus sacer, a dung beetle, is the celebrated beetle held sacred by the ancient Egyptians. They were fascinated by the beetles' strange habit of fashioning perfectly round balls from animal-droppings. These balls, larger than the insect itself, were moved backwards using the rear legs, the head being thrust against the ground to give purchase. The balls were buried with newly laid eggs and provided food for the developing larvae. The scarab was used too as a symbol of the sun god as Egyptians thought the sun was pushed round the heavens just as the beetle pushed the ball of dung.

The dung beetle is called Kheper in the Egyptian language and is associated with the verb *kheper* which means to come into being. As new beetles emerge from the ground as explained above the two words and the two actions are easily associated. Models of the beetle made in clay were supposed to have healing powers while live beetles, secured by a small chain through the wing-case, were actually worn as decoration.

The scarab seal was used to stamp letters into the clay seal on letters, bottles, wine jars etc with the owner's mark.

Scarab beetle rolls
ball of dung

Scarab seal

Sign of Scarab god
Khepri

royalty and of protection, which was worn on the pharaonic head-dress.

Further along this south wall is a deep shaft at the bottom of which lies **Zoser's Southern Tomb** which some believe held the King's entrails. More importantly there is a relief, depicting the King running the Heb-Sed race, which illustrates the purpose of the surrounding buildings and monuments. The buildings in the funerary complex, some of which are mere façades like a Hollywood film-set, simply represented a pastiche for the after-life of this crucial ceremony. Their intended purpose was to eternalize the symbol of the unification of a greater Egypt and the power of the pharaoh even in death.

This symbolism is echoed in the lotus and papyrus capitals on top of the columns fronting the **House of the South** and the **House of the North** which represent the heraldic emblems of Upper and Lower Egypt, respectively. The **House of the South** is interesting because its columns, which are precursors of the Greek Doric style, and its New Kingdom graffiti offer a fascinating reminder of the continuity of human civilization.

On the north side of the Step Pyramid there is a stone casket, known as the **Serdab** (cellar), containing a copy of a life-size statue of Zoser. The original is in the Egyptian Museum in Cairo. The Serdab has two cylindrical holes to enable the statue to communicate with the outside world and to preserve the Pharaoh's *Ka*. To the west of the Serdab the **Funerary Temple** is in ruins but some of the walls and the entrance can still be seen. A tunnel originally linked it with the royal tomb.

SOUTH OF ZOSER'S FUNERARY COMPLEX

The Pyramid of Unas, which was built for the last pharaoh of the 5th Dynasty (2494-2345 BC), appears from the outside to be a heap of rubble but the inside is still very well preserved and contains some beautiful hieroglyphs. As always, the entrance is from the north side down a passageway leading to the Burial Chamber. This is largely undecorated except for the star-covered ceiling and the sarcophagus which is made from a single block of black basalt and bears no inscriptions. The most interesting inscriptions are in the passageway, painted in green and organized in vertical lines. The hieroglyphs are magic formulae and prayers for the Pharaoh to help his passage into the after-life. They were the first to be found inside a tomb and formed the basis for the *Book of the Dead* (see Valley of the Kings, page 230). To the east, a few remnants of the **Funerary Temple** can be seen. Beyond this the remains of a causeway linking the Funerary Temple to the Valley Temple 700m away have been discovered. The pyramid was excavated and opened as a tourist attraction in 1881 by the director of antiquities Gaston Maspero with financial sponsorship from Thomas Cook & Son.

To the north of the Pyramid the **Mastaba of Queen Nebet**, who was Unas' wife, is also fascinating and well preserved. It is divided into three rooms of which the second is most interesting because it contains some rare scenes of Nebet in the women's quarters, or harem, in the palace. From here, a door leads to a gallery with beautifully decorated walls.

Opposite, to the northeast, is the **Mastaba of Princess Idout**. The tomb is divided into 10 rooms but only five are decorated. The wall paintings give us a glimpse of life in Idout's day with the many tableaux of rural and domestic scenes. Two rooms are dedicated to the offerings to the Princess and are designed to provide for her in the after-life.

Slightly to the east is the **Mastaba of Merou** containing some exceptionally well preserved paintings. In the **Grand Offerings Room** the paint scarcely seems to have faded thereby giving a good idea of the original splendour of these tombs.

South of the Pyramid of Unas a stone hut covers the access to three small **Persian Tombs** 25m underground and composed of two shafts. In order to lower the heavy sarcophagus, an ingenious system was devised involving the use of an additional smaller shaft. The main shaft was dug out, then filled with sand. The sarcophagus was then placed on top of the sand which was gradually removed from below via the smaller shaft. The tombs dating from the 27th Dynasty (525-404 BC) are interesting because they have very similar inscriptions to those found in Unas' Pyramid constructed over 2,000 years earlier.

To the southwest are the remains of the **Pyramid of Sekhemkhet** which was at the centre of an unfinished and unused funerary complex, very similar to that of his predecessor Zoser, which was only discovered in 1950 and to which there is no public access.

To the east of the Pyramid of Sekhemkhet can be seen the remains of the **Monastery of St Jeremiah** which was founded

Dash for the Altar – The Heb-sed Race

🐾   The Heb-Sed race took place during the festival held to mark the 30th anniversary of Zoser's reign. He would sprint between two altars, which represented Upper and Lower Egypt, thereby not only re-enacting his coronation in both parts of the country and symbolising the unification of the two lands but also demonstrating his continuing vigour.

in the 5th century but destroyed by the Arabs five centuries later. Following its discovery in 1907 many of the paintings and other items of interest were removed and are now on display in the Coptic Museum in Cairo.

NORTHEAST OF THE FUNERARY COMPLEX

The **Pyramid of Teti**, the founder of the 6th Dynasty (2345-2181 BC), was discovered by Mariette in 1853 but is now little more than a pile of rubble in constant danger of being submerged by sand. It is entered via a steep pathway leading to the funerary chamber in which the ceiling is decorated with stars.

Mastaba of Mereruka To the north are a number of well preserved *mastabas*. The most outstanding is that of **Mereruka**, who was Teti's visir, an important person in 6th Dynasty society. This is one of the largest Old Kingdom *mastabas* to have been found. Its 32 rooms are divided into three parts for Mereruka (21 rooms), his wife (6 rooms) and his son (5 rooms). In the main entrance passage Mereruka is depicted painting the three seasons which leads to the next room containing some interesting hunting scenes. Particularly worth noting is the indication of the types of animal that they hunted and the techniques being used. Scenes of everyday life are beautifully depicted throughout the tomb giving a valuable insight into contemporary life. The largest room, with six pillars, has a statue of Mereruka to the north and some unusual mourning scenes on the east wall. On the left are scenes of Mereruka carried by his son and surrounded by dwarfs and dogs. To enter Mereruka's wife's rooms go back to the main entrance and take the door on the left.

To the east, the **Mastaba of Kagemni** has some excellent reliefs and paintings of a much a higher standard, but unfortunately less well preserved, than those in Mereruka's tomb. Further east is the **Mastaba of Ankh-ma-hor**, the visir and overseer of the Great House in the 6th

Dynasty, which is also known as the Doctor's Tomb because of the paintings depicting circumcision and an operation on a toe! The other rooms are interesting and show the usual scenes of the preparation and transportation of the offerings and various representations of hunting and daily life.

NORTHWEST OF THE FUNERARY COMPLEX

Situated about 200m south of the road to the refreshment tent is one of the finest of all the *mastabas*. The **Double Mastaba of Ptah-Hotep & Akhiti-Hotep** contains some of the finest Old Kingdom art and some fascinating unfinished work which demonstrates the techniques used in painting reliefs. Ptah-Hotep was a priest of Maat in the reign of Djedkare, who was Unas' predecessor. His son Akhiti-Hotep was visir, judge, and the overseer of the treasury and the granaries.

The entrance leads into a long corridor decorated with unfinished agricultural scenes. The red paint indicates the preliminary drawing before the wall was carved and painted. The outstanding masterpiece, however, is in the **Sanctuary** dedicated to Ptah-Hotep. On the walls behind the entrance Ptah-Hotep is seated watching a concert while his servants wash and manicure him. Other walls bear scenes of Ptah-Hotep receiving offerings. On the left wall, which is the most interesting and impressive, the figure in the first boat is being given water by a boy. The inscription describes him as the Chief Artist, who is thought to have been Ankhen-Ptah, and this scene may well represent the first known example of an artist's signature.

The Serapeum was a burial place for the sacred Apis Bulls which were believed to be manifestations of Ptah's blessed soul and were identified with Osiris after his death. They were given full honours in a ceremony worthy of any Pharaoh or important noble and were then embalmed and the mummified body placed

Music

Music played an important part in the lives of the ancient Egyptians. This bas relief discovered in a nobleman's tomb at Saqqara is a good illustration of entertainments of that era. Here three musicians entertained the owner of this 5th Dynasty tomb while he feasted from a huge basket of fruit. Sometimes musicians played to placate an angry goddess such as Hathor. Music was produced on harps as shown here which were very common, though some had fewer string, single and double flutes, drums and by hand clapping. A number of wall reliefs show blind singers and instrumentalists.

in a sarcophagus and buried in the Serapeum. The sarcophagus was then sealed off from the main gallery by means of a richly decorated wall. The high priests would then start searching for the new Apis Bull within the sacred herd. The cult was a significant one and the Serapeum represents an important funerary complex which, besides the tombs themselves, included the priests' quarters, schools and inns catering for passing pilgrims. The cult of the Apis Bulls lasted well into the Ptolemaic period.

The Serapeum is situated 300m to the northwest of the refreshment tent and is one of the most impressive sites in Saqqara. It is reached via a long, sloping path, at the bottom of which a door leads to the three galleries. Only two are accessible, and the 24 surviving sarcophagi are set in small galleries on either side of the main one. Only three of the enormous basalt or granite sarcophagi bear inscriptions, and these are marked with the cartouches of different pharaohs. The Serapeum was discovered in 1851 but, with the exception of one tomb, most had already been looted. The artifacts discovered are now displayed in the Musée du Louvre, Paris.

The **Mastaba of Ti** is one of the wonders of the Old Kingdom, and its beautiful reliefs provide some interesting insights into life during that period. Ti was a 5th Dynasty royal hairdresser who married well and became steward of the sun temples of Neferikare and Nyuserre and whose children later bore the title of 'royal descendant'.

The *mastaba* stands 400m north of the refreshment tent, very close to the Serapeum, and is centred around a square courtyard which is surrounded by columns. The entrance is through a vestibule with portraits of Ti on the two entrance pillars. The reliefs in the courtyard have been damaged but their representations of daily life – breeding birds (north wall left), Ti on his litter with dogs and dwarfs (east wall, centre), and Ti with his wife (west wall centre) – are still worth seeing. In the centre of the courtyard an undecorated shaft leads to the tomb. A corridor leads from the southwest corner through to the main shrine. On the left of the corridor, just after the door, servants are depicted bringing offerings while on the right are musicians and dancers. Further on, to the right, is a false door bearing a representation of Ti's wife.

Further down the corridor on the right is a storage room and then the main hall of offerings and shrine which has a number of scenes depicting the offerings ceremony, the brewing of beer and the baking of bread. The main shrine is remarkable for its abundance of scenes depicting daily life including one illustrating boat construction. Note the extreme simplicity of the tools used.

The south wall holds the **Serdab**, where a copy of Ti's statue, the original being in the Cairo Museum, can be seen through the slit. Around the two slits there are scenes of daily market life, carpenters, tanners, and various other artisans. Around the second slit, Ti is entertained by musicians while servants burn incense. These paintings should be taken on one level as literal depictions of Egyptian life but it is also important to realize the importance of symbolism and allegory. The north walls show Ti in a boat observing a hippopotamus hunt in the Delta region. The hippopotamus was symbolic of evil so there is probably more to the picture than meets the eye.

The **Pyramids of Abu Sir** are situated 2½ km further northeast of the Mastaba of Ti. The site originally contained 14 5th Dynasty pyramids but only four are still standing. When arriving from the main

Saqqara complex the **Pyramid of Neferefre** is the first to be encountered. It was never finished and is now in very poor condition. The next also unfinished pyramid to the north was built for **Neferikare** and towering over the others is, at 68m, the tallest of the group. To the northeast, the **Pyramid of Nouserre** is worth noting for its **Funerary Temple** which, although originally built for the Neferikare, was used by Nouserre because of Neferikare's premature death. About 100m to the northeast lies the tomb of **Ptah-Cepses**. The *mastaba* is not in good condition but is worth seeing for the columns with lotus capitals which are the oldest so far discovered.

The remaining one, **Sahure's Pyramid**, is directly north and its **Funerary Temple** is not too severely damaged. Excavation work around it has led to the discovery of the remains of a 240m ramp which connected it to the **Valley Temple**. The Funerary Temple was originally walled with reliefs, some of which have been removed and placed in museums, but a few remain and are quite well preserved.

The Sun-Temples of Abu Ghurab, built in the 5th Dynasty when the solar cult had been declared the State religion, are about 1 km northeast of Sahure's Pyramid. Unlike earlier temples their purpose was solely devotional and the pharaohs who built them were not buried in them. There were twin temples but only the **Sun-Temple of Nyuserre** remains with the **Sun-Temple of Userkaf** being little more than rubble. Fortunately because they were identical little is lost.

At the western end of an enclosed courtyard a massive 70m obelisk once stood. The obelisk was the symbol of the primordial mound, the sun's resting place at the end of the day. An alabaster altar stands in the centre of the courtyard which would have been at the eastern side of the obelisk's base. Animals were sacrificed at the northeast corner of the courtyard from which channels cut in the paving carried the blood to 10 alabaster basins, nine of which survive.

SOUTH SAQQARA

This completely separate necropolis, founded by the pharaohs of the 6th Dynasty (2345-2181 BC), is situated about 1 km south of the Pyramid of Sekhemkhet which is the most southerly of all the pyramids in North Saqqara. It has a few interesting tombs, based on the Pyramid

of Unas as an architectural model, but sadly has been plundered by unscrupulous stone-masons or their suppliers. The pyramids of **Pepi I** and **Merenre** are in ruins.

To the east of the latter lies the **Pyramid of Djedkare**, known in Arabic as the Pyramid of the Sentinel, which is 25m tall and is open to visitors. The entrance is on the north side through a tunnel leading into the funerary chamber but there is comparatively little to see.

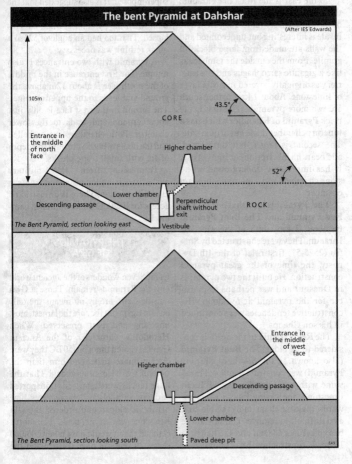

The bent Pyramid at Dahshar

(After IES Edwards)

105m

43.5°

CORE

52°

Entrance in the middle of north face

Higher chamber

Lower chamber

Descending passage

Perpendicular shaft without exit

ROCK

The Bent Pyramid, section looking east

Vestibule

Higher chamber

Entrance in the middle of west face

Descending passage

Lower chamber

Paved deep pit

The Bent Pyramid, section looking south

The most important and interesting tombs are further south. The **Pyramid of Pepi II** is surrounded by an entire funerary complex. The inside chamber is decorated with stars and funerary inscriptions. Within the complex are a number of smaller pyramids belonging to his queens. They are all based on the same design as Pepi's pyramid and contain a miniature funerary complex. The **Pyramid of Queen Neith** is interesting and has some wonderful inscriptions and decorations.

To the east is the **Mastaba Faraoun**, the tomb of **Shepseskaf**, the last Pharaoh of the 4th Dynasty (2613-2494 BC). The inside is interesting but undecorated and the walls are made from large blocks of granite. From the outside the tomb looks like a gigantic sarcophagus and the exterior was originally covered in a thin layer of limestone. About 1 km further south are two more pyramids. The first is the brick **Pyramid of Khendjer** which has a funerary chamber made out of quartzite. The second is larger, but unfinished, and bears no inscriptions or signs of use. It has impressive underground white stone chambers and a quartzite funerary chamber.

The Pyramids at Dhashur – The Red Pyramid and The Bent Pyramid lie about 2 km south of the Mastaba Faraoun. They were constructed by Snefru (2575-51) first ruler of the 4th Dynasty, the time of the great pyramid construction. He built the two pyramids in Dhashur and was perhaps responsible for the pyramid at Maidoun. His constructive tendencies were continued in his son Cheops.

The **Red Pyramid** to the north is considered to be older. The **Bent Pyramid** (also known as the Southern Shining Pyramid) was constructed of local limestone with a casing of polished Turah limestone, the casing blocks slope inwards making them more stable and also difficult to remove. The side at the base measures 188.6m and the height is 105m. If construction had continued at the original angle it would have been 128.5m high.

The pyramid is unique on two counts. First the angles change. The lower angle is 52° enclosing some 70% of the bulk of the pyramid. It then reduces to 43.5° up to the peak. There is a number of theories for the unusual shape. It is suggested that the builders got tired and changed the angle to reduce the volume and so complete sooner. It is suggested that the change in slope indicated a double pyramid – two pyramids superimposed. It is also suggested that the architect lost his nerve for this was being built when the pyramid at Maidoun collapsed. That too had an angle of 52° so a quick rethink was necessary.

A pyramid with two entrances is also unique. The first entrance in the middle of the north face is about 12m above the ground and leads to the upper chamber. The second in the west face is only just above ground and leads to the lower chamber. Both chambers are corbelled and the floors of both were built to a depth of 4m with small stone blocks.

Permission from the military authorities is no longer necessary for a closer inspection. There is unrestricted access for E£20, E£10 for students, camera E£5.

THE PYRAMIDS OF GIZA

Of the Seven Wonders of the ancient world only the **Pyramids** remain. Those at **Giza** outside Cairo are by no means the only ones in Egypt but they are the largest, most imposing and best preserved. When **Herodotus**, chronicler of the Ancient Greeks, visited them in 450 BC they were already more ancient to him than the time of Christ is to us today! That the huge blocks were quarried, transported and put into place demonstrates how highly developed and ordered the Old Kingdom was at its peak. Herodotus claimed that it would have taken 100,000 slaves 30 years to have constructed the

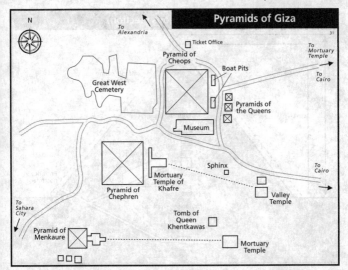

great **Pyramid of Cheops**, but it is more likely that the pyramid was built by peasants, paid in food, who were unable to work the land whilst the Nile flooded between July and November. Happily, the high waters also made it possible to transport the casing stone from Aswan and Tura, virtually to the base of the pyramids. The enormous Pyramid of Cheops, built between 2589-66 BC out of over 2,300,000 blocks of stone with an average weight of 2.5 tonnes and a total weight of 6,000,000 tonnes to a height of almost 140m, is the oldest and largest of the pyramids at Giza. The **Pyramid of Chephren** and **Pyramid of Menkaure** date from 2570 BC to 2530 BC.

A breakdown in the structure of society, and the reduction of wealth, have been proposed as reasons why other pyramids were not constructed on the same scale later in the Old Kingdom. The first thefts from tombs occurred relatively soon after the Pyramids' construction. A couple of centuries, or so, is not long when one considers that they have been standing for 4,000 years! This was undoubtedly an important factor in

the preference for hidden tombs, such as in **The Valley of the Kings**, by the time of the New Kingdom.

ACCESS One of the first things that visitors to the Pyramids will notice is their unexpected proximity to Cairo. Giza itself is now little more than a suburb. Naturally the picture-postcards do not emphasize this fact! It costs E£20 per person to enter the area and the second pyramid, an additional E£20 to enter the Pyramid of Cheops and E£10 to visit the pyramid of Menkaure, plus E£10 for cameras inside the pyramid but no flash photography is allowed. All the official guides demand a tip but most have already been tipped by the tour operator so don't give much. It is difficult but possible to avoid amateur guides who then demand money. The café has a minimum charge and should be avoided so make sure that you take water with you. The hassling camel owners will demand much more but don't pay more than E£10 for a short ride and make sure you agree the price first and don't pay until you are back on the ground. The whole complex can be fairly busy at peak times and very dusty. Claustrophobics should avoid the inside of the pyramids.

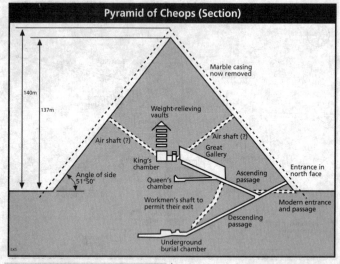

Pyramid of Cheops (Section)

140m

137m

Marble casing now removed

Weight-relieving vaults

Air shaft (?)

Air shaft (?)

Great Gallery

King's chamber

Entrance in north face

Angle of side 51°50'

Ascending passage

Queen's chamber

Workmen's shaft to permit their exit

Modern entrance and passage

Descending passage

Underground burial chamber

PYRAMID OF CHEOPS (KHUFU)

Very little is known of Cheops. His tomb, which could have provided some answers, was looted long before the archaeologists arrived. He is believed to have been the absolute ruler of a highly stratified society and his reign must have been one of great wealth in order to afford so stupendous a burial site. Although he was buried alone his wives and relations may have merited smaller *mastabas* nearby.

Originally the 230m x 230m pyramid would have stood at 140m high but 3m has been lost in all dimensions since the encasing marble was eroded or removed. The entrance, which was at the centre of the north face, has been changed in modern times and access is now 15m lower via an opening created by the plundering Khalifa Ma'mun in 820 AD. From this entrance a tunnel descends steeply for about 25m until it reaches a point where it is met by an ascending corridor which climbs at the same angle.

If one were to continue down the very long, narrow and steep descending shaft, which is closed to ordinary visitors and is

definitely not for those who are either unfit or claustrophobic, one would eventually reach a lower unfinished chamber which lies 20m beneath the bedrock of the pyramid's foundations! Even though the chamber is empty, except for a deep pit where the sarcophagus would have been lowered, the sensation of standing alone under 6 million tonnes of stone blocks is overpowering. Despite the speculation that the chamber was unfinished because of a change of plan by either Cheops or his architect the later pyramid of Chephren follows an identical pattern.

Going up the 36m long ascending corridor, which is 1.6m high and has a steep 1:2 gradient, one arrives at the start of the larger 47m long **Great Gallery** which continues upward at the same incline to the **King's Chamber** 95m beneath the pyramid's apex. The gallery, whose magnificent stonework is so well cut that it is impossible to insert a blade into the joints, narrows at the top end to a corbelled roof which is 8.5m high.

At the beginning of the gallery there is a second horizontal passage, 35m long and 1.75m high, which leads to a room misleadingly known as the **Queen's Chamber**. In fact no queen was buried there and the small room, measuring 5.2m by 5.7m with a 6.13m pointed roof, is more likely to be the Serdab which contained the icon of the Pharaoh. In 1872 two triangular holes were made by a British engineer in the chamber's north and south walls in order to discover the location of the air or ventilation shafts.

The walls of **The King's Chamber** are lined with polished red granite. The room measures 5.2m by 10.8m by 5.8m high and contains the huge lidless Aswan red granite sarcophagus which was all that remained of the treasures when archaeologists first explored the site. It was saved because it was too large to move along the entrance passage and, therefore, must have been placed in the chamber during the pyramid's construction. Above this upper chamber there is a series of five relieving chambers which are structurally essential to support the massed weight of the stones above and distribute the weight away from the burial chamber. A visit to the collapsed pyramid at Maidoum (see Fayoum, page 173) will illustrate why this was necessary! As in the Queen's Chamber the north and south walls bear air shafts but in this case they are the original ones.

One of the great mysteries of the massive Pyramid of Cheops is the four tiny meticulously crafted 20 cm square shafts, which travel, two from the King's Chamber and another two from the Queen's Chamber, at precisely maintained angles through the body of the pyramid to the outer walls. Obviously serving a significant function, they were originally thought to be ventilation shafts. However, Egyptologists now are more inclined to believe that they are of religious significance and relate to the Ancient Egyptian's belief that the stars are a heavenly counterpart to their land, inhabited by gods and souls of the departed.

The main feature of the ancient night sky was the Milky Way, the bright band of stars which was believed to be the celestial River Nile. The most conspicuous of bright stars which appeared in the night sky were those of Orion's Belt, which because their reappearance after 70 days coincided with the yearly miracle of the Nile flood, were associated with Osiris, the protector god. The brightest star in the sky, Syrius, was his consort the goddess Isis because it was bright, beautiful, and followed Osiris across the sky. Linked into the creation myth, the texts on the great pyramid's walls repeatedly tell of the dead pharoah, seen as the latest incarnation of Horus, the son of Isis and Osiris, travelling in a boat between various star constellations. At an angle of exactly 45°, the southern shaft of the King's Chamber points directly at where Orion's Belt would have been in the sky in ancient times. Meanwhile, the southern shaft of the Queen's Chamber points to Syrius, his consort Isis. The northern

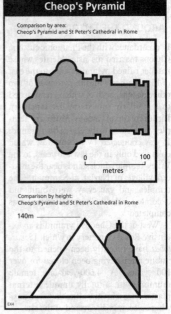

Cheop's Pyramid

Comparison by area:
Cheop's Pyramid and St Peter's Cathedral in Rome

0   100
metres

Comparison by height:
Cheop's Pyramid and St Peter's Cathedral in Rome

140m

EX4

Flinders Petrie –
The beginnings of systematic archaeology

Flinders Petrie applied the first systematic excavation techniques to archaeological sites in Egypt. He was born in 1853 in Scotland and arrived in Egypt in 1880 in search of measurements of pyramids. He stayed and excavated many sites, recording in detail each item and layer of his work with consistency and accuracy, which was in sharp contrast to the acquisitive and unscientific digging of this and earlier periods. He it was who set the chronological framework within which most archaeologists and their colleagues later worked. Petrie had the reputation even as a young man for wanting his own way and there were constant skirmishes between himself and his financing committee in London. In 1886 Petrie left his employment with the Egypt Exploration Fund but remained in Egypt for a further 37 years, actively excavating and recording his finds. He eventually left Egypt in 1923 when the law on the division of archaeological finds was changed after the discovery of the tomb of Tutankhamen by Howard Carter. He died in 1942.

shaft of the King's Chamber is directed at the circumpolar stars, important to the Ancient Egyptians as the celestial pole because these stars never disappear or die in the sky. The 'star shafts' thus appear to be directed so that the spirit of the dead pharoah could use the shafts to reach the important stars with pinpoint accuracy.

AROUND THE CHEOPS PYRAMID

In accordance with the Pharaonic custom, Cheops married his sister Merites whose smaller ruined pyramid stands to the east of his together with the pyramids of two other queens, both of which are attached to a similarly ruined smaller sanctuary. Little remains of **Cheops' Mortuary Temple** which stood to the east of the pyramid. It was connected by a causeway, which collapsed only in the last 150 years, to the Valley Temple which stands near the modern village of **Nazlat al-Samman**. The temples and causeway were built and decorated before Cheops' Pyramid was completed.

West of the Cheops Pyramid is an extensive Royal Cemetery in which 15 *mastabas* have recently been opened to the public after having been closed for over 100 years. A 4,600-year-old female mummy, with a totally unique internal plaster encasement unlike that seen anywhere else, was discovered at the site.

The **Boat Pits and Museum** (open daily 0900-1600) is located at the base of the south face of the Cheops Pyramid where five boat pits were discovered in 1982. The boat, which is encased in the stones, is amazingly intact and was held together with rope with no nails being used at all. The exact purpose of these buried boats is unclear but they may have been regarded as a means of travelling to the after-life, as can be seen in the 17th to 19th Dynasty tombs at Thebes, or possibly as a means of accompanying the Sun-God on his diurnal journey. One boat has been located at the site and can be seen in the museum. It is best to avoid visiting the sun ship at prayer time because you cannot get in.

Pyramid of Chephren (Khafre) Built for the son of Cheops and Hensuten the Pyramid of Chephren, or Khafre as he is sometimes known, stands to the southwest of the Great Pyramid of Cheops. Although, at 136.5m high, and an estimated weight of 4,880,000 tonnes, it is actually a few metres smaller than the Cheops Pyramid. The fact that it was built on a raised limestone plateau was a deliberate attempt to make it appear larger than that of his father. The top of the pyramid still retains some of the marble casing that once covered the entire surface, thus providing an idea of the original finish. The entrance to the tomb was lost for centuries until 1818 when Belzoni located and blasted open the sealed portal on the north side. Although he believed that it would still be intact, he found that it had been looted many centuries earlier. As with the Pyramid of Cheops there is an unfinished and presumed unused chamber below the bedrock. The passageway now used to enter the burial chamber heads downwards before levelling out to the granite lined passageway that leads to the chamber. To the west of the chamber is the red granite sarcophagus, built into the floor, with the lid lying nearby.

The **Mortuary Temple of Khafre** lies to the east of the pyramid and is more elaborate and better preserved than that of his father. Although the statues and riches have been stolen, the limestone walls were cased with granite which is still present in places. There are still the remains a large pillared hall, a small sanctuary, outhouses and a courtyard.

A 500m causeway linked the Mortuary Temple to the Valley Temple (open daily 0900-1600) which is better preserved than

any other because it lay hidden in the sands until Mariette rediscovered it in 1852. It is lined with red granite at roof height which protects the limestone. Two entrances to the Temple face east and lead to a T-shaped hall supported by enormous pillars. In front of these stood 23 diorite statues of Khafre. The only one which has remained intact can be found in the Egyptian Museum. Side chambers lie off to the south of the hall. A passage which joined the causeway is now closed off.

The Sphinx is next to Khafre's Valley Temple to the northeast . We are extremely lucky that it still exists because it was built of soft sandstone and would have disappeared centuries ago had the sand not covered it for so much of its history. Yet it is equally surprising that it was ever carved because its sculptor must have known that such soft stone would quickly decay. The Arabs call it *Abu'l-Hawl*, the awesome, or terrible one. Nobody can be certain who it personifies but it is possibly Khafre himself and would then be the oldest known large-scale royal portrait. Some say that it was hewn from the remaining stone after the completion

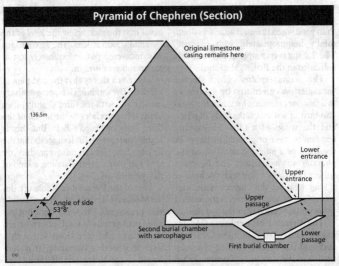

Pyramid of Chephren (Section)

Original limestone casing remains here

136.5m

Angle of side 53°8'

Lower entrance

Upper entrance

Upper passage

Second burial chamber with sarcophagus

First burial chamber

Lower passage

EXE

Save our Sphinx

The carefully planned, 6-year-long, restoration of the Sphinx programme is in its third and final stage. In the 1980s over 2,000 new limestone blocks were added to the ailing body of the sphinx and it was subjected to injections of chemicals. Unfortunately this 'treatment' flaked away taking with it parts of the original rock surface. The next attempt at restoration was certainly unkind and unscientific. Various mortars and numerous workers, untrained in restoration, carried out a 6-month repair. The result was further damage and in 1988 the crumbling of the left shoulder and falling of blocks.

The present attempts to restore the Sphinx are under the control of archaeologists from the Supreme Council of Antiquities. Work has been concentrated so far on draining away the subsoil seepage which is damaging the rock and on repairing the damaged shoulder with smaller blocks more in keeping with the original size. After all, said the Minister of Culture, "It is an *objet d'art*". We admire his sentiments and wish them every success.

of the pyramid and that, almost as an afterthought, Khafre set it, as a sort of monumental scarecrow, to guard his tomb. Others claim that the face is that of his guardian deity rather than Khafre's own. The Sphinx was first uncovered by Tuthmosis IV (1425-17 BC) thereby fulfilling a prophecy that by uncovering the great man-lion he would gain the throne. Recent efforts to conserve the Sphinx are now complete but the rising water table threatens to accelerate its decay. Earlier attempts to restore it caused more harm than good when the sandstone was filled, totally inappropriately, with concrete. The Sphinx is incomplete. The 'beard' is exhibited in the British Museum.

The name 'sphinx' which means 'strangler' was given first by the Greeks to a *fabulous creature* which had the head and bust of a woman, the body of a lion and the wings of a bird. The sphinx appears to have originated in Egypt in the form of a sun god with whom the pharaoh was associated. The Egyptian sphinx is usually a lion with the head of a king wearing the characteristic wig-cover. There are however ram-headed sphinxes associated with the god Amun.

The Pyramid of Menkaure (Mycerinus) is the smallest of the three Giza Pyramids and marks the beginning of a steep decline in the standards of workmanship

and attention to detail in the art of pyramid-building. At the time of the death of Menkaure, who was Chephren's successor and was later known by the Greek name of Mycerinus, it was unfinished and the granite encasement was never put in place by his son Shepseskaf who completed the rest of the pyramid. It stands at only 66.5m high, considerably lower than the earlier pyramids, and also differs from those of Khufu and Khafre in that the lower chamber was used as the burial tomb. The walls are lined with granite hewn into the rock below the level of the Pyramid's foundations. The sarcophagus was discovered but unfortunately lost at sea en route to Britain.

There is a theory that the odd plan of the three Pyramids of Giza, progressively smaller and with the third slightly offset to the left, correlates to the layout of the three stars of Orion's Belt. But this is highly controversial as it suggests that the Ancient Egyptians chose to reproduce, on land and over a great distance, a kind of map of the stars.

East of the Pyramid of Menkaure lies the **Mortuary Temple** which is relatively well preserved. The walls were not encased with granite or marble but with red mud bricks and then lined with a thin layer of smoother limestone. It is connected to the Valley Temple via a 660m

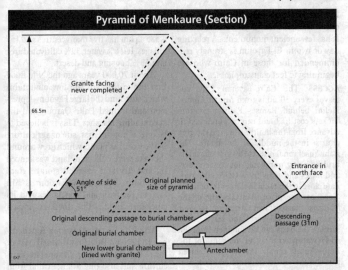

Pyramid of Menkaure (Section)

Granite facing
never completed

66.5m

Angle of side
51°

Original planned
size of pyramid

Entrance in
north face

Original descending passage to burial chamber

Descending
passage (31m)

Original burial chamber

New lower burial chamber
(lined with granite)

Antechamber

EX7

mud-brick causeway which now lies beneath the sand.

SUBSIDIARY PYRAMIDS

South of the Pyramid of Menkaure are three smaller incomplete ones. The largest, to the east, was most likely intended for Menkaure's principal wife. The granite sarcophagus of the central tomb was recovered and was found to contain the bones of a young woman.

The Tomb of Queen Khentkawes, who was an obscure but intriguing and important figure, is situated to the south of the main Giza pyramids. Although she appears to have been married to Shepseskaf, who was the last 4th Dynasty pharaoh, she subsequently married a high priest of the sun-god Re at a time when the male dynastic line was particularly weak. By going on to bear a number of later kings who are buried in Saqqara and Abu Sir, she acted as the link between the 4th and 5th Dynasties. Her tomb is an enormous sarcophagus and is linked to a Mortuary Temple cut out of the limestone.

The Zawiyat al-Aryan Pyramids are roughly halfway between Giza and North Saqqara and one has to ride through the desert to see them. A visit would probably only be rewarding to the devoted Egyptologist. There are two pyramids of which the southernmost one is probably a 3rd Dynasty (2686-13 BC) step pyramid. The granite of the more northerly suggests that it is 4th Dynasty (2613-2494 BC) but it would appear to have been abandoned after the foundations had been laid. The **Pyramids of Abu Sir** and **The Sun-Temples of Abu Ghurab** are about 3 km further south (see Saqqara, page 158).

For those researching the Coptic Monasteries look out for the **Monastery of St Mercurius** (Abu Seifein) in Tamouh just 12 km south of Giza, now used as a training centre.

EL-FAYOUM AND LAKE QAROUN

After the noise, crowds and pollution of Cairo the **El-Fayoum** oasis, which includes **Lake Qaroun**, is literally a breath of fresh air. It offers both Egyptian and foreign visitors a relaxing break from city life, a day at the beach and a chance to see oasis life without having to venture too far. It has few ancient monuments. A relaxing day or two in El-Fayoum is strongly recommended for those in Cairo who are beginning to feel claustrophobic.

ACCESS The Cairo-Fayoum City bus leaves every 30 mins from Midan Ahmad Helmi behind Ramses Railway Station. Tickets cost E£3 and can be purchased in advance from the building behind the grey church in the middle of the square. The Bahr Yusef canal bisects Fayoum, the many bridges being numbered for convenience, and buses and taxis from Cairo all terminate close to the canal in the centre of town. Negotiate the price then take one of the *hantours* (horse-drawn carriages) to your destination. Local buses and service taxis serving the oasis can be obtained from the Al-Hawatim terminal to the south of the Bahr Yusef canal. Private taxis hired through the tourist information kiosk, *Hotel Auberge du Lac* and the Kom Aushim museum, cost about E£10 per hour.

FAYOUM CITY

Although usually described as an oasis El-Fayoum is not fed by underground water, like the Western Desert oases further southwest, but by water from the Nile which is transported to this natural triangular depression by a series of canals. The water comes from the River Nile leaving the Ibrahimeya canal at Assiut as the Bahr Yusef which itself divides into a number of smaller canals west of Fayoum City. Having irrigated the oasis the water runs into Lake Qaroun which, despite having dramatically shrunk over the past few thousand years, is at about 215 sq km still Egypt's largest natural salt-water lake

ranging in depth from 5m in the east to 12m in the west. The oasis which covers 4,585 sq km has five main centres and 157 villages. It is 8% water, 39% cultivated area and 63% housing and desert.

About 70,000 years ago the Nile flood first broke through the low mountains which surround the large Fayoum depression and formed Lake Qaroun and the surrounding marshes. This is believed to be one, if not the first, site of agriculture in the world as plants which grew around the lake were collected, land was fenced in, and dry and guarded storage areas were built. Even today Fayoum is still famous for fruit and vegetables and its chickens. To describe food as *fayoum* means delicious.

The 12th Dynasty pharaoh Amenemhat I (1991-62 BC) first drained part of the marshes to develop the area for agriculture and also dug a large canal from the River Nile controlled by a regulator at El-Lahun to the northwest of Beni Suef. The result of this and further developments by Amenemhat III (1842-1797 BC), who showed great interest in the area and built a pyramid at Hawara (see page 173), was Lake Moeris (Great Lake), twice the present size and teeming with fish, and an agricultural area to the south renowned for its rich and varied crops.

The Romans, who called the area **Crocodilopolis** (because of the ever present crocodiles) changed Fayoum's previous system of crop rotation and forced the area to supply grain exclusively to the Roman market. Muslims believe that the prophet Joseph developed the area during his captivity in Egypt through the canalization of the Bahr Yusef River and

The Groaning Water-wheels of El-Fayoum

Because the land in the El-Fayoum oasis varies from +26m to -42m in three main steps, self-powered water-wheels were essential and the construction of one particular type, which is exclusive to Fayoum, began in pharaonic times. There are often whole series of these 'sawaqih al-Hadir' (or 'roaring water-wheels'), which produce a perpetual groaning noise and can last 10 years if they are properly maintained, and there are over 200 in the oasis which has adopted the water-wheel as its official symbol.

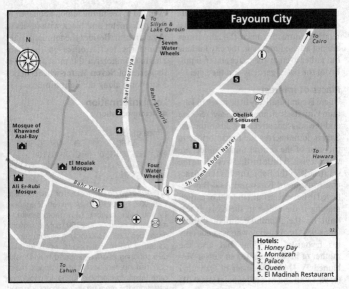

Map legend:

To Siliyin & Lake Qaroun

N

Seven Water Wheels

To Cairo

Fayoum City

Sharia Horriya

Bahr Sinnuris

2

4

5

Pol

Obelisk of Senusert

Mosque of Khawand Asal-Bay

El Moalak Mosque

1

Sh Gamal Abdel Nasser

To Hawara

Ali Er-Rubi Mosque

Bahr Yusef

Four Water Wheels

3

Pol

32

To Lahun

Hotels:
1. Honey Day
2. Montazah
3. Palace
4. Queen
5. El Madinah Restaurant

by building the world's first dam. Although Fayoum's national strategic importance diminished with the canalization of the Nile Delta it remains one of the most productive agricultural areas in the country.

The water level in Lake Qaroun had been falling for about 2,000 years as it received less and less water until the construction of the Aswan High Dam led to far greater stability in the level of the River Nile. By mediaeval times the lake had become far too salty to sustain freshwater fish and new species were introduced. The shrunken lake now lies 45m below sea level and 40m lower than its original level of 70,000 years ago and ⅙ of its original size. It is now appears that the water table is rising again as houses and fields at the lakeside have been flooded in recent years. Evidence of this is clear in notices excusing the rising damp in the walls of the Auberge du Lac and raised sills over which one must step to gain access to hotels along the lake shore.

Despite its stagnant and polluted water the beach resorts around Lake Qaroun still attract the more affluent visitors to the region. The oasis is declared free from bilharzia, a recommendation in itself. The number of visitors is increasing and while half are Egyptian about a third are European. The season runs all year round but from January to April it is considered too cold to swim. As part of its efforts to persuade tourists to visit areas outside the Nile valley the Egyptian Tourist Association is trying to encourage tours from Cairo, via Fayoum and the Middle Egypt sites, to both the Red Sea coast and Upper Egypt which would undoubtedly be a wonderful and fascinating tour.

Fayoum City is the main town in the oasis and the province's capital, 103 km southwest of central Cairo and 85 km from Giza and the Pyramids, an estimated 1 hr journey along the 4-lane carriageway. The majority of the oasis' population of 1.8 million people are not Nile Valley Egyptians but settled and semi-nomadic Berber people who are related to the Libyan Arabs. Although few reminders of its ancient past have survived it is still a relatively attractive town though visitors are not advised to stay in the city for long but rather to enjoy the peace and tranquillity of the oasis' gardens and the lake.

Places of interest

There is comparatively little to see in Fayoum City itself although the covered *souq* and the adjacent street of goldsmiths, **es-Sagha**, found across the fourth bridge to the west of the central tourist office, are worth a visit. A little further west along the south side of the Bahr Yusef is the attractive **Mosque of Khawand Asal-Bay** believed to have been built in 1490, or earlier, making it the oldest in the oasis. It was built by the Mamluke Sultan Qaitbai (1468-98) for Asal-Bay who was not only his favourite concubine but also the mother of his assassinated successor Mohamed IV (1496-98), sister of Qansuh I (1498-1500) and wife of Janbalat (1500-01) who were both deposed and murdered. When, however, Tumanbay I (1501-01) married Qaitbai's official wife Fatima he insulted and disgraced Asal-Bay but he was soon deposed and exiled. Remains of its former impressive structure, most of which fell into the Bahr Yusef in 1892, include the dome supported by ancient pillars and the gilded teak *mihrab* elaborately inlaid with ivory. Other mosques worth visiting in town, particularly during the **moulids** are the **Mosque and Mausoleum** in honour of **Ali er-Rubi** with its mud-brick dome and the so called **Hanging Mosque** or **El Moalak Mosque** constructed in 1375 by Prince Soliman Ibn Mouhamed built above five arches and with a double flight of steps leading to the main door.

The 13m red granite **Obelisk** of **Senusert I** (12th Dynasty) to the northeast of town serves as a useful point of reference. Originally it was situated in the settlement of Abgig to south.

The locals are particularly proud of their water-wheels, first introduced by the Ptolemies and used now as the official symbol of El-Fayoum province. There are over 200 to see in the region about 4m to 5m in diameter and black with layers of protective tar. Besides the four large ones behind the tourist office on the main Sharia Gumhorriya the most famous is the series of **Seven Water-wheels** about 3 km north along the Bahr Sinnuris.

Local information
● Accommodation

Price guide:			
AL	US$150+	**D**	US$25-50
A	US$100-150	**E**	US$10-25
B	US$75-100	**F**	under US$10
C	US$50-75		

B/C *Auberge du Lac*, located on Lake Qaroun, T 700002, F 700730, 81 a/c rm with telephone, TV and bath, laundry, 24-hr room service, 4 restaurants open 0600-2300 (only in season), disco open 2200-0300 (only in season), tennis, squash, 2 pools, watersports, boats for hire, duck shooting, poorly equipped gym and health club, parking, facilities for handicapped, major cards taken, comfortable but not luxurious, the view from the more expensive rooms is ruined by the cheaper chalets built in the gardens beside the lake, King Ibn Saud and Winston Churchill met here in 1945, ask to have a look at the suite used by King Farouk, now all very faded and lacking in care, someone has decorated the stairs – all over the dark red carpet, don't stay here – go to the *Oasis*; **C** *Panorama Shakshuk*, on Lake Qaroun, T 701314, F 701757, 30 a/c rm with balcony and lake view, TV room, pool, watersports, fishing, wind surfing, water, skiing, duck shooting, garden, restaurants inside and out, sea food speciality.

D *Oasis Motel*, on Lake Qaroun shore, T 701565, 28 rm, 2 restaurants, one over the lake, pool over lake, cheerful staff, caravan and camping facilities.

E *Aïn al-Siliyin*, T 327471, 32 chalets, restaurant with good range of basic foods, gardens; **E** *Palace Hotel*, on Sharia Horriya, central, 35 clean a/c rm and a friendly owner who others have claimed is a real shark so beware, plans to upgrade, cars, motorbikes and bicycles for hire.

F *El Montazah*, Minshit Lutfallah, Fayoum City, T 324633, located next to the Bahr Sinnuris canal to the north of the town centre, run by Copts; **F** *Geziret el-Bat*, Manshiet el-Sadat, Lake Qaroun, T 749288, 22 rm, lakeside location, very cheap; **F** *Honey Day Hotel*, Sharia Gamal Abdel Nasser, Fayoum Entrance,

T 341205, 25 rm, spacious and clean with 1970s decor and friendly staff, 25% discount for groups; **F Queen**, Sharia Menshat Luftallah, Fayoum City, T 326819, 32 beds, reasonable and newish hotel.

Camping *Aïn al-Siliyin Hotel, Oasis Hotel; Kom Abu Muslim* camp site and *Kom Oshim* nr Karanis.

Youth hostels *Fayoum Hostel*, in Fayoum City, T 323682; *Fayoum Stadium Hostel*, Fayoum City, T 327368; *Shakshuk Hostel*, in Shakshuk, nr Lake Qaroun, T 323164; *Siliyin Hostel and Scout Camp*, T 500062. Flats No 7 & 8, Housing Block No 7, Hadaka, 48 beds, T 323682, station 3 km, overnight fee E£3.

● **Places to eat**

♦♦♦: *Aïn el Shayr*, nr springs at Aïn Siliyin; *Café Gabal el Zinah*, on Qaroun Lake, play areas for children, boatlanding, fish is main item on menu; *El Medinah*, overlooking the 4 water wheels in Fayoum City; *Karanis Tourist Restaurant*, Kom Oshim, eat in shaded garden, T 600783; the *Auberge du Lac-Fayoum* provides average quality food in interesting surrounding.

♦♦: *Al Jowhara (Gem) Restaurant*, at Aïn Siliyin, in disappointing garden; *Café al-Louloua*, at Qaroun Lake, at major junction serving Western food; *Lake Plage Café*, overlooking Qaroun Lake and 1.5 km of beach, play areas for children, adequate but unimaginative; *Zahret el Shatea Restaurant*, at Aïn Siliyin.

♦: *Mokhimar*, 100m west of central tourist office.

● **Banks & money changers**

Bank of Alexandria, Banque du Caire, Banque Misr and National Bank of Egypt, in town centre. You may have to try all for exchange facilities.

● **Hospitals & medical services**

Hospital: T 322249.

● **Post & telecommunications**

Area code: 084.

Post Office: central post office is on the south side of the Bahr Yusef canal opp the central tourist office.

● **Shopping**

Fayoum chickens, fresh fruit and straw baskets.

● **Tourist offices**

There is a particularly active and helpful local tourist administration, which is run by the excellent Director of Tourism, Nabil Hanzal, which can be contacted at the main office (T 342313)

in the centre of town on Sharia Gumhorriya. The office by the waterwheels is T 325211.

● **Useful telephone numbers**

Ambulance: T 123; **Fire**: T 180; **Police**: T 122; **Tourist Police**: T 324048.

● **Transport**

Local Bus: to Cairo's Ahmed Helmi and Giza stations buses leave every 30 mins between 0630-1830 from the main bus station in the centre of town on Sharia el-Hadqa by bridge No 3. There are also regular buses south to Beni Suef with connections south up the Nile Valley.

Service taxis: are quicker but more hair-raising than buses and leave the depot next to the bus station for Cairo's Midan Giza, and thence on to central Cairo, and for Beni Suef.

Train These are so slow and inefficient that they are not worth taking, except to El-Wasta and Beni Suef.

EXCURSIONS FROM EL-FAYOUM

Outside town at **Aïn al-Siliyin**, 9 km north of the city towards Lake Qaroun, is a popular park which has natural springs and a stream. This is a very tatty area, the springs, Aïn Siliyin and Aïn Alshayr, rarely flow yet it is very crowded on Friday and holidays. Entrance 25 piastres. Further north is **Lake Qaroun** which, despite the stagnant and salt encrusted water, is a favourite beach resort. Although it is calm much of the time, in winter it is reported to be quite rough and teeming with ducks and geese which bring the hunters to the lakeside hotels. Qaroun means 'Lake of the Horn'. It is possible to negotiate a row boat from the *Auberge du Lac* to the barren **Golden Horn Island** or to the north shore.

Spring clean

🐦 In January each year every canal in the country undergoes cleaning and repair. The sluices are shut, silt is dredged, walls are strengthened and the water wheels are lifted and overhauled. Although the wheels are considered to be ancient in fact no part is more than about 10 years old. It is said the state of the canals is a mirror of the condition of the whole country.

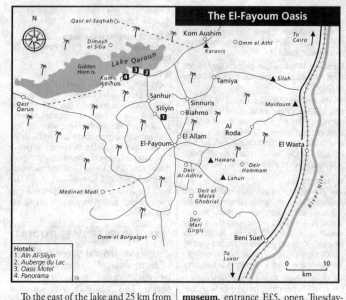

The El-Fayoum Oasis

Hotels:
1. Ain Al-Siliyin
2. Auberge du Lac
3. Oasis Motel
4. Panorama

To the east of the lake and 25 km from the city on the main road towards Cairo, **Kom Aushim** is adjacent to the site of the ancient city of **Karanis**. Karanis, founded in the 3rd century BC and inhabited by mercenaries of Ptolemy II, was once the centre of a large agricultural area exporting cereals to Rome via Alexandria. Walking to the remains of two Roman temples, the Temple of Pnepheros and Petesouchos (yet more crocodile gods) is the larger, one crunches across ground covered with broken pottery. Expect to be shown the oil/wine presses, tank for crocodiles, Roman baths with evidence of heating pipes, a row of headless sphinxes and the former residence of British High Commissioner Sir Miles Lampson. The site is very large, open 0900-1600 in winter and to 1700 in summer, entrance E£10, has café, play area and offers camping sites with 50 tents available. The results of excavations carried out in the 1920s by the University of Michigan are displayed, together with exhibits from other sites around the Fayoum, in a small circular

museum, entrance E£5, open Tuesday-Sunday 0900-1600 in winter and 1700 in summer. The most interesting exhibits are the carefully restored pottery and glassware, the central mummy, the necklaces and the minute statues. Trips to **Qasr es-Saghah** and the ruins of the Ptolemaic settlement of Soknopaiou Nesos, which used to be on the lakeside but is now 11 km away and 65m above the current lake, can be arranged at the museum and it is strongly recommended to take a guide.

Medinat Madi about 30 km southwest of Fayoum City contains the ruins of a 12th Dynasty temple, built by Amenemhat III and Amenemhat IV dedicated to Sobek the crocodile god. This site retains an attractive avenue of lions and sphinxes. Access by normal vehicle. **Dimayh el Siba** would have been situated on the north coast of the lake which is now almost 3 km away. This old Ptolemaic city with ruins of small temple dedicated to Soknopaios (crocodile) was once the starting point of a camel trade route to the oases of the Western desert. The goods first crossed the lake by boat, still a good way to reach this site. **Omm el Athl**, east of Karanis is the ruins of Bachias city, 700 mud brick houses and a small mud brick temple dedicated to a crocodile god. Pedestals of **Biahmo** – two large pedestals each about 6m high in Biahmo village some 7 km north of Fayoum – once supported a seated colossus of Amenemhat III. **Omm el Borgaigat** with the ruins of **Tebtunis** are 30 km south of Fayoum. **Qsar Qarun**, to the west end of the lake, has the remains of the Graeco-Roman city of Dionysias, and a well preserved limestone Ptolemaic temple dedicated to a crocodile god and decorated with a symbol of a winged sun.

The pyramids of El-Fayoum

There are four separate pyramid sites in the vicinity. **Hawara** pyramid, about 10 km southeast from Fayoum is a mud brick pyramid of Amenemhat III of 12th Dynasty, 58m high and side of base measures 100m. All the decorative casing has long since been removed. Contrary to normal practice the entrance was situated on the south side in an unsuccessful attempt to confuse looters. Adjacent to this pyramid is the legendary Labyrinth, a mortuary temple built by Amenemhat III, covering an area of 105,000 sq m. It was half carved into the interior of the rock and was composed of over 3,000 rooms but today few traces remain of this spectacular construction. Nearby is the tomb of his daughter Princess Sobek-Nefru Btah which was discovered intact in 1956.

The ruined **Pyramid of Senusert II** (1897-78 BC) near **Lahun** was built by Amenemhat III's grandfather. It was built on a rocky outcrop on which limestone pillars were constructed and then covered over with mud-brick and finally encased in stone. A 'sponge' made of sand and flint was placed around the base in order to prevent any flooding. Once again the unusual south facing entrance did not deter the tomb robbers who looted Senusert's sarcophagus but left some wonderful jewellery which is now in the Egyptian Museum and New York's Metropolitan Museum. The walled pyramid complex also include the ruins of a subsidiary pyramid for the queen, the mortuary temple and the mastaba tombs of other members of the royal family.

The collapsed **Maidoum Pyramid**, located to the northwest of El-Wasta on the River Nile, is most easily reached from there by a 1 hr early morning train journey followed by a 15 mins taxi ride to the village of Maidoum and a short walk. Originally it was 144m square and 42m high but over the centuries the imposing pyramid, which is built on the edge of an escarpment above the cultivated area, has collapsed leaving only a central layer of stone which looks rather like a mediaeval fort. The difficult entry is up a 30m stairway on the north side from which visitors descend into a long 57m sloping passage which levels out to reach a short vertical shaft leading to the limestone-lined and corbel roofed burial chamber which is on the same level as the pyramid's foundations.

Fayoum portraits

While excavating in a cemetery in the vicinity of the Hawara pyramid Sir Flinders Petrie found 146 quite remarkable hand painted portraits. These funeral masks or portraits were executed in tempra or encaustic – a mixture of paint and wax – on slices of cedar or other wood. They are dated from Graeco-Roman times, 30 BC to 395 AD, and are among the earliest portraits known. It is assumed that they were commissioned during the person's lifetime and used as decoration in the home until required. When the diseased was emblamed the portrait would be attached to the coffin or mummy case. Examples can be seen in the museum in Cairo.

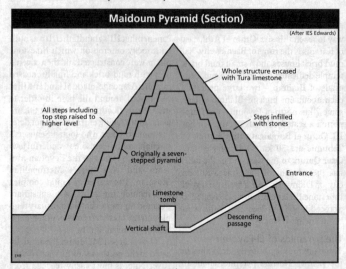

Maidoum Pyramid (Section)

(After IES Edwards)

Whole structure encased with Tura limestone

All steps including top step raised to higher level

Steps infilled with stones

Originally a seven-stepped pyramid

Entrance

Limestone tomb

Descending passage

Vertical shaft

While it is generally agreed that the Maidoum Pyramid housed the first 4th Dynasty (2613-2494 BC) pharaoh Snefru, because he also had two other pyramids at Dashur, it is now believed that it was started by his father Huni and completed by Snefru. The theory as to why it collapsed is that, unlike the pyramids at Giza which distributed the stresses inwards, the incorrectly calculated outward stresses in this progression from the early step-pyramid to the later standard pyramid caused its collapse. Slightly further north are the rubble remains of the **Seila/Silah** step pyramid of limestone from 2nd Dynasty and adjacent Christian? rock tombs. This excursion requires 4WD, a guide and a short walk.

The monasteries of El-Fayoum

Saint Anthony (251-356 AD) acted as an inspiration for hermits and there were soon numerous monasteries throughout the country including the Fayoum depression. A number still stand today. The 12th century **Deir al-Adhra (Monastery of the Virgin)** just off the road to Beni Suef about 6 km outside Fayoum City is the most accessible. It was inhabited until the 18th century then fell into disuse. Bishop Anba Abram was buried here in 1914. The *moulid* of the Virgin is celebrated here each August and the number of pilgrims, already large, is increasing each year. Further south is the beautiful 7th century Coptic **Deir Malak Ghobrial (Monastery of the Angel Gabriel)** which is located on the desert escarpment at Naqlun above the cultivated lowlands. There is a large number of cells in the area – cut into the hillside – and these were accommodation for the monks. The last rebuilding/refurbishment took place this century, so today pilgrims to the annual celebration find more comfortable places to stay in the monastery buildings which surround the church. **Deir Hammam**, which was originally built in the 6th or 8th century, is 6 km northeast of Luhun and Coptic **Deir Mari Girgis (Monastery of St George)** can be reached by boat from Sidmant al-Gabal which is 15 km southwest of Luhan. Even more isolated is **Deir Anba Samwail (Monastery of St Samuel)** which is about 30 km south of the rim of the Fayoum depression and can only be reached by pack animal or 4WD vehicle.

The Nile Valley
Middle Egypt (Cairo to Luxor)

A LTHOUGH MOST tourists tend to concentrate on Cairo and the splendours of Luxor and Aswan in Upper Egypt, the area stretching along the River Nile between Cairo and Luxor, termed Middle Egypt, should not be missed, security conditions permitting. There is a number of very interesting sites and the slower provincial pace of life is most acceptable after the noise and hassle of Cairo.

WARNING Middle Egypt in general and the towns such as Beni Suef, Assiut, Minya, Mallawi and Qena in particular are Islamic fundamentalist strongholds. Christian Copts, some 20% of the region's population, have been the target of intimidation, extortion, arson and even murder by small and unrepresentative terrorist groups who have also, on occasion, targeted tourists in an effort to harm the government's largest source of foreign currency.

The threat should not, however, be exaggerated or be allowed to deter tourists from visiting Middle Egypt provided they take precautions. In order to minimize the risks it is probably best for independent travellers to avoid staying in Beni Suef, Mallawi, Assiut and Qena which, besides any potential threat, are unpleasant towns with little or nothing to see. Instead most sites can be seen on trips from the attractive provincial capital of **Minya** once the security conditions improve (see page 176). Islamic terrorists have been driven out of surrounding villages by the police and army and have sought refuge in Minya. Therefore, although the risks are less than those in Mallawi and Assiut, it is unfortunate that

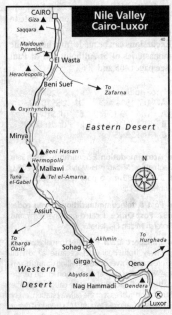

**Nile Valley
Cairo-Luxor**

CAIRO
Giza ▲
Saqqara ▲

Maidoum
Pyramids ▲
El Wasta

Heracleopolis ▲
Beni Suef

To
Zafarna

▲ Oxyrhynchus

Eastern Desert

Minya

▲ Beni Hassan
Hermopolis
Mallawi ▲
Tuna ▲ Tel el-Amarna
el-Gabel

N

Assiut

To
Kharga
Oasis

Akhmin

To
Hurghada

Sohag

Western
Desert

Girga

Qena

Abydos ▲

Nag Hammadi

Dendera

Luxor

Minya is no longer entirely risk free. The wonderful temples at Abydos and Dendera can be visited on long but worthwhile day trips from Luxor or Sohag rather than staying nearby in less pleasant circumstances.

If planning to visit Middle Egypt it is **very** important to obtain the very latest security/risk information from an unbiased source such as your embassy. **If** the security situation improves don't hesitate to visit this fascinating but neglected region.

BENI SUEF

130 km south of Cairo, with a population of 86,000, Beni Suef is the northernmost provincial capital in Middle Egypt but is best avoided (see above) if possible and the few nearby sites can be seen on day trips from Cairo or the Fayoum Oasis.

Places of interest Besides the **Maidoum Pyramid**, which is best seen on a trip from the Fayoum Oasis or even Cairo, there is little to see in Beni Suef except the ancient and very poorly preserved cities of **Heracleopolis** and **Oxyrhynchus**. They are located 15 km west of Beni Suef and 9 km west of Beni Mazar on the route to Minya.

Excursions can be made from here to the monasteries of St Anthony and St Paul (see pages 405 and 406).

Price guide:			
AL	US$150+	**D**	US$25-50
A	US$100-150	**E**	US$10-25
B	US$75-100	**F**	under US$10
C	US$50-75		

● **Accommodation E** *Semiramis*, Sharia Safir Zaghloul, Midan El-Mahat, T 322092, F 316017, 30 rm, a poor quality hotel in an unpleasant city.

● **Post & telecommunications Area code:** 082. **Post Office:** located opp the *Semiramis hotel* in Midan El-Mahat.

● **Transport Train** It is easy to make a quick getaway from Beni Suef because almost all express and slower trains travelling up and down the Nile Valley stop at the station in the centre of the city. **Road Bus:** can be caught from the bus station, just east of the railway station, every 30 mins to Cairo or Fayoum. Less frequent direct services go to Alexandria and some of the Delta towns. **Service taxis:** north to Cairo, west to Fayoum, south to Minya and east to Zafarana on the Red Sea coast can be caught from the depot west of the bus and train stations.

MINYA

Minya, 110 km south of Beni Suef and 245 km from Cairo on the West Bank of the River Nile, was until recently one of the nicest, friendliest and most relaxed towns in the whole country. At present it is to be avoided.

The centre of Minya is bounded on the east by the River Nile which here runs southeast-northwest, and the parallel railway line and Ibrahimiya Canal to the west. Beyond to the west is agricultural land.

ACCESS Train At the train station exit, across a colonial looking square, is the town's main street called Sharia Gumhorriya which runs northeast to the Corniche and the river front about 1 km away. **Road** The main service taxi depot and the bus terminal are both 5 mins walk to the right of the railway station exit along the parallel Sharia Sa'ad Zaghloul. The service taxi depot for Abu Qirkus, the jumping off point for Beni Hassan only, is 250m further south just across the railway and the canal bridge. Two buses a day from Alexandria to Assiut stop at Minya, cost E£20. Picking the bus up for return is difficult.

Places of interest

Beni Hassan, which is named after an ancient tribe, is about half way between Minya and Mallawi. It is the site of a neat row of 11th and 12th Dynasty (2050-1786 BC) tombs which were dug into the rock face of hills overlooking the River Nile. The tombs are important because they are the first to show illustrations of sports and games as well as the daily life of the people.

ACCESS Reach Beni Hassan by service taxi to the small town of Abu Qirkus on the main Minya to Mallawi road, cross over the canal and walk about 1 km straight down its main street until the road forks from where you can take a E£0.25 pick-up to the banks of the River Nile. The efficient little ferry across the river costs E£4.50 return but

Hermopolis – The City of Thoth

Hermopolis was the city of Thoth, the gods' scribe and vizier, the reckoner of time, the inventor of writing and, following his association with Khonsu, a moon-god with mastery of science and knowledge. Thoth is depicted either with a man's body and the head of a sacred ibis or as a white and very well endowed baboon. Although his cult originated further north in the Nile Delta, its greatest following was in Middle Egypt.

In the city's complex creation myth, known as the Hermopolitan cosmogony, the chaos before the world's creation was thought to have had four characteristics – water, infinity, darkness and invisibility – each represented by a male and a female god who collectively are known as the Hermopolitan Ogdoad (company of eight). A primordial mound and the cosmic egg arose from the chaos and hatched the sun god who then began to organize the world from the chaos. While most people believed that the Ogdoad itself produced the cosmic egg Thoth's devotees alone credited him with having laid it and therefore having been connected with the creation of the world. A modern interpretation of the link between his representation as a baboon and his role in the Creation is associated with the habit of baboons shrieking at sunrise thus being the first to welcome the sun. The baboon is also connected to the moon and there are often statues of baboons with moons on their head. This is probably because of the ancient Egyptians' love of puns and word-play because the word for 'to orbit' was apparently similar to that for 'baboon'. Although by the New Kingdom this Hermopolitan version of creation myth had been supplanted by the Heliopolitan cosmogony, Thoth's cult continued until the later Ptolemaic era.

this also includes the short minibus ride to the tombs. Entry is permitted to four tombs, open daily 0800-1600 costs E£8 or E£4 for students. Although the regional Ministry of Tourism is now reviewing the policy, which is set by the national rather than provincial authorities, it still costs E£10 to take photographs in each tomb which, given their simplicity compared with the wonders of Luxor's Valley of the Kings, is both a rip-off and a disincentive for tourists to visit the region.

The tombs are interesting because they mark a stage in the evolution of tomb design from the lateral Old Kingdom (2686-2181 BC) style *mastabas* to the deep New Kingdom (1567-1085 BC) royal tombs of the Valley of the Kings (see page 233). At Beni Hassan some of the earlier tombs have no vestibules and consist only of a simple chamber carved in the rock while the later ones contain a vestibule and a more intricate arrangement of the chamber. Another interesting feature is that they were not royal tombs but were built for regional rulers and military leaders. Their illustrations tend to be more personal and to depict feudal or military life rather than those of offerings and magic formulae for reaching the after-life which are more commonly associated with the royal tombs. Of the 39 tombs only 12 were decorated and only four can currently be visited.

Tomb of Amenemhat (No 2) He was the regional governor and commander-in-chief at the time of Senusert I (1971-28 BC) and his tomb has a columned portico facade and a lintel bearing a list of his titles. The texts inside the door relate to his numerous military campaigns south to Kush and praise his administrative skills. Particular reference is made to a year when there was heavy flooding of the River Nile but taxes were not increased. The main chamber has a vaulted roof which is supported by four columns and decorated in a chequered pattern. To the back of the chamber the niche once contained a statue of Amenemhat. The chamber walls are finely decorated with a cooking scene on the right of the south wall. In the middle Amenemhat is seated during an offering ceremony while the north wall has scenes of hunting and military preparations. On the east wall there are pictures of wrestling, an attack on a fortress and boats sailing towards Abydos.

Tomb of Khnumhotep (No 3) This tomb is very similar and is that of Amenemhat's successor Khnumhotep who was also governor of the Eastern Desert. The façade has a proto-Doric columned portico leading into a central chamber with a niche for his statue at the far end. Inscriptions of great historical importance about feudal life in the 12th Dynasty were discovered in the tomb. Clockwise around the tomb there are scenes of ploughing, the harvest and his voyage to Abydos. Below the next scene of desert hunting on the north wall is the lower register showing the arrival of an Asian caravan which offers gifts to the governor. All is shown in minute detail. This is followed by Khnumhotep and his wife who are shown fishing and fowling in the marshes on the left and harpooning fish from a punt on the right of the niche for the statue. On the south wall he inspects boat-building and then sails to Abydos while other registers show dyers, weavers, carpenters and other artisans.

Tomb of Baqet III (No 15), who was governor of the Oryx Nome, is much simpler than the others and dates back to the 11th Dynasty (2050-1991 BC). In the chamber are two columns with lotus capitals. On the north wall are scenes of a desert hunt with four mythological animals in the midst of the normal animals including copulating gazelles. On the east wall there are illustrations of 200 wrestling positions while the south wall illustrates scenes from Baqet's turbulent life including an attack on a fortress.

Tomb of Kheti (No 17), who was Baqet's son and heir, is quite similar to that of his father. The same wrestling scenes are to be found on the east wall and there are very similar representations of

craftsmen and desert hunts. On the south wall Kheti is shown watching agricultural scenes and receiving offerings from under a sunshade attended by his servants and a dwarf.

Local information
● **Accommodation**

C *Mercure Nefertiti & Aton*, Corniche el-Nil, T 086 341515, F 326467, river-side location about 2 km north of the town centre on both sides of the beautiful tree-lined corniche, opened 1986 and recently expanded, 96 rm (30 decent rm in main building, 24 satisfactory garden chalets without a river view, and 42 chalets adjacent to the River Nile), 3 restaurants (*La Palma*, *Banana Island* and *Darna*), a bar, tea and coffee shops, pool, tennis, sauna, small gym, efficient and very friendly staff, reduction in tourist trade has resulted in some of the facilities being closed.

E *Beach Hotel el-Shata*, 32 rm and 2 suites a/c with bath, good location.

F *El-Shatek*, 31 Sharia el-Gumhorriya, T 322307, 32 rm; **F** *Lotus*, 1 Sharia Port Said, T 324541, F 324576, 42 extremely clean rm with rather noisy a/c and bath, 92 beds, River Nile 1 km, station 1 km, pleasant hotel.

Youth hostels The youth hostel has dormitory beds and a pool, 1.5 km out of town nr the stadium.

● **Places to eat**
Besides restaurants in the *Nefertiti* and *Lotus* hotels, which offer different standard but reasonably priced good quality food, the *El-Fayrouz* restaurant on the Corniche about 150m north of Sharia Gumhorriya provides excellent meat dishes and juices. The *Ali Baba* cafeteria is not rec. Good cheap food can be bought at many of the other local cafés such as *Cafeteria Ali*.

● **Banks & money changers**
There are two banks, open Sunday-Thursday 0830-1400 and 1700-2200, next to the tourist office on the Corniche.

● **Post & telecommunications**
Area code: 086.
Post Office: in the main square called Midan Sa'a, directly outside the railway station, open Sunday-Thursday 0830-1400 and 1700-2200.

● **Shopping**
While the more up-market shops are on Sharia Gumhorriya the best and main shopping streets bisect it about half way between the station and

the river. There has been a Monday market since Ottoman times.

● **Tourist offices**

The Minya provincial government is very keen to promote tourism and the tourist information office (open daily 0800-1400 and 1700-2200, T 320150) on the Corniche is very helpful and is well worth a visit.

● **Transport**

Train Most inter-city trains stop at Minya so it is possible to travel easily north to Cairo (4 hrs, E£25 first class) via Beni Suef or south to Luxor via Assiut and Qena.

Road Bus: almost hourly buses from the terminal on Sharia Sa'ad Zaghloul to Cairo (5 hrs) or south to Assiut. **Service taxis**: which are quicker but still cheap can be caught to the same destinations from the nearby depot under the railway arch. Those for Abu Qirkus (30-45 mins), the jumping off point for Beni Hassan, can only be caught 250m further south just across the railway and the canal bridge.

MALLAWI

Mallawi is definitely not a place to stay. It is the centre of armed Islamist resistance to the government and remains under curfew for much of the day.

Mallawi was replaced by Minya as the regional capital in 1824 since when it has deteriorated sharply. Today its dirty streets and open drains make it a town to avoid particularly because Minya is just up the road. Although Mallawi is an awful town the fact that there are a number of important archaeological sites has persuaded the regional tourist authority to plan to new 3- or 4-star hotel. Located besides the River Nile, mercifully outside the town, it will have berthing facilities for nine tourist boats while the chalets will be able to accommodate 404 tourists. This remains at the planning stage.

Today little remains of the ruined 7th Dynasty (2181-73 BC) city of **Hermopolis Magna** and its necropolis at nearby **Tuna el-Gabel** which are located to the northwest of **Mallawi**, about 50 km south of Minya.

Antinopolis

It is necessary to travel north from Mallawi to take the ferry east across the River Nile to visit Sheik Abada, the ruined Roman town of Antinopolis. Construction started here in 130 AD in memory of Antinous, a favourite who was accompanying Emperor Hadrian on an official visit to the area. It is said that he drowned himself in the River Nile to prevent a danger which had been prophesied for the Emperor. Early travellers described the splendid columns and archways, now dismantled and dispersed, but the plan of the town can still be traced.

Hermopolis Magna as it was known in Ptolemaic times, was the ancient city of Khmunu the capital of the Hare Nome, and had a dual function as a secular and religious centre and was ruled by the High Priest. It was once quite large, extending to both sides of the River Nile's banks, with a temple surrounded by a 15m thick wall at its centre. The town regained importance under the Ptolemies who associated Thoth with their god Hermes and gave the town its name.

At the same time a vast necropolis, now known as **Tuna el-Gabel**, was established west of the town. Today, however, little remains of the city except a large mound of rubble and mud-bricks and 24 rose granite columns. The Tuna el-Gabel Necropolis (open daily 0900-1700 E£7) is 6 km west across a very hot and empty desert road from the small town of that name and 6 km southwest of Hermopolis. To the right of the sand-blown entrance site where the road ends, is a tree-lined government resthouse. The café has closed since tourist numbers dropped so take your own water. To the left are the administration and accommodation buildings. There is comparatively little to see above ground because most of the tombs lie below the sand dunes which would soon cover the whole site if it were not for the workers' constant efforts to keep them at bay.

The **Sacred Animal Necropolis** is to the right of the entrance and is set in catacombs, which may stretch as far as Hermopolis, but only a small area is now open to the public. Mummified baboons and ibises, which were sacred animals because they were the two representations of Thoth, were buried in these catacombs. A large number of mummified animals were found but the best have been removed to museums and the remaining ones are poorly preserved.

A few hundred metres to the south is the main part of the **City of the Dead** which was modelled on a real city with streets and some tombs which resemble houses. Egyptians traditionally went to visit their dead relatives and took a meal or spent the night in the mausoleum. Some of the tombs therefore have more than one chamber and a few have an additional floor or even a kitchen. The City of the Dead's most interesting building is the tomb-chapel of **Petosiris** who was the High Priest of Thoth at Hermopolis and whose coffin is in the Museum in Cairo. It was built in 300 BC and is strongly influenced by Hellenistic art as illustrated by the Greek clothes. The mausoleum was a family tomb divided between the vestibule, which is decorated with scenes of traditional crafts such as metalwork, wine and brick making and woodwork, and the inner shrine. On either side of the door to the shrine are offering and sacrifice scenes. In the shrine are colourful illustrations from traditional Egyptian funerary texts with the east wall depicting a funerary procession. The actual burial chambers, where three generations of high priests were buried, is 8m below the shrine.

Another interesting two storey tomb-chapel is that of **Isadora** which dates from 120 BC and still contains the well-preserved mummy of the young girl. Because she drowned in the sacred River Nile this led to the brief establishment of a cult for her. Also worth a visit is the tomb known as the **House of Graffiti** which has been restored and contains a kitchen, various rooms and a chamber where the deceased was exposed before being buried in the funerary shaft.

TELL EL-AMARNA

12 km south of Mallawi, Tell el-Amarna is the East Bank city which was headed by Pharaoh Amenhotep IV (1379-62 BC), who is better known as **Akhenaten**, after he had left Thebes (Luxor) to establish the totally new and heretical monotheistic religion. Although little remains today because most of the temples and palaces were destroyed by subsequent pharaohs who reverted back to the previous polytheistic religion, the site still has plenty of atmosphere. There is another school of archaeologists who believe that, far from introducing a radical new monotheism, Akhenaten chose to ignore a religion which through a multiplicity of myths and images was able to present a surprisingly complex view of the world.

ACCESS   In order to reach Tell el-Amarna (open daily 0700-1700), drivers should head south from Mallawi to the village of Deir el-Mawas and then east to the ferry crossing, E£1 return. The river can easily be reached by catching any southbound bus or pick-up from the depot just south of the Mallawi train station at the bridge between the canal and the railway tracks or taking a private taxi. Pick up costs 25p. The River Nile can be crossed by car ferry, motorboat or *felucca* to the rather unpleasant East Bank village of El-Till, where you will be greeted by hassling adults and children hawking basketwork and other handicrafts. The ticket kiosk is just to the left of the landing stage and there is a little café to the east of the village. On arrival independent travellers will be expected to pay a 'local tax' of a few E£ to keep El-Till functioning. Alternatively there is also a small car ferry from nearby Beni Amar to the nicer village of Hagg Qandil, to the south of El-Till, but the only tickets and transport are at El-Till. **NB** Neither ferry can be relied on to carry cars after 1600. The tractor ride to the Northern Tombs costs E£10, expensive but the only realistic option, plus E£6 (students E£3). Make sure the guide includes Tomb 6 in the itinerary. The **Northern Palace** costs a further E£5 to visit.

Places of interest

The huge site is made up of a number of different areas – the **city ruins** to the south of El-Till; the **Northern Tombs** 5 km to the east and up an 80m escarpment for which a donkey or tractor-driven trailer is almost essential; the **Royal Tomb** 5 km further away up a hidden valley and closed to the public; the rarely visited **Southern Tombs** southeast of El-Till; and the **Northern Palace** near the riverbank to the north of the village. At least half a day is required for the site and a full day if the Southern Tombs are to be included.

Amenhotep IV was the son of Amenhotep III (1417-1379) BC and his dark-skinned and possibly Nubian 'chief wife' Queen Tiy who may have ruled jointly for 12 years with her son after he ascended the throne in 1379 BC. The cult of Aten, which was one aspect of the sun-god, had been mentioned in earlier texts and shown as a human being but may have been a private and personal royal belief during his father's reign. Amenhotep IV, however, espoused it very strongly at the expense of Amun and the other gods very early in his reign which naturally upset the high priests of Amun in Thebes (Luxor).

Therefore, in the 5th year of his reign in 1374 BC, he and his wife Nefertiti moved the capital to Akhetaten ('horizon of Aten') half way between Thebes and Memphis at Tell el-Amarna in order to make a clean break with previous traditions. For those of a romantic disposition the large gully or river *wadi* cutting through the eastern cliffs have been likened to the Egyptian symbol for the horizon. It has been suggested that it was because the sun rose from behind these cliffs that Akhenaten chose this as the site for his new city of Akhetaten.

On arriving in Akhetaten he changed his name to Akhenaten or 'servant of

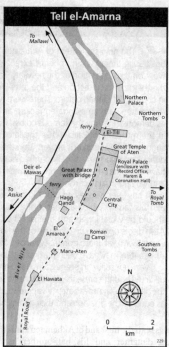

Tell el-Amarna

Aten' while Nefertiti became Nefernefruaten or 'beautiful are the beauties of the Aten'. In the 12th year of his reign he adopted a more confrontational approach to the old cults and his decision to close down all the old temples probably led to unrest because of the detrimental economic effect caused by the temple being closed. There is some evidence that Akhenaten was criticized for not defending Egypt's borders and for jeopardizing the territories previously won by his expansionist father.

How Akhenaten's reign ended is still a mystery. One theory is that Akhenaten rejected his wife Nefertiti and made his son-in-law Smenkhkare the co-regent. Some have interpreted the fact that the two men lived together and some of their poses in the murals as proof of a homosexual relationship. Smenkhkare, who

Revolutionary Art:
Akhenaten and Nefertiti's New Designs

The new settlement of Akhetaten was not only revolutionary in its religion but also in the arts. A number of excellent craftsmen and artists were recruited to work on the decoration of the new city. Rather than focusing almost exclusively on the theme of resurrection and the after-life they also depicted daily life and nature in greater detail than before. There were two main art styles with the first depicting Akhenaten with an elongated face, protruding stomach, and female-style thighs, as demonstrated by the famous colossi from his temple at Karnak which are now in the museum in Cairo, while the later style is much less distorted. It has been suggested, although not proven, that the earlier distortions were partly due to the difficulties that the artists had in radically altering their style. Alternatively it may have been that the decoration was undertaken too hastily using inferior limestone and varying quality carvings.

It has been suggested that Akhenaten intended that the depictions of himself and his family, which appear in the shrines of private houses in Tell el-Amarna, should be worshipped and that only he could directly mediate with the god. The Aten disc is only shown when he or the Royal family are present. While the pharaoh was always, at least nominally, accepted as a god or the gods it appears that Akhenaten may have been particularly literal about this convention.

Very unusually, in scenes of royal dinners both the pharaoh and his wife were depicted and the presence of both their cartouches almost as co-rulers demonstrated the difference in Amenhotep IV's approach. Wives had never previously been portrayed as equal to the pharaoh and their names had never appeared side by side.

was both the husband of Akhenaten's eldest daughter and his half-brother, is thought to have continued ruling for a year after Akhenaten's death in 1362 BC but soon died himself. The other, more contentious, interpretation of events is that, far from splitting up with Nefertiti, the pharaoh actually made her co-regent and his equal. She may then have adopted Smenkhkare as her official name and been illustrated in a different way. However only the cartouches can be used to identify the figures which makes the theory a suitably interesting alternative. The reality is that no-one knows the truth which may be very dull compared with these stories.

Worship of Aten did not long outlive its creator. In 1361 BC Smenkhkare was succeeded by Tutankhamen (1361-52 BC), another of Amenhotep III's sons and therefore Akhenaten's half-brother, who returned to the Thebes-based cult of Amun. He and his successors attempted to eradicate all traces of Akhenaten and the city of Akhetaten was subsequently destroyed and completely pillaged by Seti I (1318-04 BC) so that nothing was known of the city or its cult until the second half of this century.

Apart from the romantic story of Akhenaten, the importance of the city lies in its short history. Although about 5 km long, the city was built and occupied for no more than 25 years. When abandoned a record of life in the late 18th Dynasty was left which ranged from peasants in small houses to the official buildings and palaces. Most urban sites in Egypt have either been lost under modern towns and villages or have been badly damaged so that Tell el-Amarna offers a unique record.

Leaving El-Till one passes the remains of the massive **Great Temple of Aten** on the right which is now partly covered by the modern cemetery. There are then the vague ruins in the sand of a mixture of administrative and residential buildings until one reaches the **Small Temple of Aten** which is currently being preserved and re-excavated by the Egyptian Exploration Society. Although it is not yet open to tourists a good view of the temple can be had from a local tractor-trailor.

Just before the temple there is a large mud-brick structure on either side of the road. This is the remains of the **Bridge** which crossed the road and connected the **King's House** to the east with the so-called **Great Palace** to the west which runs along and partly under the cultivated area. This area including the palace, temple and ancillary buildings is the **Central City** which was the administrative and religious centre of the ancient city.

The Northern Tombs, which are the most interesting site at Tell el-Amarna, was the necropolis for the nobles many of whom were not originally from Thebes but were elevated to their position by Akhenaten once he arrived at Akhetaten. Most of the tombs also devote more space and decoration to Akhenaten himself than to the occupant. It is **advisable to carry a torch** but there is now electric lighting in the Northern Tombs.

Tomb of Huya (No 1) Huya was the Superintendent of the Royal Harem and Steward of Akhenaten's mother Queen Tiy and may have died during her visit to Akhetaten in 1367 BC. At the entrance he is pictured praying next to a hymn to Aten and on either side of the door are highly unusual scenes of Queen Tiy drinking wine with Akhenaten, Nefertiti and princesses. On the left wall is a scene showing Akhenaten in a procession being carried on his litter towards the Hall of Tribute where ambassadors from Kush and Syria await his arrival. To the left and right of the entrance to the shrine are somewhat damaged scenes of Huya being decorated by Akhenaten from the Window of Appearances with the sculptor's studio below. On the right hand wall Akhenaten leads Queen Tiy to see the temple he has built for his parents while the staff who worked on the temple are displayed below. The shrine is undecorated but the niche has some scenes of funerary offerings, mourning, and a curious representation of the funerary furniture.

Tomb of Mery-Re II (No 2) This tomb of the Royal Scribe, Overseer of the Two Treasuries and Overseer of the Harem of the Great Royal Wife Nefertiti was started during Akhenaten's reign but finished by Smenkhkare and follows a similar plan to Huya's tomb. After the now destroyed Hymn to the Aten at the entrance, Mery-Re is shown worshipping the Aten and then to the left Nefertiti offers Akhenaten a drink next to three young princesses. Further along the upper register depicts Mery-Re receiving a golden collar from Akhenaten while foreigners look on and then being acclaimed by his household. Further along the right wall Akhenaten, Nefertiti and their daughters are at the centre of a scene divided into three subjects. The first shows black slaves, with their faces painted red, carrying gold bars and coins. The tables are heaped with piles of gold and a number of slaves are shown carrying their children. In the second scene, Asian people pay homage to Akhenaten and bring him treasures and a number of female slaves. The last scene shows a double procession with the empty royal litter and the royal guard while treasures are offered to the Pharaoh. The rest of the tomb was never finished except for a defaced scene on the back wall of Mary-Re being rewarded by Smenkhkare and his wife.

Tomb of Ahmose (No 3), who was Akhenaten's fan bearer and therefore had the right to a noble's tomb, is with another group of four tombs just beyond the next valley. The tomb was unfinished and some of the scenes are damaged. Most of them depict aspects of the palace including the throne room, the royal apartments and some of Akhenaten's army preparing for battle.

Slaughter by The Nile

Re, the sun-god, creator of all men and all things, grew old and the men began to mock him. They criticized his appearance and even complained about his neglect. Re was very angry at their lack of reverence due to his position, after all he was their creator. He called a secret council of gods and goddesses (Geb, Shu, Tefnut, Nut and Hathor), where it was agreed to remove the unnecessary aggravation and destroy all mankind.

The task of destruction was handed to Hathor, the daughter of Re. She seems to have been happy in her work, 'wading in blood' as the story goes. The gods realized, almost too late, that without the men the tasks on earth in the temples would not be performed. It was essential therefore to protect those who remained from Hathor. The drug mandrake was mixed with freshly brewed beer and the blood of the already slain making 7,000 vessels in all. This liquid was poured out across the land (symbolic of the Nile floods) and Hathor, waking, mistook this liquid for blood, drank it all and was too stupefied to complete her task.

Tomb of Mery-Re I (No 4), the High Priest of the Aten and the father of Mery-Re II, has three chambers and is probably the best of all. On the entrance wall he is shown in adoration before the Aten while in the columned and flower decorated vestibule Mery-Re and his wife Tenro are shown in prayer. On the left hand wall of the main chamber, which now only has two of the original four columns, Mery-Re is invested with the High Priest's gold collar by Akhenaten. The royal family and escorts are then portrayed in an important scene, because it shows the height of the buildings, leaving the palace for the Great Temple in chariots. There are hymns to the Aten and offering scenes above the entrance to the unfinished inner chambers. On the right of the main chamber Akhenaten, accompanied by Nefertiti and two of their daughters, is in the Great Temple making sacrifices to the Aten. Other scenes show Akhenaten after the sacrifice with his daughters playing musical instruments while beggars await alms in the corner. Below is a scene which has given archaeologists a rare insight into the original appearance of the city. Mery-Re is seen showing the Pharaoh the stocks in the temple with views towards the port, a stable and the royal boats on the River Nile.

The nearby **Tomb of Pentu (No 5)**, the royal scribe and chief physician, is badly disfigured and it is better to see the **Tomb of Panehsi (No 6)** which is 500m to the south. This High Priest's tomb, which has four columns in each of the two chambers, was later transformed by the Copts into a chapel but many of the original decorations are still in place. In the first chamber are scenes of Akhenaten decorating Panehsi. On the left hand wall, the royal family worship the Aten in front of their household. There are further scenes of Akhenaten including one on the far wall on the left behind a Coptic baptistery and one by the stairs leading down to the funerary chamber, showing him with Nefertiti and their daughters in their chariots surrounded by troops. The rest of the tomb is either unfinished or has been damaged.

The **Royal Tomb**, which is located in a secret valley 5.5 km east of the main plain, has been closed since 1934 and cannot normally be visited although if really keen it is possible to arrange a visit beforehand with the antiquities department at Minya. Although there are electric lights, because there is no source of power, it is necessary to take your own generator. It is a very rough ride, best undertaken by tractor, because it will damage all but the strongest of 4WD vehicles.

People with their own transport can see the **Northern Palace** about 1.5 km north of El-Till which was recleared several years ago by the Egyptian Antiquities Service. Although it is only really for enthusiasts it is possible to walk around and enter this large mud-brick ruin where a section of mosaic can still be seen. There is a temple to the south called Kom el-Nana which is being excavated by a British mission but it is not accessible or currently open to the public.

ACCESS Visitors to the southern tombs usually travel on the north-south road along the edge of the cultivated area which almost exactly follows the ancient 'royal road' which linked all Akhetaten's official buildings.

The **Southern Tombs** are spread over seven low hills in two groups but only about five of the 18 tombs are of any possible interest. They include the **Tomb of Ay** (No 25) (1352-48 BC), who was Akhenaten's maternal uncle and visir to Amenhotep III, Akhenaten and Tutankhamen whom he succeeded as pharaoh when he died. There are unproven theories either that his wife Tey was Nefertiti's wet-nurse or that the couple conceived Tutankhamen. Despite this, possibly because they do not justify the effort of getting there, the southern tombs are rarely visited by tourists.

ASSIUT

Assiut, 109 km south of Minya and the largest city south of Cairo (375 km), is well worth missing. Not only is it a noisy, aggressive and unpleasant city but, as one of the Islamic fundamentalist strongholds, it has also been the scene of some of Egypt's worst communal violence (see Political Risks, page 19). Having almost nothing to offer the tourist except a few fairly decent hotels, fast trains out of town and the main road to the Western Desert oases which is 12 km north of the city it is probably best avoided. For those who have the misfortune to be stuck in the city here are a few of the essential details.

ACCESS The train, bus and service taxi stations are all located on Sharia el-Geish and most of the best hotels are situated on or near the same street. Roads in front of the stations run to the River Nile while those behind the railway station lead to the *souqs*. The airport 10 km northwest of the city has no bus connection.

Places of interest

There is comparatively little to see in Assiut itself although the **Nasser Museum** in the village of Beni Marr just to the south of the city and the very large **Convent of the Virgin** (Deir el-Adhra), where Copts believe the Holy Family sought refuge from Herod in the caves at Dirunka 12 km west of Assiut, are worth a visit. Every year in August in the presence of up to 50,000 pilgrims the icons are paraded around its cave-church during the **Moulid of the Virgin**. Further afield, 5 km out of El-Qusiya which is 42 km north of Assiut, is the **Burnt Monastery** (Deir el-Muharraq) which gets its name from its location on the edge of the burning, roasting desert but which, given the attacks on Coptic churches by the area's Islamic fundamentalists, is a particularly apt name. The Burnt Monastery is the largest and wealthiest in Middle Egypt. It is considered a place of healing and the Feast of Consecration, the annual moulid with up to 50,000 pilgrims, takes place before Easter. It is claimed that the **Church of the Blessed Virgin Mary** was the first church built in Egypt, although the current church was constructed in 1964 and badly damaged by Islamic extremists in 1988. It is better to visit Tell el-Amarna from Minya and Abydos from Sohag rather than from Assiut.

Local information
● Accommodation

If you have to stay in Assiut the decent hotels are nr the train station, but there are also some really unpleasant places.

D *Badr Touristic*, Sharia el-Thallaga, T 329811, F 322820, 44 rm, some with TV, comfortable hotel where tour groups are usually accommodated; **D** *Casa Blanca*, Sharia Mohamed Tawfik

Fundamentalism

Islam has been marked over the course of history by the emergence of rigorous revivalist movements. Most have sought a return of the faithful to the fundamentals of Islam – the basic doctrines of the Prophet Mohammed – uncluttered by the interpretations of later Islamic jurists and commentators. Behind the movements was generally the idea that Muslims should go back to the simple basics of their religion. Some, like the Wahhabi movement in Saudi Arabia were puritan in concept, demanding plain lives and an adherence to the tenets of Islam in all daily aspects of life. Others, imposed a rigorous schedule of ritual in prayer and avoidance of the 'unclean' in public life. A good example of this type of reformist tendency was the Senusi Movement in Libya which in the period from the close of the 19th century to 1969 created an educational, commercial and religious society throughout eastern Libya and northern Chad.

Until recent times the fundamentalist movements inside Islam arose from a desire to cleanse the religion of unnecessary ideology and to make all Muslims observe the basic pillars of the Islamic religion – prayer, belief and actions on a consistent and demonstrable basis. In the last 100 years there has been a growing tendency in the Islamic world for revivalist movements to be reactions to political, military and cultural setbacks experienced at the hands of the Western industrialized world. The aim of the reformers has been to make good the disadvantage and backwardness of the Muslim states in contrast with the powerful countries of Europe, America and the Far East. The matter is varied and complex, depending on the particular cases involved but the clear linkage between an increasingly dominant Western culture and economy and the growth of reactive Islamic movements is inescapable. In Egypt, the Muslim Brotherhood was an early form of revivalist movement of this kind. Founded by an Egyptian schoolteacher, Has al-Banna in 1928, it initially tried to take Islam back to its roots and therefore to its perceived strengths but was later taken over by extremists who used its organization for political ends. The development of the Muslim Brotherhood as a clandestine political group and the harnessing of religious fervour to political objectives, including the assassination of political enemies, set the pattern for most later movements of the kind.

In Egypt the Muslim Brotherhood remained the main organization though other smaller sects were also founded. Fundamentalism in Sudan has been adopted as a system of government and many of the attributes of the Iranian revolution have been copied, some with Iranian assistance. Libya has not been threatened by Islamic fundamentalism on the scale experienced elsewhere in the region.

Politically, the Egyptian government has struggled to find ways either to repress or co-opt the extreme Islamist movements which have been responsible for the murder of and injury to foreign tourists and Egyptians (including the 83-year-old novelist Naguib Mahfouz) over recent years.

This lack of any understanding between the government and the Islamist opposition gives Egypt's political system an unneeded air of fragility. President Mobarak has responded as a soldier – with violence against violence – to armed political attacks on his régime. The attack on the state by the Islamists has diminished but remains as serious and likely to be protracted unless ended by a political solution – unlikely at the present. But for the foreign tourist, there is much less to fear. They now seem to be out of the direct firing line from the Islamists and the situation is very much improved on the previous position.

Khashaba, T 324483, F 321662, 50 rm, cheaper than above.

E *Akhenaten Touristic*, Sharia Mohamed Tawfik Khashaba, T 327723, F 321600, 35 rm; **E** *Reem Touristic*, Sharia el-Nahda, T 326235, F 329102, 40 rm, very cheap.

F *El-Salam*, Sharia Thabet, T 332256, 40 rm; **F** *YMCA*, Sharia Gumhorriya, T 323218, located about 10 mins walk from the train station, clean, cheap a/c rooms, pool.

Camping It is possible but unadvisable to camp nr the Assiut barrage (built by the British in 1898-1903 and carries a wide road), at the Officers Club (T 323134) and the Sporting Club (T 233139) or on Banana Island where there are no facilities.

Youth hostels Building 503, El-Walidia, Assiut, T 324841, 40 beds, kitchen, 2 km from station, overnight fee E£3.

● **Places to eat**
All the better hotels have restaurants which offer decent food as do the various clubs which usually admit better-dressed tourists. The best is *Badr Touristic* but there is little competition. There are a number of good cheap and cheerful restaurants between the back of the station and the *souq* in the main commercial district. The cheap ones incl: *Express Restaurant* and *Mattam al-Azhar*, as well as others along Sharia Talaat Harb and Sharia 26 July.

● **Banks & money changers**
There are a number of banks, incl the **Alexandria Bank** (open Saturday-Thursday 0830-1400 and 1800-2100, Friday 0900-1230 and 1800-2100) in the commercial district around Talaat Harb.

● **Post & telecommunications**
Area code: 088.

Post Office: nr the railway station and open Sunday-Thursday 0830-1400 and 1700-2200.

● **Tourist offices**
It is best to ask for information at the better hotels.

● **Transport**
Air Internal flights to Cairo and Kharga from the airport, 10 km northwest of the town.

Train Run 12 times a day to Cairo (7 hrs) via Mallawi (2 hrs) and Minya (3 hrs), but less frequently to Luxor (6-7 hrs) via Sohag (2 hrs) and Qena (4-5 hrs).

Road Bus: 7 daily buses Cairo (7 hrs), 5 to Kharga Oasis (5 hrs) which go on to Dakhla (8-9 hrs), and 4 to Qena (4 hrs), as well as buses every 30 mins between 0600-1800 north to Minya (2 hrs) and south to Sohag. **Service taxis**: which are quicker than buses, run to every town between Minya and Sohag, as well as to Kharga (5 hrs), and are easy to catch from the depot in the mornings but are less frequent later in the day.

SOHAG

A small agricultural and university West Bank town, 97 km south of Assiut along the River Nile, Sohag has a large Coptic community amongst its 90,000 population. Although it has few minor sites it is not really geared to tourists but it does have the advantage of being relatively close to the beautiful temple at Abydos and within half a day's journey from Dendera.

ACCESS Directly outside the train station on Sharia el-Mahata (Station Rd) are the only hotels in the town while north and south bound service taxis are at either end of the street 5 mins from station. Over the bridge across the railway tracks is the main road to the River Nile.

Places of interest

The small **White Monastery** (Deir al-Abyad) and **Red Monastery** (Deir al-Ahmar), at 10 km and 14 km south of Sohag are of interest. The **White Monastery**, with light coloured walls of limestone, was founded in the 5th century by St Pjol and dedicated to St Shenuda, one of the most prominent figures in the history of the Coptic church. Moulid each July. Once it had a population of over 2,000 monks. The church which dominates the monastery is divided with decorated columns into a central nave and two aisles. The three altars are dedicated to St Shenuda (centrally placed), also St George and The Holy Virgin. St Shenuda worked in the White and Red Monasteries for over 80 years. (He is believed to have lived for well over 100 years.) He introduced both spiritual and social support for the local community including medical help. Just 3 km to the north of here is the smaller **Red Monastery** founded by St Bishoi who was a disciple of Shenuda. It is built of burnt brick, hence the name. It is said to have been the centre of a monastery of 3,000 monks. The church of St Bishai has some interesting wall paintings and a sanctuary screen with icons of St Bishai, St Shenuda and St Pjol.

Akhmin is not to be ignored, **Deir al Shuhuda** (Monastery of the Martyrs) is an important place for pilgrims. It is here that papyrus scrolls containing the Book of Proverbs was found. In the town too is **Deir al-Adra** (Convent of the Holy Virgin) with a *moulid* on 22 August

On the way south the beautiful **Temple of Seti I** at **Abydos** is an absolute must and better visited from here than from Qena.

Abydos is 10 km southwest of El-Balyana and halfway between Sohag and Qena and can be reached by service taxi from Sohag to El-Balyana (E£2) and then on to Abydos (E£0.5). It was the holiest town of all for the ancient Egyptians and pilgrims were making the journey to Abydos from the 7th Dynasty (2181-73 BC) until well into the Ptolemaic era (323-30 BC). Site open 0700-1800, entrance E£6.

It was the cult-centre for **Osiris**, the god of the dead who was known as 'Lord of Abydos', because according to legend either his head or his whole body was buried at the site (see Temple of Isis, Aswan, page 290). Abydos was considered the door to the after-life which looked out over the Western Desert where the gates were thought to be. Initially, in order to achieve resurrection it was necessary to be buried at Abydos but the requirement was later changed to a simple pilgrimage and the gift of a commemorative stele.

There are cemeteries and tombs scattered over a very wide area in Abydos but there are only a few buildings left standing. They do, however, include the **Temple of Seti I**, the **Osireon** (Cenotaph) and the **Temple of Ramses II** which are open daily 0700-1800 (entry E£6 and E£3 for students).

Next to the ticket booth is an excellent little café with green tables which is cheap and clean and serves very welcoming cold drinks.

The Temple of Seti I, was constructed in fine white marble by Seti I (1318-04 BC) as an offering in the same way that lesser individuals would come on a pilgrimage and make a gift of a stele. Most of the work on the temple and its convex bas-reliefs, which are amongst the most beautiful of all New Kingdom buildings, was carried out by Seti I but when he died his son Ramses II (1304-1237 BC) completed the courtyard and façade. This can be seen from the quality of workmanship which changes from Seti I's beautiful bas-reliefs to Ramses II's much cruder, quicker and therefore cheaper sunken reliefs. It is a very unusual temple because it is L-shaped rather than the usual rectangular and because it has seven separate chapels rather than a single one behind the hypostyle halls. This may have been because of the water table or the presence of the older Osirieon behind the temple.

The temple was originally approached via a pylon and two forecourts, built by Ramses II below the main temple so that the concept of the temple sloping upwards from the entrance to the inner sanctuary was maintained, but they have now been largely destroyed. The temple's

---

Diagnosis just 3,000 years too late ...

The German Institute of Archeology in Cairo has successfully used DNA tests on mummy tissue to diagnose a 3,000-year-old disease. The mummy from a noble's tomb suffered in life from tuberculosis of the left lung. Due to problems of contamination of ancient tissue this is the first time such a diagnosis has been possible. With this breakthrough 'a carefully controlled analysis of ancient Egyptian mummies may provide insights into infectious diseases of ancient individuals and population'. One hopes diagnosis today is completed with greater speed!

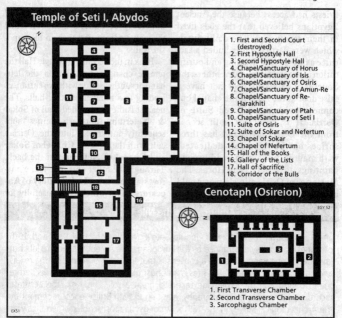

Temple of Seti I, Abydos

1. First and Second Court (destroyed)
2. First Hypostyle Hall
3. Second Hypostyle Hall
4. Chapel/Sanctuary of Horus
5. Chapel/Sanctuary of Isis
6. Chapel/Sanctuary of Osiris
7. Chapel/Sanctuary of Amun-Re
8. Chapel/Sanctuary of Re-Harakhiti
9. Chapel/Sanctuary of Ptah
10. Chapel/Sanctuary of Seti I
11. Suite of Osiris
12. Suite of Sokar and Nefertum
13. Chapel of Sokar
14. Chapel of Nefertum
15. Hall of the Books
16. Gallery of the Lists
17. Hall of Sacrifice
18. Corridor of the Bulls

Cenotaph (Osireion)

EGY 52

1. First Transverse Chamber
2. Second Transverse Chamber
3. Sarcophagus Chamber

front is now the square-columned façade behind 12 rectangular pillars decorated with Ramses welcoming Osiris, Isis and Horus. Originally there were seven doors through the façade which led on to the seven chapels but Ramses altered the construction and only the central one is now unblocked.

The theme of the seven separate chapels is evident in the **First Hypostyle Hall**, built and decorated by Ramses II's second-rate craftsmen, where the columns with papyrus capitals depict Ramses with the god represented in the corresponding sanctuary. In the much more impressive **Second Hypostyle Hall**, built by Seti, the first two rows of columns also have papyrus capitals but the last row have no capitals at all. On the right-hand wall Seti is pictured before Osiris and Horus who are pouring holy water from vases and making offerings in front of Osiris' shrine as five goddesses look on. The quality of the

work in this hall contrasts sharply with the rougher decoration in the outer hall which was probably because Ramses had ordered all the most skilled craftsmen to concentrate on his own temple!

Behind the inner hypostyle hall there are seven separate **Sanctuaries** or chapels which are dedicated to the deified Seti I, the Osiris triad of Osiris, Isis and Horus, and the Amun triad of Amun, Mut and Khonsu. Many of the wonderful bas-reliefs are still coloured, which gives a good idea of the temple's original decoration, but some of the finest are unpainted and show the precision and great artistry used in the moulding. The sanctuary to the left is dedicated to Seti and contains a beautiful scene of the Pharaoh being crowned by the goddess of Upper and Lower Egypt.

Each of these sanctuaries would have contained the god's barque as well as his stele placed in front of a false door. The sanctuary was locked and only High

EX51

Priests had access because the Ancient Egyptians believed that the gods lived in their sanctuaries. The daily rituals which were carried out included a sacrifice as well as the dressing and purification of the stele. Unlike the others, the **Sanctuary of Osiris** does not have a false door at the back of the chapel but connects with the pillared **Suite of Osiris**. It is decorated with scenes from the Osiris myth and has three shrines on the west wall dedicated, with magnificent and incredibly vivid paintings, to Seti, Isis and Horus. The Mysteries of Osiris miracle play would have been performed in the hall and in

the unfinished and partially destroyed **Sanctuary of Osiris** which is reached through a narrow entrance on the opposite wall.

Back in the Second Hypostyle Hall the temple changes direction on the lefthand or southeast side with two entrances leading to a number of other halls. The nearest is the 3-columned **Hall of Sokar & Nefertum**, northern deities subsequently integrated into the Osirian cult, with the separate **Chapel of Sokar** and **Chapel of Nefertum** at the back. Through the other entrance is the narrow star decorated **Hall/Gallery of Ancestors/Lists** which, very usefully for

Americans in the Nile Valley

📝 Although the history of enquiry into Egyptology in the 18th and 19th centuries was largely determined by the Europeans, the Americans put in a late but important appearance. There is a consensus that the work of recording the reliefs and paintings of the Nile Valley sites is amongst the most pressing of tasks before theft, looting and other damage take too great a toll. This task, the accurate recording of inscriptions or epigraphy, was begun with British encouragement by the Archaeological Survey in the 1890s. Amongst its most scholarly members was Norman de Garis Davies and his wife Nina, working first for the (British) Exploration Fund and later for the Metropolitan Museum of Art, New York. His work inspired US interest in the matter and the foundation of Chicago House at Luxor in 1924.

The arrival of US academic concern was the achievement of James Henry Breasted. He was born in Rockford USA in 1865 and rose to become the USA's first professional Egyptologist at the University of Chicago in 1894. He began a process of recording all known Egyptian hieroglyphs and continued his work in a series of scientific expeditions to Egypt and Nubia in the period 1905-07. He was particularly concerned to record all inscriptions that were at risk of damage or decay. His enthusiasm was rewarded by JD Rockefeller Jnr, who funded the establishment of an Oriental Institute at Chicago. The Institute's field centre in Egypt was sited in Luxor and a comprehensive study of a number of sites was accomplished, most famous those of Medinet Habu and the Temple of Seti I at Abydos. Breasted died in 1935 after major archaeological successes for the Institute both in Egypt and Iran.

An American businessman, Theodore Davis, became a major backer of archaeological work in Egypt, eager to find new tombs and artifacts. He was a generous sponsor of excavations but impatient of the academic requirements of good archaeology. He fell out with all the inspectors of antiquities appointed by the Antiquities Service – Carter, Quibell and Ayrton – and was responsible for more haste than discipline in the excavation of some sites, notably that of the tomb of Smenkhare, brother, it is thought, of Tutankhamen. Davis did, however, use his money to finance the publication of many books on the archaeology of the sites he paid to have excavated. Davis died in 1915 sure that the Valley of the Kings was exhausted of new archaeological finds.

Brick making in Egypt

🪶 Sun dried bricks were made from the dried Nile mud. This mud shrinks a great deal when it dries and has to be protected from the sun and the wind to prevent the brick collapsing even before it is used. To reduce the breakage rate the mud was mixed with chopped straw or reeds.

The Bible tells of the Israelites being forced to make bricks while in captivity in Egypt as the tomb painting shows. Each brickmaker had a daily target to reach, only whole bricks being counted. Forcing them to make bricks without straw meant more journeys to collect mud as it was then the only ingredient and the bricks were fragile and more frequently broken.

Painting from the Tomb of Rekhmire (see page 251).

archaeologists, lists in rows the names of the gods and 76 of Seti's predecessors although, for political reasons, some such as Hatshepsut, Akhenaten and his heirs are omitted. The gallery leads on to the **Hall of Barques** where the sacred boats were stored, the **Hall of Sacrifices** used as the slaughterhouse for the sacrifices, and other store-rooms: they are currently closed to visitors. Instead it is best to follow the side **Corridor of the Bulls**, where Ramses II is shown lassoing a bull before the jackal-headed 'opener of the ways' Wepwawet on one side and driving four dappled calves towards Khonsu and Seti I on the other, before climbing the steps to the temple's rear door and the Osirieon.

The **Osirieon**, built earlier than the main temple and at water level which has led to severe flooding, is sometimes called the Cenotaph of Seti I because it contains a sarcophagus. Although it was never used by Seti I, who is actually buried in the Valley of the Kings in Luxor, it was built as a symbol of his closeness to Osiris. Many other pharaohs built similar 'fake' tombs, which were modelled on the tombs at Luxor, in Abydos but were eventually buried elsewhere. The Osirieon is the only remaining visible tomb but is unfortunately inaccessible because of the inundation of sand and the flooding caused by the rise in the water table.

The small **Temple of Ramses II**, near the village 300m northwest from the Temple of Seti I across soft sand, is naturally an anticlimax after the scale and sheer beauty of the Temple of Seti I. It was originally a very finely built shrine which was erected in 1298 BC for Ramses' *Ka* or spirit in order to give him a close association with Osiris. The workmanship is better than in most of Ramses II's monuments because it was probably decorated by craftsmen trained in his father's era. Although the temple

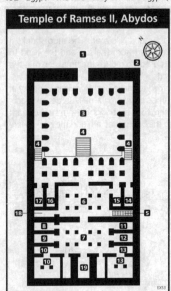

Temple of Ramses II, Abydos

1. First Pylon and First Courtyard (in ruins)
2. Second Pylon
3. Second Courtyard with square pillars
4. Steps to raised courtyard
5. Stairs to roof (no roof now)
6. First Octostyle Hall
7. Second Octostyle Hall
8. Chapel to Osiris
9. Chapel to Min
10. Chapel to Onuris
11. Room for linen
12. Room for ornaments
13. Room for offerings
14. Temple to Seti
15. Temple to Royal Ancestor
16. Temple to Ennead
17. Temple to Ramses II
18. Temple to Onuris
19. Main sanctuary

EX53

was reportedly almost intact when first seen by Napoleon's archaeologists, it has since fallen into ruin except for the lower parts of the limestone walls which are still brightly coloured.

Nag Hammadi At Hiw to the south of Nag Hammadi in the curve of a meander of the River Nile stands a complex known as the Monastery of St Palomen. This is a rich agricultural area and the bell tower can be seen from quite a distance. There are three churches, St Palomen, St Mercurius and St Damyanah. St Palomen died of excessive fasting. To the north of here in 1947 the famous Gnostic codices were discovered (see page 88, Coptic Museum).

Local information

● Accommodation
There are four hotels directly outside the railway station of which the best is **F** *Andolous*, which is a clean but noisy budget hotel which mainly caters for Egyptian train travellers, there are fans in each room but only an inadequate shared shower and toilet on each flr.

Youth hostels 5 Sharia Port Said, T 324395, 28 beds, kitchen, parking, station 1.5 km, overnight fee E£5 incl breakfast.

● Places to eat
There are a number of small cheap restaurants and cafés in the streets around the railway station incl *El-Eman* to the north of *Andolous*.

● Post & telecommunications
Area code: 093.

● Transport
Train To all regional destinations, but those to Cairo and Luxor (4 hrs) are much slower than buses or service taxis and are not worth taking.

Road Bus: 5 daily buses north to Minya and Cairo and south to Luxor, as well as much more frequent ones to Assiut (2 hrs), El-Balyana (for Abydos) and Qena (3 hrs), which can be caught from the bus depot, 5 mins to the left of railway station. **Service taxis**: run north as far as Assiut and south to Qena via El-Balyana and Nag Hammadi.

QENA

Although not as bad as Mallawi, Beni Suef or Assiut, the town of Qena, 147 km south of Sohag and 58 km north of Luxor, is another place which is best avoided. It is an unfriendly, dirty town with difficult transport connections and problems of Islamic fundamentalism (See political risks, page 19). The only reason for stopping in the town is to see the magnificent temple at Dendera about 8 km from the centre of town.

ACCESS From the train station and the southbound service taxi depot, which are on either side of the main canal, yet another Sharia el-Gumhorriya leads southeast to a major roundabout and the town's main street, to the west end of which is the bus station and the northbound service taxi depot. Tourists on excursions from Luxor may travel north to Dendera either by cruise ship or by coach. Expect delays from the additional security procedures associated with visiting this area. Coaches are driven in convoy from Luxor and the intervention of the tourist police can result in a lengthy wait (half an hour or more) at both ends of the journey.

Places of interest

Visitors should immediately head for Dendera. Because Qena's transport terminals are so far apart the easiest way of getting there is to forget about the cost, which in Western terms is still very modest, and take a taxi direct from Qena to the temple and thereby avoid a long hot walk or misdirections and total confusion. Alternatively service taxis between Qena and Sohag which can be caught next to the bus station will drop you at Dendera village which is only a 1 km walk to the temple.

Dendera was the cult-centre of Hathor since pre-dynastic times and there are signs of earlier buildings on the site dating back to Cheops in the 4th Dynasty (2613-2494 BC). Hathor, who is represented as a cow or cow-headed woman, was the goddess associated with love, joy, music, protection of the dead and, above all, of nurturing. Her great popularity was demonstrated by the huge festival held at Edfu (see page 267) when her barque symbolically sailed upstream on her annual visit to Horus to whom she was both wet-nurse and lover. As they reconsumated their union the population indulged in the Festival of Drunkenness which led the Greeks to identify Hathor with Aphrodite who was their own goddess of love and joy.

The **Temple of Hathor** (Open daily 0700-1800, Entry E£12, students E£6 (use of cameras and video recorders free), which was built between 125 BC and 60 AD by the Ptolemies and the Romans, is only the latest temple on the site with the first being built by Pepi I in the 6th Dynasty (2345-2181 BC). The huge well preserved temple dominates the walled Dendera complex which also includes a number of smaller buildings. Even although it was built by

non-Egyptian foreign conquerors it copies the earlier pharaonic temples with large hypostyle halls leading up, via a series of successively smaller vestibules and store-rooms, to the darkened sanctuary at the back of the temple. There are also two sets of steps leading up to and down from the roof sanctuaries.

At the front the pylon-shaped façade is supported by six huge Hathor-headed columns and reliefs showing the Roman emperors Tiberius and Claudius performing rituals with the gods. Through

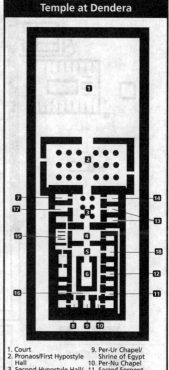

Temple at Dendera

1. Court
2. Pronaos/First Hypostyle Hall
3. Second Hypostyle Hall/ Hall of Appearances
4. First Vestibule/ Hall of Offerings
5. Second Vestibule/ Hall of Ennead
6. Sanctuary
7. Treasury
8. Per-Neser Chapel/ House of Flame
9. Per-Ur Chapel/ Shrine of Egypt
10. Per-Nu Chapel
11. Sacred Serpent
12. Seat of Repose
13. Harvest Rooms
14. Laboratory
15. Stairs to roof
16. Stairs to crypts
17. Nile Room
18. Hathor's Wardrobe

Site of Temple of Hathor at Dendera

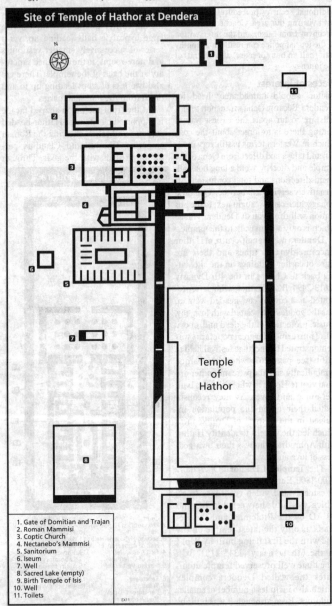

Temple of Hathor

1. Gate of Domitian and Trajan
2. Roman Mammisi
3. Coptic Church
4. Nectanebo's Mammisi
5. Sanitorium
6. Iseum
7. Well
8. Sacred Lake (empty)
9. Birth Temple of Isis
10. Well
11. Toilets

EX11

in the **Hypostyle Hall** the 18 Hathor-headed columns, organized into groups of three, are identical to those on the façade. The magnificent ceiling, which is illustrated with an astronomical theme showing the mystical significance of the sky, has retained much of its original colour. It is divided between day and night and illustrates the 14 days moon cycle, the gods of the four cardinal points, the constellations, the zodiac, and the elongated goddess Nut who swallows the sun at sunset and gives birth to it at dawn.

Holes at the base of the pillars here were reputedly used as tethering points for animals kept by the Copts whilst in hiding in the temple after Roman times.

The next room, which is known as the **Hall of Appearances** and is supported by six columns, is where the goddess 'appeared' from the depths of the temple as she was transported on her ritual barque for the annual voyage to Edfu. On either side of the doorway there are scenes of offerings and the presentation of the temple to the gods.

Around this Hall are six small rooms. The first on the left was the laboratory, used for the preparation of balms and the nine oils used to anoint the statues, which has several inscriptions with the recipes and instructions for their preparation. The next two rooms were used as store-rooms for offerings such as flowers, beer, wine and poultry. On the right of the hall's doorway is the Treasury which has scenes on the base of the walls representing the 13 mountainous countries where the precious minerals were found. The second room called the Nile Room, has river scenes and an exit to the back corridor and the well outside.

Next is the first vestibule which was known as the **Hall of Offerings** because it was there that the priests displayed the offerings for the goddess on large tables. The food and drink was then divided among the priests once the gods had savoured them. On the left a stairway leads to the roof sanctuary. **NB** All the rooms

are lit by sunlight from holes in the roof. The second vestibule called the **Hall of the Ennead** contained the statues of the kings and gods which were involved in the ceremonies to Hathor while her wardrobe was stored in the room on the left.

This leads on to the **Sanctuary of the Golden One** which contained Hathor's statue and her ceremonial barque which would be carried to the river each New Year to be transported on a boat upstream to the Temple of horus at Edfu. The south and north walls of the independently roofed sanctuary depict the Pharaoh in various phases of the ceremony. The so-called **Corridor of Mysteries** around the outside of the sanctuary has nine doors which lead to 11 small shrines with 32 closed crypts below the back shrines including crypt where the temple's valuables would have been store.

The walls of the stairway from the left of the Hall of Offerings to the **Roof Sanctuaries**, which unlike anywhere else have been completely preserved at Dendera, depict the New Year ceremony when the statue of Hathor was carried up to the roof to the small open **Chapel of the Union with the Disk** pavilion to await the sunrise. The scenes on the left of the stairs represent Hathor going up and those on the right going down. In the northwest corner of the roof terrace is **Osiris' Tomb**, where ceremonies commemorating Osiris' death and resurrection were carried out. In the east corner there are two rooms with the outer one containing a plaster-cast copy of the original **Dendera Zodiac** ceiling which was stolen and taken to the Louvre in Paris in 1820. The Zodiac was introduced to Egypt by the Romans and, although Scorpio's scorpion is replaced by a scarab beetle and the hippo-goddess Tweri was added, this circular zodiac held up by four goddesses is virtually identical to the one used today.

The views from the uppermost level of the roof terrace are superb and provide an excellent opportunity to appreciate the overall scale and layout of the temple buildings, the extensive outer walls and the intensively cultivated countryside surrounding Dendera. From the northern edge of the upper terrace there are good views looking down on to the sanitarium, the two birth houses and the Coptic basilica (see below).

Back downstairs in the temple enclosure on the exterior south wall of the temple there are two damaged reliefs depicting Cleopatra and her son Caesarion and beyond a number of small ruined buildings surround the main temple. At the back is the small **Temple of Isis** which was almost totally destroyed by the early Christians because of the fear that the worship of Isis as the universal Egyptian god might spread. At the front of the main temple to the right is the **Roman Birth House**, or Mammisi, which has some interesting carvings on its façade and south walls. It was built to replace the older 30th Dynasty **Birth House of Nectanebo** (380-362 BC) which was partially destroyed when the Romans built a wall around the temple. The **Sanatorium** between it and the main temple was where pilgrims, who came to Dendera to be healed by Hathor, were treated and washed in water from the stone-lined **Sacred Lake** to the southwest of the main temple which is now drained of water. Between the two birth-houses is a ruined 5th century **Coptic Basilica**, one of the earliest Coptic buildings in Egypt, which was built using stone from the adjacent buildings.

Local information
● Accommodation
The only semi-decent hotels are: **D** *Aluminium*, Aluminium, Naga Hammadi, Qena, T/F 581320, 72 rm.

F *Dendera*, Dendera, T 322330, also called *Happy Land*, is on the junction of the main road to Sohag and the turnoff for the temple 1 km away and is probably a much better bet than Qena's grubby hotels; **F** *New Palace*, Midan Mahata, Qena, T 322509, 75 rm, very cheap, behind the Mobil garage nr the train station.

Camping Located next to the *Hotel Dendera*, the camp site has hot showers, electricity and a kitchen.

● Places to eat
There are a few small cheap restaurants, incl the *El-Prince*, *Hamdi* and *Maradona* in and around town, but none of them is particularly good.

● Post & telecommunications
Area code: 096.
Post Office: open Saturday-Thursday 0800-1400 and 1800-2000 and is at the canal end of the main street.

● Transport
Unfortunately the transport terminals are very spread out and it may be best to take a **calèche** from one to the other provided your bargaining is pretty good.

Train: 6 daily trains from the station next to the canal both north to Cairo (11-12 hrs) via Sohag, Assiut, Minya and Beni Suef, and south to Luxor (2 hrs) and Aswan (6-7 hrs).

Road Bus: although they are slower and less convenient than service taxis, there are buses to Assiut, Sohag and Cairo, from the bus station on the main street, but the 6 daily buses to Hurghada on the Red Sea coast may be of more use. **Service taxis**: the quickest way to Luxor (1 hr) and other points south is by service taxi from the square just across the canal behind the railway station; 500m away there are taxis to Safaga and Hurghada. Northbound service taxis along the West Bank to Sohag via Nag Hammadi and El-Balyana, can be caught from the depot which is next to the bus station but one should be prepared for a long wait except in the early morning.

The Nile Valley Luxor and the West Bank

(*Pop* 40,000; *Alt* 89m)

HISTORY

On the site of the small present-day town of Luxor (676 km south of Cairo, 65 km south of Qena and 223 km north of Aswan), stood the ancient city which the Greeks called **Thebes** and which was described in Homer's *Iliad* as the 'city of a hundred gates'. Later the Arabs described it as 'el-Uqsur' or 'city of palaces' from which it gets its current name.

THE AREA around Luxor, which was the capital of the New Kingdom (1567-1085 BC), has the largest concentration of ancient tombs and monuments in the country and has been described as the world's greatest open-air museum filled with the most awe-inspiring monuments of ancient civilisations. It has been the focus of Upper Egypt's tourist industry for more than a century. Luxor is more dependent on tourism than any other town in Egypt and its fortunes have therefore fluctuated in recent years as a result of the Gulf War and the threat of Islamic fundamentalist terrorism, demonstrated by the terrible massacre of tourists on the West Bank in November 1997.

The town and the surrounding limestone hills had been settled for many centuries but during the Old Kingdom (2616-2181 BC) it was little more than a small provincial town called Waset. It first assumed importance under Menutuhotep II who reunited Egypt and made it his capital but it soon lost its position. It was during the 18th-20th Dynasty of the New Kingdom (1567-1085 BC) that Thebes reached its zenith when, except for the brief reign of Akhenaten (1379-62 BC), it was the capital of the Egyptian Empire which stretched from Palestine to Nubia. At its peak the population reached almost 1 million. Besides being the site of the largest and greatest concentration of monuments in the world it was, for the ancient Egyptians, the prototype for all future cities.

When the capital later shifted elsewhere it remained a vibrant city and the focus for the worship of Amun ('the Supreme Creator'). Although there is no obvious connection with the Greek city of Thebes the name was subsequently given to the city by the Greeks. It was a shadow of its former self during the Ptolemaic (323-30 BC) and Roman (30 BC-640 AD) periods but, unlike ancient Memphis to the south of Cairo, it was never abandoned and it became an important regional Christian settlement. In the Luxor region a number of temples became Coptic monasteries. For example at both Deir el-Medina and Deir el-Bahri Egyptian monuments have been taken over and converted for Christian use.

After the Muslim conquest in 640 AD, the town continued to decline and it was not until the beginning of the 19th century, during Napoleon's expedition to Egypt, that its historical importance began to be recognized. The display of some of its treasures in Paris' Louvre museum (see box, page 129) sparked off considerable interest from the world's archaeologists who still continue to explore the area almost 200 years later. Since 1869, when Thomas Cook took his first party of travellers to Egypt for the opening of the Suez Canal, Luxor has become the most important tourist destination in Upper Egypt. Today, although it has become an important administrative town, the economic livelihood of Luxor is, as the sudden collapse in business during the 1990/91 Gulf war and as the mass exodus of thousands of tourists in November 1997 demonstrated, almost totally dependent on the tourist industry.

ACCESS Air The airport is 7 km east of the town centre which can be reached by taxi (E£15) or bus. **Train** Those arriving at the railway station can take a *calèche*, a taxi or walk the 500m along Sharia al-Mahatta into town. **Road** The bus terminal is on Sharia Television about 10 mins walk from the centre of town, while the service taxi terminal is just off Sharia el-Karnak about 1 km from both Luxor town centre and Karnak temple. The majority of the tourist hotels and shops are located near the River Nile along the Corniche and the parallel Sharia el-Karnak.

PLACES OF INTEREST

There is so much to see in Luxor that it is best to plan your itinerary carefully. In and around the town on the East Bank of the river the **Luxor Temple** (see page 220), **Luxor Museum** (page 223) and **Karnak Temple** complex (page 224) are essential stops. Although the West Bank is dominated by the **Theban Necropolis** (page 231) and the **Valley of the Kings** (page 233) there are also important temples and monuments to see above ground and the West Bank is certainly worth 2 days. See separate details below.

WHO'S WHO IN ANCIENT EGYPT: KINGS AND QUEENS

It will certainly aid your visit to be able to recognize the personalities which dominate the area. Not all of them can be seen in Luxor but they are all highly relevant to your visit.

Akhenaten

Amenhotep IV, who later took the name of Akhenaten, ruled for 15 years around 1379-52 BC. He is remembered for the religious revolution he effected.

The authority of the priests of Amen-Re, the Sun God, the chief god of the Egyptians, had grown so great it almost rivalled that of the pharaohs. The pharaoh was regarded as the son of Amen-Re and was bound by strict religious ritual, part of a theological system understood clearly only by the priests, wherein lay their power.

Meanwhile a small religious cult was developing with the god Aten (a manifestation of the old sun-god Re of Memphis) at the centre, the sole god. This new cult

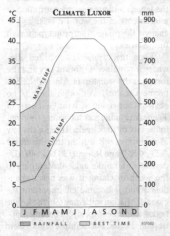

CLIMATE: LUXOR

°C / mm chart showing MAX TEMP and MIN TEMP curves across months J F M A M J J A S O N D; temperature scale 0–45°C, rainfall scale 0–900 mm.

RAINFALL   BEST TIME

appealed to the young prince Amenophis and after he succeed his father he changed his name to Akhenaten meaning 'it is well with the Aten' and moved his capital from Thebes to an entirely new city identified with the modern Tell el-Amarna, though no trace remains (see page 180).

This idea of the sole god was new in Egypt, new in the world, and Akhenaten is known as the first real monotheist. There is no evidence that the new religion appealed to the mass of the people for while the King was deeply involved in his worship his empire fell into decay. The new religious ideas were expressed in carvings. While the pharaoh as the son of god could not be portrayed and the queen rarely appeared at all in reliefs and statues, Akhenaten changed all the conventions and his artists represented him, and his wife and family, as they were, riding in chariots, bestowing gifts to his followers, even kissing.

When Akhenaten died at the age of 41, his half brother, Tutankhaton, a young boy, succeeded him. The Court returned to Thebes, the priests of Amen returned to power, the King changed his name to Tutankhamen (see page 58) and everything possible was done to wipe out Akhenaten's 'heretical' religion.

Cheops

Cheops or Khufu was an Old Kingdom pharaoh, the second king of the 4th Dynasty succeeding his father Snefru. His mother was Queen Hetepheres. He reigned between 2549 and 2526 BC. He is well known as the builder of the Great Pyramid of Giza (see page 162). He is recorded as having had four wives. Three names are given – Merityetes, Hen-utsen and Nefert-kau one of whom was his sister/half-sister, and one queen is unnamed. For Merityetes and Hen-utsen there are smaller pyramids built beside his own.

Herodotus records his reign and that of his son Chephren (Khafre) as a century of misery and oppression under wicked and tyrannical kings but in Egyptian history he is considered to have been a wise ruler. There was certainly misery. He shut all the temples and forbade the people to make sacrifices. At the same time he forced them to give up their livelihoods and assist in the construction of the pyramid being part of the team of a hundred thousand men who worked a 3 month shift. The preliminaries and actual construction took over 20 years. Part of the preparation was the construction of the oldest known paved road. Its purpose was to allow the huge granite facing blocks for his pyramid to be dragged and rolled to the site. Small fragments of the road exist today.

Cleopatra 69-30 BC

In 51 BC at the death of her father Ptolemy XIII she became joint ruler of Egypt with her younger brother. 3 years later she was ousted from the throne but reinstated by Julius Caesar. It is related that while Julius Caesar was seated in a room in the citadel in Alexandria two slaves entered bearing a magnificent carpet.

'Cleopatra, Queen of Egypt, begs you to accept this gift' says one and as the

carpet unrolls out springs 19-year-old Cleopatra. Dazzled at the sight of such loveliness, so the tale goes, the stern warrior fell in with all her plans, helping her subdue her enemies and permanently dispose of her brother.

When the daggers of the conspirators at Rome removed Caesar's protection she turned her charms on Mark Antony. Called to his presence to answer charges of assisting his enemies she came, not as a penitent, but, in a barge of beaten gold, lying under a gold embroidered canopy and fanned by 'pretty dimpled boys'. This certainly caught his attention and conveniently forgetting his wife and duties in Rome he became, we are told, her willing slave. While Cleopatra had visions of ruling in Rome as Antony's consort his enemies at Rome prevailed on the Senate to declare war on such a dangerous woman. The battle was fought at Actium in 31 BC but Cleopatra slipped away with her ships at the first opportunity leaving Antony to follow her as a hunted fugitive.

Cleopatra attempted to charm Octavian, Antony's conqueror, but he was made of sterner stuff and proof against her wiles. Antony killed himself and Cleopatra, proud and queenly to the last chose to die by the bite of a poisonous asp (this fact is unsubstantiated), rather than be taken to Rome in chains. Certainly an eventful life for a woman who never reached her fortieth birthday.

Hatshepsut

She was the first great woman in history living about 1503-1482 BC in the 18th Dynasty. She had immense power, adopted the full title of a pharaoh and was dressed in the full regalia down to the kilt and the false beard. She ruled for about 21 years.

She was the daughter of Tuthmosis I and Queen Ahmose and was married to her half brother Tuthmosis II who came to rule Egypt in 1512 at the death of his father. He was not very strong and at his death Hatshepsut who had had no sons of her own became the regent of his young son Tuthmosis III, son of a minor wife/woman in the harem. She took effective control of the government while pretending to be only the prince's regent and Tuthmosis III was made a priest of the god Amun.

Around 1503 she gave up all pretence of being subservient to her stepson and had herself crowned as pharaoh. To have reached this position and to retain it indicates the support of a number of faithful and influential officials in her government. Her steward Senenmut was well-known and may have been the father of her daughter Neferure.

Determined to expand commercially she despatched (with Amun's blessing, she said) an impressive expedition to Punt on the African coast (now part of Somalia) from which were brought gold, ebony, animal skins, live baboons, processed myrrh and live myrrh trees to decorate her temple and that of Amun in Karnak. Tributes also flooded in from Libya, Nubia and the nearer parts of Asia.

In the name of/to honour the god Amun-Re (the main god of the region and

her adopted 'father') she set about a huge construction/reconstruction programme repairing damage caused to earlier temples and building new ones. The chapels to the Thebian Triad behind the Great Pylon of Ramses II at Luxor were built by Hatshepsut and Tuthmosis III. She renovated The Great Temple of Amun, at Karnak where she introduced four huge (30m+) obelisks made of Aswan granite. At Beni Hasan she built a rock cut temple known as Speos Artemidos but her finest achievement was her own beautiful temple cut into the rock at three different levels.

The wall reliefs in the temple fortified her position of importance, her divine birth which is a very complicated set of scenes involving the god Amun, her mother and herself as a baby; her selection as pharaoh by Hathor; her coronation by Hathor and Seth watched over by her real father, Tuthmosis I.

Her expedition to the exotic land of Punt is depicted in very great detail with pictures of the scenery (stilt houses) and selected incidents from the voyages (some baboons escaping up the rigging). Items brought back are offered to Amun in another relief. She even had depicted the huge barges used to transport the four obelisks she had erected for her adopted father (Amun) in Karnak.

To continue her position as a pharaoh even after her death she had her tomb cut in the Valley of the Kings. It was the longest and deepest in the valley.

Late in his reign Tuthmosis III turned against the memory of Hatshepsut and had all her images in the reliefs erased and replaced with figures of himself or the two preceding male pharaohs. In many places her cartouches have been rewritten too. Unfortunately he had all her statues destroyed.

Ramses III

He reigned from 1198-66 BC, in the 20th Dynasty which was noted for the beginning of the great decline of Egypt. He was not part of the decline being known as a worthy monarch. He excelled himself in the earlier part of his reign with victories on land and victories at sea vanquishing the Cretans and the Carians. On land he used the military colonies established by previous rulers such as Ramses II and Seti I to conduct his missions further into Asia. He had little trouble subduing the tribes far into Asia but had problems nearer at home – having to fight to hold his position as pharaoh. A group of invaders made up of Libyans, Sardinians and Italians managed to advance as far as Memphis in the 8th year of his reign but their defeat put him in a much stronger position internally.

Having had his fill of expeditions to foreign parts and no doubt having returned with sufficient booty to have made the trips worthwhile and make him a very wealthy monarch he paid off his troops and set about adding to and constructing temples and other monumental works. Of particular note are the buildings at Medinet Habu. Here there is a magnificent temple with the walls covered in reliefs depicting the engagements on land and sea in which he had been so successful. Even the gate is inscribed with reliefs showing the despatch of prisoners and where a neat design on the pylons shows a cartouche of each vanquished country surmounted by a human head and with bound arms (see Medinet Habu, page 261). This is a valuable historical record of Egypt and the surrounding lands at this time.

Keeping everything in proportion

Production of carved reliefs for the decoration of temple walls or coloured illustrations for tombs had to follow many rigid rules. While the eye and the brain soon get used to the Egyptian representation of human and animal forms mental adjustment has to take place for the Egyptian artist was not permitted to draw what he saw but only to represent what he knew to be there. There was no place of originality. Perhaps the best artists were those who produced illustrations indistinguishable from earlier examples. The grid marked on to the wall gave the parameters and variations were not allowed. All the men in the picture were the same size, only gods or pharaohs were larger while enemies, children and sometimes women were drawn on a smaller grid. On the earlier drawings the grid was made up of 18 squares – from the hairline to soles of the feet, later (from the 19th Dynasty) the figures were slightly elongated using a 21 square grid. Measuring to the hairline gave scope for ornamental headdresses.

Examine a figure. The head was always drawn profile, more generally facing right (the preferred direction) but the eye with a very dark eyebrow looked out of the picture to the viewer, not forward. The shoulders were square and parallel to the floor while the front of the body, from the armpits, was sideways with a nipple or breast in profile. The navel was placed slightly off centre, so it could be seen. Arms were of equal length but the back of the right hand and the incurled fingers of the left hand were not necessarily on the correct arm.

Female clothing caused a problem as the tunic top hanging from square shoulders did not cover the breasts that were in profile. The legs like the head pointed to the right, the left leg in front, or it could be the right leg because both legs have left feet, feet drawn from the inside, no toes indicated. Sometimes an instep is drawn but both feet are still the same. The female figures took shorter, daintier steps.

Having produced one figure the rear outline could be repeated to indicate a host of soldiers, hostages, etc. It is interesting that the Egyptians depicted were all without blemish, did not suffer from wrinkles or spots or any deformities.

With animals conventional depiction was easier to follow. For example if it was in profile it was crocodile, if shown from above a lizard. Fish were always 2-dimensional side view but drawn swimming in a square pool.

Use of colour was restricted too, with no change of tone or shading used. Outlining in black or brown was common. Men were dark skinned while the women who were expected to be indoors all day were much lighter in colour.

A sculptor has no greater freedom of expression. The forward facing head of a figure is in almost every case at right angles to the shoulders. All seated statues have their hands on their knees. The smaller figures of children and wives always cling to the legs of their master. A standing statue has the left leg forward – no variation allowed.

Strange as they are these illustrations show us what we are meant to see, and we have no problem in comprehension or appreciating the work of the artists from such distant centuries.

In brief he restored law and order within Egypt and provided some security from outside aggression. He revived commercial prosperity. His attentions to the temples of Thebes, Memphis and Heliopolis certainly enriched Egyptian architecture. He was, however, unable to turn the slow ebb of his country's grandeur which was said to be suffering from 'fundamental decadence'.

He was assassinated. Four sons, all bearing the his name, succeeded him but their reigns were not distinguished and the decline of Egypt was hastened.

Tutankhamen

He was a pharaoh of the New Kingdom, 18th Dynasty, and reigned from 1361-52 BC. He was the son of Amenhotep III and probably his chief queen Tiy and was married to Akhenaten's daughter. He was too young to rule without a visir and regent. He died in the 9th year of his reign at about 18 years of age, leaving no surviving children, his regent Ay succeeded him by marrying his widow.

He was originally called Tutankhaton but changed name to Tutankhamen to distance himself from Atun and the cult

of Atun worship of his half brother Amenhotep IV (Akhenaten). He moved his capital back to Memphis and to eradicate the effects of the rule of his predecessor he restored the temples and the status of the old gods and their priests. His greatest claim to fame was his intact tomb discovered by Howard Carter in 1922, details of which are given on page 241, see also box, The Curse of Tutankhamen, below .

Tuthmosis I – the trend setter

He was an 18th Dynasty pharaoh who ruled from around 1525-12 BC. He is noted for his expansion of the Egyptian Empire south into Nubia and east into present day Syria. He led a river-bourne expedition into Nubia to beyond the 4th Cataract (he was after the gold there) and set up a number of defensive forts along the route. His foray across the Euphrates was part of his campaign against the Hyksos who caused many problems for the Egyptians. Tuthmosis I used the Euphrates as the border over which he did not intend these enemies to cross.

He is also noted for the building and renovation works he contracted at Karnak. Much of the inner temple of Amun at Karnak is attributed to him. In particular the sandstone 4th Pylon in front of which one of his obelisks still stands and the limestone 5th Pylon which marked the centre of the temple at the time and

The Curse of Tutankhamen

Tutankhamen tomb's fame and mystery was enhanced by the fate of those who were directly connected with its discovery. The expedition's sponsor Lord Carnarvon, who had first opened the tomb with his chief archaeologist Howard Carter, died shortly afterwards in April 1923 from an infected mosquito bite. A subsequent succession of bizarre deaths added weight to novelist Marie Corelli's totally unproven and unhistoric claim that "dire punishment follows any intruder into the tomb". Such alleged curses have, however, done nothing to deter the tens of thousands of visitors who still visit the site despite the fact that most of the treasures are now in the Egyptian Museum!

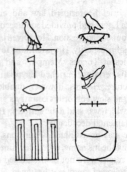

behind which was the original position of the sanctuary of Tuthmosis I.

He was born in the era when burial in a pyramid was 'out' and being buried in a secret tomb in the rocks of the surrounding hillside was just coming 'in'. It is suggested that his tomb was the first in the Valley of the Kings and he certainly set a trend. Even so his red quartzite sarcophagus was found in the tomb of his daughter Queen Hatshepsut and is now in the museum in Cairo.

Zoser

This was a king of the Old Kingdom, the second king of the 3rd Dynasty. It is hard to piece together his history. He succeeded his brother and perhaps reigned for 19 years between 2667-48. Two of his daughters were called Intkaes and Hetephernebti, their names taken from steles in the complex.

His funerary complex at Saqqara (see page 152) is an example of some of the world's most ancient architecture and it was all, not only the Step Pyramid, but also the huge enclosure wall and the subsidiary temples and structures, designed by Zoser, under the charge of his talented architect/chancellor/physician Imhotep. This building was important being the first large scale building to be made completely of stone. In addition it was of an unusual stepped design. Many of the buildings in the surrounding complex were never intended for use but were replicas of the buildings used by the pharaoh on earth so that he could use them in eternity. Eventually he was buried under his Step Pyramid. So what was the other tomb for in the complex? Perhaps it was for his entrails as it was too small for a royal person?

He made Memphis his capital which gave impetus to the growth in importance of this town which eventually became the political and cultural centre.

Travellers interested in seeing his likeness must visit room 46 in Cairo Museum which has the huge seated figure of King Zoser taken from the complex.

WHO'S WHO IN ANCIENT EGYPT: DEITIES

There were hundreds of gods and goddesses worshipped by the ancient Egyptians. Over time some grew in favour and others became less important. In addition each district of the country had its own deities. It is useful to have an idea of their role in ancient Egypt and to recognize them on the wall paintings and carvings. Unfortunately they could be represented in more than one way, being different aspects of the same god.

Aker

He was an earth god often shown with the head of a lion. He guarded the east and west gates of the afterworld.

Amun

He was first worshipped as a local deity in Khmun in Middle Egypt in Hermopolis and later when his cult reached Thebes his importance spread to all of Egypt. He was believed to be the creator of all things, to order time and the seasons. When he sailed over the heavens he controlled the wind and the direction of the clouds. His name means 'the hidden' or 'unseen one'. At times he was identified with the sun-god Re, hence Amun-Re, and as Amun-Min was the god of fertility. He was often drawn as a human form with twisted rams horns and two tall feathers as a headdress, a sceptre/crook in one hand and a ceremonial flail in the other, an erect phallus and a black pointed beard.

The sacred animals with which he was identified were the ram and the goose (the Great Cackler). As the ram-headed god he renewed the life in the souls of the departed. He was part of the Thebian Triad with Mut his wife and Khonsu his adopted son.

Anubis

This god was responsible for the ritual of embalming and looking after the place where the mummification was done. Indeed he was reputed to have invented embalming, his first attempt of this art being on the corpse of Osiris. When Anubis was drawn on the wall on either side of a tomb's entrance the mummy would be protected. He helped Isis to restore life to Osiris.

He was also included in scenes weighing the dead person's heart/soul against the 'feather of truth', which was the only way to enter the next world.

In the earlier dynasties of the Old Kingdom he held an important position as lord of the dead but was later overshadowed by Osiris. Later he was better known simply as a conductor of souls. He was closely associated with Middle Egypt and some sections of Upper Egypt.

He was depicted as a recumbent black dog/fox/jackal or a jackal-headed god. On any illustration the ears of the creature were alertly up and slightly forward. The association with a fox/ jackal was the number of jackals that were to be found in the cemeteries. Sometimes he was shown seated on a pylon.

Anukis

This was the wife of Khnum and the mother of Sartis, the third member of the Elephantine Triad. She was the goddess of the first cataract area and was depicted wearing a high crown of feathers and carrying a sceptre of papyrus plant.

Apis Bulls

The sacred bulls of Memphis were all black bulls with a white triangle on the forehead and a crescent shape on the flank. A sacred bull was believed to contain the spirit of Ptah and lived in a palace and was present as guest of honour at state functions. When it died it was mummified and buried at the huge underground tomb of the Serapeum at Saqqara and a new younger bull, its reincarnation, took its place. On illustrations it was sometimes shown with a sun disc between its horns.

Apophis

This was a symbol of unrest and chaos in the form of a large serpent. It was kept under control by the stronger powers of good, in particular the cat-goddess Bastet and by Sekhmet the fierce lioness god.

Aten

He was the sun-god depicted as the solar disc emitting long bright rays which often terminated in human hands. For a brief time, under Akhenaton, worship of Aten was the state religion. He was considered the one true god. After the demise of Akhenaton he disappeared into obscurity.

Atum

This was one of the first forms of the sun-creator god. He was originally just a local deity of Heliopolis but joined with Re, as Atum-Re, he became more popular. Re took the part of the sun at the zenith and Atum was identified with the setting sun when it goes to the underworld. As this he was represented as a man, sometimes an old man, indicating the dying of the day.

Bastet

The famous cat goddess of the Delta region was the daughter of Re. She represented the power of the sun to ripen crops and was considered to be virile, strong and agile. Her home city was Bubastis (see page 310) but her fame spread widely. She was initially a goddess of the home but in the religion of the New Kingdom she became associated with the lioness war goddess. She was regarded as a friendly deity – the goddess of joy.

She was represented as a woman with a cat's head, carried an ancient percussion instrument, the sistrum, in her right hand, a breast plate in her left hand and had a small bag hung over her left arm. Numerous small cat figures were used in the home for worship or as amulets. Mummified cats (votive offerings) were buried in a vast cemetery at Bubastis. She was loosely connected with Mut and Sekhmet.

Bes

This was a strange creature, the god of dancing, merriment and music, being capable of playing many musical instruments. He was always portrayed as a jolly dwarf with a large head, a round face, round ears, goggle eyes, protruding tongue, sprouting lion's whiskers, which later became stylized as a fancy collar, under a tall headdress of feathers. He had short bow legs and a bushy tail. He was one of the few gods drawn front face rather than profile.

It is suggested his hideousness was to drive away evil spirits and hence pain and sorrow. As the guardian of women and children he kept the house free from snakes and evil spirits. He was portrayed on vases, mirrors, perfume jars and other toilet articles and even on the pillows of mummies. He was frequently represented in birth houses as the guardian of women in childbirth. It seems that at first he just protected the Royal family but later took on the care of all Egyptians.

Buto

This deity, also known as Wadjet, was a cobra goddess whose fame spread from the Delta to all of Lower Egypt. She was known as the green goddess (the colour of papyrus) and was said to be responsible for the burning heat of the sun.

Geb/Shu/Nut

These members of the Heliopolitan ennead, are frequently depicted together. Geb (god of the earth), son of Shu (god of

the air or emptiness), was married to his sister Nut (goddess of the sky). The sun-god Re was displeased with this association although most gods seem to marry their sisters and ordered Shu to keep the two apart. Hence all three are represented together with Shu between Geb's green recumbent form and Nut arching in the sky.

Geb

As explained, this was the god of the earth, the physical support of the world. Along with his sister/wife Nut he was part of the second generation ennead of Heliopolis. He was usually drawn as a man without any distinguishing characteristics though sometimes had the head of a goose which was distinguishing enough. He could be also be depicted as a bull in contrast to Nut's cow. His recumbent form mentioned above represented the hills and valleys and the green colour the plants growing there.

He was the cause of the bitter quarrel between Osiris and his brother Seth for at his retirement he left them both to rule the world. Hence the famous myth. See box, page 64.

Hapi/Hapy

He was the god who lived next to the river because he controlled the level of Nile and was responsible for the floods. He was even responsible for the dew that fell at night. He was represented as a bearded man with a female breast wearing a bunch of papyrus on his head and carrying offerings or leading a sacrifice. There was an association here with Apis.

There was another god Hapi who was one of the sons of Horus, the baboon headed guardian of the Canopic jar of the lungs.

Harpokrates

This was the name given to Horus as a child. In illustrations he was a naked child with a finger in his mouth. The side lock of hair he wore is an indication of youth.

Hathor

This was the goddess of the sky who was also known as the golden one. Her name means 'castle of the sky-god Horus'. She was a goddess of festivity, love and dance. The original centre of her cult was Dendera and her importance spread to Thebes and Memphis. With the increase in her fame and contrary to her earlier nature she became known as a goddess of the dead and the region of the dead. She was believed to have been responsible for nearly destroying all mankind. See myths, page 184. On illustrations she was represented as a cow or a cow-headed woman or a woman with a headdress of a disc between two horns and large cow-like ears.

Heh

This lesser known god can be seen kneeling holding a palm branch notched with the number of the years in a king's life.

Heqet

This was a frog goddess who sometimes assisted at childbirth.

Horus

This was a very important god, the falcon headed sky god. Horus means 'he who is far above' and the hawk fits this image. Hence he was depicted as hawk-headed or even a full hawk often wearing the double crown of Egypt. The hawk's eyes are

thought of as the sun and the moon. Horus' left eye was damaged in his conflict with Seth and this was thought to indicate the waxing and waning of the moon. He probably originated in the Delta region and the cult spread to all of Egypt. It was only later that he became associated with Isis and Osiris as their son.

Imhotep

He was a man, one of two mortals (the other was Amenhotep) who were totally deified. He was recorded as the designer of the first temple at Edfu and the official architect of Zoser's step pyramid. When he was later deified it was as a god of healing and made the honorary son of Ptah. He was known, not as a temple builder, but, as a patron of scribes, a healer, a sage and a magician, and was worshipped as a god of medicine. He was considered to have been a physician of considerable skill.

At the time of the Persian conquest he was elevated to the position of a deity. His cult reached its peak in Greaco-Roman times where his temples at Memphis and on the island of Philae in the River Nile were often crowded with unhealthy people who slept there hoping that a cure for their problems would be revealed to them in their dreams. He was depicted on wall illustrations as a seated man holding an open papyrus.

Isis

She was one of the most important ancient Egyptian goddesses, the most popular goddess in Egypt from around 650 AD right up to the introduction of Christianity. Originally the cult was in Lower Egypt but it spread to embrace eventually the whole of Egypt and parts of Nubia. Her name means 'throne' and because the word throne is feminine it was depicted by a woman's figure. This made her the mother of the king who sat on the throne. She receives a number of mentions as the grieving widow of Osiris. She was also the sister of Osiris, Seth and Nephthys.

She was held in high esteem as the perfect wife and mother and became the goddess of protection. She was also an enchantress, using her power to bring Osiris back to life again. She was represented as a woman with the hieroglyph sign for a throne on her head, an orb or sun between two horns, and was generally sitting nursing her son Horus, or seen also kneeling at a coffin of Osiris. Her ability to give life to the dead meant she was the chief deity at all funerals.

There are temples to her at Dendera, on Philae and in the Nile Delta. Several temples were dedicated to her in Alexandria where she was the patroness of seafarers. She was guardian of the Canopic jar which held the viscera.

Khepri

He was the sun-god represented as a scarab beetle with a sun disc. As the scarab beetle rolls a ball of dung around so the Egyptians thought this was how the sun was moved. See box, page 154.

Khnum

He was represented on wall drawings as a man with a ram's head with long twisted horns. The Egyptians believed he made the first man by moulding him in clay from the River Nile on a potter's wheel. Over

time his area of responsibility changed. He lived at the first cataract on the Nile where he presided over all the cataracts of the Nile. He had the authority to decide whether or not the god Hapi 'rose' and the River Nile flooded. He was associated with temples at Elephantine and Esna.

Khonsu

He was regarded as the son of Amun and Mut. The three made up the Thebian Triad. He had the ability to cast a range of spells, dispel demons and act as an oracle. He travelled through the sky at night and sometimes assisted the scribe of the gods. As the moon god he was usually represented as a man wearing a disc of the full moon and horns on his head or the head of a falcon. He had a single lock of hair to show his youth.

Ma'at

This well loved deity was the goddess of order, truth and justice. She was the daughter of the sun-god Re and Thoth the goddess of wisdom. She can be seen at the ceremony of judgement, the balancing of the heart of the deceased against a feather. The scale was balanced by Ma'at or her ideogram the single ostrich feather as a test of truthfulness. The priests with her were judges. She often appears, confusingly, as two identical god-desses, a case of double judgement. She was very popular with the other gods. She was also depicted on wall paintings in the solar barque.

Mertseger

This was the goddess of the west, a cobra goddess from Thebes. She was said to punish those who did not come up to scratch with illness or even death.

Min

This was the god of sexual prowess, of fertility and of good harvests. He was depicted bearded, wearing a crown of two feathers, phallus erect, a ceremonial flail in his raised right hand and a ribbon from his headdress reaching down to the ground at the back. He was worshipped at Luxor. His feast day was an important festival often associated with wild orgies. He was worshipped too as the guardian of travellers as he protected the routes to the Red Sea and in the Eastern Desert. The lettuce was his sacred plant.

Montu

The war god Montu who rose to importance in the 11th Dynasty protected the king in battle. He has a temple to the north of the main temple in Karnak. His image was hawk-headed with a sun disc between two plumes.

Mut

She was originally a very ancient vulture goddess of Thebes but during the 18th Dynasty was married to the god Amun and with their adopted son Khonsu made up the Thebian Triad. The marriage of Amun and Mut was a reason for great annual celebrations in Thebes. Her role as mistress of the heavens or as sky goddess often had her appearing as a cow, standing behind her husband as he rose from the primeval sea Nu to his place in the heavens. More often she was represented with a double crown of Egypt on her head, a vulture's head or lioness's head on her forehead. Another role was as a great divine mother. She has a temple south of the main temple at Karnak.

Nefertum

He was one of the Memphis deities most often associated with perfumes. He was represented as a man with a lotus flower on his head.

Neith

This was the goddess of weaving, war and hunting, among other things. She was also protector of the dead and the Canopic jars. She wore a red crown of Lower Egypt and a shield on her head (sometimes held in her hand), held two crossed arrows and an ankh in her hand. She was connected with Sobek and was worshipped at Memphis, Esna and Fayoum.

Nekhbet

In her more important guise she was the vulture or serpent goddess, protectress of Upper Egypt and especially of its rulers. She was generally depicted with spreading wings held over the pharaoh while grasping in her claw the royal ring or other emblems. She always appeared as a woman, sometimes with a vulture's head and always wearing a white crown. Her special colour was white, in contrast to her counterpart Buto (red) who was the goddess of Lower Egypt. In another aspect she was worshipped as goddess of the River Nile and consort of the river god. She was associated too with Mut.

Nephthys

Her name was translated as 'lady of the house'. She was the sister of Seth, Osiris and Isis. She was married to Seth. She had no children by her husband but a son, Anubis, by Osiris. She wears the hieroglyphs of her name on her head. She was one of the protector guardians of the Canopic jars and a goddess of the dead.

Nut

She was goddess of the sky, the vault of the heavens. She was wife/sister of Geb. The Egyptians believed that on five special days preceding the new year she gave birth on successive days to the deities Osiris, Horus, Seth, Isis and Nephthys. This was cause for great celebrations. She was usually depicted as a naked woman arched over Shu who supported her with upraised arms. She was also represented wearing a water pot or pear shaped vessel on her head, this being the hieroglyph of her name. Sometimes she was depicted as a cow, so that she could carry the sun-god Re on her back to the sky. The cow was usually spangled with stars to represent the night sky. It was supposed that the cow swallowed the sun which journeyed through her body during the night to emerge at sunrise. This was also considered a symbol of resurrection.

Osiris

This was one of the most important gods in ancient Egypt, the god of the dead, the god of the underworld and the god of plenty. He had the power to control the vegetation (particular cereals because he began his career as a corn deity) which sprouted after the annual flooding of the River Nile. He originated in the Delta at Busiris and it is suggested that he was once a real ruler. His importance spread to the whole of Egypt.

Annual celebrations included the moulding of a clay body in the shape of Osiris, filled with soil and containing seeds. This was moistened with water from the River Nile and the sprouting grain symbolized the strength of Osiris. One of the main celebrations in the Temple at Abydos where he was very popular was associated with Osiris and it was fashionable to be buried or have a memorial on the processional road to Abydos and so absorb the blessing of Osiris. There are temples dedicated to Osiris at Edfu and on Bigah Island opposite Philae.

According to ancient Egyptian custom when a king and later any person died he became Osiris and thus through him mankind had a some hope of resurrection. The Apis bull at Memphis also represented Osiris. The names Osiris-apis and Sarapis are derived from this.

He was shown as a mummy with his arm crossed over his breast, one hand holding a royal crook the other a ceremonial flail. These crook and flail sceptres on his portraits and statues showed he was god of the underworld. He wore a narrow plaited beard and on his head the white crown of Upper Egypt and two red feathers.

Ptah

He was originally the local deity of the capital Memphis and his importance eventually spread over the whole of Egypt. He was very popular at Thebes and Abydos. He was worshipped as the creator of the gods of the Memphite theology. Ptah was the husband of Sekhmet and father of Nefertum. Only later was he associated with Osiris. He was the patron of craftsmen, especially sculptors. He was renowned for his skill as an engineer, stonemason, metal worker and artist.

He was always shown in human form, mummified or swathed in a winding sheet, with a clean shaven human head. He would be holding a staff and wearing an amulet. The Apis bull had its stall in the great temple of Ptah in Memphis.

Qebehsenuf

The falcon headed guardian of the Canopic jar of the intestines was the son of Horus.

Re

This was the sun-god of Heliopolis and the supreme judge. He was the main god at the time of the New Kingdom. His importance was great. His cult centre was Heliopolis and the cult reached the zenith in the 5th Dynasty when he had become the official god of the pharaohs and every king was both the son of Re and Re incarnate.

Re was the god who symbolized the sun. He appeared in many aspects and was portrayed in many different ways. He was found in conjunction with other gods Re-Horakhte, Amun-Re, Min-Re

etc. As Amun-Re (Amun was the god from Thebes) he was king of the gods and responsible for the pharaoh on military campaigns where he handed the scimitar of conquest to the great warriors. Re was king and father of the gods and the creator of mankind. It was believed that after death, the pharaoh in his barge joined Re in the heavens.

He was thought to travel across the sky each day in his solar boat and during the night make his passage in the underworld in another boat. He was represented as man with a hawk or falcon's head wearing a sun disc or if dead with a ram's head. See also page 58.

Sekhmet

This was another aspect of the goddess Hathor. Sekhmet the consort of Ptah was a fierce goddess of war and the destroyer of the enemies of her father the sun-god Re. She was usually depicted as a lioness or as a woman with a lion's head on which was placed the

solar disc and the uraeus. She was also the goddess who was associated with pestilence, and could bring disease and death to mankind but her task also was to do the healing and her priests were often doctors. She was said to have chained the serpent Apophis.

Selket

This was one of the four goddesses who protected the sources of the River Nile. As the guardian of the dead she was portrayed often with a scorpion on her head. She was put in charge of the bound serpent Apophis in the underworld.

Seshat

Seshat was shown as a woman with a seven point star on her head, and dressed in a panther skin. She was the goddess of writing and of recording the years. She carried a palm leaf on which she wrote her records.

Seth

Seth did not begin with such bad press. He was in favour in the 19th Dynasty especially in the Eastern Delta around Tanis but by the Late Period he was considered evil and on some monuments his image was effaced. By the Christian era he was firmly in

place as the devil. The Egyptians thought Seth who was the brother of Osiris, Isis and Nephthys tried to prevent the sun from rising each dawn. As such an enemy of mankind they represented him as a huge serpent-dragon. He was sometime depicted as a hippopotamus and sometimes took the form of a crocodile as he did to avoid the avenging Horus. More often he was depicted as an unidentified animal, a greyhound, dog, pig, ass, okapi, anteater or a man with the head of an animal. The head had an unusual long down curved snout and the ears were upstanding and square-tipped. The eyes were slanting and the tail long and forked. He was also seen in drawings standing at the prow of the sun-god's boat.

Shu

He and his twin sister and wife Tefnut were created by the sun-god Re by his own power without the aid of a woman. They were the first couple of the ennead of Heliopolis. He was father of Geb the earth god and Nut the sky goddess. He was the representation of air and emptiness, of light and space, the supporter of the sky.

He was portrayed in human form with the hieroglyph of his name, an ostrich feather on his head. Often he was drawn separating Geb and Nut for their union was not approved of by Re.

Sobek

He was known as the crocodile god, a protector of reptiles and of kings. Crocodile gods were very common in Fayoum, mainly at the time of the Middle Kingdom and also at Esna and Kom Ombo. The live crocodiles at the temples were believed to be this god incarnate and accordingly were treated very well. These sacred crocodiles were kept in a lake before the temples. They were pampered and bejewelled. After death they were mummified. Confusingly he was usually depicted with Amun's crown of rams' horns and feathers.

Taweret

This upright pregnant hippopotamus had pendant human breasts, lion's paws and a crocodile's tail. Sometimes she wore the horns of Hathor with a solar disc. She was also know as Apet/Opet.

She was the goddess of childbirth and attended both royal births and the daily rebirth of the sun. She was a goddess at Esna.

Tefnut

She was the wife/sister of Shu, the lion-headed goddess of moisture and dew, one of the Heliopolitan ennead.

Thoth

His cult originated in the Nile Delta and was then mainly centred in Upper Egypt. He was held to be the inventor of writing, the founder of social order, the creator of languages, the patron of scribes, interpreter and adviser to the gods, and (in his spare time?) representative of the sun-god Re on earth. He gave the Egyptians knowledge of medicine and mathematics. He possessed a book in which all the wisdom of the world was recorded. In another aspect he was known as the moon god. He was also associated with the birth of the earth.

Thoth protected Isis during her pregnancy and healed the injury to Horus inflicted by Seth. He too was depicted in the feather/heart weighing judgement ceremonies of the diseased and as the scribe reported the results to Osiris. His sacred animals were the ibis and the baboon. Numerous mummified bodies of these two animals were found in cemeteries in Hermopolis and Thebes.

He was usually represented as a human with an ibis' head. The curved beak of the ibis was like the crescent moon so the two were connected and the ibis became the symbol of the moon god Thoth.

Wepwawet

He was the jackal-headed god of Middle Egypt, especially popular in the Assiut region. He was know as 'the opener of the ways'.

LOCAL INFORMATION

● Accommodation

Price guide:		
AL US$150+	**D**	US$25-50
A US$100-150	**E**	US$10-25
B US$75-100	**F**	under US$10
C US$50-75		

Because Luxor attracts so many tourists there are numerous hotels, with thousands of beds, covering the widest range of accommodation. Most hotels are located on or close to the River Nile although some are a short bus ride south of the town. Rooms are cheaper if booked as part of a package. In normal circumstances, during the peak season in November-February there are no spare rooms but during the hottest months there are plenty of cut-price deals to be had if you shop around. Don't be shy to ask for a better rate or an upgrade even at the best hotels.

AL *Luxor Hilton*, New Karnak, T 374955, F 376571, 261 rm with twin beds, rather small, but magnificent views from private balcony, located to north of town with free courtesy bus, unprepossessing exterior hides an excellent interior with reportedly the best hotel management in the town, sleep may be disturbed by cruise liners which moor alongside and run engines all night, three restaurants provide wide choice of excellent food, coffee shop, heated pool (necessary for comfort in winter) with sundeck which overlooks the River Nile, casino, well stocked boutiques with items of good quality, new mini-gym, billiards; **AL** *Luxor Sheraton Hotel & Resort*, Sharia El-Awameya, PO Box 34, T 374544, F 374941, 298 rm in main building with views of River Nile (more expensive) or bungalows in garden (very comfortable), shopping arcade, hairdresser, disco, tennis courts, well managed, caters for tour groups which receive reduced rates, the service is consistently excellent, a pleasure to be a guest and our choice of the **AL** hotels; **AL** *Movenpick Jolie Ville Luxor*, Crocodile Island, T 374855, F 374936, 320 rm in 20 bungalow pavilions, the only tourist village in Luxor, beautiful location 4 km south of Luxor, connected to mainland by bridge and to town centre by free hourly ferry, under 16s can sleep free in their parents' room, good restaurants – *Movenpick, Jolie Ville, Garden Terrace, Sharazade Nile Terrace, Crocodile Bar*, and the Sobek Hall for banquets, functions and conferences, good pool; **AL** *Sofitel Winter Palace Hotel*, Corniche el-Nil, T 380422, F 374087, 110 rm in the old building and 260 in the new, 700 beds overlooking the Nile, the oldest and most famous luxury hotel in Luxor whose guests have incl heads of state, Noel Coward and Agatha Christie, the old style rooms are unusual but rather basic, 2 restaurants, terrace bar in splendid position overlooking Corniche and river, shared pool.

A *Isis Hotel Luxor*, Sharia Khalid Ibn el-Walid, T 373344, F 372923, the largest hotel in Upper Egypt with 520 large, clean, well decorated rooms set in 3 wings round the garden and 2 large pools (one is heated) where non-residents can swim for E£15, located in extensive grounds to the south of town, courtesy bus, main Italian and seafood restaurants plus 3 specialists restaurants, 2 bars, excellent facilities but slow service, sports facilities incl clay tennis courts and squash; **A** *Akhetaten Village*, Sharia Khalid Ibn el-Walid, T 380850, F 380879, 140 rm, run by Club Med with its unique and stylish atmosphere.

B *Mercure Luxor Hotel*, Corniche el-Nil, T 380944, F 373316, 306 quality rm with bath, located in town centre on river front, attractive atmosphere, very well run, 2 restaurants with live entertainment, 24-hr coffee shop, most guests are tour groups who are mainly British in summer and German in the winter high season when the hotel is always full.

C *Luxor Wena Hotel*, opp Luxor Temple, T 380018, F 380623, 86 rm, standard hotel; **C** *Mercure Inn Luxor Hotel*, 10 Sharia Maabad Luxor, T 373521, F 580817, 89 rm, caters mainly for tour groups, reportedly has excellent food; **C** *Novotel Evasion Luxor Hotel*, Sharia Khalid Ibn el-Walid, T 380925, F 380972, new hotel, 185 rm, emphasis on friendly service, 2 restaurants (1 floating), conference and fax facilities, most guests are tour groups.

D *Emilo Hotel* and *New Emilo Hotel*, Sharia Yusef Hassan, T 386666, F 374884, roof garden, in town centre, 111 a/c rm with bath and TV, 2 restaurants, 3 bars, disco, pool, small shop, exchange, international phone lines, friendly service, main guests are German and British tour groups; **D** *New Windsor Hotel*, Sharia Nefertiti, T 374306, F 373447, 40 rm, biggest and probably the best 3-star hotel in town, located just behind the Corniche, roof garden has river view, rooms in the new extension around the small pool are better choice, bar, discotheque below the restaurant, a bank and 2 international telephone lines, food good but unspectacular.

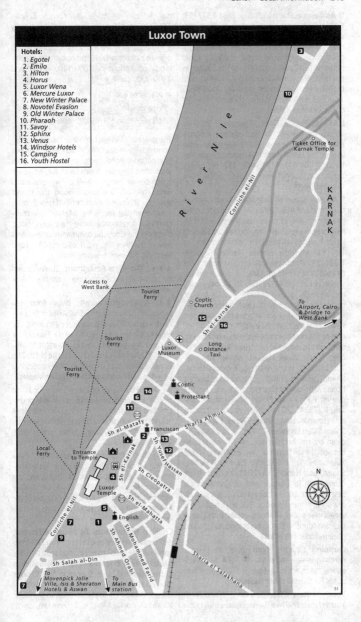

Luxor Town

Hotels:
1. Egotel
2. Emilo
3. Hilton
4. Horus
5. Luxor Wena
6. Mercure Luxor
7. New Winter Palace
8. Novotel Evasion
9. Old Winter Palace
10. Pharaoh
11. Savoy
12. Sphinx
13. Venus
14. Windsor Hotels
15. Camping
16. Youth Hostel

River Nile

KARNAK

Corniche el-Nil

Ticket Office for
Karnak Temple

To
Airport, Cairo
& bridge to
West Bank

Access to
West Bank

Tourist Ferry

Tourist Ferry

Tourist Ferry

Local Ferry

Coptic Church

Sh el-Karnak

Luxor Museum

Long Distance Taxi

Coptic

Protestant

Sh el-Mataty

Franciscan

Sharia Ahmus

Entrance to Temple

Sh el-Karnak

Venus

Sphinx

Sh Yusef Hassan

Luxor Temple

Sh Cleopatra

Sh el-Mahatta

English

Corniche el-Nil

N

Sh Salah al-Din

Sh Ahmed Orabi

Sh Mohammed Farid

Sharia el-Salathana

To
Movenpick Jolie
Ville, Isis & Sheraton
Hotels & Aswan

To
Main Bus
station

51

D *Arabesque*, Sharia Mohamed Farid, T 372193, F 372193, 36 rm, new, roof garden with impressive view of Luxor temple; **D** *Pharaon*, New Karnak, T 374924, F 376477, 50 rm, clean rooms, good pool; **D** *Philippe Hotel*, Sharia Dr Labib Habashi, T 372284, F 580060, 40 rm, located in the heart of town, swimming pool, roof garden; **D** *Savoy Hotel*, Corniche el-Nil, PO Box 83952, T 580522, F 580526, 108 rm, cheapest of Luxor's classic Victorian hotels.

E *Marwa Palace*, Sharia Television, T 580040, 40 rm, convenient for bus station; **E** *Santa Maria*, Sharia Television, T 372603, 48 rm, convenient for bus station; **E** *Windsor*, Sharia Nefertiti, T 372847, F 373447, 112 rm, clean, family run budget hotel joined to the *New Windsor Hotel*.

F *Abu el-Hagag (4 Seasons)*, Sharia Maabad Luxor and M Farid, T 372958, 15 rm, one of the cheapest hotels in town mainly frequented by long-stay budget travellers, located adjacent to Luxor Temple with excellent views from the top flrs; **F** *El-Mustafa Hotel*, Sharia Television, T 374721, 20 rm, new, nr bus station and the *Marwa Palace* and *Santa Maria* hotels; **F** *Horus*, Sharia el-Karnak, T 372165, 25 a/c rm, highly rec, centrally located but rather noisy budget hotel with friendly staff, clean a/c rooms (erratic), hot showers and a good breakfast, rec; **F** *Mina Palace*, Corniche el-Nil, T 372074, 40 rm, one of the best cheap hotels, excellent location, some rooms overlook Nile/Luxor Temple; **F** *Nobles*, Sharia Yusef Hassan, Midan Ahmose, T 372823, 40 rm, very cheap; **F** *Nour Home*, Sharia Mohamed Farid, highly rec quiet budget hotel with worn but clean rooms, helpful owner; **F** *Pyramids Hotel*, Sharia Yusef Hassan, T 373243, 20 rm, cheapest but not cleanest in town located nr *Nobles Hotel*; **F** *Ramoza*, Sharia Sa'ad Zaghloul, T 372270, Tx 23604, 48 clean a/c rm, hot showers, nr railway station but about 1 km from the river; **F** *Sphinx*, Sharia Yusef Hassan, T 372830, 33 rm; **F** *Venus*, Sharia Yusef Hassan, T 372635, 23 clean, basic rooms with fans or a/c and bath, one of the best small downtown budget hotels, good laundry service, new rooftop bar and restaurant serves meals and alcohol, popular with young German tourists, discounts for long stay guests, price includes breakfast.

Camping Opp the youth hostel, the permanently guarded camp site (T 382425), which mainly caters for noisy Egyptian families, offers space for tents and hot showers.

Youth hostels Clean, spartan 275 bed *IYHF Youth Hostel* halfway between Luxor and Kar-nak Temples at 16 Sharia Karnak Temple, T/F 372139, 275 beds, meals available, family rooms, laundry, overnight fee E£5-10. Although it is cheap, there are many cheap hotels which offer more comfortable and convenient accommodation without the 1000-1400 lockout and 2300-0600 curfew.

● **Places to eat**

Price guide:
♦♦♦Expensive; ♦♦average; ♦cheap.

The majority of the better hotels have expensive good quality restaurants, which serve standard international hotel food, and in some cases interesting Egyptian food. There are, however, a number of comparatively cheap restaurants which are concentrated around the tourist shops on Sharia el-Karnak behind Luxor Temple. Away from the shops the *Maharba Restaurant's* rooftop terrace above the town's tourist office on the Corniche commands an excellent view of the River Nile, provides decent food and beer and the service is excellent.

♦ ♦ ♦: *The Class Restaurant*, Sharia Khaled Ibn el-Walid, excellent food – continental or oriental – and service.

♦ ♦: *Amigos Restaurant*, Italian food well presented, Sharia Salah al-Din; *Anubis Restaurant*, open 24 hrs serving European food, breakfast is rec and the view of the Nile can be enjoyed any time of the day. Adjacent to Museum of Mummification on Corniche el-Nil; *The Green Palace*, Karnak Temple, offers traditional Egyptian cuisine together with Italian staples.

♦: *Ali Baba Café*, offering a view of Luxor temple and Egyptian fare at reasonable prices; *Chicken Hut*, take away chicken, adequate but not ethnic, junction of Sharia Station and El-Souq; *El-Fishawy Café*, coffee and *shisha*, Sharia Salah al-Din.

A number of cheap new restaurants have sprung up on the West Bank. *The Tutankhamun*, on the public ferry dock, highly rec, the *African Restaurant* next door, the *Valley Bloom* and *Marsam Hotel* all serve decent Egyptian food and possess good Nile views particularly at sunset.

Cruising Restaurants *Le Lotus*, at *Novotel*, well organized dinner cruises offering international cuisine, book to get a good seat, also day cruises with high quality lunch while travelling to Dendera and Esna; *Sheraton Nile Cruiser* moored at *Sheraton Hotel* for sunset and dinner cruises, also day cruise with lunch to Dendera; *Vivant-Denon* at *Movenpick*, breakfast, lunch,

Opera Egyptian style

The Temple of Queen Hatshepsut made a perfect backdrop for the staging of Giuseppe Verdi's spectacular opera Aida. The purpose built arena had seating for 3,000 and a special pontoon bridge was constructed across the River Nile for easy access. The opera was performed to celebrate the 125th anniversary of the World Premier of Aida in Cairo and the 75th anniversary of the discovery of the tomb of Tutankhamen in Luxor. The six performances were fully booked with tickets costing from US$150 to US$300. Don't miss the next event. Call Cairo Opera House on T 2023417314, F 2023417313.

afternoon tea and dinner cruises in a 105-year-old sailing boat.

● **Airline offices**
Egypt Air, T 580581.

● **Banks & money changers**
Bank of Alexandria, north of Sharia Nefertiti and Sharia el-Karnak intersection on Corniche el-Nil; Banque Misr (Sunday-Thursday 0830-2100), on Sharia Dr Habib Habashy; Egyptian American Bank in Novotel on Corniche el-Nil; National Bank of Egypt, on Corniche el-Nil (open Saturday-Thursday 0830-1400 and 1700-2000, Friday 0830-1100 and 1700-2000), just south of the Old Winter Palace Hotel.

● **Entertainment**
Balloon flights: Balloons over Egypt in British built hot air balloons holding 8 persons. Leave your hotel at 0500, total excursion time is 4 hrs, flight 45-90 mins, breakfast served in desert or leave your hotel at 1430 and return after a desert 'sundowner buffet'. Insured by Lloyds of London and full refund if weather conditions prevent flight, T/F 376515 (E£250 pp). Details available at Luxor office of Balloons over Egypt T 581584, T/F 386515 and at all leading hotels and cruise ships. Hat, sunblock and flat shoes rec.

Casino: Hilton Hotel has the only casino in Luxor offering roulette, blackjack and lots of slot machines. Open only to non-Egyptians over 18 years, have your passport available, open 2000-0200.

Discos: Aladin in Isis Hotel open from 2100; Rababa in Luxor Hilton open 2000-0200; Sabil in Mercure Luxor Hotel; Sukkareya Club in Sheraton Hotel; Club Med Disco in Club Med, open 2200-0200; King Tut in Winter Palace, live band from 1830, belly dancer 1900-2000, snake show 2100.

Nightlife: although most of the major hotels have music and floor shows they are generally mediocre compared with Cairo. Nightlife is largely restricted to promenades through the town and along the Corniche with stops for soft drinks, a water-pipe sheesha, and backgammon thowla. The sound and light show at Karnak is over melodramatic but certainly worth a visit. Rather than buy an expensive all inclusive 'tour', which can cost E£75 or more, arrange your own transport for a few E£ and pay the normal E£33 entrance at the kiosk.

Sound & light: shows daily at 1800, 1915, 2030 and 2145 (for Friday, Saturday, Sunday only) as follows:

Monday	English/French/Spanish
Tuesday	German/Japanese/English
Wednesday	German/English/French
Thursday	English/French/Arabic
Friday	Italian/English/French/Spanish
Saturday	French/Japanese/English/German
Sunday	German/English/French/Italian

Make sure to see one of these performances, not to be missed, the spotlights accentuate the carved figures.

● **Hospitals & medical services**
Hospital: T 382025/372045; General Fever Hospital, T 372474; Maged Pharmacy, 24 hr, Sharia Aly Ibn Abi Taleb, T 370524, will deliver.

● **Passport Office**
On Sharia Khaled Ibn el-Walid, just south of and opp Hotel Isis.

● **Places of worship**
Roman Catholic, The Holy Family Church, 16 Sharia Karnak Temple, holds Mass in Latin with multilingual readings each Sunday at 0900 and 1800 and Mass in Arabic on Sunday at 0730.

● **Post & telecommunications**
Area code: 095.

Post Office: main post office (Sunday-Thursday 0800-1400) is on Sharia el-Mahata on the way to the railway station. Hotels sell stamps.

Egyptian popular music

Egypt is the recording centre of the Arab world, although Lebanon is beginning to become a rival once more. Egyptian popular music dates back to pharaonic times, but it is influenced much more by the country's Arab and Islamic heritage. While Western music is popular with the cosmopolitan upper class, the vast majority of Egyptians prefer their own indigenous sounds. Arabic music is based on quarter notes rather than the Western half tone scale.

Classical Arabic Music is the traditional music of the upper class with its roots in the court music of the Ottoman empire. Sung in classical Arabic, it is highly operatic, poetic, and stylized in form. It is characterized by a soloist backed by mass ranks of violinists and cellists and a large male choir. Its most famous singer by far, and the Arab world's first singing superstar, was Umm Kalthoum who died in 1975. During her 5-hr concerts, her endless melodic variations could ensure that one song lasted up to 2½ hrs.

This tradition was lightened and popularised in the 1960s by Abdul Halim Hafez, the other 'great' of Egyptian music, whose romantic croonings in colloquial Arabic also dominated the Arab musical scene.

By contrast, **Shaabi**, or 'popular' music, is that of the working classes, particularly the urban poor. Like Algerian Rai, it has retained a traditional form but through stars such as Ahmed Adawia it broke convention by speaking in plain and often raunchy language about politics and the problems of society.

Al-Musika al-Shababeya or 'youth music' is highly popular with the middle and upper classes and is sometimes imitated in the *Shaabi*. First appearing in the late 1970s, it is a mixture of Arabic and Western influences, taking typical Arabic singing and Arabic instruments such as the *dof* drum and *oud* lute and underpinning this with a Western beat or melodies. The seminal album is Mohamed Mounir's Shababik (Windows) which, in partnership with Yehia Khalil, revolutionized Egyptian pop music in 1981 by introducing thoughtful lyrics, harmonies and a jazz-rock influence into still authentically Arabic music.

In the late 1980s Hamid al-Shaeri pioneered the offshoot **al-Jil** or '(new) generation' wave of sound whose fast handclap dance style glories in its self-proclaimed Egyptian-ness. It has spawned a new clutch of stars such as Amr Diab and Hisham Abbas but its disco style and safe lyrics have brought criticism that Egyptian pop music has become stagnant and repetitive.

Much less popular is Egyptian **ethnic music**, although it has its adherents particularly in the countryside. Of particular note are **Simsimmeya** music, named after its dominant guitar-like stringed instrument, which comes from Ismailia and around the Suez Canal zone; **Saiyidi** or Upper Egyptian music the rhythms of which are based on the wooden horn, *mismar saiyidi*, and two-sided drum nahrasan; the **Delta Fellahi** or peasant music which is calmer and less sharp; and **Nubian** music, which possesses a more African feel, and, unlike Arabic music, uses the pentatonic scale. The pre-eminent Nubian folkloric singer is Hanza Alaa Eddin, who counts among his admirers Peter Gabriel and The Grateful Dead.

Cassettes of Egyptian music are available in all major cities either from small roadside kiosks (often bootleg), market stalls, or from record shops. Try the English speaking Jet Line, 20 Sharia Mansour Mohamed, Zamalek T 3400605 or California, 2 Sharia Taher Hussein, Zamalek T 3412619.

● **Shopping**

Luxor shops are mainly divided between those for tourists found in the hotels and in the main central tourist bazaar, and the local markets. For the independent traveller good quality fruit and vegetables can be bought in the *Sharia Television Market* on Tuesday. Generally the further away from the river the lower the prices and the less the hassle. Foreign newspapers are sold in a kiosk in the middle of the street outside the *Old Winter Palace Hotel*. There is a good chance that these will also be offered for sale by street vendors along the Corniche where the cruise ships are moored. Local alabaster carved into vases (E£25 small), clay pots and tagins are cheap (E£2 medium size). An unusual collection of unpolished precious and semi-precious stones, many believe to have healing properties can be found at Zaghloul Bazaar by Luxor Temple.

Bookshops: Bookshops are found at all major hotels such as *Chez George Gaddis* at the *Hotel Sheraton* but better to go to *Aboudi Books* nr *New Winter Palace* on Corniche el-Nil, T 373390, for books in English, German and French, also a good selection of cards and a shelf of second-hand paper back novels in English. Open 0800-2000 except Friday; *Al Ahram* by the Museum of Mummification on Corniche el-Nil with a good selection of books, also maps and cards and newspapers. Open 0800-2200; *Gaddis Bookshop* by *New Winter Palace* on Corniche el-Nil, T 372142, has books in English, French and German. Open 0800-2130. Recommended as the best of the book shops in Luxor.

● **Sports**

Besides swimming pools, the main hotels have the best sporting facilities incl tennis, sailing and a wide range of indooor games. This section of the River Nile is used for international rowing championships.

Horse riding: on West Bank has become popular, usually passing through villages and some monuments towards the mountains (E£20/hr). Camel and donkey excursions can also be taken.

● **Tour companies & travel agents**

Those in the main hotels are generally very good and can arrange tickets for almost anywhere in the country. The town's travel agents incl *Eastmar Travel*, Corniche el-Nil, *Old Winter Palace*, T 376211, F 382151; *Kuoni Travel*, Sheraton Hotel, T 384544; *Abercrombie and Kent* in *Isis Hotel*; **Thomas Cook**, Corniche el-Nil T 372196; *Misr Travel* nr *Winter Palace Hotel* T 373551.

● **Tourist offices**

The official and very well meaning **Egyptian Tourist Authority (ETA)** office, T 372215, open daily 0800-2000, is on the Corniche between the Luxor Temple and the *Old Winter Palace Hotel*. It is worth a visit to check the current official prices for everything incl *calèches*, taxis and other services. The tourist police are in the same building but also have branches at the airport and the railway station.

● **Useful telephone numbers**

Airport information: T 374665; **Bus**: T 372118; **Fire**: T 180; **Passport Office**: T 380885; **Police**: T 372350; **Post Office**: T 372037; **Tourist Police**: T 376620; **Train**: T 372018.

● **Transport**

Local Cycle hire: from *Hilton Hotel* or *Mercure Inn Luxor Hotel* for E£5/hr. Cheaper and fairly roadworthy cycles can be hired from El-Hussein behind Luxor Temple.

Air There are frequent daily flights particularly in the winter high season to Cairo, Aswan and Abu Simbel and less frequently to Hurghada. **Egyptair** (office in *Winter Palace Hotel*, T 380580-380586) and the privately-owned **ZAS** (in *New Winter Palace*, T 375928), charge identical rates for their flights. There is an increasing number of charter flights to/from European cities.

Train From the station on Sharia al-Mahata there are 6 daily a/c trains to Cairo (12-14 hrs) and slower ones to Aswan (5 hrs). The first class service on the Cairo trains is good and it is a pleasant way to see the Egyptian countryside. It is essential, particularly in the high winter season, to reserve your seat at the station a few days before you travel. Trains to Aswan at 0510, 0705, 0810, 1410, 1840, 2155. Trains to Cairo, 0030, 0130, 0415, 0825, 1000, 1315, 1730, 2100, 2130.

Road Bus: from the Sharia Television bus terminal it is possible to catch 3 daily express buses to Cairo, T 372118 (10 hrs); 4 to Hurghada (4 hrs) via Qena (the left-hand seats are cooler in the Eastern Desert), 0600, 1100, 1430, 1900; and frequent slow southbound ones every hour to Aswan via Esna, Edfu and Kom Ombo between 0630-1830. **Private taxi**: sample charges E£100 to Aswan, E£160 to Hurghada, E£13 to airport. **Service taxi**: from the terminal just off Sharia el-Karnak, half way between the Luxor town centre and Karnak temple, these are quicker and more convenient than trains or buses but only go as far north

The Brooke Hospital for Animals

Dorothy Brooke arrived in Cairo in Oct 1930. 12 years earlier at the end of WW1 the British government had tragically sold off some 20,000 cavalry horses to buyers in Egypt. The condition of the surviving horses, still working in the streets of Cairo, so shocked Mrs Brooke she at once set about putting an end to their suffering. Donations from a single descriptive letter in the 'Morning Post' raised sufficient funds to purchase the remaining 5,000 horses. The vast majority, being over 20 years old and often in the final stages of collapse, had to be destroyed. However, they ended their days peacefully amid the care and attention to which they were all once so accustomed.

Mrs Brooke then turned the attention of her committee to the working conditions and hardship of the other draught animals. Their owners are, for the most part, very poor and so have the greatest difficulty in just feeding and maintaining their families. When their animals become old, lame or need treatment they cannot be released from work and many literally die in harness. This process benefits nobody.

One often hears of cruelty to animals but perhaps not enough of the love the owners feel for their charges. After all their very livelihood depends on them. Choices are very limited for a man whose income is equivalent to US$4 a day. His own life is very harsh and sometimes he has to work his animal beyond what we might consider reasonable limits. This is not malicious cruelty; it is pure survival.

Following on from the first free veterinary clinic set up in 1934 as the 'Old War Horse Memorial Hospital' and now known as the 'Brooke Hospital for Animals' millions of animals and their owners have received assistance. In Egypt today there are 14 fully qualified veterinary surgeons and 70 veterinary assistants, farriers and supporting staff working at five centres in Cairo, Alexandria, Luxor, Aswan and Edfu. The new centre in Marsa Matruh is almost complete. They provide over 182,000 treatments annually and owners are always instructed in the future care of their animal, a fundamental part of the work. Egypt has the largest network of assistance. The Brooke Hospital for Animals also has centres in Jordan, Pakistan and India.

The ultimate aim is to work until there is no job left to do. In the meantime all animals are treated free of charge; mares brought in for foaling are kept for four weeks after the birth; no animal is discharged until fit for work; all discharged animals are reshod and have their harness refitted; very poor owners receive a small subsistence while their animal is 'off the road'; owners of animals beyond assistance are often given a small contribution towards a replacement.

If the condition of working animals in the Third World concerns you, be practical, send a donation to Broadmead House, 21 Panton St, London SW1 4DR.

---

as Qena (1 hr). Change taxis there to go on to Esna (45 mins), Kom Ombo (2-3 hrs) and Aswan (4-5 hrs).

Boat *Feluccas*: are numerous on this most beautiful stretch of the Nile. Travel is limited to the southward direction, but this also has the most attractive scenery. Sunset is the best time to ride but bring a sweater and protection against mosquitoes (E£15/hr).

SITES IN LUXOR AND ON THE EAST BANK

LUXOR TEMPLE

Allow 3 or 4 hrs to see this in detail and if possible get to see it in the evening – with spotlights it looks stunning. The temple, in the centre of town on the Corniche, is open daily 0700-2100 in winter, 0700-2200 in summer and during Ramadan 0800-1100 and 2000-2300. Entry E£20 and E£10 for cameras.

Like the much larger Karnak Temple it is dedicated to the three Theban gods Amun, Mut and Khonsu. **Amun** is usually depicted as a man wearing ram's horns or a tall feathered Atef crown. His wife **Mut** was considered to be the mistress of heaven and **Khonsu** was their son who was believed to travel through the sky at night assisting the scribe god.

Because it is smaller, more compact and fewer pharaohs were involved in its construction, Luxor Temple is simpler and more coherent than Karnak Temple a few kilometres away. Although the 18th Dynasty (1537-1320 BC) pharaoh **Amenhotep III** (1417-1379 BC) began the Temple, his son **Amenhotep IV**, who changed his name to **Akhenaten** (1379-62 BC) by which he is better known, concentrated instead on building a shrine to Aten adjacent to the site. However **Tutankhamen** (1361-52 BC) and **Horemheb** (1348-20 BC) later resumed the work and decorated the peristyle court and colonnade. **Ramses II** (1304-1237 BC) completed the majority of the building by adding a second colonnade and pylon as well as a multitude of colossi. The Temple subsequently became covered with sand and silt which helped preserve it although salt encrustation has caused some damage. Because the ground level has risen 6m since its construction the temple now stands at the bottom of a gentle depression. An avenue of sphinxes, a 30th Dynasty (380-343 BC) addition, lines the approach. This avenue once stretched all the way to the Karnak Temple complex.

The entrance to the temple is through the First Pylon. In front of the pylon are the three remaining colossi of Ramses II, two seated and one standing and, to the left, a single obelisk 25m high.

The **First Pylon** gives an impression of how awe-inspiring the Temple must have looked in its prime. The 22.8m high second

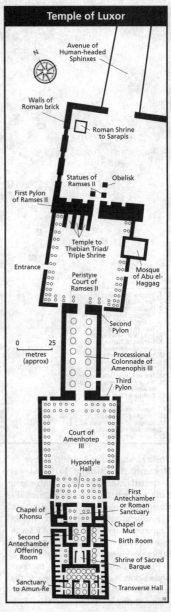

Temple of Luxor

- Avenue of Human-headed Sphinxes
- N
- Walls of Roman brick
- Roman Shrine to Sarapis
- Statues of Ramses II
- Obelisk
- First Pylon of Ramses II
- Temple to Thebian Triad/Triple Shrine
- Entrance
- Mosque of Abu el-Haggag
- Peristyle Court of Ramses II
- Second Pylon
- 0 metres (approx) 25
- Processional Colonnade of Amenophis III
- Third Pylon
- Court of Amenhotep III
- Hypostyle Hall
- First Antechamber or Roman Sanctuary
- Chapel of Khonsu
- Chapel of Mut
- Second Antechamber /Offering Room
- Birth Room
- Shrine of Sacred Barque
- Sanctuary to Amun-Re
- Transverse Hall

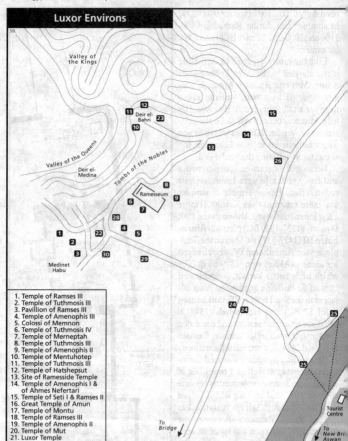

Luxor Environs

50L

Valley of the Kings

Deir el-Bahri

Valley of the Queens

Deir el-Medina

Tombs of the Nobles

Ramesseum

Medinet Habu

To Bridge

Tourist Centre

To New Bri Aswan

1. Temple of Ramses III
2. Temple of Tuthmosis III
3. Pavillion of Ramses III
4. Temple of Amenophis III
5. Colossi of Memnon
6. Temple of Tuthmosis IV
7. Temple of Merneptah
8. Temple of Tuthmosis III
9. Temple of Amenophis II
10. Temple of Mentuhotep
11. Temple of Tuthmosis III
12. Temple of Hatshepsut
13. Site of Ramesside Temple
14. Temple of Amenophis I & of Ahmes Nefertari
15. Temple of Seti I & Ramses II
16. Great Temple of Amun
17. Temple of Montu
18. Temple of Ramses III
19. Temple of Amenophis II
20. Temple of Mut
21. Luxor Temple

Obelisk, which was given to France by Mohamed Ali Pasha in 1819 and was re-erected in the Place de la Concorde in Paris, and another three of Ramses II's six original colossi have been removed. The reliefs on the First Pylon depict Ramses' victory at the Battle of Kadesh with later embellishments by Nubian and Ethiopian kings.

Passing through the pylon, the **Peristyle Court** is set at a slight angle to the rest of the Temple and encompasses the earlier shrine of **Tuthmosis III** (1504-

1450 BC) which is also dedicated to the Theban triad. The east end of the court has not been fully excavated because it is the site of the **Mosque of Abu el-Haggag**, the patron saint of Luxor and, although another mosque with the same name has been built nearby, this one is still preferred by locals. While most of the mosque is 19th century the northern minaret is very much older. At the south end of the court, the portal flanking the entrance to the colonnade supports two black granite statues bearing the name of

22. Ticket Booth
23. Hot Air Ballon
24. Checkpoint
25. Bicycle & Donkey Hire

Hotels:
26. Abul Kassem
27. Hilton
28. Marsam
29. Memnon
30. Resthouse, Queen &
    Medinet Habu Hotels

water-table has undermined the foundations of this court, an extensive restoration programme has recently been completed, the floor has been relaid and the 22 columns reassembled in their original positions. It leads to the **Hypostyle Hall** with 32 papyrus columns which were taken over by **Ramses IV** (1166-60 BC) and **Ramses VII** (1148-41 BC) who took no part in their erection but still added their cartouches!

Look out for the chamber which was converted into a **Coptic church** during the 4th century. The Pharaonic reliefs were plastered over and early Christian paintings covered the whitewash although little of these remains today. In a few places the stucco has crumbled away and some of the original reliefs are revealed.

Beyond is a smaller second vestibule, the **Offerings Chamber**, with its four columns still in place. Further on, in the **Sanctuary of the Sacred Barque**, the doors were made of acacia and inlaid with gold. **Alexander the Great** (332-323 BC) rebuilt the shrine in accordance with Amenhotep III's original plans. The east passage leads to the Birth Room built because of Amenhotep's claim that he was the son of the god Amun, who is depicted as entering the queen's chamber disguised as Tuthmosis IV (1425-17 BC) and breathing the child into her nostrils. The furthest hall has 12 poorly maintained papyrus bud columns and leads on to the small **Sanctuary** where the combined god Amun-Min is represented.

LUXOR MUSEUM

The Luxor Museum, located on the Corniche half way between Luxor and Karnak temples, is open daily – winter 0900-1300 and 1600-2100 (last tickets 1230 and 2030) summer 0900-1300 and 1700-2200 (last tickets 1230 and 2130). Prices E£30 plus E£10 for New Hall, E£10 for using a camera, 50% discount for students.

The few exhibits in this modern museum are tastefully displayed, centred around a small garden, with a large

Ramses II but the feathers of Tutankhamen.

The **Colonnade** of 14 columns with papyrus capitals was built by Amenhotep but decorated by Tutankhamen and Horemheb. Beyond it is a **Court of Amenhotep III**, which is the second peristyle court with double rows of columns flanking three of the sides. It was built by Amenhotep III for the deity Amun who he claimed was his father. None of the original roof remains, but the columns are well preserved. Because the rising

Ramses The Great

👉 Known by the Egyptians as Ramses al-Akbar (the great), a name that would no doubt have pleased him, the achievements of Ramses II, arguably Ancient Egypt's most famous king, were majestic. During his 67-year reign, the pharaoh presided over an empire stretching west from present-day Libya to Iraq in the east, as far north as Turkey, and south into Sudan. While his military feats were suitably exaggerated for posterity in the monuments of the day, Ramses also engineered a peace treaty with Egypt's age-old northern rivals, the Hittites, by a strategic marriage to a daughter of the Hittite king in 1246 BC which ended years of unrest. The peace lasted for the rest of the pharaoh's lengthy reign. Ramses II is believed to be the pharaoh of the biblical 'exodus', although Egyptian records make no mention of dealings with Israelite slaves. His massive fallen statue at the Ramesseum inspired Shelley's romantic sonnet Ozymandias, a title taken from the Greek version of Ramses' coronation name User-maat-re. Egypt's most prolific pharaoh (siring at least 80 children), he was also a prodigious builder. He began building soon after ascending the throne at the age of 25 having discovered that the great temple his father Seti I had begun at Abydos was a shambles. During the rest of his reign he erected dozens of monuments including a temple to Osiris at Abydos, expansions of temples at Luxor and Karnak, and the awe-inspiring cliff temples at Abu Simbel. In an age when life expectancy was 40 years at most, Ramses, who lived to 92, must truly have appeared to be a god.

ground floor and a smaller upper gallery. The most important and of particular interest are the New Kingdom statues which were found in a cache at Karnak in 1989 but the exhibits range from pharaonic treasures to the Mamluke period (1250-1517 AD).

Of the statues on the ground floor the most striking are the large pink granite head of Amenhotep III (1417-1379 BC), an alabaster crocodile-headed Sobek, and two memorable busts of Akhenaten. A few choice exhibits from Tutankhamen's tomb are also displayed including a gold-inlaid cow's head of the goddess Hathor, a funerary bed and two model barques. The prints showing how the sites looked in the 19th century are also interesting.

On the second floor is the wall of Akhenaten, 283 sandstone blocks found at the Ninth Pylon at Karnak. Here Akhenaten and Nefertiti are shown worshipping Aten.

Museum of Mummification – opened 1997 right on the banks of the River Nile – tells the story of mummification as practised by the ancient Egyptians as an integral part of their religious belief in the after life. This museum, considered to be the first of its kind in the world, contains a comprehensive display. Exhibits include several human, reptile and bird mummies as well as tools used in the mummification process. It is well set out and is certainly worth a visit.

KARNAK TEMPLE

Allow half a day to see this in detail and if possible return in the evening for the Sound and Light show. The Karnak Temple complex, 2.5 km north of Luxor town, is the largest pharaonic monument in the country after the Giza Pyramids and covers almost 25 ha. Open daily winter 0600-1730, summer 0600-1830, general entry E£20, student entry E£10. The site can just about be covered in 2 hrs. The evening Sound and Light Show (E£33 and E£30 for video cameras) is good with a somewhat overdramatic commentary. See Sound and light, page 217. *Calèches* and service taxis from Luxor town should officially cost about E£5 but you can expect to have to pay double and the ride along the Corniche is very pleasant.

Known in earlier times as **Iput-Isut** 'the most esteemed of places', the extent, scale and quality of the remains is astonishing. The complexes' numerous temples vary greatly in style because they were constructed over a period of 1,300 years. Their only common theme is worship of Amun, Mut and Khonsu who make up the Theban Triad of gods. In order to see as much of the site as possible, aim to arrive very early or just before sunset when it relatively cool and less crowded.

At the heart of the complex is the enormous **Temple of Amun** which was altered and extended by successive pharaohs. For example although the heretical **Akhenaten**, who converted to the world's first monotheistic religion and moved the capital from Thebes to Tell el-Amarna (see page 180), replaced the images of **Amun** with representations of **Aten**, these were later erased by his successors and Amun's images were restored! Included in and surrounding the main temple are numerous smaller but magnificent ones including the **Temple of Tuthmosis III (10)**, the **Temple of Ramses III (3)** and the smaller **Shrine of Seti II (2)**.

The **Temple of Amun** is approached via the **Avenue of Ram Headed Sphinxes (5)** which used to link it to the Temple at Luxor. The imposing **First Pylon** is 130m wide and each of the two unfinished towers are 43m high and, although incomplete, nothing else matches its enormous scale. Dynasty after dynasty added to it and one might speculate about which ruler oversaw each of the various sections. Moving towards the inner core of the temple, which is the oldest section, one is moving back in time through successive dynasties. The entry towers are thought to have been constructed by the Nubian and Ethiopian Kings of the 25th Dynasty (747-656 BC) while recent work has revealed that several levels were built during the later Greek and Roman eras. For a little *baksheesh* it may be possible to climb the stairs up the north tower and marvel at the fantastic view it offers of the complex.

Arriving through the First Pylon, you come to the **Great Forecourt** which was begun in the 20th Dynasty (1200-1085 BC) but completed somewhat later. Immediately on the left is the very thick-walled rose coloured granite and sandstone **Shrine of Seti II (1216-10 BC)** which was a way-station for the sacred barques of Amun, Mut and Khonsu as they were taken on ritual processions. The west wall had to be subsequently rebuilt because it collapsed when the First Pylon was under construction. The outer façade portrays Seti II making offerings to various deities.

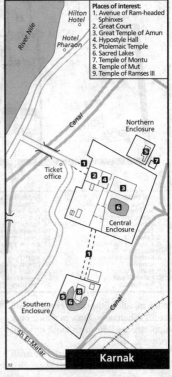

Places of interest:
1. Avenue of Ram-headed Sphinxes
2. Great Court
3. Great Temple of Amun
4. Hypostyle Hall
5. Ptolemaic Temple
6. Sacred Lakes
7. Temple of Montu
8. Temple of Mut
9. Temple of Ramses III

Karnak

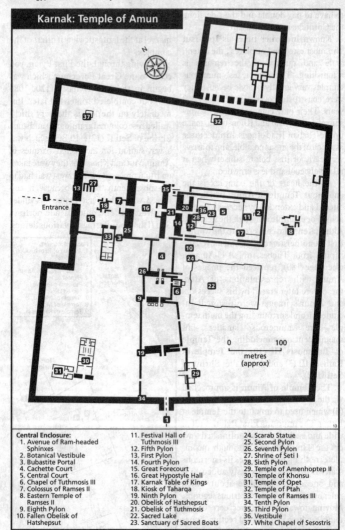

Karnak: Temple of Amun

N

0   100
metres
(approx)

Central Enclosure:
1. Avenue of Ram-headed Sphinxes
2. Botanical Vestibule
3. Bubastite Portal
4. Cachette Court
5. Central Court
6. Chapel of Tuthmosis III
7. Colossus of Ramses II
8. Eastern Temple of Ramses II
9. Eighth Pylon
10. Fallen Obelisk of Hatshepsut
11. Festival Hall of Tuthmosis III
12. Fifth Pylon
13. First Pylon
14. Fourth Pylon
15. Great Forecourt
16. Great Hypostyle Hall
17. Karnak Table of Kings
18. Kiosk of Taharqa
19. Ninth Pylon
20. Obelisk of Hatshepsut
21. Obelisk of Tuthmosis
22. Sacred Lake
23. Sanctuary of Sacred Boats
24. Scarab Statue
25. Second Pylon
26. Seventh Pylon
27. Shrine of Seti I
28. Sixth Pylon
29. Temple of Amenhoptep II
30. Temple of Khonsu
31. Temple of Opet
32. Temple of Ptah
33. Temple of Ramses III
34. Tenth Pylon
35. Third Pylon
36. Vestibule
37. White Chapel of Sesostris

Entrance

In the middle of the Great Forecourt are the 10 columns of **Taharga** which once supported a 26.5m high kiosk or small open temple.

To the right of the forecourt is the small **Temple of Ramses III** (1198-66 BC) which would have stood in solitary splendour in front of the **Second Pylon** when it was first built in honour of Amun. Like the Shrine of Seti II, it was used as another way-station for the sacred barques. Part of an inscription in the interior reads: "*I* made it for you in your city of Waset, in front of your forecourt, to the Lord of the Gods, being the Temple of Ramses in the estate of Amun, to remain as long as the heavens bear the sun. I filled its treasuries with offerings that my hands had brought."

To the left of the **Second Pylon** is the 15m high **Colossus of Ramses II** (1304-1237 BC) with his daughter Benta-anta standing in front of his legs. On the right of the pylon is the **Bubastite Portal** named after the 22nd Dynasty (945-715 BC) kings from the Delta town of Bubastis. Through the Second Pylon is the immense 5,000 sq m (102 x 53m) and spectacular **Hypostyle Hall** which is probably the best part of the whole Karnak complex. Its has 134 giant columns, which were once topped by sandstone roof slabs, of which the 12 largest making up the central processional way to the other chambers are 23m high and 15m round. The other 122 smaller columns, which have papyrus bud capitals and retain some of their original colour at the higher levels, cover the rest of the hall. They are decorated by dedications to various Gods, but particularly to the many different guises of Amun and the Theban Triad, and are also inscribed with the cartouches of the pharaohs who contributed to the hall. The south side was decorated by Ramses II with vivid but cheap and simple concave sunk-reliefs, whilst the north is attributed to Seti II whose artists painstakingly carved delicate convex bas-reliefs on the walls. Ramses is shown, on the south side of the internal wall of the Second Pylon, making offerings before the gods and seeking their guidance, while on the left is a beautiful representation of Thoth inscribing Seti's name on a holy tree.

Seti II is depicted on both sides of the **Third Pylon** but the south wall running along the right of the hall was mainly decorated by Ramses II. He is shown being crowned by Horus and Thoth and then being presented to Amun while the Theban Triad is also pictured.

The **Third Pylon** was constructed by Amenhotep III (1417-1379 BC) on the site of several earlier shrines which were moved to the Luxor Museum and the Open Air Museum within the walls of Karnak. On the inner east face is a text of tribute and a scene showing the gods' sacred boats. Amenhotep III built a small court to enclose four **Tuthmosid Obelisks** in the narrow gap between the Third and Fourth Pylon which at that time represented the entrance to the Temple. Of the four, only one pink granite obelisk (23m high, weighing 143 tonnes and originally tipped with electrum) built by Tuthmosis II (1512-04 BC) now remains and the stone bases and some blocks from two other obelisks built by Tuthmosis III (1504-1450 BC) are scattered nearby.

Moving towards the earlier centre of the temple is the limestone faced sandstone **Fourth Pylon**, built by Tuthmosis I (1525-12 BC). Texts describing later restorations are recorded on both sides by Tuthmosis IV (1425-17 BC) to the left and Shabaka (716-702 BC) to the right. Just inside is a small **Transverse Hall** which was originally a hypostyle hall before the Temple was extended outwards. Only 12 of the original papyrus bud columns and one of two 27m and 340 tonne rose-granite **Obelisk of Hatshepsut**, which once stood at the entrance, now remain. In the 16th year of the reign of Hatshepsut (1503-1482 BC), the only woman to rule Egypt as pharaoh, these two obelisks were transported from Aswan where a third unfinished one still remains (see The Unfinished Obelisk, page 288). The tip of the second obelisk, which fell to the ground, is now lying near the Sacred Lake. The surviving erect obelisk is decorated along its whole length with the following inscription – "O ye people who see this monument in years to come and speak of that which I have made, beware lest you say, 'I know not why it was done'. I did it because I wished to make a gift for my father Amun, and to gild them with electrum." Her long frustrated and usurped infant step-son Tuthmosis

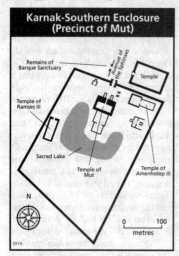

Karnak-Southern Enclosure (Precinct of Mut)

Remains of Barque Sanctuary

Avenue of the Sphinxes

Temple

Temple of Ramses III

Temple of Mut

Sacred Lake

Temple of Amenhotep III

N

0   100
metres

EX14

III (1504-1450 BC), who had plotted against her during her reign, took his revenge by hiding the obelisks behind walls almost to the ceiling which actually preserved them from later graffiti.

The east wall of the Transverse Hall is the **Fifth Pylon** which has been attributed to Hatshepsut's father Tuthmosis I. Beyond is another hall and then the badly damaged sandstone **Sixth Pylon**. The world's first imperialist Tuthmosis III inscribed it on both sides with details of his vanquished enemies and his victory at the Battle of Megiddo or Armageddon. Past the pylon is a **Vestibule** which is flanked by two courts and is dominated by two granite pillars with carvings showing Tuthmosis III being embraced by Amun, and the lotus and papyrus symbols of Upper and Lower Egypt. A seated statue of Amenhotep II (1450-25 BC) is against the west wall and on the north side are two colossi of Amun and Amunet, although their faces resemble Tutankhamen (1361-52 BC) who had had them built. The Vestibule leads to the Granite Sanctuary built by Alexander the Great's moronic half brother and successor Philip Arrhidaeus (323-317 BC). The

ceiling is covered with golden stars on a dark base while the walls depict scenes of Philip with the god Amun. The exterior walls are decorated in a similar fashion.

North of the Sanctuary beyond the granite door is a series of small chambers built by Hatshepsut but later altered by Tuthmosis III. Some of the rooms were walled up by her son to conceal Hatshepsut's influence and consequently the bright colours have been very well preserved although Hatshepsut's face has been cut away whenever it appeared.

Further to the east is Tuthmosis III's **Festival Hall** which, with its central tentpole-style columns symbolizing the tents used during his campaigns, is unlike any Egyptian building. It was built for his jubilee festivals which were intended to renew the pharaohs' temporal and spiritual authority. Access is via a small vestibule which leads to the central columned hall. The columns in the central aisle are taller than the side ones and would have supported a raised section of the roof thereby permitting sunlight to enter. The hall was later used as a Christian church and early paintings of the saints can still be seen on some of the columns.

Off to the southwest is a small chamber where the original stele, or standing block, known as the **Karnak Table of Kings** minus Hatshepsut was found. The original is in the Louvre in Paris, the one on display being a replica. The series of interconnecting chambers beyond is dedicated to the Theban Triad and further north is an attractive chamber known as the **Botanical Vestibule**. Its four columns have papyrus capitals and are carved with the unfamiliar plants and shrubs discovered by Tuthmosis III during his Syrian campaign. Surrounding the small chamber on the far east wall is the small and badly decayed **Sanctuary of Amun**, built by Hatshepsut and originally decorated with two raised obelisks on either side of the entrance – only the bases now remain. The nearby **Chapel of**

Sokar, which is dedicated to the Memphite god of darkness, is better preserved.

To the south of the main temple is the **Sacred Lake** (200m x 117m), which has been restored to its original dimensions but has become stagnant since the inundation which used to feed the lake by underground channels from the River Nile ceased after the construction of the Aswan Dam. Today the lake is totally uninteresting but it has the Sound and Light Show grandstand at the far end and a café on the north side. A Nilometer is attached to the lake and there is a statue of a giant scarab beetle which childless women walk around five times in order to ensure that they soon bear children.

While the main temple runs from west to east there is a secondary axis running south from the area between the third and fourth pylons. It begins with the **Cachette Court** which received its name after the discovery between 1903 and 1906 of 17,000 bronze statues and 780 stone ones which had been stored in the court during the Ptolemaic period and the best of which are now in the Cairo Museum. The reliefs on the outside wall of the Hypostyle Hall, northwest of the court, depict Ramses II in battle. On the east walls, close to the **Seventh Pylon**, is a replica of a stele now in the Egyptian Museum which shows the only reference to Israel during Pharaonic times. The Seventh Pylon was built by Tuthmosis III and shows him massacring his prisoners before Amun. In front of the façade are parts of two colossi of Tuthmosis and in the courtyard to the left is the small chapel of Tuthmosis III.

Although restoration work continues on the nearby **Eighth Pylon** and others further along, it may be possible to have a quick look in return for a small tip to the guard, either early or late in the day when there are fewer people. The Eighth Pylon was built by Tuthmosis II and Hatshepsut and contains extensively restored reliefs and cartouches. As in so many other places, Hatshepsut's name

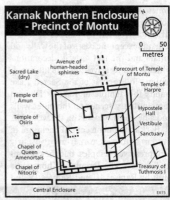

Karnak Northern Enclosure - Precinct of Montu

0   50
metres

Avenue of human-headed sphinxes

Sacred Lake (dry)

Temple of Amun

Temple of Osiris

Chapel of Queen Amenortais

Chapel of Nitocris

Central Enclosure

Forecourt of Temple of Montu

Temple of Harpre

Hypostele Hall

Vestibule

Sanctuary

Treasury of Tuthmosis I

EX15

has been erased and replaced by Tuthmosis II's name while Akhenaten's name was systematically erased by Seti I. The south side of the pylon has four of the original six **Seated Colossi**, two of which are Tuthmosis II and one is Amenhotep I.

The **Ninth Pylon** and the **Tenth Pylon** were built by Horemheb (1348-20 BC) using materials from the demolished Aten Temple. The Tenth Pylon has two colossi of Ramses II and his wife Nefertari usurping the original colossi of Amenhotep III. On the south side of the pylon there are two quartzite colossi of Amenhotep III. The pylon is part of the outer enclosure and marks the start of the ramheaded sphinx-lined road to the southern enclosure.

To the south, enclosed by a mud-brick wall are the much over-grown remains of the **Temple of Mut** and associated buildings. They are worth a quick visit. The entrance is in the centre of the north wall. Outside the enclosure and to the east are the ruins of a temple and to the west remains suggested as a barque sanctuary. Inside the enclosure, in a central position between the entrance and the Sacred Lake, and orientated north-south, stands the Temple of Mut, consort of Amun. Little remains of this construction accepted as the work of Ptolemies II and VII except a number of diorite statues of the lioness-headed god, Sekhmet. To the northeast is the Temple of Amenhotep III, later restored by Ramses II. Little remains except the bases of the walls and pillars and the feet on wall decorations which certainly leaves much to the imagination. To the west of the Sacred Lake stands the Temple of Ramses III with some military scenes on the outer walls and a headless colossus on the west side.

Back in the main central enclosure in the far southwest corner are two fairly well preserved temples, but they of limited interest. The **Temple of Khonsu** was built by Ramses III and Ramses IV and

dedicated to the son of Amun and Mut. Many of the reliefs show Herihor, high-priest of Amun, who ruled Upper Egypt after Ramses XI (1114-1085 BC) moved his capital to the Delta and delegated power to the high-priest. In the courtyard Herihor's name is inscribed on every pillar and all the scenes depict him venerating the gods and making offerings to them. The **Temple of Optet**, the hippopotamus-goddess, is normally closed to the public.

On the north side of the central enclosure, the **Temple of Ptah** leads on to Karnak's northern enclosure which includes

Theban Death Rites and the Book of the Dead

In order to fully appreciate the Theban Necropolis in the soft limestone hills opposite Luxor on the West Bank of the River Nile it is important to understand a little about the celebration and rituals of death in Ancient Egypt.

The **Book of the Dead** is the collective name given to the papyrus sheets which were included by the ancient Egyptians in their coffins. The sheets contained magic spells and small illustrations to assist the deceased in the journey through the underworld to the after-life. In total there are over 200 spells though no single papyrus contained them all. Some of the papyrus strips were specially commissioned but it was possible to buy ready-made collections with a space left for the relevant name. Some of these spells came from the **Pyramid texts**, they were the oldest written references to this passage from one life to the next. They were found on the walls of pyramids constructed during the 5th-7th Dynasties (2494-2170 BC). Later the text and descriptions of the rituals which were involved were written on the actual coffins of commoners, not kings. The spells were written in vertical columns of hieratic script. Eventually lack of space on the sarcophagi led to only the ritual prayers and offerings being listed. When papyrus began to be used during the New Kingdom (1567-1085 BC) written texts were enclosed in the coffin and they became known as the *Book of the Dead*. Many copies of the writings, including the *Book of the Caverns* and the *Litany of Re*, were subsequently discovered.

The ancient Egyptians believed that at sunset the sun-god Re descended into the underworld and voyaged through the night before emerging at dawn to sail his barque (boat) across the heavens until sunset when the whole cycle began again. This journey was believed to be replicated by the dead pharaoh who descended through the underworld and whose heart, which was believed to be the centre of intelligence, would be weighed in the **Judgment of Osiris** to determine whether or not he would be permitted to continue his journey to the after-life.

The burial ceremony was elaborate with priests performing all the necessary rites, including sacrifices, in order to ensure that the deceased had a rapid passage to the next life. The tomb, together with everything the pharaoh might need including slaves, was then closed, plastered over and stamped with the royal seal. In order to protect the royal tombs from grave-robbers, they were fitted with false burial chambers and death-traps which unfortunately did not work.

two temples, a sacred lake (now dry) and some chapels. The **Temple of Montu**, the god of war was built by Amenhotep III, some of his cartouches survive, and restored by Ramses IV. He left his mark too. Also in this small enclosure (150 sq m) to the west is a temple to Amun. At the southern wall, six small gateways gave access to six small chapels of which the chapels of Amenortais and Nitocris are the best preserved.

To the east outside the enclosure is the Treasury of Titmosis I, while to the west stand the remains of a temple to Osiris. This precinct does not have the splendours of the more famous temples and is best appreciated by real enthusiasts.

The **Open Air Museum** is situated to the northwest of the complex. It contains 1,300 blocks from the foundations of the Third Pylon and 319 stone blocks reassembled into Hatshepsut's **Sanctuary of the Barque**. Another barque sanctuary built by Amenhotep I is also on display, but the most beautiful monument is the lovely 12th Dynasty (1991-1786 BC) **White Chapel** built by Senusert I (1971-28 BC) which is divided into four rows of five pillars and includes some wonderful convex bas-reliefs and an interesting geographic list of the Middle East. The rest of the chapel is dedicated to offerings to a phallic Amun-Min who is embraced by Senusert. Open daily 0700-1800 summer, 0700-1700 winter. General entry E£10, students E£5, tickets sold at museum entrance.

THE WEST BANK AND THEBAN NECROPOLIS

Direct road access from Luxor to the West Bank is now possible following the opening of the new Nile Bridge approximately 7 km to the south of the town. A transfer time of 35-40 mins should be expected by tour parties travelling from Luxor by coach. The new bridge has been built well to the south in an attempt to ensure that the main town buildings are restricted, as far as is possible, to the East Bank by not creating a direct crossing at Luxor itself. The authorities are

Throw some light on the subject

There was obviously no need, originally, for light in the tombs and today the authorities maintain the lowest possible illumination necessary. **Take a torch** which will enable you to read the explanation and diagrams in this book, to admire the outstanding wall decorations and illustrations, to avoid tripping on the uneven ground.

making strong efforts to restrict buildings on the West Bank to ensure that the development of water, drainage and sewerage systems does not have a detrimental effect on the condition of the tombs as a result of capillary action and alterations to the water table.

TRAVEL TO THE WEST BANK An organized tour booked through an agent relieves you of all the hassle but confines you by time spent at the venue and choice of tombs. It is not difficult nor expensive (no more than E£150 a day) to arrange for independent travel from Luxor with a guide. Tickets for the tombs are extra of course. Less expensive, cross by ferry and pick up a guide at each site. You will need some sort of transport to get to the different areas so hire a bicycle in Luxor or on the West Bank or more comfortably hire a taxi (be clear where you want to go and bargain from about E£55) once you have crossed. Access aross the River Nile is by ferry (E£3 single) from beside the *Mercure Luxor Hotel* and the ticket booths are a long uphill walk away.

VISITING THE TOMBS Although so far a total of 62 tombs have been opened many, including some of the most remarkable such as that of Seti I (1318-04 BC) (No 17), are closed to the public because they suffered so badly from mass tourism that they have had to be resealed for restoration work. The combination of long queues and the hot and stuffy atmosphere in some of the most popular tombs make it impractical to try and visit all of the tombs on one visit. In order to avoid the heat and the rush it is best to go as early as possible, particularly during the summer, take a bottle of water and a torch both because there are occasional

Books of the Afterlife

The Egyptians believed that the journey to the afterlife was through *Duat* the underworld and to combat the monsters and other evils there, a series of prayers and some magic spells were necessary. These were written in the *Book of the Dead* which also contained a map of Duat. (Was this the first guide book?)

Book of the Dead – called by the Egyptians The Book of Coming Forth by Day. This is a collection of mortuary texts, a collection of spells or magic formulas which were placed in tombs and intended to be of aid in the next world. They are thought to have been compiled and perhaps edited during the 16th century BC. They included texts dating back to around 2000 BC (Coffin Texts) and 2400 BC (Pyramid Texts). Selected sections were copied on papyrus by scribes, illustrated versions cost more, and sold for inclusion in one's coffin. Many selections were found and it is estimated that there were approximately 200 chapters. Extracts appear on many of the antechamber walls of the Ramessid tombs. Nearly 12 chapters are given over to special spells – to turn the deceased into any animal shape.

Book of Am-Duat – called by the Egyptians The Book of the Secret Chamber. It deals with the sun's journey through the underworld during the 12 hrs of the night. Selections are found in many tombs. Full versions are inscribed on the walls of the burial chambers of Tuthmosis III and Amenhotep II.

Book of Gates refers to the twelve gates which separate the hours of the night and first appears on tombs of the 18th Dynasty. The inscriptions in the tomb of Ramses VI give the most complete version. This has the same journeying theme as the book of Am-Duat but the Duat is not comparable other than having 12 segments.

Book of Caverns A full version of this is found in the tomb of Ramses VI.

Litany of Re This deals with Re in his 75 different forms.

Books of the Heavens which describes the passage of the sun through the 24 hrs of the day includes the Book of the Day, the Book of Night and the Book of the Divine Cow. These texts were first used during the New Kingdom and there are several pieces inscribed in the tomb of Ramses VI.

For further details refer to book by RO Faulkner, see page 501.

power cuts and the lighting in some of the tombs is inadequate.

NB TICKETS It is very important to note that tickets for all of the sites on the West Bank of the Nile **must** be bought in advance at the main booths which are clearly marked. The booths also sell non-refundable photograph permits at E£10 per tomb (flash photography is strictly forbidden because it damages the pigment), are open from 0600-1600. The use of video cameras is not permitted in the Valley of the Kings. Sites are open 0700-1800 summer, 0700-1700 winter. Entry for the Valley of the Kings is E£20 for three tombs and E£40 extra for Tutankhamen's tomb. Entry for

other sites is E£6. Some tombs are individually priced at E£6, others E£6 for two or three tombs. A system has been devised to reduce wear and tear on the more popular tombs – by closing them at intervals. Always check if you have a particular destination in mind.

In the Valley of the Queens the tickets for Nefertari's tomb cost E£100 and are limited to 200 sold on the day and one ticket for E£12 will give access to the other three tombs there that are open to the public.

The Tombs of the Nobles are divided into four groups and a separate ticket costing E£12 is needed for each group. The most important group of tombs is 100, 96, 55 and

52: the next important is 69, 56, and 57. Students with a card should always ask for a discount.

THE VALLEY OF THE KINGS

Also known as Wadi Biban el-Muluk. Allow a day to do this in some comfort and a little depth. One of many necropoli in the limestone hills on the West Bank of the River Nile, the area first became a burial site during the New Kingdom rule of Tuthmosis I (1525-1512 BC) in the hope that the tombs would be safe from looters. The kings' tombs are not actually confined to the single valley and it is believed that there may be others still waiting to be discovered. Those already discovered are numbered in the chronological order of their discovery rather than by location. Although some are simple and comparatively crude the best are incredibly well preserved, stunningly decorated and illustrate their intricate craftsmanship.

The tombs generally follow two designs. The early 18th Dynasty (1567-1320 BC) tombs are a series of descending galleries followed by a well or rock pit which was intended to both collect any rain water and deter thieves. On the other side of the pit there were sealed offering chambers and then the rectangular burial chamber built at right angles to the descending galleries. The later tombs, from the late 18th to the 20th Dynasties (1360-

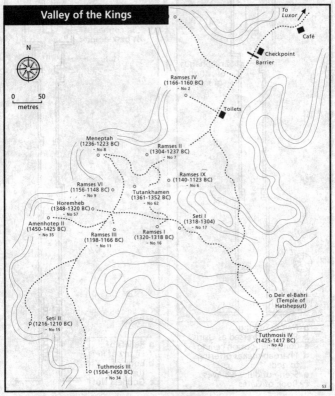

Valley of the Kings

N

0   50
metres

To Luxor

Café

Checkpoint Barrier

Toilets

Ramses IV (1166-1160 BC) - No 2

Meneptah (1236-1223 BC) - No 8

Ramses II (1304-1237 BC) - No 7

Ramses IX (1140-1123 BC) - No 6

Ramses VI (1156-1148 BC) - No 9

Tutankhamen (1361-1352 BC) - No 62

Horemheb (1348-1320 BC) - No 57

Amenhotep II (1450-1425 BC) - No 35

Ramses III (1198-1166 BC) - No 11

Ramses I (1320-1318 BC) - No 16

Seti I (1318-1304) - No 17

Deir el-Bahri (Temple of Hatshepsut)

Seti II (1216-1210 BC) - No 15

Tuthmosis IV (1425-1417 BC) - No 43

Tuthmosis III (1504-1450 BC) - No 34

53

1085 BC), were built in the same way but the galleries and burial chambers were on the same axis being cut horizontally but deeper straight into the rock face.

Ramses VII (1148-41 BC) (No 1)

This later style, single horizontal plane, and poorly preserved tomb lies in a small valley to the right after the entrance gate and is seldom visited by tourists. Above the outer door Ramses VII's names are displayed with a scabbard and disc. The walls are lined with scenes from the *Book of Gates*. The most interesting area is the Burial Chamber with its granite sarcophagus still in place. The picture on the ceiling portrays the constellations and calendar of feasts while the sky goddess Nut spans the area. The inner chamber contains scenes of Ramses making offerings to the gods.

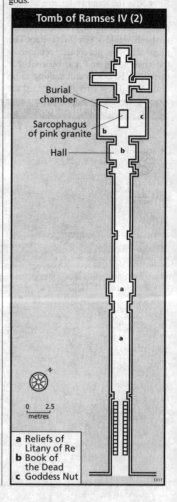

Tomb of Ramses VII (1)

Inner chamber — d

Burial chamber — e

Sarcophagus of rough granite

a Names of king
b Pharoah dressed as Osiris
c Constellations on ceiling
d Pharoah makes offerings to gods
e Scene of deity & slaves
f Book of Gates

0   2.5
metres

Tomb of Ramses IV (2)

Burial chamber

Sarcophagus of pink granite — c

Hall — b

a Reliefs of Litany of Re
b Book of the Dead
c Goddess Nut

0   2.5
metres

Ramses IV (1166-60 BC) (No 2)

Nearer is the looted tomb but not the body of Ramses IV, although his coffin was re-buried in Amenhotep II's tomb. Do not be discouraged by the Coptic and Greek graffiti because the colours of the inner tomb are truly fantastic. The first two corridors contain poorly preserved reliefs of the *Litany of Re*, while the Hall and Burial Chamber are decorated with parts of the *Book of the Dead* and Nut spans the ceiling. The sarcophagus lid shows Ramses IV protected by images of Isis and Nephthys and the pink granite sarcophagus is inscribed with magical texts. This is the only tomb for which the original plans, drawn on papyrus, now in the Turin Museum, still survive. Currently closed to the public.

Tuthmosis IV (1425-17) (No 43)

This large tomb was discovered in 1903 by Carter, but others had been there before and everything moveable had been taken. Many of the walls and pillars are undecorated and the impression is rather austere.

The well shaft has scenes of Tuthmosis paying homage to various gods and receiving the key of life from various deities including Hathor. The antechamber has illustrations of a similar theme and both have a ceiling of yellow stars on a dark blue sky.

Ramses IX (1140-23 BC) (No 6)

Situated immediately to the left of the barrier, it is of the typical later long deep style which became the established style by the end of the New Kingdom. The reliefs on the corridor walls depict Ramses before the gods and this is followed by three chambers. The four pillared Offerings

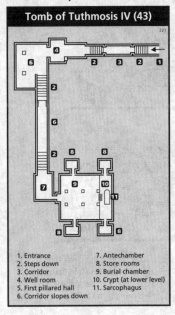

Tomb of Tuthmosis IV (43)

1. Entrance
2. Steps down
3. Corridor
4. Well room
5. First pillared hall
6. Corridor slopes down
7. Antechamber
8. Store rooms
9. Burial chamber
10. Crypt (at lower level)
11. Sarcophagus

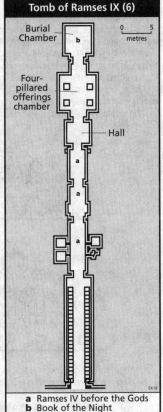

Tomb of Ramses IX (6)

Burial Chamber — b

0 — 5 metres

Four-pillared offerings chamber

Hall

a Ramses IV before the Gods
b Book of the Night

Mummification

The ritual of Mummification reached its zenith during the New Kingdom at the same time as the Luxor and Karnak temple complexes were built. It was developed because the Ancient Egyptians believed that in order for a person to reach their heavenly aspect or **Ak** in the after-life, it was essential that both their name and body survive thereby sustaining their cosmic double or **Ka** which was transported from one life to the next. In order to achieve this, the mummification ritual developed into an extremely complex means of preserving bodies. The dead were placed in tombs together with any food and utensils thought necessary to accompany the pharaoh's Ka for the journey to the underworld. Although we know the most commonly used New Kingdom mummification methods, others are still being revealed. For example a recently opened princess' tomb in Giza revealed that the body had been hollowed out and lined with very fine plaster. However, the most common mummification method found in and around the Valley of the Kings is described below.

The brain was removed through the nose and was discarded because the heart was thought to be the centre of intelligence. The entrails and organs were then extracted and stored in jars, known as Canopic jars, while the corpse was soaked in natrun salts for 40 days until it was dehydrated, when the embalming process began. In an attempt to recreate its original appearance the body was packed and then painted red for men and yellow for women, artificial eyes were inserted and the face was then made up before the body was wrapped in gum-coated linen bandages and placed in its coffin.

We recommend a visit to the Museum of Mummification in Luxor (see page 224).

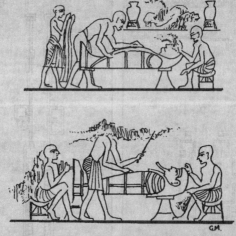

This wall painting found at Thebes shows events during mummification. Bandages are brought in to wind round the body which takes place in the centre of the first picture. The assistant at the head end is fixing the hair. In the second picture the mummy case is being drilled, painted and polished.

Chamber leads to the richly decorated Burial Room but the sarcophagus is missing. The ceiling in yellow on a dark blue background depicts a scene from the *Book of the Night* with jackals, watched by Nut, drawing the barque through the skies to the after-life.

Meneptah (1236-23 BC) (No 8)

Set back against the cliff face on the other side of the road is a long steep 80m tomb with a wonderfully preserved false Burial Chamber. The ceilings of the five corridors are decorated with flying vultures and other forbidding reliefs. Looters abandoned the

sarcophagus lid, which portrays scenes taken from the *Book of Gates* and the *Book of Am-Duat* similar to those in the hallway, in the antechamber. Steep steps lead down to the Burial Chamber where the pink granite inner sarcophagus lies, decorated with intricate designs from the *Book of Gates*. It is claimed that Meneptah was pharaoh during the time of the Exodus.

Ramses VI (1156-48 BC) (No 9)

The discovery of this tomb, which was usurped and enlarged from his predecessor Ramses V (1160-56 BC) and is one of the longest in the valley, shed light on some

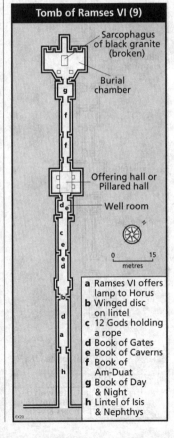

Tomb of Meneptah (8)

- Lid of Sarcophagus
- Steps
- Burial chamber
- Antechamber
- False burial chamber
- Steps

0   10
metres

EX19

Tomb of Ramses VI (9)

- Sarcophagus of black granite (broken)
- Burial chamber
- g
- f
- f
- Offering hall or Pillared hall
- Well room
- e
- d
- c
- e
- d
- b
- d
- a
- h

0   15
metres

a Ramses VI offers lamp to Horus
b Winged disc on lintel
c 12 Gods holding a rope
d Book of Gates
e Book of Caverns
f Book of Am-Duat
g Book of Day & Night
h Lintel of Isis & Nephthys

EX20

aspects of pharaonic beliefs which were not previously understood. The corridor displays reliefs from unknown and long since lost *Books*. Egyptologists were fascinated at their revelation of Pharaonic concepts, more usually associated with India, of re-incarnation birth into a new life. One does not, however, have to be an expert to appreciate the graphic designs and the colours beyond the graffiti drawings in the first two corridors.

The themes on the corridor ceilings are predominantly astronomical while the walls are largely devoted to the *Book of Gates* and the entire version of the *Book of Caverns*. In the Offerings Hall there is a relief of Ramses making libations before Osiris. The pillars are devoted to the Pharaoh making offerings to other gods including Amun. Descending deeper within the tomb the passage leading to the Burial Chamber is guarded by serpents of Nekhbet, Neith, Meretseger and Selket. Further on illustrations from the *Book of the Dead* predominate. Just before the entrance to the Burial Chamber, cryptographic texts adorn the ceiling. The Burial Chamber is supported by four pillars but two are damaged. Astronomical scenes from the *Book of Day* and the *Book of Night* cover the ceiling and the sky goddess Nut observes from above. The

Tomb of Ramses III (11)

0 5 metres

Burial chamber

Pillared hall

Realigned tomb corridor

Hathor-headed pilasters

a Lintel with disc
b Musicians, Nile boats & vases

EX21

Tomb of Ramses I (16)

Burial chamber   Sarcophagus

Corridor   a

0 5 metres

EX22

a Twelve Goddesses depicting hours of the night

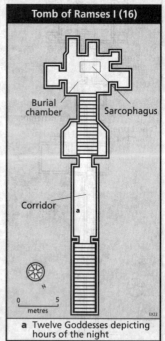

sarcophagus, shattered by grave robbers centuries ago, lies broken in the centre of the room.

Ramses III (1198-66 BC) (No 11)

This particularly beautiful and exceptionally large tomb is unusual because, unlike those of most Pharaohs, it illustrates scenes from everyday life as well as a wonderful scene of two harpists from which the tomb's other name is derived. It was originally intended for Sethnakht (1200-1185 BC), but the angle of digging was such that it coincided with another tomb and it was abandoned. Later Ramses III restarted the work by digging into the rock face from a different angle. The lintel with a disc and Re shown with a ram's head accompanied by Isis and Nephthys can be seen at the entrance. 10-side chambers – five to the left and five to the right – which were for storing objects that the Pharaoh would require after his death, lead off from the entrance corridor. Only part of this tomb has lighting. One section of the tomb is closed because of a collapsed ceiling.

Ramses I (1320-18 BC) (No 16)

Despite being the founder of the 19th Dynasty, his short reign meant that this Ramses did not merit a larger tomb but it still has beautifully ornate and sophisticated designs which are preserved on the blue-grey foundation. The granite sarcophagus is decorated with yellow while the wall relief depicts scenes of the Pharaoh with local deities and divisions from the *Book of Gates*. This is one tomb not to be missed

Tomb of Tuthmosis III (1504-1450 BC) (No 34)

Hidden away high up a side valley furthest from the main gate this is one of the oldest tombs. The approach by wooden staircase is steep. Its simple design is balanced by the interesting layout because, after the first steep corridor, it veers sharply to the left at the antechamber. The walls are lined with lists of 741 deities who are portrayed as tiny stick figures. The walls of the unusually shaped tomb chamber, like a cartouche,

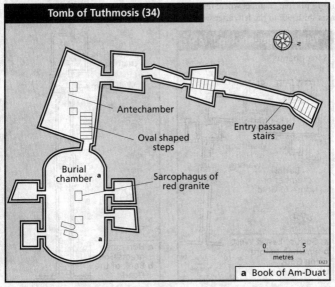

Tomb of Tuthmosis (34)

Antechamber

Oval shaped steps

Entry passage/ stairs

Burial chamber a

Sarcophagus of red granite

0   5
metres

a Book of Am-Duat

entered by a set of oval shaped steps, are dominated by sections of the *Book of Am-Duat* with an abridged version also inscribed on two pillars. The Pharaoh is depicted on one of the pillars with his mother standing behind him in his boat. A beautiful carving of Nut, effectively embracing the mummified Tuthmosis with her outstretched arms, lines the inside of the red granite sarcophagus. His mummy is in the museum of Cairo.

Amenhotep II (1450-25 BC) (No 35)

Over 90 steps lead down to the Burial Chamber which is in one of the deepest tombs in the valley. Here for once the tactics of building false chambers and sunken pits actually worked and the mummified body was found in the sarcophagus, together with another nine royal mummies which had been removed from their original tombs for safety's sake, when the tomb was opened in 1898. Amenhotep's mummy was originally kept in the tomb but after a nearby theft it was removed to the Egyptian Museum in Cairo. Steep steps and a descending corridor lead into a pillared chamber where the tomb's axis shifts 90° to the left, after which the

walls and ceiling are decorated. Further steps and a short passage lead to the enormous Burial Chamber. The delicate bluegrey of the roof is covered with clustered stars and adorned with the entire *Book of Am-Duat* on a yellow background as well as images of the Pharaoh before the gods.

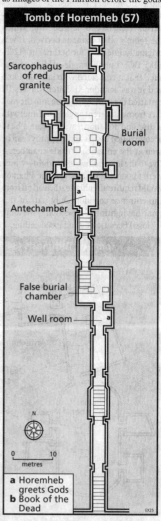

Tomb of Horemheb (57)

Sarcophagus of red granite

Burial room

Antechamber

False burial chamber

Well room

N

0   10

metres

a Horemheb greets Gods
b Book of the Dead

EX25

Tomb of Amenhotep II (35)

Sarcophagus

Ante room/ pillared chamber

Well room or Hall of waiting

Burial chamber or House of Gold

EX24

a Gods of East & West
b Pharoah before the Gods
c Ceiling of stars

0   10

metres

The sarcophagus is still in place in the centre of the pillared chamber.

Horemheb (1348-20 BC) (No 57)

After the long, steep and undecorated descent is the Well Room where the reliefs begin. Colourful scenes portray General Horemheb, who despite lacking royal blood was the effective regent during Tutankhamen's short rule and leader of the Theban counter-revolution against Akhenaten's mono-theistic religion, being introduced to Isis, Osiris, Horus, Hathor and Anubis. The scenes are repeated in the antechamber which is dominated by the huge red granite sarcophagus.

Tutankhamen (1361-52 BC) (No 62)

The tomb owes its worldwide fame not to its size or decoration, which is small and ordinary, but to the multitude of fabulous treasures that were revealed when it was opened in November 1922. The scale of the discovery was so vast that it took 10 years to fully remove, catalogue and photograph all of the 1,700 pieces.

The short entrance corridor leads to four chambers but only the Burial Chamber, which is the second on the right, is decorated. Around the room from left to right murals display Tutankhamen's coffin being moved to the shrine by mourners and officials after which his successor Ay (1352-48 BC) performs the ceremony

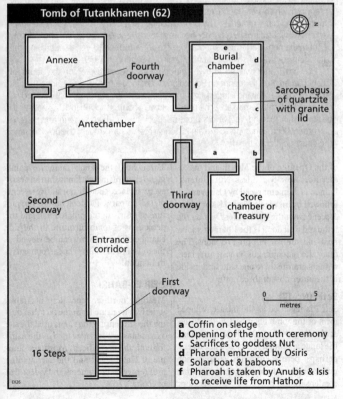

Tomb of Tutankhamen (62)

Annexe

Fourth doorway

Burial chamber

Sarcophagus of quartzite with granite lid

Antechamber

Second doorway

Third doorway

Store chamber or Treasury

Entrance corridor

First doorway

16 Steps

0   5
metres

a Coffin on sledge
b Opening of the mouth ceremony
c Sacrifices to goddess Nut
d Pharoah embraced by Osiris
e Solar boat & baboons
f Pharoah is taken by Anubis & Isis
   to receive life from Hathor

Howard Carter – discoverer of the Tomb of Tutankhamen

Howard Carter was born at Swaffham in Great Britain in 1873. When only 17 years of age he was taken on by the Archaeological Survey of Egypt under Flinders Petrie and later became inspector general of antiquities in Upper Egypt in 1899 for the Antiquities Service. Carter was responsible for excavation of the Valley of the Kings and discovered the tombs of Hatshepsut and Tuthmosis IV in 1902 for the American Theodore Davis. After a dispute with Davis he moved to Saqqara in 1903 but then left the Archaeological Service to open a studio in Luxor where in 1907 he met and began his archaeological association with the wealthy Earl of Carnarvon, whose own efforts at excavation had failed. When Theodore Davis gave up his concession to excavate in the Valley of the Kings in 1914 Carter, backed by the Earl of Carnarvon, took it up and continued digging, locating six more royal tombs. In 1922, Carter's last year of sponsorship by Lord Carnarvon, he came across a set of remains of workmen's houses built across a stairway to a tomb. Howard Carter waited for Lord Carnarvon to arrive at the site and then dug away the remaining rubble to reveal the entrance to the Tomb of Tutankhamen. Eventually Carter's men cleared the way to the ante-room which was found ransacked in antiquity but full of interesting cloths, furniture and other materials. The burial chamber that Carter found was once again packed with valuable objects but none more so than the gold-laden coffins and mummy of Tutankhamen. Carter remained at the site for a further 10 years supervising the cataloguing activity of so great a find. He died in London in 1939.

Howard Carter will be known principally as the discoverer of the Tomb of Tutankhamen. But his imprint on Egyptology went far deeper. He was among the first archaeologists, following Flinders Petrie, to apply scientific principles to the recording of his excavations. Remarkably, the treasure trove of objects found in 1922 has still to be studied in full and, to Carter's great disappointment, there were in any case no parchments or manuscripts to explain historical events surrounding the boy king and the court politics of the day.

of the Opening of the Mouth and makes sacrifices to sky-goddess Nut. Tutankhamen is then embraced by Osiris and is followed by his black-wigged Ka or spirit. A scene from the *Book of Am-Duat* on the left hand wall depicts the Pharaoh's solar boat and sun-worshipping baboons. The quartzite sarcophagus is still in place, with its granite lid to one side, and inside is the outermost of three coffins.

Seti I (No 17)

Seti I is regarded as the most developed form of the tomb chambers in the Valley of the Kings. At some 100m it is among the longest, though it is closed at present, perhaps permanently for conservation purposes since its decorations suffer from condensation produced by visitors.

Throughout the tomb there are paintings/reliefs of fine workmanship on nearly every surface, though not all were completed. In particular look out for the picture of Osiris in the pillared hall and the depictions of tomb furniture in the side chamber. The mummy can be viewed in the museum in Cairo. The sarcophagus is in London.

DEIR EL-BAHRI

Meaning 'northern monastery' in Arabic, it derives its name from the fact that during the 7th century the Copts used the site as a monastery. It is now used as the name for both the magnificent **Mortuary Temple of Hatshepsut** and the surrounding area (entry E£12, cameras and videos free of charge).

Queen Hatshepsut was not only the only female Pharaoh to reign over ancient Egypt (1503-1482 BC) but also one of its most fascinating personalities. She was Tuthmosis I's (1525-12 BC) daughter and was married to his successor Tuthmosis II (1512-04 BC) but was widowed before she could bear a son. Rather than give up power to the son of one of her husband's minor wives she assumed the throne first as regent for the infant Tuthmosis III but then as queen. Tuthmosis III, who later hugely expanded the Egyptian Kingdom

The 'Lost' Tomb

Explored and looted decades ago, dismissed as uninteresting by Egyptologists and used as a dump for debris from the excavation of Tutankhamen's tomb, Tomb 5 in the Valley of the Kings was about to become a car park. However the final exploration in May 1995 unearthed a major discovery, certainly the largest and most complex tomb ever found in Egypt and possibly the resting place of up to 50 sons of Ramses II. Excavations are expected to take at least another 5 years, but the tomb's unusual design is already apparent. Instead of plunging down into the steep hillside, Tomb 5 is more like an octopus with at least 62 chambers branching off from the central structure. There may be more chambers on a lower level where it is hoped some of the mummies may still be entombed. No treasure is expected, robbery of the tomb was documented as early as 1150 BC, but the elaborate carvings and inscriptions along with the thousands of artifacts littering the floor, including beads and fragments of jars used to store the organs of the deceased, nevertheless offer a wealth of information about the reign of one of Ancient Egypt's most important kings. Egyptologists have never before found a multiple burial of a pharaoh's children and in most cases have no idea what happened to them. This find thus raises the question of whether Ramses buried his children in a unique way or that archaelogists have overlooked a major type of royal tomb. And where are Ramses' dozens of daughters? Are they buried in a similar mausoleum perhaps in the Valley of the Queens?

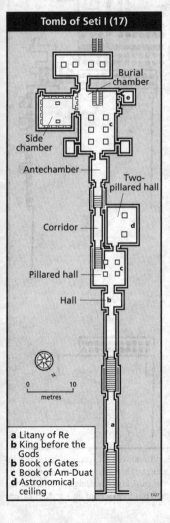

Tomb of Seti I (17)

- Burial chamber
- e
- Side chamber
- c
- Antechamber
- Two-pillared hall
- d
- Corridor
- Pillared hall
- c
- Hall
- b
- a

N

0   10
metres

a Litany of Re
b King before the Gods
b Book of Gates
c Book of Am-Duat
d Astronomical ceiling

EX27

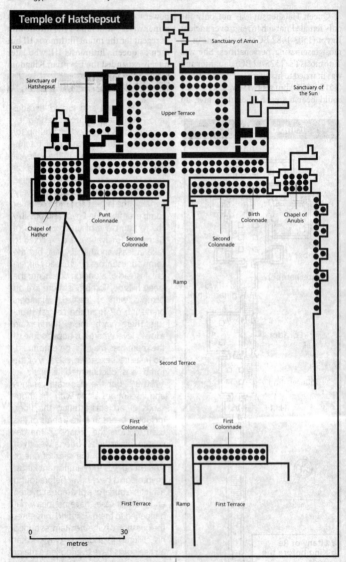

Temple of Hatshepsut

EX28

Sanctuary of Amun

Sanctuary of Hatshepsut

Sanctuary of the Sun

Upper Terrace

Punt Colonnade

Second Colonnade

Birth Colonnade

Chapel of Anubis

Chapel of Hathor

Second Colonnade

Ramp

Second Terrace

First Colonnade

First Colonnade

First Terrace

Ramp

First Terrace

0   30

metres

and was the first imperialist, was only able to assume office when Hatshepsut died 21 years later in 1482 BC. He naturally resented her usurping his position and removed all traces of her reign including her cartouches. Consequently the truth about her reign and the temples she built both here and at Karnak was only fully appreciated by archaeologists relatively recently. As a woman she legitimized her rule by being depicted with the short kilt and the false beard worn by the male pharaohs.

Hatshepsut's imposing temple which was only dug out of the sand in 1905 was designed and built in the Theban hills over an 8-year period between the 8th-16th year of her reign, by **Senenmut** who was her architect, steward, favourite courtier and possibly the father of her daughter Neferure. The temple's three rising terraces, the lower two terraces lined with fountains and myrrh trees, were originally linked to the River Nile by an avenue of sphinxes which was aligned exactly to Karnak. A pair of lions stood at the top and another at the bottom of the ramp which leads from the ground level first terrace over the first colonnade to the large second terrace.

The scenes on the restored left hand south side of the first colonnade columns depict the transportation of the two obelisks from Aswan to Karnak temple. Behind its columns on the right hand north side is a relief defaced by Tuthmosis III in which Amun can be seen receiving an offering of four calves from Hatshepsut whose face has been erased. The original stairs from the second terrace to the second colonnade have now been replaced by a ramp. Hatshepsut's famous voyage to **Punt**, which was known as 'God's Land' by the ancient Egyptians, and various texts to Amun are depicted on the left hand or south side of the second colonnade. Voyages to Punt, now believed to be modern-day Somalia, had been undertaken since the Old Kingdom (2686-2181 BC) in order to find the incense and myrrh which was required for temple rituals.

Further to the left is the large **Chapel of Hathor** where the goddess is depicted both as a cow and as a human with cow's ears suckling Hatshepsut. This area was badly damaged because Tuthmosis removed most but not all traces of Hatshep-

sut and Akhenaten later erased Amun. The reliefs on the colonnade to the right hand or north side of the ramp portray Hatshepsut's apparent divine conception and birth. She claimed that her father was the supreme god Amun who visited her mother Ahmose disguised as Tuthmosis I just as Amenhotep III (1417-1379 BC) made similar claims later on (see Luxor Temple, page 220). Further to the right is the fluted colonnade and the colourfully decorated **Chapel of Anubis**, who is portrayed in the customary way as a man with a jackal mask, but the images of Hatshepsut are once again defaced.

The ramp leading to the smaller and recently restored upper terrace (unfortunately closed) is decorated with emblems of Upper and Lower Egypt with vultures' heads guarding the entrance. There are suggestions that this was originally a Hypostyle Hall and not a terrace. The columns were originally round but were squared off by Tuthmosis III in an attempt to replace her name with his own and that of his father Tuthmosis II. Beyond the Osiride portico to the left is the **Sanctuary of Hatshepsut** with its enormous altar and to the right is the **Sanctuary of the Sun**. In the middle at the back of the whole temple is the **Sanctuary of Amun** which is dug into the cliff-face and is therefore connected to the Valley of the Kings which lies on the other side of the hill. Hatshepsut's burial chamber lies underneath but it is unclear whether she was actually ever buried there.

TOMBS OF THE NOBLES

While the pharaoh's tombs were hidden away in the Valley of the Kings and were dug deep into the valley rock those of the most important nobles were ostentatiously built at surface level overlooking the temples of Luxor and Karnak across the river. Their shrines were highly decorated but the poor quality limestone made carved reliefs impossible so the façades were painted on plaster. Freed from the restricted subject matter of the royal

Tomb decoration - offerings of wine

tombs the artists and craftsmen dedicated less space to rituals from the *Books* and more to representations of everyday life and their impressions of the after-life. Because, unlike the royal tombs, they were exposed to the elements many of the nobles' shrines have deteriorated badly over time. Although some were subsequently used as store rooms and even accommodation others are still in relatively good condition and give a clear impression of how they must originally have looked.

The tombs of the nobles are found at a variety of sites throughout Egypt but no better preserved than on the West Bank of the River Nile at Luxor. Two groups of tombs are worth visiting for their wealth of vernacular paintings – quite as interesting as the formal sculptures of the great tombs of the Kings and Queens. The tombs of Rekhmire, Sennofer, Ramoza, Userhat, Khaemet, Nakht and Mena are located in the area known as Shaikh abd al-Qurna, north and northwest of the Ramesseum and the tombs of Sennedjem and Inherkhau are just above Deir al-Medina, an archaeological site where the housing of the workmen on the West Bank has been excavated. If time is limited, see the tomb of either Sennedjem or Sennofer for a taste of this form of art. The entry fee for each pair of tombs is E£12. There are cafes and shops throughout the area, which also still has local modern village housing – inhabitants sell bric-a-brac and genuine artefacts to passing tourists.

Tomb of Nakht (No 52)

Set in the entrance of the tomb is an interesting display of representations of the statue of Nakht as originally photographed together with hunting and offer-

ing scenes and a plan of the tomb. Inside the tomb is well lit and the decoration protected by glass screens. The tomb is small and is best visited early when not many visitors are about.

Nakht was Tuthmosis IV's astronomer, vineyard keeper and chief of his granaries. He and his wife Tawi were buried is this small shrine with its well preserved and colourful antechamber which depicts the harvest in intricate detail. On its west wall in the centre is a painting illustrating what is known of Nakht's life together with the goddess of the west. On the left of the far wall is a depiction of a funeral banquet is which Nakht, his top half having been badly defaced, is shown seated beside his wife with a cat eating a fish at his feet while being entertained by a blind harpist and beautiful dancing girls. Opposite, on the east wall, in one of the most individual of paintings is grape picking where peasants are shown treading grapes while empty wine jars await filling. Here the ceiling is brightly deco-

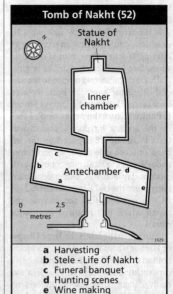

Tomb of Nakht (52)

Statue of Nakht

Inner chamber

c

b

Antechamber d

a

e

0   2.5
metres

a Harvesting
b Stele - Life of Nakht
c Funeral banquet
d Hunting scenes
e Wine making

rated with designs representing woven mats. The marshland scenes on the right-hand, south-facing section of the ante-chamber are exceptionally fine, with fish wonderfully depicted. In the inner chamber there is a small niche with a statue of Nakht bearing a stele with a hymn to Re. Unfortunately the original was lost in 1917 when the SS Arabia, which was transporting it to the USA, was torpedoed by the Germans in the Atlantic. There is a deep shaft leading to the inaccessible burial chamber.

Tomb of Ramoza (No 55)

Ramoza was Visir and Governor of Thebes at the beginning of the Akhenaten's heretical rule in 1379 BC and the tomb illustrates the transition in style between the worship of Amun and Aten (see Tell el-Amarna, page 180). The impressive and excellent quality workmanship of the shrine is probably because it was built by Ramoza's brother Amenhotep who was the chief of works at the family's home-town of Memphis. Only

the main columned hall can be entered, since the inner hall and false sarcophagus area are separated. This is one of the few tombs where the forecourt is still pre-served and the central entrance leads into a broad columned hall. The tomb was carved out of solid limestone and all the decoration carved on polished rock. On the wall to the right are depictions of Ramoza with his wife and opposite on the back wall Akhenaten and Nefertiti stand at their palace windows giving a golden chain to Ramoza. On the left hand wall are scenes of Ramoza and his wife worshipping Osiris. Beyond is an undecorated inner hall with eight columns and the shrine at the far end. There is a second gap on the left of the end wall leading to the actual sarcophagus chamber. Within each hall are the gated entrances to dark and dangerous tunnels which end with a 15m drop to the burial chamber.

Tomb of Userhat (No 56)

Userhat who, in the reign of Amenhotep II (1450-25 BC), was a royal tutor and scribe was buried in a small but pinkishly decorated tomb which was partially damaged by early Christian hermits. At the extremity of the outer hall on the left is a small stela showing the purification by opening of the mouth. At the opposite end of this hall look out for the representation

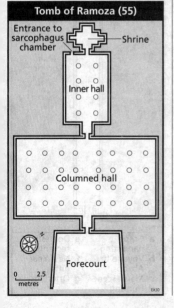

Tomb of Ramoza (55)

Entrance to sarcophagus chamber — Shrine

Inner hall

Columned hall

Forecourt

0   2,5
metres

EX30

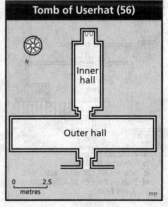

Tomb of Userhat (56)

N

Inner hall

Outer hall

0   2,5
metres

EX31

of the double python, a symbol of protection. **NB** The interesting representation of rural life on the left on the way into the hall, the façade of the snake-headed harvest goddess Renehat on the right of the back wall, and a realistic hunting scene in the desert on the left of the inner hall.

Khaemhet (No 57)

Khaemhet, another royal scribe and overseer of the granaries in the period Amenhotep III in the 18th Dynasty, adopted a raised relief system for the carved an painted decoration of his tomb-chapel which is well worth seeing for its variety. The tomb is entered through a courtyard off which there are other tomb entrances largely blocked off. The Khaemhet tomb is made up of two transverse chambers joined by a wide passage. In the outer chamber there are rich reliefs depicting rural scenes, some of the originals now only to be seen in Berlin. The passage has funeral scenes (south wall) and the voyage to Abydos (north wall), while both the transverse chambers, though mainly the far one, have statue niches of Khaemhet and his family. There is a small room annexed to the inner transverse chamber, possibly added later.

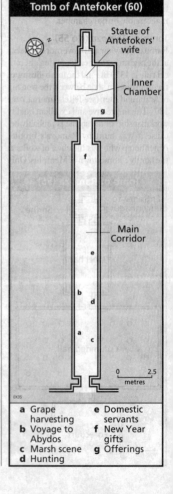

Tomb of Khaemhet (57)

- Inner chamber
- Passage
- Outer chamber
- Stele of jars
- Entrance with tombs

0   2.5
metres

EX40

a	Funeral Scenes
b	Voyage to Abydos
c	Scenes of farming activities
d	Statue niches of Khaemhet & his family

Tomb of Antefoker (60)

- Statue of Antefokers' wife
- Inner Chamber
- g
- f
- Main Corridor
- e
- b
- d
- a
- c

0   2.5
metres

EX35

a	Grape harvesting	e	Domestic servants
b	Voyage to Abydos	f	New Year gifts
c	Marsh scene	g	Offerings
d	Hunting		

Antefoker (No 60)

Antefoker was the Governor of Thebes and his tomb-chapel deserves a visit. The tomb is structured as a main corridor which carries a series of scenes of farming, the life of the marshes and hunting at the time of the 12th Dynasty at the time of Senosert 1. Domestic scenes of servants and gifts for the New Year are all contained within the main corridor. The inner chamber has figures carrying offerings and in front of the niche at the head of the tomb is a statue of Antefoker's wife.

Tomb of Mena (No 69)

This tomb has been undergoing restoration and, although Mena's eyes have been gouged out by rivals to prevent him seeing in the afterlife, the paintings are in good condition. He was an 18th Dynasty scribe or inspector of the estates in both Upper and Lower Egypt. In particular visit this tomb to see the following items: on the end wall on the right hand side of the outer hall is a depiction of a series of gods, notably, Hathor and Isis. On the adjacent wall is a fine painting of Mena and his wife giving flowers. Opposite is as vignette of the younger members of the family making gifts to their father. In the left hand limb of the outer hall note the depiction of Mena's wife in an elegant dress and jewellery as she stands with her husband before Osiris. In

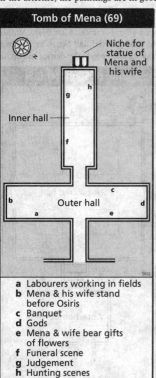

Tomb of Mena (69)

Niche for statue of Mena and his wife

Inner hall

Outer hall

- **a** Labourers working in fields
- **b** Mena & his wife stand before Osiris
- **c** Banquet
- **d** Gods
- **e** Mena & wife bear gifts of flowers
- **f** Funeral scene
- **g** Judgement
- **h** Hunting scenes

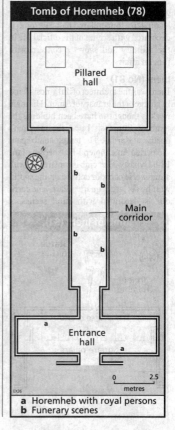

Tomb of Horemheb (78)

Pillared hall

Main corridor

Entrance hall

0   2.5
metres

- **a** Horemheb with royal persons
- **b** Funerary scenes

the inner hall there is a niche for a statue of Mena and his wife. Elsewhere in the inner hall are well-preserved paintings of the gods, presentation of gifts, funeral and judgement scenes. Look out for the finely executed paintings of hunting and fishing scenes on the right hand wall close to the statue niche, which are extremely well done with crocodiles, wild cats and fish. The ceilings are brightly coloured and represent woven cloth.

Horemheb (No 78)

Horemheb was a scribe of the recruits in the reign of Tuthmosis III-Amenhotep III. His tomb-chapel is made up of a rectangular entrance hall and a main corridor leading to a four-pillared hall. His tomb is decorated with scenes of his official life in the military and shows a concern with funeral affairs.

Ineni (No 81)

Ineni was the architect of Tuthmosis I and in charge of the granary of Amun. His main work is thought to have been building the tomb of Tuthmosis I and the monarch's obelisk at Karnak. The temple-tomb spans the period Amenhotep I-Hatshepsut of the 18th Dynasty. The tomb is constructed with a transverse corridor defined on the southwest by six large square pillars. The corridor is decorated with rural scenes of farming and hunting. The inner chamber has the normal offering, banqueting and funeral procession. Additionally at the northern end it has statue niches for Ineni, his wife and family.

Tomb of Sennofer (No 96)

At the time of Amenhotep II (1450-25 BC) amongst other positions Sennofer was Mayor of Thebes, overseer of the granaries and gardens, and chief vintner. In the antechamber of this tomb there is an excellently clear set of diagrams etched on the glass showing the layout of the tomb and its decorations, accompanied by explanations. Look at these first. The entire tomb has discrete electric lighting. The ceiling is covered in illustrations of vines and the tomb is known locally as the 'Tomb of Vines'. The antechamber is rough and irregular in shape. Pass into the pillared main chamber under a low beam. Within the four pillared hall Sennofer is shown making offerings to the deities and on his

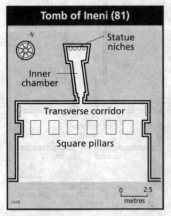

Tomb of Ineni (81)

N

Statue niches

Inner chamber

Transverse corridor

Square pillars

0   2.5
metres

EX39

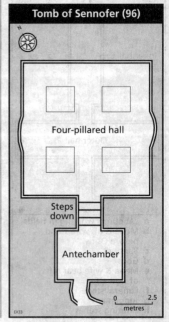

Tomb of Sennofer (96)

N

Four-pillared hall

Steps down

Antechamber

0   2.5
metres

EX33

Sennofer and his wife Meryt

journey into the after-life he is accompanied by his wife Meryt. A double figure of the jackal-headed Anubis looks down on the whole chamber from above the entrance. There is a false door painted on the east (right hand) wall with the god Anubis, the jackal and the goddess Isis. Facing the entrance arch look to the right for a depiction of Sennofer's wife, son and daughters. On the north (end) wall Sennofer and his wife cross to the west bank of the river by boat, accompanied by a funeral offering of wine and food. On the west wall are the goddess Hathor and Osiris in dark colours of the dead. On the same wall to the left is the funeral furniture for use in the after-life. There is a small niche for a statue now absent. Above note the vultures with wings spread for protection of the tomb. On the pillars are formal representations of mummification, cleansing rites and offerings.

Tomb of Rekhmire (No 100)

This crucifix-shaped tomb should not be missed because its highly decorative paintings and inscriptions reveal some of

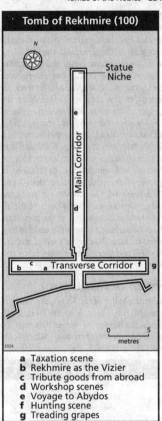

Tomb of Rekhmire (100)

N

Statue Niche

Main Corridor

e

d

b c a Transverse Corridor f g

0   5
metres

a Taxation scene
b Rekhmire as the Vizier
c Tribute goods from abroad
d Workshop scenes
e Voyage to Abydos
f Hunting scene
g Treading grapes

the secrets of Egypt's judicial, taxation and foreign policy at that time. Rekhmire, who came from a long line of viziers and governors, was the visir at the time of Tuthmosis III's death in 1450 BC when he then served his successor Amenhotep II. The tomb is in good order, though lit only by a hand-held mirrors (held by the man at the door who will require a tip), which means that the vision is only fair. Walking left or clockwise around the whole tomb from the entrance wall of the transverse corridor one sees – Egyptian taxes, Rekhmire being installed as visir, foreign tributes being received from Punt, Crete,

Nubia, Syria and Kush, then along the main corridor the inspection of the various workshops, the voyage to Abydos, the various gods of the dead, and the end niche which would have contained a statue of Rekhmire. The ceiling has deteriorated but some of the original plaster work remains, with a continuous line down the centre of the main north-pointing chamber. Look out too for the splendid marsh/woodland scene which, with a small lake and trees, has a warmth and realism to it that contrasts nicely with the formal and predictable decoration in praise of the gods (notably Osiris) and Tuthmosis III. On the way out along the other corridor wall are pictures of the after-world and then, back in the transverse hall, illustrations of hunting and fowling, wine-making, Rakhmire's wives and ancestors, and finally more taxes being collected.

VALLEY OF THE QUEENS

Like the Valley of the Kings, the Valley of the Queens, which is about 3 km south from the tombs of the nobles, can be reached via another road which cuts northwest through the main northeast-

southwest escarpment. It was once known as the 'Place of Beauty' and was used as a burial site for officials long before the queens and their offspring, who had previously been buried with their husbands, began to be buried there in the 19th Dynasty (1320-1200 BC). It contains more than 80 tombs but many are still unidentified. The tombs are generally quite simple with a long corridor, several antechambers branching off and the burial chamber at the end. The most famous tomb is that of Ramses II's wife Nefertari newly reopened to the public.

At present four tombs are open to the public; one ticket costing E£12 will give entry to tombs 44, 52, 55 and separate ticket costing E£100 for tomb 66 (Nefertari). See page 232 for ticket purchase information.

Queen Sit-re (No 38)

Queen Sit-re's tomb-chapel is situated in the south quadrant of the Valley of the Queens. The tomb is normally closed and official permission must be sought to gain entry. The Queen was the wife of Ramses I and is amongst the earliest tomb-chapels built in the valley. The elemental structure

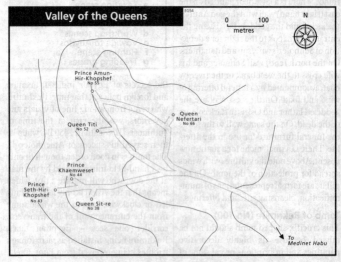

Valley of the Queens

EG54

0   100 metres

N

Prince Amun-Hir-Khopshef
No 55

Queen Nefertari
No 66

Queen Titi
No 52

Prince Khaemweset
No 44

Prince Seth-Hir-Khopshef
No 43

Queen Sit-re
No 38

To Medinet Habu

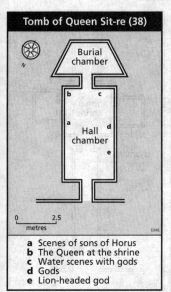

Tomb of Queen Sit-re (38)

a Scenes of sons of Horus
b The Queen at the shrine
c Water scenes with gods
d Gods
e Lion-headed god

comprises an outer hall chamber and an unfinished burial chamber. The decorations include in clockwise order in the hall chamber scenes of the sons of Horus, the queen at a shrine, a water scene with gods, gods and Lion-headed god.

Prince Seth-Hir-Khopshef (No 43)

Prince Seth-Hir-Khopshef was a son of Ramses III who died of small pox when very young. He was ceremonial charioteer of the great stables. His tomb-chapel is decorated with a series of scenes of the gods, clockwise from the entrance to the corridor including Ramses III and Seth-Hir-Khopshef in front of Osiris and other deities, the sons of Horus, Osiris enthroned, Ramses III and Prince Seth-Hir-Khopshef offering gifts, Ramses and the prince before a set of deities. At present this tomb is closed.

Prince Khaemweset (No 44)

Although the tomb is dedicated to one of Ramses III's (1198-66 BC) young sons who died of smallpox, it is dominated by the pharaoh himself. The reliefs depict the

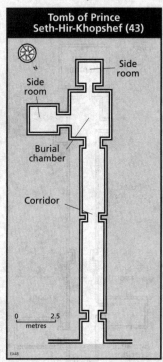

Tomb of Prince Seth-Hir-Khopshef (43)

young boy being led to the underworld by his father who is offering sacrifices and helping his son through the underworld and the judgement of Osiris to the Fields of Yaru.

Queen Titi (No 52)

Queen Titi was the daughter, wife and mother of a succession of the 20th Dynasty (1200-1085 BC) pharaohs called Ramses but it is uncertain to which one she was married. Although the tomb is open to the public the reliefs are faded and damaged. A corridor leads to a square shrine which branches into three antechambers with the badly preserved burial chamber on the left being dedicated to the four sons of Horus and Osiris. The central chamber features the Queen before the gods and the

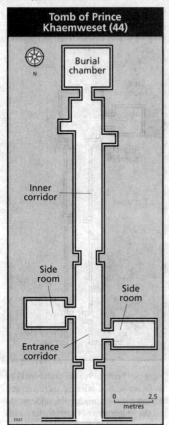

Tomb of Prince Khaemweset (44)

Burial chamber

Inner corridor

Side room

Side room

Entrance corridor

0   2.5
metres

EX47

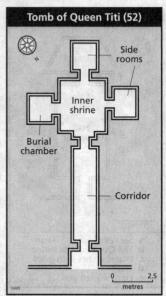

Tomb of Queen Titi (52)

Side rooms

Inner shrine

Burial chamber

Corridor

0   2.5
metres

EX45

shrine is dominated by animal deities with pictures of jackals, baboons and guardian lions. The right hand chamber is the best preserved and depicts the tree goddess and Hathor as a the cow goddess rejuvenating the Queen with Nile water.

Prince Amun-Hir-Khopshef (No 55)

Prince Amun-Hir-Khopshef was the eldest son of Ramses III who like his younger brother Seth-Hir-Khopshef (43) died young. Descent to the tomb is via a stairway into the main hall from which there is a corridor to the burial chamber. The tomb is elaborately decorated with fine illustrations which remain in good condition. The scenes show excerpts from the *Book of the Gates* and Ramses III leading his son in a course around the stations of the gods. An oddity is the sarcophagus which contained the remains of a foetus, thought to be one of the prince's stillborn infants. This foetus is displayed in a glass cabinet in one corner of the burial chamber.

Nefertari's Tomb (No 66)

The most famous and outstanding tomb is that of Nefertari, the favourite wife of Ramses II, which in November 1995 was opened to the public for the first time since its discovery in 1904. Even the most tomb resistent visitor to Egypt should try to see this for the bright clear paintings are a sheer delight. One of the most sophisticated pieces of artwork created during the New Kingdom, it stands, like the Taj Mahal, as a final testament to a king's love for his wife. Small compared to the tombs in the Valley of the Kings, its 430 sq m of fine reliefs were nearly completely destroyed

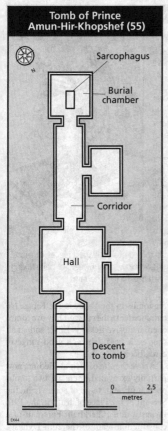

Tomb of Prince Amun-Hir-Khopshef (55)

- Sarcophagus
- Burial chamber
- Corridor
- Hall
- Descent to tomb

0 — 2.5 metres

EX44

Tomb of Nefertari (66)

N

- Side room
- Burial chamber
- Side room
- Side room
- Staircase to burial chamber
- Main outer chamber
- Flanking chamber
- Entrance corridor

0 — 2.5 metres

EX43

by flood damage and leaching of the salt crystals in the tomb's limestone bedrock which caused the plaster to buckle and crack. After a US$6mn 6-year restoration project by the Getty Conservation Institute, the tomb is ready for public display. But in order to control humidity levels, only 200 visitors are allowed inside per day. Separate tickets are required from a separate booth (E£100 or E£50 for students).

The entrance corridor leads to a main outer chamber and a small flanking chamber, the former dominated by the image of a smiling Nefertari holding hands with

Horus and being acknowledged by Isis, the vivid colours splendidly preserved. The stress here is on her beauty rather than good works. The staircase descends to the burial chamber and three small side rooms. Among the immensely rich illustrations to be seen are Queen Nefertari bearing gifts and the Queen hand in hand with the goddess Hathor and the god Horus. Unfortunately the downstairs reliefs are badly damaged but it is still possible to see that in the burial chamber Nefertari, offering sacrifices to the gods, becomes

Calling on Nefertari

Although this tomb was discovered in 1904 the delicate condition of the tomb walls and fragile nature of the ornate reliefs have prevented Nefertari from receiving visitors. At last the tomb is open but visitors are restricted to 200 per day. Visitors may be asked to wear masks to reduce moisture in the atmosphere and shoe pads to protect the stone from wear and tear. Nefertari was the favourite wife of Ramses II and her tomb was decorated with 430 sq m of the finest wall paintings ever produced. Sodium chloride seeped into the plaster which covered the limestone walls and salt crystals developed. As they grew in the damp atmosphere they forced the painted plaster off the walls and the murals fell to the floor in fragments. With the help of photographs from the museum in Turin and those taken by

Queen Nefertari

Ernesto Schiaparelli who discovered the tomb the carefully cleaned pieces of mural were replaced on the wall, a huge Egyptian jigsaw. Now, after 6 years of painstaking labour and the outlay of over US$2mn, Nefertari is fit to entertain.

solemn and her fashionable clothes are replaced by more sombre attire. The wall texts are chapters from the *Book of the Dead*.

PRIVATE TOMBS

QURNAT MURAI

Amenhoptep (Huy) (No 40)

Amenhoptep (Huy) was the Viceroy of Kush in the reign of Tutankhamen. The tomb-chapel is cruciform with a transverse chamber and an unfinished or damaged inner chamber. The decoration of the transverse chamber is very pleasing, showing scenes of Nubians offering gifts to Tutankhamen, and Amenhoptep is depicted among the Nubians and also with Tutankhamen. Almost all the worthwhile decorations are in the west wing of the transverse chamber.

DEIR EL-MEDINA

Here the neat remains of the village can be examined. The original occupants were the workers who excavated and decorated

the tombs in the Valley of the Kings. No entrance fee to the village. Only two tombs open, inclusive ticket is E£12, and small shop sells cold drinks, a good range of cards/book.

Above the site of Deir al-Medina, now partially excavated, there are two tombs open at present, those of Sennedjem, the Servant of the Place of Truth in the 19th Dynasty, and Inherkhau, Foreman of a construction team of the 20th Dynasty. Both, but especially the tomb of Sennedjem, are beautifully preserved with outstanding paintings to be seen. Normally guides are not allowed to conduct their groups into the comparatively small chambers.

Sennedjem (No 1)

Sennedjem's tomb was found undamaged in 1886 by Gaston Maspero, then head of the Antiquities Service. It is a small, simple, rectangular burial chamber, 6m by 3m, with narrow stairs leading into it and a slightly domed ceiling. On discovery it held intact the mummies of Sennedjem,

Agricultural scene from Tomb of Sennedjem

his wife, son and two daughters-in-law. There was a handsome range of funeral materials. Unfortunately, the mummies and funerary objects were dispersed across the museums of the world so that a comprehensive view is no longer possible. The wall decorations shown in the burial chamber and now protected by glass are first rate in colour, style and present condition and are worth travelling to see. The domed ceiling is wonderfully decorated with snakes, pictures of the gods and a golden orb. Clockwise round the chamber are hunting/forest scenes in the lower register and above a mummy on a bier with the goddesses Isis and Nephthys protecting it. Sennedjem and his wife stand before the gods and, the masterpiece of the tomb, the body of Sennedjem lying on an

Tomb of Amenhoptep (40)

EX41

Inner chamber

N

Transverse chamber

a Hymn to Ptah

0   2.5
metres

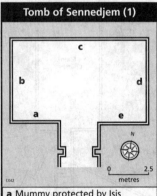

Tomb of Sennedjem (1)

c

b   d

a   e

N

EX42

0   2.5
metres

a Mummy protected by Isis and Nephthys
b Sennedjem and wife before the gods
c Sennedjem embalmed by Anubis
d Paintings: barque of Re (above) and life in eternity (below)
e Sennedjem and wife facing the Deities of the Gates

ornamental bier is embalmed by Anubis opposite to the entrance. On the east wall is a double painting of the barque of Re above and a view of life in eternity below. The south wall (right of the door) shows Sennedjem and his wife, Iyneferty, face the Deities of the Gates. The usual offering scenes are shown. Of great appeal is the depiction of the tree of life from which a goddess is appearing bearing an offering table.

Inherkhau (No 359)

This is another brilliantly painted tomb in excellent order and accessible down a steep flight of steps to a small ante-room with a low ceiling into a chamber with decorated plastered walls bearing coloured paintings, now considerably damaged by efflorescence and exfoliation of the limestone rock. From this chamber are two exits, one into a rough rock-cut burial chamber. The second exit leads down steps under a low lintel to the main decorated chamber itself. This room is vaulted and is approximately 5m by 2m. On the left hand side is a painting of a stork, the god Anubis and a fine depiction of the family with hair left down in funeral form. At the north end, slightly damaged is a full-scale representation of Inherkhau and his family with offerings. The right hand side wall also carries more pictures of Inherkhau's family, children naked and with hair curled round their ears to denote immaturity. The ceiling is vaulted and painted in bright colours – ochre, yellow, gold, bearing cartouches and a detailed list of events in the life of Inherkhau.

OTHER TEMPLES AND SITES

The Ramesseum

While most tourists confine themselves to the two valleys and Hatshepsut's temple there are a number of other interesting West Bank ruins closer to the river. Of these amongst the most impressive was the Ramesseum, a 19th century name for what was effectively a state cult-temple, on the opposite side of the road near the tombs of the nobles. Today only scattered remains and faded reliefs suggest the great temple which once stood there and reportedly rivalled the splendours of the temples at Abu Simbel.

Ramses II (1304-1237 BC) built this mortuary temple, on the consecrated site of Seti I's (1318-04 BC) much smaller but collapsing temple, in order to impress his subjects but he failed to take account of the annual flooding of the River Nile. The result was that this enormous tribute to Amun and himself was less eternal than he expected!

The first two pylons collapsed and only a single colonnade remains of what would have been the First Courtyard. On its south side is a palace where Ramses stayed when he attended religious festivals on the West Bank. In front of the ruins of the Second Pylon is the base of the enormous colossus of Ramses which was originally over 17m high but it is now

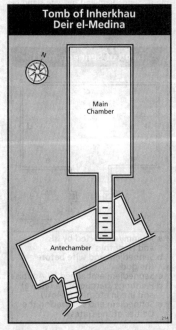

Tomb of Inherkhau
Deir el-Medina

N

Main Chamber

Antechamber

much eroded and various parts of his anatomy are scattered throughout the world's museums. The forefinger alone measures more than 1m in length. The upper part of the body crashed into the second court where the head and torso remain. Three smaller colossi stood next to the three stairways leading to the Hypostyle Hall but only one fragmented one now remains.

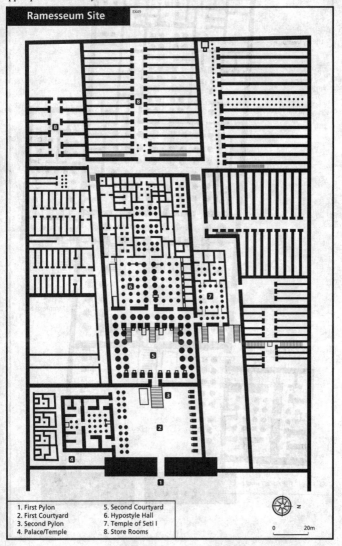

Ramesseum Site EK49

1. First Pylon
2. First Courtyard
3. Second Pylon
4. Palace/Temple
5. Second Courtyard
6. Hypostyle Hall
7. Temple of Seti I
8. Store Rooms

0   20m

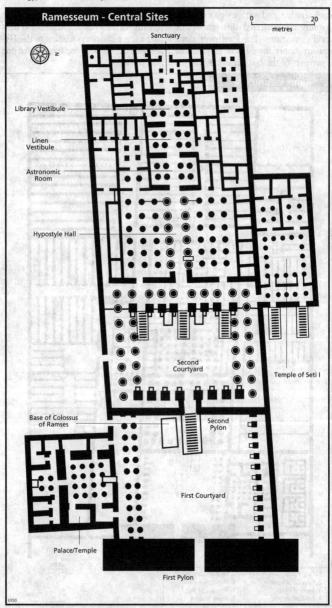

Ramesseum - Central Sites

0   20
metres

N

Sanctuary

Library Vestibule

Linen Vestibule

Astronomic Room

Hypostyle Hall

Temple of Seti I

Second Courtyard

Base of Colossus of Ramses

Second Pylon

First Courtyard

Palace/Temple

First Pylon

EX50

Although it is now roofless, 29 of the original 48 columns still stand in the Hypostyle Hall. The centre of the roof would have been higher than the sides in order to allow shafts of sunlight to enter the hall. To the left of the entrance is the famous relief of the Egyptian victory over the Hittite city of Dapur in the battle of Kadesh. Around the base of the west walls some of Ramses' many sons are depicted. At the far end of the hall a central door leads into the Astronomical Room renowned for its ceiling which is illustrated with the oldest known 12 months calendar. Because the temple was dedicated to Amun it is thought to represent a solar year. Two other vestibules, a library and a linen room, lead to the ruined sanctuary which is the temple's highest point.

The Mortuary Temple of Ramses III

The Mortuary Temple of Ramses III (1198-1166 BC), which lies west of the Colossi of Memnon and south of the Valley of the Queens at a place known in Arabic as **Medinet Habu**, was modelled on that built by his forefather Ramses II (1304-27) near by. It is second only to Karnak in terms of its size and complexity and within the enormous enclosing walls are a palace, a Nilometer and several smaller shrines with some pre-dating the temple itself.

When Thebes was threatened, such as during the 20th Dynasty's Libyan invasions, the enclosing walls sheltered the entire population. Although Ramses III named his temple the 'House of a Million Years', the smaller shrine that already occupied the site next to the south enclosure walls was in use long after the main temple shrine had fallen into disuse.

The small temple, which was constructed by Hatshepsut but later altered by Tuthmosis III who, as ever, erased her cartouche, was built on a platform from which there are good views in all directions. Until the 18th century a grove of acacia trees led to the Colossi of Memnon. The site, known as Jeser Ast or 'Sacred Place', was venerated because it was thought that the waters of chaos had divided and the primeval

mound erupted here. During Akhenaten's rule, Amun's images were destroyed but they were later replaced by those of Horemheb and Seti I.

The whole temple complex is entered via the 3-storey southeast gatehouse which is built like a fortified Syrian pavilion and was originally 22m high. Arriving through it into the large forecourt one sees the small temple to the right, the huge main temple directly ahead, and the small Chapels of the Votressess, dating from the 25th Dynasty (747-656 BC) kings of Kush, just to the left.

The remarkable homogeneity of the main temple's structure reflects the fact that it was designed and built by Ramses III alone rather than being expanded and altered by successive pharaohs. The immense and wonderfully preserved First Pylon, which is 65m long by 27m high, was originally dedicated to Amun but was also used by Ramses II as a memorial to his Libyan and Asiatic campaigns. It would originally have been larger than the one at Luxor, standing 27m high and 65m long, but now the north corner and cornice are missing. The images on the left of the Pylon show Ramses slaying Nubian prisoners watched by Amun and Ptah while Syrians are slain on the right hand side. Although the illustrations are based on genuine wars Ramses III never actually fought either nation!

On the left of the entrance way through the first Pylon, before arriving in the large 48m x 34m first court, also known as the palace, Ramses III is shown worshipping the deities Ptah, Osiris and Sokar. The west of the great court is flanked by eight columns and the east by seven Osiride pillars. On the Second Pylon the Pharaoh is depicted marching rows of prisoners, the third row being Philistines (or Palestinians) wearing feathered head-dresses, towards Amun and Mut. The second court is also made up of a combination of Osiride pillars and columns. Eight pillars line the back and front of the hall while the sides are flanked by six columns. One scene depicts the Feast of Sokar while the lower register of the back wall is dedicated to the Ramses III's sons and daughters. At the far right end of the hall is a small entrance which has two interesting illustrations. One shows the Pharaoh before Seth, but this was later defaced to change him into Horus, while above the door Ramses is shown kneeling on the symbol of the united Upper and Lower Egypt.

The west door connects to the ruins of the severely damaged Hypostyle Hall. Above the door the Pharaoh can again be seen kneeling over the symbol of Upper and Lower Egypt and at the base of the entry wall are 13 princesses and 10 princes. The central aisle of the hall

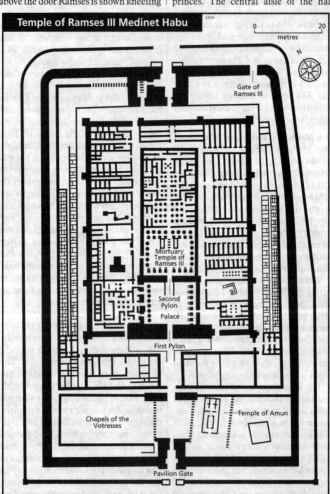

Temple of Ramses III Medinet Habu

0 — 20 metres

Gate of Ramses III

Mortuary Temple of Ramses III

Second Pylon

Palace

First Pylon

Chapels of the Votresses

Temple of Amun

Pavilion Gate

The Singing Colossus of Memnon

The northern gigantic sandstone colossus was broken off at the waist by the earthquake in 27 BC after which it was reputed to sing at dawn. This phenomenon, which was most likely caused by the wind or the expansion of the broken stone in the morning sunlight, attracted many visitors including the Roman emperors Hadrian in 130 AD and Septimus Severus (193-211 AD). The latter decided it should be repaired, after which time it never sang again.

would have been raised, in the same way as at Karnak, to allow Re's sunlight to enter.

A multitude of side rooms would originally have led off from the hypostyle hall but little now remains because of the severe damage caused by the major earthquake in 27 BC. The best preserved room is the Treasury to the north where the walls are adorned with scenes of the Pharaoh making offerings of gold to Amun. Another small room shows the Pharaoh wearing the Osiride symbols of the Atef feathered crown, a crook and flail.

The outer walls are better preserved and some of the reliefs are clearly visible. At the far end of the south wall is a calendar of religious feasts which is believed to be the longest such inscription. Further along is a portrayal of all the benefits with which Ramses III was blessed by Amun. The rear west wall is dedicated to the Pharaoh's victories in battle. In the northeast corner of the enclosure near the small temple is a small sacred lake where childless women came to bathe at night and pray to Isis that they might conceive. Close by stand the remains of the Nilometer that was originally fed by a canal which branched off from the Nile.

Colossi of Memnon

These two gigantic sandstone colossi, which are located on the main road 1.65 km from the river and next to the student ticket kiosk, represent Amenhotep III (1417-1379 BC). They once stood in front of his mortuary temple which collapsed and was plundered for stone long ago. Although the faces and crowns have been eroded the two colossi make a strange spectacle seated in splendour in the midst of the desert and are well worth a visit (see box, page 263).

On a more modern theme – the **Monastery of St Theodore** lies to the southwest of the Temple of Medinet Habu (see page 261) and is within easy reach. The religious pictures are quite modern. Theodore was one of the many Christian soldiers who fell foul of Diocletian's oppression.

The Nile Valley
Luxor to Aswan

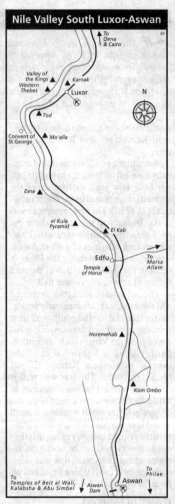

Nile Valley South Luxor-Aswan

To Qena & Cairo

Valley of the Kings
Western Thebes

Karnak

Luxor

Tod

Convent of St George

Mo'alla

Esna

el Kula Pyramid

El Kab

Edfu
Temple of Horus

To Marsa Allam

Horemehab

Kom Ombo

To Temples of Beit al Wali, Kalabsha & Abu Simbel

Aswan Dam

To Philae

Aswan

N

ALTHOUGH THE majority of tourists travel non-stop from Luxor to Aswan there is a number of interesting and beautiful temples en route of which Edfu and Kom Ombo are well worth visiting. What is so extraordinary about the generally unspectacular road journey is the fact that the strip of cultivated land between the Nile and the desert is so narrow. On one side is lush vegetation and the river and on the other the harsh and arid desert.

The main road follows the River Nile along its East Bank from Luxor, past Edfu (115 km) which is on the West Bank about half way to Aswan, before continuing via Kom Ombo (176 km) to Aswan (216 km). There is an alternative less crowded but less scenic route along the West Bank from the Valley of the Kings to Esna (55 km) and Edfu before having to cross the river to continue the journey along the East Bank to Aswan.

Increasing numbers of visitors are now making this journey by river in one of the many floating hotels which moor at the sites along the way (see box, page 274).

Egyptian village life, which is often obscured from the road and cannot be appreciated from the window of a speeding car, can be seen on this relaxing journey which is thoroughly recommended.

The **Temple of Montu** at **Tod** which dates from the 5th Dynasty is 21 km south of Luxor on the east side of the River Nile.

Travelling along the Nile

There is always a choice. In addition to the hundreds of cruisers on the river between Luxor and Aswan consider a voyage by paddlesteamer. Paddlesteamer SS Karim was built in UK in 1917 for the then sultan who became King Ahmed Faud I in 1922. It became the property of King Farouk his successor from 1936-52. After the formation of the Arab Republic in 1952 it was the property of the Ministry of Irrigation and was used by the presidents Nasser and Sadat. It has been fully refurbished (there are just 17 double cabins) making a careful attempt to evoke the atmosphere of the early 1900s with the comfort of the 1990s. Contact *Spring Tours*, T 3415972 for further details.

Motor Yachts such as Doma run by the Imaginative Traveller are another option. 14 simple cabins with bunk beds, bed linen provided, 2 bathrooms each with w/c and shower. Comfort levels are lower but the sights/sites are the same.

At the cheap end try the *felucca*, the traditional sailing boat about 10m long and 3m wide, driven by one large triangular sail. Travel is totally dependent on wind and current. The wind is stronger in the winter and blows from the north so helping the sailors against the flow of the river. As progress is at the mercy of the elements particular night stops and destinations cannot be guaranteed. There are cushions to sit on and a canopy for shade over most of the boat leaving the bow end unshaded for sunbathing. With eight passengers and a crew of two there is room to move about. The luggage is stowed below and only available morning and evening so a daysac is essential.

Traditional meals, soft drinks and beer are available on board, tea and coffee are served with the meals. There are no toilets on these boats – the boat pulls to the bank near a bush if possible and a spade is provided. For the night stops a latrine is dug. Washing is done in the river using ecofriendly soap and shampoo. Germicide soap is provided and we are assured that the utensils are disinfected after being washed in the River Nile.

It appears on the specialist tour itineraries. Stones from the original temples have been recycled. Parts of the shrine erected by Tuthmosis III remain. The site is perhaps better known for the collection of silver found here in 1936 (one of the most valuable finds of silver in Egypt) and now on display in the Egyptian Museum in Cairo.

Further south also on the east side of the River Nile at Mo'alla are two rock cut tombs of the First Intermediate Period. They belong to Ankhtifi and Sebekhotpe.

Half-way between Tod and Mo'alla on the other side of the River Nile to the edge of the desert is the Convent of St George. It is not easy to miss as the surrounding walls are about 2m high. The annual feast day is celebrated in November when thousands of pilgrims including the Bishop of Luxor attend. The main church which has 21 domes also has 6 altars dedicated (from north-south) to St Pachom, St Mercurius, The Virgin Mary, Saint George, Saint Paul of Thebes and Saint Michael.

Going through the locks at Esna can be a fascinating experience, well worth the wait. See page 267.

ESNA

This small market town lies about 55 km south of Luxor on the West Bank of the Nile which, besides its **Temple of Khnum**, is mainly known for the sandstone dam across the river. This was built in 1906 at about the same time as the first Aswan dam and today cruise ships and barges usually have to queue for a number of hours for their turn to pass through its locks. The town and the temple are certainly worth a couple of hour's visit.

Service taxis and buses stop about 10 mins walk from the temple which is in the centre of town. Walk to the river and then south along the Corniche to the ticket kiosk. The railway station is in the centre of town and is a short *calèche* ride to the temple.

Places of interest

The **Temple of Khnum**, open daily 0700-1800, entrance E£8, lies partially exposed in a deep depression in the centre of town. The excavation began in the 1860s but did not continue because the area above was covered in houses. Over the centuries since its construction the annual Nile flood has deposited 10m of silt over the temple site so that all that is visible today is the **Hypostyle Hall**. The part of the temple that can be seen today is Ptolemaic/Roman and was built on the foundations of a much older shrine which was also dedicated to the ram-headed deity Khnum. He was believed to have created man by moulding him from River Nile clay on a potter's wheel. Later, when Amun became the principal deity, Khnum's image changed and, in conjunction with Hapy, he came to be regarded as the guardian of the source of the River Nile.

The hypostyle hall's **Outer Façade** is decorated from left to right with the cartouches of three Roman emperors Claudius (41-54 AD), Titus (79-81 AD) and Vespasion (69-79 AD) (a, b and c). Above the entrance, at the very top, on the lintel, is the winged sun disc. Inside the tall hall 18 columns with capitals of varying floral designs support the **Astronomical Ceiling** which, although once a beautiful and complex spectacle, is barely visible today because it was blackened by the wood fires of a Coptic village which was once housed within the temple. In places various deities and animals, including winged dogs, two-headed snakes and the pregnant hippo-goddess Taweret (see page 213), can be seen intermingled with signs of the zodiac. Enter and turn left passing a tiny enclosed space built into the walls (d), perhaps the doorkeeper's chamber. In the first corner the pillar is decorated with rams (e) and the side wall on the second register Roman emperors Septimus Severus (he is second from the left), Caracella and Greta make offerings to Khnum (f). At the back, opposite the entrance, the walls of the original Ptolemaic temple (g) are incorporated in this hypostyle hall. The hall's columns are inscribed with texts detailing the temple's various festivals. On the lighter side look out for the cross-legged pharoah (h), frogs on top of the capital (i) representing the goddess Heqet (see page 207) and a god being offered a laurel wreath (j) showing Greek influence here. On the right hand wall pharoah with Horus and Khnum netting fowl and demons is illustrated (k) and in the last corner the column has countless crocodiles (l). Around the northern outer walls at the back of the temple are texts of Marcus Aurelius (161-180 AD) (m) while Titus, Domitian and Trajan slay their Egyptian enemies on the eastern and western outer walls (n and o).

The **Convent of the Holy Martyrs** lies 6 km to the southwest of Esna. It commemorates 3,600 Christians who refused to sacrifice to the Roman gods and died for their faith c.249-251. The older church in the complex dedicated to the martyrs was first built in 786 but has been destroyed and rebuilt on a number of occasions. It has some interesting wall

Temple of Khnum, Esna

225

paintings. The Church of the Holy Virgin Mary is of more recent construction (1931).

Local information
● **Accommodation**

The town's only hotel is the **F** *Haramin* about 1 km south of the ticket kiosk along the Corniche but it is best avoided unless stuck in town at night.

● **Places to eat**

There are a few cafés and stalls in the central square but there are no restaurants.

● **Banks & money changers**

One bank open Saturday-Thursday 0830-1400, Sunday 1800-2100, and Wednesday 1700-2000. 1000-1330 during Ramadan.

● **Post & telecommunications**
Area code: 097.

● **Shopping**

Esna style: when the cruise ships reach the locks here the traders appear in a flotilla of small rowing boats and attempt to sell a wide variety of clothing, table clothes etc. Goods are hurled from the small boats in a polythene bag with great accuracy on to the top deck of the ship for the purchaser to examine and then barter over the price by shouting to and fro. Rejected goods are expected to be thrown back, although these are not always dispatched with the same accuracy as they were received! If a price is agreed and a purchase made, a small garment to act as ballast, again in a bag, is then thrown up on deck with the expectation that payment will be placed inside the package and returned to the sender below.

● **Transport**

Train To Luxor and Aswan stop at Esna but only very slow and crowded second and third class service.

Road Bus: north to Luxor or south to Edfu, Kom Ombo and Aswan are frequent but crowded in the morning. **Service taxis**: to Luxor (1 hr), Edfu (1 hr) and Aswan (2-3 hrs) are quicker but marginally more expensive than the buses.

EL KAB

32 km south of Esna the mud-brick walls of El Kab stand on the western bank of the River Nile. The ramparts are very solid and in places measure 12m thick. The important ruins here are the **Temple of Thoth** (see page 213) built by Ramses II and the later **Temple of Nekhbet** the vulture goddess (see page 210) who was worshipped on this site. The inclusion of stone blocks from earlier periods in the building of these temples is an example of pharaonic recyling! Cut into the hills to the west of the old town are a number of tombs. The keys are held in Edfu so make arrangements to visit in advance.

EDFU

Edfu, which is 60 km south along the West Bank and almost equidistant between Luxor (115 km) and Aswan (106 km), is the site of the huge, well preserved Ptolemaic cult **Temple of Horus** which, as the most complete in the whole country, is certainly worth a visit.

ACCESS The temple is west or inland from the river along Sharia al-Maglis and can be reached by *calèche*, many of which are drawn by emaciated and badly treated horses, or taxis which await the arrival of the tourist cruise ships. Expect, in addition, to be approached by the ubiquitous photographer who will be keen to take a picture of your *calèche* party and to offer the developed photograph for sale as you return to your cruise ship. Taxis and pick-ups to the temple can be caught from the train station, which is just across the Nile bridge, while the service taxi terminal at the town-side west end of the bridge is a 20 mins walk or short ride to the temple. Inter-city buses drop their passengers on Sharia Tahrir or the parallel Sharia Gumhorriya about half way between the bridge and the temple.

Places of interest

Edfu Temple, open summer 0700-1800, winter 0700-1600, general entry E£20, student entry E£10, E£6 charge for cameras or videos used for commercial photography, is the name given to the enormous **Temple of Horus** which was the focus of the ancient city of Djeba. It was begun in August 237 BC by Ptolemy III and took 25 years to complete, with the decoration taking another 5 years. Because of a revolt in Upper Egypt it was not until February 176 BC that the opening ceremony took place under Ptolemy VII, but there were

Temple of Horus at Edfu

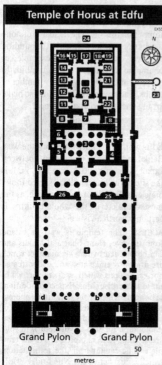

0   metres   50

1. Court of Offerings
2. First Hypostyle Hall
3. Second Hypostyle Hall/
   Festival Hall
4. Offering Hall: liquid
   offerings
5. Offering Hall: solid offerings
6. Laboratory
7. First Vestibule
   /Hall of Offerings
8. Stairs downup to roof
9. Second Vestibule/
   Sanctuary of Horus
10. Main Sanctuary dedicated
    to Horus with altar
11. Chapel of Min
12. Chamber of Linen
13. Chamber of the Throne
    of the Gods
14. Chamber of Osiris
15. Tomb of Osiris
16. Chamber of the West
17. Chamber of the Victor
    (Horus)
18. Chapel of Khonsu
19. Chapel of Hathor
20. Chapel of the Throne of Re
21. Chapel of the Spread Wings
22. Sun Court
23. Nilometer & well
24. Passage of Victory/
    Ambulatory
25. Library
26. Chamber of Ungents

further additions until Ptolemy XIII. Like Esna's **Temple of Khnum**, it was completely buried except for its huge pylons under silt and sand and its top was covered with houses until the 1860s but, unlike Esna, the whole site has been excavated. It had been severely damaged by the town's inhabitants and it was not until 1903 that the excavation work was finally completed.

The whole complex is entered from the ticket office in the northwest corner at the rear of the main north-south axis temple, which one walks along to reach the entrance at its south end. Along the base of the enclosing walls look for the images of vultures representing the goddess Nekhbet and falcons representing Horus. Just to the southwest is the small east-west axis birth house called the **Mammisi of Horus**, which was built by Ptolemy VII and VIII. The inner sanctuary is surrounded by a peristyle of foliage capped columns, topped by pilaster capitals showing the grotesque figures of Bes, god of joy and birth. His frightening appearance was thought to dispel evil and to protect women in labour (see page 206). Each year there is a performance of the miracle play which represents Horus' birth at the same time as the birth of the divine heir to the throne of Egypt. At the southwest corner of the birth house there are reliefs of Isis suckling Horus and an erect Amun. On the pillars of the colonnades in the forecourt Hathor beats tambourine, plays the harp and suckles Horus.

The main **Temple of Horus** is entered through a gateway in the huge **Grand Pylon** on either side of which are statues of the hawk-god Horus. A tiny Ptolemy stands in front of him. On the left outer wall of the pylon Ptolemy XIII (88-51 BC), who was also known as Neos Dionysus and had usurped the pylon from its original builder Ptolemy IX (170-116 BC), is shown killing his enemies before Horus and Hathor (a). The right wall has the same illustration in mirror image. Above are carved decorations and niches which were cut into the walls, as supports for the flagpoles. On its inner wall the barge of Horus tows the barque of Hathor (b) and at the other side (c) the water bourne procession continues. No sails are required as the journey is downstream. Celebrations for the gods' arrival are seen at (d).

The pylon contains the usual guardians' quarters and stairs up to the roof.

The giant **Court of Offerings**, at a slightly lower level, is lined with 32 columns with paired capitals behind which on the west side Ptolemy IX makes offerings to Horus, Hathor and Ihy, their son (e), and on the right Ptolemy X appears before the same three (f). At the north end of the court is the **First Hypostyle Hall**, built by Ptolemy VII (180-145 BC), with its 18 once brightly painted columns supporting the roof. There are three different types of capital, repeated on either side of the hall. Before the entrance of the Hall stands another large statue of Horus, in grey granite. At the entrance to the Hypostyle Hall is the small Chamber of Ungents to the left with reliefs of flowers and recipes for consecrations and a small Library, where the names of the guests for the day's festival would be kept, to the right. Here many rolls of papyrus were found. The foundation ceremonies are illustrated on the walls of the hall.

Leading north from the hall is a smaller 12 slender columned hypostyle hall, known as the **Festival Hall**, the oldest part of the building dating back to Ptolemy III (246-222 BC) and completed by his son, where offerings entered the temple and were prepared. Recipes for offerings are found on the walls of the laboratory. These were then carried through into the **Hall of Offerings**, or first vestibule, where the daily offerings would have been made at the many altars and tables bearing incense, juices, fruit and meat. From here there are steps to the east which were used for the procession up to the roof where a **Chapel of the Disc** once stood. The stairs are illustrated with pictures of the priests carrying the statues of the gods to the roof to be revitalized before returning down a separate staircase, not safe to climb, to arrive back on the west side of the Hall of Offerings. Today all the roof offers is an excellent view of the surrounding area.

The Offerings Hall leads to the inner vestibule called the **Sanctuary of Horus**, where engravings show Ptolemy IV (222-205 BC) making offerings to the deities while others show Horus and Hathor in their sacred vessels. The sanctuary holds a low altar of dark syenite on which stood the barque and behind is the large upright shrine of Aswan granite where statue of the god was placed. The sanctuary is virtually a separate temple within the main temple and is surrounded by a series of 10 minor chambers with doors, then immediately behind the sanctuary containing a lifesize model of the sacred barque. The chapel of the Throne of Re shows Horus with a serpent, Horus in the sacred tree and Horus with monkeys. These chambers, many of which originally served as vestries and store rooms, are better examined with a torch. On the dimly lit northeast wall of the outer corridor are the remains of a Nilometer. Horus' defeat of Seth, who is portrayed as a hippopotamus, is illustrated in the middle of the west wall of the ambulatory (g). Note how the hippo gets smaller and

Horus – The First Living God-King

Horus who was originally the Egyptian sky-god and falcon-god was later identified as the son of Osiris and his sister Isis. He subsequently avenged his father's murder by his uncle Seth in an epic fight at Edfu in which Horus lost an eye and Seth his testicles. It was not until Isis intervened that Horus prevailed as good triumphed over evil. Osiris pronounced his judgment by banishing Seth to the underworld and enthroning Horus as the first living god-king. Each Pharaoh claimed to be an incarnation of Horus and the annual Festival of the Coronation, at Edfu's now destroyed Temple of the Falcon in front of the main temple's grand pylon, followed by a crowning ceremony in the temple's main forecourt, symbolized the renewal of royal power.

How to survive a Nile cruise

Selecting a tour operator and cruise ship

The quality of operator and cruise ship will, of course, be largely dependent on the price paid. If the cruise is taken as an all-inclusive package, it is recommended that, if possible, one is chosen where the overall itinerary is under the day to day control of a tour manager who is a direct employee of the travel company. The local management of cruises can be sub-contracted to Egyptian travel agents who, should difficulties arise with the tour, may consider themselves primarily as guides and show marked reluctance to take on any wider responsibility or be fully accountable for solving problems of a more challenging nature. For health and safety reasons it is also recommended that travellers use only the best grade 5-star Nile cruise boats (see table on pages 274-276).

Typical cruise itineraries

Most popular is between **Luxor and Aswan**, with the journey sometimes in reverse, or a trip both ways. The itinerary will offer the following typical popular features:

Luxor: visits to the West Bank (Valley of the Kings, Valley of the Queens, Colossi of Memnon, Temple of Queen Hapshetsut), Luxor and Karnak Temples (plus at least one alabaster factory shop!). Option of sound and light show at Karnak.

Esna: Temple of Khnum.

Edfu: Temple of Horus – access by *calèche*.

Kom Ombu: Temple of Horus and Sobek.

Aswan: *Felucca* boat outing to Kitchener Island, trip to Nubian village on Elephantine Island, Unfinished Obelisk, High Dam, Temple of Philae (plus at least one papyrus factory shop!!). Option of sound and light show at Philae.

Dendera: Temple of Hathor – may not be on all itineraries.

The difference in the educational quality of the cruise will depend heavily on the calibre of the guides, library facilities on board and the availability of the evening lectures. It seems pointless to visit such spectacular historic sites without adequate instruction. Expect early starts to some excursions eg 0700 with opportunities to relax later in the heat of the day.

Esna lock closures

Cruises from Luxor to Aswan can be disrupted by the twice-yearly closure of the lock at Esna for maintenance. Closures usually in June and December and prospective travellers are strongly advised to check these dates beforehand. When the lock is closed, ships are moored at Esna and passengers are transported by coach to those points on the itinerary inaccessible by river. These makeshift arrangements can significantly reduce the pleasure and relaxation of a cruising holiday.

Meals

Expect three good meals per day, often buffet style, although there can be some variation with *table de hote* menus. Some meals served on covered deck. Meal times likely to operate to a fairly inflexible timetable. Free tea, coffee and soft drinks available at any time. Bar open most of day. Special menus can usually be organized.

Social life and entertainment

Almost inevitably at some stage during the cruise there will be an evening dinner at which travellers will be encouraged to dress in local Egyptian costume – a *jallabah* party. A local photographer will be on hand to record the event for your family album. Prints are available for purchase within 24 hrs. A good range of costumes may be available both for hire or purchase on board ship (expect hire prices in the range E£25-40) but there are also opportunities to buy these cheaply at tourist bazaars on route, for example at Edfu and Kom Ombu. An entertaining alternative to these bazaars may be to buy from the traders who congregate around the cruise ships as they queue to pass through the lock at Esna (see page 267). This is an evening to enjoy.

Other evening entertainment may include discos, live Egyptian/Nubian music and performances by belly dancers, jugglers and acrobats. These do not last long and certainly won't interfere with plans for an early night.

Banking arrangements

Access to banks for obtaining local Egyptian currency can be somewhat limited. Whilst moored in Luxor and Aswan, for example, banks in the towns are accessible, although tour itineraries do not always allow convenient spare time during banking hours. Remember, too, that banks are usually closed on Fridays, so plan ahead. Do not forget that banks will want to see your passport unless you are exchanging cash for local currency. Cruise ship operators may make arrangements for a local banker to come on board whilst boats are moored at Luxor and Aswan. Rates of exchange using this facility can be disappointing, however, despite the fact that Egypt is supposed to have a fixed rate system.

Payments on board ship

It is very probable that the ship will operate a system by which all extras, for example drinks, laundry and any purchases from shops on board, can be signed for and the bills settled at the end of the cruise. The advantages of requiring less ready cash should be balanced with the need to keep a reasonable check on items being accurately debited to your cabin account. Although it is likely that payment of this account by credit card, in TCs or cash (hard or local currencies) will be fully acceptable, personal cheques will almost certainly not be.

Dress code

Shorts and beachwear acceptable on board ship but take note of the advice on page 13 for visits ashore. Casual dress for mealtimes is likely to be acceptable (no beachwear), with something smarter for evening dinner.

Tipping

In an attempt to ease the problem of when and who to tip on board ship, tour managers may suggest paying an amount per traveller (suggestion E£100) direct to the Boat Manager at the end of the cruise for distribution amongst all the staff working on the vessel. Tipping of tour managers (suggestion E£50) and drivers, porters, temple guards, *felucca* sailors (suggestion E£35) would be additional to this. Although such systems exist, this does not preclude travellers from ignoring them and dealing with this issue personally as they see fit.

Medical assistance

Most ships have a resident doctor in attendance throughout the cruise. Given that access to pharmacies may be difficult during a cruise itinerary, it is recommended that travellers take a well stocked personal medical kit (see page 432).

Cabin accommodation

Cabins at water level will offer limited views and, depending on position, may be more affected by engine noise and fumes. A supplement can be paid for a cabin on an upper deck. Top level cabins may have a sun deck as their roof. Obtain a plan of the vessel before you book. Bear in mind that when the ship is moored there may not be a view from the cabin whatever its level. Ships can often be berthed six or seven abreast and access to the shore is gained by walking through one ship after another. Expect to be issued with a boarding pass when going ashore.

Shopping facilities

There are likely to be some limited shopping opportunities on board at reasonable prices for buying postcards, stamps and some souvenirs, jewellery, books and perhaps items of clothing. Other options may include a hairdressing salon.

Telephone and fax

Do not expect these facilities to be as good as those on shore. Availability may be erratic and unpredictable and charges expensive. Minimum fax/phone charges to the UK are around E£50 per call.

Safe deposit boxes

If safety and security of valuables, passports and money is a concern, check whether the ship offers safe deposit boxes for passenger use.

Enjoying the cruise life

One of the great pleasures of cruising on the River Nile is just sitting and watching the landscape glide gently by. The scenery is ever changing, albeit at an undemanding pace which gives a unique opportunity to take a leisurely look at village settlements which slip in and out of view and the cultivation of the narrow strip of green fertile land close to the river's banks. Dusk brings the contrast of vivid sunset colours and perhaps the graceful sight of *felucca* boats silhouetted against the water. Useful things to have to hand are a pair of binoculars and perhaps a book to help with the identification of the many birds which can be seen on the islands and river banks.

If enjoyment extends to taking exercise to keep fit, despite the heat, then exercise bicycles and rowing machines may be found on the top deck (no privacy here!). Don't expect swimming pools to be, in effect, anything more than a large plunge bath. With a gentle breeze coming off the river, the heat of the sun can often be misjudged whilst cruising. A ship with a good area of awning on the top deck might be a preferred choice.

smaller as the tale is repeated to the north. On the same side where the ambulatory narrows to the south the pharoah helped by gods pulls close a clap net containing evil spirits portrayed as fish, birds and men (h). There are some interesting water spouts jutting into this area, some in better repair than others, carved as lions' heads.

Outside the wall to the north-east are the remains of a Nilometer (see Aswan, see page 283) and a well.

The **Monastery of St Pachom** is in the desert about 6 km to the west of Edfu. It is worth a visit if you are in the area – but not worth a special journey.

Local information
● Accommodation

There are no good hotels in town and most tourists are either only passing through or are staying on cruise ships which moor on the river bank from where *calèches* take them to the temple.

There are a few cheap hotels incl the relatively clean F *Dar es-Salaam*, nr the temple; the friendly but shabby F *El-Medina*, just off the main roundabout on Sharia Gumhorriya; F *El-Magdi*, further down Sharia al-Maglis; the fairly awful F *Semiramis*.

● Places to eat

The *Happy Land Restaurant* is on the Corniche between the bridge and Sharia al-Maglis where the *Zahrat el-Medina Restaurant* is located: neither of these cheap restaurants are very good.

● Banks & money changers

Sharia Gumhorriya in the centre of town is open Sunday-Thursday 0830-1400.

● Post & telecommunications
Area code: 095.

Post Office: located nr the temple on Sharia Tahrir on the south side of the main roundabout.

● Shopping

The main tourist bazaar is next to the Edfu temple complex and offers a colourful selection of cheaply priced goods, particularly jellabahs, scarves, tablecloths and other local souvenirs. Not surprisingly, the *calèche* drivers taking tourists from the cruise ships will drop you and collect you from this area. When bargaining for goods here, as elsewhere, take care to establish whether the price is in Egyptian pounds or sterling; local traders are adept at switching between the two and attempting to cause confusion!

● Transport

Train To Luxor and Aswan stop at Edfu but only very slow and crowded second and third class service.

Road Bus: north to Esna and Luxor or south to Kom Ombo and Aswan, caught from Sharia Tahrir half way between the bridge and the temple, are slow but very cheap. **Service taxis**: north to Esna (1 hr) and Luxor (1 hr), or south to Kom Ombo (45 mins) and Aswan (1½ hrs, E£3.50), can be caught from the west end of the bridge.

KOM OMBO

Kom Ombo, 66 km south of Edfu and only about 40 km north of Aswan, is a small East Bank town known today for its sugar refinery which processes the cane grown in the surrounding area. It is home for many of the Nubians who were displaced by the flooding which followed the construction of the Aswan High Dam. Kom Ombo was the ancient crossroads where the '40 Days Road' caravan route from western Sudan met the route from the eastern desert gold mines. It was also the site of the training ground for the war elephants used in the Ptolemaic army. Most tourists stop here to visit the **Temple of Sobek and Horus**, which stands on the banks of the River Nile 4 km from the town.

ACCESS To reach the temple, leave the service taxi to Aswan at the turnoff 2 km south of Kom Ombo town from where the signposted 'tembel' is only 1.5 km away. In the town itself both buses and service taxis stop on the north-south Sharia 26th July but 300m apart. Cheap pick-ups to the temple can be caught from behind the white mosque which is one block away from the Luxor-Aswan road on the east-west axis Sharia Gamhorriya. These days the vast majority of visitors arrive by coach or by

cruise ships which dock on the river bank directly below the temple itself.

Places of interest

Kom Ombo Temple, open daily 0600-1800 (general entry E£10, students E£5 and E£30 for commercial photography permit) is the more usual name given to the small but beautiful **Temple of Sobek and Horus**. It faces the Nile at a bend in the river. The temple is unusual because it is dedicated to two gods rather than a single deity. Sobek was the crocodile god which, given the fact that the nearby sandbanks were a favourite basking ground for crocodiles until the construction of the Aswan Dam, was particularly appropriate. On its right hand side Sobek-Re, who is identified with the sun, his wife in another form of Hathor, and their moon-god son Khonsu are honoured. The left hand side is devoted to a form of Horus the Elder or Haroeris known as the 'Good doctor', his consort Ta-Sent-Nefer ('good sister') and his son Horus the Younger who was known as Pa-Heb-Tawy ('Lord of the Two

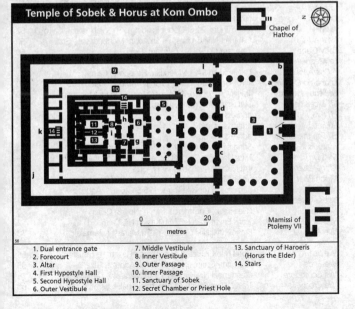

Temple of Sobek & Horus at Kom Ombo

1. Dual entrance gate	7. Middle Vestibule
2. Forecourt	8. Inner Vestibule
3. Altar	9. Outer Passage
4. First Hypostyle Hall	10. Inner Passage
5. Second Hypostyle Hall	11. Sanctuary of Sobek
6. Outer Vestibule	12. Secret Chamber or Priest Hole
	13. Sanctuary of Haroeris (Horus the Elder)
	14. Stairs

Chapel of Hathor

Mamissi of Ptolemy VII

0   20
metres

Nile Cruisers

It is recommended for health and safety reasons that travellers use only the best grade Nile Cruise boats. The following list gives the names of Egyptian Government 5-Star grade Nile cruisers:

Boat	Operator/Owner	No of Cabins
Abercrombie Sun Boats	Abercrombie and Kent, 18 Sh Youssef el-Guindy, Cairo	32+
Aida III	Nile Valley Hotels, 80 Gamet el Dowal, Mohandessin, Giza	92
Alexander the Great	Jolleys Travel & Tours, 4th Flr, 23 Sh Kasr El Nil, Cairo	74
Anni	Sheraton Corp, 4 Sh Ahmed Naguib Pasha, Garden City, Cairo	74
Aton	Sheraton Corp, address as above	80
Aurora	European Floating Hotels, 87 Sh Ramses, Cairo	42
Cairo	Shalakani Tours, 36a Sh Bahgal Ali, Zamalek	65
Cheops	International Co for Nile Cruising, 23b Sh Ismael Mohamed, Zamalek	80
Cheops III	address as above	68
Cleopatra	Nile Cruising Co, 3 Abu El-Fada Tower, Zamalek	47
Coral II	Isis Tours Co, 48 Sh Giza, Dokki	73
Diamond Boat	Egyptian Italian Co, 15 Sh Hassan Sabri, Zamalek	75
Florence	Florence & Maria Co, 15 Sh El Shaheid Gala, Heliopolis	74
Giza	Shalakani Tours, 36a Sh Bahgat Ali, Zamalek	60
Glorey	Inter Egypt, 10 Sh Syria, Giza	55
Helio	Heliopolis Tours, 26a Anower, El Mofty, Nasr City, Cairo	52
Horizon	Egyptian Cruise Lines, 21 Sh Giza, Nile Tower, Giza	105
Hotp	4 Sh Ahmed Naguib Pasha, Garden City, Cairo	74
Imperial	Travcotels, 112 Sh 26 July, Zamalek	43
Isis	Nile Hilton, Commercial Centre No 18, Cairo	48
Jasmin	Wing Tours, 21 El-Oboor Buildings, Sh Salah Salem, Cairo	62
Kasr el Nil	Cataract Nile Cruises, 26 Sh Adan, Mohandessin, Giza	50
Lady Diana	Zamzam Co, 23 Sh Zamzam, Dokki	60
Le Meridien Champollion	Le Meridien SA, Le Meridien Heliopolis, Cairo	51
Leonardo Da Vinci	Tarot Garranah Tours, 15 Sh Mahmoud Talaat, Giza	70
Le Scribe Papyrus	Travel Cruises Co, 47 Abdel Monaim Riad, Mohandessin	70
LTI Excelsior	Seti First Nile Cruises, 16 Ismail Mohamed, Zamalek	25
LTI Kira	address as above	65
LTI Seti I	address as above	55
LTI Seti the Great	address as above	65
Marquis II	Song of Egypt Co, 32 Sh Riad, Mohandessin, Giza	74
Miss Universe	Miss Universe Co, 18 Gamet el Dowal, Mohandessin	59
Monatasseri	Inter Travel, 122 Sh El Tahrir, Giza	76
Moon River	Silver Moon Nile Cruises, 20 Sh Mathaf Zerae, Giza	50
Nabila Queen	Ramses Co for Nile Tours, 195 Sh 26 July, Agouza	62
Nabila Queen II	address as above	82
Nephos	Nile Hilton, Commercia Centre No 18, Cairo	60
Neptune	Trans Egypt Travel, 37 Sh Kasr El Nil, Cairo	52
Nile Admiral	Presidential Nile Cruises, 13 Sh Marasshi, Zamalek	78
Nile Beauty	Flotel Nile Cruises, 17 Sh Ahmad Heshmat, Zamalek	55
Nile Bride	Nile Bride Cruises, 150 Sh El Nil, Agouza	65
Nile Comodore	Presidential Nile Cruises, 13 Sh Maraashi, Zamalek	78
Nile Crocodile	Travel Ways Egypt, 41 Sh Abdel Khalek Sarat, Cairo	60

Nile Elegant	Memnon Nile Cruises, 49 Sh Nobar, Cairo	65
Nile Emerald	Nile Sun Cuises, 1 Sh Gezirah El Wosta, Tower A, Zamalek	72
Nile Empress	Travcotels, 112 26 Sh July, Zamalek	31
Nile Jewel	Nile Sun Cruises, 1 Sh Gezire El-Wosta, Zamalek	56
Nile Legend	Presidential Nile Cruises, 13 Sh Marasshi, Zamalek	75
Nile Majesty I	Mo Hotel Travel & Nile, 41 Sh Sharif, Cairo	52
Nile Majesty II	Mo Hotel Travel & Nile, 41 Sh Sharif, Cairo	95
Nile Marquis	Song of Egypt Co, 32 Sh Riad, Mohandessin, Giza	74
Nile Monarch	Travcotels, 112 Sh 26 July, Zamalek	45
Nile Plaza	Presidential Nile Cruises, 13 Sh Marasshi, Zamalek	78
Nile President	Presidential Nile Cruises, 13 Sh Marasshi, Zamalek	75
Nile Quality	Memnon Nile Cruises, 49 Sh Nobar, Cairo	67
Nile Queen	Sphinx Tours & Cruises, 2 Behle Passage, Kasr El Nil, Cairo	50
Nile Queen II	address as above	64
Nile Ritz	Presidential Nile Cruises, 13 Sh Marasshi, Zamalek	78
Nile Romance	Flotel Nile Cruises, 17 Sh Ahmad Heshmat, Zamalek	35
Nile Secret	Spring Tours, 3 Sh El Sayed Bakri, Zamalek	54
Nile Smart	Memnon Nile Cruises, 49 Sh Nobar, Cairo	65
Nile Supreme	address as above	74
Nile Symphony	Presidential Nile Cruises, 13 Sh Marasshi, Zamalek	75
Nora	Noratel Hotels & Tourism, 4 Sh Mehdi, Heliopolis	74
Nubia Queen	Naggar Tourist Co, 195 Sh 26 July, Giza	62
Oberoi Philae		
Nile Cruiser	Oberoi Investments, 6 Sh Pyramids, Giza	58
Oberoi Shehrayar	Oberoi Corporation, Mena House Hotel, Sh Ahram, Giza	69
Oberoi Shehrazad	Oberoi Corporation, Mena House Hotel, Sh Ahram, Giza	71
Orchid	Wing Tours, 14 El-Oboor Buildings, Sh Salah Salem, Cairo	64
Osiris Hilton	Nile Hilton, Commercial Centre No 18, Cairo	48
Papyrus	Rey Vacances Travel, 47 Sh Abdel Monaim, Mohandessin	44
Prince Omar	Zamalek Nile Cruises, 21 Sh Behgat Ali, Zamalek	70
Princess Amira	Cataract Cruises, 27 Sh Hassan Assemi, Zamalek	67
Queen Isis	Isis Tours Co, 48 Sh Giza, Dokki	53
Queen Nefer	Nefer Tours, 5 Sh Kasr El Nil	53
Queen of Sheba	Salakamy & Naggar Tours, 195 Sh 26 July, Giza	76
Ra	Egyptian Co for Nile Cruises, 13 Sh Kasr El Nil, Cairo	72
Ra II	address as above	83
Ramses Egypt	Nile Co for Tours & Floating Hotels, 195 Sh 26 July, Giza	40
Ramses		
King of the Nile	Nile Co for Tours & Floating Hotels, 195 26 Sh July, Giza	83
Redamis	Movenpick Nile Cruises, Crocodile Island, Luxor	72
Regency	Tavcotels, 112 Sh 26 July, Zamalek	52
Regina	address as above	63
Royale	Travcotels, 112 Sh 26 July, Zamalek	52
Royal Orchid	Nlle Exploration Co, 8 Sh Maragil, Zamalek	31
Royal Rhapsody	address as above	31
Royal Serenade	address as above	31
Salacia	Trans Egypt Travel, 37 Sh Kasr El Nil, Cairo	57
Serenade	Inter Egypt Co, 10 Sh Syria, Mohandessin	64
Sherry Boat	Sherry Nile Cruises, 33 Sh Abdel Khalek Sarwat	63
Sinouhe II	Pan Egypt Hotels and Cruises, 3 Fouda Shafik, Abbassia	86
Seti II	Seti First Nile Cruises, 16 Ismail Mohamed, Zamalek	
Seti III	Seti First Nile Cruises, 16 Ismail Mohamed, Zamalek	
Seti the Great	Seti First Nile Cruises, 16 Ismail Mohamed, Zamalek	

Sobek	Cataract Nile Cruises, 26 Sh Adan, Mohandessin	48
Solaris I	Solaris Cruises, 6 Sh Kasr El Nil	62
Soleil	Five Star Travel, 49 Sh Mohey El Din Abu El Ezz	34
Sonesta Nile Goddess	Sonesta International, 4 Sh El-Tayaran, Nasr City, Heliopolis	65
Sonesta Sun Goddess	address as above	62
Spring I	Spring Tours, 3 Sh El-Seyyed Bakry, Zamalek	42
Star of Luxor	Tarot Garranah Tours, 15 Sh Mahmoud Talaat, Cairo	55
Tag El Nil	Isis Tours, 48 Sh Giza, Giza	53
Tarot	Tarot Garranah Tours, 15 Sh Mahmoud Talaat, Giza	70
Triton	Trans Egypt Travel, 37 Ksar El Nil, Cairo	20
Tut	Sheraton Corp, 4 Sh Ahmed Naguib Pasha, Garden City, Cairo	80
Vitto Rai	Pyramisa Hotels & Resorts Co, 60 Sh Giza, Giza	67
Voyageur	Solaris Nile Cruisers, 2 Sh Abdel Azem Rashed, Dokki	64

Lands'). A healing cult developed and pilgrims who came to be cured would fast for a night in the temple precinct before participating in a complex ceremony with the priest of Horus in the heart of the temple.

The present temple, like many others along this stretch of the River Nile, is a Greco-Roman construction, built of sandstone. Ptolemy VI started the temple, Neo Dionysus oversaw most of the construction while Emperor Augustus added some of the finishing touches. Its proximity to the Nile was a mixed blessing because, while its silt assisted in preserving the building, the flood waters eroded the First Pylon and Forecourt which were falling into the Nile before they were strengthened by the Department of Antiquities in 1893.

Like so many others the temple lies on a north-south axis with the main entrance at the south end. In front of it to the west on the riverbank itself is the **Mamissi of Ptolemy VII** (180-145 BC) which has been virtually destroyed by flooding. To the east of the main temple is the **Gate of Neos Dionysus**, who is believed to have been Ptolemy XIII (88-51 BC) and the father of Cleopatra, and the tiny two-room **Chapel of Hathor** which is now used to display mummified crocodiles found near the site.

With the Pylon and much of the **Forecourt** now destroyed by water erosion, one enters the main temple at the forecourt which was built by Tiberius (14-37 AD). Unfortunately only the stumps of the colourful columns, with a high-water mark clearly visible at about 2.5m, and a few pieces of its walls now remain. Continuing the theme from the rest of the temple the twin deities are divided so that the left-hand columns are dedicated to Horus the Elder and the right-hand ones to Sobek-Re. In the centre of the forecourt is the base of a huge square altar which is flanked by two granite basins set into the paving. On the column in the far corner (a) note the eye socket in the relief of Horus. Once this was inlayed for greater decoration. Behind this column, right in the corner (b), a staircase rose up to the roof level. At the north end is the double entrance of the **First Hypostyle Hall** with one door for each deity. On the left wall of which (c) Neos Dionysus undergoes the purification rutual overseen by Horus and on the right (d) the same ritual is overseen by Sobek. The capitals are brightly decorated with floral arrays while the bases are decorated with lilies. The reliefs on the lintel and door jambs show the Nile gods binding Upper and Lower Egypt together.

The five entrance columns and the 10 columns inside the Hypostyle Hall and its wall reliefs are attractively decorated and the curious mixture of the two deities

Easy to recognize – The Pied Kingfisher

The Pied Kingfisher (*Ceryle rudis*) is very common in Egypt – wherever there is water. Like all kingfishers it is recognized by a larger than expected head with a rather insignificant crest, a long, sturdy, sharp beak and by its short tail and short legs. The Pied Kingfisher, 25 cm long, is found in both salt and fresh water. It is a superb diver, fishing from a hovering position over the water or from a perch on a convenient branch. The sexes are similar in sizes in colouring, being black and white

– a white band over the eye reaching to the back of the head, a mottled crest, a white throat and neck. The back is mottled, the feathers being black with white edges, the wings are mainly black with a white central band. It has a white breast and under surface except for two black bands (only one black band on the female). It nests in holes in the river bank.

continues. Part of the roof has survived on the east side of the Hall and flying vultures are clearly depicted on the ceiling (e). The rear walls leading to the older **Second** or **Inner Hypostyle Hall**, which has two entrances and 15 columns, five incorporated in the front wall, show Ptolemy VII holding hymnal texts before the Nile gods. Inside he is shown offering sacrifices to the god. The most striking relief is adjacent on the left of the north wall where Horus the Elder presents the *Hps*, the curved sword of victory to Ptolemy VII, while Cleopatra II and Cleopatra III, his wife and sister respectively, stand behind him (f).

This is then followed by three double **Entrance Vestibules**, each progressively smaller and higher than the last, also built by Ptolemy VII. The outer vestibule shows the goddess of writing Sheshat measuring the layout of the temple's foundations (g), while the middle chamber served as an **Offering Hall** to which only priests were allowed entrance. Look for the long list or calendar detailing the temple gods' various festivals, one for each day (n). Two small side rooms originally served as the Library for the sacred texts and the other as a vestry for the altar clothes and the priests' robes. As in Edfu,

a staircase originally led to the now destroyed Chapel of the Disk on the roof.

The inner vestibule has two doors leading to the two separate **Sanctuaries of Horus and Sobek** and between the doors the gods give a Macedonian cloaked Ptolemy a notched palm branch from which the Heb Sed, or jubilee sign displaying the number of years of his reign, is suspended (i). Khonsu, who is wearing a blue crescent around a red disk, is followed by Horus in blue symbolizing the air, and Sobek in green representing the water. The sanctuaries, built by Ptolemy XIII (88-51 BC), are in a bad state and are much smaller than those at Edfu. Within each was an altar upon which a portable shrine would have stood. Beneath the sanctuary are the crypts which are empty but, unusually, are open to the public.

A small secret chamber or priest hole lies between the two sanctuaries, in what would have appeared as a very thick wall. This chamber was connected to the small room behind and to a space above the altars.

On the inner wall of the outer corridor (j) is the first known illustration of instruments, including bone-saws, scalpels, suction caps and dental tools, which date from the 2nd century AD. A seated figure of a god accepts these as offerings. While

Feluccas on the River Nile

your guide may tell you that complicated operations were carried out 1,800 years ago it is most probable that these were instruments used in the mummification process. Adjacent to the left is a repeated relief of Isis on a birthing stool. Nearby the temple corridor floor is marked with graffiti which were drawn by patients and pilgrims as they spent the night there before the next day's healing ceremonies.

In the outer corridor, at the back of the temple (k), Horus and Sebek stand either side of a small niche/shrine now empty. Above and around are mystic symbols of eyes, ears and animals and birds each sporting four pairs of wings. Continue round the corridor to (l) where the traditional killing of the enemies scene, much eroded, this time includes a lion.

In the northwest corner of the temple complex is a large circular well which has a stairway, cistern and rectangular basin which are believed to be connected in some ways with the worship of the crocodile god Sobek. The temple is particularly attractive to visit at dusk when it is floodlit and many of the beautiful reliefs are shown at their best, especially in the first and second hypostyle halls. Taking a torch with you at this time of day is essential, however, because the floors are uneven and there are many small steps and depressions waiting to catch out the unwary and footweary traveller.

Local information

● Accommodation
The cheap and clean **F** *Cleopatra Hotel* is located nr the service taxi depot on Sharia 26th July.

● Places to eat
Besides the small stalls which serve *'ful'* (beans) there is the cheap and clean *El-Noba Restaurant* just to the south of the white mosque on the main Luxor-Aswan road.

● Banks & money changers
Next to the mosque, open Sunday-Thursday 0830-1400 but 1000-1330 during Ramadan.

● Post & telecommunications
Area code: 097.

● Shopping
There is a small but colourful tourist bazaar in the street below the entrance to the temple. Scarves seem to be the speciality here and bargaining with the stallholders tends to be a more relaxed and good-natured experience as you travel further south towards Aswan.

● Transport
Train To Luxor and Aswan stop at Kom Ombo station just across the highway but only the very slow and crowded second and third class service.

Road Bus: north to Edfu, Esna and Luxor or south to Aswan, leave the bus terminal on Sharia 26th July about 350m south of Sharia Gumhorriya. **Service taxis**: north to Edfu (1 hr) or south to Aswan (45 mins) can be caught from the terminal on Sharia 26 July just south of Sharia Gumhorriya.

The Nile Valley South of Aswan

FOR MANY visitors to Egypt the highlight of their trip is Aswan and Abu Simbel which, after the noise and crowds of Cairo and the over-commercialization of Luxor, is wonderfully relaxing. The combination of the magnificent sites, the reliable weather, the breathtaking sunsets and the friendliness of the indigenous Nubian population make Egypt's deep south an experience which must not be missed. It has been a popular winter resort for cold blooded Europeans since Victorian times.

ASWAN

(*Pop* 350,000; *Alt* 193m) Aswan, Egypt's southern frontier town, in its delightful river setting is the highlight of any Nile cruise. It is stunningly beautiful, charmingly romantic, and wonderfully relaxing, an escape from the over-commercialization of **Luxor's** hordes of tourists and

vendors. This is the sunniest city in Egypt, hence the popularity. It is not too large to walk around in the cooler part of the day, pace of life is slow and so relaxing. From the corniche observe the tall masted *feluccas* handled so masterfully by a tiny crew, listen to the Nubian musicians, in the late evening watch the flocks of egrets skimming the surface of the Nile as they go to roost, in the early morning watch the sun rise behind the city and hear the call of the muezzin. Feast on freshly caught Nile fish.

Aswan's indigenous inhabitants are the ethnically, linguistically and culturally distinct **Nubians** who are undoubtedly African rather than Arab. Despite being frequently invaded and conquered by their northern Egyptian neighbours, the Nubians actually controlled Egypt during the 25th Dynasty (747-656 BC). Cleopatra was a Nubian from the modern-day Sudanese town of Wadi Halfa. Indeed, the term Nubian is equally applicable to the Sudanese who live along the Nile as far south as Khartoum. The later Nubian kingdom of Kush, whose capital was the Sudanese town of Merowe and which included Aswan, remained largely independent from Egypt. Having been the last region to adopt the Christian faith Nubia became a sanctuary for Coptic

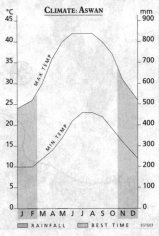

CLIMATE: ASWAN

°C / mm

MAX TEMP

MIN TEMP

J F M A M J J A S O N D

RAINFALL   BEST TIME

EGTG03

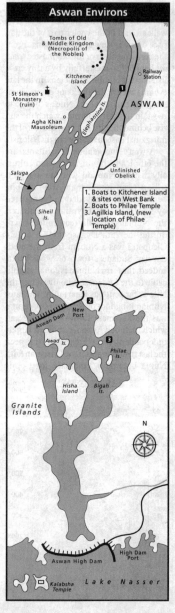

Aswan Environs

Tombs of Old
& Middle Kingdom
(Necropolis of
the Nobles)

*Kitchener
Island*

Railway
Station

ASWAN

St Simeon's
Monastery
(ruin)

Agha Khan
Mausoleum

Elephantine Is

Unfinished
Obelisk

*Saluga
Is.*

1. Boats to Kitchener Island
   & sites on West Bank
2. Boats to Philae Temple
3. Agilkia Island, (new
   location of Philae
   Temple)

*Siheil
Is.*

Aswan Dam

New Port

Awad Is.

*Philae
Is.*

*Hisha
Island*

*Bigah
Is.*

*Granite
Islands*

N

High Dam
Port

Kalabsha
Temple

Aswan High Dam

Lake Nasser

Christians fleeing the advance of Islam and it remains a Christian stronghold today.

For many centuries a sleepy backwater, Aswan assumed national importance when it became the headquarters for the successful 1898 Anglo-Egyptian reconquest of Sudan. With the 1902 construction of the first **Aswan Dam** the town became a fashionable winter resort for rich Europeans who relished its dry heat, luxury hotels and stunning views, particularly from the *feluccas* sailing on the River Nile at sunset. With the completion of the **Aswan High Dam** in 1970, the Nubian villages to the south of Aswan were submerged by the rising waters of Lake Nasser and many of those who were displaced joined in swelling the population of that ever expanding town. Despite the subsequent construction of a number of heavy industries in Aswan, to take advantage of the cheap hydro-electric power generated at the dam, the town has retained its attractive charm and relaxed atmosphere.

ACCESS The railway station is at the north end of the town, about 5 mins walk from the Corniche where most of the tourist hotels are found. The inter-city taxi depot is nearby, just one block to the south of the railway station. The inter-city bus station is even more conveniently located in the town centre behind the Corniche on Sharia Abtal el-Tahrir and *feluccas* and cruise boats moor at many places along the Corniche. Aswan's desert airport is 24 km south of the town. There is no bus service connecting the airport and town. A hired taxi will cost about E£30 but bargain like mad.

Places of interest

In the town itself, besides watching the beautiful sunset either from the **Corniche** or from the terrace of the **Old Cataract Hotel**, it is well worth visiting the exotic *souq* which, with the exception of Cairo, is probably the best in the country. Running parallel to the Corniche there are stalls selling food and a wide range of fresh produce, best bought in the morning, as well as jewellery, textiles and a host of

The *Souq*

The *souq* or bazaar economy of North Africa has distinctive characteristics. In Egypt a series of large *souqs* continues successfully to exist while bazaar economies elsewhere are faltering. In Egyptian cities as a whole, such as Aswan (see **Sh Sa'ad Zaghloul**), Islamic ideas and traditional trading habits have remained strong.

The bazaar originally functioned as an integral part of the economic and political systems. Traditional activities in financing trade and social organizations were reinforced by the bazaar's successful role in running international commodity trade. The bazaar merchants' long-term raising of credits for funding property, agricultural and manufacturing activities was strengthened by this same trend.

There is a view among orientalists that there is an Egyptian/Islamic city of specific social structure and physical shape. The crafts, trades and goods were located by their 'clean' or 'unclean' status in an Islamic sense, and whether these goods could be sold close to the mosque or *medersa*. Valuable objects were on sale near to the main thoroughfares with lesser trades needing more and cheaper land pushed to the edge of the bazaar. There was a concentration of similar crafts in specific locations within the bazaar so that all shoe-sellers for example were in the same street. These ground rules do not apply in all Egyptian bazaars but in many cases they are relevant in different combinations. Thus, there is a hierarchy of crafts, modified at times by social custom and Islamic practice, which gives highest priority to book making, perfumes, gold and silver jewellery over carpet-selling and thence through a graded scale of commodities through metal work, ceramics, sale of agricultural goods and ultimately low grade crafts such as tanning and dyeing.

oriental herbs and spices which are best bought after sunset.

The recently opened **Nubian Museum** which cost E£30 million stands on a granite hill to the south of the town. It covers an internal area of 7,000 sq m and and has an open air display of a further 50,000 sq m.

There are 2,000 artefacts tracing the area's history since early times. There are 86 explanatory panels and a huge diorama. The displays include the oldest skeleton – unearthed in the southern area of Toshka. The pre-history cave depicts the first attempts at rock carvings and the use of tools. Here the animals portrayed include elephant and giraffe. The Pharaonic period demonstrates the importance of this region to the rulers of Egypt, it being the gateway to the south and thus an important routeway. There are statues of Ramses II (one over 8m high) who maintained a very positive presence in Nubia. There are sections devoted to the Graeco-Roman, Coptic and Islamic influences.

The colourful exhibition of the folk heritage emphasizes the individuality of Nubian culture. The most common crafts are pottery and the weaving of baskets and mats from palm fronds. Hand weaving is less well developed.

Outside the features in the garden can be translated into the journey of the River Nile across desert and cataracts – bringing life to Egypt.

As yet no guide book has been produced. Entrance E£30, students E£15. No photography permitted.

Opposite the Corniche and only a short ferry ride away in the middle of the Nile is **Elephantine Island**. Measuring 2 km long and 500m at its widest point the island which gets its name from the large black rocks off its south tip which look, perhaps, like bathing elephants, is worth visiting. Public ferries run every 15 mins between 0600-2400 from the landing dock opposite the Egyptair office and dock just next to the island's **Aswan Museum**, like the *feluccas* which can be hired at negotiable rates (see Transport below).

NB The free ferry to the *Aswan Oberoi Hotel* does not give access to the rest of the island.

The Great Dams of Aswan

Although it has since become a cliché, the River Nile really is 'the lifeblood of Egypt' and the combination of a restricted area of agricultural land and an ever expanding population has necessitated the very careful management of what limited water is available. The theory behind the construction of the Aswan dams was that, rather than years of low water levels, drought and famine being followed by years when the Nile flooded and washed half the agricultural soil into the Mediterranean, the flow of the River Nile could be regulated and thereby provide a much more stable flow of water. Unfortunately, although the two dams did control the Nile waters and thereby boost both hydro-electric-power and agricultural production, the mushrooming population outstripped the gains and Egypt now imports almost half of its cereal requirements. At the same time it is now recognized that the **High Dam** was planned and built when the level of the River Nile was particularly high. Whether it is because of climatic change or simply part of an apparent 20-30 year cycle the volume of water reaching Aswan is decreasing and if the trend continues it may be necessary to pipe natural gas from the Gulf of Suez to generate the electricity at the giant 2,100 mw power station at Aswan.

The original **Aswan Dam** was built by the British between 1898-1902 and was then raised twice in 20 years to make it the largest dam in the world. Although no longer used for storage or irrigation the dam, which is crossed by the road to the airport, is now mainly used to provide local power. After the 1952 Revolution, the new leaders recognized that massive population pressure meant that a more radical solution was required both to control the waters of the River Nile and generate sufficient electricity for the new industrial sector and bring power to every Egyptian village. To finance the construction of the planned **High Dam**, following the withdrawal of a World Bank loan under US pressure, Nasser nationalized the Suez Canal and persuaded the USSR to help build the dam. Construction started in 1960 and was completed in 1971 after Nasser's death in September 1970.

Although it took a number of years to fill, the most visible effect of the dam was the creation of **Lake Nasser** which, covering an area of about 6,000 sq km and being over 180m deep in places, is the world's largest reservoir. This has enabled Egypt, unlike Sudan or Ethiopia, to save water during times of plenty and have an adequate strategic reserve for times of shortage. The extra water from the dam significantly increased the area of land under permanent irrigation and allowed over 1 million feddans (about 400,000 ha) of desert to be reclaimed. In addition, the extra electric power facilitated the expansion of the industrial sector not only around Aswan but throughout the country.

There were, however, major environmental implications of the dam's construction because the rise of Lake Nasser flooded the homeland of the Nubians who were forced to migrate north to other towns and cities: to date they have been offered negligible compensation. Another drawback is that the lake accumulates the Nile's natural silt which used to fertilize the agricultural land downstream from Aswan. Consequently farmers in Lower Egypt are now having to rely heavily on chemical fertilizers which destabilizes the whole food chain. In view of its expanding population, however, Egypt would be in an absolutely hopeless situation without the dams.

The region's first inhabitants lived on this island long before Aswan itself was occupied. It was reputed to be the home of Hapy, the god of the Nile flood, and the goddess of fertility Satet, who were both locally revered, and the regional god Khnum, who was represented by a ram's head. The **Temple of Khnum** (30th Dynasty) once accounted for over two-thirds of the island's 2 sq km fortress town of **Yebu**, the word for both elephant and ivory in ancient Egyptian and which for centuries was the main trade and security border post between Egypt and Nubia. The ruined temple, at the south end of the island boasts a gateway portraying Alexander II worshipping Khnum which suggests that the Greeks added to this temple complex. The German Archeology Institute are at present excavating the region round the Temple of Khnum and while visits are not permitted there is plenty to see from the sidelines. The island has a number of less impressive ruins, and temples have been built here for 4 millennia. Make time when visiting this site to take advantage of an outstanding high viewpoint from which to enjoy the beautiful panorama of the Aswan corniche to the east, including the picturesque *Old Cataract Hotel*, the islands and the River Nile itself. To the west the Aga Khan Mausoleum (see page 284) is clearly visible and to the south, look for the pink fronted *Hotel Amun* set on its own island amongst palm trees and exotic gardens.

You will be unlikely to visit the ruins of the Temple of Khnum without being intercepted by a local 'custodian' anxious to impart a severely limited English translation of his knowledge of the monument in return for the inevitable *baksheesh*.

The **Roman Nilometer** is reached by taking the pathway southwards to the left of the museum entrance. This fascinating device, rediscovered on the southeast tip of Elephantine Island in 1822, was designed to measure the height of the annual River Nile flood. This enabled the coming season's potential crop yield to be estimated and the level of crop taxation to be fixed. Besides Roman and very faint pharaonic numerals, there are also more recent tablets inscribed in both French and Arabic, on the 90 walled stairs which lead down to a riverside shaft.

The **Aswan Museum**, was established in order to display relics salvaged from the flooded areas behind the Aswan dams, which is ironic because the villa and gardens originally belonged to Sir William Willcocks, the designer of the first Aswan Dam. Its brief was subsequently expanded to act as a museum of the region's heritage. It offers a spread of exhibits of phaoronic material, Roman and Islamic pottery, jewellery, and funerary artefacts. The arrangement is logical and names are clear. When the Nubian material is transferrred to the newly open Nubian museum there will space to display the wealth of material found of Elephantine island itself. The ground floor is arranged in chronological order with items from the Middle and New kingdoms, including pottery, combs and some jewellery, while the basement displays a series of human and animal mummies and an impressive gold sheathed statue of Khnum.

Nilometer

Open daily winter 0800-1700, summer 0800-1800, E£10 entrance, students E£5 and E£15 for camera. Price includes entrance to the museum, view of ruins and walk down steps of the nilometer.

Besides the museum, Nilometer and temple ruins in the south and the *Aswan Oberoi Hotel* in the north, there are also three small typical **Nubian villages** in the middle of Elephantine Island. Although it is suggested that the villagers prefer not to become a tourist attraction, visits are organized for foreigners including hospitality in the houses.

Kitchener's Island which lies north of the larger Elephantine Island, originally known as the 'Island of Plants' has a magnificent **Botanical Garden**. The beautiful island was presented to Lord Kitchener, who had a passion for exotic plants and flowers from around the world, in gratitude for his successful Sudan campaign and the gardens have been maintained in their original style. The atmosphere on the island, which is almost completely shielded from the bustle of Aswan by Elephantine Island, is very relaxed and its lush vegetation, animals and birds make it an ideal place to watch the sunset. There is an expensive café at the south end of the island. Open daily from 0800 until sunset, entrance E£10. Can be reached by *felucca*, start bargaining at E£5 return. The local motorized ferry boat is a bargain. It costs E£1 each way and the company is much more interesting.

The beautiful **Agha Khan Mausoleum**, which is situated on a hill on the West Bank of the River Nile opposite the town, was built of solid marble for the 3rd Agha Khan (1877-1957) who was the 48th Imam of the Ismaili sect of Shi'a Muslims. He was renowned for his wealth and was given his body-weight in jewels by his followers for his 1945 diamond jubilee. As an adult he visited Aswan every winter for its therapeutic climate, having fallen in love with its beauty and built a villa on the West Bank. His widow, who still lives in the villa every winter, erected the mausoleum on the barren hill above the villa. Its is a brilliant white marble building, closely resembling a miniature version of the Fatimids' mausoleums in Cairo, with virtually the only hint of colour the fresh red rose placed daily on the sarcophagus. Outside, the views of the desert and of Aswan across the Nile are particularly breathtaking at sunset. There is free entry to the mausoleum for respectably dressed tourists and pilgrims on Tuesday-Sunday 0900-1645. Can by reached by local ferry E£2 return or *felucca*, start bargaining at E£20 return.

The **Necropolis of the Nobles** at Qubbet al-Hawwa (dome of the wind) is located further north along the West Bank of the River Nile, west being the world of the dead and east the world of the living. The necropolis is illuminated at night by hidden spotlights, magnificent when viewed from the Aswan side of the River Nile. The riverside cliff is lined with tombs from various periods which have been discovered during the last century. These tombs, open from 0800-1600, entrance E£12, camera E£5, can be reached by ferries, E£1 return, from the Corniche near Seti Tours which run every 30 mins from 0600-1800 and every hour from 1800-2100. Just above the water-line are the Roman tombs, a little higher are earlier ones and in the highest more durable rock are those of the Old and Middle kingdoms. The ceremonial stairways from the river bank to the tomb entrances can be easily seen, but this is not now the access. The majority of the dead are believed to have been priests or officials responsible for water transport between Egypt and Nubia.

Wear a strong pair of shoes and take a torch. Entrance fee E£12, students E£6, camera E£5 and video camera E£30. The site is open daily between 0700-1700 in summer and 0700-1600 in winter. The ticket office is above the ferry landing. There is a guide on duty to show the way, unlock the tombs and turn on the electric lights. His services are part of the entry fee but a small tip is recommended. Most tours begin at the southern end with the tombs of Mekhu and Sabni. Take care in negotiating the terrace from which the rock-cut tombs were mined since the going is uneven and stands above a steep drop. Most of the tombs are numbered in ascending order from south to north with the more interesting ones including the following:

Mekhu (No 25) was a chief overseer in Upper Egypt at the time of the 6th Dynasty and was killed while on official duties. His son **Sabni** mounted an expedition to reclaim his father's body and successfully returned to Aswan to give **Mekhu** a ceremonial burial. The tomb of **Mekhu** comprises two chambers, a narrow antechamber roughly decorated with family and farming scenes (1 and 2). The main chamber is cut out of solid rock leaving 18 slightly tapering columns,

themselves decorated with reliefs of the family and fragments of other funeral scenes. The inner wall to the left carries a series of false doors (3) and (4) inscribed to **Mekhu**. There is an offering table in the middle of this main chamber (5).

Also accessed from here (the original entry is blocked) is a memorial to **Sabni** (No 26) son of Mekhu. To the right of the main chamber is a large false door (6) and a depiction of fishing and fowling from river craft.

Sarenput II (No 31), who was governor or Guardian of the South at the height of the Middle Kingdom, has the largest, most elaborate and best preserved tomb in this necropolis. It is well lit and comprises two axial chambers, linked by a corridor with niches. The first hall is rectangular with six rock-cut pillars and a small granite offering table (1). The ceiling is decorated and

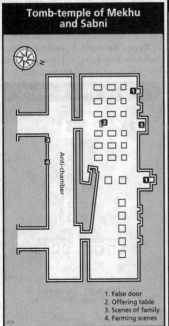

Tomb-temple of Mekhu and Sabni

Anti-chamber

1. False door
2. Offering table
3. Scenes of family
4. Farming scenes

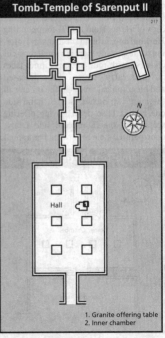

Tomb-temple of Sarenput II

Hall

1. Granite offering table
2. Inner chamber

there is a distinctive stripped, coloured door lintel. Steps lead to a narrow connecting corridor which has six niches with statues of **Sarenput II**. In the inner chamber there are four pillars with the deceased represented on the inward facing sides of each. A niche at the head of the tomb is surrounded with depictions of **Sarenput** and his family. In a small recess at the rear of the tomb there is an elaborate relief portraying him with his wife, son and mother in a beautiful garden.

Harkhuf (unnumbered, alongside No 32) This tomb has no artificial lighting. He was Guardian of southern Egypt and a royal registrar in the 6th Dynasty. He achieved great fame as a noble of Elephantine and leader of diplomatic/military expeditions in the south and west of Aswan. His tomb-temple is modest, being made up of a (now) open entrance area with a doorway centrally placed. On this entrance wall to the main chamber is (right hand side) remains of a verbatim copy of a letter from Pepi II commending **Harkhuf** and (around the doorway) offering scenes. Inside there is a small rock-cut chamber with four columns, inner faces of which carry pictures of the deceased and biographical texts. On the inner wall there are two niches, the left hand side one with a false door bearing offering scenes and the right hand side a false door/painted stele below which is a small offering table. An inclined shaft leads to the burial chamber, while to the left hand side is a second passage, thought to have been used for a later burial.

The tomb-temple of **Pepinakht**, which lies adjacent to that of **Harkhuf** is currently closed while a German excavation is in progress.

Sarenput I (No 36), the grandfather of Sarenput II in No 31, was both Guardian of the South and also the overseer of the priests of Khnum and Satet during the 12th Dynasty (1991-1786 BC). The tomb is one of the largest consisting of three major chambers with joining corridors, but unfortunately the reliefs are badly decayed. The tomb-temple is well lit. Enter through a doorway decorated with excellent reliefs carved on polished limestone, on either side of the doorway are damaged depictions of a seated **Sarenput I**. Pass into an antechamber with six columns in a line close to the inner wall, which originally carried a finely decorated portico. On the right column there are carvings on all faces of a like picture of **Prince Sarenput I**. There are small niches in the side walls of this antechamber which contain representations of

Tomb-Temple of Harkhuf

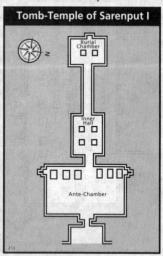

Tomb-Temple of Sarenput I

Sarenput I and his wife. The inner wall carries important scenes in good condition. On the left is a scene of the deceased spearing fish, his wife clutching him, apparently lest he fall and his son on the adjacent bank. Above are farming scenes with oxen. On the right of the inner wall are pictures of **Sarenput**, his wife, mother and family. An inner hall is entered through a narrow doorway, a modest room with four pillars. The pillar decorations have almost vanished in this room and the paintings on the plaster work of the walls have also all but disappeared. Fragments show scenes of fowling, boating and women at work. A narrow corridor has been cut into the west wall rising a little to the small burial chamber with two columns. In this room is a niche and shrine for **Sarenput I**. Two breaks in the rock in the walls of this chamber have no access.

To the north of these tombs is a separate tomb-temple, **Ka-Gem-Em-Ahu**, reached by a sandy path. **Ka-Gem-Em-Ahu** was the high priest of Khnum in the

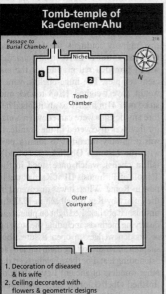

Tomb-temple of Ka-Gem-em-Ahu

Passage to Burial Chamber

Niche

N

1 **2**

Tomb Chamber

Outer Courtyard

1. Decoration of diseased & his wife
2. Ceiling decorated with flowers & geometric designs

late New Empire. His tomb was discovered by Lady William Cecil in 1902. The outer courtyard measures 10m wide with a depth of some 7m. Most of the plaster work has been lost from this six-pillared area but scenes of boats on the Nile can still be made out with one or two residual depictions of funeral scenes such as the weighing of the heart. The main tomb chamber is 7m square with a low entrance doorway and four pillars. The ceiling is quite ornately decorated with flowers, birds and geometric designs. Although the walls of the main chamber are quite plain, the left hand side inner pillar carries painted plaster with a representation of the deceased's wife. A sloping passage leads from the main chamber to the burial chamber below which is difficult of access.

The ruined desert **Monastery of St Simeon**, which lies on the West Bank inland from the Agha Khan's Mausoleum, was built and dedicated in the 7th century to a 4th century monk Anba Hadra, who was later ordained bishop. The monastery was rebuilt in the 10th century. It can be reached by *felucca* (E£30 wait and return) and then either by a 20 mins walk through soft sand or a 10 mins camel ride (which carries two) hired near the landing stage. Pay around E£25 for a return trip, open daily from 0900-1600, entrance E£5. Following an encounter with a funeral procession on the day after his own wedding Simeon decided, presumably without consulting his wife, to remain celibate. He became a student of St Balmar, rejected urban life and chose to become a desert hermit. The fortress monastery stands at the head of a desert valley looking towards the River Nile and from where the dramatic sunsets appears to turn the sand to flames. Until Salah al-Din destroyed the building in 1173 it was used by monks, including Saint Simeon about whom very little else is known, as a base for proselytising expeditions first south into Nubia and then, after the Muslim conquest, north into Egypt.

David Roberts – painter of Egypt

David Roberts was a remarkable man whose oriental paintings brought to life Egypt and its heritage for many people in the Western world. His pictures are full of atmosphere and wonderful colour. Among the most famous are the **Temple of Dendera**, **Island of Philae**, **Nubia** and **A Street in Cairo** together with his paintings of the **Temple of Ramses II** at Abu Simbel.

Roberts, born in 1796, had a difficult childhood as the son of an impecunious Edinburgh (Stockbridge) cobbler. He eventually became known as a painter of theatrical scenery at the Old Vic and Covent Garden before making his name as a picture painter with items such as **The Israelites leaving Egypt** and scenes of his travels in Spain.

David Roberts arrived in Egypt in 1838 and spent 11 months travelling through the Nile Valley and visiting the Holy Land. He was a prolific sketcher of sites and left six volumes of lithographs of this visit, including several scenes of Cairo where he terminated his Egyptian travels. Many of these and other scenes were later translated into oil paintings. Roberts returned to Great Britain where, in his absence, he had been made an associate of the Royal Academy. He lived to 69 years and produced many masterpieces based on his travels in Egypt, incidentally providing a wonderful record of the state of Egyptian monuments of the time.

There are many inexpensive cards and books with copies of his illustrations. It is certainly useful to have these with you when visiting the major sites as they show very clearly parts that have disappeared, parts that are now too high to view easily and give an excellent idea of the coloured decorations.

Although the monastery is uninhabitable its main feature the surrounding walls, the lower storeys of hewn stone and upper ones of mud-brick, have been preserved. At intervals along the walls there are remains of towers. Visitors are admitted through a small gateway in the east tower which leads to a church with a partially collapsed basilica but the nave and aisles are still accessible. There is a painting of the ascended Christ near the domed altar recess. By him are four angels in splendid robes. The walls of a small cave chapel, which can be entered via the church, are richly painted with pictures of the Apostles which were partially defaced by Muslim iconoclasts. The cave chapel leads to the upper enclosure from which the living quarters can be entered. Up to 300 monks lived in simple cells with some hewn into the rock and others in the main building to the north of the enclosure, with kitchens and stables to the south.

The guide here is well known for his ability to communicate to any nationality as he practically mimes his account. A most memorable experience in its own right.

Back on the East Bank of the Nile on the outskirts of Aswan about 2 km along the highway south, is the **Unfinished Obelisk**, entrance E£10, in the quarries which provided red granite for the ancient temples. The huge obelisk, which would have weighed 1,168 tonnes and stood over 41m high, was abandoned before any designs were carved when a major flaw was discovered in the granite. It was originally intended to form a pair with the **Lateran Obelisk**, the world's tallest obelisk which once stood in the Temple of Tuthmosis III at Karnak but is now in Rome. When it was discovered in the quarry by Rex Engelbach in 1922 the unfinished obelisk shed light on pharaonic quarrying methods, including the soaking of wooden wedges to open fissures, but shaping and transporting them remains an astounding feat. For those having seen the other wonders of ancient Egypt the Unfinished Obelisk, open daily 0600-1800, entrance E£10, students E£5, is a little

Well established as one of the UK's leading tour operators Hayes & Jarvis has been selling long haul holidays to the discerning traveller for over 40 years. Every Hayes & Jarvis holiday is the product of careful and meticulous planning where good quality and reliability go hand in hand with value for money.

To enter the Footprint Handbooks Prize Draw to win a sensational trip to Peru all you have to do is to fill in the form below and send it back to us. Fooprint Handbooks has grown rapidly in the last couple of years and now has over 35 travel guides in the series.

For more information about Footprint Handbooks
T +44 (0) 1225 469141
Email handbooks@footprint.cix.co.uk

Fill in this form using a ball-point pen and return to us as soon as possible.

Mr ☐ Mrs ☐ Miss ☐ Ms ☐

First name   Surname

Permanent Address

Postcode/Zip   Country

Email

Occupation   Age

Title of Handbook

Got any friends who would like to hear about Footprint? Please fill in their details

Mr ☐ Mrs ☐ Miss ☐ Ms ☐

First name   Surname

Permanent Address

Postcode/Zip   Country

Win

a 7 night 'Essential Peru' tour for two courtesy of Hayes & Jarvis

50 runners up to win a Footprint Handbook of their choice

HAYES and JARVIS
HOLIDAYS WORLDWIDE

Win

Footprint Handbooks
6 Riverside Court
Lower Bristol Road
Bath
BA2 3DZ
England

Affix
Stamp
Here

Which two destinations would you most like to visit in the next two years?

How did you hear about us?

| Recommended ☐ | Used before ☐ | Media/press article ☐ |
| Library ☐ | Bookshop ☐ | Internet ☐ |

There is a complete list of Footprint Handbooks at the back of this book.
Which other countries would you like to see us cover?

a 7 night 'Essential Peru' tour for two
courtesy of Hayes & Jarvis

If you do not wish to receive information from other reputable businesses, please tick box ☐

Temple of Isis- Philae

disappointing and it is probably better combining it with a trip to the Aswan Dams or the Philae Temple. Hire a taxi to the High Dam for E£35.

There are in fact two **Aswan Dams** but it is the so-called High Dam, just upstream from the original 1902 British-built Aswan Dam, that is Egypt's pride and joy and which created Lake Nasser, the world's largest reservoir. In fact the High Dam is so big – 111m high, 3,830m long, 980m wide at its base and 40m at its top – that it is almost impossible to realize its scale except from the observation deck of the lotus-shaped Soviet-Egyptian Friendship tower or from the air when landing at nearby Aswan airport. It is claimed that the structure of stones, sand, clay and facing concrete give it a volume 17 times that of the Pyramid of Cheops. To help appreciate the scale and consequences of the dam's construction the visitors' pavilion, which includes a 15m high model of the dam and photographs of the relocation of the Abu Simbel temple, is worth a visit. Occasionally, crossing the dam is prevented for security reasons. The contrast, however, between the view of the narrow river channel looking towards Aswan on the downstream side of the dam and the vast area of Lake Nasser, almost like an open sea, as you look upstream could not be more marked. It costs E£4 per person to cross the High Dam between 0700-1700 and it may be necessary to show your passport to prove that you are not a Israeli spy. Photography of the snap-shot variety is permitted, but the use of video recorders is prohibited for security reasons. A taxi here from Aswan will cost E£40 return.

For many tourists the most beautiful and romantic monuments in Aswan, if not in the whole of Egypt, are the **Philae Temples** which were built in the Ptolemaic era (332-30 BC) as an offering to Isis. In fact, the **Temple of Isis** and the rest of the monuments were moved to the neighbouring Agilkia island by UNESCO in 1972-1980 when the construction of the High Dam threatened to submerge Philae forever. They were then reconstructed to imitate the original as closely as possible but the new position no longer faces neighbouring Bigah island, one of the burial sites of Osiris and closed to all but the priesthood, which was the whole raison d'être for the Temple of Isis being on Philae island in the first place.

ACCESS Although it is possible to catch a bus and then walk 2 km to the lakeside motorboat dock, unless on a organized tour the island is most easily reached by taking a E£10 taxi ride from Aswan to the dock and a motorboat across to the island. They seat 8 people and cost E£3 per person or E£20 per boat for the return journey including a 1-hr wait at the temple although 1½ hrs is preferable. Open summer 0700-1700; winter 0700-1600. Entrance E£20, students E£10, permit for commercial photography E£10. There is no charge for video recorders.

Temples of Philae, Agilkia Island

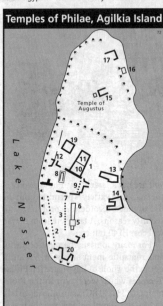

1. Temple of Isis
2. Colonnade of Augustus & Tiberius
3. First East Colonnade
4. Temple of Arensnuphis
5. Chapel of Mandulis
6. Temple of Imhotep
7. Gate of Nectanebo II
8. Mammisi
9. Second East Colonnade
10. Hypostele Hall
11. Sanctuary
12. Hadrian's Gate
13. Temple of Hathor
14. Kiosk of Trajan
15. Temple of Augustus
16. Roman Arch
17. Gate of Diocletian
18. Temple of Harendotes
19. Kiosk of Nektanebis

Although there are other smaller temples on the island it is dominated by the **Temple of Isis (1)**. She was the consort of her brother Osiris and eventually became the 'Great Mother of All Gods and Nature', 'Goddess of Ten Thousand Names', and represented women, purity and sexuality. Isis is attributed with reconstructing Osiris' dismembered body and creating his son Horus who became the model of a man and king. In the 3rd-5th century the worship of Isis became Christianity's greatest rival throughout the Mediterranean. There have even been claims that the early Christians developed the cult of the Virgin Mary to replace Isis in order to attract new converts.

Different parts of the Temple of Isis, which occupies over a quarter of the new island, were constructed over an 800 years period by Ptolemaic (332-30 BC) and Roman (30 BC-395 AD) rulers. At the top of the steps where the motorboats arrive is a Roman colonnaded court which leads to the main temple. On the west or lakeside side of the court the **Colonnade of Augustus and Tiberius (2)** is well preserved and contains 31 columns with individual capitals. There are still traces of paint on some of the columns and the starred ceiling. On the right is the plainer **First East Colonnade (3)** behind which are first the foundations of the **Temple of Arensnuphis (4)** (Nubian God), the ruined **Chapel of Mandulis (5)** (Nubian God of Kalabsha) and the **Temple of Imhotep (6)** (the architect of Zoser's step pyramid at Saqqara who was later deified as a healing God).

The main Temple of Isis at the end of the court is entered through the **First Pylon of Ptolemy XIII Neos Dionysus** which show him slaying his enemies as Isis, Horus and Hathor look on. The pylon was originally flanked by two obelisks, since looted and transported to the UK, but today only two lions at the base guarding the entrance remain. The **Gate of Ptolemy II Philadelphus**, just to the right of the pylon's main **Gate of Nectanebo II (7)**, is from the earlier 30th Dynasty (380-343 BC). On its right is graffiti written by Napoleon's troops after their victory over the Mamlukes in 1799.

Arriving in a large forecourt to the left is the colonnaded **Mammisi (8)**, used for mammisi rituals, which was originally built by Ptolemy VII and expanded by the Romans which explains why images of Isis with Horus as a baby are intermingled with the figures of contemporary Roman emperors. In the inner sanctum of the Mammisi itself are historically important scenes of Isis giving birth to Horus in the marshes and others of her suckling the child-pharaoh. A curiosity to note on the outer western wall of the birth house is a memorial to men of the Heavy Camel Regiment who lost their lives in the Sudanese Campaign of 1884-85. The tablet commemorates the nine officers and 92 men who were killed in action or died of disease. On the opposite side of the forecourt from the Birth House is the late Ptolemaic **Second East Colonnade (9)** behind which are a number of attractive reliefs and six small function rooms including a library.

The axis of the temple is changed by the **Second Pylon**, set at an angle to the first, which was built by Ptolemy XIII Neos Dionysos and which shows him presenting offerings to Horus and Hathor on the right tower but some of the scenes on the left tower were defaced by the early Christians. Beyond the Pylon a court containing ten columns opens onto the **Hypostyle Hall (10)**. These have retained few traces of their original colour although the capitals are better preserved. The ceiling in the central aisle has representations of vultures which were symbolic of the union of Lower and Upper Egypt. The rest of the ceilings have astronomical motifs and two representations of the goddess Nut. On either side of the wall, backing onto the Second Pylon, Ptolemy VII and Cleopatra II can be seen presenting offerings to Hathor and Khnum. The crosses carved on pillars and walls here provide evidence of the Coptic occupation. From the entrance at the far end of the Hypostyle Hall is a chamber which gives access to the roof. The interconnecting roof chambers are all dedicated to Osiris and lead to his shrine. Vivid reliefs portray the reconstruction of his body.

Continuing upwards and north from the chamber, linked to the Hypostyle Hall, are three rooms decorated with sacrificial reliefs representing the deities. The central room leads to a further three rooms linked to the **Sanctuary (11)** in which is a stone pedestal dedicated by Ptolemy III which formerly supported the holy barque (boat) of Isis. Reliefs portray Isis and her son surrounded by

Nubian deities. The temple's exterior was decorated at the direction of the Emperor Augustus.

Hadrian's Gate (12), which is west of the Second Pylon, has some very interesting reliefs. The north wall on the right depicts Isis, Nephthys, Horus and Amun in adoration before Osiris in the form of a bird. Behind is the source of the Nile which is depicted emerging from a cavern and Hapy, a Nile god, is shown pouring water from two jars, indicating the Egyptians' knowledge that the Nile had more than one source. The south wall depicts a mummified Osiris lying on a crocodile together with another image of the reconstructed Osiris seated on his throne with his son Horus.

Smaller shrines can be seen throughout the island dedicated to both Nubian and local deities. East of the temple of Isis is the small **Temple of Hathor (13)**. Two columns depict the head of Hathor at their capital while, in a famous relief, the local deities play musical instruments. The **Kiosk of Trajan (14)**, built in 167 AD, further south has 14 columns with floral motifs. Only two walls have been decorated and these depict Osiris, Horus and Isis receiving offerings from the Emperor Trajan. It is thought that the Kiosk originally had a wooden roof. From here looking southeast towards the original Philae Island it is possible to see the remains of the coffer dam which was built around it to reduce the water level and protect the temple ruins before they were moved to Agilkia. At the northeast end of the island is the ruined **Temple of Augustus (15)** and the **Gate of Diocletian** which were next to a mud brick Roman village which was abandoned by the archaeologists when Philae was moved because the water had already caused such severe erosion.

Although it is wonderful to visit Philae in the late afternoon, when the light is most attractive, many tourists attend the **Sound and Light Show** which involves a 1 hr floodlit tour through the ruins. As in Karnak and the

Cairo Pyramids the visual beauty of the place is more impressive than the historically informative but melodramatic soundtrack. This visit to the temple at sunset in time for the first evening show can be especially memorable. Travelling out from the harbour in a small flotilla of boats, watching the stars come out and tracing the dark shapes of the islands in the river silhouetted against the orange sunset sky is a stunning prelude to the beauty of the ancient floodlit ruins. Tour companies, obviously keen to sell you a package deal including transport to and from the show, can provide full details of the times of each show which is in a different language. Inclusive charge from Aswan E£45.

Sound and Light Shows daily at 2000, 2115 and 2230 in summer (end April-end September) and 1800, 1915 and 2030 in winter as follows:

Monday	English/Italian
Tuesday	French/English
Wednesday	English/Spanish/French
Thursday	French/Arabic
Friday	English/French
Saturday	English/French
Sunday	French/German

Local information
● Accommodation

AL *Aswan Oberoi*, Elephantine Island, PO Box 62, T 314667, F 323485, 160 rm with balcony, 38 suites and 16 villas, excellent location in middle of river Nile, reached by a free ferry which runs to/from the *Isis Hotel*, stunning views particularly at sunset, restaurants offering Indian, Egyptian and continental food, coffee shop, bar, nightclub, health spa, gym, also tennis and pool which non-residents can use; **AL** *Isis Island Aswan Hotel*, T 317002, F 317405, 382 rm spread over own island situated to south of town at the first cataract, access by private ferry, every facility incl a 9 hole mini golf course, picturesque setting, most relaxing atmosphere, an excellent place to 'get away from it all'; **AL** *New Cataract*, Sharia Abtal el-Tahrir, T 323377, F 323510, 144 rm, an unfortunate slab of a building overlooking the Nile about 5 mins walk south from town centre, connected by a series of gardens to and shares many facilities incl the pool with the *Kalabsha Hotel*, and the famous *Old Cataract Hotel*, choice of restaurants, 24-hr

coffee shop, bar and discotheque; **AL** *Sofitel Cataract Hotel*, Sharia Abtal el-Tahrir, T 323434, F 323510, 136 rm, Edwardian Moorish-style hotel, universally known as the *Old Cataract Hotel* and featured in Agatha Christie's book *Death on the Nile*, located opp Elephantine Island, about 5 mins walk south from town centre, connected to *New Cataract Hotel* and *Kalabsha Hotel*, opened in 1899, is one of Egypt's oldest and most famous hotels, large a/c rooms, some with river view, friendly service but faults due to age are reported, full range of facilities incl classic *1902 Restaurant*, nightclub, lounge bar, shops, tennis, croquet. There are minimum charges for non-residents taking drinks on the terrace (E£25) and in the Elephantine Bar (E£15). Afternoon tea which incl sandwiches and cakes is rec as better value for these minimum charges than morning coffee.

A *Amun Tourist Village*, PO Box 118, Sahara City, T 480438, F 480440, 252 rm, located nr airport, about 18 km from the attractions of Aswan and the Nile, less busy in low season, restaurants, pool, tennis; **A** *Isis Hotel*, Corniche el-Nil, T 324905, 100 rm, excellent location between river and Corniche next to *Hotel Oberoi's* landing stage, a/c bungalows, pool, riverside terrace and restaurant.

C *Amun*, Amun Island, T 313800, F 317190, 56 rm, excellent location on its own lush island in the middle of the River Nile, opp *Old Cataract Hotel*, free ferry operates to/from the Egyptair office, a Club Mediterranée resort with excellent standard of food, service and facilities; **C** *Kalabsha Hotel*, Sharia Abtal el-Tahrir, T 323434, F 325974, 120 rm, on hill overlooking the Nile, about 5 mins walk south from town centre, shares many facilities with *New Cataract* and *Old Cataract Hotel*, built in 1963 for Russians working at the High Dam, good reception and public rooms, poorly decorated bedrooms, starkly furnished restaurant serves a good breakfast, friendly and helpful service.

D *Cleopatra*, Sharia Sa'ad Zaghloul, Aswan, T 314001, F 314002, 130 rm, located downtown nr bus station and *souq*, pool on top floor, restaurant and juice bar.

E *Horus*, T 323323, located on Corniche el Nil south of the *Isis Hotel*, 41 pleasant a/c rooms, with balconies overlooking the Nile, daily clean linen and a relaxed atmosphere, many tour groups; **E** *Oskar Hotel*, Sharia Abbas Mahmoud el-Akad, T/F 326066, 54 rm, located in a crowded downtown area with Egyptian life all around it, see the real Egypt!; **E** *Philae*, Corniche el-Nil, T 322117, 70 small rm with

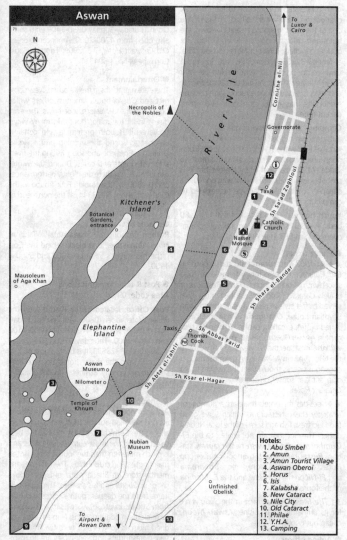

Aswan

N

River Nile

Necropolis
of the Nobles ▲

Governorate

ⓘ

⑫

Taxis ①

Catholic
Church

*Kitchener's
Island*

Botanical
Gardens,
entrance

④

⑥

Nasser
Mosque ②

Ⓢ

Mausoleum
of Aga Khan

⑤

⑪

Taxis ○ Sh Abbas Farid

*Elephantine
Island*

Thomas
Cook

Sh Abtal el-Tahrir

Pol

③

Aswan
Museum ○

Nilometer ○

Sh Ksar el-Hagar

⑩

Temple of
Khnum ○

⑧

⑦

Nubian
Museum

Unfinished
Obelisk ○

⑨

*To
Airport &
Aswan Dam* ↓

⑬

To Luxor &
Cairo

Corniche el-Nil

Sh Sa'ad Zaghloul

Sh Shara el-Bandar

Hotels:
1. *Abu Simbel*
2. *Amun*
3. *Amun Tourist Village*
4. *Aswan Oberoi*
5. *Horus*
6. *Isis*
7. *Kalabsha*
8. *New Cataract*
9. *Nile City*
10. *Old Cataract*
11. *Philae*
12. *Y.H.A.*
13. *Camping*

bath, small fan or a/c, view of the Nile; **E** *Ramses Hotel*, Sharia Abtal el-Tahrir, T 324000, 112 rm with bath, unspectacular but comfortable, small balconies overlooking Nile, friendly staff serve breakfast in the basement restaurant also bar and discotheque.

F *Abu Simbel*, Corniche el-Nil, T 322888, renowned for its reasonable prices, nr bus station, 66 a/c rm have a good view of the Nile, restaurant, bar, discotheque, laundry, bank, garden, oriental dancing and nightclub; **F** *Continental*, Sharia Abbas Farid, T 322311, located nr the main police station and close to the Corniche overlooking the Nile is the oldest, cheapest and one of the most infamous fleapits in town, the hotel and café in front are a rendezvous for budget travellers; **F Happi Hotel**, Sharia Abtal el-Tahrir, T 322028, 60 rm, 126 beds, located in town centre nr the Corniche behind the Misr Bank, Nile views from the rather cramped single and more spacious double rooms with bath on higher flrs, has good reputation and serves decent food.

Camping   Official site with guards is located outside town nr the Unfinished Obelisk, rather inconvenient without your own transport. Compound has showers and toilets but almost no shade. At E£5/car and E£3 pp/night but it is probably far more sensible to stay at one of the cheaper hotels unless you are determined to camp out.

Youth hostels   96 Sharia Abtal el-Tahrir, 80 beds, T 322313, 3 mins from railway station, overnight fee E£3, free kitchen.

● **Places to eat**

◆◆◆: *1902 Restaurant* with classic decor in *Old Cataract Hotel* offers international food spiced with Nubian dancers; *Darna Restaurant* in *New Cataract Hotel*, excellent Egyptian meal served buffet style in restaurant designed as an Egyptian house; *Orangerie* in *Aswan Oberoi*, varied buffet, excellent choice; *Tower Restaurant* in *Aswan Oberoi*, has international cuisine with the most spectacular views over Aswan and the Nile. While in Aswan even the most budget conscious visitors should treat themselves to tea or a drink at sunset on the terrace of the *Old Cataract Hotel*.

◆◆: besides the hotels there are a number of relatively cheap restaurants which serve good food incl fresh fish and some of the local Nubian dishes. They incl but are not limited to the *El-Gumhorriya* and *Darwish* nr the railway station, *Restaurant Shatti* overlooking river opp *Hotel Continental*, highly rec; *Bonarama* and *El-Nil* on the Corniche and the *El-Medina* nr the tourist office.

◆: *The Masry Restaurant* in the *Souq* is rec for its authentic local cuisine; *Aswan Moon*, cheap but good.

● **Airline offices**
Egypt Air, T 22400/22364.

● **Banks & money changers**
Besides the major hotels which change money, there are numerous branches of most of the Egyptian banks on the Corniche or Sharia Abtal el-Tahrir. Recommended are **Bank of Alexandria, National Bank of Egypt, Bank Du Caire.** Open Thursday-Sunday 0830-1400 with some also open from 1700-2000; American Express, *Old Cataract Hotel*, T 302909; Thomas Cook, Corniche el-Nil, T 304011.

● **Entertainment**
There are nightclubs in the *Kalabsha*, *New Cataract* and *Oberoi* hotels amongst others which offer Nubian and Western floorshows. There are discos in all the major hotels. In many ways, however, it is both preferable and certainly cheaper to spend the evening promenading along the Corniche and *souq* visiting the riverside restaurants and cafés. During the winter except on Friday there are nightly performances (2130-2300) by the Nubian Folk Troupe at the Cultural Centre, T 323344, at the north end of the Corniche.

● **Places of worship**
Roman Catholic, 89 Sharia Abtal el-Tahir, nr *Hotel Abu Simbel*, one block behind the Corniche has services Saturday 1800 and Sunday 1900.

● **Post & telecommunications**
Area code: 097.

Post Office: located in the road behind the *Philae Hotel*, open 0800-1400 except Friday. Post restante Saturday-Wednesday 0700-1100 and 1700-2000, Thursday 0700-1100, Friday 1700-2000, T 323533. It is best to post outgoing mail from the major hotels because they seem to get priority. Business services available at *Isis Island*.

● **Shopping**
Aswan is now a large city and it has shops of every description but the *souq*, which runs parallel to the Corniche probably still has the best selection and the most competitive prices and is much more fun than the tourist shops nr the major hotels and cruise ships. There is a departmental store on Sharia Abtal el-Tahrir. Books shops in *Oberoi* and *Isis* arcades. The *souq* sells items from the deeper south – spices and nuts from Sudan, lovely shawls of silk and cotton, table cloths in bright designs, Nubian artefacts, dried hibiscus flowers as a herb tea. The stalls selling fresh fruits and vegetables are an inspiration to castle builders, towering displays.

● **Sports**
The major hotels have good sports facilities but remember that with temperatures as high as 50°C (122°F) in the summer Aswan is not the

place to be engaging in very active sports, particularly in the middle of the day.

Horse riding: on a short or long term basis can be arranged. Try at the large hotels for the safest mounts.

Watersports: are available at the Rowing Club on the Corniche above the *Isis Hotel*.

● **Tour companies & travel agents**

There are numerous travel agencies and guide companies throughout the town who are all touting for your booking. *Eastmar Travel*, Corniche el-Nil, T 323787; *Misr Travel*, one block behind Corniche on way to railway station, adjacent to Tourist Information.

● **Tourist offices**

Located behind the gardens towards the north end of the Corniche next to *Misr Travel*. The Tourist Authority office is manned by the wonderfully helpful Shoukry Sa'ad and his excellent staff who are the nicest, most polite and well informed officials you will meet in Egypt. Although the official opening times are 0830-1600 and 1800-2000 during the high season it is manned from 0800-2000.

● **Useful numbers**

Airport: T 480307; **Emergency Police**: T 22147; **Fire**: T 303058; **Hospital**: T 322912; **Passport Office**: T 22238; **Tourist Police**: T 323163.

● **Transport**

Local Bicycles: are becoming very popular for short distances. There are many hire shops. Try on the Corniche nr Misr Bank at E£5/hr.

Air Airport T 480307, for those who can afford it the easiest, if not the most adventurous, way to leave Aswan is by air. (Taxi to the airport E£20.) There are regular daily **Egyptair** and **ZAS** flights both to Luxor and Cairo which take about 30 mins and 1½ hrs, respectively. Single fare Aswan to Luxor E£250. Allow plenty of time. Don't expect any flight announcements. When the gates open for a flight push forward, if it is not your flight you will be turned back.

Train Train information T 314754, for long distance travel to Luxor (5 hrs), Cairo (17 hrs) and Alexandria (approximately 24 hrs) train is the most comfortable method. Trains range from the deluxe first class sleeper service to crowded and dirty third class cattle trucks. The a/c night train from Aswan to Cairo is highly rec as being safe and comfortable and providing a meal and drinks service and an early breakfast. The cabins, which have large windows with blinds, are small but easily turn into room with bunks, a sink and table, and there are clean communal toilets along the corridor. Departures to Cairo at 0600, 0700, 0800 (with a/c first class coaches), 1500, 1600, 1800 and 1900 (these 3 have sleeping compartments), 2030 and 2230. Tickets cost about E£216 for dinner, bed

Worship of the Nile crocodile – Crocodylus niloticus

These huge creatures, the largest reptile in Africa, were worshipped as the god Sobek (see page 213) depicted as a man with a crocodile's head. The Ancient Egyptians kept them in lakes by the temples which were dedicated to Crocodile gods (see page 173) and fed them the best meat, geese and fish and even wine. Special creatures were decked with jewels, earrings, gold bracelets and necklaces. The bodies were embalmed after death. (Some crocodiles live for a 100 years.) Really they were very ugly creatures to be held in such high esteem. It is suggested that they were worshipped out of fear, in the hopes that offerings and prayers would make them less vicious and reduce the dangers to man and beast.

The problem was these cold blooded creatures needed to come out of the river to bask in the sunshine and they could move at a surprising speed on land. They could stay almost submerged for long periods. The long muscular tail was used as a rudder and on land could be used to fell large animals at a single blow. Small humans were easy prey.

In other regions they were hunted, eaten and considered a protector as they prevented anyone from swimming across the River Nile.

It is fortunate that today these 900 kg creatures can no longer reach the major part of Egypt. They cannot pass the Aswan dam but they exist to the south of this barrier in large numbers.

Burckhardt the Explorer

The Anglo/Swiss geographer and explorer, Johann (John) Ludwig Burckhardt was born in Lausanne, Switzerland on 24 November 1784. He studied at London and Cambridge between 1806-9 and lived in Syria where he learned Arabic and became a follower of Islam taking the Muslim name Ibrahim Ibn Abd Allah. He left Syria, en-route for Cairo and the Fezzan (Libya) from where he was to attempt to cross the Sahara. Local Bedouin spoke of the ruins of a 'lost city', located in the mountains. Knowing that the legendary lost city of Petra was in the vacinity of Aaron,;s tomb on Jebel Harun he persuaded his guides of a desire ti sacrifice a goat in honour of Aaron at his tomb. His scheme succeeded and on 22 August 1812 he was guided through the Siq and into the valley where he saw the Al-Khazneh and the Urn Tomb and thus saw enough to recognize the City of Petra.

When he arrived in Cairo he could find no immediate transport to Fezzan (nothings seems to change). Instead he journeyed up the Nile and discovered the **Temple of Ramses II** at **Abu Simbal**. He next travelled to Saudi Arabia, visiting Mecca. He returned to Cairo where he died on 15 October 1817,before he was able to complete his journey.

and breakfast; E£40 first class and E£23 second class. Trains just to Luxor at 0500, 2000, 2100, 2400.

Road Bus: Bus station T 303225, very regular slow buses and less frequent express buses, stopping only at Kom Ombo (E£1), Edfu (E£2) and Esna, go to Luxor (E£5) which takes 4 hrs. There are also 3 daily buses of very varying quality and price to Cairo (the best at 1530) but, given the distance, the train is a more comfortable option. There is now also a daily a/c bus to Hurghada on the Red Sea coast which continues to Cairo via Suez which is a good stopping off point for travellers to Sinai. **Service taxi**: usually quicker than bus or train can be picked up from the stand south of the railway station. Places served incl Kom Ombo (E£1.50 pp), Edfu (E£2.50) and to Luxor which takes 3½-4 hrs and costs E£6. The 220 km road to Luxor is good in places! The speed limit is 90 km/hr and petrol costs E£14/gallon. Taxi travel can be a heart-stopping experience and with some drivers it is difficult not to close your eyes and start praying.

Boat Feluccas: official prices, regulated by the government, for 1-10 passengers incl waiting time from the Corniche are: Kitchener Island and Agha Khan Mausoleum, E£20, 2 hrs; Kitchener Island, Elephantine Island and Agha Khan Mausoleum, E£25, 2½ hrs; St Simeon's monastery and Nobles Tombs, E£35, 3 hrs; St Simeon's monastery, Kitchener Island and Agha Khan's Mausoleum, E£50, 3 hrs; Nubian village, E£40, 2½ hrs; Elephantine Island only, E£15/hr, 1½ hrs; Elephantine Island and the Nobles' Tombs, E£50, 4 hrs; Elephantine Island and St Simeon's monastery, E£50, 4 hrs; Elephantine Island, St Simeon's monastery and back via Kitchener island, E£40, 3 hrs. Alternatively a 1 hr tour around the islands costs E£18. Hire your own felucca for E£25/hr and go where you like. The per person prices for long distance feluccas from Aswan, which carry a minimum of 6 people and where the group pays for and buys their own food and pays the E£5 pp required to obtain permission to travel are as follows: Kom Ombo, E£25, 1 day and 1 night; Edfu, E£45, 2 days and 2 nights; Esna, E£50, 3 days and 3 nights; and Luxor, E£60, 4 days and 4 nights. The Tourist Office should be able to rec the best captains and is often a place to meet potential fellow passengers.

LOWER NUBIA

Sometimes a trip to **Abu Simbel** and other Lake Nasser temples is offered as an 'extra' on a tour or an excursion from the hotel in Aswan. Do not miss the opportunity to see this amazing site.

Abu Simbel, which lies 280 km south of Aswan and only 40 km north of the Sudanese border (virtually closed to all traffic), is the site of the magnificent **Sun Temple of Ramses II** and the smaller **Temple of Queen Nefertari**. With the exception of the temples and the homes of tourist industry employees, there is almost nothing else in Abu Simbel.

ACCESS For tourists arriving by plane there are free buses from Abu Simbel airport to the site of the temples while the coach tours from Aswan go direct to the site.

Places of interest

Temples of Abu Simbel Open 0600 until the departure of the last plane. The two temples, which were rediscovered in 1813 completely buried by sand, were built by the most egotistical pharaoh of all, Ramses II (1304-1237 BC) during the 19th Dynasty of the New Kingdom. Although he built a smaller temple for his queen Nefertari, it is the four gigantic statues of himself, which were carved out of the mountainside, which dominate Abu Simbel. It was intended that his magnificent and unblinking stare would be the first thing that travellers, visitors and enemies alike, saw as they entered Egypt from the south. Behind the statues is **Ramses II's Temple of the Sun** which was originally built to venerate Amun and Re-Harakhte but really is dominated by and dedicated to the pharaoh-god Ramses II himself.

Although it had become the highlight of the trip for the relatively few intrepid travellers who ventured so far south, it was not until the monuments were threatened by the rising waters of Lake Nasser that international attention focused on Abu Simbel. UNESCO financed and organized the ambitious, costly (US$40mn) and ultimately successful 1964-68 operation, to reassemble the monuments 61m above and 210m behind their original site.

The entrance steps lead up to a terrace where the imposing façade of the main temple (35m wide by 30m high) is dominated by the 4-seated **Colossi of Ramses II**, each wearing the double crown. Each figure was originally 21m high but the second from the left lost its top during an earthquake in 27 BC. There are smaller statues of some of the members of the royal family standing at Ramses' rather crudely sculptured feet which contrast with the ornately chiselled and beautiful

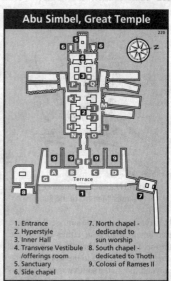

Abu Simbel, Great Temple

220

1. Entrance
2. Hyperstyle
3. Inner Hall
4. Transverse Vestibule /offerings room
5. Sanctuary
6. Side chapel
7. North chapel - dedicated to sun worship
8. South chapel - dedicated to Thoth
9. Colossi of Ramses II

faces of Ramses. The smaller statues are (a) to the left, Princess Bant Anta, to the right Princes Nebtawi, and central (perhaps) Princess Esenofre; (b) Queen Nefertari by his left leg, his mother Queen Muttuya by his right leg and a son Prince Amenhirkhopshef central front; (c) Princess Beketmut by his left leg, Queen Nefertari by his right leg and Prince Ramessesu central; (d) Queen mother Muttuya, Queen Nefertari and Princess Merytamun. There is graffiti, written by Greek mercenaries about their expeditions into Nubia, on the left leg of the damaged statue. The sides of the huge thrones at the entrance to the temple are decorated with the Nile gods entwining the plants representing Upper and Lower Egypt around the hieroglyph 'to unite'. Below are reliefs, called the Nine Bows of bound Nubians on the south side (e) and bound Asiatics to the north side (f), representing Egypt's vanquished foes. In the niche above the main doorway is a figure of Re-Harakhte. Lining the façade, above the heads of the four Ramses, is a row of

Bound Nubian from entrance to
Ramses II Temple of the Sun

baboons smiling at the sunrise. There are two small chapels at either end of the façade. The smaller chapel with altar to the north was dedicated to the worship of the sun and that to the south was dedicated to Thoth. A marriage stele (g) commemorates the union of Ramses II with Ma'at-Her-Neferure, daughter of the Hittite king.

At the entrance into the temple's rock **Hypostyle Hall** is a door bearing Ramses II's cartouche. Having entered the temple the eye is immediately drawn to eight statues of Ramses, 10m high and clad in a short kilt typical of the Nubian Osiride form, which are carved in the front of the eight enormous square pillars which support the roof. The four statues on the right bear the double crown and those on the left the white crown of Upper Egypt. Each pillar depicts the kings before the gods. See where he is presenting flowers to Min and incense to Isis (h), wine to Horus and flowers to Mut (i), flowers to Thoth and bread to Anubis (j), wine to Re-Harakhte (k). The hall's ceiling is crowded with vultures in the central aisle and star spangled elsewhere. The reliefs on the walls are colourful and well preserved. The north wall is the most dramatic with four different scenes depicting the Battle of Kadesh against the Hittites in 1300 BC (l and m) which, despite the scenes on the wall, was not an unqualified Egyptian

success. The depictions of chariots and camps are particularly revealing of ancient battle methods but, more interestingly, Ramses's double arm lancing a Libyan may have been an attempt at animation. The slaughter of prisoners, generally small in size, is a common theme (n and o).

There are also side chambers, probably originally used to store vases, temple linen, cult objects and Nubian gifts, branching off from the hall. Their walls are lined with reliefs of sacrifices and offerings being made by Ramses to the major gods including Amun.

The **Inner Hall** has four columns depicting the pharaoh participating in rituals before the deities. On the far left, Ramses can be seen before Amun (p). Lettuces, considered an aphrodisiac, are being offered to Amun (q). Two sandstone sphinxes, which originally stood at the entrance to the hall, are now in London's British Museum.

Further in and in front of the inner sanctuary is the **Transverse Vestibule** where offerings of wine, fruits and flowers were made. The **Sanctuary** itself, which was originally cased in gold, has an altar to Ramses at its centre behind which are now, unfortunately mutilated, statues of left to right Ptah, Amun-Re, Ramses II and Re-Harakhte. Ramses is deified with his patron gods. Before the temple's relocation the dawn sunrays would shine on

Bound Asiatic from entrance to
Ramses II Temple of the Sun

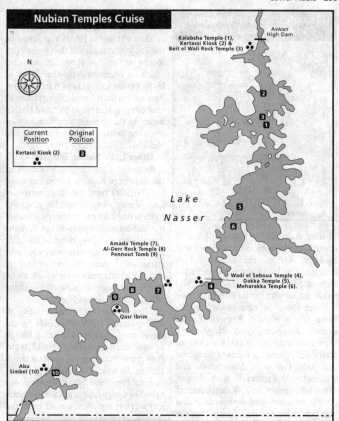

Nubian Temples Cruise

N

Kalabsha Temple (1),
Kertassi Kiosk (2) &
Beit el Wali Rock Temple (3)

Aswan
High Dam

Current Position	Original Position
Kertassi Kiosk (2)	2

Lake Nasser

Amada Temple (7),
Al-Derr Rock Temple (8)
Pennout Tomb (9)

Wadi el Seboua Temple (4),
Dakka Temple (5),
Meharakka Temple (6).

Qasr Ibrim

Abu Simbel (10)

all but Ptah, who was linked with death-cults, on 22 February and 22 October. Despite what your guide will say there is no scholastic evidence to connect these two dates to Ramses' birthday and coronation day. A sacred barque (boat) would have rested on the altar and the walls beside the door portray the barque of Amun and Ramses. The adjoining side chapels were not decorated.

Despite its magnificence and beauty for many visitors to Abu Simbel there is a slight tinge of disappointment because of the combination of a sense of familiarity and artificiality. The latter is heightened when at the end of the official tour one is led through a door and into the hollow mountain on which the temple was reconstructed when it was moved. At the same time, however, the combination of Ramses' egoism and the scale of the magnificent feat of saving the temple from the rising waters of the Nile make the trip from Aswan worthwhile.

The **Temple of Queen Nefertari** is situated 120m north of Ramses II's Temple. Although dedicated to the goddess Hathor, like that of her husband, the temple virtually deifies the human queen Nefertari. Unsurprisingly it is much

Temple of Queen Nefertari in Abu Simbel, Nubia

1. Entrance
2. Square Hall
3. Vestibule
4. Sanctuary

smaller than that of Ramses II but is nevertheless both imposing and very very beautiful. The external façade is 12m high and lined with three colossi 11.5m high on either side of the entrance. Nefertari stands with her husband and their children cluster in pairs at their knees. From left to right – Ramses II with Princes Meryatum and Meryre (a), Queen Nefertari shown as Hathor has the solar disc between the horns of the sacred cow with Princesses Merytamun and Henwati (b), Ramses II with Princes Amunhikhopshef and Rahrirwemenef (c). The same groupings appear in reverse order on the other side. Just within the entrance are the cartouches of Ramses II and Nefertari. There is one simple **Hall**, with six square pillars depicting the pharaoh and queen making their offerings to the gods. The ceiling bears a well preserved dedication inscription from Ramses to Nefertari. The reliefs on the hall walls are rather gruesome with the pharaoh slaying his enemies while Nefertari and the god Amun look on. The walls backing the entrance depict Ramses killing a Nubian and a Libyan.

Three corridors lead from the rear of the hall into the **Vestibule**, the central one passing directly into the **Sanctuary**. The back walls of the Vestibule portray reliefs of Ramses and Nefertari offering wine and flowers to Khnum and Re-Harakhte on the right and to Horus and Amun on the left. Vultures protect the Queen's cartouche on the door above the sanctuary which is dominated by the figure of Hathor in the form of a cow watching over Ramses. On the left wall, Nefertari can be seen offering incense to Mut and Hathor whilst on the opposite side Ramses worships the deified images of himself and Nefertari.

Other Lake Nasser Temples Originally spread along the length of the Nile, the important Nubian antiquities saved by UNESCO from the rising waters of Lake Nasser were clustered in groups of three to make for easier visiting. Many of the Nubian monuments do not have the magnificence of those north of the High Dam though their new sites are more attractive. A number were erected in haste with little concern for artistic merit, for the sole reason of inspiring awe in the conquered people's of Nubia.

These monuments were previously almost inaccessible. However, *Belle Epoque Travel*, now organizes a relaxing tour of Lower Nubian antiquities aboard its elegant cruiseboat *Eugenie*, constructed in 1993 in the style of a Mississippi paddle steamer. Pampered by the luxurious surroundings, high calibre guides and excellent service, travellers can sit back and

Temple of Kalabsha

1. 30m stone causeway to lake
2. First Pylon
3. Colonnaded Court
4. Second Pylon
5. Hypostele Hall
6. First Vestibule
7. Second Vestibule
8. Sanctuary
9. Staircase to roof
10. Chapel
11. Chapel
12. Altar
13. Nileometer

Fishing on Lake Nasser – an old sport in a new area

Lake Nasser is the result of flooding 496 km of the Nile valley with the construction of the Aswan Dam. There are over 6,000 sq km of lake here to fish in – enough space for all. There are 32 species of fish in the lake. The two most popular sport fish are Nile perch and Tiger fish.

Nile Perch

Nile perch (*Lates niloticus*) are found in the River Nile and other rivers in Africa, but grow to their greatest size in large bodies of water like Lake Nasser. They are large mouthed fish, green/brown above and silver below. They have an elongated body, a protruding lower jaw, a round tail and two dorsal fins. They are one of the largest freshwater fish in the world and can be over 1.9m in length and 1.5m in girth. The record catch in Lake Nasser is a massive 176 kg.

The most common of the **Tiger fish** caught is *Hydrocynus forskaalii*. They have dagger teeth that protrude when the mouth is closed. They resemble a tiger in appearance with several lengthwise stripes and resemble a tiger in habit being swift and voracious. They can grow to 5.5 kg.

Catfish are represented by 18 different species in the lake but the two of interest to anglers are Bagrus and Vundu of which the largest caught in Lake Nasser to date is 34 kg.

There are two species of **Tilapia**.

The main methods of fishing are: trolling restricted on safari to 6 hrs a day which covers a wide area and can result in a bigger catch of bigger fish and spinning or fly fishing from the shore generally in the cool of the morning which is a delight and a challenge as it requires more skill as well as a strong line and heavy duty gloves.

All fishing on Lake Nasser is on a catch and release policy, except those needed for the evening meal. Conservation is very important.

appreciate the sheer vastness of desert and lake, a sharp contrast to the lush scenery and teeming villages of the Nile valley. Few more tranquil places exist. The boat's passengers have the monuments to themselves. Memorable features include a private sunset tour of Abu Simbel followed by a candlelit dinner on board for which the temples are specially lit.

Kalabsha Temple, open 0600-1800, which was also relocated when the High Dam was built and is now semi-marooned on an island or promontory (depending on the water level) near the west end of dam, is rarely visited by tourists. The easiest way to reach the temple is by taxi from Aswan or possibly as part of a half-day tour which would include the Unfinished Obelisk, the Aswan Dams and Philae. Negotiate with the boatmen if the waters of the lake cover the pathway from the shore. Pay at the end of the return trip after about an hour on the site.

The original site of the temple, which was built in the 18th Dynasty (1567-1320 BC) in honour of Marul (Greek =Mandulis) a Nubian fertility god, was about 50 km south of Aswan at Talmis which was subsequently renamed Kalabsha. Over the centuries the later **Temple of Mandulis**, a Ptolemaic-Roman version of the earlier one, developed a healing cult as did those of Edfu and Dendera. It was moved from Kalabsha to its present site in 1970 by West German engineers in order to save it from the rising waters of Lake Nasser.

Leading up to the First Pylon is an impressive 30m causeway, used by pilgrims arriving by boat, but it is not known why the causeway and first pylon are at an angle to the temple. In order to align the structure, the first court is in the shape of a trapezium, with the pillars on the south side grouped closer together.

The left portico, beside the entrance to the Hypostyle Hall, portrays the pharaoh being purified and anointed by Thoth and Horus, while on the right is inscribed a decree from Aurelius Besarion who was Governor of Ombos and Elephantine ordering the expulsion of pigs from the temple precincts. The Hypostyle Hall has lost its roof, but the eight columns are still in good condition. The capitals are ornate and flowered, some paintings having been preserved with their original colours, though not all are complete. On either side of the doorway leading to the vestibule is a relief of Trajan making offerings to Isis, Osiris and Marul.

Beyond that are the inner vestibules each with two columns and south access to the roof. Most of the decoration has survived and on the entrance wall the pharaoh can be seen offering incense to Marul and Wadjet, and milk to Isis and Osiris. The south wall depicts the emperor making libations to Osiris, Isis, Horus, Wadjet and Marul. The statue of Marul has long since vanished, though he is pictured on the walls amongst the other deities.

Near the lakeside is the Ptolemaic-Roman **Kiosk of Kertassi** rescued by UNESCO from its original site 40 km south of Aswan. It is a single chamber with two Hathor-headed columns surviving. Dedicated to Isis, the temple is undecorated except for one column whose reliefs depict the pharaoh standing before Isis and Horus.

In the hillside behind the Kalabsha Temple stands a small rock temple, **Beit el-Wali** (House of the Governor), again part of the UNESCO rescue mission. This was originally situated northwest of Kalabsha Temple and possessed a long causeway to the river. Built during Ramses II's youth by the Viceroy of Kush, the reliefs in the temple's narrow forecourt depict Ramses victorious against the Nubians and Ethiopians (left wall) and defeating the Asiatics, Libyans and Syrians (right wall).

The isolated oasis of Wadi El Seboua, 135 km from the High Dam, contains the Temple of Wadi El Seboua, the Temple of Dakka and the Temple of Maharakka. The giant **Temple of Wadi El Seboua** (valley of the lion) named after the row of sphinxes which line its approach is dedicated to Amun, Re-Harakhte and the deified Ramses II. The massive statue on the left of the first pylon is of the royal wife and daughter, while the corresponding statue of Ramses now lies in the sand outside, damaged when the temple was converted into a church. The carved reliefs by local artists in poor quality sandstone, are crude but much remains of their original colour. Around the court are roughly carved statues of Ramses II displayed against the ten pillars. Unusually he is portrayed as a Nubian. Beyond here the interior of the temple is carved into the rock face. Beyond is the vestibule with 12 square columns and then the antechamber. Last comes the sanctuary where a relief on the wall shows Ramses presenting a bouquet to the godly triad but early Christians defaced the figures and Ramses now appears to be offering lotus flowers to St Peter. Unfortunately a number of the sphinxes have been decapitated and the heads sold to illegal treasure hunters.

Uphill is the Ptolemaic-Roman **Temple of Dakka**, reconstructed on the site of an earlier sanctuary. In fact several rulers contributed to its construction and decoration. It was started by the Meroitic King Arqamani, adapted by the Ptolemies Philopator and Euergetes II and changed again by Emperors Augustus and Tiberius (see key). What a history!

Like many temples it was used for a time by the Christians as a church and in some places fragments of their decorations remain. This is the only temple in Egypt facing north, an orientation preserved by UNESCO, pointing to the home of Thoth but perhaps an error by the foreign-born Ptolemaic builders. The pylon is still in good condition, standing some 13m in height. The gateway has a curved cornice with a central winged disc and a high level niche at each side (a) intended to hold a flag pole while on the left of the doorway is graffiti in Greek, Roman and Meriotic (ancient Nubian). Inside the doorway a king makes offerings to Thoth, Tefnut and Isis (b). Stairs in either side of the pylon lead to guard rooms and the roof from which a fine view is obtained. Deep incisions in the inner pylon wall were probably made by locals

Dakka, Temple of Thoth of Pnubs, Nubia

1. Pylon
2. First chamber
3. Vestibule (Euergetes)
4. Sanctuary (Argamani)
5. Sanctuary (Augustus)
6. Granite casket
7. Stairs

convinced that the stone possessed healing properties. The main temple building is across an open courtyard but before you enter, turn back and admire the view to the north. There are four interconnecting rooms, many of the decorations being of deities receiving assorted offerings. A staircase leads off the vestibule on the west side up to the roof. Off the first sanctuary is a small room to the east side leading, it is thought, to a now choked crypt. Here the decorations are in quite good condition, two seated ibises, two hawks and two lions. The lioness being approached by the baboons (c) needs some interpretation. As an animal could approach a lioness without danger except if she was hungry but a human was in danger at any time the humans assumed animal form to worship in safety. The king is seen worshipping gods including Osiris and Isis (d) and Horus and Hathor (e). The large pink granite casket in the sanctuary once held the cult statue of Thoth.

Less impressive is the unfinished Roman **Temple of Meharakka**, dedicated to Isis and Serapis. This stood on the southern border of Egypt in Ptolemaic and Roman times. Rather plain inside, bar the Roman graffiti from travellers and soldiers fighting Nubian troops in 23 BC, the temple illustrates the union of Egyptian and Roman styles. Isis is depicted full frontal, instead of the more common profile, while her son Horus wears a toga. For stair access to roof from which there are spectacular views enter temple and turn right. Look east to the pharaohs' gold mines.

Some 40 km further south in the Amada Oasis, is the oldest temple in Nubia, the sandstone **Temple of Amada**, dedicated to Amun-Re and Re-Harakhte. It was built by Tuthmosis III and Amenhotep II, with the pillared court added by Tuthmosis IV. At the left of the entrance hieroglyphics detail the victorious campaigns of Merneptah (a) against the Libyans. Opposite is the cartouche of Ramses

II (b). Before entering the next doorway look up at the Berber grafiti of animals high on the wall at both sides (c). Inside turn right. Reliefs show the Pharaoh running the Heb-Sed race (d) (see page 155), cattle being slaughtered and presented as offerings as heads and haunches (e). Opposite (f) are the foundation ceremonies, an interesting depiction of the way a site for a building was marked out, foundations dug, bricks manufactured and the construction eventually completed and handed over to the owner. In the central section are more offering, of pomegranates, very realistic ducks and cakes (g). The stela at the back of the the sanctuary tells of the temple's foundation during Amenhotep II's time. The holes in the roof allow light in so one can see, also on the back wall, Amenhotep dispensing justice to six Syrian captives (h), a prisoner turned upside down and crucified (i), a grisly reminder to his remote Nubian subjects of pharaoh's treatment of enemies.

Here too is the **Rock Temple of Al-Derr**, in honour of Amun-Re, Re-Harakhte and the divine aspect of the pharaoh, notable for the excellent colour and preservation of its reliefs. In the first hypostyle hall the temple's builder Ramses II stands in the Tree of Life and presents libations to Amun. Ibis, the eternal scribe, behind, records the pharaoh's years and achievements. The decorations here are, however, very damaged and only small pieces of these scenes can now be made out. The four large statues of Ramses II as Osiris, guarding the entrance, incorporated in the last row of columns

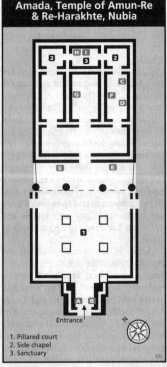

Amada, Temple of Amun-Re & Re-Harakhte, Nubia

Entrance

1. Pillared court
2. Side chapel
3. Sanctuary

222

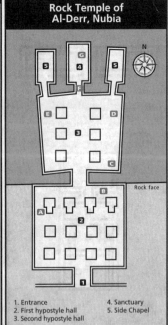

Rock Temple of Al-Derr, Nubia

N

Rock face

1. Entrance
2. First hypostyle hall
3. Second hypostyle hall
4. Sanctuary
5. Side Chapel

235

here, are reduced to legs only (a). The majority of the reliefs on the outer walls boast of the pharaoh's military triumphs (b) and warn the Nubians that his might is unassailable. However, inside the sanctuary, the pharaoh, depicted as a high priest, becomes a humble servant of the gods. On the right hand wall he gives flowers, offers wine, escorts the barque, receives jubillees from Amun-Re and Mut (c) and further along the Heb-Sed emblem is produced nine times (d). On the opposite wall he has his name recorded on the leaves of a tall acacia tree. Entering the sanctuary on the left Ramses is putting in a plea to live for ever (f). In the sanctuary on the back wall there were originally four statues as in the larger temple at Abu Simbel (see page 299), now nothing, but on the wall decorations the king continues to offer perfumes, cake and flowers.

The rock-cut **Tomb of Pennout**, viceroy of Wawat (northern Nubia) under Ramses VI, is a rare example of a high official buried south of Aswan. The ancient Egyptians believed that their souls were only secure if their bodies were carried back and buried in Egyptian soil. The tomb's wall paintings rather poignantly reflect this conviction, expressing Pennout's desire to be laid to rest in the hills of Thebes. The walls are decorated with traditional themes, including the deceased and his family. On entering on the left the deceased and his wife in adulation (a), on the main wall the judgement

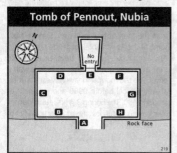

Tomb of Pennout, Nubia

scene with the weighing of the heart against a feather and below the traditional mourners pouring sand on their heads (b), Horus leads the deceased and wife to Osiris for his blessing but the lower register has all disappeared (c), representation of the solar cult (d). There is no entry into the inner chamber but the three badly mutilated statues of Pennout, his mother and his wife Takha can be viewed. The actual burial chamber lies 3m below. Above on the lintel is the sun-god barge and howling baboons (e). What is left of the decoration on the wall shows Pennout with his wife and six children while at (f) Pennout in golden colours is in his illustrated biography which continues on to the next wall (h). It is very disappointing to note that almost all the wall decorations were intact when this temple was moved here and even more disappointing to note that the damage had been caused by illegal removal from the monument.

The fortress of **Qasr Ibrim** (no access permitted), 40 km north of Abu Simbel is on its original suite, once a plateau, now an island. It is noted for an exceptional length of continuous occupation, from 1000 BC to 1812 AD. The ancient city included seven temples to Isis and a mud-brick temple built by the Nubian king Taharka, ruins of which are visible in the centre of the island. In the pre-Roman period construction of a massive stone temple, similar to the structures at Kalabsha, turned the garrison city into a major religious centre. A healing cult developed and Qasr Ibrim became 'the Philae of the south'. Footprints, carved by pilgrims to commemorate their visit, are still visible in the temple floor. A tavern, 400 BC, on the north side of the island is recognizable by the large piles of pottery shards. The temple was destroyed by early Christians who built an orthodox cathedral on the site in the 10th century AD in honour of the Virgin Mary, the Christian version of Isis. Three walls remain standing. By the steps to the burial crypt are numerous fragments of red (Roman) and glazed (Ottoman) pottery. Bosnian troops loyal to the Ottoman Sultan invaded the site in 1517 whereupon the cathedral was converted into a mosque, and their descendants inhabited the site for the next 300 years. The fortress was brought under central control in 1812.

Local information
● Accommodation
B *Nefertari Abu Simbel*, T 316403, F 316404, 122 a/c rm, built in 1960s, located nr the temples, best hotel in town but has few guests because most tourists only spend 2 hrs in Abu Simbel before returning to Aswan, there is sometimes a problem over the limited choice of food in the restaurant, offers pool and tennis.

C *Nobaleh Ramses Hotel*, T 324735, F 3484821, 40 rm, good but spartan hotel which sometimes has problems with the limited choice of food.

Floating accommodation – cruise boats on Lake Nasser Since the construction of the High Dam the upper part of the Nile has been effectively cut off to navigation from the lower reaches. The only solution to getting a good vessel on the lake was to set up a shipyard and build one. Vessels on the lake are not hampered by lack of depth as on the River Nile and can be especially designed for these deeper waters.

A *MS Eugenie*, 50 a/c cabins with balcony, 2 suites, pre-Revolution decor, 2 bars, 2 large saloons, 2 sundecks, pool, jaccuzi, health club, excellent food, no enforced entertainment, cabins are US$240 double, US$190 single incl of meals and sightseeing, peak period supplement of 10%, contact *Belle Epoque Travel*, 17 Sharia Tunis, New Maadi, Cairo, T 3528754/4775, F 3536114.

The only other cruise boats on Lake Nasser are *Kasr Ibrim* owned by Eugenie Investment Group, see above, of a similar excellent standard but without the ancient charm; *MS Nubian Sea* owned by High Dam Cruises, 15 Sharia El Shahud Mohammed Tallat, Dokki, Giza T (2) 3613680, F 3610023 which has 66 cabins and suites and *MS Tanya*, good quality but our last choice.

Camping The *Nefertari Abu Simbel* has a campground where tents can be pitched but camping at the temples is illegal.

● Places to eat
Because of Abu Simbel's position in the middle of the desert, most supplies come from Aswan and consequently there are often problems with the range of foods available. Indeed, with the exception of the hotels, there are few if any places to eat and only a few poorly equipped stores.

● Post & telecommunications
Area code: 097.

● Shopping
Because there are only a few poorly stocked stores it is essential to bring your own supplies if intending to stay in Abu Simbel.

● Sports
Swimming and tennis at the *Nefertari Abu Simbel*.

● Transport
Air Numerous daily services to Abu Simbel from Cairo (2 hrs) via Luxor (1 hr) and Aswan (30 mins) during the winter high season and about 3 during the summer low season. It is absolutely essential to book a ticket as early as possible. Most tickets are sold on the assumption that you will return the same day but it is possible to incl overnight stopovers. Seats on the left hand side of the aircraft usually offer the best views as it circles the temples before landing at Abu Simbel.

Road Bus: although most tourists travel by air or coach tour there is a service from Aswan which leaves at 0800 and arrives at around 1130, returning from the *Nefertari Abu Simbel* hotel at 1330-1400. It is best to buy a ticket at least a day in advance from the Aswan bus station with the ticket for the return journey being bought on board the bus. **Coach**: there are a number of companies which operate daily luxury return coach services from Aswan to Abu Simbel. Details and schedules can be obtained from the tourist office in Aswan. **Service taxi**: some of the Aswan hotels organize taxi tours to Abu Simbel but groups of travellers can make their own arrangements the day before with a driver. The taxis normally leave very early arriving at Abu Simbel before 0900 and returning at around 1400. The boring 3-4 hrs return journey over baking featureless desert is particularly hot and uncomfortable.

The Nile Delta

NORTH OF CAIRO, the two main distributaries of the River Nile continue northnortheast and northnorthwest to meet the Mediterranean near Damietta and Rosetta, respectively. On either side and between the two branches the very flat, green and fertile land fans out to create, with the help of some of the world's oldest and most efficient irrigation systems, the Nile delta, Egypt's agricultural heartland and most heavily populated region. The fertility of this region has enabled this scorched desert country, with under 4% of its land cultivatable, to support a huge population and to export large quantities of fruits and vegetables, albeit while having to import huge volumes of cereals. Confusingly, because of its position north rather than south of Upper Egypt, this area was known as Lower Egypt. Because of the lack of hard stone and the very high population density, successive generations plundered old buildings for stone and built new ones on top of ancient sites. As a result there are no monuments to match the splendours of Upper Egypt. This is no reason, however, for visitors to ignore the region which personifies Egypt's calm and relaxing but industrious village life and is the region of many *moulids* or popular religious festivals.

The branching of the River Nile divides the Delta into three interlocking areas. The best pharaonic ruins including **Tanis** and **Bubastis** are in the Eastern Delta. The Central Delta includes **El-Mahalla el-Kubra** and **Tanta** which are Egypt's fourth and fifth largest cities, while Tanta is the location of Egypt's largest *moulid*. If heading for Alexandria, in preference to the more direct desert route, take the more scenic 'agricultural route' on highway H1 from Cairo through the cotton growing region of the Western Delta which includes the coastal town of

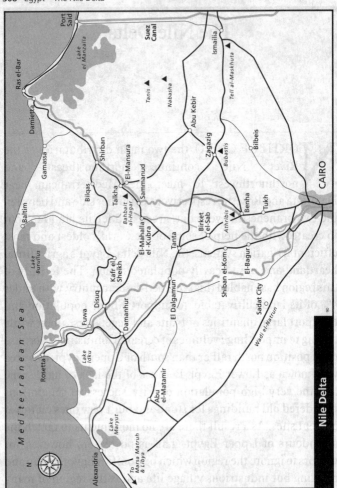

Nile Delta

Rosetta. Although technically in the Central Delta the small coastal resorts of Gamassa and Ras el-Bar can be reached more easily from the Eastern Delta coastal town of Damietta.

EASTERN DELTA

The main road (H1) from Cairo to **Damietta** runs north through the Central

Delta via **Tanta** before striking northeast through **El-Mansura** but there are other routes which offer more interest to the traveller. Turning east in **Benha**, a road goes through **Zagazig** to the ancient sites of **Nabasha** and **Tanis** from which a minor road continues to the coast or north through the intensive cultivation to El-Mansura. Damietta gives access along the

Herodotus – The Historian

Herodotus lived in Greece in the 5th century BC. His great achievement was a history of the Greek wars against the Persian Empire. His origins are obscure but it is believed that he was a Greek born in Asia Minor in approximately 485 BC. He developed the great tradition of Greek historical research in which questions were asked and answers to them sought in the available written evidence. He became an avid collector of information – stories and travel data – which he eventually assembled into his **History** – writings on the wars against the Persians. He travelled widely in Asia Minor, the Black Sea region and the Mediterranean islands.

Perhaps his most famous journey was to Egypt. He began in the Nile delta and voyaged to Memphis, Thebes and the first cataract. He was deeply interested in the topography of the Nile Valley and in the nature of the Nile flood. He is attributed with the saying that, "Egypt is the gift of the Nile". Like all geographer-historians of the early period, he mixed scientific evidence and serious observation with myths, fables and tall tales. His readers were given all the excitement of the grotesque and supernatural wonders of the world, though he rarely entirely gave up rational explanations for historical events he wrote about including those in Egypt. His works were widely accepted in Athenian society and today are regarded as an important development in the establishment of history as an academic study. He was a contemporary and companion of Sophocles. In his later life he moved to a new Greek city colony in Thurii, Italy where he is buried.

coast either east to **Port Said** (see page 368) at the northern end of the Suez Canal or west to the coastal resorts of **Ras el-Bar, Gamassa** and even the isolated **Baltim**.

The main road is normally very busy with a mixture of agricultural traffic and vehicles bound for the ports. On Fridays and holidays it can be even busier with private cars. Shamut Oranges between Tukh and Benha is a very popular spot for picnics. Pigeon towers of varying designs are common in the delta region. The pigeons provide free fertilizer and are the main ingredient in 'pigeon sweet and sour', a speciality dish.

BENHA

48 km north of Cairo and the first major town on the H1 highway, can be reached by bus which runs every 30 mins from Cairo's Koulali Terminal (0600-2100). Close by lie the remains of the ancient town of **Athribis** which was once the capital of the 10th Nome and associated with the worship of the black bull. Although it pre-dates the Greeks, its greatest importance was during the Roman period. Its

orderly layout, like that of many Delta towns, was built around two intersecting roads. Little remains of the town today except traces of 18th-26th Dynasty temples and an extensive Graeco-Roman cemetery. A cache of 26th-30th Dynasty silver ingots and jewellery from the site is now in the Egyptian Museum in Cairo.

From Benha via Minyet el Qamh the railway lies to north of road. The tall chimney decorated with white bricks and the huge cereal stores indicate you have arrived.

ZAGAZIG

The provincial capital, 36 km northeast of Benha and 80 km from Cairo, was founded in 1830 and was the birthplace of the nationalist Col Ahmed Orabi who led the 1882 revolt against the British. It can be reached by bus or service taxi from Cairo and trains to Port Said stop at the local station. The small **Orabi Museum** (open daily 0900-1300 except Tuesday) contains some interesting archaeological exhibits. Most visitors stop in Zagazig to see the

Price guide:			
AL	US$150+	**D**	US$25-50
A	US$100-150	**E**	US$10-25
B	US$75-100	**F**	under US$10
C	US$50-75		

large ruins of Bubastis which lie 3 km southeast of the town.

● **Accommodation** Try **F** *Funduk Sharah Farouk*, said to be none better in town.

● **Places to eat** There are numerous local coffee houses or eat at the *Arak Restaurant* in Sharia Tahrir.

BUBASTIS

This was the capital of the 18th Nome of Lower Egypt and was known to the Ancient Egyptians as Pr Baset (House of Baset). The name is derived from the worship of the Egyptian cat goddess Baset who was believed to be the daughter of the sun-god Re. During the Old Kingdom she was originally associated with the destructive forces of his eye and she was symbolized as a lion. Later, during the Middle Kingdom, this image was tamed and she was represented with a brood of kittens and carrying the sacred rattle. The ancient Egyptians worshipped cats and mummified them at a number of sites including Bubastis because they believed that they would be protected by Baset.

The town was begun during the 6th Dynasty (2345-2181 BC) with the granite **Temple of Baset** which was enlarged over the centuries until the 18th Dynasty (1567-1320 BC) and was excavated in the 19th century. Herodotus described it as the most pleasing in the whole of Egypt but also criticized the antics of up to 700,000 pilgrims who attended the licentious festivals. Near the site is an underground **cat cemetery** where many statues of Baset have survived. You may find a guide to get you in – but unlikely.

EL-MANSURA

About 55 km north of Zagazig, El-Mansura is an attractive River Nile city which was founded comparatively recently (1220

AD) by the great Salah al-Din's nephew Sultan al-Kamil (1218-38 AD) during the Siege of Damietta by the Crusader forces during the 6th Crusade. Despite its name, which means 'the victorious', the Crusaders reoccupied Damietta in 1249 and then, following the death in El-Mansura of Kamil's son Sultan Ayyub (1240-49), which was concealed by his widow in order not to demoralize his troops, the Crusaders captured the town. However when the Crusaders were weakened by a vicious bout of food poisoning, the Muslims counter-attacked and captured not only El-Mansura but also France's King Louis IX before he was eventually ransomed for the return of Damietta.

● **Accommodation** There are a few cheap and simple hotels in El-Mansura incl: **D** *Marshal el Gezirah*, Sharia Gezirah el Ward, T/F 36888, 34 beds is the best hotel in town; **E** *Cleopatra*, 13 Souq Toggar, El-Gharby, T 341234, 55 rm; **E** *Marshal*, Midan Om Kalsoum, T 324380, 57 rm; **F** *Abu Shama Hotel*, Sharia Bank Misr, T 354227, 20 rm; **F** *Mecca Touristic*, Sharia el-Abbas, Corniche, T 349910, 54 rm.

● **Post & telecommunications** Area code: 050.

● **Transport** Road Bus & service taxis: there are very frequent buses and service taxis to/from Zagazig and Cairo to the south and Damietta to the north and links to various towns in the Eastern and Central Delta.

TANIS

While most travellers from Zagazig head north to El-Mansura, those going east towards the Suez Canal might make a detour to the ruins of an Old Kingdom city better known by its Greek name of **Tanis** (**Djane**). It is located near the modern village of San el-Hagar, 167 km from Zagazig, and once lay alongside and got its name from the now dry Tanite branch of the River Nile. In the **Second Intermediate Period** (1786-1567 BC) Asiatic settlers to the region, known as the Hyksos kings or 'princes of foreign lands', established the 15th Dynasty (1674-1567 BC) until they were expelled from Egypt and chased

Sacred cats

Cats were first domesticated by the Egyptians and it seems probable that the breed they domesticated was the *Kaffir* cat, a thin, poorly striped, grey cat common all over Africa. Numerous tomb drawings and mummified bodies have been discovered which date from the very early Egyptian dynasties.

The cat was held in great awe and worshipped in the form of the cat-headed goddess Bast or Pasht from which it has been suggested the word 'puss' is derived. Egyptians believed that all cats went to heaven, a choice of two heavens, the more aristocratic creatures having a better class destination. If a family cat died the household members would all go into mourning and shave off their eyebrows.

back to Asia by indigenous Theban kings from Luxor.

Until earlier this century it was believed that Tanis was Avaris which was the capital of the Hyksos Kingdom but Avaris has now been discovered further to the southwest at the modern day site of Tell el-Dab'a. Instead Tanis was the birth place of Ramses I (1320-18 BC) an ambitious local prince who become pharaoh and founded the 19th Dynasty (see page 239.) The area is dotted with ruins, scattered and broken statues and stones which are the only remnants of the **Temple of Amun**. To the south of the temple is the **Royal Necropolis** which is closed to the public. Six tombs of the 11th and 22nd Dynasties were found here. They were almost intact.

TELL AL-MASKHUTA

Another ruined site on the eastern edge of the Delta is **Tell al-Maskhuta** which lies just south of the main Zagazig (70 km) to Ismailia (11 km) road. It has been identified as the site of the ancient town of **Tjehu** which was the capital of the 8th Nome of Lower Egypt and was often known by its Biblical name of **Pithom**. Archaeological excavations have revealed the foundations of the ancient city, a temple structure and brick chambers for single and multiple burials together with children's bodies buried in amporae. A well preserved sphinx and a statue of Ramses II were also uncovered and are now in a museum in Ismailia.

DAMIETTA

Back near the River Nile the easiest way north from El-Mansura is to cross the river to the Central Delta town of Talkha and head up the main H8 highway to the coastal town of **Damietta** (or **Dumyat**). It is located on the east bank almost at the mouth of the Damietta branch of the River Nile and is 191 km from Cairo, 122 km from Zagazig and 66 km from El-Mansura.

The town is in many ways similar to Rosetta, 50 km east of Alexandria (see page 319). Indeed Damietta flourished as a trading port throughout the Middle

Sacred Cat

Bird watching in Egypt

Why Egypt? Egypt stands in a special position as a bridge between the continents of Europe, Asia and Africa. Migrating birds, the larger birds in particular like **storks**, **pelicans** and **raptors**, depend on thermals which only occur over land. This restricts their routes and provides birdwatchers in Egypt with some awesome sights. In addition Sinai as the only land link to the east is specially important.

Egypt is the over wintering quarters for a wide range of birds, visitors such as the **White Stork**, **Spoonbill**, **Greater Flamingo**, **Great Crested Grebe**, **Ringed Plover**. The Nile Delta is a major resting place and the watering holes in the oases life saving halts.

Egypt is interesting too as the most northern limit for some species which include **Senegal Thick-knee**, **Painted Snipe**, **Kittlitz's Plover**, **Senegal Coucal** and **Nile Valley Sunbird**.

One delightful resident is the Nile Valley Sunbird already mentioned. The male has iridescent purple/green plumage, a yellow breast and a long slender tailfeather. It is only a small bird (10 cm) attracted into gardens by the nectar in flowers. Another attractive resident is the **Purple Gallinule**, sporting red beak and legs along with plumage of blue, purple and green. It is about half the size of a duck. There are many, many more.

Bird watching locations:

1. **Lake Burullus**, a good location for delta birds – thousands of Wigeon, Coot and Whiskered Tern and other water birds. Access can be difficult.

2. **Lake el Manzalah** is in the Eastern Delta with access from Port Said. It is an important over wintering area for water/shore birds.

3. **Lake Bardweel** on the north Sinai coast is well known for migratory birds in their thousands, especially in the autumn, and in particular water birds, ducks and herons. Shore birds too like Avocet and Flamingo can be seen here.

4. **Wadi el-Natrun**. Here in the shallow lagoons may be found Kittlitz's Plover and Blue-cheeked Bee-eaters but don't expect an instant sighting.

5. Near Cairo airport at **Gabel Asfar** the recycling plant provides a mixed habitat with opportunities to see Painted Snipe, Senegal Coucal and the White-breasted Kingfisher. The Egyptian Nightjar may be heard but is unlikely to be seen. Cairo Zoo at Giza is recommended – for the song birds in the gardens. In Cairo, in the city, or any settlement for that matter, the Black Kite acts as a scavenger. Near Cairo, at the Pyramids look out for the Pharaoh Eagle Owl.

6. **Suez** in the perfect position for observing migratory birds – for Raptors in particular which pass over in their thousands, also Gulls, Waders and Terns. Look for the Greater Sand Plover and Broad-billed Sandpiper also White-eyed Gull and Lesser Crested Tern more often associated with the Red Sea. All these resident and migratory birds are attracted by the mud flats and conditions in Suez Basin.

7. **Taba** region residents include Namaqua Dove, Little Green Bee-eater, Mourning, Hooded and White-crowned Black Wheatears. Migrants include Olivaceous and Orphean Warblers. White-cheeked and Bridle Tern can be seen off the coast between Taba and Sharm el-Sheikh.

8. At **Mt Sinai** look for Verreaux's Eagle which nest in this area. Residents include Lammergeier, Sinai Rosefinch frequently sighted near St Catherine's Monastery, Barbary

Painted Snipe

Falcon, Sand Partridge, Little Green Bee-eater, Rock Martin, Desert and Hoopoe Larks, Scrub Warbler, White-crowned Black and Hooded Wheatears, Blackstart, Tristram's Grackle, Brown-necked Raven and House Bunting. There are special migrants to be observed such as Masked and Red-backed Shrikes, Olive-tree and Orphean Warblers. Look also for Hulme's Tawny Owl.

9. Try the tip of Sinai round **Ras Mohammed** where the Nabq protected area is recommended (see page 376). Mark up Sooty Falcon seen on the cliffs nest here, Lichtenstein's Sandgrouse further

Bee-eater

inland near the recycling plant, White-eyed Gull, Bridled Tern, White-cheeked and Lesser Crested Tern (less common are Brown Booby and Crested Tern). Osprey nest in this region too. Migratory birds include White Storks which are very abundant. There is a White Stork sanctuary near Sharm el-Sheikh.

10. **El-Fayoum oasis** is noted for water birds and waders. It has been associated with duck hunting from ancient times. Over wintering duck, Coot and Grebe gather here in great numbers. Lake Qaroun in El-Fayoum oasis is a salt water lake and the whole area is now a protected region. In winter it is covered with water fowl. On the north shores of the lake falcons and hawks quarter the ground and in the trees see the Green Bee-eater, Bulbul and Grey Shrike. Note too Lapwing, Swallow and Senegal Thick-knee. Shore birds include Sandpipers, Curlew, Coot (never seen so many) and Grebe.

11. The Red Sea off **Hurghada** is a rich habitat supporting fifteen species of breeding birds, both water birds and sea birds. Brown Booby, Western Reef Egret, White-eyed and Sooty Gulls, Crested, Lesser Crested and White-cheeked Terns, Red-billed Tropicbird, Bridled Tern are on the list. The islands in the Red Sea provide a safer habitat for the birds. Such is Isle of Tiran, approach only by boat, not to land. Osprey nest here, in places quite common. Sooty (a few) and White-eyed Gulls (more common) are found on the uninhabited islands further south.

12. Around **Luxor** look for Black-shouldered Kite, Black Kite, Egyptian Vulture, Senegal Thick-knee, Purple Gallinule with perhaps a Painted Snipe or a Nile Valley Sunbird on Crocodile Island where Hotel Movenpick has made an effort to protect the environment for these birds. On the other side of the River Nile in the Valleys of the Kings and Queens are Rock Martin, Trumpeter Finch, Little Green Bee-eater. Desert birds found anywhere in desert are represented here by Hoopoe and Bar-tailed Larks.

13. **Dakhla Oasis** has a large lake called the Fishpond the surface almost obscured by birds, Avocet, Stilt, coot.

14. **Aswan** is one of the best places for herons and kingfishers, best viewed from the river itself. Pied Kingfishers and Egyptian Geese are common. At Aswan try Saluga Island which has been designated as a protected area.

15. **Abu Simbel** is important due to its southerly location. After viewing the monuments take time to look for rarities including Long-tailed Cormorant, Pink-backed Pelican, Yellow-billed stork, African Skimmer, Pink-headed Dove and African Pied Wagtail.

16. **Jebel Elba** in the very south-east corner of Egypt has samples of sub-Saharan birds – Verreaux's eagles, Pink headed Doves and perhaps even Ostrich. This region cannot be visited without a permit, which is not likely to be forthcoming.

A study of the birds of ancient Egypt can be done at leisure by examining the hieroglyphics and carvings in the tombs and temples. Here they cannot fly away before the glasses are focussed. Sunbird Tours (see page 504) have identified a total of 45 species ranging from the predynastic rock carvings of Ostrich to the Common and Demoiselle Cranes in the Mastaba of Ti at Saqqara. Certainly different.

Birdwatching Sites in Egypt

Mediterranean Sea

Sollum
Marsa Matruh
Alexandria 1
Port Said
2
3

Qattara Depression
CAIRO 5
4
Suez
6
Taba
7

El-Fayoum Oasis 10
Beni Suef
8
Mt. Sinai

Bahariya Oasis
Minya
9
Sharm el-Sheikh

Farafra Oasis
Assiut
Hurghada 11

Libyan
Sohag
Qena

Desert
Dakhla Oasis 13
12 Luxor
Esna

Kharga Oasis
Edfu
Kom Ombo

N
14 Aswan
Red Sea

Sahara Desert
Abu Simbel 15
Lake Nasser
16

Ages but suffered greatly during the Crusades. The Christian forces occupied the town in 1167-68 and again in 1218-21 when St Francis of Assisi accompanied the invaders. Sultan al-Kamil's attempts to recapture it followed. (See El-Mansura, page 310.) Worse was yet to come, for the Mamlukes destroyed the city in 1250 and made the river impassable as a punishment for suspected disloyalty and to prevent further invasions. The Ottomans revived the town and, as in the case of Rosetta, many of their attractive buildings are still in good condition. The last Ottoman Pasha here surrendered to the Beys in 1801 before the time of Mohamed Ali. Although the construction of the Suez Canal shifted trade to Port Said, 70 km to the east, Damietta is still a small and successful port although it has little to attract visitors.

Places of interest Besides its Otto-

man buildings there is little to see in Damietta itself. Out of town, however is the huge **Lake el Manzalla** which in winter teems with migrating birds including flamingoes, spoonbills and herons (see box on birdwatching, page 312). On the other side of the branch of the River Nile there are three beach resorts, **Ras el-Bar**, **Gamassa** and **Baltim** which, although technically in the Central Delta, are most easily reached from Damietta.

● **Accommodation** The only government registered hotel is **F** *El-Manshi Hotel*, 5 Sharia el-Nokrashy, T 323308, 20 rm, which is barely comfortable but there are a few other cheaper hotels along the Corniche.

● **Post & telecommunications Area code**: 057.

● **Transport Train** Although they are slower, there are trains to Cairo, Alexandria, Tanta and Zagazig. **Road Bus & service taxis**: there are hourly buses and service taxis to Cairo either down the main H8 highway via Tanta and Benha or the east route via El-Mansura and Zagazig. Port Said, 70 km east along the causeway which divides the lake from the Mediterranean, is only easily reached by service taxi.

RAS EL-BAR

Located on the west bank of the Damietta branch of River Nile only a few kilometres north of the city at the point where the river meets the sea. It is a favourite resort for middle-class Egyptians who want to get away from Cairo's summer heat. It is an attractive resort, popular without too much bustle. It can be reached very easily either from Damietta or by special a/c buses direct from Cairo's Koulali bus station or service taxis. Al-Jirbi, just 2 km from Ras el-Bar has a therapy centre for the treatment of gout, sciatica, polio and rheumatism. This is only open in the summer months.

● **Accommodation** There a lots of cheap beach hotels which cater for the Egyptian tourists. The best of a mediocre bunch are: **E** *Beau Sejour*, 40 Sharia 67, T 528368, 36 rm and **E** *El-Mina Hotel*, end of Sharia 61, El-Shatee, T 529290, 53 rm. It is impossible to rec any of the very cheap hotels as the standard changes with staff and management. Choose from these listed below after you have inspected the room: **F** *Abu Tabl*, 4 Sharia 17, T 528166, 26 rm; **F** *El-Madina el-Monawara*, 1 Sharia 29, T 527261, 34 rm; **F** *El-Mobasher*, 1 Sharia 56, T 527097, 34 rm; **F** *El-Mogharbel*, 23 Sharia 51, T 528697, 56 rm; **F** *El-Riad*, 4 Sharia 47, T 5280919, 20 rm; **F** *El-Salam*, 6 Sharia 44, First Area, T 528156, 37 rm; **F** *El-Shatee*, 39 Sharia 63, T 528029, 48 rm; **F** *Marine el-Nil*, 1 Sharia el-Mohafza, T 528006, 49 rm; **F** *Marine Ras el-Bar*, 4 Sharia el-Mohafza, T 528728, 32 rm; **F** *Mira Hotel*, 2 Sharia 33, T 529868, 21 rm.

GAMASSA

Further west along the coast about 20 km from Damietta, Gamassa is another quiet and beautiful resort with a long beach, some 25 km, of fine sand. It can be reached, either by bus from Damietta or directly from Cairo. Alternatively catch a train to El-Mansura or Shirban from where a bus can be caught.

● **Accommodation** There is a number of hotels which range from those detailed below to unofficially registered ones with cabin-like chalets. **D** *Amun*, El-Souq area, Gamassa, T 760660, 82 rm, located on the beach, best in town; **F** *Beau Rivage*, Gamassa, T 760268, 76 rm; **F** *Hannoville*, Shagaret el-Dor Area, Gamassa, T 760750, 54 rm.

BALTIM

The most inaccessible and quietest of the three resorts, is actually about half way between Damietta and Rosetta and, although it can be reached from Damietta it may be easier by direct coach from Cairo. Take a Delta East bus or the train to El-Mansura and complete the journey by bus.

● **Accommodation** There are two officially registered hotels but neither have many Western visitors and mainly cater for Egyptian summer tourists. **F** *Baltim Beach*, El-Narguess Area, Baltim, T 501541, 30 rm; **F** *Cleopatra Touristic*, Baltim Beach, Baltim, 28 rm, charges E£10 per night.

CENTRAL DELTA

There are fewer sites in the Central Delta but it does include two of Egypt's largest cities and has some of the largest annual *moulids*. Assuming that most tourists to the northern beach resorts will probably either travel to Damietta or take special coaches direct from Cairo it is probably best for visitors to the Central Delta region to base themselves in the centrally situated, large but charming town of **Tanta**, which has excellent communications, and then from there make day trips to the various sites.

TANTA

This town maintains its rural atmosphere despite being the fifth largest city in Egypt with a major university. It is located 94 km north of Cairo and 130 km southeast of Alexandria on the main agricultural route between the two cities. The H1 highway from Cairo to Benha crosses the Damietta branch of the River Nile and continues northwest via Birket el-Sab to Tanta. In late October the biggest *moulid* of all, attracting up to 2 million visitors (see page 316) is held here.

Places of interest Although it is an interesting city, which is worth visiting to soak up the atmosphere of modern life for most Egyptian without the glories of past eras and masses of tourists, there is little or nothing to see in Tanta itself for most of the year. It really comes alive, however, in October at the end of the cotton harvest during the 8-day festival or **Moulid of Sayid Ahmed el-Badawi** when the population swells to over 2 million as pilgrims pour in from throughout Egypt and the Muslim world.

Sayid Ahmed el-Badawi (1199-1276 AD) was the founder of one of Egypt's largest Sufi *tariqas* (brotherhoods/orders) which is known as the Badawiya. Born in Fes in Morocco he emigrated to Arabia and then travelled to Iraq where he joined the Rifaiyah brotherhood. He was sent to Tanta in 1234 as its representative but then received permission to establish his own *tariqa* which soon flourished. Although the mosque built by his successor and containing his tomb was demolished in the mid-19th century a large, new, rather undistinguished one was built by

pasha Abbas I (1848-54 AD) and is the focus of Badawi's annual *moulid*.

● **Accommodation** There are few facilities for Western tourists here but, unless you are visiting specifically for the *moulid* when it is essential to book well in advance, there should be no problem in finding a room. Although there are many other small establishments there are only two officially registered hotels. **D** *Arafa Hotel*, Midan Station, First Tanta, Tanta, T 336952, F 331800, 43 rm, directly outside the station; **D** *Green House*, Sharia el-Borsa, Midan Gumhorriya, Tanta, T 330761, F 330320, 30 good a/c rm, restaurant, splendid central location, parking, rec. **Youth hostels** Sharia Mahala el Kobra, T 337978, 24 beds, parking.

● **Places to eat** There are numerous cheap food stalls during the moulids, otherwise eat at the restaurant in *Green House*, which is clean and comfortable.

EL-MAHALLA EL-KUBRA

The fourth largest city in Egypt, is 25 km northeast of Tanta and 120 km north of Cairo. The only decent hotel is **E** *Omar el-Khayyam*, Midan July 23rd, T 334866, 36 rm. To the west of the nearby riverside town of **Sammanud** is the remains of the red and black granite **Temple of Onuris-**

Moulids – Festivals in the Delta

🦶 Officially, *moulids* are festivals in commemoration of a specific saint when pilgrims obtain their *baraka* or blessing by visiting their shrine. There is usually a parade of devotees, carrying banners and dressed in turbans and sashes in the colours of their saint, which is followed by chanting and dancing that goes on for hours. In addition, however, the most important *moulids* are like a giant mediaeval fair where pilgrims meet their friends and eat, drink and have fun together. They stroll amongst the stalls and rides watching the magicians, jugglers, acrobats, snake charmers, animal trainers and other traditional entertainers.

High Noon at Damyanah – Martyrs' Calendar

🦶 Damyanah, who was the daughter of Rome's regional governor in the time of **Diocletian** (284-305 AD), chose celibacy rather than marriage and took refuge with 40 other virgins in a palace built for her by her father. When her father renounced the worship of the Roman gods and converted to Christianity both he and all of the women were executed on the orders of Diocletian. His persecution of the Christians was so great that the Copts date their era, known as the Martyrs' Calendar, from the massacres of 284 AD. The first shrine to Damyanah is believed to have been built by St Helena who was the mother of emperor Constantine (306-337 AD).

Easy to recognize – The Hoopoe

The Hoopoe *Upupa epopsis* is like no other bird – it is the only one in its species.

It is a resident breeder, fairly common especially in the Delta area. The sexes are similar, both 28 cm in length. It is in evidence on lawns and in parks and oases where it disturbs the ground searching for grubs. It also eats locusts, moths, spiders and ants. It nests in holes in old trees or ruins (plenty of scope in Egypt) laying up to six eggs.

In general the colouring is buff/pink with very distinctive black and white bars in a striped pattern (like a zebra) on the wings and tail. It has a long and slender down-curving bill with a black tip, a square tail and broad rounded wings, striped with black tips. A distinctive, large erect crest runs from front to back of the head, the feathers having quite marked black tips. This crest is raised when it alights and is evident in mating displays.

The call is a distinct Hoo-poo-oo.

Shu which was rebuilt by Nectanebo II (360-343 BC) for Tjeboutjes which was the capital of the 12th Nome of Lower Egypt. Further northeast some 10 km from Sammanud along the main H8 highway towards **Talkha** there is the modern town of **Bahbait al-Hagar** and what little remains of the great **Temple of Isis** in the ancient town of **Iseum** or **Pr-Hebeit** as it was known to the ancient Egyptians.

Continuing further along the H8 highway 25 km past Talkha, is the town of **Shirban** which has a bridge to the east bank of the Rosetta branch of the River Nile. Leaving H8 and travelling 12 km west along H7 is **Bilqas** where, 3 km to the north, is the **Monastery of St Damyanah** (Deir Sitt Damyanah). St Damyanah was put to death, along with another 40 maidens, under Diocletian's purges against the Christians. Normally it is isolated and difficult to reach except during the annual **Moulid of Damyanah** between 15-20 May, which is one of the country's largest Christian *moulids*. Thousands of pilgrims flock to the four 19th and 20th century churches on the site in the hope of being healed. Women praying for increased fertility and those who have lost young children are common visitors here.

The only claim to fame of **El-Bagur**, which lies at the extremity of the Central Delta to the south of **Shiban el-Kom**, is that it is President Mubarak's small home town. The only place to stay is **E** *Nice Tourist Village*, El-Bagur Minufiya, T 384073, 25 rm. Mubarak's predecessor President Anwar Sadat, who was assassinated by Islamic fundamentalists in 1981, came from the nearby village of **Mit Abu el-Kom** which is close to Quweisna on the main Benha-Tanta highway.

● **Post & telecommunications Area code**: 040.

● **Transport Road & Train** The Central Delta region is well served by public transport and there are buses and service taxis between all the major and most of the minor towns. From Tanta there are very frequent services to Cairo and Alexandria, while the train journeys take 1½ hrs and 2 hrs, respectively. Although they are less frequent there are also train services from Tanta to the other major cities but a service taxi may be easiest given the comparatively short distances.

WESTERN DELTA

The main H1 continues on to Alexandria and there are many clean roadside restaurants catering for the weekend travellers –

More a land of buffalo than camels

The conventional view of Egypt is that the camel is king. Far from it. Although no self-respecting tourist will leave without having sampled the riding qualities of the camel, it only makes up a small part of the domesticated animals in Egypt. There are a mere 100,000 camels reported against 3,250,000 buffalo and 3,400,000 sheep. Like the ancient Egyptians, the modern dwellers in the delta and valley prefer birds to animals. Some 39 million chickens and 10 million pigeons populate the country as commercial livestock for eating and egg production. In Egypt's rambling urban areas, where recent migrants from the countryside gather, there are great numbers of sheep, goats and cattle kept for milk and meat by every family that can afford to. The animals scavenge among the refuse tips and graze every available scrap of roadside vegetation, giving even city areas a rustic appearance and a distinctly rural smell! Their value is however undisputed – animal output accounts for as much as 7.5% of gross domestic product (GDP), about half the value of all agricultural production (E£30,000mn) in 1995.

Stylized camel design common on tribal rugs

strangely there are more on the north bound carriageway. On the outskirts of Tanta going north try the *Pearl* café (where the waiters wear bow ties) for tea or Turkish coffee and a clean toilet.

Across the wider Rosetta branch of the River Nile is the **Western Delta** which has fewer ancient remains than either the Eastern or Central Delta. The main attractions are the port of **Rosetta** and a couple of *moulids* held in and around the town of **Damanhur**. This route, like most in the delta, goes through an interesting mixture of scenery: fields of cotton, sugar cane and pocket-sized areas of vegetables, tiny clusters of houses, old fashioned water lifting devices (see delu well, page 482) and the whole area is busy with carts, donkeys, and men and women working in the fields. It is an ever-changing scene of rural Egypt, absolutely fascinating, yet most travellers rush straight on to Alexandria. The taming of the River Nile in

the late 19th century, changing the water supply from uncontrolled annual flood to perennial irrigation, enables the cultivation of three or four crops a year in this extremely fertile region.

DAMANHUR

Mid-way between Tanta and Alexandria, Damanhur lies in the middle of the Western Delta, 160 km northwest of Cairo. This sleepy provincial capital and textile town, which was once the site of the ancient city of Tmn-Hor dedicated to Horus, normally has nothing to offer the visitor. In November, however, there is the **Moulid of Sheikh Abu Rish** which follows the more important one in Tanta. Extending over 2 days in January is Egypt's only **Jewish moulid** at the shrine of a 19th century mystic called **Abu Khatzeira**. Because of the security problems, non-Jewish Egyptians are kept out of the festival by the police and most of those who attend are

Europeans and Israelis who bring sick relatives or bottled water to be blessed at the shrine.

• **Accommodation Youth hostels** 9 Sharia el Shaheed Gawad, T 324056, 30 beds, kitchen, station 2 km, overnight fee E£3.

ROSETTA

64 km east of Alexandria on the H18 at the coast on the mouth of the major distributary of the River Nile, stands Rosetta (Rashid). It is famous for the discovery, in 1799, of the **Rosetta Stone**, which was the key to our understanding of Hieroglyphics and, consequently, much of what we know of Egypt's ancient civilization. The stone is inscribed, in Greek, hieroglyphics and demotic Egyptian with a proclamation by Ptolemy V Epiphanes. Today the stone is in the British Museum in London.

HIEROGLYPHS

The writings of the ancient Egyptians were in hieroglyphs, the word meaning in Greek 'sacred carving' and originally applied only to Egyptian signs though is now used as a general word for all pictorial writing. The evolution of the ancient Egyptian language was complex and more or less continuous from Semitic and other elements. In the Ptolomaic period there was a rapid development of the language through loan-words from Greek leading to the emergence of Coptic, which made use of Greek script. The continuity provided by this transition was a major aid in the ultimate deciphering of hieroglyphs.

There is continuing argument concerning the origins of the hieroglyphs. Some experts believe that hieroglyphs began with a picture writing phase, others that they started as phonetic symbols and never went through a pictorial phase. Certainly, the hieroglyphs became a phonetic alphabet and were designed to enable scribes to distinguish particular dates and events. Kings, important figures of state, time and place were designated with their own sign signature or

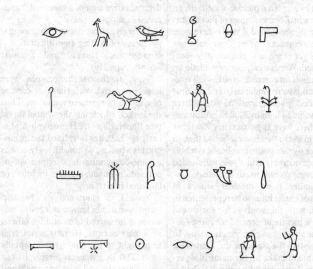

Pictograms

Champollion – Founder of Scientific Egyptology

Jean-Francois Champollion was born in the village of Figeac in France in December 1790. He was a precocious learner of difficult foreign languages and from an early age became involved with studies of Greek, Latin and the Coptic languages.

Like other scholars before him, in the 1820s he began deciphering Egyptian hieroglyphs and by 1822 evolved a virtually complete set of hieroglyphic signs and their Greek equivalent, using the information on the **Rosetta Stone**. The Rosetta Stone was found near Rashid in 1799 by members of Napoleon's expedition to Egypt. The inscriptions on the Rosetta Stone were in Greek script below and hieroglyphs, demotic and cursive Egyptian languages above, all however proclaiming the same message. The Swede Akerblad and the Englishman Thomas Young had made some progress in deciphering the Rosetta Stone but it was Champollion, using his knowledge of Egyptology, Greek and Coptic languages, who finally broke the code. He was unique in understanding that individual Egyptian hieroglyphs stood for individual letters, groups of letters and even for entire objects.

Champollion undertook archaeological work in Egypt in 1828 with the Italian Ippolito Rosellini, recording a whole series of sites in the Nile Valley. He died suddenly in 1832 age 42 years having been curator of the Egyptian collection of the Louvre and professor of Egyptian antiquities at the highly esteemed Collège de France. His brother Jacques-Joseph prepared and published his works after Jean-Francois's death.

---

cartouche. Some objects such as the giraffe or the eye or bread would be rendered by a stylized picture of a giraffe, an eye or a loaf. See examples of pictograms below. By the second dynasty there were whole sentences rather than only key words in use, all phonetically constructed. Words were, however, made up of symbols for consonants only – full vowels sounds were unmarked – and can thus be called 'phonograms', of which there were some 24 signs by 3000 BC. Additionally, there were approximately 700 other signs in use in the classical period though in later dynasties the number of symbols rose considerably as new ones were added to encompass new words and ideas.

Another trend brought groups of words or entire ideas to be represented in script, with the symbols for each word given a picture of general meaning (determinatives) but no phonetic value. In this system the signs for the sounds for example to make up the name of a particular flower would be given, followed by a general picture of a flower so that any uncertainty of the meaning would be removed. Similarly, the phonetic signs for prayer would be given follower by the determinative sign of a man with hands raised in supplication.

Hieroglyphs developed into three major forms of writing (see illustration – Hieroglyphic, Hieratic and Demotic Scripts, page 319).

First, traditional hieroglyphs were largely pictorial, with elaborate carving of symbols in representational art. Thus the basket, which was the symbol for 'k' (see illustration – A Hieroglyph Alphabet, page 322), was fully lined and unmistakably a basket. Writing hieroglyphs was a time-consuming task either colour painted on smooth surfaces by brush or chiselled into stone.

Second, a shortened or 'hieratic' script, sometimes known as 'cursive' was adopted for sacred texts and for official state manuscripts. Hieratic script read from right to left (though horizontally from 2000 BC) whereas hierglyphs can also occur to be read from left to right and vertically. In both forms the direction of writing can be detected since the symbols

◄──── Hieroglyphic ────►◄── Hieratic ──►◄─Demotic─►

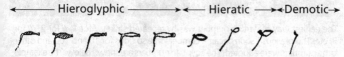

Hieroglyphic, Heiratic, Demotic Scripts

for humans, animals and birds always face towards the beginning of a line of script. The cursive script enabled scribes to join up two letters in a single brush stroke.

A third form of script evolved called 'demotic' since it was the common or popular means of writing. It came into use in the 7th century BC. In it a type of shorthand was used with joined up characters though it was mainly applied to symbols carved in stone and was applied to official state papers. Although demotic script was in popular use, in reality it was hieratic script – easily written using ink on papyrus – which was the principal means of conveying information.

Most visitors to Egypt see hieroglyphs in their various forms on tombs, temple and chapel monuments. These symbols are often repeated in this formal setting, especially the signs for kings, queens, princes and gods. Tutankhamen, for example, carries two names in his cartouche, the first "NB-HPRW-R" and a second "TWT-'NH-'IMN-HKs-'LWNW RSY" so that he can be distinguished from other kings with similar representational symbols (see illustration – Tutankhamen's Cartouche, page 323).

The gods similarly have symbol signatures, notably the Re, God of the Sun (see symbol of Re on page 57).

Hieroglyphic writing survived at least until the 5th century AD but the Christian period brought change and from the 3rd century AD there was extensive use of Greek script to write the Egyptian language of the time (Coptic) for religious and eventually all purposes. Hieroglyphics fell from use and understanding of it was entirely lost. It was not until Thomas Young in England and, more completely,

Jean-Francois Champollion in France deciphered hieroglyphic writing in the 19th century that there was a re-awakening of interest in the ancient Egyptian language.

Like many towns in Egypt that can claim a flourishing and varied past, there is relatively little to see in Rosetta today. Since ancient times its fortunes have been linked with the ebb and flow of those of it's neighbour Alexandria. When one waxed, the other would wane. Mohamed Ali's Mahmudiya Canal project linking the River Nile to Alexandria marked the end of Rosetta's significance as a port. Whilst Alexandria is now Egypt's second city, Rosetta is little more than a fishing village.

There are some interesting older (early 17th century) buildings in the town, houses of the merchants in this once important trading centre. The Department of Egyptian Antiquities began a programme of restoration here in 1985. Many of these houses are made of distinctive red and black brick and incorporate recycled stones and columns from earlier eras. Many too have delicately carved *mashrabiyyas*. In particular are those of El Fatatri just off the main street to the north of the town and Arab Keli (18th century) at the west end of Midan Gumhurriya. The latter is now a museum noted for its delicately handcrafted woodwork. Other buildings to look out for are Thabet House, Mekki House and Abu Shahin Mill. The mosques are worth a visit for their coloured tilework. The huge Zagloul mosque one block north of the main road to Alexandria, is a double mosque, that to the west is brighter and smarter and remembered for its arched courtyard while that to the west (founded

Egyptian numbers

The earliest way of writing number was by repeated strikes: / for 1, // for 2, /// for 3, etc. This obviously soon became cumbersome so signs for 10 and 100 and other large numbers were adopted. The Egyptian numbers are shown below. The example drawn out is a great advance on writing and then counting 1,343 separate strokes.

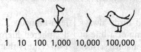

1 10 100 1,000 10,000 100,000

Example: = 1343

Heiroglyph Alphabet

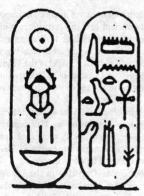

Tutankhamen's Cartouche

around 1600) with over 300 columns is unfortunately suffering from partial submersion. The Mohammed al-Abassi mosque (1809) stands to the south of the town by the River Nile and has a distinctive minaret. A lively market is held in the main street to the north of the town towards the station.

The H11 Desert road is a fast dual carriageway and the distance from Cairo to Alexandria (224 km) can be covered easily in 3 hrs. Express coaches of the West Delta Bus Co follow this route (see page 151). It is not busy as most drivers begrudge the E£1.5 toll per car. There is plenty of fuel available and accommodation: try the *Sahara Inn Motel* 117 km before Alexandria for a long or a short rest. Agriculture along here is large scale, comprising huge developments of bananas, dates and deciduous trees all dependent on underground water supplies. There is a large new town, **Sadat City**, off the road to the east.

WADI EL NATRUN

Wadi El Natrun is a natural depression of salt lakes and salt flats lying in the desert to the west of the Nile delta (30°25'north, 30°20'east). The *wadi* is aligned on an axis northwest to southeast to the immediate west of the direct desert road from Giza to

Alexandria at approximately Km 100. Access is either from the desert road at approximately 90 km from Giza turning west just before the outskirts of Sadat City, which stands to the east of the road, or from just north of the resthouse at Km 103.

Wadi El Natrun became the centre of a series of monastic groups principally in the 4th century AD. Insecurity, the plague and attacks by Bedouin led to the decline of some scattered communities but also led to some centralization of Christians into monasteries, of which four remain populated to the present day. The **Monastery of St Makarios** (Deir Abu Maqar) lies 3 km off the desert highway. It comprises the meagre set of remains of a once-great site in which a hasty and not entirely aesthetically pleasing reconstruction programme is under way. Its importance arises from the importance of St Makarios (St Makarios the Egyptian, c300-390 AD) the son of a village priest who came to the Wadi El Natrun in 330 AD and became the spiritual leader of the Christian hermits and monks in the area. He was ordained and made his name as a prophet and preacher of the ascetic way of life. He was buried at the monastery in the Wadi El Natrun. Another nine patriarchs of the Church are also interred at the site. This monastery is not open to visitors.

The site itself is made up of several churches, frequently destroyed and re-

Wadi El Natrun

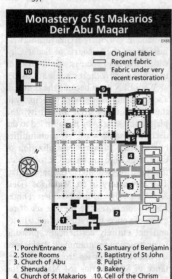

Monastery of St Makarios
Deir Abu Maqar

■ Original fabric
□ Recent fabric
■ Fabric under very recent restoration

0   10
metres

1. Porch/Entrance
2. Store Rooms
3. Church of Abu Shenuda
4. Church of St Makarios
5. Cell of the Council
6. Santuary of Benjamin
7. Baptistry of St John
8. Pulpit
9. Bakery
10. Cell of the Chrism

built. The main church, that of St Makarios, is basically a much-restored building on ancient foundations with some small survivals such as the 11th century dome and vestiges of the side chapels which are 7th-9th centuries. Those of St Benjamin and St John are among the most ancient of the original fabric. The main site contains the Cell of the Chrism, the fluid used to embalm Jesus Christ, and there is a belief that some of this original material was stored here at Deir Abu Maqar. A small bakery for making the host is located in a small room still standing in its original form on the north wall. An 11th century 3-storey defensive tower can be found behind the churches. Note the religious paintings in the smaller chapels in the tower.

To the northwest lie two other living monasteries – **Deir Anba Bishoi (Pschoi)** and **Deir el-Suriani**. These two sites are easily reached and offer no problems for visitors who wish to walk around. The buildings at Deir Anba Bishoi are mainly 20th century and are run for a thoroughly

modern community of monks. The layout of the ancient church is cruciform, with a central nave leading to a choir and through doors to the altar sanctuary. Small side chapels (Chapel of the Virgin to the left and Chapel of St Istkhirun or Ischyrion to the right) lie either side of the sanctuary.

Deir el-Suriani (Monastery of the Syrians) is thought to be an 11th century foundation by orthodox monks who resisted a schismatic movement at Deir Anba Bishoi. The site was acquired by a devout Syrian Christian in the 8th-9th centuries and thus took its now popular name since the schism had ended and the monks had returned to their centre at Bishoi. The Church of the Virgin Mary, the main structure at Deir el-Suriani is built over the cave used by St Bishoi. It is possible to visit this. The church has two main sections – the nave and the choir-sanctuary separated by buttresses and a doorway. The nave has a basin for the washing of feet, a stone screen and houses some religious relics, reputedly including hair from the head of Mary Magdalene, in a niche on the place where St Bishoi

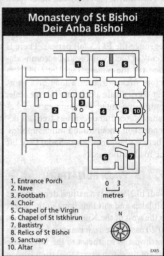

Monastery of St Bishoi
Deir Anba Bishoi

0   3
metres

N

1. Entrance Porch
2. Nave
3. Footbath
4. Choir
5. Chapel of the Virgin
6. Chapel of St Istkhirun
7. Bastistry
8. Relics of St Bishoi
9. Sanctuary
10. Altar

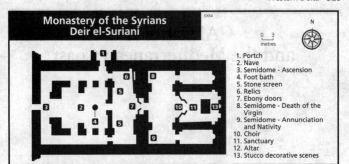

**Monastery of the Syrians
Deir el-Suriani**

EX64

0   3
metres

N

1. Portch
2. Nave
3. Semidome - Ascension
4. Foot bath
5. Stone screen
6. Relics
7. Ebony doors
8. Semidome - Death of the Virgin
9. Semidome - Annunciation and Nativity
10. Choir
11. Sanctuary
12. Altar
13. Stucco decorative scenes

lived in ascetic contemplation. In a semi-dome above the west door there is a picture of the Ascension. The altar is a very dark marble.

It is the choir which is most famous, however, for its wonderful 10th century black wood doors with their ivory inlays. Unfortunately the two three-panel doors between the choir and the sanctuary are in poor condition. There are paintings in the semi-domes in the choir, the death of the Virgin to the left and the annunciation and the nativity to the right. There are interesting stucco decorations behind the central altar. There is a library of over 3,000 books and many valuable manuscripts. There is also a small museum of 16th-17th century icons. Check before visiting as the monastery is closed to the public at times of important religious ceremonies.

Deir el-Baramous is the fourth monastery of the group, somewhat isolated to the north end of the Wadi El Natrun. Gaining entry is not always possible to this, the oldest of the sites. Legend has it that Maximus and Domitius, two sons of the Roman Emperor Valentinian died young of self-imposed fasting at this place and that St Makarios set up the new monastery to commemorate them. The five churches are dedicated to the Virgin Mary, St Theodore, St George, St John the Baptist and St Michael. The present day structures have been recently restored and have little of aesthetic merit to recommend them to the traveller.

Alexandria
and the Mediterranean Coast

A LEXANDRIA (El-Iskandariya), 224 km northwest of
Cairo, is Egypt's second largest city and a great cultural
centre, rich in classical remains, without the bustle and
hassle of the capital city. It extends 20 km along Egypt's
northern coast at the western edge of the Nile Delta and has
become a popular summer retreat for folk from Cairo. From
Alexandria, the Mediterranean Coast stretches 500 km west to
the Libyan border, passing the city's local beach resorts of
El-Agami and Hannoville, the site of the huge WW2 battle at
El-Alamein, and the new beach resorts of Sidi Abdel Rahman
and Marsa Matruh from which a road leads inland to the Siwa
oasis, before finally arriving at the Libyan border near Sollum.

For details on El-Agami and Hannoville see
El-Alamein, page 349 and for the Siwa oasis, which is accessible only from the coast,
see **Marsa Matruh**, page 352.

ALEXANDRIA

(*Pop* 3.7 million; *Alt* 7m)

History
Having conquered Egypt by 332 BC, **Alexander The Great**, who was then only 25
years old, commissioned his architect De-
inocrates to construct a new capital city on
the coast. He chose a site near the small
fishing village of Rhakotis for its natural
harbour and its proximity to his native
Macedonia, that had significant strategic
and commercial advantages over Mem-

phis (near modern-day Cairo). It was the
first Egyptian city to be built to the Greek

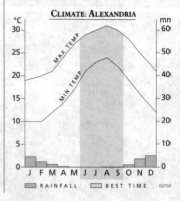

CLIMATE: ALEXANDRIA

MAX TEMP

MIN TEMP

J F M A M J J A S O N D

☐ RAINFALL ☐ BEST TIME

The Ptolemy Dynasty in Brief

Following the death of Alexander the Great, Ptolemy, satrap (governor) of Egypt soon gained control of the country. He took the title of king and founded a dynasty that lasted from 323 BC to 30 BC. There were 14 monarchs in all, ending with Cleopatra's son. The first three members of the dynasty were the most important.

Ptolemy I 367-283 BC known as Ptolemy Soter (saviour) was a great soldier with administrative ability who built roads and canals, founded the famous Library of Alexandria, wrote a scholarly account of Alexander's campaigns and abdicated at 82 in favour of Ptolemy II 309-246 BC, surnamed Philadelphus, a cultivated man whose court has been compared to that of Louis XIV at Versailles. He was not a soldier but supported Rome against her foes. Ptolemy III 281-221 BC, like his grandfather, was a vigorous warrior, supreme controller of the eastern Mediterranean who reopened the war against the Seleucids. He was a just ruler and was specially noted for his leniency towards Egyptian religion and customs.

The later members of the dynasty were described as decadent and dissolute, due largely to the convention for the king to marry his own sister.

design, with the two major roads running north-south and east-west intersecting in the city centre, and the rest of the town built around them in rectangular blocks, as can be seen in almost any modern North American city. A causeway linking the city to the island of **Pharos** created two huge harbours and Alexandria became a major port.

Alexander never saw his city. He travelled to Asia after instructing his architects and 8 years later he was dead. The priests at Memphis refused him burial, so his body was sent to Alexandria instead.

After Alexander's death his whole empire was divided amongst his various generals. **Ptolemy 1 Soter** (323-282 BC) started the Ptolemaic Dynasty (323-30 BC) in Egypt, and Alexandria became a major centre of Hellenistic culture, attracting many of the great and good, acquiring significant social, historical, and commercial importance throughout the Graeco-Roman period.

The Greeks integrated well with the Egyptians and created a new hybrid religion known as the cult of Serapis. The Romans, however, were more reserved. The influence of later Ptolemies declined steadily and they relied on the Romans for support. **Cleopatra VII** (51-30 BC),

the last of the Ptolemies, seduced first Julius Caesar and then his successor Mark Anthony in order to retain her crown. Mark Anthony and Cleopatra held sway in Egypt for 14 years until they were deposed by Octavian who became the Emperor Augustus.

Tradition has it that the Gospel was first preached in Alexandria by Saint Mark in 62 AD. Whatever the accuracy of this date, **Christianity** was certainly established around this time and Alexandria remained the centre of its theology for 3 centuries. However, its presence was still sufficiently threatening to the Muslim conquerors 3 centuries later to make them move their administration and theological capital inland to Cairo. Although Alexandria was still important as a centre of trade it's decline as a city was inevitable when the power base, along with the customary baggage of wealth, learning and culture went south.

With the 16th century discovery of America and the sea route around Africa to India and the Orient, which made the land route via Egypt virtually redundant, Alexandria lost its former magnificence. The decline during the Ottoman period was so great that while Cairo continued to flourish, the population of Alexandria fell to a mere 5,000 people by 1800.

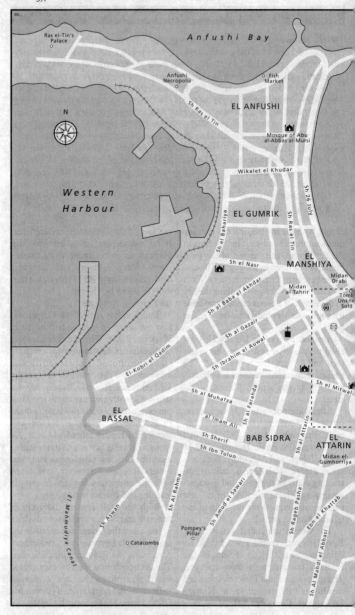

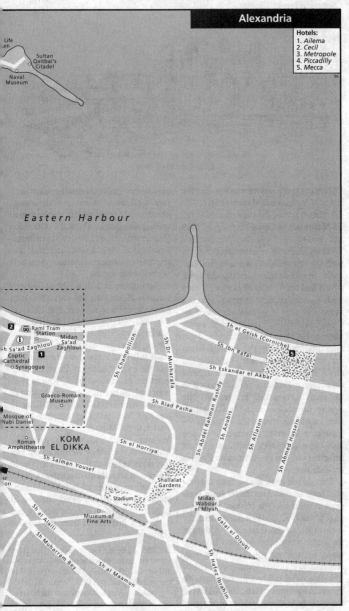

Alexandria

Life
um

Sultan
Qaitbai's
Citadel

Naval
Museum

Eastern Harbour

2 🚐 Raml Tram
Station
ℹ️
Midan
Sh Sa'ad Zaghloul   Sa'ad
1   Zaghloul
Coptic
Cathedral
○ Synagogue

Sh el Geish (Corniche)

Sh Ibn Rafai

Sh Eskandar el Akbar   **5**

Graeco-Roman
Museum ○

Sh Champollion

Sh Dr Musharafa

Sh Riad Pasha

Mosque of
Nabi Daniel

Roman
Amphitheatre

**KOM
EL DIKKA**

Sh el Horriya

Sh Abdel Rahman Rushdy

Sh Anubis

Sh Aflaton

Sh Ahmed Hussein

Sh Salman Yousef

st
on

Shallalat
Gardens

Midan
Wabour
el Miyah

Galal el Disuqi

Stadium

Museum of
Fine Arts

Sh al Aｌａili

Sh Muharram Bey

Sh al Maamun

Sh Hafez Ibrahim

Sultan Qaitbai's Citadel

Just in time, a saviour was found in the shape of **Mohamed (Mehmet) Ali** (1805-48). He organized the construction of the **El-Mahmudiya Canal** starting in 1819 and linked the Nile and Alexandria's Western Harbour, reconnecting the city with the rest of Egypt, whilst simultaneously irrigating the surrounding land, which had been badly neglected. With a trade route open, the city prospered once more and now it is only surpassed by Cairo itself. Foreign trade grew at a pace with the Egyptian merchant fleet and was later maintained by the British. Being further north and nearer to the sea, the city is cooler than Cairo in summer and each year the administration moved to the coast during this hot season. The British invested in many building projects including, true to the Victorian obsession, a sea-front promenade. If you half close your eyes, and use a bit of imagination, you could be in an English sea-side resort!

Population growth and industrialization have altered Alexandria since **Nasser's** revolution (see History of Egypt, page 65) in 1952. Today it is a modern city with much to recommend it. Although the outer areas have suffered from too rapid rural-urban migration, the busy central area is small enough for the visitor to walk around and become familiar with the main squares and landmarks. Having the coast to the north makes orientation easy. Although Alexandria's opulent heritage is no longer so obvious, the atmosphere of the town which inspired such literary classics as Durrell's *Alexandria Quartet* still remains. So don't rush immediately to all the places of interest. It is as important to absorb the atmosphere as it is to view the sights.

Alexandria is a thin ribbon-like city which is 20 km long but only a few kilometres wide because the residential areas are still largely bound by the El-Mahmudiya canal and Lake Maryut. At the city's western end is the El-Anfushi peninsula which now links the mainland and the former island of Pharos and divides the giant functional Western Harbour and the beautiful sweeping curve of the Eastern Harbour and its Corniche. To the east is a series of beaches which stretch to the Montazah Palace and on to Ma'mura beach and eventually Abu Qir which was the site of Nelson's 1798 victory over the French fleet. The city's main downtown area, its main transport terminals and many of the hotels are in the blocks around Midan Sa'ad Zaghloul in El-Manshiya which is in the western end of the city just inland from the Eastern Harbour.

ACCESS The airport is about 10 km from the town centre which is reached by bus No 307 or No 310 to Midan Orabi or No 203 to the nearby Midan Sa'ad Zaghloul. Intercity buses to Alexandria stop in the heart of the downtown area in Midan Sa'ad

Seeing the Light – Ancient Alexandria

The **Mouseion**, from which the word *museum* is derived, meaning Temple of the Muses, was a vast centre of learning standing at the main crossroads of the city. As well as laboratories, lodgings and a refectory for hundreds of scholars, it housed the famous library which by Caesar's day contained nearly a million papyrus volumes. Tragically, it was sacked and burned by Christian mobs in the 7th century AD. Recently, however, the international community has pledged US$64mn to build a new one and the phoenix of the Alexandrine Library is scheduled to rise gloriously from its ashes, beginning sometime in 1998.

The Lighthouse of Pharos The fire from this immense lighthouse could be seen from 55 km across the open sea. It was 135m high and stood at the mouth of the Eastern Harbour where Sultan Qaitbai's fort now stands. It was still in use at the time of the Muslim invasion over 900 years after its construction. The idea for the lighthouse may have come from Alexander the Great but it was actually built in 279 BC by Sostratus, an Asiatic Greek, during the reign of Ptolemy II (284-246 BC). According to popular myth an immense mirror lens made it possible to view ships far out at sea while the fuel to feed the fire is said to have been hydraulically lifted to the top of the lighthouse. The great earthquakes of 1100 and 1307 destroyed the ancient foundations and the stones lay abandoned until the Ottoman Sultan Qaitbai decided to build the fort on the site in 1479 AD.

Zaghloul while buses from the Delta towns sometimes stop 1 km further south at the huge Midan El-Gumhorriya outside the main Misr railway station. Service taxis stop at either of the two squares or at Midan Orabi which is 750m west of Midan Sa'ad Zaghloul. Traffic flow directions change on the Corniche depending on the time and the day. Follow police instructions.

Alexandria – the port

About 75% of the country's foreign trade passed through the port of Alexandria, Egypt's main port. The facilities are most impressive. The 62 quays provide enormous capacity for cereals, refrigerated items and general cargoes. The container area, also enormous, has winching and RO-RO facilities.

Places of interest

Historical remains in Alexandria today are such pale shadows of their former glories, chief amongst which were the **Mouseion** and the **Lighthouse of Pharos**, one of **the seven wonders of the ancient world**. For a city with such a magnificent past history there is, unlike Cairo, comparatively little to see today because the modern city overlies

the ancient one. Most visitors come to Alexandria for its Mediterranean beaches and cool and cosmopolitan atmosphere.

The description of places of interest begins in Central Alexandria at the harbour and works south and east.

At the very end of the peninsula, in a most imposing position stands the **Citadel of Qaitbai**. It was built in 1479 by Sultan Qaitbai (1468-96 AD) on the ancient site of, and probably with the stones of, the Lighthouse of Pharos stands at the far end of the Eastern Harbour as one of a series of coastal forts. It is one of the city's major landmarks and is now the property of the Egyptian Navy. The Citadel is approached up a wide causeway which ends at the original gateway between two half-round towers, both with interior rooms. Unfortunately today's entrance, further to the east, is less impressive. From the causeway notice the antique granite and marble columns incorporated in the fabric of the west facing wall. Three sides of the enclosed courtyard were given over to storage and accommodation for animals and troops. The north facing wall has emplacements for a score of cannon and

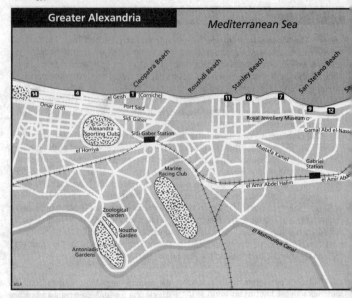

the higher look-out tower gives a commanding view over the Mediterranean. The keep houses a small mosque which, unusually for the Delta region, is built in the shape of a cross. The entrance to this mosque is through a huge gateway flanked by pillars of red Aswan granite. To the side of the mosque a complex cistern stored water in case of siege. The fort's greatest attraction is the view from the battlements back over the open sea toward Alexandria. It can be reached from downtown Alexandria by taking the No 15 tram from Raml tram station. Open Saturday-Thursday 0900-1600, Friday 0900-1200 and 1400-1600, Ramadan daily 1000-1430. Entrance E£6, students E£3, camera E£10 and video camera E£50. Its **Naval Museum** contains artifacts from Roman and Napoleonic sea battles which are likely to appeal more to specialists than to the casual tourist. Open daily 0900-1500 except Friday.

The **Marine Life Museum** and Hydro-Biological Institute near Sultan Qaitbai's Fort on Anfushi Bay houses a rare collection of fish and marine life. Open daily 0900-1600, price 10 piastres.

The **Fish Market** further west on Anfushi Bay is easy to find, just follow your nose. Go early to see this small area teeming with fish and people.

The **Anfushi Necropolis** (open daily 0900-1600, Friday 0900-1130 and 1300-1600, entrance E£12) is located to the west of the fort near the sweep of the small Anfushi Bay. This is a set of 3rd and 2nd century tombs in which there are some Roman additions. The complex is cut into the limestone with the main tombs entered down flights of steps. The right hand stairway is decorated at the turn with scenes of Horus, Isis and Anubis. Below off an open hall lie two principal chambers with vestibules each distinctively decorated. The right hand room bears Greek graffiti and naval scenes while the left hand chamber is more colourful with scenes of deities and a chequer-board pattern above. The burial chamber, with matching wall decoration, is guarded by sphinxes. Inside the left

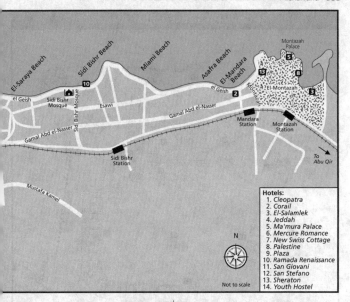

Hotels:
1. *Cleopatra*
2. *Corail*
3. *El-Salamlek*
4. *Jeddah*
5. *Ma'mura Palace*
6. *Mercure Romance*
7. *New Swiss Cottage*
8. *Palestine*
9. *Plaza*
10. *Ramada Renaissance*
11. *San Giovani*
12. *San Stefano*
13. *Sheraton*
14. *Youth Hostel*

N

Not to scale

hand group there is an entrance hall off which are two vestibules and tomb chambers. The right hand vestibule has benches and leads to a chamber with a red granite sarcophagus. In the left hand room the layout was modified in the Roman period to take a series of sarcophagi.

Further west along the peninsula are formal gardens and then **Ras el-Tin's Palace** (Cape of Figs Palace) which overlooks the Western harbour but which is now the Admiralty Headquarters and is unfortunately closed to the public. It was built so that Mohamed Ali (1805-48) could review his fleet and was reconstructed in the European Turkish style by Fouad I (1917-36) to serve as the government's summer seat. It was therefore ironic that his son King Farouk signed his abdication at the palace on 26 July 1952 before boarding a yacht bound for exile in Italy.

Inland from the peninsula towards the city centre is the old Ottoman area of Anfushi and some of the most important mosques including the **Mosque of Abu al-Abbas al-Mursi** north off Sharia Ras el

Tin. Ahmed Abu al-Abbas al-Mursi (1219-87) was an Andalusian who came to Alexandria to join and eventually lead the Shadhali brotherhood. He is the patron saint of Alexandria's fishermen and sailors. His mosque and tomb were renovated in 1775 by a rich Maghrebi merchant but was then demolished and rebuilt in 1943 and is now the largest mosque in Alexandria. The current layout is octagonal with Italian granite supporting the roof arches, four decorated domes and the slender 73m minaret rising in tiers which gives the modern mosque a pleasing weightless aspect. This is one of Alexandria's foremost religious buildings and is well worth a visit but visitors are advised that women are only permitted entry into a room at the back of the mosque.

Further south in this Ottoman part of the city is the **Al-Tarbana Mosque** which is situated on Sharia Farnasa to the east of Sharia al-Shahid. It has undergone major alterations since it was built in 1685 by Hajji Ibrahim Tarbana. The

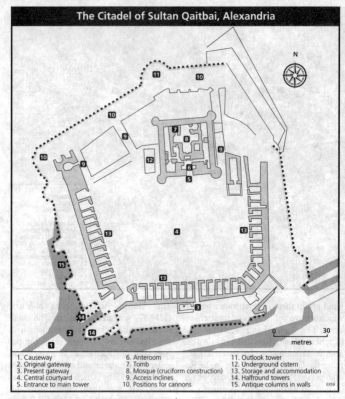

The Citadel of Sultan Qaitbai, Alexandria

1. Causeway	6. Anteroom	11. Outlook tower
2. Original gateway	7. Tomb	12. Underground cistern
3. Present gateway	8. Mosque (cruciform construction)	13. Storage and accommodation
4. Central courtyard	9. Access inclines	14. Halfround towers
5. Entrance to main tower	10. Positions for cannons	15. Antique columns in walls

0   30
metres

minaret is supported by two antique columns which stand above the entrance whilst a further eight columns support the ornamental ceiling. The original Delta style façade is almost completely obscured by plastering.

The **Attarine Mosque** dates from the 14th century and stands on the site of the once famous Mosque of a Thousand Columns. It was from here that Napoleon removed the 7 tonne sarcophagus which now is displayed in the British Museum.

The **Ibrahim al-Shurbaji Mosque**, to the east of Midan Sa'ad Zaghloul, was built in 1757. The internal layout is similar to that of the Al-Tarbana Mosque. A courtyard to the rear creates a pleasant impression of

space. There have been many modifications, but the *mihrab* is still decorated with the original Kufic inscriptions.

The **Tomb of the Unknown Soldier**, about half way round the Eastern Harbour on Midan Obari, is worth noting as a good landmark.

Turn south from the sea to Midan Sa'ad Zaghloul and walk down Sharia Nabi Daniel to the **Coptic Orthodox Cathedral**. This is a very recent establishment (1950-87) and presented as a large arched vault is a fine example of ecclesiastical architecture. It is dedicated to five saints, in particular St Mark whose head is reputed to be buried at this site together with the remains of early

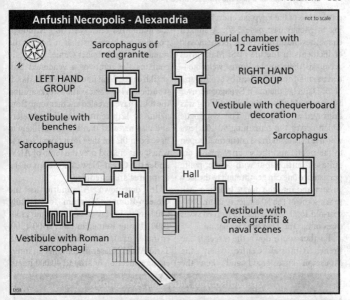

Anfushi Necropolis - Alexandria   not to scale

LEFT HAND GROUP
Sarcophagus of red granite
Vestibule with benches
Sarcophagus
Hall
Vestibule with Roman sarcophagi

Burial chamber with 12 cavities
RIGHT HAND GROUP
Vestibule with chequerboard decoration
Sarcophagus
Hall
Vestibule with Greek graffiti & naval scenes

Alexander The Great – Greek King of Egypt

Alexander the Great and his army entered Egypt in November 332 BC. He made a sacrifice to Apis in Memphis, taking at that time the twin crowns of Lower and Upper Egypt. He remained in Egypt for some months setting up control of the Egyptian army and founding the city of Alexandria on the coast of the northwest of the Nile delta. In the spring of 331 he marched along the Mediterranean coast to Paraetonium (present-day Marsa Matruh) and thence through the Western Desert to Siwa.

His visit to Siwa was to consult the oracle of Zeus-Amun. The Temple of the oracle at Siwa (see page 355) is situated to the west of Shali, the new town, at the old site of Aghurmi. There are elaborate stories of Alexander's visit to the oracle temple of Amun but what is clear is that he was received by the priests at Siwa as a pharoah and had a private audience at the oracle. His concern was his expedition against his enemies, the Persians, but he gave no word to his followers on the outcome though in a letter to his mother he promised to tell all when he saw her again (which he never did!). Much later it was reported that Alexander was saluted by the oracle as the son of Zeus which effectively led to his deification and assured him of success in Asia. Certainly, Alexander retained a deep belief in the powers of the god Amun and a flow of gifts continued to come during Alexander's lifetime to the temple priests at Siwa.

He went on in 331 to attack Babylon and by 330 had control of the Persian empire and thereafter moved his armies into Central Asia and in 327 to India. Within 10 years he was master of the known world. He died unchallenged in this role aged 33 on 13 June 323. He was buried in the Egyptian city of Alexandria. (See also page 354.)

patriarches of the Egyptian church including St Menas (see page 347). A sunken chapel beyond an interesting recent mosaic of incidents in the life of St Mark gives access to their tombs. Entry welcome – leave a small donation. Nearby at 69 Sharia Nabi Daniel is the main **Synagogue**, over 145 years old. The previous building was destroyed by Napoleon. The synagogue which serves the remaining 90-100 Jews who live in Alexandria is not normally open to the public and the security guards are quite off-putting: but with gentle, polite persistence one can get through to the lady curator and into the ornate building. Ask to see some of the 50 ancient 500 to 1,000-year-old Torah scrolls held in worked silver cases in the arc. They are fascinating.

Further south down the street is the French Cultural Centre where the Mouseion once stood and then the **Mosque al-Nabi Daniel** which is near the main Misr railway station. Although popular myth claims that it houses the remains of the prophet Daniel it actually contains the tomb of a venerated Sufi sheikh called Mohamed Danyal al-Maridi who died in 1497. Excavation works around the tomb have revealed another tomb from a 10th or 12th century Muslim cemetery and also revealed that the site is likely to have been that of the Great Soma Temple which was erected over the tomb of **Alexander the Great**. New excavations of the crypt area are scheduled.

In downtown Alexandria is the **Graeco-Roman Museum** (open daily 0900-1600, Friday 0900-1130 and 1330-1600, during Ramadan daily 0900-1500, entrance E£8), in Sharia Amin Fikri and Tariq Abdel Nasser. It contains an interesting collection of around 40,000 items,

Graeco-Roman Museum, Alexandria

North garden   Verandah   South garden

Entrance

EX60a

1-2. Coptic earthenware and architectural elements	10. Late Pharaonic - Sir John Antoniadis collection	18a. Miniature Tanagra terracotta figures
3. Jewellery	11. Statues of and fragments from Athribus near Benha	19. Statues, funerary urns and pottery
4. Textiles		20. Chatby collection
5. Coptic Stucco	12-14. Miscellaneous sculptures of Graeco-Roman period	21. Ibrahimeya collection
6. Cult of Serapis	15. Tomb paintings	22. Coloured glassware
7. Artifacts from Ancient Canopus	16-16a. Hellenistic sculpture	22a. Bronze and other metals
8. Mummies and sarcophagi	17. Monolith and sarcophagi	23. Coins
9. Crocodile worship in el-Fayoum	18. Pottery and glass	

20th century pirates

Are we likely to see raids with sabres clashing under the emblem of Salah al-Din's golden eagle? Perhaps not. However, while it is hard to believe, pirates do exist in this day and age and Sharon Bailey, anti-piracy manager for Africa, the Middle East and Mediterranean regions has a special interest in activities in Egypt. It is claimed that pirated software accounts for 88% of software use in Egypt, and Microsoft are not impressed. They estimate that Arabic versions of its software could be produced 20% more cheaply in Egypt than in Europe but plans to contract out the work depend on controlling the pirates.

mainly taken from local tombs dating from about 300 BC to AD 300, of relics from the Graeco-Roman period. The most significant cult was that of Serapis which was a hybrid of the Greek god Dionysus and the Nile god Osiris. The Serapis was depicted as a bull and is directly associated with the ancient Egyptian cult of the Apis bull. Take the rooms in chronological order, beginning in **Room 6** with the centrally placed magnificent sculpture of the black granite Apis bull (see Deities, page 205). The inscription dates it at 117-138 AD. The white marble sculpture of Serapis was, like the bull, found near Pompey's Column. This room has some attractive mosaics.

Canopus, now reduced to rubble, was situated on the coast to the east of Alexandria and the artefacts from there in **Room 7** seem to be a collection of headless statues, sandstone sphinxes and basalt goddesses. Ramses II put his name on the huge red granite statue. **Room 8** has mummies differently decorated and an example of a Fayoum portrait (see box, page 173 Fayoum portraits) while **Room 9** has a mummified crocodile and other pieces from the Temple of Pnepheros, all connected with the crocodile worship practised there. **Room 11** – the mixture of Greek and Egyptian influences produced some interesting sculptures excavated from Athribus near Benha in the Central Delta. On the fragments of tomb paintings in **Room 15** is a *saqiya* or water-wheel with jars to collect and lift the water (see section on the Nile and man, page 50). The sculptures in **Rooms 16-16A** are

some of the most worthwhile exhibits in the museum. Look particularly at the Persian god, the lion-headed Mithras; the giant eagle from the Aegean; the graceful figure of Aphrodite and the carefully executed male and female torsos. There are six marble sarcophagi in **Room 17**, most with intricate carvings and one with scenes from the Greek myths, keeping company with what is claimed to be the largest statue ever carved in porphyry (even though it has no head). The tiny terracotta figures from Greece displayed in **Room 18a** were associated with burials of young people and provide interesting detail about the dress and fashions of the time. Local Alexandrian excavations provide the displays in **Rooms 19-21**. Look particularly at the figures of the happy god Bes and Min (see Deities, page 204). **Room 22** is a reminder that Alexandria was a centre for glass making. **Room 23** has an interesting display of coins.

Rooms 1-5 are devoted to Coptic artefacts. There are objects relating to St Menas' Monastery (see Abu Mina, page 347), including numerous pilgrim's flasks. The textiles have delightful designs, the Copts being recognized as fine weavers. Take time to examine the larger items displayed in the garden. Some of the statues are very fine. There are rock-cut tombs in the South Garden and the parts of the Temple of Pnepheros (Room 9) in the North Garden.

Royal Jewellery Museum, 21 Sharia Ahmed Yehia Pasha, Gleem, T 5868348 (behind the Governor's residence). The palace, originally belonging to Fatma el-Zahra, granddaughter of Ibrahim Pasha, was formerly one of King Farouk's palaces which with its garden covers an area of over 4,000 sq m. It now houses a glittering collection of treasures from the time of Mohamed Ali through to King Farouk. There are jewels on everything in cases clearly labelled in Arabic and English. Statues and paintings are also on display. The mansion in which these are housed is almost of equal interest. It contains ten stained glass doors and many stained glass windows depicting stories of European history. The bathrooms, cordoned off but on view to the public, are an inspiration. Lift your eyes from the jewels to admire the ceilings. The items

Western artists in Egypt

Egypt has rarely been an independent country. The Ottoman empire lasted until 1805, though the first direct intervention in Egypt began in 1798 with the Napoleonic invasion. A great entourage of scientists, writers and artists accompanied the French occupation of Egypt, which went on until 1801 opening this hitherto largely protected Islamic country to a new and interested audience.

The orientalist artists and writers of the 19th century were confronted in Egypt and elsewhere in North Africa with sights and scenes of what appeared to be a startlingly different culture. They recorded what they saw for an audience at home that was eager to catch glimpses of these unknown lands. By the end of the century, a new breed of artists found their way to the new territorial possessions that their countries had acquired in the great grab for colonial purposes. France was the military power in Egypt and much of the Maghreb and it was from here that inspiration came to many of the great French and other artists – though to indulge their art and their own senses rather than to convey impressions of exotic lands. Some artists such as Baron Gros and Jean-Augustine-Dominique Ingres never actually got as far as Egypt but none the less produced fine paintings of the Napoleonic campaigns (viz The Battle of Nazareth by Gros).

In addition to the French, the British imperial mission was important in 19th century Egypt and brought its own harvest of 'orientalist' works of art. John Frederick Lewis (1805-75) spent 10 years in Egypt and was a prolific painter of watercolours of ancient monuments such as Edfou, Upper Egypt and scenes of contemporary Cairo life such as A Turkish School in the vicinity of Cairo.

David Roberts (1796-1864) was another master of the sketch and oil painting who voyaged along the Nile in 1839. His sketches, reproduced as lithographs, are still popular and provide a wonderful catalogue of the major Nilotic sites in the mid-19th century. Temple at Dendereh and The Island of Philae are fine examples of his work.

Later comers to Egypt were William Holman Hunt (1827-1910), who was a founder member of the Pre-Raphaelite Brotherhood and who visited Egypt in 1854-56. His paintings were enlightened by his view of the archaeological sites of Egypt and the Levant, with notable pieces such as The Great Pyramid and Entrance to the Temple of Amun. In the 20th century a modern artist, Paul Klee (1879-1940), was deeply influenced by his travels in Egypt in 1928-29, from which he took not merely symbols into his paintings but ideas of a holistic universe. His Legend of the Nile encapsulated his Egyptian experiences in a single modern picture in pastel.

Today, keen painters can still take advantage of a brilliantly unique Nile landscape and highly individualistic local architecture and dress in Egypt and Libya to develop their expertise through an accompanied tour with organisations such as The Prospect Music and Art Tours, 454-458 Chiswick High Road, London, W4 5TT, T 0181-995 2151.

in the collection considered the most important include – from Mohammed Ali, a gold plated, enamelled and inscribed snuff box; from King Fuad, a gold knob inlaid with diamonds, gold medals and decorations, a platinum crown inlaid with diamonds and sapphires with other pieces of jewellery to match; from King Farouk, a gold chess set enamelled and inlaid with diamonds, a gold tray inscribed with the signatures of 110 pashas; from Queen Safinaz, her crown of platinum inlaid with diamonds, gold and platinum brooches inlaid with diamonds. This is just the beginning of the catalogue. Open daily 1900-1600, Friday 0900-1130 and 1330-1600, entrance E£10.

Cavafy Museum has recently moved from the Greek Consulate building. It is now housed at 4 Sharia Sharm el-Sheikh, in the building where the great Alexandrian poet Constantine Cavafy lived for the last 25 years of his life. He died in 1933. It is marked with a plaque. It lies to the east of Sharia Nabi Daniel in the street parallel to and just north of Sharia el Horriya. Two of the rooms have been arranged with his household furniture, books and manuscripts to give an idea of the place when he was in occupation. Open 0900-1400 daily, also 1800-2000 on Tuesday and Thursday, closed Monday. Entrance free.

The **Naval Museum** is situated at the end of the peninsula, at the west end of the Corniche, open 0900-1500 daily except Friday and adjacent is the **Marine Life Museum** (same times as above) with live specimens of Egyptian marine life in aquaria.

To the east of the mosque and to the north of the Misr railway station is the Kom al-Dikkah (Hill of Rubble), thought to be the ancient site of the Paneion ('Park of Pan', a hilly pleasure garden), which has been excavated since 1959. Instead a small semi-circular 700-800 seat **Roman Amphitheatre**, Kom el-Dikka, behind Cinema Amir (open Saturday-Thursday 0900-1600, Friday 0900-1600, Ramadan

A famous citizen of Alexandria misleads Columbus

Claudius Ptolemy the famous Greek astronomer and geographer lived in Alexandria. According to the Ptolemaic system the sun and moon rotated round the earth which was believed to be the centre of the universe. In his *Geography*, eight books which contained many maps, he greatly under-estimated the distances between continents and left out the Americas altogether. This miscalculation led Columbus, 15 centuries later, to seek a route to India by travelling west from Spain.

daily 0900-1500, entrance E£6), was discovered with 12 rows of marble seats focussing on a columned stage which still has the remains of its mosaic flooring. A residential quarter with Roman baths is being excavated to the north. The site is one of the few in Alexandria to indicate the wealth of the city's heritage and it is well worth a visit. An annex of the Graeco-Roman Museum displays local discoveries.

Fine Art Museum (open 0800-1400, closed Friday, entrance free) is located at 18 Sharia Menasce. On the ground floor there is a permanent exhibition of 20th century Egyptian painting while the upper floor is dedicated to temporary exhibitions which are generally of modern Egyptian art. Film club meets here every Wednesday.

Further southeast on the way to the El-Mahmudiya Canal and Lake Maryut in an area of cheap markets is **Pompey's Pillar** (open daily 0900-1600, closes at 1500 in Ramadan, entrance E£6), just to the east of Sharia al Rahman. It is a 27m high and 9m thick column of red Aswan granite topped by an impressive Corinthian capital. This pillar, Alexandria's tallest ancient monument, is a rather bizarre spectacle and its origins are the subject of speculation. It certainly does not originate from Pompey and is thought to have come from the **Sarupis Temple**

(40 km to the west) and to have been erected in honour of **Diocletian** (AD 284-305). It may have supported his statue. Extensive archaeological excavations surround the site. See the three granite sphinxes and some underground cisterns to the west of the ridge.

Nearby in an area where many of the houses are 120-200 years old are the **Catacombs of Kom el-Shoqafa** (Mounds of Shards), located in Karmouz (open daily 0900-1600, closes 1500 in Ramadan, entrance E£12 plus E£10 for camera), originally 2nd century private tombs which were later extended in order to serve the whole community. They have been extensively excavated since their rediscovery in 1900 but sadly, water has flooded the lowest level and caused some deterioration. A large spiral staircase serves as the entrance to the tombs, below which passages lead to interconnecting tomb shafts.

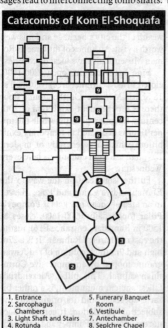

Catacombs of Kom El-Shoquafa

1. Entrance	5. Funerary Banquet Room
2. Sarcophagus Chambers	6. Vestibule
3. Light Shaft and Stairs	7. Antechamber
4. Rotunda	8. Seplchre Chapel
	9. Gallery

EX60

Immediately to the left of the entrance is a corridor leading to the more recent tombs. The main passage from the stairwell runs into a large rotunda with a domed roof. Branching from this is a banqueting hall for those visiting the deceased! A burial chamber leads off the rotunda opposite the dining area. Within the chamber are many niches in which one or more bodies were sealed. A fourth passage leads to another stairway from which further ornate chambers branch off. In places red paint can be found below the niches bearing the name of those encased within. The eerie atmosphere is intensified by the ornate serpents and medusa heads that lurk above doorways and passage entrances. Also on the site is a **Hypogeum** containing over 30 murals.

Other tombs Tombs of Chatby, Sharia Port Said, dates from 3rd century. Believed to be the most ancient tombs to be found in Alexandria. Entrance E£6. Tombs of Mustafa Kamel, Sharia Moasker Romani, Rushdi. Here there are four tombs dating from the 2nd and 3rd centuries. Entrance E£12.

To the east of downtown Alexandria lie 17 km of beaches stretching to the beautiful 160 ha gardens of **Montazah Palace** (see gardens, page 341), which is now a state guesthouse. It was constructed in the 19th century by the visionary Mohamed Ali as a palace for the engineers who built the barrages which are so important for the irrigation of the Delta. It was later inhabited by King Farouk. The original construction had been halted, and was completed later in the century, on a grander scale, by Sir Colin Scott-Moncrieff.

Further to the east and 5 km along Ma'mura Bay is **Canopus** which bears few traces of the Delta's chief port which flourished before the development of Alexandria. The motivation for building a city in the area was the Canopic branch of the River Nile which has long since dried up. The city is claimed to have been built by Menalaeus' pilot Canopus on his

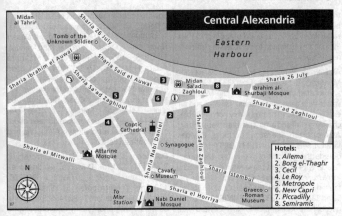

Central Alexandria

Midan al Tahrir
Tomb of the Unknown Soldier
Sharia 26 July
Sharia Ibrahim el Auwal
Sharia Said el Auwal
Sharia Sa'ad Zaghloul
Eastern Harbour
Sharia 26 July
Midan Sa'ad Zaghloul
Ibrahim al-Shurbaji Mosque
Sharia Sa'ad Zaghloul
Coptic Cathedral
Sharia Nabi Daniel
Synagogue
Sharia Safia Zaghloul
Sharia el Mitwalli
Attarine Mosque
Cavafy Museum
Sharia Istambul
Sharia el Horriya
N
To Misr Station
Nabi Daniel Mosque
Graeco-Roman Museum

Hotels:
1. Ailema
2. Borg el-Thaghr
3. Cecil
4. Le Roy
5. Metropole
6. New Capri
7. Piccadilly
8. Semiramis

return from the Trojan wars who was venerated by the local population after his death from snakebite. Today little remains of the site. The destruction is a recent phenomenon, apparently mainly caused by British occupation during WW1 and WW2. The ancient remains which have survived, including several statues of Ramses II, are now in the Graeco-Roman Museum in Alexandria. Two abandoned forts to the east of Canopus can be explored.

Beaches

Anywhere along the Corniche the beach is very pleasant and there are all the facilities nearby. Ask for Stanley Beach which is one of the best in town. To the east is the beach of the Montazah gardens and another at Ma'amoura. Abu Qir, a small fishing village further east again offers a good beach and the opportunity to sample the extremely fresh fish and shell fish.

Gardens

The **Montazah Palace Gardens** cover almost 160 ha. A very large area is formal gardens, a welcome respite from the bustle of the city. Originally built in 1892, this palace only dates from 1926 being the summer residence of the Egyptian royal family. The adjacent beautiful beach makes this the most popular of the gardens

here. Open 24 hrs, entrance E£4. **Nouzha Gardens and Zoo**, Sharia Smouha, Smouha has many interesting birds and animals in the zoo. Adjacent gardens have picnic areas. Entrance to zoo and gardens 50pt. Both open daily 0800-1600. The **Antoniadis Gardens** are near the El-Mahmudiya Canal and the zoo. The house, originally owned by a wealthy Greek family is now used for meetings of state. The gardens contain beautiful arrangements of trees and flower beds as well as several marble statues. Well maintained gardens and walkways, several Greek statues, open daily 0800-1600, entrance 50pt. **Shallalat Gardens** to east of city centre, varying levels, rockeries and waterways, lovely.

The Yacht Club beside Qaitbai's Fort hires boats, so why not end your tour of Alexandria by seeing it from the sea?

Local information
● Accommodation

Price guide:			
AL	US$150+	**D**	US$25-50
A	US$100-150	**E**	US$10-25
B	US$75-100	**F**	under US$10
C	US$50-75		

Alexandria is Egypt's second largest city and the major domestic resort for Egyptian tourists and has hotels to suit every taste. Besides the main downtown hotels there are others east along the coast to the exclusive El-Montazah area and beyond. **NB** That all hotels on the Corniche suffer from traffic noise – day and night. They incl but are not limited to the following officially registered hotels.

AL *Helnan Palestine*, Montazah Palace, El-Montazah, T 5474033, F 5473378, 210 rm, also located in the grounds of the Montazah Palace with a lagoon, beautiful gardens and an excellent beach nearby. Very comfortable, charming staff and a most pleasant place to stay; **AL** *Montazah Sheraton*, Corniche, El-Montazah, T 5480550, F 5401331, 305 rm, located outside the grounds of the walled Montazah Palace, with excellent sea-views, private beach, for luxury and convenience this cannot be faulted. Highly rec; **AL** *Pullman Cecil*, 16 Midan Sa'ad Zaghloul, T 4837173, F 4836401, 86 rm, guests have incl Churchill, Noel Coward and Lawrence Durrell, 5 restaurants and casino open 2000-0400. Pseudo Moorish style. While this has the convenience of being in the centre of town, situated in the former European quarter close to the Old Eastern Harbour, it lacks the peace of the other high quality hotels in El-Montazah. Weigh up the attractions before you decide.

A *Mercure Alexandria Romance*, 313 Sharia el-Geish, Saba Pasha, T 5876804, F 5870526, 64 rm; **A** *Plaza*, 394 Sharia el-Geish, Zizinia, T 5878714, F 5875399, 180 rm, good standard, modern, sea view; **A** *Ramada Renaissance*, 544 Sharia el-Geish, Sidi Bishr, T 5490935, F 5497690, 20 suites and 150 very comfortable double rm, located on coast road 12-15 km from town centre, try excellent restaurant with panoramic view of the Mediterranean. This has all the comforts of a good international hotel and the charm of well trained staff. Check your room for traffic noise. This is certainly the best choice of the A grade hotels.

B *El-Salamlek San Giovanni*, Montazah Palace, T 5473585, F 5464408, 33 rm, built like an Alpine chalet for the Khedive's Austrian mistress, still being renovated; **B** *Landmark*, 163 Sharia Abdel Salam Aref, San Stefano, T 5880500, F 5880515, 150 rm, located about half way between downtown Alexandria and the Montazah Palace.

The quality of hotel varies considerably in this price range. A change of management or staff makes a bigger difference here. Always ask to see the room first.

C *Alexandria*, 23 Midan El-Nasr, El-Manshiya, T 4837694, F 4823113, 108 rm, family run downtown hotel with good personal service; **C** *Delta*, 14 Sharia Champollion, Mazarita, T 4829053, F 4825630, 63 rm; **C** *Desert Home*, Sharia Omar el-Mokhtar, King Mariout, T 981315, F 4914939, 14 rm, cosy; **C** *Ma'mura Palace*, El-Ma'mura, T/F 5473108, 80 rm, good standard, modern, good views, located in the exclusive El-Ma'mura area to the east of the Montazah Palace, rec; **C** *San Giovanni*, 205 Sharia el-Geish, Stanley, T 5467774, F 5464408, 30 rm, beach hotel located about half way between downtown Alexandria and the Montazah Palace.

D *Amun*, 32 Midan el-Nasr, El-Manshiya, T 807131, 120 rm; **D** *Mecca*, 44 Sharia el-Geish, Camp Caesar, T 5973925, F 5969935, 120 rm; **D** *Metropole*, 52 Sharia Sa'ad Zaghloul, Raml Station, T 4821466, F 4822040, 82 rm, all with phones and TV, worth staying for the wonderful Art Deco and Art Nouveau decor; **D** *New Swiss Cottage*, 384 Sharia el-Geish, Gleem, T 5875830, F 5870455, on coast road about half way between downtown Alexandria and the Montazah Palace, next door to the original *Swiss Cottage*; **D** *San Stefano*, Sharia Abdel Salam Aref, San Stefano, T 5863587, F 5865935, 120 rm, good position, on beach; **D** *Semiramis*, 80 Sharia el-Geish, Raml Station, T 4830824, 64 rm, many with sea view, rooftop restaurant; **D** *Venezia*, 21 Sharia el-Nasr, El-Manshiya, T 802322, F 4824664, 120 rm, good value for money.

E *Admiral*, 24 Sharia Amin Fikri, Raml Station, T 4831787, 68 rm, generally clean, some rooms with bath, good value, breakfast incl; **E** *Ailema*, 21 Sharia Amin Fikri, Raml Station, T 4837011, 38 rm, rather faded Greek-run downtown hotel; **E** *Borg el-Thaghr*, Sharia Safeya Zaghloul, Raml Station, T 4924519, 33 rm, 69 beds; **E** *Corail*, 802 Sharia el-Geish, El-Mandara, T 5480996, F 5407746, 28 rm, beach hotel just to west of Montazah Palace; **E** *Deauville*, 274 Sharia el-Geish, Stanley, T 5454804, F 5454806, 41 rm, on beach; **E** *Holiday*, 6 Midan Orabi, El-Manshiya, T 8014559, 44 double rm, 80 beds, comfortable; **E** *Jeddah*, 137 Sharia el-Geish, Sporting, T 857643, 69 rm, 125 beds, just north of the Alexandria Sporting Club.

F *Cleopatra*, 160 Sharia el-Geish, Cleopatra, T 852409, 60 rm, on beach at Cleopatra bay; **F** *El-Mehrek*, 133 Sharia el-Geish, Sporting, T 854513, 99 rm, just north of the Alexandria Sporting Club; **F** *Hyde Park House*, 21 Sharia Amin Fikri, Raml Station, T 4835667, 58 rm, rather run down, one flr above the *Ailema hotel*; **F** *Le Roy*, 25 Sharia Talaat Harb, Raml Station,

T 4833439, 65 rm, a shadow of its former Art Deco self; **F** *New Capri*, 23 El-Mina, Sharia el-Sharkia, Raml Station, T 809310, 32 rm, downtown hotel located in tourist police building; **F** *Piccadilly*, 11 Sharia el-Horriya, El-Nabi Daniel, 32 rm, a 6th flr exceedingly cheap hotel, nr the railway station, a very good bargain.

Camping At Sharia Bahr al-Mait in Abu Qir which is about 20 km from downtown Alexandria about 5 km east of the Montazah Palace.

Youth hostels 32 Sharia Port Said, Shatbi, Raml, T/F 5975459, 2 km northeast of city centre, 200 beds, meals available, train 3 km, ferry 5 km, overnight fee E£5.

● **Places to eat**

Price guide:
♦♦♦Expensive; ♦♦average; ♦cheap.

For the greatest concentration of restaurants and cafés, try the area bounded by Sharia Sa'ad Zaghloul, Raml station and Eastern Harbour by Midan Sa'ad Zaghloul. The restaurants in the higher grade hotels are reliable and serve Western and Egyptian cuisine.

♦♦♦: *Alexander's* at the *Ramada Renaissance*, 544 Sharia el-Geish, Sidi Bishr, T 866111, elegant service, excellent fish food, has a panoramic view of the Mediterranean; *San Giovanni*, on Corniche in Stanley, excellent fish, sea views, from E£30/head; *Santa Lucia*, 40 Sharia Safeya Zaghloul, T 4824240, excellent seafood, serves wine and beer, open 1200-1600 and 1900-0100.

♦♦: *Denise*, Sharia Ibn Bassam, off Raml tram station, T 4830457, select your own fish from the freezer, alcohol, open 0900-0100; *Elite*, 43 Sharia Safeya Zaghloul, T 4823592, opp *Santa Lucia*, large helpings, alcohol, open 0900-2400; *New China Restaurant* in *Corail Hotel*, T 5470996, 802 Sharia el-Geish, Chinese food, spicy shrimps and beef served in lovely setting, alcohol, open 1200-1600 and 1800-2300; *Seagull*, Sharia el Agami, T 4455575, highly rec but way out of town to west in industrial area; *Tikka Grill*, T 805119, nr Al-Mursi's Mosque, views overlooking Eastern Harbour, beautifully served, spicy Indian food, salad bar, open 1300-1700 and 2000-0200, from E£40/head.

♦: *Cafeteria Asteria*, T 4822293, next door to *Santa Lucia* in Sharia Safeya Zaghloul, serves a range of tasty, cheap meals, open until 2400; *Fuul Mohamed Ahmed*, T 4833576, a block east of Midan Sa'ad Zaghloul, beyond Bank of Alexandria and a block south of Sharia Safeya Zaghloul, very cheap, very tasty, open 0600-

2400; *La Pizzeria*, T 4838082, 14 Sharia el-Horriya, filling rather than fancy; *Taverna Restaurants*, T 4928189, at Raml station, Greek owned tasty fish dishes and pizzas with salad bar, open 0730-0200, rec. For those lacking in initiative there are 3 *Kentucky Fried Chicken* and 2 *Pizza Huts*.

Coffee houses: 24-hr service in better hotels incl *Sheraton*, *Ramada Renaissance*, *Plaza*, *Landmark* and *San Giovanni*. Good atmosphere at *Cecil Hotel* by bus station, minimum charge E£8 pp, mouthwatering pastries. *Athineos* by the station, classical decor, gets noisy in the evenings; *Brazilian Coffee Shop* by the Tourist Office on Sharia Sa'ad Zaghloul, open 0630-1500, excellent coffee and pastries; *Délices*, T 4825657, 46 Sa'ad Zaghloul, faded charm; *Pastroudis*, T 4929609, 39 Sharia el-Horriya, behind Roman amphitheatre, enjoy the atmosphere, watch the crowds and try the excellent cakes; *Trianon*, T 4828539, east end of Midan Sa'ad Zaghloul by station under *Hotel Metropole*, elegant, pricey, excellent coffee.

● **Airline offices**
Air France, 22 Sharia Salah Salam, T 4836311; **Air Maroc**, 15 Midan Sa'ad Zaghloul, T 4816638; **British Airways**, 15 Midan Sa'ad Zaghloul, T 4821565; **Egyptair**, 19 Midan Sa'ad Zaghloul, T 4828937; **Lufthansa**, 6 Sharia Talaat Harb, T 4835983; **Sudan Airways**, 6 Sharia Talaat Harb, T 4824834.

● **Banks & money changers**
There are branches of most domestic banks. The downtown branches of **Bank of Alexandria**, 1 Sharia Mahmoud Azmy, 59 Sharia Sa'ad Zaghloul and 6 Sharia Salah Salam are open Sunday-Thursday 0830-1400 and 1030-1300 during Ramadan. **Bank Misr**, 9 & 18 Sharia Talaat Harb, T 807429/807031, and *Pullman Cecil*; **Banque du Caire**, 16 Sharia Sisostris and 5 Sharia Salah Salam. Foreign banks incl **Bank of America**, T 4921257, on Sharia Lomomba, **Barclays**, T 4921307, at 10 Sharia Fawoteur, **Chase Manhattan**, 19 Sharia Dr Ibrahim Abdel el-Said, **Citibank**, T 806376, 95 Sharia 26th July, takes all Visas and Mastercard, as well as money changing outlets in most of the major hotels.

● **Cultural Centres**
American 3 Sharia Pharana, T 4821009; **British Council** 9 Sharia Batalsa, Bab Sharaqi, T 48220199; **French** 30 Sharia Nabi Daniel, T 4920804; **German** 10 Sharia Batalsa, Bab Sharaqi, T 4839870; **Italian** Italian Consulate, Midan Sa'ad Zaghloul, T 4820258; **Russian** 5

Sharia Batalsa, Bab Sharaqi, T 4825645; **Spanish** 101 Sharia el Horriya, T 4920214, open 1700-2000.

● **Embassies & consulates**
Denmark and Norway, 20 Sharia Lumumba, T 4921818; **France**, 2 Midan Orabi, T 4827950, Sunday-Thursday 0900-1400; **Germany**, 5 Sharia Kafr Abdu, Roushdi, T 4845443; **Netherlands**, 35 Sharia el-Shaheed Salah Mustafa, T 4823999; **Spain**, 101 Sharia el Horriya, T 4838346; **Sudan**, Silsila Bldg, Sharia 26th July, Azharita, T 483920; **Switzerland**, 8 Sharia Mokhtar Adbel-Hamid Khalifa, T 5872978; **UK**, 3 Mena Kafr Abdu, Roushdi, T 4847166, open Sunday-Thursday 0800-1300; **USA**, 110-111 Sharia el Horriya, T 4821911, Sunday-Thursday 0900$1200. Please note Libyan consulate is for Arab nations only.

● **Entertainment**
Cinemas: *Amir* 42 Sharia el Horriya, T 4917972; *Metro* 26 Sharia Safia Zaghloul, T 4830432; *Radio* 22 Midan Sa'ad Zaghloul, T 4830282; *Rialto* 46 Sharia Safia Zaghloul, T 4824694; *Rio* 37 Sharia el Horriya, T 4929036.

Concerts: *Alexandria Conference Centre*, in Great Hall – contact Les Amis de la Musique et Des Arts, T 5862325 for programme.

Nightclubs: most of the large hotels have some evening entertainment, though not with the style of the capital. Try *Aquarius* at *Montazah Sheraton Hotel*; *Crazy Horse*, Midan Sa'ad Zaghloul; *Dolphin Nightclub* at *Palestine Hotel*, open 2200-0330; *El-Phanar* at the *Montazah Sheraton Hotel*, open 2230-0300 except Monday; *Monte Carlo*, 34 Sharia el Geish; *Palace Suite* at the *Plaza Hotel*, open 2200-0430; *Queen's Hall Nightclub* in the *San Giovanni Hotel*.

● **Hospitals & medical services**
Chemists: *El-Issaf*, 55 Sharia el-Sayed Mohammed Korayem; *El-Zahaby*, 157 Sharia Gamal

The tax man plays the tune

Nothing escapes the tax man. Egypt's 12 highest earning belly dancers pay a total in annual taxes equivalent to US$250mn. This makes them the country's fifth largest source of income. Only the receipts from traffic on the Suez Canal, tourism, oil exports and cotton exports are more important.

Abd el-Nasser; *Hisham*, 40 Sharia Moharram Bay; *Oxford*, 10 Sharia Kolleyet el-Teb; *Rushdi*, 423 Sharia el Horriya.

Hospitals: *Coptic Hospital*, Moharam Bey, T 4921404; *Egyptian-British Hospital*, Sharia el-Ghatori, Semouha, T 4227722; *Egypt Denmark Hospital*, Sharia el-Gaberti, T 4913417; *German Hospital*, 56 Sharia Abd el-Salam Arif, T 5881806; *International Hospital*, 8 Sharia Mustafah Kamel, Semouha, T 4425017; *Italian Hospital*, El-Hadarah, T 4921459; *Medical Care Advisory Team* 97 Sharia Abdel Salam Aref, Glym Beach, T 5862323; *Medical Centre*, Sharia 14th May, Semouha, T 4202652; *Medical Research Institute*, Sharia el Horriya, T 4212373; *Sharia el-Horriya*, T 4212886; *Poison Hospital*, Downtown T 4822244; *University Hospital*, T 4820029.

● **Places of worship**
Anglican/Episcopal in *All Saint's Church*, Stanley Bay, services Sunday 1800 (in Arabic) and Friday 1030 (in English) and St Mark's, Midan el-Tahrir, El-Mansheya at 1030 each Sunday; **Catholic** at *Sacred Heart Convent*, opp *Lord's Inn*, Roushdi, Friday 1700 and Saturday 0830; **Protestant**, interdenominational worship, Schutz American School, details on T 5873591; **Synagogue**, 69 Sharia Nabi Daniel, Friday pm and Saturday am, T 4821426. Please check as temporarily closed.

● **Post & telecommunications**
Area code: 03.

International calls: from the exchange at Midan Raml, open 24 hrs. International calls from hotels are trouble free but slightly more expensive. Cheaper calls 2000-0800.

Post Office: open daily 0800-2000 at Midan Raml, Misr station which has an express mail service, and Sharia Iskander al-Akbar with a post restante service. American Express (c/o *Eyeress Travel*, 26 Sharia el-Horriya, Monday-Thursday 0830-1300 and 1730-1800, Friday and Saturday 0830-1300), also does post restante.

● **Shipping Agencies**
Abu Simbel Agency 3 Sharia Adib, T 808935; *Alexandria Agency, Amoun Agency and Thebes Agency*, 71 Sharia el Horriya, T 4937109; *Egyptian Agency*, 1 Sharia el Horriya, T 4920824; *Mena Tours Agency*, Midan Sa'ad Zaghloul, T 808407; *North Africa Agency*, 63 Sharia Nabi Daniel, T 4830059.

● **Shopping**
Alexandria has a wide range of shops but lacks the famous specific *souqs* of Cairo. The main

area is south and west of Midan Sa'ad Zaghloul. Leather goods incl shoes are of good quality and rec as best bargins. Look also for silk and cotton material and clothes. The public sector chain stores are well represented, for example Omar Effendi Stores, Haute Couture Co. and Couture Moderne Co.

Bookshops: *Al-Ahram*, 10 Sharia el-Horriya; *Book Bazaar* in *Ramada Renaissance*, open 0900-2300 daily; *Book Centre*, 49 Sharia Sa'ad Zaghloul, has best choice of books in English, French and German; *Dar el-Mostakbal*, 32 Sharia Safeya Zaghloul, books and magazines in English, French and German; *International Language Bookshop*, 18 Sharia Abd el-Hamid El-Dib, Tharwat; *Nile Christian Bookshop*, 4 Sharia Anglican Church, Attarine.

● **Sports**
Beach and watersports facilities are available at all major hotels. Non residents can, with permission, use pools at major hotels like *Sheraton* and *Ramada Renaissance*. *Alexandria Sporting Club* has golf, tennis, bowling and horse riding. *Alexandria Yacht Club*, adjacent Sultan Qaitbai's Fort, gives sailing lessons and holds an annual regatta each November, boats available for hire. *Delta Harriers* run or jog each Friday evening, about 1 hr before sunset, T 4847054.

● **Tour companies & travel agents**
Atlantic Tours, 40 Sharia Safeya Zaghloul, T 4821109; *Egyptian International Travel*, 16 Sharia Talaat Harb, T 4825426; *Fayed Travel*, 7 Sharia el-Fath, Wezarah Station, Fleming, T 5870579; *Misr Tours*, 28 Sharia Sa'ad Zaghloul, T 4809617, F 4808776; *North African Shipping Co*, 63 Sharia Nabi Daniel, T 4830050; *Passant Travel*, 164 Sharia el-Horriya, Camp Caesar, T 5966091; *Sporting Tours*, 178 Sharia Omar Lutfi, Sporting, T 5952778; *Thomas Cook*, 15 Midan Sa'ad Zaghloul, T 4828077 and in hotels *Pullman Cecil*, *Palestine*, *Metropole* and *San Stephano*.

● **Tourist offices**
Open daily 0800-1800 but 0900-1600 during Ramadan, located right in the city centre on southwest corner of Midan Sa'ad Zaghloul, T 4807611. There are also tourist offices at the Misr railway station (T 4925985), the airport (T 852021) and the port (T 803494). For practical advice visit *Misr Tours*. **Tourist Friends Association**, offers all services needed by tourists, introduces them to local customs, provides multi-lingual guides, T 5962108/5866115.

● **Useful addresses**
Archaeology Society: 6 Shari Mahmoud Mukhtar, behind Graeco-Roman museum.
Passport Office: 28 Sharia Talaat Harb, T 4824366, for registering arrival and renewing visas, open Saturday-Thursday 0830-1400, Friday 1000-1300 and 1900-2100.
Tourist Police: on Midan Sa'ad Zaghloul, T 5473814, and in grounds of Montazah Palace, T 863804.

● **Useful telephone numbers**
Airport: T 4202021
Ambulance: T 123.
Fire: T 180.
Police: T 122.
Port: T 4803494
Tourist police: T 807611.

● **Transport**
Local Car hire: Avis, T 807532, in *Pullman Cecil*; **Budget**, 59 Tariq el-Geish, T 5971273. A/c Fiat costs E£125/day incl tax and insurance, deposit of E£300 required; **Limousine**, 25 Sharia Talaat Harb T 4825253. **Service taxis**: run quick and relatively cheap services from Midan El-Gumhorriya, which is next to the Misr railway station and about 1 km south of the Corniche, to most places within a few hundred kilometres radius. Drivers call out their destinations. **Taxis & calèches**: metered black and orange city taxis can be caught throughout the downtown and many other areas but a tip will be expected. E£25 to ride full length of Corniche. A ride in a horse-drawn *calèche* along the Corniche or from outside the Misr railway station for a pre-negotiated price is an alternative. **Trams & city buses**: from Raml station just to the east of Midan Sa'ad Zaghloul there are very

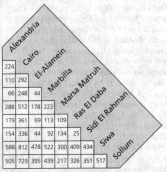

Alexandria	Cairo	El-Alamein	Marbilla	Marsa Matruh	Ras El Daba	Sidi El Rahman	Siwa	Sollum
224								
110	292							
66	248	44						
288	512	178	222					
179	361	69	113	109				
154	336	44	92	134	25			
588	812	478	522	300	409	434		
505	729	395	439	217	326	351	517	

Distances between main towns in NW Egypt in kilometres

cheap but crowded trams from dawn until 2400 incl: east to Sidi Bishr beach (No 1-No 4), west to the Maritime Station (No 6) in the Western Harbour, north to Qaitbai Fort (No 5) via El-Gomruk and El-Anfushi, and south from Midan Orabi which is west of Midan Sa'ad Zaghloul to Karmous and Pompey's Pillar (No 5 and No 15). As a general rule blue trams to middle class areas and yellow to poorer areas. Local buses, which are fast but very crowded and dirty, operate throughout the city from the main squares. The main services incl the following: Midan Sa'ad Zaghloul to the airport (No 203), Midan Orabi to the airport (No 307 and No 310), Montazah and Abu Qir (No 129), Raml to Pompey's Pillar (No 209), along the Corniche to Montazah (No 120, No 220 and No 300), Ma'mura (No 725), Abu Qir (No 729), or to El-Agami and Hannoville beaches (No 455 or No 500), Misr station to the Zoo (No 41).

Air The airport, which is southeast of the city on land reclaimed from Lake Maryut off the main Delta road to Cairo, has regular daily flights to Cairo, Athens (4 a week) and Paris (1 a week). For information T 420201. *Egypt Air*, 19 Midan Sa'ad Zaghloul, T 4820778.

Train The main Misr station in Midan El-Gumhorriya has inter-city services south to Cairo via Sidi Gaber, Damanhur, Tanta and Benha (11 a day, 2½-3 hrs) and some a/c which go onward to Luxor and Aswan. Although less frequent, there are trains west to El-Alamein and Marsa Matruh. For information T 4923207.

Road Bus: the main terminal at Midan Sa'ad Zaghloul operates very regular a/c express Superjet buses to Cairo (3 hrs), T 4824391, and a twice daily service to Ismailia (5 hrs), on *West Delta Buses*, T 809685. There are also 3-4 daily services from Midan El-Gumhorriya, which is next to the Misr train station and about 1 km south of Midan Sa'ad Zaghloul, incl the express service to Marsa Matruh (4 hrs) and Siwa (7 hrs) and the regular non-express bus which goes to Marsa via El-Alamein. Seats for these services, however, have to be booked at Midan Sa'ad Zaghloul. Non-scheduled buses east along the coast to Rosetta and Damietta can be caught from nr the Roman Theatre in Midan El-Gumhorriya. International departures from outside *Cecil Hotel* to Tunisia, Libya, Syria and Abu Dhabi. Payment on these superjet services required in hard currency. Where *Western Delta Buses* have equivalent departure this can be paid for in local currency. *Superjet* daily 0530-2400 every half hour to Giza, Ramses station and

Heliopolis; 0010 direct to Cairo airport; 2000 to Hurghada and 0645 to Marsa Matruh.

Trains All trains leave from Misr station and call at Sidi Gaber Station 10 mins later. Trains daily to direct to Cairo at 0815, 1400, 1900; calling at Tanta at 1100 and 1730, calling at Banha, Tanta and Damanhour at 0600, 0610, 1000, 1210, 1300, 1520, 1700, 2000.

Boat There are sailings on Adriatica Lines (main office at 33 Sharia Salem) from the Maritime Station to Piraeus and Venice via Crete every 8-12 days. Bookings should be made in advance with *Menatours* (T 806909) in Midan Sa'ad Zaghloul. *Alexandria Navigation Agencies*, 71 Sharia el Horriya, T 4837113/5. For information at port T 4803494.

WEST TO LIBYA

The **Mediterranean Coast** stretches 500 km west to the Libyan border passing through Alexandria's local beach resorts of **El-Agami** and **Hannoville**, and the new beach resorts of **Maraqia**, **Marabilla**, **Sidi Abdel Rahman** and **Marsa Matruh** from which a road leads inland to the **Siwa** oasis (see page 355), before finally arriving at the Libyan border near Sollum.

The first few kilometres are the worst as the road west out of Alexandria is complicated and very badly signposted. There are two roads going west: it is best to take the more scenic coastal route. For the first 30 km a series of developments, more attractive to stay in than to look at, lie between the road and the sea. Petrol is easily available.

ACCESS **Egypt Air** operates a daily service from Cairo all the year and through the summer month to/from Marsa Matruh. **Trains** including the express Turbini leave from Ramses Station. **Buses** – Superjet, West Delta Bus Co, Golden Arrow from Abd el Mouneem Riyad terminal near *Ramses Hilton*. Some buses depart directly from Cairo Airport. Regular departures too from Midan Sa'ad Zaghloul in Alexandria. **Service taxis** from in front of *Nile Hilton*, near Ramses Station or Ahmed Helmi Station.

Places of interest

El-Agami and **Hannoville**, 20-25 km west of Alexandria, are beach resorts which are packed at weekends and during the high

Mediterranean Sea

LIBYA
Sollum · Sidi Barrani
Marsa Matruh
El Daba · Sidi Abdel Rahman
El-Alamein · El Hammam
Rosetta
Alexandria
To Siwa
Qattara Depression
To Cairo
0 50 km
N

Mediterranean Coast

season with the result that litter and pollution are a growing problem. They can be reached both easily and cheaply from Alexandria by bus (No 455 from Midan Sa'ad Zaghloul or No 760 and No 600 from Misr Station and Midan Orabi); service taxi; or micro buses which leave El-Gumhorriya every 10-30 mins.

Abu Sir, 43 km from Alexandria is further along the coast halfway between Alexandria and El-Alamein. Here an important but neglected archeological site dating back to the 27th Dynasty stands to the south of the road. Remains include that of a necropolis, two temples, a 10th century church and the **lighthouse**. In the Ptolemaic period a string of beacons lit up the coast from Pharos in Alexandria to Cyrenaica in Libya. The **Burg al-Arab** (Arab Tower) just to the east of Abu Sir, is the sole survivor. The 17m high lighthouse has the same 3-tier construction as Pharos but is just a tenth of the size. The cylindrical top has collapsed but it does give an accurate impression of the appearance, if not the scale, of the Wonder at Pharos. The ancient temple dedicated to Osiris was of Ptolemaic design except for the gate at the east which had a more traditional Pharaonic structure. The series of colonnades were thought to resemble Karnak temple.

A second temple was discovered here at the beginning of the century by Italian archeologists. This was dedicated to Ibis the sacred bird of Egypt. This was hewn out of the rock and is well enough preserved for the illustrations of birds and animals on the walls to be quite clear today. There is much concern, however, about the continuing deterioration of the buildings due to erosion, the dampness and salt in the atmosphere being harsh enough to make some places critical. There is grave concern too about the stability of the remains of the church. Many damaged stones have been replaced and a safe walkway for visitors has been cleared.

The mound or tell has been excavated – following the discovery during WW2 of an engraving – and it is here the necropolis is buried, parts dated as Graeco-Roman and others going back to the 27th Dynasty. All the sarcophagi found here were anthropoidal in shape. Abu Sir was once an important coastal town, surrounded by great walls which have long since crumbled, so now only the gates remain. From the top there is a beautiful view over the Maryut marshes to the sea.

Abu Mina lies 48 km westsouthwest from Alexandria and about 15 km inland from Abu Sir, beyond the new town of Mobarak. It is black top all the way. It was once the most important destination in the east for Christian pilgrims as **Deir Mari Mina** is one of the largest Coptic monasteries. **St Menas**, who was an Egyptian-born Roman legionnaire, was martyred in Asia Minor in 296 AD for refusing to renounce Christ. He had rather a bad time. Legend says that first they tore off the soles of his feet, then they poked out his eyes before pulling out his tongue. None of these assaults prevented him from standing up to address the crowd. In the end the Emperor himself

The Desert War 1940-1943

Italy, the colonial power in Libya at the outbreak of WW2, invaded Egypt in the closing weeks of 1940 thus beginning a long period of fighting between the Axis powers and Great Britain in North Africa. Italian and later German strategic plans were the displacement of Britain from Egypt, destruction of Britain's imperial communications links through Suez and the opening up of the Middle East oilfields to Axis penetration. The local Arab and Berber peoples of North Africa played a remarkably small role in events, though royalist Libyan troops joined the British in the final liberation of their country. The damage and disruption of the war were considerable and their negative effects persisted long after the end of hostilities.

The Italians were soon expelled from Egypt and much of eastern Libya but were powerfully reinforced in Tripolitania in February 1941 by the arrival of German troops and armour which rapidly drove the British back to the Egyptian frontier by April. The German formations were led by Rommel with skill and audacity. Air power favoured the joint German-Italian armies in the earlier part of the campaign. Rommel's eastward advance was slowed by the protracted resistance of the garrisons, first Australian then British and Polish, at Tobruk. Meanwhile, the main armies fought pitched battles around the Libyan-Egyptian border until Rommel withdrew temporarily in December 1941. He used his improved lines of communications in the west to prepare a counter attack and pushed east again as far as Gazala, near Derna, in January and February 1942 and, after a pause, into Tobruk and deep into Egypt in June though his advance was finally held at El-Alamein after a fierce battle. Rommel made a final attempt at Alam Halfa, east of El-Alamein, to push aside British and Commonwealth forces and break through to the Nile Valley in August 1942 but failed in the face of a strong defensive effort and his own growing losses of men and equipment.

The balance in the desert war was changing in mid-1942 as the Allies gradually won superiority in the air and had more freedom of movement at sea. The Germans and Italians began increasingly to suffer from shortages of equipment, while the health of Field Marshal Rommel gave rise for concern. On the Allied side General Montgomery took over leadership and began a build-up of the Eighth Army sufficient to overwhelm the well trained and experienced Afrika Korps. Montgomery opened his attack at El-Alamein on 23 October 1942 and after 11 days of hard fighting the Axis army was beaten back and retreated by rapid stages to the west to make a last stand in Tunisian territory.

The German attempt to hold on in North Africa was made difficult by sea and airborne landings by Allied, including American, troops in Morocco and Algeria in November 1942. These two countries were liberated with ease when French Vichy units, formerly collaborating with the Germans, were brought round to supporting the invasion. German and Italian reinforcements were rushed to Tunis and a battle began to stop the advance of allied units from the west as they fought their way in from Algeria and from the south through Libya. German attacks in the Battle of Kasserine in the hills north of Gafsa during January and February 1943 almost succeeded in halting Allied progress but when Rommel's final assault on Montgomery's advancing Eighth Army arriving from Libya failed in early March, the Axis forces retreated northwards behind the Mareth Line on the Gulf of Gabès before being outflanked and being forced to withdraw by Montgomery's troops. A final set of battles in Northern Tunisia saw the Allies push through the Medjerda Valley to Tunis and Bizerte in May 1943, effectively ending Axis resistance in North Africa.

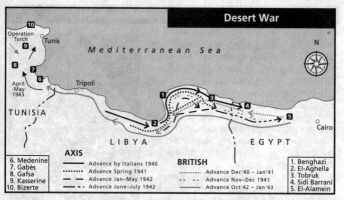

Desert War

AXIS	
——	Advance by Italians 1940
········	Advance Spring 1941
– – –	Advance Jan–May 1942
–·–·–	Advance June–July 1942

BRITISH	
··········	Advance Dec'40 – Jan'41
–·· –··	Advance Nov–Dec 1941
——	Advance Oct'42 – Jan'43

6. Medenine	1. Benghazi
7. Gabès	2. El-Aghella
8. Gafsa	3. Tobruk
9. Kasserine	4. Sidi Barrani
10. Bizerte	5. El-Alamein

struck the fatal blow and the body was placed in a lead coffin and sunk out at sea. The coffin was washed ashore, discovered by passing bedouins and loaded on to a camel. He was buried here when the camel carrying his coffin would go no further. When miracles occurred at the site of his tomb the news travelled across Christendom, via the camel trains, that the tomb of Abu Mina and the Holy Waters nearby could cure sickness and suffering, and his sanctity was assured. Successive emperors built temples and basilicas around the shrine but when the waters dried up in the 12th century the town fell into decay. Excavations have revealed the remains of the basilicas and shrines and much of the surrounding pilgrim town. Saint Menas's day is now celebrated on 11 November and the town is the site of an austere concrete Coptic monastery which was built in 1959, easily recognized by its two white towers.

Coastal resorts west from Alexandria

At 51 km out of Alexandria is **Maraqia**, built by the public sector Maraqia Co in 1982. There are chalets, villas and small cabins. Units can be rented by the night, week or month. There is a huge shopping area, banks, restaurants and a medical centre. There are four swimming pools and most other sports are catered for. The beach is splendid but not the place for a quiet stay. Stay at **D** *Maraqia Village*, T 991313/2 as there is little choice.

Marabilla, also built by Maraqia Co and very similar in style but less strident is mainly villas and no apartments. The beach is smaller but it is very private, just for those in residence.

Aida Beach located 30 km east of El-Alamein has become very popular despite being 77 km west of Alexandria. Easy access by Super Jet bus from Alex or Cairo. (See transport entry, page 352.) **B-C** *Aida Beach Hotel*, Km 77 on Alexandria to Marsa Matruh road, T 3603888/3611888 has 100 rooms in the hotel, 40 apartments and 22 villas. Sports equipment and courts to hire, jet skis and windsurfing. Not as close to the beach as the name suggests. Recommended for its high quality service and entertainment facilities. No real competition.

EL-ALAMEIN

106 km west of Alexandria, owes its fame to what was, until the 1967 Arab-Israeli war, the largest tank battle in history. In July 1942 the Allies under Field Marshal Montgomery halted the German-Italian advance towards the River Nile and, in British eyes if not in those of the Soviet troops at Stalingrad, turned the course of WW2. Winston Churchill later wrote, not

Instruments for navigation in the desert

The Arabs are thought to have been amongst the great navigators and certainly the Middle East and North Africa were the sources of invention of many means of navigation such as by the stars. Its people invented a fascinating range of instruments for determining locations and directions, most notably the astrolabe. It was the Babylonians who as early as 1700 BC used systems of numbering, algebra and geometry and who combined their mathematical knowledge to develop astronomy to a fine art by 100 BC. Further expansion of mathematics were made by the Greeks, notably in the 8th and 7th centuries BC by individuals such as Pythagoras and, later, Archimedes.

Astrolabe of Esfahan, 1715

The Arabs were very early students of mathematics and algebra (the English name of which was derived from the Arabic *al-gebit*) was widely developed, a book on the subject by Mohammed ben Moosa being printed in the 9th century AD at the instigation of the Caliph Mam'un. Most importantly the Islamic period witnessed the tabulation of information, much of it of direct value to navigation in difficult or featureless desert terrain. The astrolabe, invented by the Greeks, was developed in Egypt by Ptolemy of Alexandria and was perfected by the Muslims as an accurate fixer of angles. The earliest known astrolabe was manufactured in the Iranian city of Esfahan in 984 AD. The astrolabe was made from a circular brass plate, some as large as 500 mm in diameter, with a movable pointer or finger called an alidade pinned at the centre of the plate. The astrolabe would be suspended from a ring and the angle to a given star or planet fixed from gradations marked on the rim of the plate which could indicate latitude and even time of day. Instruments of this kind were often wonderfully ornate, often those in Egypt imported from Iberia or Persia.

Egyptian astrolabe, with Zodiac signs

One of the earliest references to use of a magnetic compass in navigation was in the Middle East in the 13th century. The sun compass is still a useful instrument for desert navigation. With this the direction of the sun is picked out on a form of gnomon on a plate that gives an approximation of north.

The arrival of satellite aided navigation and location systems has finally made safe desert travel possible – but not in all cases. The local knowledge of the Arab nomads in desert areas is still invaluable, especially in sand sea areas such as the Western Desert, where electronic devices might tell you where you are geographically speaking but not how to escape the maze of sand.

entirely accurately that, "Before Alamein we never had a victory. After Alamein we never had a defeat". (See The North Africa campaign, page 348.) Unless you are a military historian or have a personal interest in the battle, there is little to see and it is probably best to combine a visit here with other sights on the journey from Alexandria to El-Alamein.

ACCESS El-Alamein is only a short car or bus ride away from Alexandria but the trains are slow and it is a 2 hrs return journey and then a 2 km walk north from the station to the town. The buses and taxis doing the journey between Alexandria and Marsa Matruh stop at *Alamein Rest House*.

El-Alamein was the site of the battle between Germany's Afrika Korps and the Allied Eighth Army which turned WW2 in the latter's favour and marks the closest that the Axis forces got to the Nile valley. The results of the encounter can be seen adjacent to the town in the huge **war cemeteries**. The Greek war memorial is passed first. The **Commonwealth cemetery** (entry free, open daily 0700-1630 but books of remembrance not available Friday) lies to the east of the town to the south of the road. Through the arch and beyond the gardens sombre lines of over 7,000 white headstones commemorate those who fought and died supporting the Allied cause. The **German cemetery** lies about 4 km to the west of the town between the road and the sea. Here in a sand coloured building resembling a castle there are 4,200 graves. The man with the key will see you coming. He lives nearby. The **Italian cemetery**, the only one in North Africa, lies a further 6 km west of the town on seaside. Just walk in.

A **museum** to the west of the settlement contains maps of the campaign and some of the uniforms and weaponry used in Egypt by both sides. A clever map/model display with lights and commentary (choose your language) explains the North Africa campaign. There is also information here about the war between Egypt and Israel in 1973. Open daily 0800-1800, 0900-1500 in Ramadan, entrance E£5 plus E£5 for camera. El-Alamein has a fairly good beach but heed the danger signs for unexploded mines!

Local information
● **Accommodation**

For something a little different try the resort of Marina, just 10 km beyond *Aida Beach*. This is a 3 km stretch of up-market 2-storey villas. Some of these villas are for rent at about E£4,500 a month. The beach is beautiful but the reason the beach is so clean is the strong sea currents – be warned. **A** *Seagull Resort Hotel* overlooking the artificial lake in the middle of the complex rents out jet skis. A very smart place to stay. **B** *Atic Hotel*, Km 90, Alexandria to Marsa Matruh road, T 4921349, F 4938313, 64 double rm, located 16 km east of El-Alamein, good standard of service, pool, private beach, mainly Egyptian guests. This hotel is rec as it has plenty of space – the rooms are large, the beds are large and so are the dining room and the pool and the beach is huge. The sports facilities are not up to the standard of *Aida Beach*. Compensate by enjoying the lively night life, the good food (try the fish food, the pizzeria or the coffee shop in addition to the main Omda restaurant). Used by day guests who are not quite so restrained.

C *El-Alamein*, Sidi Abdel Rahman, El-Dabaa Center, T 4921228, 209 rm and villas with own seaside barbecue, very good standard, located on the beautiful white sands of the isolated up-market resort of Sidi Abdel Rahman about 25 km west of El-Alamein, early reservations essential, open April-November. Prices have been reduced slightly but rooms and general facilities are not really up to price standard. Day use of beautiful beach E£350.

D *Agami Palace*, Al-Bittash Beach, El-Agami, T 4330230, F 4309364, 56 rm, located 20 km west of Alexandria, tasteful decor, pool; **D** *Hannoville*, Hannoville Beach, El-Agami, T 4303258, 157 rm, located on rather polluted and crowded Hannoville beach about 25 km west of Alexandria, day-trippers from Alexandria flock here every weekend.

E *New Admiral*, Hannoville, El-Agami, T 4303038, 44 rm, on beach.

F *Alamein Rest House*, Km 105, Alexandria to Marsa Matruh road, El-Alamein, T 4302785, 8 rm, small, mainly Egyptian guests, serves decent meals, incl such local specialities as armadillo eggs, undergoing restoration, please check; F *Costa Blanca*, Sharia Hannoville, El-Agami, T 4303112, 36 rm, on beach, see comment for *Hannoville Hotel*; F *Menas Agami*, Agami Beach, El-Agami, T 4300150, 55 rm; F *Monoco*, Abu Talaat, Km 25, Alexandria to Marsa Matruh road, T 4321100, 33 rm, on beach; F *New Talaat* Hannoville, El-Agami, T 4891039, 25 rm, see comment for *Hannoville Hotel*.

Camping There are no specific camp sites but the *El-Alamein Hotel* has a tourist camp equipped with all necessary services.

WARNING As with the Red Sea coast, large parts of the coast and the desert are fenced off because they are still littered with unexploded mines and shells. It is **essential** to obey signs, use common sense and keep to the main roads and beaches.

● **Places to eat**
These are tiny places and except for the hotels there are few restaurants in and around El-Alamein. 8 km beyond the Italian cemetery, turn right at roadblock for a good coffee stop at *El-Alamein* hotel.

● **Post & telecommunications**
Area code: 03.

● **Transport**
Road & Train Besides private transport there are regular buses and irregular trains from El-Alamein either east to Alexandria or west to Marsa Matruh.

MARSA MATRUH

Marsa Matruh (178 km west of El-Alamein, 288 km west of Alexandria and 512 km northwest of Cairo), has been transformed from a sleepy fishing village and minor port into a popular, low grade, summer resort for domestic tourists with a plethora of tatty beach side tented areas belonging to trade and government groups. Despite the government's attempts it has not, and is unlikely to be, turned into the new mass tourist Mediterranean beach destination for European tourists. Although there are some good beaches in the area and the lagoon has potential if correctly developed, the dull little town with a population of around 25,000 has few of the holiday facilities and nightlife that tourists expect.

ACCESS Marsa Matruh's streets are on a grid pattern with most of the hotels being located on the streets behind and parallel to the Corniche. Buses and service taxis stop at Sharia Cleopatra about 1 km south of the beach and the hotels which can be reached by one of the *carettas*, cheap donkey carts, which are the main type of transport within the town. Airport close to south of town.

Places of interest

There are really only two reasons for visiting Marsa Matruh, either to travel to the magnificent desert oasis at Siwa (see page 355) or a rest en route to Libya. The area's much advertised beaches are a severe disappointment. Except for the *Beau Site* hotel's private beach, almost all beaches are public. Western women can still experience problems from both voyeurs and exhibitionists who are more used to seeing fully-clothed Egyptian women swimming and sunbathing, although the situation is improving as the locals become more used to visitors. No serious attempt has been made to solve the major litter problem on those beaches closest to town.

The beaches in the town's bay are protected by two sand spits which will eventually meet and form a lagoon. The water is shallow and stagnant, NOT a place to swim. **Lido Beach** and **Beach of Lovers** curve around the bay to the west of the town while in the other direction **Rommel's Beach** and its small military museum in a cave hewn in the rock, are beyond the small port and are almost facing the town on the landward side of the east spit. The approach, past rusting pipework which once served as the naval pier, is depressing even in the sunshine. **The Rommel Museum** (open summer 0930-1600) gives details of this famous field marshal in the WW2 campaign. Offshore from the beach is a red buoy, 25m beyond which is a sunken German U-boat, which can be seen if you have suitable underwater swimming gear.

The better and cleaner beaches are those to the west of the town: in order they are **Cleopatra's Bath** (7 km) which is surrounded by cliffs and gets deep very

Marsa Matruh

Mediterranean Sea

To Rommel's Cave

Sharia Corniche

Sharia Galaa

Sharia el Tahrir

Sharia Cleopatra

To Solum & Siwa

To Airport

Market

Sharia Iskandariya

Taxis

Passport Office

To Alexandria

Hotels:
1. Adriatika
2. Arouss el-Bahr
3. Beach House & Beau Site
4. Blue Gulf
5. El Lido
6. Hamada
7. Matrouh
8. Negresco
9. New Royal Palace
10. Radi
11. Reem
12. Riviera Palace
13. Rommel House
14. Semiramis
15. Youth Hostel

suddenly; **Al-Nasr City Beach** (10 km); **El-Obeid City Beach** (20 km) with beautiful white sand and **Agibah Beach** (28 km), best of all, the name means 'a wonder', which is set in the middle of a cove.

The nearby beaches can be reached from town by hiring a bicycle for 24 hrs from the hire shop (open 0600-2400) E£10 or by donkey cart for a negotiated price. Donkey carts carry two people and cost E£3 out to Rommel Museum. The more distant beaches to the west can be reached in summer by service taxi, microbus or Tuf-Tuf which shuttle back and forth (0800-1700) from near the bus station. In the winter the seaside areas are dead but the town life continues as normal.

Local information
● Accommodation

Many hotels are closed in winter. Hotels may have a problem of fresh water supplies. There are no really first class hotels and it is best to avoid the very cheap ones nr the bus station. This leaves, in addition to a number of cheap and cheerful hotels to the south, away from the beach, a wide range of officially registered hotels in and around Marsa Matruh incl the following.

A *Badr Tourist Village*, El-Obeid, T 945348, F 730443, 130 rm, large hotel located on El-Obeid beach about 20 km west of town; **A** *Beach House Hotel*, Sharia el-Shatee, T 934011/2, F 933319, 20 suites here sleeping 3/4, very expensive but not international standard.

B/C *Beau Site*, Sharia el-Shatee, T 933319, F 2599484, 90 rm, open May-October only, highly rec, located 2 km west of Sharia Iskandariya on the Corniche, full board is compulsory, but the food is reported as excellent, also rents out chalets for 3-8 persons; **C** *New Beau Site* nearing completion has 88 rm and splendid views from the Corniche.

B *Negresco*, Corniche, T 934492, 68 rm, breakfast incl.

D *Miami Hotel*, Corniche, T 935891, F 935892, rather large with 200 rm; **D** *New Royal Palace*, Corniche, T 933406, 170 rm; **D** *Radi*, Corniche, Old Port, T 934827, F 934828, 72 rm, disco in summer, pleasant staff, lots of hot water, food ok, very warm welcome; **D** *Riviera Palace*, Sharia Galaa, Market Area, T 943045, 32 rm, a downtown hotel, good restaurant, no alcohol, closed in winter; **D** *Rommel House*, Sharia Galaa, T 945466, 60 rm, good café, a good standard; **D** *Royal Palace*, Corniche, T 934295, largish with 126 rm;

A long lost tomb?

First it was, then it wasn't and now it probably isn't – the long lost tomb of Alexander the Great. The recent announcement by Greek archaeologist, Liana Souvaltzi, that she had uncovered at Maraqi in Siwa possibly the most important archaeological find since that of Tutankhamun's tomb created a storm of controversy. Her claim centres around a 50m above-ground 'tomb' which Souvaltzi says bears the same markings as that of Alexander's father King Philip of Macedonia including his royal symbol, an 8-pointed star. Just 18m away, lies an entrance to a tunnel guarded by two royal lion statues and three steles. The inscriptions, she claims, describe Alexander's funeral procession to Siwa. The find, if authentic, would rewrite history. According to ancient texts, the conqueror, who died possibly through poison in 323 BC, expressed a wish to be buried in Siwa, where he was deified in 331 BC, but was finally laid to rest in Alexandria. A team of Greek experts, who flew out immediately to assess the find, concluded that there was "no evidence" of Alexander's tomb: the inscriptions were from the late Roman rather than earlier Hellenistic period, and the 'royal' 8-pointed star was a common theme in Macedonian monuments. Meanwhile, the burial chamber, at 76 cm wide, is too narrow for a sarcophagus to pass through. Excavations are still continuing but so far the only point of agreement is that the tomb, unusually large by Macedonian standards, is an important discovery – but of whom has yet to be decisively determined.

D *Semiramis*, Corniche, T 934091, 64 rm, good standard.

E *Adriatika*, Sharia Galaa, T 945195, 55 rm with bath and balcony, good, located just north of the tourist office, closed in winter, inexpensive, yet facilities incl 24-hr room service, laundry, bar, cafeteria and TV; **E** *Arouss el-Bahr*, Corniche, T 942419, 54 rm, some bungalows for 4 persons, small hotel, sea views, helpful staff, restaurant; **E** *El-Khalig el-Azrak*, Corniche, T 942981, 57 rm, recently expanded; **E** *Reem*, Corniche, T 943605, 58 rm, very cheap, good value.

Camping It is essential to obtain permission to camp on the beach from the Military Intelligence Office on Sharia Galaa because they patrol the beaches at night. There is camping on the beach at *Badr Tourist Village* and on El-Obeid beach.

Youth hostels Behind 4 Sharia Galaa, Sollum Rd, T 932331, 60 beds, kitchen, overnight fee E£5, train 2 km.

● **Places to eat**
Besides the hotel restaurants incl those at the *Beau Site* and *Riviera Palace*, there are a few cheap downtown restaurants nr the Corniche incl the *Alexandria Tourist Restaurant*, *Mansour Fish Restaurant*, *Restaurant Panayotis* which serves cheap beer and salads, and the bargain *Hani el-Onda*. Choose carefully remembering the fresh water problems.

● **Airline offices**
Egyptair, Sharia Galaa, nr Tourist office.

● **Banks & money changers**
Most of the town's banks are west of the Egyptair office and are open daily 0900-1400 and 1800-2000. The **Banque du Caire** branch, located east of the main north-south Sharia Iskandariya is open 0830-1430 and 1800-2100; **National Bank of Egypt** to west of town. There are no banks in Siwa so make sure that you have enough or change your money in Marsa Matruh.

● **Entertainment**
Nightclubs: there are nightclubs in the larger hotels and discotheques at the *Beau Site* and *Radi* hotels, in summer.

● **Post & telecommunications**
Area code: 094.

Post Office: on Sharia Galaa to east of Sharia Iskandariya, open daily 0900-1500.

Telephones: 24-hr telephones are just opp the post office on Sharia Galaa.

● **Tourist offices**
On Sharia Galaa open daily 0900-1400 and 2000-2200 has limited material. You are advised to get information from one of the better hotels.

● **Transport**
Air There are three flights a week by Egyptair

from Marsa Matruh to Cairo. Book in advance during the summer high season.

Train Although in summer there is a daily train service to Cairo (5-15 hrs) it is very slow and is not really worth the effort.

Road Bus: local transport to the beaches of Cleopatra, El-Obeid and Agibah leave every 15 mins during daylight. The best long distance services are the 3 daily Golden Rocket buses to Alexandria (3-4 hrs) and Cairo (8 hrs) which should be booked in advance. There are also slower blue buses to Alexandria (5 hrs) which stop at Sidi Abdel Rahman and El-Alamein, E£8. There is an early morning non-stop 5 hrs a/c daily service to Siwa, E£10, which is better than the afternoon service which, because it originates in Alexandria, is usually very crowded by the time it reaches Marsa Matruh. **Service taxis**: are quicker and cheaper but less comfortable than the express buses to Alexandria. Taxis to Siwa (5 hrs) leave early morning or in the afternoon to avoid the midday heat. It is difficult but not impossible to take one of the service taxis, which carry Egyptian expatriate workers, to the Libyan border (230 km east of Marsa Matruh) via Sidi Barrani (150 km) and Sollum (220 km) but it is essential to have a Libyan visa.

SIWA OASIS

Siwa Oasis is 82 km long east-west and 20 km north-south at its widest point and includes a number of large lakes. It is 300 km southwest from Marsa Matruh, a journey by car of 4 hrs along a black top road built in 1986. Traffic is sparse. The half-way stop for tea or coffee is the Badwy 'hotel'. Scenery is limited until the escarpment is crossed and the trees of Siwa, 300,000 date palms and 70,000 olive trees come into view. This magnificent oasis is recommended for those who want a break from the beach and want another type of sand. Comparatively few travellers visit the oasis because of its isolation and very limited facilities, but with the improved road and the encouragement of tour companies, the sense of 'away from it all' has been lost. Siwa is further from the Nile Delta, the source of Egyptian civilization and the point of contact with those civilizations which superseded it, than any of the oases along the Great Desert Circuit. With Siwa's customs unchanged for centuries, untouched by the world around, and its position on the shores of the Great Sand Sea, it is geographically and culturally remote, and the closest to every romantic's notion of what a *real* desert should be like. It is not surprising then that there is a potential clash of cultures and visitors would do well to respect local customs by dressing modestly. Women are requested to keep legs and upper arms covered. Alcohol and affection are forbidden in public!

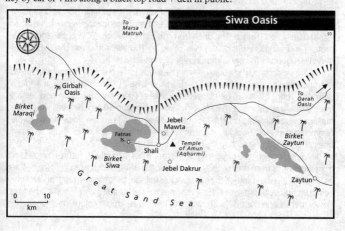

The 'sacred aunt' of the Arabs – the date palm

Egypt produces about half a million tons of dates each year, though only a small portion of the total is made up of top quality dessert fruit. Even so, dates are important parts of the Egyptian rural diet and each year some 62,000 tons of dates are produced from scattered palmeries in the Delta and valley areas, though principally in the commercial plantations of the true desert or the oases such as Siwa. The date palm is amongst the longest established orchard trees in Egypt and was a favoured symbol on monuments from pre-dynastic times.

The prophet Mohammed called on the Islamic faithful to protect the date palm, which he called their 'sacred aunt' because of its many uses as a food, building material and provider of shade (see below). The Swedish naturalist Carl Linnaeus rendered homage to the beauty and generosity of the palm tree when he classified it in the order of Principes, 'The Order of Princes'. The green and yellow foliage of the date palm is also a fine decoration in the otherwise vegetation-less squares and avenues of many Egyptian cities. In the western oases of Egypt, the palm is the tree of life, its fruit, leaves and wood the basis of the local economy. The Latin name of the date palm, *Phoenix dactylifera*, may be translated as "the Phoenician tree with fruit resembling fingers". Egypt's top variety of date from the Western desert is the *sa'idi*, which has a delicate translucent appearance. Other favourite dates are the *ghazali*, known in Siwa for its energy giving properties, and the *frihi*, a succulent date with a good flavour. The *izzawai* date is a low grade crop used as human food but also for feeding to animals and for making into alcoholic beverages.

The date palm is a close relation to the grasses. The tree has neither branches nor twigs. Its trunk is in fact a stem: it has no bark; being simply covered by the base of the old fallen leaves. A cross-section of a palm trunk reveals a multitude of rigid tubes containing sap bearing vessels, rather than the annual growth rings of a true tree. Due to the activity of a single bud hidden at the heart of the palm leaves, this trunk grows continuously.

The *phoenix dactylifera* grows to 23m. The top delicate, pinnate leaves grow to some 5m long. Flowers spring from the axils of the leaves and today most cultivated palms are hand pollinated. The date fruit (trees bear fruit at 5 years of age) is a berry – with one long seed or pit and an individual palm can have up to 1,000 dates in one bunch. The dried fruit contains by weight 50% sugar and a little protein and fat. Date palms can live for up to 100 years, though the older trees become ragged in foliage and gradually yield less fruits.

In the wild state, the young palm tree tends to resemble a hedgehog due to the uncontrolled development of buds at the base of the initial trunk. If severed with skill, these buds can be planted elsewhere. There are both male and female trees. Broadly speaking, a male tree can pollinate some 50 female trees. To ensure maximum fruit production, the farmer will place a sprig of male flowers next to the female flowers – or should he have only a small orchard, he will not grow any male trees at all, preferring to buy male sprigs at the market.

In March or April, the tiny green date is round like a marble. Its future is uncertain: if the hot winds from the south are too fierce, it may be blown from the tree before its time. During the summer, the date reaches full size, becoming smooth and yellow, rich in vitamins but bitter to taste. In the heat of the summer and autumn, the fruit slowly matures on the tree, softening and turning an amber colour, deep brown or black, depending on the variety. The date sugars change as well and, little by little, the date dries out and becomes a preserved fruit if left on the tree.

For the oasis dwellers, the date is so precious that they have a name for each stage of its growth. The date palm may produce up to 100 kg of dates annually for a whole century. However, in order to do this, it needs manure and a lot of water, anything up to 300 litres a day!

The palm tree provides many essentials for its owner. The trunks are used to support roofs of houses, strengthen walls and in slices are used to make doors. One or two trunks make an adequate bridge over an irrigation channel, and with pieces cut out can be used as steps. The fibres on the trunk are removed and used as stuffing for saddles while the base of the palm frond, stripped of its leafy part, makes a beater for the washer woman and a trowel for the mason. Palm fronds are used to make baskets and a variety of mats such as the famous *margunah* or covered basket of Siwa. Midribs have enough strength to be used to make crates and furniture. Leaf bases are used for fuel and fibre for packing. The sap is drained and consumed as a rough but intoxicating beer *laghbi* or even as a distilled liqueur. This practice is banned for Muslims,

who are forbidden alcohol and in any case drawing the sap can also kill the tree and is therefore discouraged by the authorities. The flesh of fruit which is rich in sugar and vitamins is eaten by man and the stone is eaten by the camel. Date stones can even be ground and used to supplement coffee. Best quality fresh dates are a delicacy for the rich. Dried and pressed dates stay edible for long periods and can be taken on journeys or used to sustain the nomads in their wanderings.

It is possible to buy fresh dates in Egypt or special packs for the tourist trade. Date purchased from an open market stall, must be washed thoroughly before they are eaten.

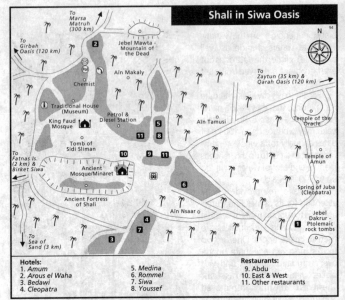

Shali in Siwa Oasis

To Marsa Matruh (300 km)
To Girbah Oasis (120 km)
Jebel Mawta – Mountain of the Dead
Aïn Makaly
Pol
Chemist
Traditional House (Museum)
King Faud Mosque
Petrol & Diesel Station
Aïn Tamusi
Temple of the Oracle
Tomb of Sidi Sliman
Temple of Amun
Ancient Mosque/Minaret
To Fatnas Is. (2 km) & Birket Siwa
Ancient Fortress of Shali
Spring of Juba (Cleopatra)
Aïn Nsaar
To Zaytun (35 km) & Qarah Oasis (120 km)
Jebel Dakrur – Ptolemaic rock tombs
To Sea of Sand (3 km)
N 94

Hotels:
1. Amum
2. Arous el Waha
3. Bedawi
4. Cleopatra
5. Medina
6. Rommel
7. Siwa
8. Youssef

Restaurants:
9. Abdu
10. East & West
11. Other restaurants

Siwans, currently numbering 30,000, have always been fiercely independent, in fact this oasis only officially became part of Egypt in the 19th century. It has been inhabited, with reliance on the 200 or so fresh, salt, warm and cold springs, since Palaeolithic times.

South from Siwa the Sudanese border lies across 700 km of desert. Of this 400 km is **The Great Sand Sea**, which like a frozen storm with waves 100m high, has rolling sand dunes in every direction. Legend tells of a **lost oasis**, but it has never (obviously) been found. Perhaps the descendants of Cambyses live on! (See box, page 359.)

The main settlement is **Shali**, until recently straddling two low hills within the depression, but now abandoned. The ruins of the old town established in 1203 are still impressive. The minaret of the 17th century mosque remains. The mud brick walls and towers are floodlit at night, a splendid sight. New stone dwellings, mainly single storey, have been constructed. They are certainly not so attractive but probably much more comfortable. The new mosque of Faud I, a solidly built structure of stone in the pleasant style of the late 19th/early 20th century, is the natural centre of the new town. Adjacent to it is the tomb of Sidi Sliman, a local saint.

The economy is based on agriculture, dates and olives. The Sa'idi date is preferred for eating. Water supply is from natural springs. No pumping is necessary but the springs are capped to provide some control. Surplus water is a serious problem and the water level is rising at about 9 mm annually. New land is taken into cultivation if demand increases, the olives bearing fruit in 5 years and the date palms in 10 years. Quarrying, transport, trade (and smuggling?) are also important with increasing revenue from tourism. Labour costs are high as labourers have to be brought in and need food and accommodation.

The Oracle of Amun

It was **The Oracle of Amun** which brought Siwa to the attention of the world, from the 26th Dynasty (664-525 BC) onward. **Alexander the Great** is known to have consulted the Oracle in 331 BC after wresting control of the country from its Persian rulers in order to ask it if, as he suspected, he was indeed the son of Zeus. His arrival with a large party of friends and an even larger number of soldiers must have caused quite a stir in sleepy Siwa. Unfortunately posterity does not record the Oracle's response. Nearly 200 years earlier, Egypt's Persian ruler Cambyses (525-522 BC) is said to have carelessly lost an army of 50,000 men who were dispatched from Aïn Dalla near the Farafra Oasis to Siwa in order to destroy the Oracle. The army was simply never seen again having been either buried by a sandstorm or snatched by aliens.

ACCESS Permits are no longer required. The bus station and taxi halt are in the south of the town only a short walk from the centre.

Places of interest

Siwa is such a wonderful place that rather than going to see anything specific most tourists visit Siwa simply to soak up the experience and the atmosphere of life in the oasis which is totally surrounded by the majesty of the desert. Its isolation from the rest of Egypt is increased by the fact that the inhabitants speak Siwa, which is a Berber dialect, rather than Arabic, and have their own festivals and customs.

Birket Siwa salt lake and **Fantis Island** reached by a newly built causeway are a popular picnic spot and on all itineraries. Recommended for an afternoon swim and later for the spectacular sunsets. Take precautions against the many mosquitoes.

Temples of Amun There are two temples to Amun here, both at the deserted village of Aghurmi 3 km to east. The **Temple of the Oracle** (see box, page 359) is built on a large rock amidst the remains of the village. The ascent is quite steep and in summer when temperatures reach 44 °C almost impossible. The Temple which dates back to the 26th Dynasty is fairly well preserved and some attempts have been made to clear the debris and reveal the original façade. There are views to the adjacent Temple of Umm 'Ubayda, Jebel Matwa and across the palm groves to the shimmering salt lakes. The site of the second temple **Umm 'Ubayda**, from the 30th Dynasty, is marked by an area of fallen blocks in which one wall, carefully inscribed, still stands.

Juba's Spring, also called Cleopatra's Pool although it has nothing at all to do with the lady, was mentioned by Heroditus. It is supposed to change temperature during the day but the reality is the relative difference between air temperature and the temperature of the person dipping in, and many people do... On a practical note, the spring produces enough water to irrigate 121 ha every 14 days.

Tombs of Gebel Mawta or Mountain of the Dead is a conical hill about 1½ km from the centre of Shali. It is honeycombed with tombs from 26th Dynasty to the Roman period, varying from small chambers to large composite excavations complete with columns and wall paintings. Anything worth stealing has long since been removed. During 1940 many items were 'sold' to the visiting troops by Siwans who had moved into the tombs for security. Splendid views from the summit, open 0900-1400, closed Friday. No photographs allowed inside. Tombs open to visitors: that of Si-Amun is the most important with wall paintings of the Si-Amun and his family, of Nut the goddess of the sky, and a very recognizable maple tree; Tomb of Mesu-Isis; Tomb of the crocodile; and Tomb of Niperpathot which is in very poor condition.

Sexism in Siwa

Female donkeys are not allowed in Siwa oasis.

Traditional Siwan House, exhibition financed by Canadians, shows in great detail the artefacts and decorations used until very recently in the houses of the oasis. Open 0900-1200 on request – best to give some notice – visitors book is almost as fascinating as the house. No entrance fee, just a tip.

Siwa Festival in October just before date harvest, lasts 3 days and over 3,000 people come to celebrate with prayers and sing some religious songs.

Olive press This old press, driven by donkey power, is in operation only at the end of the olive season around the first week of December. Arrangements can be made at the Tourist Office. No fee but do tip as it is the man's livelihood.

Siwa water bottling plant is run by an Italian company on the outskirts of Shali. An excellent way to exploit an area with too much water.

Sulphur Springs and **Oasis Garden** in desert, contact Ahmed in *Café Abdou*. Cost E£35 day trip.

Local information
● **Accommodation**
There are 8 small cheap hotels in Siwa. Price for double rooms give range of comfort. All basic facilities, tiled floors, a/c of sorts. Always ask to see the room. *Amun Hotel*, government run, E£8; *Arouss el Waha*, rather run down, all rooms bath and balcony, hot shower, E£20; *Bedawi Hotel*, hot showers, E£6; *Cleopatra*, front view over ruins of Shali with shower, E£15-20, rear view with shower, E£10, dormitory E£5 each, roof E£1, hot showers, clean spartan rooms, friendly staff, rec; *Medina Hotel*, E£6; *Rommel Garden Hotel*, under construction; *Siwa Hotel*, E£6; *Youssef Hotel*, E£10.

Camping This is a sensitive area close to the Libyan border, so despite the good relations, don't camp out without permission from the tourist office. Hotels are so cheap camping is really unnecessary but is allowed at the springs called Cleopatra's Baths. *Hotel Cleopatra* permits sleeping on the roof for E£1/night.

● **Places to eat**
The only places to eat in town are 2 or 3 small cafés in the area around the market and new mosque in the centre of town. *Abdou*, which is cheerful and welcoming, is considered 'one of the best' but there is not much competition. Prices cheap, omelette and chips with Pepsi E£2.

● **Banks & money changers**
There is no bank in town.

● **Post & telecommunications**
Post Office: located with the police station just south of the *Arouss el-Waha Hotel*.

● **Shopping**
Market: every Friday.

● **Tourist offices**
Located to the west of the new mosque, the tourist office run by English speaking Mahdi Mohamed Hweti (open sat-Thursday 0900-1300, Friday 1800-2000), is a very helpful first stop for any information. A guide for the main sites of Siwa will cost around E£25. Try Mohammed Ali Herdi on T 6033.

● **Transport**
Local Most places are within cycling distance – *Youssef Hotel* and *Cleopatra Hotel*, hire cycles at E£3/hr or E£5/day. *Abdou Café* or your hotel can organize a donkey cart.

Road Bus: besides a reliable private car, the only way to and from the oasis are the 2 daily buses from Siwa to Marsa Matruh at 0630 and 1300, costs E£6, goes on to Alexandria \(extra E£6.50), a/c bus to Alex from Siwa Sunday, Tuesday and Thursday, E£20, leaves at 1000, book the night before travelling and wait next to the new mosque. **Service taxis**: there are service taxis back to the coast which leave mid-morning and late afternoon.

The Suez Canal Zone

ALTHOUGH THE Suez Canal Zone may not be the most attractive or interesting region in Egypt, it is certainly worth a detour to Ismailia when crossing between Sinai and the rest of Egypt. We may live in an age when it is difficult to be impressed by something as mundane as a canal but it should not be forgotten that the Suez Canal was as great a feat of engineering in the 19th century as the Pyramids were in their day.

Most visitors who head east from Cairo cross the desert and go under the Suez Canal through the Ahmed Hamdi Tunnel, 12 km north of the town of Suez. From there they go into the Sinai peninsula, ignoring not only Suez itself which is not a pleasant town but also the relatively tedious journey north past the Great Bitter Lakes to Ismailia and Qantara and to Port Said on the Mediterranean. Although these towns may not have the attractions of either Cairo or the Sinai resorts, the route is used by those travelling overland to Israel or to catch the ferry to Cyprus and Greece.

SUEZ

Suez (*Pop* 458,000; *Alt* 11m), at the southern end of the Suez Canal, just 134 km from Cairo, was known as Klysma during the Ptolemaic period. It was the spice trade and the pilgrims travelling to Mecca that made the walled city, then known as Qulzum, so prosperous in the Middle Ages. In the 15th century it became a naval base and the opening of the Suez Canal in 1869 ensured its survival and development. It was almost totally destroyed during the 1948 and other wars with Israel, after which it was rebuilt with Gulf funds. Today it is one of Egypt's largest ports and an important industrial centre producing cement, fertilizers and petrochemicals using domestic oil from the offshore fields in the Gulf of Suez. Besides a new ferry

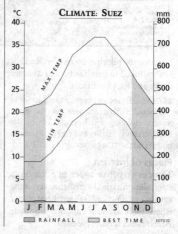

CLIMATE: SUEZ

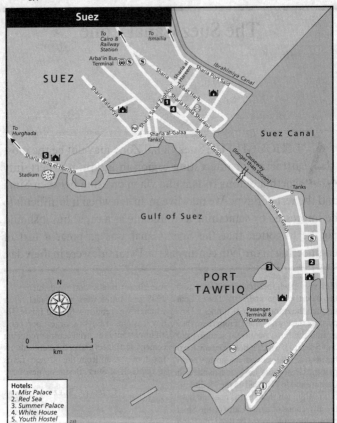

Hotels:
1. *Misr Palace*
2. *Red Sea*
3. *Summer Palace*
4. *White House*
5. *Youth Hostel*

terminal for pilgrims bound for Mecca it is also linked to Port Tawfiq and its other docks and ferry terminals.

ACCESS Buses and service taxis arrive at the Arba'in Terminal just off the main Sharia el-Geish which leads left to the nearby railway station and right to the main hotels and then the causeway to Port Tawfiq.

Places of interest

There is very little to see in Suez, but a stroll along Sharia el-Geish then across the causeway to Port Tawfiq's northeast corner where there are four captured US-made Israeli tanks is quite pleasant.

Excursions are organized from here to the Monasteries of St Anthony and St Paul. (See page 405.)

Local information
● Accommodation

Price guide:

AL	US$150+	D	US$25-50
A	US$100-150	E	US$10-25
B	US$75-100	F	under US$10
C	US$50-75		

D *Green House*, Sharia Port Said, T 223337, F 223330, 54 rm, like most of the hotels in Suez the majority of the guests are Egyptians and oil company workers; **D** *Red Sea Hotel*, 13 Sharia

Riad, Port Tawfiq, T 223334, F 227761, 81 rm, TV a/c, comfortable, good choice in restaurant; **D** *Summer Palace*, Port Tawfiq, T 224475, F 321944, 90 rm.

F *Misr Palace*, 2 Sharia Sa'ad Zaghloul, T 223031, 30 rm; **F** *White House*, 322 Sharia el-Geish, T 227599, F 223330, 45 rm, all rooms have bath, a/c, TV.

Youth hostels Sharia Tariq el-Horriya (nr sports stadium), PO 171, Suez, 100 beds, kitchen, station 2 km, T 21945, overnight fee E£5.

● **Places to eat**
There is a decent fish restaurant on Sharia el-Geish nr the bus station. Beer can only be found in one or two of the hotels and the average *El-Magharbel Restaurant* nr the *White House Hotel*. Try also the cheaper *El-Tayib* on Sharia Hoda Sharawi.

● **Banks & money changers**
Both the **Bank of Alexandria** and **Bank Misr** are on Sharia el-Geish just east of the bus station.

● **Post & telecommunications**
Area code: 062.

Post Office: on Sharia Hoda Sharawi which is one block away from the main Sharia el-Geish, nr the causeway to Port Tawfiq. Open Saturday-Thursday 0830-1400. The telephone office is further south on Sharia Sa'ad Zaghloul.

● **Tourist offices**
There is a **Tourist Friends** booth at the bus station manned by friendly volunteer students who want to be helpful while improving their English. The Tourist Information is right across by the canal on Sharia Sa'ad Zaghloul.

● **Useful addresses**
Passport office: for registration or extending a visa is on Sharia Tariq el-Horriya.

● **Transport**
Train Trains run to/from Cairo (Ramses railway station) but it is better to take the direct express (3 hrs) train which runs 4 times a day rather than the much slower ones via Ismailia.

Road Bus: buses leave the terminal every 30 mins between 0600-2030 for the 2 hrs journey for Cairo (nr Ramses railway station) and north along the canal to Ismailia and Port Said. Other buses incl 2 a day east to Sharm el-Sheikh and Dahab, St Catherine's monastery and Nuweiba, and Taba, and north to Alexandria, 5 a day south along the Red Sea coast to Hurghada and on to Luxor. **Service taxis**: from the main Arba'in terminal off Sharia el-Geish these travel to all of the same destinations as the buses. Besides the

very frequent services to Cairo and north along the canal, travellers going east and south to more remote destinations must split the pre-arranged cost of the journey.

Boat Ferry: the vehicle ferry service, taking 2-3 days, from Port Tawfiq to Port Sudan is supposed to be weekly but because of both operational and political problems it is often less frequent. During the Hadj season, the ferries shuttle instead to and from Jeddah in Saudi Arabia.

AIN SUKHNA

This is a region of hot springs, hence its name, on the Gulf of Suez about 55 km south of Suez on road/route 44. It is a very attractive area, popular with bird watchers as it is on the raptor migration route. These sulphur springs have become the centre of a popular weekend resort for the people of Cairo. There are some fine beaches (quieter during the week), a coral reef close to shore, fishing and opportunities for most watersports.

● **Accommodation** **C** *El Aïn el Sukhna*, T/F 775226. Transport here from Suez by bus or service taxi.

FAYED

This small beach resort is located just to the west of the Great Bitter Lakes about 60 km north of Suez and 30 km north of Ismailia.

● **Accommodation** **B** *Helnan Morgan Village*, Km 54, Ismailia/Suez Rd, Fayed, T 661718, F 661719, 124 good double rm, excellent views, good pool and beach, a real 'find' in this area, rec; **D** *Bonita Village* is a new resort hotel in Kabrit, T 6604341 with 60 rm, a/c and good choice in restaurant; **D** *Shamoussa*, Km 59, Suez Canal Rd, Great Bitter Lakes, T 661525, F 661009, 60 rm of good standard; **E** *El Safa Hotel*, Farana, T 661659, 30 rm, cheapest place in town.

● **Transport Road Buses & service**: taxis running between Suez and Ismailia stop at Fayed.

ISMAILIA

Ismailia is 120 km east of Cairo, 90 km north of Suez and 85 km south of Port Said, is the largest and certainly the most attractive of the three main Canal Zone cities.

The Suez Canal

🦶 Since its completion in 1869 the **Suez Canal**, which at 167 km is the third longest in the world, has enabled ships to pass from the Mediterranean to the Indian Ocean via the Red Sea without sailing around the southern tip of the African continent. There had been many previous attempts to build a canal including those in the 26th Dynasty by Necho II (610-595 BC) and the Persian Emperor Darius I (521-486 BC). Napoleon's engineers vetoed their own plan to build the canal after calculating (incorrectly) that the sea level in the Red Sea was 10m lower than in the Mediterranean. Although it was the British who discovered their error in the 1840s it was **Ferdinand de Lesseps**, a young French vice-consul in Egypt, who finally persuaded the Khedive Said Pasha (1854-63), son of the great Mohamed Ali Pasha, to begin work at the north end of the canal in 1859. Thousands of the workers died moving over 97 million cu m of earth, before its eventual completion in 1869 during the rule of his successor the Khedive Ismail whose name is given to Ismailia midway along the canal.

The lavish opening ceremony on 17 November 1869 was attended by many European dignitaries and a party of tourists organized by Thomas Cook who travelled in their wake, but things soon began to go wrong. Given Britain's constant opposition to the project it was ironic that it was to her that the bankrupt Ismail was forced to sell his 44% holding in the Suez Canal Company for £4mn, the amount loaned to Disraeli's government by the Rothschild bankers, before the much more enthusiastic France could make an offer. The canal, the main route between Europe and India, soon produced very significant profits which were remitted to Britain rather than being ploughed back into Egypt. In the 1920s and 1930s the strategically vital Canal Zone was one of the world's largest military bases.

Since 1945 the canal has been the subject of both important political disputes and serious armed conflicts. Britain reluctantly agreed to remove its troops in 1954 but refused to give a larger share of the revenues to Egypt. The West vetoed World Bank loans to help finance the construction of the Aswan Dam because of the Soviet Union's offer to rearm Egypt after its 1948 defeat by Israel. In reply Colonel Gamal Abdel Nasser nationalized the Suez Canal on 26 July 1956. Britain and France used the pretext of an agreed and pre-planned Israeli invasion of Sinai in October 1956 in an attempt to reoccupy the Canal Zone but were forced to withdraw when the US, opposed to imperialism but wanting to break Britain's stranglehold on the Middle East and get a slice of the action in the region itself, threatened to destabilize the British economy.

The Six Day War with Israel in 1967 caused new damage to the recently rebuilt canal cities and the canal itself was blocked by sunken ships. Egyptian forces briefly broke through the Israeli's Bar-Lev Line on the east bank of the canal during the Yom Kippur war of October 1973 before being forced back and it was not until 1982 that the Israelis withdrew from the East Bank and the canal could be reopened.

With access via the canal denied, super-tankers were built to carry vast quantities of crude oil around Africa. These huge vessels are unable to pass through the reopened Suez Canal which, in order to face increasingly fierce competition from other routes, is now to be widened. It will accommodate vessels up to 180,000 dwt and 20m draft compared with the current 150,000 dwt and 19m draft. In 1994 canal receipts brought in US$1.9bn (with about 35-40% from oil tankers), making it one of the largest sources of foreign currency after tourism, oil and expatriate remittances.

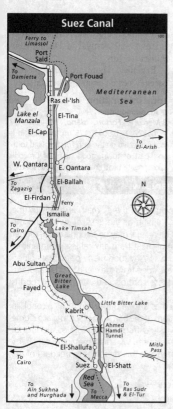

Suez Canal

Ferry to Limassol

Port Said

To Damietta

Port Fouad

Ras el-'Ish

Mediterranean Sea

Lake el Manzala

El-Tina

El-Cap

To El-Arish

W. Qantara

E. Qantara

El-Ballah

To Zagazig

El-Firdan

Ferry

N

Ismailia

To Cairo

Lake Timsah

Abu Sultan

Great Bitter Lake

Fayed

Little Bitter Lake

Kabrit

Ahmed Hamdi Tunnel

Mitla Pass

El-Shallufa

To Cairo

Suez

El-Shatt

Red Sea

To Ain Sukhna and Hurghada

To Ras Sudr & El-Tur

To Mecca

It was built as a depot by the Suez Canal Company in 1861 on the west shore of **Lake Timsah** (Crocodile Lake), one of Egypt's largest lakes. It is divided by the railway track with the attractive and calm Garden City, which was built for the company's European employees to the south towards the Sweetwater Canal and the lake, and the poorly constructed apartment blocks, which were financed with Gulf money, and slums to the north. The Sweetwater Canal was dug from its source in Lake Timsah to provide fresh water during the construction of the Suez Canal. Desert weary travellers find the orchard gardens and trees a delight. There is very little night life but blissful days can be

spent sitting on the beach on Forsan Island watching the ships go by.

ACCESS Travellers arriving by public transport from the Canal Zone and the Delta will be dropped at the depot on Sharia Gumhorriya on the wrong side of the railway tracks. Cross the line to reach the decent end of town and head for the railway station on Midan Orabi. Buses from Alexandria and Cairo drop passengers at the terminal on Midan Orabi. Sharia Ahmed Orabi outside the station runs straight down to the lake and most of the hotels are to be found to the north or left of the street in the Garden City area.

Places of interest

Located in the attractive Garden City are a number of minor sites which, although comparatively unimportant, are worth visiting while in town.

The **Ismailia Museum** near Fountain Park in the north of the Garden City is open 0900-1600 on Saturday-Thursday, 0900-1100 and 1400-1600 on Friday, and 0900-1400 daily during Ramadan, entrance E£6, E£3 for students. Although it has some minor ancient Egyptian pieces it is the mosaics and other pieces amongst its collection of 4,000 Graeco-Roman artifacts which are the museum's highlights. There is also an interesting exhibit illustrating the construction of the Suez Canal. Permission is necessary from the Museum to visit the Garden of Stelae nearby which holds a number of pharonic artifacts and obelisks, mainly from the period of Ramses II.

Left off Sharia Ahmed Orabi on Mohammed Ali Quay next to the Sweetwater Canal is the **House of Ferdinand de Lesseps** which, although officially a museum, open Wednesday-Monday 0900-1600, is sometimes used as a government guesthouse at which times it is closed to the public.

About 7 km north of the city is the main car-ferry across the Suez Canal to Sinai and the **Bar-Lev Line** which is the impressive 25m high embankment built by the occupying Israelis to stall any Egyptian advance across the canal and into Sinai. Although Egyptian forces managed to break through the line at the beginning of the October 1973 war, by using the element of total surprise and high pressure water hoses, the Israeli counter-attack across the Great Bitter Lakes virtually succeeded in surrounding the Egyptian army and, under pressure from the super-powers, both sides were forced to the negotiating table.

Bicycles can be rented from the streets off Mohamed Ali Quay. Picnic in the park between Lake Timsah and Sweetwater Canal. The International Folklore Dance Festival takes place each August and the International Festival of Documentary Films each July.

Beaches There are some pleasant beaches located around Lake Timsah.

Local information
● **Accommodation**

B *Mercure Forsan Island*, PO Box 77, T 765322, F 338043, 175 rm, the best in Ismailia, located on the lush Forsan Island to the northeast of town, good views of Crocodile Lake, private beach, tennis and watersports, a

Islamic dietary laws

🦶 Islam has important rules governing what things may be eaten by the faithful. The Koran specifically forbids the eating of the flesh of swine and the drinking of wine. Other rules dictate how an animal may be slaughtered in proper Islamic manner and ban the consumption of meat from any carcass of an animal that perished other than in the approved way. Any food made of animal's blood such as black pudding or boudin is strictly excluded from the diet of a good Muslim. Non-muslim visitors are not included in these controls and international food is provided in all quality hotels.

The ban on wine has been interpreted as a total outlawing of all alcohol. In practice, local traditions have led to relaxations of the ban from place to place. Some areas, such as much of Turkey forbad Muslims from trading in alcohol but not necessarily from drinking it. Indeed sufi poets used wine as a metaphor for liberty and the ecstasy of truth – and perhaps often as a real stimulant to freedom of the soul! As the poet Hafez wrote:

"From monkish cell and lying garb released,
Oh heart of mine,
Where is the Tavern fane, the Tavern priest,
Where is the wine?"

In Egypt sufism was a road to spiritual understanding, but the tradition of wine imbibing was never well developed here. Wine is produced in Egypt though the quality varies round the 'only fair' standard. No alcohol is available in Libya.

Fasting is a pillar of Islam, as originally of Judaism and Christianity. It demands that Muslims desist from eating, drinking and smoking for the month of Ramadan during the hours of daylight. The Ramadan fast, always followed by the faithful in Libya and Egypt, is now rigorously enforced by social influence.

Travellers are unlikely to be disconcerted by Islamic taboos on food and during Ramadan meals will be provided at normal times. However, the Ramadan fast can be very inconvenient for the uninitiated western traveller. Quite apart from a rising tide of irascibility in some of the Egyptian population, the break of fast in the evening can mean that service in transport, hotels and restaurants can be discontinuous or erratic. The holidays that follow the fast have a similar impact as most local people meet with their extended families and leave their places of work for several days. Check the calendar on page 446 with care.

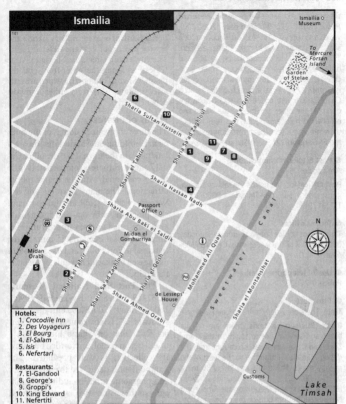

Ismailia

Hotels:
1. Crocodile Inn
2. Des Voyageurs
3. El Bourg
4. El-Salam
5. Isis
6. Nefertari

Restaurants:
7. El-Gandool
8. George's
9. Groppi's
10. King Edward
11. Nefertiti

lunchtime buffet on Friday and Saturday and a nightly barbecue, all facilities available to non-residents for E£20/day, excellent value.

B *Palma Abu Sultan Village*, Abu Sultan, T 400421, F 400862, 98 rm; **B** *Six Corners Resort*, Km 32, Abu Sultan, T 400232, F 400849, 70 rm, a new hotel, well up to standard, deserves patronage.

D *El Bourg Hotel*, off Midan Orabi, T 226327, large colonial style hotel, rooms a/c, friendly service.

F *Crocodile Inn*, 179 Sharia Sa'ad Zaghloul, T 222724, 39 rm; **F** *El-Salam Hotel*, Sharia el-Geish, PO Box 50, T 224401, 50 rm; **F** *Hotel de Voyageurs*, 22 Sharia Ahmed Orabi, T 228304, 25 rm, atmospheric but cheap colonial style hotel; **F** *Isis*, 32 Sharia Adli, Midan

Station, T 227821, 51 rm, façade more impressive than service, favoured by Egyptian honeymoon couples; **F** *Nefertari Hotel*, 41 Sharia Sultan Hussein, T 322822, 32 rm, excellent value with good rooms and facilities.

Youth hostels *Sea Scout's Building*, Temsah Lake, Ismailia, T/F 322850, 200 beds, meals available, family rooms, kitchen, laundry, parking, station 5 km, overnight fee E£5-12.

● **Places to eat**
Although there are many other places to eat, besides the hotels, the best restaurants are the *King Edward* on Sharia Tahrir just off Sharia Sultan Hussein which is the site of the *Nefertari* and *George's*. Popular with visitors from Cairo for the day, *George's*, T 288363 (open daily 1100-2300), is famous for its seafood. Across

the road is the cheaper family-owned **Nefertiti Restaurant** (T 220494, open daily 1200-2400), which also specializes in seafood. If looking for a snack or takeaway **Zahran**, Sharia el-Geish, T 229037, has an outdoor barbecue grill and rotisserie and often cheap decent kofta, lamb chops and chicken. Across the road from **George's** is **Groppi's Patisserie**, a branch of the famous Cairo Café, where coffee and sticky cakes are good. At the other extreme are the kebab and other food stalls around the bus terminal but there are also a few cheap restaurants such as the **El-Gandool** off Sharia Sultan Hussein.

● **Post & telecommunications**
Area code: 064.

Post Office: located beside the railway station, it is open Saturday-Thursday 0900-1500. T 228179.

● **Tourist offices**
The tourist office open Saturday-Thursday 0800-1400 is nr the Sweetwater Canal on Mohamed Ali Quay.

● **Useful telephone numbers**
Police: T 270008.

● **Transport**
Train There are 7 daily trains to Cairo (3-4 hrs).

Road Bus/service taxis: there are regular buses and service taxis to towns in the Canal Zone and Delta which can be caught from the depot in Sharia Gumhorriya to the west of the railway tracks. Those to Cairo (every 30 mins, 0630-2000, 2½ hrs), Alexandria 2/day (E£10/4½ hrs) and El-Arish on the Sinai coast can be caught from outside the railway station.

PORT SAID

Port Said (*Pop* 526,000), 225 km from Cairo and 85 km north of Ismailia at the Mediterranean end of the Suez Canal, was founded in 1859 and named after Said Pasha (1854-63) who began the construction of the canal. It used to be synonymous with smuggling, drugs and every vice under the sun but today it is a slightly seedy beach resort, predominantly for Egyptians, and a free port since 1976. Although it has almost no sites, because of the lack of Western tourists it is a relaxing place to sit on the beach for a few days. As this is a duty free zone have passports ready to enter and leave.

ACCESS Most visitors arrive either at the bus terminal in the centre of town near Ferial Gardens or at the railway station and service taxi depot near the Arsenal Basin. The city's main streets are Sharia Filistine (Palestine) along the water-front and the parallel Sharia Gumhorriya which are only a few minutes walk from either transport depot.

Places of interest

The three shiny green domes of the Suez Canal Building on Sharia Filistine are a landmark in the town. Like the other Canal Zone cities there is comparatively little to see compared with the major tourist attractions. The many Egyptian and few Western visitors stroll around the main shopping streets by day and promenade along the canal and sea-front in the evening. There is a free ferry 15 mins across the canal to Port Fouad and its yacht basin on the east bank which is quieter than the main city.

The **Port Said National Museum**, T 237419, open Saturday-Thursday 0900-1600, Friday 1200-1400, entrance E£6, students E£3, is located near *Nora's Floating Restaurant* on Sharia Filistine in a brand new and cool, uncrowded building. Its collection is well presented. The ground floor is dedicated to early history and pharaonic times including sarcophagi, statues, and two well preserved pharaonic mummies beside utensils and pots. The second floor is Islamic and Coptic material, textiles, coins and manuscripts. The coach used by Khedive Ismail at the inauguration of the Suez Canal in 1869.

The **Military Museum**, open daily 0800-1500, entrance E£2, is located on Sharia 23rd July near the Corniche and displays exhibits from the various conflicts fought along the length of the Suez Canal. These include not only the 1956 Suez crisis with some very lurid paintings (look for the headless figures), but also the successive wars with Israel: the 1973 storming of the Bar-Lev line receives pride of place and is on display in a separate room.

The base of the statue of **Ferdinand de Lesseps** stands on the quay by the canal he constructed. Take a Port Cruise to see the ship convoys going through De Lesseps's canal.

Port Said is the access point for Lake el Manzalah, an excellent spot for watching migrating birds and those that overwinter on the shores.

Christian monuments Church of St Eugenie founded 1869, Sharia Ahmed Shawki; Roman Catholic Cathedral founded 1931, Sharia 23rd July Church of St George (Mari Girgis), founded 1946, Sharia Mohammed Ali.

Local information
● Accommodation

There are expensive hotels and cheap hotels, but no happy medium. If possible, for comfort's sake, go up-market.

A *Helnan Port Said*, El-Corniche, PO Box 1110, T 320890, F 323762, 70 good rm, private beach overlooking the Mediterranean, best hotel in town; **A** *Nora's Tourist Village*, El-Corniche, PO Box 75, T 329834, F 329841, 192 rm, the first tourist village in Port Said and still very good. *Sonesta Port Said Hotel*, Sharia Sultan Hussein, T 325511, F 324825, 90 rm yet another high quality hotel.

D *Holiday*, Sharia Gumhorriya, PO Box 204, T 220713, F 220710, 81 rm; **D** *New Concorde*,

Ferdinand de Lesseps – builder of the Suez Canal

Ferdinand de Lesseps was a French citizen through whose vision and perseverance the Suez Canal was constructed. He was born in France in 1805 and served as a senior diplomat in the French Foreign Service. His first visit to Egypt was in 1832 when he was the French consul in Alexandria. At this time he became acquainted with proposals for a canal across the Isthmus of Suez by a French engineer, Le Père, with whom he had served in Egypt during the Napoleonic invasion. De Lesseps was deeply convinced of the economic and strategic utility of a Suez Canal and was encouraged to press the scheme's merits by the then ruler of Egypt, Mohammed Ali. De Lesseps transferred to Cairo as French consul in the years 1833-37 when he became a friend of the ruler's eldest son, Said Pasha. Said Pasha it was who in 1854 invited de Lesseps back to Cairo to pursue the Suez Canal scheme, granting him a concession for construction of the canal in that same year.

Within 2 years de Lesseps had engineering designs prepared, raised the necessary capital and overcome British political reservations. On 25 April 1859 the project for the Suez Canal (Qanat es-Suways) was begun. The canal ran for 168 km from Port Said to Suez, using the path of Lake Menzala and the Bitter Lakes. It was 8m deep and 22m wide with passing places every 25.5 km. The project saw the excavation of great volumes of material and the building of port and ship handling facilities at sites along the canal. Although de Lesseps had hoped to finish the scheme in 6 years, it took 10 years to complete, delayed by environmental difficulties, labour problems and disease.

The Suez Canal came into full use in 1869 run by the Suez Canal Company which had a 99-year concession to manage it. The new company was 52% French, 44% Egyptian and 4% internationally owned. In 1875 financial troubles of the Egyptian government led to its holding being bought out by the British. De Lesseps welcomed the British involvement and kept a close interest in the affairs of the company. De Lesseps sponsored the construction of the Panama Canal but his company was caught up in engineering and commercial problems and failed. Despite this shadow, de Lesseps remains a monumental figure in Egyptian history for his foresight and determination in creating the Suez Canal which still contributes generously to Egypt's foreign exchange earnings, employs thousands of workers and which brings prosperity to the entire zone along its banks.

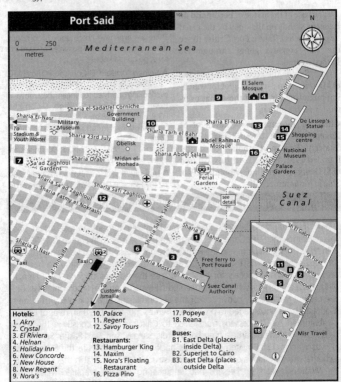

Port Said

Mediterranean Sea

0 250 metres

Hotels:
1. Akry
2. Crystal
3. El Riviera
4. Helnan
5. Holiday Inn
6. New Concorde
7. New House
8. New Regent
9. Nora's
10. Palace
11. Regent
12. Savoy Tours

Restaurants:
13. Hamburger King
14. Maxim
15. Nora's Floating Restaurant
16. Pizza Pino
17. Popeye
18. Reana

Buses:
B1. East Delta (places inside Delta)
B2. Superjet to Cairo
B3. East Delta (places outside Delta)

corner of Sharia, Salah Salam & Sharia Mustafa Kamel, T 235341, Tx 235930, 60 rm; **D** *New Regent Hotel*, 27 Sharia Gumhorriya, T 223802, F 224891, 36 rm; **D** *Palace Hotel*, 19 Sharia Ghandy, T 239990, F 239464, 72 rm, nr the governorate building just off the main coast road and good access to the beach.

F *Akry Hotel*, 24 Sharia Gumhorriya, T 221013, 26 rm; **F** *Crystal*, 12 Sharia Mohamed Mahmoud, T 222961, Tx 53159, 70 a/c rm; **F** *De La Poste*, 42 Sharia Gumhorriya, T 224048, 46 rm; **F** *New House*, 128 Sharia Orabi, T 220515, 40 rm, each with 3 or 4 beds; **F** *Regent*, 27 Sharia Gumhorriya, T 223802, 16 rm, TV; **F** *El Riviera*, 30 Sharia Ramses, T 228836, 48 rm; **F** *Savoy Tours Hotel*, Sharia Mohamed Ali, El-Shohada, T 222197, 30 rm.

Youth Hostels Sharia el-Amin and El-Corniche (nr sports stadium), T 226433, 210 beds, family rooms, kitchen, meals available,

parking, train 2 km, bus 3 km, overnight fee E£5 incl breakfast.

● **Places to eat**

There are numerous restaurants serving decent if unspectacular Western food with the best being on Sharia Gumhorriya and the Corniche coast road, such as the *Seahorse* which serves good seafood. The reasonably priced lunch and dinner cruises on the *Nora's Floating Restaurant*, which operates from Sharia Filistine in front of the National Museum, provide a good view of the Canal. The most fashionable place in town is the *Pizza Pino*, Sharia Gumhorriya, T 239949, serving standard Italian fare, which is nearby just behind the National Museum on Sharia Gumhorriya. Further south along the street is *Popeye's Café*, T 224877, which is really a burger bar, past which is *Reana House* which serves large helpings of Korean food.

● **Banks & money changers**
There are numerous banks: **Central Bank**, **Bank of Cairo** or Thomas Cook all on Sharia Gumhorriya, open 0900-1800.

● **Embassies & consulates**
A number here as it is an important port: **Belgium**, in main shopping centre, T 238513; **France**, in main shopping centre, T 323860; **Greece**, 52 Sharia Gumhorriya; **India**, 12 Sharia El Gisr; **Italy**, Sharia Salah Salem; **Norway/Sweden/Denmark**, 30 Sharia Filistine, T 224706; **Spain**, 19 Al-Gabarty/El Geish; **UK**, in main shopping centre; **USA**, 11 Sharia Gumhorriya, T 226691.

● **Post & telecommunications**
Area code: 066.

Post Office: T 225918, the main post office, with International Telex and Fax, open daily 0700-1700, is on the corner of Ferial Gardens nr the bus station.

● **Shopping**
As Port Said is a free port visitors, excluding ship's passengers, are supposed to pass through customs when entering and leaving and it is therefore necessary to declare all valuable items on arrival to avoid being charged a hefty tax when leaving. The town is a delight for shoppers offering many imported goods at very competitive prices. Places to visit are:

Sharia El Togary which is organized like a typical Egyptian market but sells a wide variety of goods; *Sharia Filistine* where the Shopping Centre has a wide range of high quality imported goods. This is a European style shopping centre with parking, restaurant and café; *Sharia Gumhorriya* and *Sharia El Nahda* further west are important commercial streets with some shops.

Items on sale of Egyptian origin of interest to visitors incl oriental dresses and fine scarves, silver and gold jewellery, leather work and paintings on papyrus. Avoid the ivory items which cannot be imported into Europe.

● **Sports**
Sporting clubs: *El Uonani Club*, by Yacht Club, T 240926; *Fishing Club*, north end of Sharia Gumhorriya, T 236870 (Places to fish – Al-Jameel bridge, Hagar Said, Lake el Manzalah,

Al-Tafri'a and Port Fouad bridge, prepare for the National Fishing Competition each October); *Port Said Club*, west end of Sharia 23 July by stadium, T 221718; *Yacht Club*, Sharia El Tirsana/El Baharia, across canal in Port Fouad, T 240926.

● **Tour companies & travel agents**
EgyptAir, Sharia Gumhorriya, T 220921; *Misr Travel*, 16 Sharia Filistine, T 226610; *Port Said Tourist*, Sharia Filistine, T 329834; *Thomas Cook*, 43 Sharia Gumhorriya, T 227559.

● **Tourist offices**
The tourist office is at the south end of Sharia Filistine, T 23868.

● **Useful numbers**
Bus station, T 226883; Passport office in Government Building, T 226720; Passport office in Port Police Building, T 224811; Port Said Harbour Authority, Sharia Filistine, T 223783; Railway station, T 221861.

Shipping agencies: Aswan Shipping Agency, 8 Sharia Gumhorriya, T 220790; Assiut Shipping Agency, 20 Sharia Mostafah Kamal, T 220523; Canal Shipping Agency, Sharia Filistine, T 220662; Damanhour Shipping Agency, west end of Sharia Safi Zaghloul, T 222804; El Menia Shipping Agency, 40 Sharia Gumhorriya, T 220675.

● **Transport**
Train There are 5 slow and dirty trains a day to and from Cairo which take 4-5 hrs via Ismailia (details T 221861). Buses and service taxis may be preferable.

Road Bus: there are both regular express and normal a/c buses from the bus station at Ferial Gardens to Cairo (3 hrs) and Alexandria (7 hrs) (details T 228793 for superjet and T 226883 for regular buses). There are also buses south along the canal, west to the Delta and east to El-Arish. **Service taxis**: regular and quick service taxis can be caught to Cairo and Alexandria from the depot on Sharia El Sbah, nr the railway station as well as to other destinations in the Canal Zone, Delta and across the canal to El-Arish.

Boat Ferry: a weekly ferry service to Limassol in Cyprus usually leaves Port Said on Tuesday while its sister ship sometimes goes on to Athens via Rhodes (details T 223783).

The Sinai Peninsula

ALTHOUGH SOME hardy travellers wish to encounter the isolation of the harsh but stunning landscapes of the desert interior, most tourists come to the Sinai peninsula to visit the remote St Catherine's Monastery and experience some of the world's finest diving and snorkelling grounds off the Gulf of Aqaba coast around Sharm el-Sheikh, whilst others are part of the rapidly expanding sector of sun, sea and sand tourism that the region is trying so hard to promote. Since the area reverted to Egyptian control in 1982 and the chance of yet another war with Israel receded, the government has succeeded in encouraging the private sector to invest in the area and it is now Egypt's major tourist destination outside the Nile Valley.

Sinai is a very sparsely populated 62,000 sq km desert peninsula which throughout history has acted as both a land bridge linking, and a hostile but spectacular wilderness dividing, Africa and the Middle East. It was the route by which the Israelites reputedly reached the Promised Land and Islam arrived in Africa. It is divided from the rest of Egypt both literally, by the geographical barrier of the Suez Canal and Gulf of Suez, and metaphorically, by successive Israeli occupations between 1948 and 1989 when the dispute over the ownership of the Taba enclave was finally resolved in Egypt's favour. While many tourists still travel overland, either from Cairo or Israel, or by ship from Hurghada or Jordan, the majority now fly to Sinai direct to Sharm el-Sheikh airport.

WARNING Never allow your driver to stray off the tracks in the desert because in the National Parks it is illegal and because many areas still have MINES. Maps of mined areas are unreliable, mines are moved in flood waters and remain hidden. This is a general warning for all desert-border areas of Egypt and the Western Desert but is especially pertinent in the Sinai.

THE EAST COAST

The east coast of Sinai from Ras Mohammed to Taba boasts the most attractive shoreline coral reefs in the northern hemisphere. The climate, tempered by the sea, varies from pleasant in winter to hot but bearable in summer. There are white sand beaches, rugged cliffs and views east to Saudi Arabia and Jordan while to the west lies the barren interior.

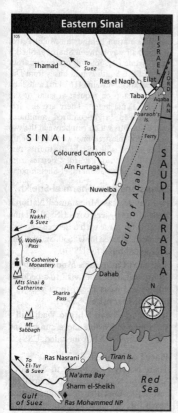

Eastern Sinai

Thamad
To Suez
Ras el Naqb
Taba
Eilat
ISRAEL
JORDAN
Aqaba
Pharaoh's Is.
Ferry
SINAI
Coloured Canyon
Aïn Furtaga
Nuweiba
To Nakhl & Suez
Watiya Pass
St Catherine's Monastery
Mts Sinai & Catherine
Sharira Pass
Mt. Sabbagh
To El-Tur & Suez
Ras Nasrani
Tiran Is.
Na'ama Bay
Sharm el-Sheikh
Gulf of Suez
Ras Mohammed NP
SAUDI ARABIA
Gulf of Aqaba
Red Sea

	Abu Rudeis	Cairo	Dahab	El Shatt	El-Tur	Nuweiba	Ras Sudr	Sharm el-Sheikh	St Catherines	Taba
	272									
	459	570								
	161	111	459							
	104	376	194	265						
	367	639	69	528	263					
	98	174	396	63	202	465				
	200	472	98	361	66	167	298			
	149	412	361	301	167	430	247	263		
	431	703	133	592	327	64	529	231	494	

Distances in Sinai in kilometres

SHARM EL-SHEIKH

This is the usual name given for the twin resorts of Sharm el-Sheikh and Na'ama Bay (some 7 km further north) which lie about 470 km from Cairo. The area has developed rapidly in recent years. Ten years ago there were only two hotels, now (1998) there are 75 and 40 more are under construction. It has certainly become an international resort with the development of a spectacular and now exceedingly popular diving area. There are over 60 km of reef providing dramatic drop offs and breathtaking formations claimed to be unparalleled anywhere else in the diving world. The location takes advantage of the coasts for the divers, the beaches for the holiday makers and the interior for the more adventurous. Being in the lee of the desert highlands the site is protected from the winds most likely to disturb the waters for divers. One of the great advantages to visitors is the lack of hassle on the beaches. There are no hawkers on these carefully controlled stretches of sand.

Sharm itself, which existed pre-1967 as a closed military zone was used by the Israelis. This small town, which is rapidly shedding its previous dilapidated image, has a bus station, docks, 3 banks, post office, telephone exchange, hospital, police station, supermarket, poorly stocked local shops, a couple of seedy cafés, two garages with welding facilities, a row of souvenir shops, a sports club and the rather run down Tentoria Dive Club which is popular with Israelis in the summer season. Although most tourists stay in adjacent Na'ama Bay, Sharm has a youth hostel, a couple of cheap hotels, the excellent *Fayrouz Residence* hotel belonging to the Hilton chain and the 5-star *Seti Sharm Beach Hotel*.

Purely a tourist resort, **Na'ama Bay**, which gets its name from the Arabic for 'God's Blessing', is much more attractive than Sharm and has an excellent sandy beach, good quality modern hotels, an attractive Corniche and some of the best diving facilities in the world (see **Sports**,

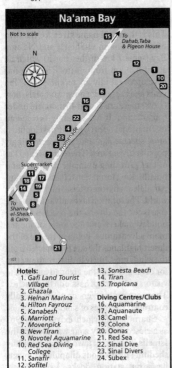

Na'ama Bay

Not to scale

N

15 → To Dahab, Taba & Pigeon House

12

13

1
10
20

6

16
9

22

4
23
2
7
7

Promenade

Supermarket

11
18
14
19
5

8

To Sharma el-Sheikh & Cairo

3

21

107

Hotels:
1. Gafi Land Tourist Village
2. Ghazala
3. Helnan Marina
4. Hilton Fayrouz
5. Kanabesh
6. Marriott
7. Movenpick
8. New Tiran
9. Novotel Aquamarine
10. Red Sea Diving College
11. Sanafir
12. Sofitel
13. Sonesta Beach
14. Tiran
15. Tropicana

Diving Centres/Clubs
16. Aquamarine
17. Aquanaute
18. Camel
19. Colona
20. Oonas
21. Red Sea
22. Sinai Dive
23. Sinai Divers
24. Subex

page 381). There are restaurants and shops for divers and other tourists but little or no indigenous Egyptian life. Indeed the vast majority of the hotel workers come not from Sinai but from elsewhere in Egypt. There are spectacular views across the clear blue waters of the Red Sea to the mountains of Saudi Arabia. It is an excellent place for relaxation and for the variety of watersports available. You don't have to be interested in diving but it helps.

ACCESS Package tours lay on a bus to the hotel from Sharm el-Sheikh airport, about 10 km north of Na'ama and 17 km north of Sharm, but individual travellers must rely on service taxis (around E£30) into town. Buses from Cairo (470 km) to Sharm via Suez (336 km) and the rest of Sinai can be caught from Cairo's Sinai Bus Terminal in Abbassia (T 824753), and terminate in the new bus station behind the Mobil Petrol station half way between Sharm el-Sheikh and Na'ama Bay. You will need a taxi from here (E£10). South bound buses from Dahab (98 km), Nuweiba (167 km) and Taba (231 km) stop on request at some of the major Na'ama hotels. There are also frequent cheap bright-coloured minibuses called Tuf-Tufs which run between the two resorts (50 piastres one way, 0630-2400). While a taxi will cost E£10 (tourist rate E£20!) for the same journey. Ferries from Hurghada arrive at Sharm el-Sheikh port.

Excursions from Sharm el-Sheikh

Full day to **Ras Mohammed National Park** – 8 hrs by jeep costs US$60. Diving possible for those with a licence – equipment can be hired for US$30. Snorkelling equipment hired for US$10.

Tour to **St Catherine's Monastery** takes 10 hrs – also includes visit to a bedouin village and oasis Feran for a visit to a convent. Tour price US$90.

Jeep safari ride of 5 hrs to **Wadi Kid** – short hike so sensible shoes, sun hat and sun screen, lunch box included, US$45.

Places of interest

There is very little to see in Sharm el-Sheikh or Na'ama Bay and tourist life revolves around the diving and typical beach life. See Sinai's desert interior by taking an organized day trip to **St Catherine's Monastery**, for E£150 (see page 391), which is breathtaking, a visit to Mount Sinai to climb to the summit (see page 394), a boat trip out to the coral reefs or a desert safari to Wadi el-Aat for E£150, which includes a camel ride and possibly supper under the stars at a bedouin encampment. The *Tourist Scene* centre at *Sanafir Hotel* offers a selection of package deals including a 1-day safari US$55, St Catherine's US$49, Camel sunset including dinner US$35. A helicopter or a glider can be rented for a tour of the area from Cessna or the *Siag Travel Agency* offices in Sharm, T 600860 (helicopter, 5-seater, US$70 an hour), or through the *Movenpick*

Hotel (glider). *Spring Tours*, office at Sharm port, offer daily boat trips, except Friday, between Sharm el-Sheikh and Hurghada, E£65. Day trips to Luxor 0600-2130 are organized by *Sonesta Hotel*.

A visit to nearby **Ras Mohammed National Park** to see the marine life from the shark observatory is well worth the effort. Ras Mohammed is a small peninsula which juts out from Sinai's most southerly tip and is the point where the waters of the shallow (95m) Gulf of Suez meet the deep waters (1,800m max) of the Gulf of Aqaba. The result is that, while the land is barren desert, the waters teem with exotic marine life. Besides the huge variety of brightly coloured fish which live on the coral reef normally deep water species such as sharks, tuna, barracuda and turtles come to the reef to feed. Ras Mohammed has clean, shallow beaches, some sheltered but others very windy, from which the snorkelling is excellent, but beware the strong currents.

Taxis to Ras Mohammed from Sharm el-Sheikh cost E£60 one way but it is advisable to keep the taxi for the day –

around E£150 – as there are no taxis at Ras Mohammed. Vehicles pass through UN checkposts. Passports are scrutinized at the Egyptian checkpost where Israelis or any non-Egyptians who came in through Taba may experience delays. Beyond deserted Israeli trenches are the gates of the national park and nature reserve, entrance fee US$5 equivalent plus US$5 per car. The National Park is open from sunrise to sunset while the visitors' centre, which includes a restaurant, audiovisual presentations, first aid, shops and toilets, is open from 1000 to sunset. It is currently closed but toilets are still available. Also crude toilets between Main Beach and Observatory Beach. There is very limited water so bring your own bottles from Sharm el-Sheikh. There are around 100,000 visitors per year.

Camping is permitted in designated areas (US$5 per person per night) but numbers are strictly limited to preserve the environment. Permits are available from the park office at Sharm el-Sheik. Booking: T 600559, F 600668. Collection of or damage to any natural resource,

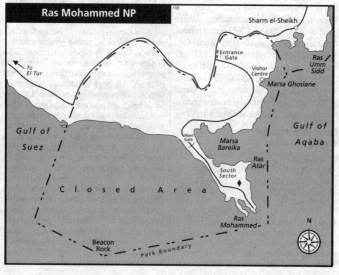

Ras Mohammed NP

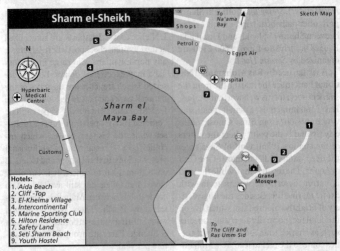

Sharm el-Sheikh

Sketch Map

To Na'ama Bay

Shops

Petrol

Egypt Air

Hospital

Sharm el Maya Bay

Hyperbaric Medical Centre

Customs

Pol

Grand Mosque

To The Cliff and Ras Umm Sid

Hotels:
1. Aida Beach
2. Cliff -Top
3. El-Kheima Village
4. Intercontinental
5. Marine Sporting Club
6. Hilton Residence
7. Safety Land
8. Seti Sharm Beach
9. Youth Hostel

hunting, driving on vegetation or in a prohibited area, spear fishing or fish feeding are prohibited. Rules are strictly enforced by the park's English-speaking Rangers.

The **Nabq Protected Area** 40 km north of Sharm though popular with safari groups is less crowded. There are two permanent Bedouin settlements, Ghargana on the coast and Kherieza, inland from the main coastal valley Wadi Kid. Entrance free. Taxis from Sharm E£60-80 one way but it is advisable to keep the taxi for the day at around E£200. The wildlife is outstanding, storks, kites, ospreys and raptors are quite common but mammals like foxes and gazelles are much rarer.

Local information
● Accommodation

Price guide:			
AL	US$150+	**D**	US$25-50
A	US$100-150	**E**	US$10-25
B	US$75-100	**F**	under US$10
C	US$50-75		

There is accommodation to suit all pockets. A few hotels are in Sharm el-Sheik but most are in Na'ama Bay and it is advisable to make advance bookings for all but the winter season. Rooms are much cheaper if they are booked as part of a package. Attempts are being made to popularise Sharm Maya Bay offering cheaper accommodation plus the traditional shopping area of Sharm el-Sheikh which provides lots of local colour. Good value for money restaurants. Lies 6.5 km south of Na'ama Bay, on a cliff top area.

The hotels in **Sharm el-Sheikh** itself are: **A** *Hilton Residence*, T 600266-8, F 600270, stunning views from cliff top position. All 150 rm a/c, self-catering apartments have one/two bedrooms, satellite TV, phone, private facilities, fridge, kitchen for light cooking, hair dryer, patio or balcony. Choice of bars and restaurants, large pool with children's section, fitness centre, free children's club open 0800-2000, baby-sitting service, arrangements can be made for B&B. Sandy beach and adjacent coral gardens reached by staircase or outdoor elevator. Shuttle buses run to *Fayrouz Hilton* every 30 mins (E£1 residents, E£3 non-residents), reported as too quiet in the low season; **A** *Intercontinental*, new 1996, something for everyone at a very high standard, free shuttle from airport, wonderful views from position on cliff top, extensive landscaped grounds, nearby sandy beaches, easy walk to town centre. Junior, Executive and Royal suites available, 254 rm with a/c and private facilities, terrace or balcony, satellite TV, telephone, personal safe, casino and disco. International restaurant, Italian and Grill restaurants, Terrace café, beachside barbecue. Private beach, large outdoor pool, indoor pool, children's pool, sports centre with extensive watersports, volley ball, snooker, 2 floodlit clay tennis courts, health club, fitness room, children's club for the over 4's, baby sitting. Rooms overlooking pool can be noisy; **A** Seti Sharm Beach, T 600870-9, F 600147, brand new, 231 rm, 7 suites, beach location, 5 restaurants, 2 swimming pools, tennis courts, watersports and diving centre; **B** Aida Beach Hotel, hilltop location, wonderful views, overlooking Sharm el-Maya Bay, 147 large split-level rm, seating area, TV, minibar, phone, shower etc, several restaurants, coffee shop, bars, shops, pool, tennis and squash, snooker and pool, bowling alley, free transport to hotel beach about 5 mins away; **C** Cliff-Top Hotel, T 600251, F 600253, 30 rm, part of Sinai Hotel & Dive Club; **D** El-Kheima Village, T 600167, F 600166, 33 rm of which 20 double rm have a/c, nr harbour.

The number of hotels in **Na'ama Bay** continues to grow rapidly. They incl: **A** Ghazala Hotel, T 600150, F 600155, smart modern hotel, 80 twin rm with balcony in the 2-storey main building, 88 twin rm in the garden chalets and 12 family chalets which sleep 4, all have TV etc, main restaurant, also Grill Room, Franco's Pizzeria, Tam Tam (Egyptian cuisine) and Ice Cream corner, bars in lobby and by pool which is said to be the largest in the region, separate children's pool, easy access to beach and all facilities, restaurants, beach location; **A** Hilton Fayrouz Village, T 600137-9, F 770726, 150 double a/c bungalow rm, in lovely gardens, private beach location, bar, choice of restaurants, excellent meals, first class watersports, yacht, glass-bottom boat, pool, tennis, minigolf, volley ball, horse riding, massage, aerobics, discotheque, games room, play area for children, bus (E£1) to and from Na'ama Bay every hour until midnight; **A** Marriott Beach Resort, spacious, modern hotel. large free-form pool, connected by wooden bridges and surrounded by sun terrace and gardens. All mod cons, dining room, restaurant, 2 bars, pub, health club, gym, volley ball, horse riding, being greeted by a spectacular waterfall in the central courtyard is a wonderful experience, refreshing and very impressive, modern, spacious, comfortable, on sandy beach approximately 10 mins from airport (ie 10 mins from town centre), 206 rm, balcony, Saturday TV, choice of cuisine, pool dive centre, watersports (pay locally) fully equipped health club; **A** Movenpick Hotel Jolie Ville, T 600100-5, F 600111, very large low level building, spreads on both sides of desert road, most extensive hotel in Na'ama Bay so not suitable for those with walking difficulties, 337 rm and 10 suites,

the cheaper rooms on far side of desert road are 5 mins to walk from beach. Large circular pool, children's pool, children's club. excellent service, good food, modern facilities but soulless; **A** Sofitel, T 600725-7, F 600733, a beautiful, sophisticated hotel, 312 rm on 5 floors, all with private facilities, TV, a/c, balcony, satellite TV, telephone, choice of restaurants and bars, café, large pool, children's pool, diving centre for beginners and advance level skills, health club with gym, aerobics, sauna, jacuzzi, Turkish bath and massage, table tennis, archery (pay locally) and mountain bikes for hire. Shows and entertainments provide by in-house professional team, has the coral gardens called Nir Gardens just off shore. Not rec for the elderly; **A** Sonesta Beach, T 600725-7, F 600733, just 10 km from airport and 10 mins from centre, at north end of the bay. A cool collection of white domes in extensive gardens, attractive and spacious, 3 pools of which one salt water, diving centre, shops and boutique. 228 split level rm decorated in bedouin style with either balcony or patio, TV, radio, telephone, shower, a/c. Selection of cuisine, main dining room known as the Citadel plus La Gondola Italian restaurant, 3 cafés, 3 bars, children's club 5-12 years runs daily 1000-1600, tennis, squash, spa, 24 hr baby sitting service; **B** Novotel Aquamarine Hotel, T 600178, F 600193, 152 rm, with terrace or balcony, central position, landscaped gardens, choice of restaurants (Al Dente is rec), tennis, pool, Aquamarine Diving Centre in complex, all watersports; **C** Helnan Marina Hotel, T 600170-1, F 600170, 150 rm, the first hotel here, beach location, good sea views, helpful and efficient staff, bar service, clean rooms, buffet; **C** Tiran Village, T 600221, F 600220, currently 75 a/c clean rm with bath, 155 beds, 150 seat restaurant open to non-residents, bank, shops, diving centre, snack bars, pleasant open air areas, mainly European tourists in winter and Israelis in summer; **C** New Tiran Village, T 600225-7, F 600220, newly constructed to high standard with 50 rm; **D** Gafi Land Tourist Village, T 600210, F 600210, 45 rm, 135 beds, beach restaurant open to non-guests, special dinners, loud disco, relaxed, friendly, clean, welcoming, credit cards accepted, plans for pool; **D** Kanabesh Hotel, T/F 600185, 64 double rm with a/c and bath, restaurant, café, snackbar, bar, live music, small kiosks, travel agent, dive club (see **Sports**, page 381); **D** Rosetta Hotel about 10 mins from airport, owned by same management as Tropicana, friendly, high standard, all 108 rm have usual facilities and terrace, main restaurant, pizza, Egyptian tent, bank,

National Parks and Protected Areas of the South Sinai and Gulf of Aqaba

👣 The Sinai has been a new experience for Egypt's tourism industry which has previously orientated around the nation's rich cultural heritage. When travellers started coming to the Sinai in greater numbers during the 1980s they were looking for something different, something that they found in the wilderness of the desert and the abundance of life along the coast. Although the concept of eco-tourist was as yet unheard of, the Egyptian authorities were sufficiently far-sighted to start planning the protection of the area, so that people could visit in great numbers and yet still experience a largely untouched area of natural beauty.

This protection has taken the form of a network of protected areas along the coast from Ras Mohammed National Park to the Taba Managed Resource Protected Area, and St Catherine's National Park covering a huge swathe of the southern mountains. The Department of Protectorates has responsibility for conservation and natural resource management, education and the enforcement of environmental planning law for all developments in the area of their control.

It is of course, the fringing coral reefs that line the Gulf of Aqaba that make Sinai, especially Ras Mohammed, so popular with divers. As well as the stunning variety of forms and colours in the corals and reef fish, areas such as the Straits of Tiran and Ras Mohammed are also famous for shark, manta ray and turtle. Two of the reefs in the Straits of Tiran, which falls under the Ras Mohammed National Park, are the permanent residences of Hawksbill Turtles and there are also turtle nesting beaches within the restricted areas of the National Park. Particularly good fossil reefs dating back 2,000 to 15,000 years can be found all around Ras Mohammed but especially vivid around the mangrove channel and the visitors' centre.

Ras Mohammed is also remarkable too for its rare northerly mangroves which lie in a shallow channel at the tip of the peninsula, in an area with many rock pools and crevices in the fossil reef which hold shrimp – and much stranger creatures too. The famous Hidden Bay confuses visitors, because it appears and disappears with the changing tide, and the Saline or Solar Lake is also interesting for the associated salt loving plants.

Although the land appears to be barren and hostile it is in fact home to a variety of life, from insects to small mammals, Nubian ibex and Desert foxes. The foxes are often seen near the main beaches and cubs can be seen at sunset in late spring. They are harmless if approached but should not be fed. The Park is an important area for resident bird populations including four heron species, gulls, terns and ospreys and during the late summer for migrating birds, especially White Storks.

Nabq, to the north of Na'ama, is also an outstanding area, containing a dense area of mangroves, the most northerly in the world and also rare sand dune habitats.

doctor, 3 pools, laundry; **D** *Red Sea Diving College Sultana* run by the Sinai Hotel & Dive Clubs, has 12 double a/c rm with bath, fridge and phone; **D** *Sanafir*, T 600197, F 600196, 90 rm/huts, 150 beds, all creditcards accepted, highly rec by all the guests of whom about 80% are divers, relaxed, friendly authentic Egyptian atmosphere, *Divers Den* bar, Egyptian, fish and South Korean restaurants, snackbar, own private beach.

E *Emperor Diving Village*, forms part of the newly built Rosetta Hotel with which it shares facilities, at Na'ama Bay purpose built for divers – 18 small rm and 16 slightly larger. Pool is central and built for diving training, a very basic, quite ugly hotel; **E** *Pigeon House*, 5 mins walk to beach, small, basic, **A** rooms have a/c, bath, double bed (small) and single bed, mini bar and terrace; **B** rooms in the main hotel complex have fan and share wc and showers. **C**

As well as the birds of the area, ibex and gazelle can be seen. The Hyrax, a small rodent-like mammal which is actually the closest living relative to the elephant, can be found here in Wadi Khereiza. The diving here is superb, though little is done these days as the reefs lie at some distance.

Much of the 600 sq km of Nabq is a restricted area to prevent critical damage by 4WD vehicles but there is much to see here for the careful viewer. A small bedouin settlement lies on the cost where the tribesmen continue to fish in a traditional manner. The Parks make a sincere effort to involve the bedouin in their work and to protect their traditional lifestyle currently under much pressure from the rapid development in the area. Near the settlement is a more modern establishment, a shrimp farm that supplies much of the produce for the hotels and restaurants in Sharm el-Sheikh.

Ras Abu Galum, which lies between Dahab and Nuweiba, has yet no entry fee or visitors' centre, although one is planned to the north of the protectorate. This is an area of stunning scenery, with high mountains and long winding valleys running right down to the sea. Safaris with camels and bedouins can be arranged to visit these areas where wheeled vehicles cannot venture. It is strongly recommended not to visit without a guide and certainly never to leave the marked trails. Although the Protectorate is valued mainly for its rare plant life, the diving here is superb. It should be noted, however, that access to the underwater cave network at Ras Mamlah is strictly forbidden. Many divers have died here and their bodies remain unrecovered, as the caves which exceed 100m in depth are very unstable.

Taba is the newest and largest in the network of coastal protected areas (declared January 1998). Already known are the wealth of ancient writings and carvings on rock walls in the area that span the history of Sinai as the crossroads between Asia and Africa. The scripts include Arabic, Semetic, Greek, Nabatean and other, unknown, languages.

The largest single protected area in Sinai is St Catherine's National Park, which covers a roughly triangular area of the mountains from the monastery south. As well as containing the cultural sites of the monastery of St Catherine and Mount Sinai, a site holy to Christians, Muslims and Jews, the Park also contains ibex, gazelle and hyena, hyrax, leopards and possibly cheetahs. Bedouin have been recruited as community guards to help the Rangers patrol this immense expanse of mountains, *wadis* and desert. Although the Park has not been long established, it has already had noticeable success, particularly in cleaning the area of the previously abundant rubbish and providing information and nature trails.

Although the ecosystems of the Sinai are being subjected to the effects of rapid development due to its success as a tourist destination, it is hoped that the National Parks will preserve the natural beauty of the area for interested visitors.

grade in straw huts have 2 beds and cupboard and share the same WC and showers. For the laid back budget conscious diver; **E** *Tropicana*, T 600596-7, just 5 mins walk from beach, 60 rm built in Moorish citadel style, white with domes, small, friendly, pool has slide, but is deep and has no shallow end – not suitable for children, restaurant, billiards, all watersports available nearby.

Camping *Safety-Land*, large, cheap camp site next to Sharm el-Sheikh's *Tentoria Diving Centre*, T 600373, F 600334. Is particularly popular with young Israeli tourists, US$12 pp. Divers should be warned that, although cheaper than the Na'ama Bay clubs, the diving safety record is generally not so good at Sharm el-Sheikh. 38 bungalows for 2-4 people at about E£25 pp for half board and 60 large army tents sleeping 4 at the same price, an indoor winter and outdoor summer restaurant with a E£5 breakfast and a E£12 lunch/supper. Nearby *Sharks Bay* camp, 5 km to north of Na'ama Bay, about 10 mins from airport by taxi, offers very basic accommodation, Bedouin style huts (bamboo cabins) with communal toilet/showers. There is a diving centre. Meals are taken in the Shark's Bay open air restaurant where the speciality is sea food or in a Bedouin style tent by the beach. Friendly and informal, coral garden for diving or snorkelling is directly off the beach, dive centre on site with diving programme, very popular, run by Bedouin, rec for budget travellers.

Youth hostels *Sharm el-Sheikh*, PO 46619, T/F 600317, 105 beds in a/c dormitories, with double bunks, no lockers, open 0600-0900 and 1400-2200, kitchen, food available, laundry, parking, members E£5/night, incl breakfast.

● **Places to eat**

♦ ♦ ♦: pick from the multitude of restaurants, which cater for all pockets and tastes, both along the Na'ama Bay beach-front and in all the major hotels which are open to non-residents. Most serve huge buffet meals. *Wings and Things*, at *Oonas Divers Inn* for a special occasion meal.

♦ ♦: *Al Dente Restaurant* in *Azur Aquamarine Hotel*, open 1200-1600 and 1800-2200, also does takeaways; *Bedouin Restaurant*, T 600826, at foot of Ras Umm Sid light house, 1 km from *Hilton Residence*, offers charcoal grill, Bedouin entertainment and torchlight camel rides; *Franco Pizzaria*, at *Ghazala Hotel*, serves good Italian food; *The Ship Restaurant* in Sharm El Maya is actually on a grounded ship – how about that for local colour and the sea food is excellent; *Viva La Vista* at the *Divers College* (Sultana), serves reasonably priced, no nonsense, food; *Viva Restaurant*, beach location, friendly, new and spacious a/c restaurant and bar which serves good quality French food; *Wadi Restaurant* in *Hilton Fayrouz Village*, lunch E£40, restaurant dinner E£46, with belly dancer at 2100; *Yong Jong*, South Korean restaurant at *Sanafir Hotel*.

♦: in addition there are beach-front stalls serving most varieties of takeaway food. The *Tam Tam*, in front of the *Gazala Hotel* is still on our highly rec list, also *Sinai Star*, T 600393, in market area of Sharm which offers cheap, decent fish and *Safsafa*, in the same area, excellent seafood, meals starting at around E£25.

● **Airline offices**

Egyptair, *Hotel Movenpick*, T 600409; Sharm market area, T 601057; airport, T 600408/664. The office of the local independent airline **ZAS** is in the Gafi Mall, T 601909.

● **Banks & money changers**

At the top of the hill nr the *Hilton Residence* in Sharm el-Sheikh there are three banks and two banks in the Na'ama Shopping Mall (Monday-Saturday 0800-1400 and 1800-2100, Sunday 1000-1200). Most hotels have banking facilities exchanging money at the normal rate.

● **Entertainment**

Filmshow: every Friday evening at **Spot** at the *Gazala Hotel*, entry E£15, first drink free.

Folk music: The traditional *El Fishawy Café* in Sharm Mall has lively Egyptian folk music.

Nightclubs: oriental floorshows, which are open to non-residents, are largely confined to the major hotels but new independent bars and restaurants are being opened all the time in Na'ama Bay. *Pirates Bar* in *Fayrouz Hilton*; the *Cactus Disco* at the *Movenpick*; *Bus Stop* the *Sanafir* E£20 entry incl a drink and is open until 0400 with lots of noise, dancing and billiards down stairs; *Salsa* same house and admission as above is mainly 80s music but lots of fun; the *Spot American Bar*, dark (dingy) but popular with the local youth looking for excitement.

● **Post & telecommunications**

Area code: 062.

All numbers in Sharm el-Sheikh are to be changed to begin with either 660 or 661. Numbers in Na'ama bay remain unchanged.

Post Office: at the top of the hill nr the *Hilton Residence* in Sharm el-Sheikh there is a post office (Saturday-Thursday 0800-1500) but all the major hotels have mail services. The main telephone exchange is up on the Hataba, opp the Grand Mosque. Sinaint, the local internet service is behind *Hilton Residence*, T 661090. They can provide a short term connection for your own computer or rent theirs at hourly rates.

● **Hospitals & medical services**

Ambulance: Sharm, T 600425.

Medical: *Movenpick Hotel* runs a daily clinic (1900-2000) and their doctors are on 24-hr call, reached through hotel reception. *Fayrouz Hilton* has a doctor living on the premises. The *Red Sea Diving Club* has 2 doctors, T 600343. The *Hyperbaric Medical Centre*, T 661011/660922/3 (very modern facilities) deals with diving accidents and also with emergencies needing cardiology, intensive care and minor surgery. *Air*

Medivacs can be arranged by helicopter at Cessna, open 0900-1800, T 600922/3, F 601011 or after hours at the *Hilton Residence*, Room 2012 or 3008. The Egyptian Army operates a 'flying ambulance' to take serious cases to Cairo, T (02) 665663/668472. *Sharm Hospital*, T 600425, nr the bus station (which looks like a glass pyramid), has very limited facilities but will help in an emergency. Better medical care is available from Dr Adel Taher at the Hyperbaric Medical Centre or for non-emergency cases there are doctors on call at the larger hotels.

Pharmacy: in Sharm Mall: *Towa Pharmacy*, T 600779; In Sharm town: *Dr Sherif Pharmacy*, T 600388.

● **Shopping**

Most shops in Na'ama Bay are linked to the hotels and are small but well stocked with provisions for a beach or diving holiday. Two shopping malls offer a variety of fashionable shops incl *Adidas*, *Benetton*, *Next* and *Naf Naf*. With expansion of the town the services have expanded too and shops have a wider selection of fresher produce.

Bookshops: bookshops in *Sharm Mall, Movenpick, Sanafir, Ghazala* and *Fayrouz Hilton* hotels.

Photography: hire an underwater camera at *Hilton Fayrouz Village. Sanafir Hotel* has a shop where film can be developed within 1 hr. *Movenpick, Fayrouz Hilton* and *Tiran Village* all have photo shops.

● **Sports**

Bowling: the *Aida Beach* has a bowling alley.

Diving: watersports in general, and diving in particular, are the main attractions in south Sinai. The reefs off the Gulf of Aqaba coast are acknowledged as some of the best in the world with incomparable coral reefs and colourful marine life. The main dive centres, which are based in Na'ama Bay but which organize dive trips to all of the region's major reefs, incl the following: *Aquanaute Diving Center*, T 600187, F 600619, located in Na'ama Bay next to the *Kanabesh Hotel*, comes **very** highly rec by our correspondents, 11 instructors, 3-6 boats, good underwater photo facilities. Aquanaute has lots of return customers. Back packers are welcome and helped with accommodation while booked groups receive discount rates. Bookings through *Regal Diving*, Station Rd, Sutton in the Isle, Ely, Cambridgeshire CB6 2RL, T 01353-778096, F 01353-777897. *Camel Dive Club*, Na'ama Bay, T 600700, F 600601, which claims to be the largest in town, slick and friendly service. In winter the

majority of the divers are Italians, Swiss and Germans while British and French predominate in summer. The club runs 4-7 boats, has 10 European instructors who provide a flexible range of CMAS, PADI and NAUI courses. Provides free camping for divers who should bring their tents and sleeping bags. Operates dive safaris to Sudan for a maximum of 12 passengers at US$140 a night. *Novotel Aquamarine Diving Center*, Na'ama Bay, T 600178-182, F 600193, is hidden away in the *Novotel Aquamarine Hotel* from where its 9 instructors operate friendly PADI, NAUI and CMAS diving courses using 4 boats. *Oona Diving Centre*, Na'ama Bay, T 600581, F 600582. Residential diving club whose guests come exclusively via tour operators, accommodates up to 48 divers in self-catering room over diving centre, which has full equipment and repair facilities, at about US$20 a night. Oona runs land safaris in 2 Mercedes trucks at US$90 a day and sea safaris for 6-8 people at US$100 a day. Mainly European instructors and divers. Egyptian office at 32 Sharia Baron, Heliopolis, Cairo, T 02 668747, F 02 674153, overseas bookings which incl flights can be made through *Oonas Divers UK*, 23 Enys Rd, Eastbourne, Sussex, T 01323-648924, F 01323-738356. *Red Sea Diving College*, Na'ama Bay, T 600145, F 600144, located in the centre of the beach next to *Kanabesh Hotel*, is a PADI 5-star fully equipped IDC centre joint project between Sinai Hotels & Diving Clubs and Scubapro Europe. Opened 1991, 10 multi-lingual PADI instructors from a good purpose built facility. Courses which incl all the gear but excludes certification fees are US$40 for an introductory dive, US$265 for a standard open water course, US$360 for a 3 days underwater photography course and US$550 for a dive masters' course. The college caters for up to 40 divers incl British (35%), German (30%), Italians and other Europeans. *Sinai Divers Club*, Na'ama Bay, T 600150-4, F 600158, in *Gazala Hotel*. Claims to be the largest diving centre in Na'ama Bay and handles 40-110 divers on 2 dives a day. Germans make

Blacktail Butterfly Fish

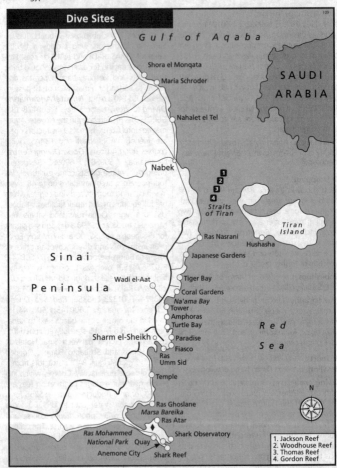

Dive Sites

Gulf of Aqaba

SAUDI ARABIA

Shora el Monqata

Maria Schroder

Nahalet el Tel

Nabek

Straits of Tiran

1 **2** **3** **4**

Tiran Island

Ras Nasrani

Hushasha

Japanese Gardens

Sinai Peninsula

Wadi el-Aat

Tiger Bay

Coral Gardens

Na'ama Bay

Tower

Amphoras

Turtle Bay

Sharm el-Sheikh

Paradise

Fiasco

Ras Umm Sid

Red Sea

Temple

Ras Ghoslane

Marsa Bareika

Ras Atar

Ras Mohammed National Park

Quay

Shark Observatory

Anemone City

Shark Reef

N

1. Jackson Reef
2. Woodhouse Reef
3. Thomas Reef
4. Gordon Reef

up half the divers in summer (May-October) while about 60% of the winter divers are British. Book in advance in the winter high season. Sinai runs 8-day boats and 2 live aboard boats, has 10 qualified instructors, runs a full range of courses, has daily excursions and dive cruises for the keen diver with everything under one roof and trips to all the major reefs. *Umbarak Diving Resort* (Umbarak was the first bedouin to learn to dive) – local style architecture, right on beach, very basic, very laid back, bamboo bungalows sleep 2, shared shower and facilities, fish restaurant,

the only PADI dive centre with its own private jetty, ideal for the more adventurous who can live without today's luxuries. For **non-divers** there are many other watersports.

Horse riding: the *Sanafir* offers horse riding excursions incl sunset rides. Lessons E£10/hr; hire E£20/hr and E£70/day and good stables at *Sofitel*.

Ice skating: yes, believe it or not, a new rink has opened in Na'ama Bay.

Parasailing: the *Movenpick* offers parasailing.

Quadrunners (4WD bikes for short desert rides): available at most hotels.

Snorkelling: is practised in many places but the headland of Ras-um-Sid has possibly the best snorkelling drop-offs in the world.

Watersports: on the beach outside the *Marina Sharm Hotel* you can rent masks and fins (E£16/day), windsurf board (E£31.5/day), jetski (E£150/hr, E£75/30 mins, E£40/15 mins), glass-bottom boat E£20 for 30 mins. At *Fayrouz Village* snorkelling equipment E£15, motor boat E£30 for 15 mins, windsurf board E£30/hr, pedal boat or canoe E£15/hr. Glass bottom boat trip E£20 for 30 mins.

● **Useful telephone numbers**
Area code: 062; **Fire**: T 600633; **Hospital**: T 600425; **Police**: T 600415; **Tourist Police**: (Na'ama) T 600517 (Sharm), T 600311.

● **Tour companies & travel agents**
There are travel agents attached to almost all the major hotels, as well as a few independent ones, which can book transport, hotels, sight-seeing and other excursions.

● **Tourist offices**
The **Egyptian Tourist Authority (ETA)** office is at the top of the hill nr the youth hostel in Sharm el-Sheikh, T 768385. In addition all the major hotels can provide detailed tourist information.

● **Transport**
Local Car hire: Avis from *Sonesta Hotel*; **Europe Car** from *Fayrouz Hilton* or *Ghazala* hotels; **Hertz** from *Movenpick Hotel*. **Taxi**: T 600357.

Air Ras Nasrani Airport, T 600314, F 600416, is further along the coast 10 km north of Na'ama Bay with direct flights to and from an increasing number of European cities as well as internal flights to Cairo (daily at 0645), Hurghada, Luxor and St Catherine.

Road The bus station Sharm, T 600660, is at the bottom of the hill in Sharm el-Sheikh. Buses to Cairo cost E£25-E£50 depending on which you take, go at 0700, 1000, 1300, 1630, 2330 and 2400, and take 6 hrs. Other destinations incl: Zagazig, E£15, 1200, 7 hrs; Suez, E£12, 0900, 1100, 5 hrs; Mansura, E£27, 0900, 1100, 8 hrs; Taba, E£10, 0900, 3½ hrs; St Catherine's Monastery, E£10, 0800, 4 hrs; Nuweiba, E£7, 0900, 2½ hrs; and Dahab, E£5, 0900, 1½ hrs.

Boat Ferry: ferry to Hurghada (Sunday, Tuesday and Thursday at 0900, Return Monday, Wednesday and Friday at 0800), takes 5-15 hrs,

costs E£100, T 544702. Harbour Master in reply to a query of when the ferry would run, "this week, if God wills it", so do check.

Private vessels: Entry procedures for Sharm el-Sheikh port. Visas may be obtained for boats and crews from Egyptian consulates in country of origin. It is possible but more hassle to get one in Sharm el-Sheikh. It is as well to give clear advance (at least 1 week) notification of your intention to berth. The Port Commander must be notified upon arrival. The course of the vessel, in national waters, must be filed and approved by the Port Authority.

Dive Sites

Straits of Tiran: Jackson, Woodhouse, Thomas and Gordon (wreck of *Loulica* lies here) Reefs, currents can be strong here. Wrecks of Sangria and Laura. Coral reef at 10-15m, large pelagic fish and perhaps shark. Hushasha south west off island, shallow with sand floor and sea grass. Ras Nasrani (The Light): 40m drop off, large pelagic fish, watch the currents. Ras Nasrani (The Point) hard coral boulders. Tower: steep wall, 60m, large caves. Ras Nasrani (End of the Road Reef). Amphoras: Unnamed Turkish wreck, cargo of mercury still evident, sandy floor at 25m.

Shark Observatory: wall with vertical drop to 90m.

Shark Reef: sandy slope with two submerged islands, open sea and pelagic fish, sharks.

Quay: steep slope, pelagic and reef fish, sharks.

Liveboards available at Sharm el Shiekh: Recommend M V Sea Surveyor – 18 divers in 9 rooms, with a/c and wash basins. 7 toilets and shower. Tutors for underwater photography and dark room facilities. Very comfortable. Was a Danish oceanic research vessel – equipped for serious diving – long range cruises. Small boats available at Sharm el Sheikh, Freedom II, Freedom III and Seagull – from 18m-24m long, holding 8-14 persons, limited a/c.

NORTH FROM SHARM EL-SHEIKH

The road journey north from Sharm el-Sheikh to Dahab (98 km) takes 1-1½ hrs and passes the airport before turning inland through beautifully rugged scenery past a bedouin school, a water drilling camp, a manganese quarry, the tomb of an Israeli general and the remains of his bombed out car before entering Dahab.

DAHAB

98 km north of Sharm el-Sheikh, 82 km from Sharm el-Sheikh airport, 133 km from Taba and 570 km from Cairo, Dahab made its name which means 'gold' in Arabic, as Egypt's hippy capital after Israeli troops started visiting the bedouin village for rest and recreation on its golden beaches in the 1960s. Although it is a rather commercialized shadow of its past it is still a primary destination for would-be hippies and beach bums. In recent years the government has tried to clean up Dahab's image, by cracking down on drugs and discouraging back-packers and turn it into a more conventional resort to cater for 'normal' tourists. It is not a mainstream tourist stop – but now more likely to be patronized by divers and windsurfers. There is an splendid coral garden along the shore line and excellent wind conditions due to its position in a wide *wadi* mouth, make it an important windsurfing centre.

Dahab can be divided into three distinct areas. About 1 km inland from the beach is the dull little administrative town of Dahab which seems covered in windblown rubbish from the local tip. Bedouin village, Asla, 3 km up the coast, is where the hippies hang out in the beach campgrounds and restaurants although there are now two 3-star hotels in the village. Meanwhile the impressive new and totally self-contained holiday village on the beach is deliberately isolated from the two other parts of the town.

ACCESS There are daily buses north from Sharm el-Sheikh and south from Taba and Nuweiba, or shared taxis can be hired from anywhere along the Gulf of Aqaba coast. Because of Dahab's split site, make sure you know where you want to be set down. A taxi from one section of town to the other will cost as much as the bus fare from Sharm el-Sheikh.

Places of interest

On land there is little or nothing to see in Dahab itself, but camel trips can be organized to one or two bedouin villages in the beautiful interior. Jeep and horseback safaris can be taken into the mountains. An aerial tour can be taken by helicopter or cessna, through Siag Travel in the Novotel, T 640301.

Local information
● Accommodation

The options are the tourist holiday village, the 2 new hotels in the Bedouin village or the numerous campgrounds along the beach in the bedouin village.

A *Helnan Dahab Hotel*, Dahab village, T 640425, F 640428, 200 rm, a/c, brand new, private beach, 2 swimming pools, 2 restaurants, café, bar, tennis, squash, pool hall, diving centre, watersports; **B** *Nemissa*, takes 1½ hrs by taxi from Sharm el-Sheikh, breathtaking views across the Gulf, 51 spacious rm with a/c, private facilities, some are designed for wheel chair access, pool, has dive centre on site and first class snorkelling. A small hotel, friendly, built in traditional style, public rooms directly on to the beach. Main sea front of Dahab is about 10 mins walk, full service restaurant, pub, roof garden, doctor on call, bank and post office in village. Access to dive sites is by jeep; **B** *Novotel Dahab Holiday Village*, Dahab Village, PO Box 23, Dahab, T/F 640301-5, 141 a/c rm with private terrace, incl 40 divers' cabanas, 1 2-bedroom suite and 4 1-bedroom suites, new, spotlessly clean, very attractive, excellent beach, best beach in Dahab, 'A' rooms are on the beach are larger and have a sea view, 'B' rooms in the middle of the village, have a garden view and 'C' rooms at the back are more basic, 2 restaurants, café, bar, discotheque, bank, the *Inmo Diving Centre*, windsurfing, a glass boat, pedalos, canoes, tennis courts, bicycle hire, volley ball, jet skis, speed boats, horseback riding, safari and desert trips, shops, satellite TV, non-residents can enjoy the facilities for E£40. NB pool has no shallow end.

D *Nesima Dive Club and Hotel*, Oriental style with arches and domes ceilings, simple but comfortable. Very new, confirm hotel and pool are complete before you go. **D** *The Sphinx*, T 640032, in Bedovin village, offers cheaper rooms without en suite bathroom, pleasant,

clean, close to centre. Other cheap places incl: **E Gulf Hotel**, T 640147, 21 rm; **E Lagouna**, T 640353, 45 rm; **E Sarah Hotel**, T 640315, 20 rm.

Camping The contrast could not be greater than with the multitude of cheap campgrounds, which have names like *Crazy House*, *Fighting Kangaroo* and *Lazy Days Camp* along the beach-front in the nearby Bedouin village. For the sake of security it is best to opt for thatched-roofed but stone-walled huts which can be padlocked while avoiding the baking tin-roofed shacks. Most have showers, sinks, primitive toilets, but no electricity. Like the *Hilton Camp* most charge around E£4 a night or about E£15 for full board. While some campgrounds, such as *Mohamed Ali*, *Reef & Coral* and *Star of Sinai* are more popular than others and some should be avoided, they change from year to year and it is probably best to ask around and see which ones are rec. More hygenic, if more expensive, is the *Sheikh Ali and William Camp*, E£10 a night, which still retains its original Bedouin simplicity and beauty.

● **Places to eat**
In the *Dahab Holiday Village* restaurants are: ♦♦♦ : *Zeitouna*, main restaurant. ♦♦ : *Aqamarina*, diving centre cafeteria; *Bar-A-Cuda*, bar; *Bedouin Corner*; *Lagoon*, beach café.

In addition there are lots of beach-front restaurants in the Bedouin village incl: ♦ : *Hard Rock Café*, *Scorpions Restaurant* and the Australian run vegetarian *Fighting Kangaroo*.

In Asla: *Ali Baba*, which incl vegetarian dishes, a Chinese and a Korean restaurant; *Neptune's*, Egyptian food, sparkling clean, cost E£15 each; *Tota* is the most highly rec eaterie in Asla, easily recognized by its boat shaped façade, good quality, and almost the only place selling beer.

● **Banks & money changers**
Bank of Egypt (open daily 0830-1400 and 1800-2100), nr the bus station, in Dahab town accepts TCs. There is also a bank in the holiday village.

● **Entertainment**
Nightclubs: besides the holiday village's *Where-Else* discotheque and bar, nightlife mainly revolves around the restaurants and cafés in the Bedouin village which are open until around midnight. Most popular by far, is the *Black Prince Disco* in the *Gulf Hotel*. A shuttle bus to the camp sites is provided by the hotel free of charge.

● **Post & telecommunications**
Area code: 062.
Post Office: in Dahab town centre is open Saturday-Thursday 0830-1500.

● **Shopping**
In Dahab town and a few very small supermarkets in the Bedouin village which are open 0730-2400 and stock most of the basics incl bottled water. *Hano's Madness* in Asla is the only tattoo parlour in Egypt.

● **Sports**
Although the reefs are not as good as in Na'ama Bay there are diving centres in the holiday village and in the Bedouin village which rent equipment and run PADI diving courses. Overnight trips to see the nocturnal lobsters at the Blue Hole, 2 km north of the village, and possibly eat one the next day are rec. Be advised the Blue Hole is difficult and dangerous and is only for very experienced divers. The holiday village also offers a wide range of sporting activities incl the *Inmo Diving Centre*, windsurfing, a glass boat, pedalos, canoes, tennis courts, free bicycles, volley ball.

Dive sites in vicinity of Dahab: the coral is so close here that the dive sites have shore access.
  North from the lighthouse: Lighthouse, by lighthouse in Dahab Bay Eel Garden north of lighthouse, off Bedouin Village; north again is Small Canyon; Canyon, opp Canyon Dive centre, north of Small Canyon – one of the deep sites to be dived appropriately; Blue Hole – another deep dive to treat with respect; The Bells – north of Blue Hole.
  South from the lighthouse: Off *Lagouna Hotel* is The islands, a very beautiful location. The Caves some 5 km south of the lighthouse Gabr el Bint south of the Caves, access from road to be arranged by camel.

● **Tourist offices**
There is no tourist office in town. Drivers should be warned that there is only one petrol station on the 81 km route between Dahab and Sharm el-Sheikh which also has the nearest hospital.

Parrot Fish

● **Transport**
Road Bus: the bus station, T 640250, is outside the Bank of Egypt in Dahab and there are a number of daily buses south to Cairo via Na'ama Bay and Sharm el-Sheikh, north to Nuweiba and Taba, and east to St Catherine. **Taxis**: are a necessary expense for getting between Dahab town and the beaches and unfortunately tourists are usually charged more than Egyptians.

NUWEIBA

This town, 69 km north of Dahab and 64 km south of the Israeli border at Taba, and its Moshav or cooperative village used to be a major destination for Israeli tourists during its occupation, but it has long since been surpassed by Na'ama Bay and has now lost most of its tourist business. Nuweiba is divided between the tourist village with its fine white sandy beaches, and the small town around the port, some 8 km south used both for fishing and as a port for boats which ferry Saudi Arabia bound Egyptian expatriate workers and pilgrims to the Jordanian port of Aqaba. From Nuweiba you can see Saudi Arabia across the water as the Gulf of Aqaba narrows towards the north. There can be strong southerly winds but not sandstorms for a few days in January, February, April and October. Guests of Nuweiba hotels entering from Israel must pay Israeli departure tax locally, US$17, and Egyptian Tax US$6 on leaving. Access time from Ovda 2½ hrs.

ACCESS All the buses arrive at Nuweiba port and most continue on to the tourist village or vice versa. Arriving at the port – the only means of transport is taxi.

Places of interest

Apart from the beachlife there is little to see or do in Nuweiba which is a boring little town. Enterprising locals, however, organize camel treks and jeep safaris from the resort to the magnificent Coloured Canyon and elsewhere in the interior. Many take short trips to Petra in Jordan via the ferry to Aqaba. Swimming with a wild dolphin which has adopted a local Bedouin has become a tourist attraction (E£5 for 15 mins), by the beach front *Abdullah's Café*

in the Bedouin village at the entrance to Nuweiba. It is important not to wear any suntan lotion or cream as this can harm the dolphin.

Local information
● **Accommodation**
Nuweiba has a number of mid-range to cheap hotels and camp sites mainly in the tourist village but also in the port and further along the coast towards Taba.

A *Nuweiba Hilton Coral Village*, T 520321-6, F 520327, new, 200 rm, 6 suites, 20 'superior' bungalows sleeps 4, choice of restaurants, spread over 115,000 sq m of beach front, watersports, camel and horseriding, safaris, bicycles, squash, tennis, children's facilities, 2 heated pools, diving centre, travel agency, disco. A stylish resort, very relaxing, ideal for recuperating, rather isolated from rest of Sinai resorts. Excellent snorkling just 30m off shore where there is a coral garden. Aquasport Dive and Watersport Centre on the beach.

B *Nuweiba Holiday Village*, Nuweiba, T 500401-410, F 768832, 172 rm, Egyptian run, 60% of guests are on package tours, clean, comfortable a/c chalets with bath, beach location, shuttle bus to/from Nuweiba, restaurant, sports facilities.

C *Bawaki Beach Hotel*, 18 km north of Nuweiba, T 500470-1, F 3526123, 36 rm, beach location, 1 km from Nuweiba-Taba road and 47 km from Taba, attractive, well built chalet hotel, friendly and helpful staff, cheap restaurant, bar, beach café, seawater pool, mainly European guests in winter and locals in summer, some problems with fresh water, power and telephone facilities, hire of fishing boat, cruise boat (E£100/hr), speed boat for water skiing (E£40/hr), windsurfing, and good snorkelling with submerged coral reef just offshore.

D *El-Sayadeen Touristic Village*, Nuweiba, T 520340, F 2476535, 99 a/c twin bed chalets with bath, poorly located nr (but outside) the port, adequate but rather old and spartan, restaurant, pool, pebbly beach with windsurf boards and pedalos, European guests in winter and locals in summer. **D** *El-Salam Village*, Nuweiba, T 500441, F 500440, 89 rm; **D** *Helnan Hotel*, T 500402, 127 large rm, a/c, bath, TV, there is a pool, shops and nearby dive centre; **D** *La Sirene*, T 500701/2, just down the road from *Hilton*, simple, no pool but right on the beach with excellent snorkelling on the coral reef.

Responsible diving

There has been a great deal of unnecessary damage caused to the beautiful coral reefs around the coast. Divers taking trophies, anchors being dropped on to the living corals, rubbish being thrown into the water. The regulatory bodies set up to prevent this damage to the environment have had little effect – it is up to those who delight in this area to preserve it for the future.

Code of responsibility for reef divers

1. Check you have the correct weights. As the Red Sea is a semi-enclosed basin it has a greater salt content than the open ocean. The extra salinity requires heavy weights thus bouyancy checks are essential.

2. Avoid all contact with coral. These living creatures can be damaged by the slightest touch. Many reef fish are inedible or poisonous – but the reef needs them to survive.

3. Remove nothing from the reef. Shells and pieces of coral are an integral part of the reef. In Egypt this is taken so seriously that boat captains can lose their licence if either shells or pieces or coral are brought on board.

4. Move with care. Careless finning stirs the sand and can smother and kill the softer corals.

5. Do not feed the fish. Introducing an unnatural imbalance in food chain can be fatal and is thus prohibited.

6. Air bubbles trapped in caves can kill the marine creatures who extract their oxygen from the water.

7. Do not purchase souvenirs of marine origin. Aid conservation, do not encourage trade in dead marine objects which is illegal in Egypt.

8. Take back only memories and photographs

E *Sally Land Tourist Village*, Taba-Nuweiba Rd, Nuweiba, T 530380, F 530381, located off coast road half way between Nuweiba and Taba (36 km), highly rec, tastefully planned, 68 attractive chalets, beautiful white sandy beach, courteous and efficient staff, mainly European guests, restaurant, café, bar, shop and beach snack bar, snorkelling and windsurfing equipment for hire.

Camping *Nuweiba Helnan Camp*, bamboo cabins allow breezes to flow (and sand and hot air) comfortable interiors, dive centre, use of facilities at *Helnan Hotel*; *Nuweiba Camping* located next to *Nuweiba Holiday Village*, simple huts with 3 beds, a mirror, cupboard, table and chairs (E£24 pp), E£12 to pitch your own tent or E£3 to sleep on the beach, large clean communal cold showers, self-catering facilities and also nr to a range of restaurants, cheerful staff who will organize camel and other trips.

● **Places to eat**
♦ ♦ : The *Nuweiba Holiday Village's* main restaurant provides adequate but unspectacular breakfast (E£8), lunch (E£21) and dinner (E£23) as well as a special barbecue (E£25), and fish restaurant dinner (E£23). At *Bawaki Village* restaurant the prices are slightly less. Besides the hotels there are a number of places to eat such as the average *Macondo's* fish restaurant next to the Holiday Village and the cheaper *Sharkawi* which is one of 3 cheap restaurants nr the former Moshav and along the beach towards the village of Tarbeen, 2 km north of the resort.

● **Banks & money changers**
There is a bank inside Nuweiba port, but you need your passport to get into the port, and the tourist village will change cash.

● **Entertainment**
Nightclubs: nightlife in Nuweiba is very limited and revolves around the hotel beach bars. *Pool*

Cave Bar with live music and darts at *Nuweiba Hilton Coral Village* is the most popular.

● **Post & telecommunications**
Area code: 062.

Post Office: in the tourist resort.

● **Shopping**
There are a few small stores and bakeries in and around Nuweiba town and the tourist resort.

● **Sports**
Although the Holiday Village has some facilities incl tennis courts, bicycles for hire and horse riding E£150 for 8 hrs, sports are otherwise limited to watersports with equipment being hired out at the hotel. The *Nuweiba Diving Centre* is run by good European divers who are rec as being particularly helpful for beginners. Nuweiba itself is not the best site on the coast for diving but, because it is quiet, it is ideal for beginners and a 45 mins introductory course costs US$40 while a full diving course costs US$240 pp. Trips to other and better dive sites can also be organized. Aquasport has a 'Hobycat' at Nuweiba. Learning to dive for 12 years and over is just US$185.

● **Tour companies & travel agents**
Hilton Coral Village, Nuweiba; also *Abanoub Travel*, T 520201, F 520206.

● **Tourist offices**
Best at the hotels.

● **Transport**
Road Bus: T 520370-1. There are various daily buses from Cairo, Suez, Sharm el-Sheikh and Taba which call at the port and the tourist village. Buses leave for Sharm el-Sheik at 0700 and 1500. **Service taxis**: with passengers sharing the cost of the journey, are available from Nuweiba port to Taba and other towns in the region and prices should be negotiated before setting off.

Boat Ferry: there are 2 ferries a day (except on Saturday, when there is one) between Nuweiba port and the Jordanian port of Aqaba which is 4 hrs further up the coast. Although there are

some tourists the service is mainly used by Egyptian expatriate workers and also pilgrims who have to queue for hours outside the port during Ramadan, when a third sailing is often added to the schedule. Having checked their passports, foreigners are usually encouraged to jump the queue and proceed into the port to the ticket office and through customs. 2 weeks or 1 month Jordanian visas (£23 equivalent) are issued on board or immediately on arrival in Aqaba, with charges varying according to nationality.

TABA

This town has a special place in the hearts of most Egyptians because, although it is only tiny, it was the last piece of territory which was occupied by the Israelis. The fact that the luxury *Sonesta hotel*, one of Israel's best and most popular hotels, was located in the Taba enclave no doubt complicated the dispute. Despite having to pay compensation to the Sonesta's owners, before handing the hotel over to the Hilton group to manage and despite the very small size of the area in dispute, Cairo had been determined to retrieve every centimetre of Egyptian land and was satisfied at the outcome.

Taba is unusual, an international border town between an empty desert and the bright lights of Eilat. The coastline is attractive but although shelter from the wind is sought by sunbathers, windsurfers have no complaints. Besides the hotel there is little else in the tiny enclave except barracks and facilities for the border guards and customs officials. There are, however, major plans for the area and a danger of too much development. Land is very cheap at only E£5 per sq metre to be paid over a 10 years period. The result is that at **Taba Heights** just 9 km southwest of Taba five beach side hotels are under construction with plans for an international airport there. Having won Taba back from Israel, the government is now concentrating tourist development in the region and is building power stations and other infrastructual facilities to support the planned tourist influx.

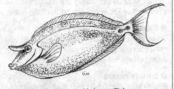

Longnose Unicorn Fish

ACCESS The easiest way to reach Taba, which is 390 km from Cairo and 260 km from Sharm el-Sheikh, is via Israel's Eilat airport which is only 15 km across the border. However, few flights come directly here, most come in through Ovda. Time from Ovda to Taba Hilton at least 1 hr depending on border controls. Guests of the Taba Hilton and Nelson Village do not have to pay Israeli Departure Tax. These hotels will provide a pass to allow free movement through the border during time of stay. Taxis and buses run to the border and the hotel is just a few steps on.

Places of interest

Sightseeing in Taba is limited to trips to the beautiful interior, **Pharaoh's Island** with the ruins of Salah al-Din's (Saladin's) fortress (the most important Islamic remains in Sinai) and across the Israeli border to Eilat. A visit to the island, which is a short boat ride (400m) from the *Salah el-Din* hotel, where refreshments are available, is well worth the trip especially around sunset when it is particularly beautiful. The fortress was originally built by the Crusaders to guard the head of the Gulf of Aqaba and protect pilgrims travelling between Jerusalem and St Catherine's monastery: it was also used to levy taxes on Arab merchants travelling to and from Aqaba. Although Eilat, which is Israel's main holiday resort has many obvious attractions, it should be remembered that a visit could cause passport problems in other Arab countries (see Transport into Israel, page 390). There are helicopter rides available from Taba (also Dahab and Sharm el-Sheikh), max five passengers, range 600 km. For information Siag at *Taba Hilton*, T 530300-1, also Sharm el-Sheikh, T 600860.

Local information
● Accommodation

A *Taba Hilton*, Taba Beach, Taba, T 530300-1, F 5787044 (address via Israel which is far more efficient is PO Box 892, Eilat 88107, Israel, T 059 79222, F 059 79660), 10 storey hotel with 251 double rm, 53 twin bed rm and 12 suites, private beach, pool, watersports, a 150 hp motorboat, a diving yacht with 14 berths for extended trips, 5 floodlit tennis courts, volley ball, table tennis, billiards room, games room, and video games, use of facilities at the sister hotel *Club Inn* just across the border in Eilat, there are 5 restaurants and 3 bars – the *Taba Lounge, Papo's Pub, Fantasy Island*, pool bar and *Nelson Village* bar, in addition there is the *End of the World* nightclub and a gambling casino attracting cross-border business from Israel, a variety of shops, bank, travel agency and car rental service. There is an excellent coral reef just off the shore with Aquasport Dive and Watersport Centre on the site, Aquasport has a 'Hobycat' at Taba – learning to dive available for those over 12 years old for just US$180.

B *Nelson Village*, designed using natural materials to blend in with the surroundings. An extension of the Taba hotel, with a private beach, 84 rm on 3 floors all with a/c, private facilities, satellite TV, radio, telephone, tea and coffee making facilities. All rooms have 1 double and 1 single bed, garden and sea view. Lounge and coffee bar, restaurant offers Tex/Mex cuisine, also more standard fare. Guests have use of facilities of Taba hotel.

C *Salah el-Din Hotel*, Taba, T 530340-2, F 530343, 50 double well equipped chalets, located 5 km south of Taba, view of Pharaoh's Island, large portions of simple food, friendly staff.

Camping F *Basata Camping*, at Ras al-Bourg, T 500481 or 3501829, beach location 42 km south of Taba, peaceful, well run, caters for a maximum of 300 people in single/double/family huts but 80-90 is normal, especially popular with

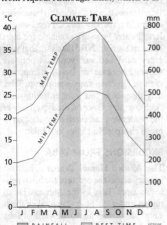

°C   **CLIMATE: TABA**   mm
40 — MAX TEMP — 800
35 — — 700
30 — — 600
25 — — 500
20 — MIN TEMP — 400
15 — — 300
10 — — 200
5 — — 100
0 — J F M A M J J A S O N D — 0

▢ RAINFALL   ▢ BEST TIME   EGTG05

Pharaoh's Island

Germans, Israelis, Egyptians, Dutch, British and French incl many diplomats from Cairo embassies, strict policy of no drugs, alcohol or loud music, only natural food, no diving which would damage the coral, communal evening meal (E£7-E£10), clean and well run communal kitchen, facilities incl a small desalination plant, showers, snorkelling, safari trips by camel and jeep, and 2 taxis for hire.

● **Places to eat**
Expensive in the *Taba Hilton* restaurants – *Palm Court*, *Marhaba Oriental*, *Casa Taba Italian*, *Surfer's Deck*. Average at the *Taba Hilton*, outdoor *Nelson Village Grill* and cheap and cheerful meals in the *Salah el-Din*, breakfast E£6, lunch E£14 and dinner E£16.

● **Banks & money changers**
Taba Hilton in Taba open 24 hrs, only bank in Egypt that changes Israeli money.

● **Entertainment**
Nightclubs: the *End of the World* and gambling casino at *Taba Hilton*. *Nelson Village Disco* under the stars, also at *Taba Hilton*.

● **Post & telecommunications**
Area code: 062.
Post Office: use *Taba Hilton* which sends mail via adjacent Eilat rather than distant Cairo.

● **Shopping**
Except for a few local food shops the only other ones are in the hotel.

● **Sports**
See *Taba Hilton* above.

● **Tour companies & travel agents**
In *Taba Hilton* are very efficient and can arrange onward travel.

● **Tourist offices**
Available at hotels.

● **Transport**
Air Nearest airport is Eilat (15 km) with direct daily flights to major European cities. (No problem at Egyptian border but customs officials at airport are very thorough.) By comparison the local Ras el-Naqb airport 39 km away only has a few flights a week from Cairo.

Road Bus: there are daily buses to and from Cairo, Sharm el-Sheikh via Nuweiba and Dahab, and Eilat across the border in Israel.

Transport into Israel

Although the checkpoints are always open it is better to cross between 0700-2100 and to avoid crossing on Friday just before the Israeli sabbath when almost all businesses close and transport ceases. Free 1-month Israeli entry visas are available for most Western tourists. **NB** Make sure that your **entry card** and **not** your passport are stamped because an Israeli stamp, and even an Egyptian entry stamp from Taba, may disqualify you from entering some Arab counties. Once on the Israeli side of the border you can catch a service-taxi or much cheaper No 15 bus into Eilat.

EXCURSIONS FROM TABA

The Ahmed Hamdi Tunnel The road journey across the centre of the Sinai peninsula from Taba to the Ahmed Hamdi tunnel under the Suez Canal takes about 4 hrs. The turnoff just to the south of Taba is the main road, which is good except for

Taba and the Realigned Border Post

🐾 Taba is an enclave of land of no more than 1 sq km on the Gulf of Aqaba seized by the Israelis in the war of 1956 but, unlike the rest of Sinai, not returned to Egypt. Assuming that the Taba strip would be forever Israeli, an international hotel complex was built there (now the *Taba Hilton*). In 1986 agitation by Egypt for a final settlement of the international border at Taba led the dispute being put to an arbitration panel of three persons.

The arbitration revealed that the border post at Ras Taba, one of fourteen put in place after the 1906 Anglo-Turkish agreement, had been moved by the Israeli side. This was discovered from searches made by specialists from the **School of Oriental & African Studies, London University,** of the Ottoman archives in Istanbul and through evidence taken from the notes of the original British survey team in the early part of the 20th century.

In one of the oddest of cases concerning the delimitation of an international border this century, it was found that the Israeli army had cut away part of the hill at Ras Taba to enable Israeli artillery to have a good sweep of the Sinai coast road as it approached the port of Eilat. At the same time the Israeli military engineers removed the border post which rested on the top of Ras Taba. This gave the Israeli government the excuse to claim that, despite Israeli maps to the contrary, the old border had always run south of the Taba strip. In 1989 the arbitrators returned Taba to Egypt, though it remains virtually an enclave with border posts on all sides.

the first 17 km which is very steep and suffers from regular flooding, to the tunnel 270 km away. Ras el-Naqb airport, 20 km further on, serves Taba and Nuweiba which is 80 km away but only has a few flights a week from Cairo. From the airport the road proceeds onto a flat plain and to both UN and Egyptian checkpoints. About 190 km from the tunnel there is a small, dirty site which includes a petrol station, mosque, restaurant, radio mast and semi-finished houses. Further along the route there are pillboxes, burnt out trucks from the fleeing Egyptian army in 1967, and lots of road building. At **Nakhl** there is a petrol station, police post, garage, mosque, as well as cafés and stalls which have fresh fruit. At a crossroads 126 km from the tunnel there are turnoffs to El-Arish (151 km) and El-Hasana (63 km). The maximum speed limit is 90 km per hour for cars and 80 km per hour for buses. About 70 km from the tunnel there is turnoff for Ras Sudr one way and El-Hasana the other way. Further on is the **Mitla Pass** and its trenches, pillboxes and other war debris, which was the site of one

of the largest tank battles in history. Closer to the tunnel there are turnoffs for Ras Sudr, Wadi el-Giddi, El-Tur and Qantara. The tunnel under the Suez Canal costs E£1.50 for cars and E£3 for buses.

Immediately after the Ahmed Hamdi Tunnel there is a crossroads to Ismailia, Suez and Cairo where there are some rather dirty cafés and a petrol station. The road to Cairo across a empty featureless desert plain passes lots of quarries, a coal stockpile and army camps, including one with candy striped huts, and follows the railway line from Suez to Cairo. After a major traffic police checkpoint the dual carriageway is a very good road. About 100 km from Cairo there is a Red Crescent station. The east of Cairo has some very large industrial works and the air becomes noticeably more polluted.

THE INTERIOR

St Catherine's Monastery (Cairo 450 km, Sharm el-Sheikh, Dahab 140 km, Nuweiba 110 km, Taba 188 km, Ras Sudr 260 km), despite its location in the heart of the

Sinai wilderness, is one of the most important tourist sites in the country. This Greek orthodox monastery located at the base of **Mount Sinai**, where God is believed to have revealed the Ten Commandments to Moses, has attracted pilgrims and visitors for centuries.

The **Burning Bush**, through which God is said to have spoken to Moses, holds religious significance for Jews, Christians and Muslims and in 337 AD **Empress Helena**, mother of **Constantine**, decreed that a sanctuary was be built around what was thought to be the site of the bush. It became a refuge for an increasing number of hermits and pilgrims who sought the wilderness of the Sinai Valley over the following centuries. Between 537 and 562, **Emperor Justinian** expanded the site considerably by building fortifications to protect the residents and adding the **Church of the Virgin** and the **Basilica of the Transfiguration**. The monastery and its community which then, as today, was controlled by the Byzantine Church was tolerated by the subsequent Muslim conquerors. The number of pilgrims dwindled until a body, claimed to be that of the Egyptian born St Catherine, was 'discovered' in the 10th century and was brought to the monastery which attracted many pilgrims during the period of Crusader occupation (1099-1270). The numbers of both pilgrims and monks, who are now restricted to Greeks mainly from the Mt Athos area, subsequently waxed and waned until today there are only 25 monks, but the thousands of international pilgrims and tourists actually make the monastery too crowded in the high season.

The road journey from Dahab to St Catherine, which is generally very good with little traffic, takes about 1½ hrs. On the way, at the top of a very steep hill there is a breathtaking view over the desert. The coaches and taxis stop here and bedouins attempt to sell fossils, sand-roses and other souvenirs. You then pass through one UN and then two Egyptian checkpoints. There is a small run down cafeteria 55 km from St Catherine, trenches (25 km), the *El-Salam hotel* (15 km), Green Lodge camping and restaurant and Masr petrol station (10 km), Morganland camping (8 km) and a bedouin village and encampment just before arriving in St Catherine.

ACCESS While all of the organized tours to St Catherine stop at the monastery itself, the normal buses services stop in the small village of St Catherine about 2 km below the monastery. **NB Climate**: St Catherine's is very cold in winter with a metre of snow a few times a year and snow sometimes until March but it is very hot in summer. Despite the environment there are no problems with water or electricity.

ST CATHERINE'S MONASTERY

Entry to the monastery, which is open Monday-Thursday and Saturday 0900-1200 but closed Friday, Sunday and public holidays is free. Visitors to the interior of the Monastery must dress modestly. Shorts are not allowed – for either men or women. There is no dress code for outside visiting. Although an official tour guide, who will explain the history and symbolism of each part of the monastery, is a bonus he is not essential if you buy the monastery's guide book in the small bookshop near the entrance.

The highlight of the walled monastery, which includes the monks' quarters and gardens which are not open to the public, is the highly decorative and incense-perfumed **St Catherine's Church** which includes **St Helena's Chapel of the Burning Bush**. The church was built between 542-551 AD in memory of **Emperor Justinian**'s wife. The building is of granite. It has a wide central nave and two side aisles reduced by the construction of side chapels and a vestry. Its 12 enormous pillars are free standing decorated with beautiful icons representing the saints which are venerated in each of the 12 months of the year. A candle is lit below the relevant icon on each saint's day. Examine the capitals for their Christian symbols. The walls, pillars and cedarwood doors of the church are all original.

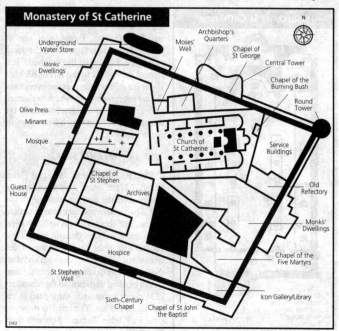

Monastery of St Catherine

Underground Water Store

Monks' Dwellings

Moses' Well

Archbishop's Quarters

Chapel of St George

Central Tower

Chapel of the Burning Bush

Round Tower

Olive Press

Minaret

Mosque

Church of St Catherine

Service Buildings

Chapel of St Stephen

Archives

Old Refectory

Guest House

Monks' Dwellings

Hospice

Chapel of the Five Martyrs

St Stephen's Well

Sixth-Century Chapel

Chapel of St John the Baptist

Icon Gallery/Library

EX62

The *iconostasis* is dated at 1612. In the apse is one of the delights of this building, a magnificent mosaic illustrating the Transfiguration. The figure of Jesus stands in the centre with Moses and Elijah on either side and Peter, James and John sitting at his feet. Around the edge are further figures identified as the apostles – and the abbot in charge at the time the monastery was built. At the far side of the north aisle is **St Helena's Chapel of the Burning Bush** which, although it was the site of the original sanctuary, was not included in Justinian's original building but was only enclosed later on. A silver plate below the altar marks the site where the bush is supposed to have stood.

West of the church is a small 11th century **Mosque** which was apparently built in order to placate the Muslim invaders and to encourage them to tolerate

the monastery. Significantly, however, the church steeple is considerably taller than the minaret of the mosque.

The **Library**, which is unfortunately closed to most of the public, is one of the monastery's most unique features with an almost unrivalled collection of precious Greek, Arabic, Syrian, Georgian, Armenian and Slavonic manuscripts reputedly second only to that of the Vatican. An extra US$8 is charged to see the library and refectory.

The monastery's small **Museum** contains a collection of the gifts presented to the monastery over the centuries. The treasures were randomly scattered throughout the monastery until their accumulated worth was calculated by Friar Pachomius who then carefully gathered and preserved them in one place but many of the more interesting items have been lost over the ages.

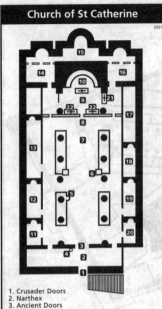

Church of St Catherine

EX61

1. Crusader Doors
2. Narthex
3. Ancient Doors
4. Holy Water
5. Pulpit
6. Archbishop's Chair
7. Basilica
8. Iconostasis
9. Holy Altar
10. Apse
11. Chapel of St Marina
12. Chapel of Sts Constantine and Helena
13. Chapel of St Antipas
14. Chapel of St James
15. Chapel of the Burning Bush
16. Chapel of Martyrs of Sinai
17. Vestry
18. Chapel of Sts Anna and Joachim
19. Chapel of St Simeon Stylites
20. Chapel of St Cosmas Damian
21. Marble Coffin of St Catherine
22. Sarcophagi of St Catherine

Because the monastery's **Cemetery** in the gardens was so small the custom was developed of storing the overflow of monks' bodies in the **Charnel House** which is in the monastery gardens. When a monk died his body was buried in the cemetery place of the oldest body which is then removed to the Charnel House. Visitors can visit this rather macabre room which is full of skeletons and skulls.

Immediately to the right of the monastery's main entrance at **Kleber's Tower**, which is about 15m high and 3m thick, is **Jacob's Well** which it is claimed has never dried up. It is supposed to be the site where the 40-year-old Moses, who was fleeing from Egypt, met one of Jethro's seven daughters called Zipporah whom he subsequently married. Just around the corner to the left of Kleber's Tower is a rather unimpressive overgrown thorny evergreen bush which is claimed to be a transplanted descendant of the **Burning Bush** from which God allegedly spoke to Moses.

MOUNT SINAI

If time permits, climb Mt Sinai (Jebel Musa), 2,285m, where Moses is alleged to have received the Ten Commandments. The view is particularly spectacular at sunset and sunrise. The shortest way is up 3,000 steps, tough going and very difficult in the dark. The stiff walk up the steep camel track, which takes about 2½ hrs, is quite rough and stout shoes and warm clothing are essential. Camels can be hired from behind the monastery E£35 one way takes you three parts of the way up in 1½ hrs. The last 700 steps you must walk takes 30 mins. Although there are refreshment stalls on the way up, which get more expensive nearer the summit, it is advisable to take at least 2 litres of water per person if making the ascent during the day but it is best to start the ascent at about 1700, or earlier in winter, in order to arrive at the summit at sunset.

A summit meeting of Christians, Jews and Muslims is planned here in 2000. Go now and avoid the rush.

MOUNT CATHERINE

At 2,642m Mt Catherine or Jebel Katrinahht is Egypt's highest peak. It is about 6 km south of Mt Sinai and is a 5-6 hrs exhausting climb. On the summit there is a small chapel with water, a 2-room hostel for overnight pilgrims and a meteorological station.

Local information
● Accommodation
A *St Catherine Tourist Village*, Wadi el-Raha, St Catherine, T/F 770221, in the Wadi el-Raha or 'Valley of Repose', unrestricted views of the

Blazing Bushes and Catherine Wheels

Mount Sinai marked the half way point of the flight of the Jews from Egypt to the 'promised land'. Moses was clearly an inspirational leader for the incident of the burning bush led him to return to Egypt to lead his people to the land of milk and honey. Despite calling down from God the 10 plagues (frogs, lice, locusts, hail and fire among them), he failed to persuade the Pharaoh to release them from their slave labour. Finally the 80-year-old Moses asked God to strike the Egyptians with the passover when the Jews marked their houses with lamb's blood and were spared the massacre of all first born children. As a result, the Pharaoh banished the 600,000 Israelite men, women and children from Egypt. Their epic journey is related in the Book of Exodus in the Bible. They were pursued by the Egyptians (drowned after the Red Sea divided to allow the Israelites across), faced starvation (rescued with manna from heaven) and thirst (saved when a spring flowed from a rock Moses had struck with his staff) and defeated an attack by the Amaleks.

On Mount Sinai, Moses received the wisdom of the Ten Commandments which have formed the code of practice for human behaviour for centuries.

The supposed site of the burning bush was developed into a monastery and in the 10th century named after Saint Catherine. According to legend Saint Catherine, who was born in AD 294 and was from a noble family in Alexandria, was a Christian convert who was martyred in the early 4th century for refusing to renounce her faith. She herself converted hundreds of people to Christianity and accused Emperor Maxentius of idolatry. When he tried to have her broken it was claimed that she shattered the spiked (Catherine) wheel by touching it, so Maxentius resorted to having her beheaded in Alexandria. Her body was alleged to have been found centuries later at Egypt's highest point on top of Mount Catherine (2,642m), where angels were said to have laid it, but others believe that the myth was created by mediaeval Western Catholicism.

monastery 2 km up the road, 130 clean twin-bed chalets of local stone the shape of a Bedouin tent, mainly European, US and Japanese guests who stay 1 night, normally full in high season, restaurant, coffee shop, gift shop, library, video hall, tennis, billiards, and table-tennis.

C *Danielli*, T 749772, F 3607750, St Catherine, 54 rm, nice grounds, simple, comfortable but not enough blankets in winter, overpriced, provides good packed lunch for climbing mountains!; **C** *El-Salam*, St Catherine Airport, St Catherine, T 771409, F 2476535, 35 rm, expensive 2-star hotel.

Cheaper accommodation at **E** *Zeitouna Camp*, T 771409, 50 double rm, and **E** *Morgan Land Village*, T 470331, with 92 rm each sleeping 3/4.

Camping There is no specific camp site at St Catherine but it is possible to spend the night on Mt Sinai to see the sunrise but, because of the altitude, its sub-zero night-time temperatures for much of the year make a torch, sleeping bag and warm clothing absolutely essential.

Hostel The hostel at the monastery, E£30+ a night for a bed in a simple and cramped dormitory, communal showers, incl simple breakfast. Reserve a room by asking at the monastery between 1700-1900, T 770945.

● **Places to eat**
Besides the more expensive hotel restaurants like *El-Safsafa* at *St Catherine's Tourist Village* there are 2 cafés serving decent food in town and the El-Monagah snack bar.

● **Banks & money changers**
Bank **Misr** branch on the main street in St Catherine town is open daily from 1000-1400 and 1800-2100.

● **Post & telecommunications**
Area code: 062.

Post Office: is opp the bank in town and open Saturday-Thursday 0800-1400.

Telephone: there is an international telephone exchange in town open from 0800-2400 nr the post office.

● **Shopping**
In the town there is the *Supermarket Katreen* and another supermarket, a grocery store, bakery, bazaar and petrol station.

● **Sports**
Mainly limited to tennis and a few indoor games at the tourist village.

● **Transport**
Air Reservations must be made well in advance for the direct Air Sinai flights between St Catherine airport, 15 km from the town, and Cairo (2 flights a week), Hurghada and Sharm el-Sheikh which offer in addition spectacular views of the Sinai peninsula.

Road Bus: there are direct buses for the 8 hrs journey between St Catherine town and Cairo's Sinai terminal via Suez and others to Dahab, Nuweiba and Sharm el-Sheikh. **Service taxis**: travellers can share the cost of hiring a 7 seat service taxi to Dahab, Sharm el-Sheikh, Taba, Suez or other towns in the peninsula, but the prices almost double once the last bus has left St Catherine.

Keen travellers/campers could extend the journey westwards to **Serbit El-Khadim** which, in the Pharaonic period was an area well known for the mining of the semi-precious stone turquoise. Here on the summit of Jebel Serabit (850m) are the ruins of the Temple of Hathor which they erected to the 'Lady of Turquoise' with a small chapel to Sopdu, who was guardian of the desert ways. The views over the desert region from here are outstanding. Other turquoise mines in the area include Jebel Maghara.

THE WEST COAST

The west coast of Sinai on the Gulf of Suez is far less attractive than the Gulf of Aqaba coast. It has been spoilt by the oil industry which, while being one of Egypt's sources of foreign exchange, has transformed this region into a mass of oil rigs and gas flares and made it unsuitable for another foreign exchange earner – tourism. The largely featureless coast has become polluted with oil industry debris and is far more interesting to the industrialist than to the tourist.

EL-TUR

Although it is the administrative capital of south Sinai the seedy and dilapidated coastal town of El-Tur, which is 108 km from Sharm el-Sheikh and 170 km from Suez, has little to commend it. The best hospitals are located here as it was the quarantine stop for pilgrims from Mecca.

● **Accommodation** E *Jolie Valley Hotel*, by Port El-Tur, T 771111, 43 rm; **E** *Lido Hotel*, Moon Beach, T 771700/Cairo T 2906496, F 771780, 32 rm.

● **Places to eat** Only the restaurants in the hotels can be rec.

● **Hospitals & medical services Ambulance**: T 770350. **Hospital**: T 770320 (0900-1400).

● **Post & telecommunications Area code**: 062.

● **Transport Road Bus**: T 770029. The most important information about El-Tur is how to get out of town. There are daily buses to Sharm el-Sheikh and Suez.

RAS SUDR

Cairo (190 km), Sharm el-Sheikh (290 km), Nuweiba (365 km), Dahab (385 km), St Catherine's (250 km), Taba (433 km), near the northern end of the Gulf of Suez is both an oil company town and the site of a noxious oil refinery but also a destination for middle class Egyptian tourists.

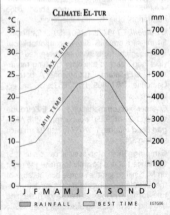

CLIMATE: EL-TUR

RAINFALL   BEST TIME   EGTG06

Places of interest Nearby sites include **El-Shatt point** (41 km), **Oyoun Moussa** (31 km), the 494m high natural pyramid at **Hammamat Pharaoun** (50 km), and the rock temple at **Sarabit el-Khadem** 'Heights of the Slave' (130 km).

• **Accommodation** Two new hotels – **D** *Mesalla Beach Resort*, T 400427, 150 rm and *Moon Beach Resort*, T 2915023, on the road out to El Tor, 52 rm, have upgraded the accommodation here, but not much; **E** *Sudr Beach Inn*, PO Box 119, Cairo, T 770752 or Cairo, T 2828113, F 770752, 20 rm with bath and balcony (12 double and 8 triples), good accommodation overlooking the Gulf of Suez, restaurant and gift shop; **E** *Ras Sudr Tourist Village*, T 770752, 12 villas, 100 chalets, and a 20 rm hotel, 2 restaurants, shops, watersports, tennis, squash and volley ball, childrens' playground, video hall, billiards, chess and table tennis, information/reservations from Misr-Sinai Tourist Company, *Misr Travel*, Tower Building, Abbassia, Cairo; **F** *Daghash Land Tourist Village*, T 777049 or Cairo, T 609672, 60 rm, located 19 km from Ras Sudr, often space available, restaurant, café, table tennis, video hall and private beach with 2 bars, information/reservations, Cairo, T 609672.

• **Places to eat** Only the restaurants in the hotels are rec.

• **Post & telecommunications Area code**: 062.

• **Sports** Some facilities at the tourist village.

• **Transport Road Bus**: the daily buses between Suez and Sharm el-Sheikh stop at Rus Sudr.

NORTHERN SINAI

Although the majority of tourists only visit the Gulf of Aqaba coastline and St Catherine's Monastery, the northern part of the peninsula has a number of attractions both in El-Arish and along the 210 km Mediterranean coastline which stretches from Port Said to the Israeli border at Rafa. Unfortunately, while the region is beginning to be appreciated by Egyptian tourists, most foreigners only see the area from the bus window as they speed to or from the Israeli border.

The main beaches on the north coast of Sinai are at El-Arish, Oruba, further east, beside Rafa near the border and Lake Bardweel really a lagoon on the central north coast famous for its fishing.

If you have your own transport visit **Pelusium**. This ancient city was situated on a now dry distributary of the River Nile. It guarded the access from the east and acted as a customs post. It is mentioned in the Bible as "the stronghold of Egypt", the Persians came through while both Pompey and Baldwin I ended their days here in tragic circumstances. The ruins date from Roman times and are open 0900-1600 daily.

EL-ARISH

This town 180 km east of the Suez Canal is the governorate capital of North Sinai and is noted for its 30 km of palm-lined beach of fine white sand. From the bus station in Midan Baladiya it is a 2-3 km walk or minibus ride along the main road north to the beach which is the site of most of the hotels. This area is very popular at weekends. Al-Nakheel is the best beach at El-Arish with palm trees extending the length of the beach. Also try Al-Masa'ed and Rumana.

Places of interest You can visit **El-Arish Castle**, which is located on a plateau to the southwest of the town on the remains of an ancient pharaonic castle. Otherwise life in town revolves around the beach. Out on the Rafa road there is a small **museum** of handicrafts and stuffed Sinai wildlife but its opening hours are very irregular and the exhibits disappointing. Thursday market (Souq el-Khamees) bedouin market in the oldest part of town selling north Sinai embroidered cloth, plants, produce, bedouin handicrafts.

• **Accommodation** Hotels along the beach range from the luxurious **A** *Hotel Egoth Oberoi*, T 351321/7, F 352352, Sharia Fouad Abu Zakry, sports and recreation facilities incl health spa, tennis and squash courts, windsurfing, pedal boats, private beach, which is the only place in town which sells alcohol to a

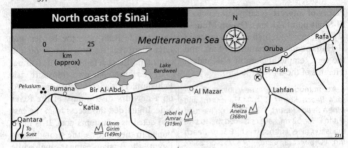

number of more simple tourist hotels. During the July-September high season it may be difficult to find a room without booking. **C** *Semiramis Hotel*, Sharia Fouad Abu Zakry, T 344166, F 344168, 90 rm; **D** *Sinai Beach Hotel*, Sharia Fouad Abu Zakry, T 341713, 30 rm some with sea view; **D** *Sinai Sun Hotel*, Sharia 23 July, T 341855, all rooms with a/c and shower; **E** *Mecca Hotel*, Sharia Fouad Abu Zakry, T 344909, 36 rm, used almost exclusively by Egyptians; **E** *Zahret Sinai*, Sharia Fouad Abu Zakry, T 340051, 40 rm. **Youth Hostel** adjacent to Governorate Building. **Camping** It is possible to camp on the beach with permission from the police. *El-Arish Camping*, about 7 km west of the town has 2-man tents or you can pitch your own.

● **Places to eat** Besides the hotels there is an outdoor restaurant nr the *Egoth Oberoi* and a number of cheap restaurants and sheesha (water-pipe) cafés in and around Midan Baladiya such as *Maxim's* on the beach or *Sammar* and *Aziz*, T 340345, highly rec.

● **Banks & money changers** Bank of Alexandria, T 40169, Misr Bank, T 40036, National Bank of Egypt, T 40414, and Sinai National Bank for Development, T 40952, in town and the main hotels will also change money.

● **Entertainment** Besides the main hotels there is almost no nightlife except the cafés in Midan Baladiya.

● **Hospitals & medical services Ambulance**: T 340123. **Hospital**: *El-Arish General Hospital*, Sharia el-Geish, T 340010. **Pharmacies**: *Pharmacy Fouad*, T 341541, open 0800-2400 except Friday.

● **Post & telecommunications Area code**: 068. **Post Office**: the post office and the international telephone exchange are located off Sharia 23rd July between the *Sinai Sun Hotel* and Midan Baladiya.

● **Shopping** There are some rather sleazy tourist shops on Sharia 23rd July but for quality items it is better to bargain at the Bedouin market on Thursday.

● **Tour companies & travel agents** *Misr Travel Office*, T 41241/41049.

● **Tourist offices** There is an Egyptian General Authority for the Promotion of Tourism office in El-Arish, T 41016, in the same office as the Tourist Police station, T 41016, which is located just before the beach on Sharia Fouad Abu Zakry.

● **Useful addresses** The main **police station** and **hospital** are on Sharia el-Geish on the way to Rafa. **Police**: T 340049 and T 340202; **Tourist Police**: T 341016.

● **Transport Air** There are two Air Sinai flights a week from Cairo on Sunday and Thursday, takes 1 hr. The airport is along the Bir Lahfan road to the south of the town. **Road Bus**: there are frequent daily buses between El-Arish and Cairo (6 hrs), which should be booked the day before, and others to the Suez Canal cities of Qantara and Ismailia. Bus station off Midan Baladiya nr the mosque. **Service taxis**: to/from Midan Koulali Terminal in Cairo (takes 5-6 hrs, E£20); Midan el Gomhurriya in Ismailia (takes 3 hrs, E£10) or by the Suez Canal in Qantara (takes 2½ hrs, E£8). Taxis to Cairo leave early morning. **Taxis**: run from here to the beach.

Transport into Israel

There are very frequent buses and service taxis east to the international border with Israel at **Rafa**, 41 km from El-Arish, open winter 0900-1700 and summer 1000-1800. It is best to avoid crossing on Friday.

Whenever you cross it is advisable to leave El-Arish in the morning to avoid getting caught in the Gaza Strip during the 2000-0400 curfew. There is a free 1 month Israeli visa for most Western tourists. **NB** Make sure that your **entry card** and **not** your passport are stamped because an Israeli stamp, and even an Egyptian entry stamp from Rafa, disqualifies you from entering some Arab countries. Occasionally there are major luggage searches of tourists but this is usually reserved for Arab travellers. Once on the Israeli side of the border you can catch a service-taxi into the Israeli side of the divided town of Rafa and then on to Khan Yunis and Gaza City's Palestine Square from where there are service taxis to Jerusalem and Tel Aviv.

The Red Sea Coast and Eastern Desert

THE EASTERN DESERT lies in a belt between the River Nile and the Red Sea which stretches for about 1,250 km from the southern end of the Suez Canal to the Sudanese border. The slowly widening major fault line running along the whole length of the Red Sea has created the Red Sea Mountains, including Jebel Shaayib ell-Banat (2,184m), which are the highest in Egypt outside the Sinai peninsula. Most visitors simply traverse this scorchingly hot, inhospitable and virtually uninhabited region to get to the Red Sea Coast which is one of the fastest growing tourist regions in the country. The mountain region is very remote and the occasional ibex and gazelle can still be seen. The red colour of these mountain ranges is said to have inspired the name for the adjacent sea. As the closest tropical sea to Europe the Red Sea is the perfect choice for divers and snorkellers. The tropical waters offer an amazing variety of marine fauna – with over 1,000 species of fish feeding on the coral. The species of flora, though less in number, are no less in interest. This is indeed an underwater paradise. The comfortable temperatures of the sea all year round encourage such visitors.

The Ministry of Tourism is trying to encourage tourists to visit not just Cairo, Luxor and Aswan but also other regions of the country. This will reduce the burden, particularly during the high winter season, on the overloaded infrastructure of the main tourist centres and spread the financial benefits of the tourist industry more evenly throughout the country. For this reason the ministry is promoting the Sinai peninsula, which is already a major tourist destination, the Western Desert and, above all, Hurghada on the Red Sea coast. Nevertheless this region is not completely isolated and trips are available westward to the Luxor region of the River

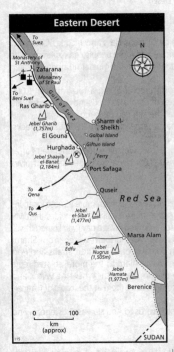

Eastern Desert

To Suez

Monastery of St Anthony
Zafarana
Monastery of St Paul
To Beni Suef
Ras Gharib

Gulf of Suez

Jebel Gharib (1,757m)
El Gouna
Sharm el-Sheikh
Golbal Island
Hurghada
Giftun Island
Jebel Shaayib el-Banat (2,184m)
Ferry
Port Safaga

To Qena

Quseir

Red Sea

To Qus
Jebel el-Siba'i (1,477m)

Marsa Alam

To Edfu
Jebel Nugrus (1,505m)

Jebel Hamata (1,977m)
Berenice

0   100
km
(approx)

SUDAN

---

with the exception of fresh water which is supplied from the Nile valley, are largely self-contained. They employ workers from the major cities. Unfortunately, although there are many very good hotels, in its dash for growth the government has allowed the 'get-rich-quick' private sector to erect some less attractive accommodation. In truth the area has been developed too quickly since the first constructions in 1992 and frequently without adequate controls and has thus repeated the mistakes of some resorts on the northern Mediterranean shores but with maturity the region has gained its own character. While Hurghada's facilities undoubtedly offer good cheap beach holidays it has been partially achieved by removing any trace of local Egyptian culture. The Egyptian government has pledged considerable investment to create further leisure facilities here. Hurghada itself has about 50,000 permanent residents employed in tourism and its related activities, in fishing and in boat construction and repair. There are two harbours, one for the local fishing boats and in the other, the marina, boats associated with sporting activities, excursions and the ferry to Sharm el-Sheikh.

Nile or north to the monasteries of St Paul and St Anthony and even to Suez and Cairo. See the local agencies for a full range of excursions.

HURGHADA

529 km southeast of Cairo, 395 km south of Suez and 299 km northeast of Luxor, Hurghada lies on the Red Sea about half way between Suez and the Sudanese border. It extends along the coast for 25 km. In some ways it is an ideal location for a new tourist development because it is in a virtually uninhabited region, its origins a small fishing village, and a long way from the Islamic fundamentalist strongholds. This means that the hotels and their guests do not overburden the local infrastructure or offend the sensibilities of the local population. Instead hotels and holiday villages have been built which,

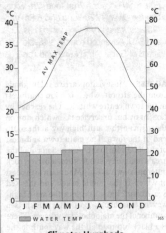

°C
40
35
30
25
20
15
10
5
0

AV MAX TEMP

°C
80
70
60
50
40
30
20
10
0

J F M A M J J A S O N D

WATER TEMP

Climate: Hurghada

Diving in the Red Sea

Diving here was pioneered in the 1950s by Dr Hans Hass and Jacques Cousteau. Today the popularity of this sport means more and more people can experience the wonders of this special environment and that greater and greater numbers threaten this fragile habitat.

A mixture of deep water fish and surface coral giving a total of over 1,000 species of fish to observe, some 500 species of coral and thousands of invertebrate reef dwellers. The clear waters ensure that the fish can be 'caught' on film.

Sites to visit include sheer drop-offs, sea grass meadows, coral encrusted wrecks, gullies and pinnacles, a new world.

Water temperatures vary. A 3 mm or 5 mm wetsuit is recommended for all year but something thicker for winter wear (18°C) or a prolonged series of dives may be needed.

Liveboard

This method of accessing the dive sights permits divers to reach more remote locations in smaller groups so less disturbance is caused at these locations. It provides the diver with accommodation and the opportunity for unlimited dives a day with limited travel.

Most liveboard agents extend all year over the northern waters from Sharm el-Sheikh and Hurghada to Ras Mohammed, Gulf of Suez, Tiran Straits and Port Sudan. In summer they chart south from Marsa Alam to the more isolated reefs and islands. Summer is the best time to dive in the south when the winds and currents are not so strong and the water temperature (here at the tropic of Cancer) reaches about 30°C.

Boats from Hurghada tend to head northwards to Abu Nawas, Thistegorm and Ras Mohammed or southwards to Safaga.

Accommodation

Emperor Divers – 20-25m long, limited facilities, civilized and comfortable with tolerance.

Emperor Pegasus – 24m long, 7m wide, max 16 persons in twin cabins.

Golden Diver – 22m long and 6.5m wide, 14 persons in twin cabins.

Crusade Travel – VIP One which has 7 cabins, with private facilities, professional crew and PADI Advanced courses available – departs from Sharm el Maya – to Straits of Tira, Straits of Gubal, Abu Nuwas and Thistlegorm and to Ras Mohammed marine park.

ACCESS Most visitors arrive at Hurghada from the airport, which is 6 km southwest of the town centre which can be reached by taxi, or by bus or service taxi which stop on the main north-south 'highway' at the south end of the town. The main town and most of the hotels lie to the west and north of the area's main physical feature, a barren rock outcrop known as Ugly Mountain to the east of which is the public beach and the Red Sea. About 2 km south along the main highway is Hurghada's port after which is a number of the major holiday villages. There is a black top road all the way south to the Sudanese border.

Although it is easy to walk around the relatively compact town it is necessary, when trying to get to the port or the holiday villages to the south of town, to take cheap local buses and minibuses or the town's taxis which are amongst the most expensive in the country. Alternatively cars and bicycles can be hired from some of the hotels.

Places of interest

This is not just another place to toast on the beach. It is now an international resort for water sports – if you can do it in the water, you can do it here. A few hotels have very fine coral gardens actually on their

From Sharm el-Sheikh – *Ghazala I, Ghazala II* and *Freedom II*.
From Hurghada – *Emperor Fleet, Golden Diver, Alexandria, Sabrina, Amira* and *Loveman*.
From Marsa Alam – *Shadia*. Sailing out of Marsa Alum gives speedier access to the southern area.

Diving Prices

6/12 days diving	US$200-400
5/10 days diving	US$175-350

Diving courses

The prices quoted for PADI diving courses (for which the minimum age is 12 years) should include all diving equipment and materials for the course which should take just five days, three days of theory and work in confined water/deep swimming pool to put the theory into practice and two days in the ocean completing four open-water dives. After which a new underwater world waits you.

There are three main sections:
● theory – written test after reading the manual and watching a training video
● pool work – confined water training
● open water qualifying dives – in the sea

Courses requiring certification are an extra US$30 per certificate for which you will require two passport photographs. You will also need a log book (on sale in diving resorts) to record your dives (US$8).

Open Water Certification	US$230-275
Advanced Open Water Certification	US$190-210
Medic First Aid	US$100
Rescue Diver Certification	US$300-320
Dive Master Certification	US$530-580
Also Under Water Naturalist	US$50
Night Diver	US$60
Multi-level Diver	US$65
Reef Diver	US$65
Wreck Diver	US$100

site and there are plenty of coral islands offshore from which to study the hidden life below the warm blue waters. The best hotels with coral gardens are *Safir, Arabia Beach, Three Corners* and *Shedwan*. In Hurghada life revolves around the beach, watersports and nightlife. All-day boat excursions to **Giftun Island**, now often overcrowded with boats anchored offshore, are available from most hotels which usually add a 20%-25% commission to include rental of snorkelling equipment. Expect your tour to include a fish barbecue and perhaps a trip in a glass bottomed boat.

The same operators, including Flying Dolphin Sea Trips, Nefertiti Diving Centre and Sunshine Sea Trips also organize longer boat trips including 3-day trips to **Gobal Island**, overnight excursions to Giftun, and expeditions to the deeper reefs such as the **House of Sharks** (20 km south) where the experienced divers can see hammerheads and tiger sharks and other exotic marine life. To view marine life and keep dry there is the Finnish-built a/c 44 seat **Sinbad Submarine** offering a 2 hrs round trip including 1 hr underwater which should be booked the day before.

Hurghada Islands, Reefs & Dive Sites

Dive Sites:

1. Abu Ramada North	12. Gota Abu Ramada
2. Abu Ramada South (The Aquarium)	13. Little Giftun
	14. Shaab Disha
3. Careless Reef	15. Shaab Eshta
4. El Aruk	16. Shaab Farasha
5. El Fandur	17. Shaab Sabina
6. Erg Abu Ramada	18. Shaab Tiffany
7. Erg Sabina	19. Shaab Torf
8. Erg Somaya	20. Shaab Rur
9. Fanous East	21. Stone Beach
10. Fanous West	22. Turtle Bay
11. Giftun Police	23. Um Gamar North
	24. Um Gamar South

about the marine life of the area with stuffed examples of coral reef fish, shark, manta rays and associated bird life as well as samples of coral and shells. Entrance daily 0800-1700 E£5 for this and its adjacent **Red Sea Aquarium**. The **Aquarium** on Sharia el Corniche adjacent to *Three Corners Village* is quite small but has live specimens in well marked tanks and is well worth the E£5. Open daily 0900-2100. The ruined Roman settlement of Jebel Abu Dukhan about 55 km west of Hurghada may prove of interest. Hire suitable transport, take sensible provisions and hire a local guide.

Much further afield, back north towards Cairo on highway H44, hidden in the folds of the Red Sea Mountains, are two neighbouring isolated monasteries, **St Anthony's** and **St Paul's**, the oldest monasteries in Egypt (also on itineraries from Beni Suef or Suez and from Minya, Assiut and Luxor.) Pilgrim tours to these monasteries are organized through the YMCA in Cairo, T 917360, and by the Coptic Patriachate in Cairo, T 960025. Day tours there with lunch are offered by a number of Hurghada travel agents including Misr Travel. Otherwise a group can negotiate a single price with a local taxi in Hurghada. Provided it is not too hot and you take enough water and only light luggage it is also possible to get out of a Beni Suef to Zafarana service taxi or the Hurghada to Cairo or Suez bus at the turn offs for the respective monasteries, and then hitch or walk the remaining distance. For St Paul's turn off the north-south desert road approximately 24 km south of Zafarana at the small blue and white signs indicating the monastery and follow the rough track for about 13 km. For St Anthony's drive inland from Zafarana and after 32 km turn left at the blue and white sign which indicates the monastery. There are still 15 km more to go. Please note that advanced booking is required for accommodation in these monasteries.

Transfer by boat 30 mins, out to submarine, goes down to 22m with diver in front attracting fish with food (not a recommended procedure). Carries 44 passengers. Reservations on T 444688-90. Trips every hour between 0900 and 1600. Price US$50 for adults and US$25 for children under 12. **Aquascope** has a deep hull with glass sides. Transfer to it from the Marine Sports Club near the *Grand Hotel*. It travels to Magawish Island and back. Operates 1000-1400 and each trip takes 2 hrs, costs US$40, reservations necessary, T 548249. **Marine Museum** is about 7 km to the north of the town centre and is associated with the *National Institute of Oceanography and Fisheries*. A good place to start to learn

Wrecked ships

🐟 By far the most wrecks are to be found around the dangerous Straits of Gubal at the mouth of the Gulf of Suez. Access easiest from Hurghada or Sharm el-Sheikh.

SS Thistlegorm, was a 126m long, 5,000-tonne English cargo ship which was damaged on 6 October 1941 by a long range German bomber and sank without firing a defensive shot or delivering her goods to the awaiting British troops fighting in the North Africa campaign. Nine of the crew lost their lives. She lies on the massive Shaab Ali reef, on the northern edge of the Straits of Gubal, under 30m of water just as she went down complete with an incredible cargo of armaments. There are jeeps, trucks, motorbikes, tanks, train cars, a locomotive and an 'explosive' collection of ammunition ranging from rifle bullets to mortar shells, along with uniforms and regulation boots. She was 'discovered' by Jacques Cousteau in 1956 but visits by casual divers only began in the last 5 years.

S/S Dunraven, a 82m sail-equipped steam ship has been lying on the reef just south of Beacon rock since 1876 and is now covered with corals and each year looks more attractive. She lies bottom up with the bow 15m and the stern (propeller still in place) 28m below the surface. Her journey from Bombay to Newcastle on Tyne remains incomplete.

Carnatic, once a 90m luxurious Greek steamship is a sad tale. With a passenger list numbering 230 and a cargo of gold reported to be then worth £40,000 she hit the reef at Shab Abu Nuas on 13 September 1869. The conditons were calm, the ship remained upright and life for the passengers remained as normal until the vessel snapped in two without warning. Survivors were taken to Shadwan island but 27 people were drowned. £32,000 worth of gold was rescued, but where is the rest? Perhaps it is still there waiting for the lucky diver.

Giannis D was another Greek vessel, 99m long and full of cargo. She ran aground on the reef at Shab Abu Nuas on 19 April 1983 and later broke in two and sank. The shallowest remains are just 8m under the surface allowing easy access to the bridge and the engine room in the stern.

Chrisoula K was a 106m Greek cargo ship carrying Italian tiles which struck the northwest corner of Shab Abu Nuas reef at full speed. The wreck remains upright but at an angle with the bow nearer the surface. The hull and much of the superstructure can be visited with safety but the badly damaged bow section should be avoided in rough weather.

St Anthony's Monastery (open daily 0900-1700 except during Lent and between 25 November-7 January), known locally as Deir Amba Antonyus is the more important. It has recently reopened to the public having been closed for a year for cleaning and restoration of the ceiling and entrances to the church. In particular the fabulous wall paintings have been carefully preserved. St Anthony, (251-356 AD), was born in the small village of **Koma al Arus**. He became a hermit after he was orphaned at 18 just before the height of the persecution against the Christians by emperor Diocletian (284-305 AD). By 313 AD not only was Christianity tolerated but it had also been corrupted by becoming the state religion. This led to increasing numbers of hermits following Anthony's example and seeking isolation in desert retreats (see St Catherine's monastery, page 391 and El-Fayoum, page 167). After his death, at the reported age of 105, the location of his grave was kept secret but a small chapel was erected which became the foundation of the monastery. St John the Short sought refuge at the monastery 200 years later and died there.

In the course of its history it has been subject to attacks from the bedouin tribes in the 8th and 9th centuries and the Nasir al-Dawla who destroyed it in the 11th century. It was restored in the 12th century by monks from throughout the Coptic world, only to be attacked again in the 15th century when the monks were massacred and the buildings badly damaged by rebellious servants. Syrian monks were sent to rebuild it in the mid-16th century and it was then inhabited by a mixture of Coptic, Ethiopian and Syrian monks. Its importance rose and many 17th-19th century Coptic patriarchs were chosen from amongst its monks: by the 18th century it was receiving increasing numbers of European visitors. The result has been that the 5-church monastery has developed into a large and virtually self-sufficient modern village which draws water from an ancient spring and grows most of its own food, mills its own grain and bakes its own bread. Rituals observed here have hardly changed in the last 16 centuries.

St Anthony's Church, parts of which date back to the 13th century, is the oldest church in the complex. It consists of a central nave, two side chapels and an antechamber. While inside try to identify the apostles in the picture on the south wall! There are four other churches in the complex. **St Mark's Church** dates from 1766 and is reputed to contain the relics of St Mark the Evangelist in a chest on the north wall.

The whole complex is enormous with the outer walls spanning 2 km. In addition to the churches and chapels there is a library which contains over 1,700 hand written manuscripts, a large garden, flour mills and a bakery.

Cave of St Anthony, 276m above and 2 km northeast of the monastery, is a steep 1-2 hrs walk but the view alone from the cave, 690m above the Red Sea, justifies the climb. The cave, where St Anthony is supposed to have spent the last 25 years of his life, consists of a terrace, chamber, tunnel and balcony. The decorations on the walls are mediaeval graffiti often complemented by more recent additions in the shape of supplications stuck into the cracks of the walls by visiting pilgrims.

The smaller **Monastery of St Paul**, (open daily 0900-1700 except during Lent and 25 November-7 January), which lies to the southeast of St Anthony's monastery, and is reached via the main coastal road, was built around the cave where St Paul the Theban (228-348 AD) spent his life. Although the dates do not actually match, he is supposed to have fled the persecution of **Decius** (249-251 AD) and arrived in the eastern Desert from Alexandria at the age of 16. He is the earliest hermit on record and was visited by St Anthony to whom he gave a tunic of palm leaves. St Paul apparently acknowledged him as his spiritual superior and St Anthony's Monastery has always overshadowed that of St Paul both theologically and architecturally.

The larger of the two churches is dedicated to St Michael and there are two sanctuaries. The south one is dedicated to St John the Baptist where a strange 18th century gilded icon depicts the saint's head on a dish. The **Church of St Paul** contains the actual cave where he lived and what are claimed to be his relics which were preserved during the raids on the monastery. On the third floor of the keep is the **Church of the Virgin** which is unfortunately closed to the public because its wooden floor is dangerous.

Local information
● Accommodation

Price guide:		
AL US$150+	**D**	US$25-50
A US$100-150	**E**	US$10-25
B US$75-100	**F**	under US$10
C US$50-75		

There are many officially registered hotels and many other non-registered ones and new ones are being erected all the time. Although most visitors pre-book their accommodation as part of a package with their flight there should be no problem, except perhaps during the winter high season, for independent travellers to find a room. All of the hotels have roof tanks to store fresh water which is piped in from the Nile Valley but, depending on their capacity and electricity supplies, there can be problems with the water provisions at certain times. If the promised tourist developments along the coast towards Safaga do go ahead it will be necessary to build at least one desalination plant because the water supply is the main obstacle to any major expansion in tourist numbers in the area. There are 98 good quality hotels listed in the latest tourist information literature. Here is our selection:

AL Conrad International Resort, T 443250-6, F 443258-9, just 10 mins from airport and 15 mins from downtown areas, has shuttle bus to centre, many restaurants – *La Palma* for breakfast and buffet dinner; Chinese menu in *Ginger House*; El Khan for local flavour and colour; Sunrise pool-side bar; *Café Trottoir* a French style coffee house overlooking gardens and sea; *Posidon* for fish and sea food, disco bar and *Trocadero* piano bar for relaxation. Sports incl volleyball, a huge pool, billiards, 2 all-weather tennis courts, basketball, health club, with all usual facilities, 260 rm all with sea view and 9 special 4 bedroomed villas, hair dryer, mini bar, satellite TV, telephone, money exchange, shops. same day laundry, medical clinic. Also diving centre. Very friendly staff; **AL Hurghada Hilton**, T 442116-8, F 442113, 10-15 mins from airport and from town centre, good range of high standard facilities, 161 rm located round the main pool and nr the beach, 40 garden rm in the hotel block on the desert side of the road all with a/c, bath/shower. All Hilton facilities, free day time shuttle to town centre, 2 pools, private marina, tennis, squash, health club, dive centre. Selection of restaurants, bars, tennis, pool. Good service one would expect from this chain of hotels; **AL Intercontinental**, T 443911, F 443910, highly rec as the best in town – and one of the best in Egypt, Very new, opened 1996, secluded bay, all rooms have bath, a/c, TV, telephone, minibar and sea view from terrace, large pool, 3 restaurants, bars, health club, 3 floodlit tennis courts, 2 squash courts, billiards, medical centre, horse riding, shops, diving centre. – sheer luxury; **AL Marriott**, T 443950, F 443970, tranquil and relaxed, all rooms have a/c, bath, TV, mini bar and balcony, large pool, 3 bars, shops, water sport and dive centre, health club, 2 floodlit tennis courts, 2 a/c squash courts; **AL Sonesta Beach**, PO Box 18, T 547934-6, F 547933, 120 rm, new, private beach, 3 restaurants, good food, guests are 80% German and 20% British tour groups, *Sonesta Diving Centre* with 8 instructors, easy access to beach for disabled, rec as one of the best hotels in Hurghada.

A Coral Beach Village, Km 22, Hurghada-Safaga Rd, T 442160-2, F 443577, 178 rm; **A Grand Hotel**, T 443748/9, F 443577, just 10 mins drive from airport, on own sandy beach, 549 rm, all have balcony/terrace, standard rooms have shower, superior rooms are larger and have bath and shower, several restaurants, coffee shop, bars, disco, tennis, health club, water sports on beach, very comfortable and lively beach resort; **A Intercontinental**, T 443911, F 443910, 285 a/c rm with terrace and sea view, **all** facilities incl casino and health club; **A Magawish Tourist Village**, south of the airport, T 442620-2, F 442759, 314 rm, excellent standard, private bay and beach to south of port, offers all the normal facilities plus a wide range of watersports and children's activities; **A Sheraton**, T 442000-2, F 442333, 130 rm, to south of town, 8 km from airport, 65 rm in distinctive circular main building, 9 pool-side cabanas and 10 2-storey 4 rm chalets on two very good beaches, all luxury facilities, 3 restaurants, bars, large pool, tennis, watersports, boat cruises, glass bottomed boat, fishing trips and barbecue; **A Sofitel Club**, T 447261-69, F 447260, El Corniche, directly on beach, just 20 mins drive from airport, 312 rm with balcony, many interconnecting, most have sea view, all facilities, various restaurants, bars, disco, fitness club, spa with jacuzzi and steam bath, tennis, squash, shops, outdoor amphitheatre for entertainments, kids club, pool, horse riding. Free activities incl archery, gymnastics, kayaking, water gym. To pay – water skiing, wind surfing, catamaran sailing, ideal for families, very cosmopolitan. Restaurants incl *The Terrace* with German food, German music and German beer, also *O'Reilly's Irish Pub* with Irish beer (Guinness) and Irish food.

B Arabia Beach Tourist Village, T 441790, F 441792, 9 km from centre, 348 rm, 700 beds, very large, well equipped, new, mainly German guests, saltwater pools, tennis, squash, courts, jetski and water-skiing, fitness centre, *Nautico Diving Centre* with 6 instructors; **B Hilton Villas** on desert side of the road opp main Hilton, 22

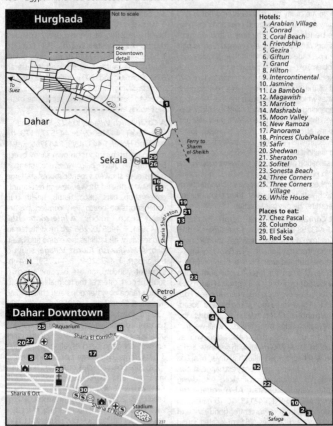

Hurghada

Not to scale

To Suez

Dahar

see Downtown detail

Sekala

Ferry to Sharm el-Sheikh

Sharia Sheraton

Petrol

Dahar: Downtown

Aquarium

Sharia El Corniche

Sharia 6 Oct

Sharia El Nasr

Stadium

To Safaga

N

Hotels:
1. Arabian Village
2. Conrad
3. Coral Beach
4. Friendship
5. Gezira
6. Giftun
7. Grand
8. Hilton
9. Intercontinental
10. Jasmine
11. La Bambola
12. Magawish
13. Marriott
14. Mashrabia
15. Moon Valley
16. New Ramoza
17. Panorama
18. Princess Club/Palace
19. Safir
20. Shedwan
21. Sheraton
22. Sofitel
23. Sonesta Beach
24. Three Corners
25. Three Corners Village
26. White House

Places to eat:
27. Chez Pascal
28. Columbo
29. El Sakia
30. Red Sea

2-storey villas with 4 bedrooms, 3 bathrooms (shower) and 2 lounges and a kitchen sleeping up to 12 people, built round the second pool, bar plus full use of all facilities at *Hilton Hotel*, excellent value for groups. See Hurghada Hilton for more details; **B** *Mashrabia Village*, Sharia Sheraton, T 443330-1, F 443344, 140 rm, very good Moorish style 4-star hotel, located to south of port, 3 pools, parasailing and excellent watersports, guests 75% German; **B** *Safir*, El Corniche, T 442901-3, F 442904, on its own beach-front lagoon, 10 mins drive from airport, 123 rm with usual facilities, variety of restaurants, bars, shops, billiards, pool with sun deck and a marina with aqua sports centre, a lively hotel, comfortable.

C *Giftun Village*, T 442666-7, F 442666, 391 comfortable bungalows set in a vast private sandy beach a little out of town, pool, squash, tennis, all water sports are free except diving, windsurfing and tennis lessons, main restaurant provides buffet meals and there are bars and discos for evening entertainment. Barakuda Dive centre within the hotel; **C** *Jasmine Holiday Village*, 6 km south of airport, T 442442, F 442441, 362 rm, good standard, so large that it is a long walk from the main building to the beach. Has own diving centre; **C** *Three Corners Village*, El Corniche, T 547816-7, F 547514, Belgian management, central location, situated on a beautiful sandy beach, 136 rm with magnificent views and good facilities, 2 restaurants,

2 bars, fresh water pool, dive centre, windsurfing centre, volley ball, minigolf. Use of beach E£10 per day for non-guests.

D *Gezira*, off Sharia El Bahr, T 447785, F 443708, 30 good rm built around a courtyard, located in northeast of town nr the poor public beach, restaurant, bar and discotheque; **D** *La Bambola*, El Corniche, T 44085, 56 en suite rm with balconies, clean, good, up-market, highly rec budget hotel, located in town centre, 200m from beach, restaurant, rooftop bar, pool, barbecue, discotheque; **D** *Moon Valley*, Sharia Sheraton, T 440074, 30 rm, former backpackers retreat which moved up-market, located to south of port, private beach, diving courses around a small coral reef; **D** *Princess Club/Palace*, T 443100, F 443109, 160 spacious rm, 2 separate parts directly opp one another about 3 km south of town, *Palace* offers better accommodation than the cheaper *Club*, both offer good service, cool, relaxing atmosphere, main building has European and Egyptian buffet restaurants, eat also at hotel's private beach or by main swimming pool. The *Fox and Hounds* serves drinks and the *Vienna* serves snacks, bar, shops, bank, squash, tennis, (floodlit), gym, pool, private beach, windsurfing with instruction, hire of jetskis, waterskiing, pedalos, British managed *Red Sea Scuba School* located in Princess Village, *Emperor Divers* located within the complex; **D** *Shedwan Golden Beach*, T 447044, F 448045, 152 rm, reasonable standard, town centre location, restaurant, bar, disco, banking, private beach, pool, tennis, squash, dive centre, guests mainly French, Belgian and German.

E *Friendship Village*, T 443100-2, F 447800, 129 rm, budget hotel, use of facilities at *Princess Club*, large open-air restaurant, pizzeria, shop and laundry service, clean rooms, 2 tennis courts, pool table, doctor on call; **E** *Mena House*, T 442303, 20 rm, budget hotel which caters mainly for students, restaurant, bar, oriental cabaret and belly dancing, private beach, windsurfing, diving with multi-lingual instructors, and day trips to Giftun Island.

F *New Ramoza*, Hurghada, 43 rm with a/c or fans and balconies, good value, popular with students, small private beach, TV lobby, and discotheque; The *Old Ramoza*, just next door, has 24 rm with fans, communal showers, guests are students or Egyptians; *Panorama Hotel*, T 447890, F 443045, poor views but what's in a name! Clean and very cheap, excellent service, use of pool at *Three Corners Village*, good food; **F** *Sunshine Hotel*, T 441463, located off main road nr minibus stand, cheap and tatty but clean

community style hotel with shared kitchen and showers, restaurant and diving centre, has been highly rec; **F** *White House*, Sheraton, T 443688, nr old harbour, very clean, up-market budget hotel, German owned, 45 comfortable a/c rm with bath and balconies, decent restaurant, TV lounge, guests can use facilities of *Giftun Village* which is a short taxi ride away – for divers this transfer is free. There are numerous small, cheap, unclassified hotels too.

Camping There are so many cheap hotels that camping is unnecessary. The site most rec is the *National Youth Camp*, 5 km north of town. **BEWARE If camping on the coast, large areas of shoreline are still mined, enter fenced-off areas at your peril**.

Youth hostels *New Tourist Centre*, T 442432, 45 beds, kitchen, overnight fee E£5 incl breakfast.

● **Places to eat**
Besides the hotels there are a number of places to eat in Hurghada.

♦ ♦ ♦ : *Lacost de Mirette*, beach restaurant.

♦ ♦ : *Chez Pascal*, Belgium run restaurant, fresh lobster, seafood and pizzas, adjacent to *Shedwan*; *El Sakia* in *Sekala*, T 442497, fish specialities – choose your own from the pond, oriental meals too, highly rec for the atmosphere; *Felfel*, Sharia Sheraton, Egyptian food, T 442410; *Lagoona* at *Hilton Resort*, a fish restaurant and international dishes, open aspect gives breathtaking views, open daily 1930-2330, T 443567; *Portofino* Italian seafood and specialities, by General Hospital, Downtown, T 546250; *Sharivari Bavarian Restaurant*, Hurghada downtown.

There are lots of ♦ restaurants, cafés and food stalls in the centre of town of which the best are probably the *Red Sea Restaurant*, for good fish dishes; *Columbo Restaurant* at the south end of Sharia Abdel Aziz Mustafa and *Golden Spur Restaurant*, steaks and burgers and Mexican food, opp *Marriott Hotel* T 444414.

Fast food outlets incl: *Rossi Pizzeria*, Sekala, T 446012; *Pizza Hut* and *KFC* on village road beside *Sindbad*.

● **Bars**
At the last count there were almost 100 bars in Hurghada. They incl: *Cheers* open 24 hrs at the *Shedwan Hotel*; *Peanuts Bar* next to *Empire Hotel*; *The Pub*, Hilton Resort with a variety of draught beers, and local drinks, open 1700-0200, T 443567; *Daoud's Pub and Indian restaurant*

– authentic Indian food, many vegetarian dishes; *Fisherman's Pub* in *Giftun Village*.

● **Banks & money changers**
Commercial International Bank in front of *Grand Hotel*. Other banks on the main road in Hurghada are **Bank of Alexandria**, **Banque Misr**, **Islamic Investment Bank** and **National Bank of Egypt**, Sharia Sheraton. Banks open from Sunday-Thursday 0830-2100, Friday and Saturday 0900-1330 with an irregular lunch break. Money transfer can be arranged through *Thomas Cook* and *Western Union* T 442772, both in Sakala shopping centre.

Business services available at *Hilton Resort*.

● **Entertainment**
Casino: at *Intercontinental Hotel*.

Nightclubs: as a major tourist resort there is less concern about offending Islamic sensibilities. As a result, besides the main hotel restaurants which serve beer, there are many discotheques in town incl the **Cha Cha Disco**, next to *Shedwan*, which is open until 0300, and those at the major hotels. *Peanuts* nr *Three Corners Hotel*.

● **Places of worship**
Coptic Church, Friday and Sunday 1000, at El-Anba Shenouda.

● **Post & telecommunications**
Area code: 065.

Post Office: is located next to the tourist police on Sharia al-Centeral to the south of the new mosque. Open 0800-1400 daily except Friday. Special post by Federal Express – T 442772, in Sakala shopping centre.

Telephone: it is quite easy to make international telephone calls from most hotels.

● **Shopping**
Hurghada has very few local shops although all of the major hotels and holiday villages have shopping arcades which cater for the tourists' requirements.

Bookshops: *Al Ahram* in *Hotel Intercontinental* with daily newspapers in Arabic and English (sometimes just one day old); *Jetline* in *Arabia Beach* with a good selection of books on the Red Sea; *Pyramid Bookshop* in *Jasmine Village* with international newspapers; bookshop in *Conran Hotel* has good range.

● **Sports**
Deep-sea fishing: in the particularly rich fishing grounds of the Red Sea is very popular with rich

European and Japanese businessmen but it is also comparatively expensive.

Spear fishing: is becoming more common. This region is noted especially for shark, barracuda, swordfish, sailfish, mullet and grouper. It is forbidden to catch coloured fish (which lose their colour once out of the water) or rare fish.

Diving: visitors come to Hurghada for the diving as the Red Sea has a high world ranking for this sport and all the major hotels either have an affiliation to one of the main diving centres or have their own.

Diving Clubs in Hurghada: this is a selection of the Diving Clubs available, choose with care, diving is a dangerous sport, check the qualifications, see what safety precautions are in place. Cheap may not be best. *Abu Saad Diving Centre*, T 546578; *Aquanaut* at *Shedwan Golden Beach*, T 549891; *Barakuda Diving Centre* in *Marriott Beach*, T 446950 and *Giftun Village*; *Blue Lagoon Diving Centre* in *Grand Hotel*, T 443751; *Blue Water Centre* and *Nautico Diving and Surfing Centre* at *Arabian Beach*; *Dive Point* at *Coral Beach*, T 447160; *Divers Lodge*, *Intercontinental*; *Divers World*, Sheraton, T 442000; *Dolphin Aqua Centre*; El Samaka Club Hotel; *Emperor Divers* at *Princess Palace* and *Hilton*, T/F 444854; *Hani Minyawi Dive Co*; *Hurghada Beach Hotel*; *Masters Club* in *Sonesta Beach Resort*, T 443660; *Orso Diving Club* in *Mashrabia Hotel*, T 443332; *Scuba-Doo Hotel and Dive Centre*, T 549314; *Stingray Diving Centre* at *Sinbad Resort*; *Sub Aqua* at *Sofitel* and *Conrad*, T/F 442473. (See box 402 for details about diving.)

Watersports: windsurfing is particularly good at Hurghada because of the gusty winds usually 4-8 on Beaufort Scale and equipment of varying weights can be hired from a number of outlets, try your own hotel first. Jet skis can be hired for E£200/hr and waterskis from E£220. Boats with motors to tow or for fishing or snorkelling can be hired from E£800/hr depending on size. Sailing boats are available too.

Emperor Angel Fish

Lunartail Grouper

● **Tour companies & travel agents**
Besides the independent travel agents there is at least one in each major hotel. *Egypt Air Offices*, at Tourist Centre, T 443591-4; *Misr Travel* at Tourist Centre, T 442130; *Seti First Travel*, beside *Shedwan Hotel*.

● **Tourist offices**
Open daily 0900-1400, managed by Omar Soliman Aly with exceedingly helpful staff is now in a smart new building opp the *Marine Sports Club* on the west side of main road. Given the intense competition between travel agencies and dive centres, there is probably little additional information that the office can provide.

● **Useful telephone numbers**
Airport: T 442831/442594; **Ambulance**: T 546490; **Bus station**: T 548582; **Egyptair**: T 443591/4; **Fire**: T 549814; **Hospital**: T 546740; **Police**: T 546723; **Post Office**: T 546372; **Super jet bus**: T 546768; **Tourist Information**: T 44420; **Tourist Police**: T 546765.

● **Transport**
Air There are regular daily **Egyptair** flights and ZAS flights from Hurghada airport to Cairo (1 hr) daily at 0715 and 1600 plus additional flights during the week, and 3 times a week to Luxor. Egyptair, T 443591/4 (open 0800-2000) and ZAS, T 440019 (open 1000-2100) have offices almost next to each other in the square with the new mosque. **Air Sinai Company** at *Nile Hilton*, T 776893/760948 has weekly flights to Sharm el-Sheikh and St Catherine's monastery.

Road Bus: the new bus station is on the main north-south road to the south of the main town. Regular daily buses north go to Suez (6-8 hrs, E£20) and Cairo (6-12 hrs depending on the service) and southeast to Luxor (4-5 hrs, E£15) and Aswan via Qena (7-8 hrs) which are very full in the winter high season. Bus (incl Superjets) or service taxis to Hurghada from Cairo from Ahmed Helmi terminal, T 746658, nr Ramses railway station or from Abdel

Mounim Riyad terminal nr the *Ramses Hilton Hotel*. Buses to Cairo 1000, 1300, 1500, 1900, 2130, 2200, 2400; Superjet to Cairo 1200, 1800 contact T 546767; to Luxor 1200, 2400, returning at 0600, 1100, 1430, 1900. **Service taxis**: (quicker but more expensive than buses), can be caught from either the minibus stand on the main road or the square next to the old mosque. Go early in the morning for the 7-seat taxis to Suez (4 hrs) and Cairo (5-7 hrs) or Luxor (4 hrs) and Aswan (6 hrs). Group hire of a taxi to Sharm el-Sheikh (700 km about 10-14 hrs) avoids the 18 hrs bus journey with a long wait in Suez. **Car rental**: Budget in *Sofitel*, T 442261 and *Marriot Beach*, T 446950; Eurocar in *Sonesta Beach*, T 443660 plus many more along Sharia Sheraton.

Boat Ferry: ferry to Sharm el-Sheikh on the Sinai peninsula (5-15 hrs depending on the weather and the boat), costs E£100 one way and booking is essential through your own hotel or Spring Tours on Tariq el-Nsr. Hurghada to Sharm el-Sheikh Monday, Wednesday and Friday at 0800; Sharm el-Sheikh to Hurghada Sunday, Tuesday and Thursday at 0900; contact in Hurghada T 444003/546282 and in Sharm el-Sheikh T 544702. Take food and water for the journey.

Ras Abu Soma – projected tourist complex

A new tourist complex is under construction just 48 km, 1-hr drive, south of Hurghada on the peninsula of Abu Soma. 13 luxury hotels are planned including a Sheraton, its buildings inspired by Pharaonic architecture (the mind boggles) and a Robinson-Hyatt expected to attract German customers. The 18 hole golf course covering 400,000 sq m and designed by Gary Player, is situated on the highest point of the peninsula, almost 22m above sea level and offers good views. The first 9 holes are already complete. The intention is to attract 'well to do' visitors such as Japanese who love golf into their 60 room club house. Other activities are provided by a fresh water swimming pool and the seven coral reefs in the vicinity. A 4 km long promenade is planned and a marina to accommodate 50 vessels. This could be a splendid place to stay.

EL GOUNA

This is a new up-market resort, with a very attractive coastline, situated just 30 km (45 mins in a taxi) north of Hurghada. Compared with the bustle of Hurghada this is a very peaceful place to visit. The coastline is a series of lagoons giving privacy for the hotel developments and private villas all of which have been constructed in a style best described as Nubian/Arabesque. There are many uninhabited islands and coral reefs which are exposed only at low tide. The development boasts its own private airport, a museum, an observatory, an aquarium and an amphitheatre. There is also a marina, a casino, a hospital including a very important hyperbaric chamber.

Local information
● **Accommodation**

A *Movenpick*, T 545160, F 544503, shuttle bus 30 km from airport, private airfield. Built in terracotta, in tropical gardens with tropical plants and palms framed by the desert behind and the lagoon in front. The accommodation is a village setting has a/c, extra large beds, satellite TV and video, phone, minibar, 2 large pools, health club, Turkish bath, disco, a selection of bars and restaurants incl El Sayadin on the beach, children's club, children's pool, baby sitting, 298 rm, 20 for families, 13 suites. Associated within the hotel complex is *Nautic Dive Centre* with the latest facilities. Non-divers may join the day boats at US$22/day. Parasailing, pedalos, snorkelling and water skiing; A *Sheraton*, T 545606, F 545608, 282 rm, beach front on nine separate islands in the lagoon, diving centre in the hotel, health club, beauty salon, choice of restaurants, golf course; A *Sonesta*

Paradiso, T 547934/9, F 547933, a sprawling beach-front resort 20 mins from the airport at Hurghada, own private strip for small planes, 225 rm and suites with balconies and sea view, satellite TV, direct dial telephone, 3 restaurants, 2 lounges, private beach, 3 pools, water sports, tennis, horse riding.

Very new accommodation: *Dawar el Omda*, T 545060 and *El Khan*, T 545162.

● **Places to eat**

Tower Café; *Zeytuna Beach Bar*; *All Seasons*, T 547934; *Morgan Fish*, T 547934; *Chez Pascal*, T 545162; *Palavrion*, T 545160; *Piazza Terrace*, in *Movenpick*.

● **Bars**

Gallery Bar at *Movenpick*; *Zeytuna Beach Bar*; *Lobby Bar* at *Sonesta Paradiso* or the *Patio Bar* at *Dwar el Omda*.

● **Entertainment**

Cinema: at El Arena twice a week, also theatrical performances.

Discos: *Movenpick*, *Jazz Bar* next to *El Khan*; *El Arena* – open-air, built in Greco-Roman style, dancing Thursday and Friday nights; *Desires* in *Paradiso Sonesta*.

● **Sports**

Diving: this location provides for the visitor some flora and fauna not normally found any further north and gives opportunity for day boats to reach dives normally accessed only by liveboards. Dives may incl the two wreck sites as well as the coral gardens, pinnacles and other diverse reef structures.

Other than watersports there is horse riding, tennis and an 18-hole golf course.

● **Post & telecommunications**

Area code: 065.

● **Useful telephone numbers**

Emergency numbers as for Hurghada. See above.

SAFAGA

Safaga stands a long 567 km from Cairo but just 65 km (45 min by taxi) south from Hurghada airport, where the coastal road meets the main road across the Eastern Desert to Qena. This region does not rely totally on tourism. It has local phosphate mines and the mineral is exported from the small port which imports grain, much of it US food aid, which is currently

El Gouna

N

To Suez

El Arena
Disco &
Cinema

To Hurghada (25 km)

Hotels:
1. *El Khan*
2. *Dwar el Omda*
3. *Movenpick*
4. *Sheraton*
5. *Sonesta Paradiso*

trucked inland to the Nile Valley although a disused freight railway line to Qena may soon be reopened.

There is less pressure of people but more hotels are planned. The stiff breezes which favoured the trading vessels along these shores now provide excellent conditions for wind surfing, generally cross-shore in the morning and side-shore in the early afternoon. The Windsurfing World Championships were held here in 1993. Good for diving with noted (recommended) sites of Panorama and Abu Kafana. The prolific marine life is an underwater photographer's dream. There are frequent sightings of dolphin, ray, barracuda, reef and leopard shark.

Most travellers simply pass through in a convoy on their way between Hurghada and the Nile Valley. There is very little to visit other than a small fort which overlooks the town and offers good views. Suggested day trips to Tobia Island or Mons Claudianus in the Red Sea Mountains.

Local information
● Accommodation

The officially registered hotels all addressed as Safaga, Red Sea, are: **A** *Holiday Inn*, T 452821/3, usual facilities associated with this hotel chain, spacious, well tended gardens, perfect for sports enthusiasts, health club, tennis, volley ball, large pool, 2 restaurants, bars, shopping arcade. Most expensive hotel in town; **B** *Menaville Village*, T 451761/4, F 451765 is a better choice, about 5 km north of Safaga port, 100 hotel/villa rm, 48 chalets and 33 suites, villas in gardens, by pool or adjacent to the very good beach, all rooms a/c, telephone, minibar and terrace or balcony, villas sleep 4/5 and have lounge and small kitchen. Shops, bank, laundry, clinic. TV lounge, 24 hr cafe, private beach, cycle hire, billiards, table tennis. Our choice. Has own Barakuda Dive Club (German management) with private jetty. Unlimited shore diving from hotel reef and boat dives available with all equipment for hire; **C** *Lotus Bay Club and Villas*, T 451040, whitewashed clusters with gardens between yet all rooms sea view; **C** *Safaga Paradise Village*, T 451633, F 451630, 244 rm, similar to *Menaville* but larger and less cosy; **C** *Shams Safaga Village*, T 451783, F 451780, designed and built in local style, 135

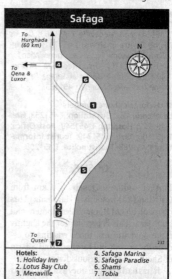

bungalow rm and 150 hotel rm with a/c, bath, terrace/balcony, TV, private sandy beach within a protected, secluded, natural bay, and spacious, well tended gardens, restaurant, 3 bars, tennis, squash, mini golf, health club, para sailing, all water sports, large pool, small children's pool, play area and baby sitting. Shams diving centre on site. Club Mistral for windsurfing with full range of instruction from beginners to slalom stylists. A rescue boat is on hand. Advantage for disabled is flat access to beach; **E** *Cleopatra Hotel*, T 451544, 48 rm, more than adequate; **F** *Sea Land Village*, Sharm el-Naga, T 3545756, F 3545060, 15 rm, value for money.

● Places to eat

The resort is so new that really all the best places to eat are in the hotels, as are the only bars. Try *Layalina*, *Lord's Pub* and *Splash Bar* in the Holiday Inn; *Moon & Sun* and *Beach Bar* at Menaville; *Omar Khayam* in Safaga Paradise or the *Dolphin Bar* at Shams.

● Banks & money changers

Banque Misr, Quseir-Hurghada Road, T 541552.

● Entertainment

Discos: *Albano* in *Menaville*; *Black Cat* in *Holiday Inn*; *Serpent* in *Shams*; *Paradise* in *Safaga Paradise*.

● **Sports**
Diving clubs: *Barakuda* at *Lotus Bay*
T 451041 and *Menaville* T 451763; *Duck's
Diving Centre* in *Shams*, T 451781; *El Okby
Village* (with some F grade accommodation for
divers) T 452116; *Orca Red Sea Diving*,
T 442357; *Safaga Divers* at *Safaga Paradise
Village* and *Safaga Marina* T 451133.

● **Useful telephone numbers**
Local code: 065; **Bus station**: T 451253; **Fire**:
T 451227; **Hospital**: T 451549; **Post Office**:
T 451206; **Taxi**: T 451349; **Tourist informa-
tion**: T 451785; **Tourist police**: T 451208.

QUSEIR

Further south is **Quseir**, 650 km from
Cairo and 80 km south of Harghada (2 hrs
by road), an old Roman encampment and
busy port. This is popular for the slightly
more adventurous, those wishing to escape the crowds of Hurghada and Sharm
el-Sheikh and for serious divers.

It has had a long history as a major port
of the Red Sea. It was from here that
Queen Hatshepsut departed on her famous expedition to the Land of Punt (see
page 201). This was also once the most
important Muslim port on the Red Sea
and was the main transit point for Egyptian pilgrims bound for Mecca. In the
10th century it was superseded first by
Aydhab, which is the ancient name for the
Halaib in the currently disputed triangle
on the Egyptian-Sudanese border, and
then by Suez after the canal was opened
in 1869. The port has recently been reopened, its main function for the export
of phosphates. The 16th century fortress
of Sultan Selim (rebuilt by the French in
1798) which still stands in the centre of
the town (see below) indicates its earlier
importance. Today the influx of tourists
and fortifications are not required. All the
activity here is based on diving, scuba
diving or serious snorkelling.

It is a very peaceful place located in a
small inlet sheltered by a coral reef. The
town, however, remains sleepy dominated by the Fort of Sultan Selim originally built in the 16th century. The road
inland from Quseir to Qift, which is just

south of Qena, a distance of 164 km,
follows the ancient pharaonic road which
was built at a time when almost a hundred
small but very rich gold mines operated
in the region. Many of these mines have
been reopened using modern technology.

When sitting in the sun loses its appeal
there are other things to do. Visit the
Sultan Semil fortress. The partly ruined
fortress was built by Sultan Selim to protect the Nile Valley from attacks from the
sea – and was in use between 1122 and
1710. At that time it became the main
departure point for Egyptian pilgrims on
their annual journey to Mecca.

There was conflict here too at the end
of the 18th century – during the French
campaign. Also between the British Indian Army coming in from Bombay and
the Egyptian campaign to the Arabian
Peninsula headed by Ibrahim Pasha in
1816. (See box on Mohammed Ali and
family.) During the Ottoman era it had
been used as an administrative office and
today the ancient structure is sufficiently
repaired to be used as a police station. Some
of the inscribed verses from the Koran can
still be read. There are other buildings from
this earlier period including the mosques
of Al-Faroah, Abdel-Rehim Al-Qenay and
Al-Sanussi and a number of tombs, mainly
by the fortress, of holy men considered
important by the inhabitants.

Jeep and horseback safaris can be
taken into the mountains to visit nearby
oases and a number of ghost cities created
when the mines were abandoned. *Quseir
Movenpick* offers escorted excursions to
Luxor and Hurghada.

Local information
● **Accommodation**
Sample of hotels officially addressed as Quseir,
Red Sea, are: **A** *Movenpick Serena Beach*, El
Quadim Bay, T 432100-120, F 4321290, unbeat-
able value with a coral reef running the entire
length of the private beach. You can almost snorkel
from your room. Moorish style, lovely gardens,
beautiful beach, large pool, 3 restaurants of which
Orangerie is rec, 4 bars especially Jolie Bar, 2 floodlit
tennis courts, squash, archery ranges with coach,
gym, mountain bikes to hire, horse and camel

riding. Children's pool, children's club, supervised play area. All 175 rm have usual facilities from sea view to hair dryer. Close by, but completely isolated, is the *Utopia Beach Club*. Also Pensee – the Nile cruise boat used as a hotel ship. Excellent diving but no nightlife. Subex Diving Centre, see **Sport**. Often windy, spotless, friendly service, good food, fitness centre, wide variety of sports available; **A** *Utopia Beach Club*, a bus is needed to get into Quseir but taxis are available. New – right on the beach, restaurant, pool with snack bar, lobby bar, disco, billiards, volleyball, tennis, table tennis, windsurfing and pedalo hire, children's pool and small size tennis court, play area, cots and pens free, mini kids club, room with bath, a/c, Saturday TV, fridge, terrace/balcony, doctor on call. Some spectacular dives just off the beach, others reached by jeep.

New accommodation – **B** *Fanadir Beach Hotel and resort*.

D *Daly Dive Resort*, El Hamrawein, T 430039, F 430720, 30 rm with bath, sea views, beach site, clean, basic.

● **Places to eat**
The resort is so new that the best places to eat are at the restaurants in the hotels.

● **Entertainment**
No nightlife except in hotels, so try *Jolie Bar* in *Movenpick*.

● **Useful telephone numbers**
Area code: 065; **Fire brigade**: T 430067; **Hospital**: T 430070; **Police**: T 430017

Diving off Quseir

Shallow dives Off the shore at *Movenpick's* Subex Dive Centre is El Qadima Bay with a variety of topography and fauna; about 10 km further south is the more sheltered El Kaf.

Deep dives The islands Big Brother and Little Brother are about 1 km apart, 67 km off the shore to the northeast of Quseir. They are two exposed parts of the same reef. Access by liveboard. The walls are a vertical 900m. On the larger island, Big Brother, is a stone built light house constructed by the British in 1883 (and still working) and to the northwest of Big Brother are two wrecks. The unnamed cargo vessel with its shattered bow can be reached at 5m (and then deeper as it is at

an incline). The other wreck, Aida II, about 100m to the south, was a military vessel which went down in 1957 and as the corals encrust it is becoming part of the reef which caused it to sink. The wreck remains upright but the depth (30-40m) makes this inaccessible for the average diver.

These two dives offer a wealth of corals and an impressive range of fish. *Subex Diving Centre* very expensive at US$100 per dive including equipment rental. *Daly Dive Resort* is more basic with dives made at the resort from US$15 per dive, US$44 per day. *Coral Cove* offers 2 dives for E£240 including equipment rental.

Recipe for Falafel

These tiny chick pea pancakes served with tahini sauce have been served at meals in Egypt since the time of the Pharaohs.

250 gm dried chick peas
1 small onion finely chopped
25 gm of soft bread crumbs
2 cloves of garlic, crushed
25 gm chopped parsley
large pinch of ground coriander
large pinch of ground cumin
olive oil for frying

The chick peas must be soaked overnight, rinsed in fresh water and drained. Blend the chick peas, bread crumbs, onion and crushed garlic with 50 ml of water in the mixer until quite smooth. Add the spices and parsley into the bowl and knead together. Make the mixture into small balls the size of a date, flatten with the hand and deep fry in batches until golden brown – about 4 mins. Drain off excess oil. Serve with the tahini sauce.

Sauce

50 ml of tahini (sesami seed paste)
juice of a lemon
1 clove of garlic, crushed
5 gm chopped parsley
pinch of ground cumin
pinch of salt
pepper to taste

Mix the ingredients with water to a smooth creamy paste.

Both the pancakes and the sauce can be frozen.

MARSA SHAGRA

This remote bay located 113 km south of Quesir and 13 km north of **Marsa Alam** has become a small village well known to divers. It has good opportunities for a variety of coastal shore dives, day and night. There is a very extensive cave system which can be explored and some outstanding coral formations. It is near to a group of offshore reefs with walls such as the Elphinstone Reef.

There is just one accommodation complex set back from the beach to the west of the coast road (so as not to spoil the view). The construction in local red sandstone is very sympathetic. A central domed area containing all the main facilities is surrounded by separate villas with lots of space. Prices around £800 a week for the diver and £700 for non-diver including full board. This is the first complex to be constructed here and it is to be hoped that the precident of style and position is copied so that this tranquil area is not spoilt. This is also an excellent spot for fishing.

Live-board dive locations south from Marsa Alam: Elphinstone Reef, 12 km off shore; Daedalus Reef, 96 km off shore; Shaab Sharm; Dolphine Reef, 15 km to the northwest of Ras Banas; Zabargad Island, 45 km southeast of Berenice.

ACCESS Flights to Hurghada or Luxor – plus 3-hr coach journey. There is also a fairly good surface, direct road from the River Nile at Edfu, 280 km. You would need to hire a taxi.

BERENICE

908 km from Cairo, 400 km from Hurghada and 178 km from Quesir. Sometimes a permit is required for this area. This was a very ancient city – named by Ptolemy II. It became a trading port around 275 BC. The ruined temple of Semiramis is near the modern town and inland there are remains of the emerald mines of Wadi Sakait which were worked from Pharonic to Roman times.

The coast is lined with mangrove swamps and there are some beautiful coves which are completely isolated.

Offshore is the Zabargad, a most unusual volcanic island. Evidence of its origin is found in the (olive-green) olivine mined as a semi-precious gem stone. Mining which has not long been discontinued has been active here on and off since 1500 BC. Peridot Hill (named after another semi-precious stone) offers breathtaking views of the surrounding area. A wonderful place to watch the dolphins and, in season, the migrating birds. Recommended as a place for remedial tourism.

ACCESS Access by road only. Nearest airports are Hurghada and Luxor.

Marsa Alam about 35 km south of Quesir and best reached from the Nile Valley by the paved road from Edfu, is also destined for development. At present it is the domain of the *Egyptian Shooting Club* who cannot hope to keep this lovely area for themselves.

There is one interesting excursion possible from here into the interior, but a guide is essential. The tomb and mosque of Sidi Abul Hassan Al-Shazli lies some distance inland. The track/road is a distance of 110 km southwards off the main road west towards Edfu. Al-Shazli (1196-1258) was an influential sufi sheikh originating in the northwest of Africa but spending much of his life in Egypt. He had a large and important following and was noted for his piety and unselfishness. He travelled annually to Mecca for which Marsa Alam was convenient. His moulid is popular despite the isolation of the site. The buildings are modern, being last restored on the instructions of King Farouk after his visit in 1947.

Camping at *Coral Cove*, Sharia Marsa Alam, T (02) 3647970, beach location 8 km north of Marsa Alam, tents for 2, 3 or 10 persons, peaceful, clean, popular with divers.

The Western Desert and
The Great Desert Circuit

THIS SECTION concentrates on the journey along the 'great desert circuit' rather than on individual towns, because it is the journey itself and not the oases towns which is of greatest importance.

"It is not easy to conceive the sterile grandeur of the scene ... I may truly say, I never enjoyed myself more, despite the thermometer at 105 degrees, and the numerous petty inconveniences I was necessarily obliged to submit to. Certainly, no fine lady, who could not do without her everyday luxuries and comforts, should attempt the desert ... but I was born under a wandering star ..."
Anne Katherine Elwood 1830.

Wherever you are in Egypt, the desert is not far away, and its presence can always be felt. The Western Desert alone constitutes two-thirds of Egypt's total area. Its significance in any travel itinerary depends upon how much of a traveller you are and how much a tourist. Desert travel presents its inconveniences and its hazards, but the rewards are beyond measure.

Depending upon the time available and personal preference there are various choices. They range from a day trip from Cairo to **El-Fayoum** (see page 167) or to **Wadi El Natrun** (see page 323), to **The Great Desert Circuit** of Bahariya, Farafra, **Dakhla** and **Kharga Oases**, or **Siwa** (see page 352) and **The Great Sand Sea**. Although it is undoubtedly part of the Western Desert, the wonderful oasis of **Siwa** is dealt with in the section on Alexandria and the Mediterranean because it is most easily accessible from Marsa Matruh and is not linked directly to the Great Desert circuit.

Many areas in the vicinity of the oases are set aside for military use, so for detours from the main road a **permit** may be necessary. The **Travel Permits Department** (T 3556301/3548661) at the Ministry of the Interior in Cairo in the Abdin district is open Saturday-Thursday 0900-1400. In order to get your permit, which can take anything from 1-7 days, it is essential to take photocopies of the first three pages of your passport and the Egyptian entry stamp and two passport photos.

Spring is the best time to visit the desert, when the daytime temperatures are still bearable and the nights are cool but not cold, and the summer desert winds and sand storms, which can be very uncomfortable, have not yet arrived. Take enough money with you. Credit cards will *not* do, indeed, you will be lucky to find a bank. When planning a drive NEVER underestimate the potential dangers of the desert. It is said that in 524 BC Cambyses, the Persian conqueror of Egypt, managed to lose an entire army of 50,000

men without a trace! Always carry more than enough fuel, food and water. There are no service stations between towns. You need the right type of vehicle, and the necessary driving skills to handle it in this terrain. See Travel and Survival in the Desert, page 34 and read further on the subject before you throw yourself into a potentially lethal environment. Other options include service buses and organized desert safaris. The latter could be the most rewarding if you are anything but meticulously prepared and equipped.

THE GREAT DESERT CIRCUIT

The Great Desert Circuit became accessible in the 1980s, when a road was built linking the oases of **Bahariya**, **Farafra**, **Dakhla** and **Kharga**. These are all situated on a dead branch of the River Nile, and depend, for their livelihood on the massive fossil water reservoirs beneath the Libyan Desert. The area was designated as the **New Valley** in 1958 with a scheme to tap this subterranean water-source and relocate landless peasants from the overcrowded Nile Valley and Delta. However the lack of resources and a reassessment of the long-term viability of the water supply led to the virtual abandonment of the project and to the area's inevitable stagnation.

Coming from Cairo, the natural choice is an anti-clockwise journey round the circuit beginning by going into the desert past the Pyramids at Giza on Route 341. This gives the option of a refreshing last leg of your journey back down the River Nile. Driving conditions are not ideal, with pot-holed roads and few opportunities for petrol, food or water. You may have to stand for hours waiting for and on crowded buses, and accommodation along the route is pretty basic. Lacking the time or the inclination for all this you can fly direct from Cairo to New Valley Airport at Kharga, where you can get a taste of the desert, but you will be missing far more than you experience. It may be true that Kharga has more interesting monuments than some of its neighbours, but the desert itself is the star of this piece and Kharga, with it's sprawling modern town, is undoubtedly a disappointment.

Depending on the level of security precautions taken by the Egyptian authorities you may find yourself accompanied by armed guards for part of your journey. Generally these concern themselves with travellers in self-drive vehicles or cars with hired drivers. They cause no problems though the effectiveness of their protection may be questioned. Use it as an opportunity to educate, take them into the museums and round the monuments.

BAHARIYA

The journey to Bahariya, 310 km west of the Pyramids of Giza, along Route 341 takes 6-7 hrs by bus, with one stop en route, 5-6 hrs by service taxi or 4-4½ hrs in 4WD vehicle.

After taking the turn to October 6th City the dual carriageway becomes a new black top 3-lane highway. A new oil rig – Santa Fé rig no 94 – stands on the right and new road signs, big yellow markers, give distances from Cairo. Running parallel to the road is a private railway which takes iron ore from the country's most important mine at Managum to the giant

Camels – Ships of the Desert

There are two kinds of camel, *Camelus Dromedarius*, the Arabian camel with one hump and *Camelus Bactrianus*, the Bactrian which has two. Arabian camels, found in North Africa, though only as domestic animals, are about 3m long and about 2m high at the shoulder. They range in colour from white to black.

They are not the most attractive of creatures, looking particularly ragged and scruffy at the spring moult. Large bare leathery areas on legs and chest look like some serious skin complaint but are normal and act as cushions when the animal kneels down.

Interesting physical characteristics which allow these animals to survive in the desert include hairs inside the ear opening as well as the ability to close the nostrils between breaths, both preventing sand penetration; thick eyebrows to shade the eyes from the sun's glare; a pad of skin between the two large toes on each foot forming a broad, tough 'slipper' which spreads the animal's weight over a larger area and prevents sinking in the loose sand; the ability to store a reserve of fat in the hump and to go for days without water. Each eye has three eyelids, the upper and lower lids have very long eyelashes to protect the eyes from sand whipped up by desert winds, while a third, thinner lid blinks away dust from the eyeball. The skin inside a camel's mouth is so tough that cactus thorns do not penetrate, hence a camel can eat anything, 'even its owner's tent'.

Camels can go for many days without food as the hump can store up to 35 kilos of fat as emergency rations. They can go without water for even longer, depending on the weather and the kind of food available. As camels do not sweat but instead function at a higher body temperature without brain damage, their demands of fluid are less. At a water hole they drink only enough to balance their body moisture content.

Less pleasant characteristics include a most unpredictable nature, especially in the mating season, which includes nasty habits like using its long sharp teeth to bite people and other camels, viciously kicking with the back legs, spitting and being generally awkward. When a camel stands up it moves in a series of violent jerks as it straightens first its hind legs then its front legs. When a camel walks, it moves both the legs at one side at the same time, giving a very rolling motion which can give the rider travel sickness.

Camels are unwilling beasts of burden, grunting and groaning as they are loaded and generally complaining at being made to lie down or stand up. Once underway though, they move without further protest.

These large, strong beasts are used to pull ploughs, turn water wheels and carry large loads for long distances across difficult terrain. They can carry up to 400 kg but usually the load is nearer 200 kg. Despite moving at a mere 6 or 7 km an hour, camels can travel 100 km in a day. They also provide their owners with hair for cloth, rich milk and cheese, dried dung fuel and eventually meat, bones for utensils and hides for shoes, bags and tenting.

The Arabian dromedary, bred for riding and racing, is of a slighter build but can cover 160 km in a day and reach speeds of up to 15 km per hour.

Asses, donkeys and mules

There is a certain amount of confusion when naming the normally overladen and generally undernourished beasts of burden found in the countries of North Africa. While there can be no confusion as to what is a **horse**, *Equus caballus*, or even an **ass**, *Equus asinus*, despite the fact that it is most commonly called a **donkey**, a **mule** requires some definition.

The term **mule** can refer to any hybrid but as a beast of burden it is the offspring of a male donkey (jack) and a female horse (mare), while the offspring of a male horse (stallion) and a female donkey (jenny) is correctly termed a **hinny**.

A mule is a horse in the middle with a donkey at either end. It has longer ears, and a thinner mane and tail than its mother and carries the typical 'cross' markings on the shoulders and back. The hinny is less popular, being nearer the size of a donkey and has the shorter ears and thicker mane and tail of its father.

A mule is stronger than a horse, has a much longer working life under the right circumstances, can withstand extremes of temperature without long-term ill effects, is less vulnerable to sickness and can survive on a very limited diet. Mules are noted for being surefooted and for being fast and accurate kickers. Mules are generally considered to be infertile though instances of offspring are recorded.

The Algerian wild ass originally roamed the Atlas Ranges. The Romans carefully preserved them on mosaics but are held responsible for their demise. The Nubian wild ass, of a distinctive reddish hue, roamed the semi-desert areas between the River Nile and the Red Sea shores. It survived into the 20th century.

The Egyptians used asses. Illustrations from 2500 BC show us that even then these domesticated beasts were carrying loads and passengers out of all proportion to their size. They also had mules which are thought to have first been bred around 1750 BC. Models of this hybrid were found in the pyramids and a mule drawing a chariot is depicted on a vase found in Thebes.

The Romans placed heavy reliance on the mule, for riding, to draw carts and farm implements and to carry equipment. To assist copulation they devised a wooden cage with a ramp to enable the shorter jack ass reach the taller mare.

Helwan steelworks near Cairo. This was the catalyst for Egypt's industrial development in the 1950s.

At 155 km from Giza is a resthouse with petrol. The bus and service taxis stop here. No soft drinks, just tea. Don't rely on the 'new' resthouse mentioned in some guides about 11 km further on. This is not open, it is still incomplete. 31 km after the resthouse is the new road north to El-Alamein marked by five signs – of the petrol companies involved.

81 km from the resthouse the road becomes narrower, the surface rougher and the railway swings away to left. The telegraph poles march alongside the road – but there are no wires between them! As the road begins its descent towards the

oasis the first huge black topped inselburgs appear, protruding through the yellow sands. The Managum mines are announced by a sign at 150 km from the resthouse but it is a further 10 km before houses for the workers appear on the right. The head office of the mines, down the road to the left is reported to have a museum but getting beyond the guard at the gate could prove very difficult.

Pause at the top of the scarp for a really magnificent view of the Bahariya depression, the smallest of the four depressions but 2,000 sq km in area, with 33,000 inhabitants. **Bawati** is the main settlement. The farmed areas are owned by small landowners. The main crops are dates, olives and wheat. Problems of falling water tables in the oases were solved by tapping the subterranean aquifers held in the Cretaceous sandstones, but the interesting underground water channels (similar to those found as far afield as Morocco and Iran) formerly used in Bawati are dry and a very depressing sight.

Throughout their history the people of the oasis have prevaricated between independence and co-operation with the current régime. They converted to Islam soon after the Muslim invasion but returned to a Berber Emirate during the 10th century before being incorporated once more into the Islamic state by the Fatimids a century later. In the last few centuries they have co-operated fully with the ruling régimes but have maintained a slightly independent stance. They are generally very welcoming to visitors.

The small settlements are all worth visiting to see how these sturdy people combat the elements. Once on the floor of the depression take the track to the south of the road which continues beyond **El Harrah** (rock cut tombs) and its ponds which are used by the locals for duck breeding to the gardens round the spring of **Eïn Yousef**. Further west along the main road the ruins of **Muhrib** are out of bounds at present but a black top road opposite on the right leads to **Gabala** where the encroaching sands have been spreading over the oasis gardens for the last 20 years and have covered the rest of the road. Approaching closer to Bawati, again on the right, is **Eïn Hemma** with **Mandesha** beyond, also fighting a losing battle against the encroaching sand. The last turn right before Bawati leads to **Agouz**. A guide from the village is an asset when visiting these small settlements. Ask for school teacher Badry Macpool.

BAWATI

Bawati is built along the main road and the parallel oasis road to the south. South of the village in a dominant position stands Jebel Hafuf, Bahar's highest mountain, made of dolerite and basalt.

A circular walk along the main road and the oasis road through the gardens, by Al Bishmu, the Roman springs, where the hot water is used for bathing and washing clothes and by the shafts to the now dry underground water channels will take an hour. Cultivation of fruit takes place in these gardens, apricots, dates, figs and melons. In some places oranges struggle to survive. The women work in the gardens and also contribute to the household finances by selling embroidery which is of high quality.

Places of interest
Oasis Heritage Museum at entrance to

Bawati

1. Hotel Alpenblick
2. Oasis Hotel
3. Paradise Hotel
4. Hamid Restaurant
5. Paradise Café
6. Popular Restaurant

village by artist Mahmoud Eed is well worth a visit. An opportunity to learn more about the bedouin and their way of life. Here the traditional handicrafts and artefacts from a typical bedouin home are on display. In fact the main hall of the display is set up as the principal living area of the family – a low bench, a bread oven and some associated implements. Here one can purchase embroidered dresses and locally made pieces of silver jewellery.

Local information
● **Accommodation**

Price guide:		
AL US$150+	**D**	US$25-50
A US$100-150	**E**	US$10-25
B US$75-100	**F**	under US$10
C US$50-75		

The hotel provision is not constant. The government closes those 'not up to standard' but they reopen very soon. Accommodation incl: **F** *Alpenblick Hotel*, double room with shower E£50, budget room E£16.5, breakfast E£5, lunch E£8, dinner E£12, are based on large helpings of bread, evening tea round the fire in the courtyard make it a special place; **F** *Oasis* and *Popular* are slightly cheaper and even less comfortable than *Alpenblick*.

Camping *Pyramid Mountain Camp*, 17 km from Bawati, hot water spring of 42°C, huts, guard, E£6 pp/night incl mattress and blankets, ask at *Alpenblick Hotel* for details.

● **Places to eat**
There is a number of small shops and small cheap places to eat. None is outstanding.

● **Hospitals & medical services**
A doctor lives beside the post office.

● **Tour companies & travel agents**
Tours of the White desert are organized by *Alpenblick Hotel*.

● **Transport**
Road Bus: buses from Bawati for Cairo leave daily at 0700, Sunday, Tuesday and Friday at 1000, Monday, Wednesday and Thursday at 1200. Buses to Farafra leave Saturday, Monday and Thursday at 1330.
   Service Taxi: leave for Cairo around 0800 from the *Popular Restaurant*.

Al-Qasr lying west on the road to Siwa, is Bawati's sister village, beneath which lies Bahariya's ancient capital. Here you will see stones from a 26th Dynasty (664-525 BC) temple reused for house building and the remains of a Roman triumphal arch which stayed intact until the 19th century.

A much improved but still fairly uncomfortable track leads west from here to **Siwa** (see page 355). A 4WD and guide are recommended. Check at Tourist Information before you leave.

Before moving on from Bahariya, drivers must fill up with fuel and water as the nearest service station is in Dakhla which is 490 km away. The 180 km road between Bahariya and Farafra is in a very bad state. At best it will take 4 hrs to travel so it is a good opportunity to admire the scenery. Just 12 km beyond the outskirts of Bawati is the Runi shrine of Rene Michael, the Swiss explorer who lived in the village for 7 years, rediscovered the area and was so enchanted by the beauty of the place that he wanted to be buried there in the desert. Beyond lies the black desert, the pebbles of dolerite darkening the land. The road begins to rise out of the Bahariya depression through a colourful 'Rainbow' canyon and a checkpoint. A second checkpoint is just beyond the village of **Eïn el Izza**, a place to stop for a drink. On the plateau are numerous erosion features known locally as *lions*. Of special note are the small mountains of calcite. One just 10m to the left of the road is called *Jebel el Izza* or Crystal Mountain and it is worth spending some time here. The road cuts through the escarpment and descends towards the Farafra depression. Of the flat topped outliers two are particularly prominent to the east of the road, and are known as Twin Peaks.

Beyond is the fabled **White Desert** where many travellers stop for the night. By moonlight, the eerie windshaped landscape has been compared to the Arctic wasteland, and sunrise here could be the highlight of your trip. These strange shaped rocks have caught the imagination of countless travellers – intrigued them and inspired them. Geologists will

Landforms in White Desert

delight in the huge calcite crystals, the chalk fossils and the accumulations of pyrites. To the north of Jebel Gunna a road goes west to Eïn Della (Spring of the Shade). An extra permit is required for this journey and rarely provided.

FARAFRA OASIS

This is the smallest and most isolated of the oases in the Western Desert but the deep depression in which it lies suggests that it was once larger. To the northwest steep cliffs rise dramatically out of the desert whilst to the south there is a gentle incline. In spite of its isolation the residents of the region, who now number about 2,500 and are mainly from two extended families, have been involved in trade and contact with the Nile Valley since earliest times. The village of Qasr el-Farafra had a large 116 room mud brick qasr (fort, or castle) from which it got it's name. This was used by all the villagers when they were under attack until it collapsed in 1958. The village is generally pleasing with palm-lined roads and decorated houses, although some less attractive concrete buildings are now being constructed.

Places of interest

Badr's Museum with its eccentric displays must not be missed. The small oases to the east of the village are intensively cultivated and pleasant to walk through.

Local information
● Accommodation

There are two check points before Qasr Farafra and immediately on the left after the second is the New Resthouse, 5 rm each with 3 beds,

E£9/bed, shower with warm water, no flyscreen, no curtains, electricity erratic, take your own sleeping bag and a torch and use their blanket to cover the window. No other accommodation currently available.

Camping Campsite at Bir Setta, 4 km from village has a hot spring, straw shacks in compound, used by 'Explore', etc.

● Places to eat

Hussein's Café serves fuul, omelette or tinned tuna with chips or bread with coca cola or tea; Sa'ad Restaurant and residents at the New Resthouse have similar menu with tinned fig jam. White Desert Restaurant keeps very irregular opening days. There is a small bakery and goods like eggs sold from dwellings.

● Tour companies & travel agents

Ask at Sa'ad restaurant for excursions into the desert.

● Useful information

There is no petrol station but fuel from cans is available.

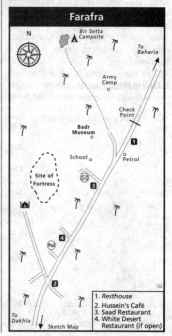

Farafra

To Baharia

To Dakhla Sketch Map

1. Resthouse
2. Hussein's Café
3. Saad Restaurant
4. White Desert Restaurant (if open)

● **Transport**

Road Bus: a/c bus to Cairo is supposed to leave Sunday, Tuesday, Friday at 0600; Saturday, Monday, Thursday at 1000; costs E£8 to Bahariya; E£20 to Cairo. To Dakhla daily except Wednesday at whatever time the bus from Cairo reaches the village.

Service Taxis: to Cairo are very irregular – depends on a returning vehicle. To Dakhla daily, very early.

DAKHLA OASIS

(*Pop* 70,000; *Alt* 111m) Moving on southeast from Farafra, the much larger **Dakhla** oasis, with a population of around 70,000 in 14 settlements, is 310 km from Farafra, and buses make the journey in 4-5 hrs and a car in 3-4 hrs.

The first 100 km of the journey are through unoccupied oases and open areas of sand which in places extend over the road. The check point at Abu Minguan has a resthouse offering tea. Beyond, the sand dunes increase in size and after a huge vegetation filled *wadi* crosses the route and then the check point stands at Maghoub, sheltering under Jebel Edmonstone.

Just 1 km directly south of Maghoub is **Deir el Haga**, a small sandstone temple dating from the Roman period which was

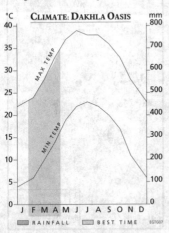

built in honour of the triad of Thebian gods, Amun Ra', Mut and Khonsu. It is a remote and very tranquil location. The site, surrounded by a wall, is well preserved due to being enveloped by the sand for much of its more recent history and may have been rebuilt during the reigns of Nero (54-68 AD) and Titus (79-81 AD). This ancient wall, just the mudbrick capping is new, is designed to deflect the drifting sand, and is fairly effective. There are some interesting inscriptions representing religious life. It was officially closed to visitors while Canadian specialists did renovations under the Dakhla Oasis Project. The responsibility for the site now lies in the hands of the Supreme Council of Antiquities, who are actively encouraging visitors. In the corner of the surrounding windbreak was the site workshop, now converted into a simple but instructive visitors' centre. Here there are nine framed panels. The central bilingual (English and Arabic) panel describes the site before restoration. The four to the right (in English) and the left (in Arabic) show a plan, describe the history, introduce the gods and emperors and explain the conservation process. The route is not direct but the temple can be seen from Maghoub or from the Muzawaka tombs and reached across country in the right kind of vehicle. The **Muzawaka Tombs** (Hill of Decoration), one of Petosiris and the other of Sadosiris are clearly signed to the south of the road, access by normal vehicle along piste to car park, but everything here is firmly shut. One is thus unable to see the murals depicting contemporary myths relating to the afterlife.

Set in a striking landscape, **Mut** (pronounced moot), the capital, is pretty in a shabby faded way. It is a lively town and the people are very friendly.

Places of interest

Ethnographic Museum, official times 0800-1400 and 1800-2100 except Friday.

Oasis Cultivation

Date Palms

Olive tree

Prickly pear on wall

Prickly pear on wall

Pomegranate

Pomegranate

Peppers, wheat and broadbeans

Local information

● Accommodation

D *Dakhla Muhariz Hotel* on Sharia el Tharwa, T 941524, organized for package tours, quite clean, avoid taking a room over TV lounge or kitchen if you want some rest, large double room, hot shower, netting and shutters on window. Two restaurants, but little choice.

E *Garden Hotel*, T 941577, nr to bus station, clean and fairly comfortable for budget travellers.

F *Dar el Wafdeen Hotel* has 9 rm; **F** *Hot Spring Resthouse* at El Douhous has 6 chalets for E£5 each and 6 rm in resthouse, all have private bathrooms.

Camping At *Hot Springs Resthouse*. Mosquitoes can be a problem here.

● Places to eat

Everywhere is cheap, some just cheaper than others. *Dakhla Hotel*, most uninspiring and highest prices; *Hamdy's Restaurant*, popular with tourists and locals; *Alhag Restaurant* noted for shish kebab; *Abu Mohammed* comes last on our list.

● Banks & money changers

Misr Bank, open 0830-1400 and 1800-2100 each day, takes TCs and cash.

● Hospitals & medical services

General Hospital, T 941333.

● Post & telecommunications

Post Offices: both open Saturday-Thursday 0800-1400.

Telephone: international calls are best made from the *Dakhla Muhariz Hotel*.

● Tourist offices

Tourist Office open Sunday-Thursday 0900-1400, T 940407. Ask here for trips into the desert, and overnight stays.

● Useful telephone numbers

Police: T 941500/941100.

● Transport

Local Bicycles: can be hired from *Abu Mohammed's Café* E£5 or *Garden Hotel* for E£8. Where are you going to ride to? **Service taxis & bus**: run to Al-Qasr, 50 piastres, and a local bus four times a day.

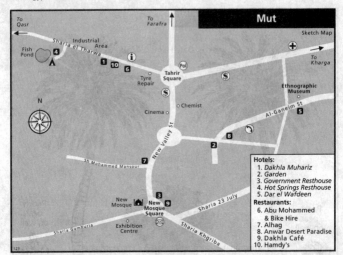

Circular excursion from Mut

Travelling northwest from Mut the Hot Springs are on the left. Here water temperatures reach 43°C and the well is 1,224m deep. After 1 km are the lakes known as the **Fish Pond**, a haven for water fowl and at times the surface is crowded with birds. Continuing north for 3 km is Rashda where there are Roman ruins at the east end of the village. As the villagers don't call them Roman, or indeed anything in particular, asking directions leads to a great deal of amusing confusion and disagreement. Ezbet Abu Asman has a white mosque and Deir Abuf Matta has Deir el Seba'a Banat Monastery of the Seven Virgins on the left. Look out for the Sheiks tomb and a single tree. Bud Khulu is an agricultural village with an old minaret on the left and the new village further on the right.

The next village is Ezbet Fiteima. Beyond this Bir el Gebel is signposted. This is about 5 km off the main road to the resthouse and well/spring.

Al-Qasr was a Roman settlement and Dakhla's fortified mediaeval capital. The narrow streets, covered as protection from the sand and sun, found in the old quarter reflect the antiquity of the area. Ancient wooden lintels at doorways are decorated with carved inscriptions from the Koran. It is possible to see inside these houses. The houses of Abu Nafri and Abu Misid are commonly used by guides. An ancient mosque no longer in use dates back to the Ayyubid period and alongside is Nasr el Din, a 3-storey wooden minaret 21m high. The saqiya, an ancient water wheel, near the two high pigeon towers and the sheikh's tomb, is a disappointment. No longer in use due to falling water levels it stands in a litter filled ravine and is rapidly falling to pieces. El Kasr Hotel and restaurant on the main road is the only comfortable place to stay or eat.

Beyond Al-Qasr the road turns left and south and a large site on the right is **Amheidah** where the tombs date from 22nd century BC. The road continues by the Ottoman village of Qalamun back to Mut.

● **Transport Road Bus**: buses from Dakhla (Mut): to Cairo at 0600 E£25, at 1700 and 1900 E£35; to Assiut at 0830 and 1600 E£17; to Kharga at 0830 E£8, 1600 E£7, 1700 E£8. Buses to Cairo go via Farafra E£10 and Bahariya E£15.

Taxi: there are also service taxis from the bus station to all the above destinations.

DAKHLA TO KHARGA

The journey from Dakhla to Kharga, 195 km in a generally easterly direction, takes about 3 hrs. The road, good surface, passes the villages of Sheikh Wali and Masara, Asmant (Smint) a fortress town at 11 km, at 16 km Sheikh Mufta can be seen from the road on the right and at 20 km Qasr el Kassaba. To reach the ruins of Asmant el Khorab (**Kellis**) turn right off the road at the sign which says Kharga 170 km and drive directly into the desert for 1 km.

Balat, an interesting village with narrow covered streets and fertile gardens with vines and palms, dates back to the Turkish period. There are tombs from the 6th Dynasty and a Greek cemetery but fresh supplies from the bakery at the west side of the village or refreshment at the tea shop are perhaps more attractive.

Bashendi, on a huge arch at its entrance, describes itself as a model village. To see the internal decorations of the Roman period 1st century BC Tomb of Kitnes you need to ask around for the key. The Tomb of Bash Endi has a Roman base and a much more recent Islamic dome.

The French have been working at **Aïn Asil** for 14 years. To reach the site turn towards Bashendi through the triumphal arch, swing left before the mosque and then right at the next through-way into the desert. The track turns off to the left to a brick hut, the excavations are behind the hut, ie going back towards the main road. **Qila el Dabba** visible from the Aïn Asil site with 6th Dynasty pyramids is also being worked by the French. Approaching these excavations from Aïn Asil avoids checks for permits.

Immediately beyond **Tineida** and its tombs on the left of the road is a checkpoint. Look out now for the sandstone outcrops very near the road and on the closest, to the south, are a number of inscriptions – some purporting to be very old.

45 km west of Kharga a new town is being constructed by the road to the phosphate mine. Your next point of interest is a single tree. The road into Kharga for the last 20 km has been replaced at intervals with another to the south due to the contiuing march of the dunes. There is a very poor entrance to Kharga from the west, through a rubbish tip.

KHARGA OASIS

Pre-industrial Kharga was very different from the city of today. At that time the water level was considerably higher and the route was vital for the caravan trade. The New Valley scheme has converted this attractive oasis into a modern concrete town thereby removing almost all traces of its former charm. Nevertheless, two sites of interest remain in the surrounding area.

The **Temple of Hibis**, about 2 km to the north of the town, was erected in 510-490 BC at the beginning of the Persian occupation, and is one of the few remains from that period. It is dedicated to the triad of Thebian gods, Amun Ra', Mut and Khons. Unfortunately it was built on clay and suffers from subsidence. Several attempts have been made to restore the planks and reinforce the foundations. It is relatively well preserved from the **Third Pylon** onwards. The remains demonstrate the prevailing influence of the Pharaonic era on the later empires. The ornamentation and designs within the temple are mainly animals, showing vultures, dogs and serpents intertwined with Persian and Egyptian deities. No entry charge.

The **Necropolis of El-Baqawat**, covering an area 500m x 200m and situated approximately 5 km north of the town, can be reached by taking a dirt track from the Hibis Temple road through a palm grove and a short distance into the desert. This was once so far from civilization that hermits came for the seclusion it offered. In the 4th century the Christian theologian St Athanasius was banished here.

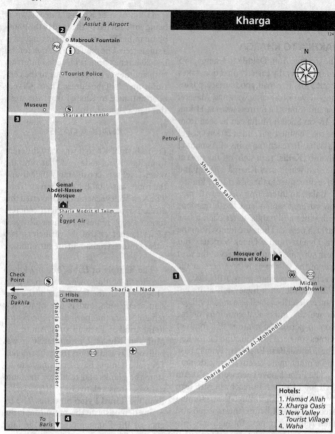

To Assiut & Airport

Kharga

124

Pol

Mabrouk Fountain

Tourist Police

Museum

Sharia el Khenesso

Petrol

Sharia Port Said

N

Gemal Abdel-Nasser Mosque

Sharia Modrit el Talim

Egypt Air

Mosque of Gamma el Kebir

Midan Ash-Showla

Check Point

To Dakhla

Sharia Gamal Abdul Nasser

Hibis Cinema

Sharia el Nada

1

Sharia An-Nabawy Al-Mohandis

To Baris

4

Hotels:
1. *Hamad Allah*
2. *Kharga Oasis*
3. *New Valley Tourist Village*
4. *Waha*

Open daily 0800-1800 summer, 0800-1700 winter. Entrance E£20. About 500 baked brick tombs, originating from an early Christian burial site, and dating from 3rd-7th centuries lie crumbling in the desert. Small chapels cover some of the tombs. The most interesting features of the burial ground are the vivid wall paintings of biblical scenes. Some are fairly crudely executed and others were defaced by the ancient Greeks. The chapels are known by the illustrations they contain which are mainly of Old Testament scenes depicting

Adam and Eve, the Exodus, Daniel in the lion's den, Noah's Ark, Abraham and Isaac. Look out for Jonah being vomited out of the whale's stomach. From the New Testament the Virgin Mary and St Paul feature most often. Takla Hamanout (see page 85) is shown here with St Paul. Some of the best preserved paintings are in locked chapels but, by negotiating with the guard, you may be allowed in to see them.

In the centre is a church dating from the 5th century AD – one of the oldest in Egypt.

Temple of Nadoura, go north from town and turn right at the triumphal arch. This small temple of sandstone was built by Antonius Pius in 138 AD and commands a splendid view of the Temple of Hibis.

Places of interest

Alwadi Algadeed Museum on Sharia Gamal Abdel Nasser opened 1993, £E10 for foreigners – open 0800-1500 every day. In particular look at the mummies, the painted sphynx and the selection of gold coins upstairs. This is a very good museum, well laid out and most of the items are named in English or French.

Local information
● **Accommodation**

E *El Kharga Oasis*, Sharia Gamal Abdel Nasser, T 901500, Tx 93766, 30 rm, best hotel in town; **E** *Hamad Allah Hotel*, T 900638, F 905017, 32 rm with phone and shower, restaurant, bar, shop, garden, lunch £E15, dinner £E20.

F *Hamadalla Hotel*, El-Kharga, El-Wadi Guedid, T 900638, 54 rm with a/c; **F** *Waha*, T 900393, cheap, fairly comfortable, hot water supply is erratic.

Camping At *El Kharga Oasis* where use of hotel facilities is permitted. *Nasr Wells*, south of Kharga, is in a beautiful site. Although there are only a few official camping there is no problem camping along the route. Indeed one of the highlights of the trip, albeit for properly equipped campers with sufficient water, is a night spent under the stars.

● **Places to eat**

Besides the hotels and the few local cafés the choice is limited.

● **Banks & money changers**

Misr Bank, open Sunday-Thursday 0800-1400 and 1700-2000, Friday-Saturday opens at 1030.

● **Hospitals & medical services**

General Hospital, T 900777.

● **Tourist offices**

Tourist office, opp *Kharga Oasis Hotel*, open Sunday-Thursday 1000-1500 and 1900-2200.

● **Useful telephone numbers**

Airport: T 901695.
Police: T 122.
Tourist information: T 900728.

Tourist police: T 901502.

● **Transport**

Air There are direct flights on Wednesday and Sunday to Cairo, leaves at 0800, takes 50 mins. Airport is 5 km northeast of town on road to Assiut.

Road Bus: from Midan Ash-Showla to Cairo via Assiut, 2 each day (10 hrs). The evening bus has a/c and costs more. There are frequent buses to Dakhla. *Upper Egypt Bus Co*, T 900838. **Service taxis**: usually caught from nr the bus station are marginally more expensive than the bus but are quicker taking 5 hrs to Assiut. Some only travel at night when it is cooler – this means missing the searing heat and the magnificent scenery which are the two things which make the Great Desert Circuit the great experience that it is! **Taxis**: which are supposed to cover the whole of the area, T 900029.

Excursion south

To the south of Kharga, on the road to Darfur is the Nasser Resthouse and Tourist Wells with campsite; Bulaq village with wells/springs with temperatures reaching 39°C and a primitive resthouse; Baris with a Roman Temple of Dush dedicated to the God Serapis, also a mud-brick Turkish fortress, an ancient church and some Coptic pottery. Service taxis and buses operate on this route.

ASSIUT

Arriving back in the Nile Valley at **Assiut** (see page 185) one can either continue the circuit back to Cairo or take the opportunity to travel south via the Abydos and Dendera temples to the wonders of Luxor and the Valley of the Kings.

● **Transport** Transport is certainly no problem. **Air** There are direct flights to Cairo and Kharga from the airport 10 km northwest of the town. **Train** Trains run 12 times a day to Cairo (7 hrs) via Mallawi (2 hrs) and Minya (3 hrs), but less frequently to Luxor (6-7 hrs) via Sohag (2 hrs) and Qena (4-5 hrs). **Road Bus**: there are 7 daily buses Cairo (7 hrs) as well as buses every 30 mins between 0600-1800 north to Minya (2 hrs) and south to Sohag. **Service taxis**: run to every town between Minya and Sohag and are easy to catch from the main depot in the mornings but are less frequent later in the day.

Information for travellers

The advice given below relates to Egypt. For detailed information relating to Libya see page 491.

BEFORE TRAVELLING

ENTRY REQUIREMENTS

Passports
Passports are required by all and should be valid for at least 6 months beyond the period of intended stay in Egypt.

Special permits
There are few closed areas in this region but certain sensitive border zones can be mined or be restricted to military personnel. Do not stray into clearly marked boundary or no-go areas. Details of any known sensitive areas are given in appropriate sections of this Handbook.

Visas
Visas are required by all except nationals of Ghana, Guinea and Malta and most Arab countries. Tourist visas cost around US$20 equivalent. In UK this is £15 for a single entry and £18 for up to three entries. Business visas cost £53 and £91 accompanied by a letter of authorization. Payment must be by cash or postal order, cheques are not accepted. Visas are valid for 3 months from date of issue and 1 month from date of arrival and cannot be post dated.

Emergency visas may be granted at the point of entry other than Sinai. A renewable 30 day tourist visa can be obtained at airport points of entry and ports, and even on the boat. Entrance without a visa is permitted for visits of up to a week to South Sinai and St Catherine when entering through Sinai entry points of Taba, St Catherine and Sharm el-Sheikh airports, Nuweiba and Sharm el-Sheikh seaports. Do not permit officials to stamp your passport at these entry points.

As part of the easing of controls on travellers in this area, most countries will issue entry visas at principal border posts.

Visas for travel into Libya are available only from their embassy in Cairo: their consulate in Alexandria deals only with Arab nationals. At present visas are issued on an individual basis. A letter of recommendation is required from the traveller's own embassy (£27.50 from UK embassy in Cairo). The Sudanese embassy also requires a letter of recommendation. Presenting the application in modest dress and a courteous manner aids the process.

Identity & membership cards
If you are in full-time education you will be entitled to an International Student Identity Card (ISIC), which is distributed by student travel offices and travel agencies in 77 countries. The ISIC gives you

Main UK Tour Operators featuring Egypt

Name	Telephone	Fax
Abercrombie and Kent*#	0171 730 9600	0171 730 9376
African Safari Tours	0181 941 7400	0181 941 5168
Amoun Travel#	0171 402 3100	0171 402 3424
Ancient World Tours	07071 222950	01328 823293
Bales Tours	01306 885991	01306 740048
British Museum Traveller	0171 323 8895	0171 580 8677
Destination Red Sea*#	0181 440 9900	0181 440 9905
Diving World#	0171 407 0017	0171 378 1108
Egyptian Encounter*#	01590 677665	01590 677373
El-Sawy Travel Ltd*#	0171 258 1901	0171 724 8003
Exodus Travels	0181 675 5550	0181 673 0779
Explore Worldwide	01252 316016	01252 315935
Explorers Tours#	01753 681999	01753 682660
Gerba World Adventures	01373 826611	01373 858351
Global Encounter#	01273 473455	01273 483089
Goodwood Travel	01227 763336	01227 762417
Hayes and Jarvis*#	0181 222 7800	0181 741 0299
The Imaginative Traveller#	0181 742 8612	0181 742 3045
Jasmin Tours*#	0181 675 8886	0181 673 1204
Kuoni Travel*#	01306 743000	01306 744222
Longwood Holidays#	0181 551 4494	0181 550 0086
MISR Travel*#	0171 255 1087	0171 255 1089
Oonasdivers*#	01323 648924	01323 738356
Peltours Ltd#	0181 343 0590	0181 343 0579
Regal Holidays*#	01353 778096	01353 777897
Seafarer Cruising and Sailing	0171 234 0500	0171 234 0700
Skybus Holidays	0171 631 3444	0171 631 3338
Soliman Travel#	0171 244 6855	0171 835 1394
Somak Holidays	0181 423 3000	0181 423 7700
Swan Hellenic	0171 800 2200	0171 831 1280
Tailor Made Holidays*#	0181 398 4464	0181 398 6007
Thomas Cook		
Thomson Holidays#	0171 383 1020	0171 383 1767
Top Deck Travel	0171 370 4555	0171 373 6201
Travelbag Adventures#	01420 541007	01420 541022
Travelscope Worldwide#	01483 569453	01483 569466

* = provision for disabled   # = diving holidays

special prices on all forms of transport (air, sea, rail etc) and access to a variety of other concessions and services. Contact ISIC, Box 9048, 1000 Copenhagen, Denmark, T (+45) 33939303.

Vaccinations

Vaccinations are not required unless travelling from a country where yellow fever or cholera frequently occurs. You are advised to be up to date with polio, tetanus and hepatitis protection. Evidence of an AIDS test is required for visits over 30 days – although this requirement is not always enforced (see Health, page 505).

WHAT TO TAKE

Travellers tend to take more than they need though requirements vary with the destination and the type of travel that is to be undertaken. Laundry services are generally cheap and speedy. A travelpack, a hybrid backpack/suitcase, rather than a rigid suitcase, covers most eventualities and survives bus boot, roof rack and plane/ship hold travel with ease. Serious trekkers will need a framed backpack.

Clothing of light cotton or cotton/polyester with a a woollen sweater for evenings, more northern regions, higher altitudes and the clear desert nights. Comfortable shoes with socks as feet may swell in hot weather. Modest dress for women including (see page 13) a sunhat and headscarf. See hints in country sections.

Checklist:

Air cushions for hard seating
Bumbag
Earplugs
Eye mask
Insect repellent and/or mosquito net, electric mosquito mats, coils
Neck pillow
International driving licence
Photocopies of essential documents
Short wave radio
Spare passport photographs
Sun hat
Sun protection cream
Sunglasses
Swiss Army knife
Tissues/toilet paper
Torch
Umbrella (excellent protection from sun and unfriendly dogs)
Wipes (*Damp Ones*, *Baby Wipes*)
Zip-lock bags

Those intending to stay in budget accommodation might also include:

Cotton sheet sleeping bag
Money belt
Padlock (for hotel room and pack)
Soap
Student card
Towel
Toilet paper
Universal bath plug

Health kit

Antiacid tablets
Anti-diarrhoea tablets
Anti-malaria tablets
Anti-infective ointment
Condoms
Contraceptives
Dusting powder for feet
First aid kit and disposable needles
Flea powder
Sachets of rehydration salts
Tampons
Travel sickness pills
Water sterilizing tablets

WHEN TO GO

Best time to visit

The sun shines the whole year round and rainy days are the exception. The temperature increases as one travels south with Luxor being about 10°C warmer than Cairo. The high summer temperatures in the desert will be of greatest concern for visitors. See page 53 and individual climatic statistics in the text.

Each section has at least one climatic table with the best season(s) shaded for easy reference.

HEALTH

Staying healthy

Mosquitoes and flies can be a problem in certain areas. Buy a fly spray, take good repellent creams and antihistamine cream if you are prone to bites. Raw food is best avoided unless you can wash it or peel it. The sun is hot all year round so take adequate precautions.

Water

Bottled water is easily available, cheap and safer to drink, but cleaning your teeth with tap water will not be harmful.

Further health information

Read the section on Health (see page 505) and be prepared for some stomach upsets due to heat and change of diet.

MONEY

Banks

There are five national banks and more than 78 branches of foreign banks. Banking hours are 0830-1400 Sunday-Thursday.

Cost of living

Egypt is very cheap. Depending on the standards of comfort and cleanliness one is prepared to accept for accommodation, food and travel, it is possible to survive on as little as E£25-30 pp per day. Petrol (super) 100 piastres per litre, coffee or tea E£0.50, soft drink E£0.75-E£1, medium beer E£1.50.

Exchange rates (September 1998)					
	US$	**£**	**Ffr**	**DM**	**Ptas**
Egypt (Pound)	3.40	5.7	0.60	2.02	0.02
Libya (Dinar)	0.39	0.65	0.07	0.23	0.002

Credit cards

Access/Mastercard, American Express, Diners Club and Visa are accepted in all major hotels, larger restaurants and shops but, in the main, Egypt is still a cash economy.

Currency

E£1 = 100 Piastres. Notes are in denominations of E£1, E£5, E£10, E£20, E£50, E£100 and 5, 10, 25 and 50 Piastres. Coins (which are not worth carrying) are 5 and 10 Piastres.

Regulations and money changing

Visitors can enter and leave Egypt with a maximum of E£10,000. There are no restrictions on the import of foreign currency provided it is declared on an official customs form. Export of foreign currency may not exceed the amount imported. All cash, TCs, credit cards and gold over E£500 must be declared on arrival.

Travellers' cheques

Travellers' cheques can be honoured in most banks and *bureaux de change*. US$ are the easiest to exchange particularly if they are well-known like Visa, Thomas Cook or American Express. There is always a transaction charge so it is a balance between using high value cheques and paying one charge and carrying extra cash or using lower value cheques and paying more charges. A small amount of cash, again in US$, is useful in an emergency.

Egypt has a fixed exchange rate – wherever the transaction is carried out.

GETTING THERE

AIR

It is possible to fly direct to Egypt from Europe, the Middle East, North Africa, most adjacent African countries and also from the USA and Canada. Libya, which is currently suffering a UN embargo on international flights is an exception.

There are regular flights from and to USA: New York (4) and Los Angeles (2). Flights from and to Asia: Tokyo, Karachi (2). Flights from and to Europe: Paris, Rome, London (daily), Barcelona, Madrid (3), Berlin (1), Copenhagen, Milan (2), Frankfurt (5), Geneva, Zurich (4). Flights from and to Middle East/North Africa: Abu Dhabi, Amman, Dubai, Jeddah, Kuwait (daily); Bahrain, Beirut, Tunis, Tripoli (2/3/week); Khartoum, Algiers (1); Casablanca (3).

Air Sinai operates return services: Cairo-Tel Aviv; Cairo-El-Arish, Cairo-St Catherine-Eilat; Cairo-Ras el-Nakab-Luxor-Sharm el-Sheikh. Details from *Nile Hilton Hotels*, T 760948/776893.

Egypt's international airports are Cairo International (CAI) 22 km northeast of the city (travel time 30 mins); Alexandria Airport (ALY) 5 km southeast of the city; Luxor Airport (LXR) 5.5 km from the town. The national airline is Egyptair. Flight times to Cairo: from London about 4 hrs 40 mins, £240 return; from Paris 4½ hrs; from Athens 2 hrs; from Tunis 1¾ hrs. The major destinations are the national capitals and an increasing number of tourist airports such as Sharm el-Sheikh and Hurghada. The scheduled flying times from London are Cairo 5 hrs and Luxor 7 hrs. From Paris flying times are approximately half an hour less than those from London. Package tours which frequently offer cheaper flight – only deals generally operate smaller planes which take longer.

Airline restrictions

General airline restrictions apply with regard to luggage weight allowances before surcharge; normally 30 kg for first class and 20 kg for business and economy class. An understanding of the term 'limited' with regard to amount of hand luggage varies greatly. Some airlines can be strict and will decline to permit large or in some cases more than one item of hand luggage on board with the passenger.

Discounts

It is possible to obtain significantly cheaper tickets by avoiding school vacation times, by flying at night, by shopping around and by booking early to obtain one of the quota of discounted fares. Group discounts apply in many instances.

Airline security

International airlines vary in their arrangements and requirements for security over electrical items such as radios, tape recorders and lap-top computers (as does the interest of the customs officials on arrival and departure). Check in advance if you can, carry the items in your hand luggage for convenience and have them wrapped for safety but available for inspection.

TRAIN AND STEAMER

There is no international rail link either east to Israel or west to Libya (Libya has no railway) and the ferry connection across Lake Nasser between Aswan and Wadi Halfa in Sudan has been suspended due to political tensions.

ROAD

Bus and taxi

For coaches to Israel (Tel Aviv and Jerusalem) contact *Travco Travel Agency*, T 403448; the *East Delta Bus Company* (Sinai International Station) runs a/c buses daily except Saturday to Tel-Aviv. Contact Sinai International Station, T 824753 or East Delta Buses, 14, Sharia Mustafa Abu Hef, Cairo, T 743027. Service taxis run between Marsa Matruh and Sollum on the Libyan border. Reach Marsa Matruh by bus (a/c or service) from Midan Sa'ad Zaghloul, Alexandria. Arab Union superjet

buses leave from Midan Almaza, Cairo at 0200 for Amman, Jeddah, Damascus, Kuwait, Bahrain and Qatar; at 0700 for Libya. Regular departures from Alexandria to Benghazi (15-20 hrs) and Tripoli (30 hrs).

Motoring

Vehicles drive on the right in Egypt. Road signs are international with Arabic script. The main international road west goes to Libya and to the east over the Suez Canal and via El-Arish to Israel. Other international routes are along the Nile Valley or along the northern Sinai and the Red Sea coasts. Entry for private cars requirments – a Carnet de Passage en Douane and an International Driving Licence. Contact Egyptian Automobile Club, 1 Sharia Kasr el-Nil, Cairo, T 743355. Vehicles must be petrol, not diesel, lead-free petrol is not available, and 4WD vehicles require permission from the Ministry of Defence. Extra vehicle insurance may be required at the border.

SEA

Ferries

The region is served by a number of ferry services, particularly across the Red Sea/Gulf of Aqaba, most catering for both vehicles and foot passengers. Most ferries are reliable and moderately comfortable.

The main coastal ports are Alexandria, Port Said and Suez. Ferries operating in this area can be contacted in UK at: *Viamare Travel*, Graphic House, 2 Sumatra Rd, London NW6 1PU, T 071 431 4560 or *CTC Lines*, 1 Regent St, London SW1Y 4NN, T 071 930 9962.

For connections to Italy, Greece, Cyprus contact Adriatica's represntive at *Mena Tours Agency*, 14 Sharia Talaat Harb, Cairo, T 740955/740864; 28 Sharia al-Ghorfa al-Tigariya, Alexandria, T 809676.

For connections with Jordan, from Nuweiba to Aqaba contact *Egyptian Shipping Co*, Cairo, T 758278, daily from Aqaba at 1300 and 1800 – except Saturday, only one sailing so check carefully.

Cruise ships calling in at ports in

Ferry Routes

Mediterranean Sea

To Heraklion & Athens
To Limassol
To Rhodes & Athens
To Heraklion & Genoa
Aqaba
Port Said
Alexandria
Nuweiba
Suez
To Port Sudan & Jeddah
Sharm el-Sheikh
Hurghada

Egypt: Airtours Cruises, Wavell House, Helmshore, Rossendale, Lancs, BB4 4NB, T 0170 6260000, call in at Alexandria. Cargo Ship Voyages, Strand Cruise Travel Centre, Charing Cross Shopping Concourse, Strand, London, WC2N 4HZ, call in at Port Said, Damietta, Suez, Port Sudan, Alexandria. Crystal Cruises, 11 Quadrant Arcade, Regent Street, London W1R 6JB, T 0171 287 9040, F 0171 434 1410, call in at Alexandria and Port Said. P&O Cruises, 77 New Oxford St, London, WC1A 1PP, T 0171 800 2222, F 0171 800 1280, call in at Port Said. Titan Travel/Costa Cruises, HiTours House, 26-30 Holmethorpe Ave, Redhill, Surrey, RH1 2NL, T 01737 760033, F 01737 779288, call in at Alexandria and Port Said.

Ferries ply between Suez and Jeddah in Saudi Arabia via Aqaba, contact *Mena Tours Agency*, 14 Sharia Talaat Harb, Cairo, T 740955 or *Misr Travel*, 1 Sharia Talaat Harb, Cairo, T 3930010.

In the case of Libya, entry by ferry from Italy or Malta is important in view of the suspension of air services.

CUSTOMS

Declarations On arrival declare video cameras and computers on the D form. In case of theft report to police or they will assume you have sold them and charge duty.

Departure There is no departure tax.

Confirm airline flights at least 48 hrs in advance. Have all currency exchange receipts easily available. Before passing into the departure lounge/area it is necessary to fill in an embarkation card. Only a limited amount of currency can be reconverted before you leave. This is a tedious process and is not possible at Luxor airport. Sometimes suitable foreign currency is not available. It is better to budget with care, have no excess cash and save all the trouble. A maximum of E£1,000 may be carried into or out of Egypt.

Duty free allowances Goods may be imported into Egypt as follows: 200 cigarettes or 50 cigars or 250 gm of tobacco, 1 litre of spirit, 1 litre of perfume or toilet water, gifts up to the value of E£500. Duty free export of purchases can be arranged through the larger shops and tourist agencies.

Entry into Israel, Libya and Sudan With the appropriate visas entry is comparatively straight forward although bilateral relations with Sudan are currently very strained.

Insurance Comprehensive travel insurance is essential. Consider one which offers immediate repatriation for illness or accident. Claims for lost or stolen items must be backed by evidence of reporting the matter to the police.

Prohibited goods include drugs and firearms. Permits can be obtained for hunting guns through the hotel/tour organizer. It is forbidden to take into UK – ivory, crocodile, snake or lizard skin. It is forbidden to take from Egypt genuine Egyptian artifacts.

Registration All visitors to Egypt must register with the police within 7 days of arrival. This is generally done by the hotel. Independent travellers are responsible for their own registration which can be done at a main police station or the Mogamma building off Cairo's Medan Tahrir. If you do not register be prepared for a fine.

ON ARRIVAL

General note

The countries adjacent to the River Nile are principally Islamic. Day to day travel is inevitably tempered by bureaucracy, religion and politics. Even the terrain, much of it desert away from the river, will make travelling quite different. The points below are essentially practical in nature but a study of the larger issues, outlined in the Regional Introduction on page 13, will undoubtedly lead to a hassle-free and enjoyable trip.

Airline offices

British Airways, 1 Abdel Salam Aref, Cairo, T 759977, at airport 671741; Air France, 2 Talaat Harb, Cairo, T 5743300, at airport 661028; Air India, 1 Talaat Harb, Cairo, T 3934873; Alitalia, Nile Hilton Commercial Complex, Cairo, T 5743488, at airport 665143; Iberia, 15 Midan Tahrir, Cairo, T 3910828; KLM, 11 Kasr el-Nil, Cairo, T 5740999, at airport 662226; Lufthansa, 6 El-Sheikh el-Marsafi, Zamalek, Cairo, T 3420471, at airport 666975; Royal Air Maroc, 16 Bustan, T 3934574; Swissair, 22 Kasr el-Nil, Cairo, T 3937955, at airport 669537; Tunis Air, 14 Talaat Harb, Cairo, T 769726.

Bargaining

Bargaining is expected in the bazaars. Start lower than you would expect to pay, be polite and good humoured, enjoy the experience and if the final price doesn't suit – walk away. There are plenty more shops. Once you have gained confidence, try it on the taxi drivers and when negotiating a room.

Beggars

Beggars are a fact of life in Muslim countries where alms-giving is a personal duty. It is unlikely that they will be too persistent. Have a few very small coins ready. You will be unable to help many and your donation will most probably be passed on to the syndicate organizer!

Clothing

Cotton clothes in summer, warmer garments for winter and desert evenings. Egyptian cotton garments are good value. Trousers and long sleeved shirts provide protection from the sun and insects. A wide brimmed hat or sun glasses will offer protection from the glare of the sun. Comfortable shoes are necessary for sightseeing. Open sandals let the sand and dust in. Egypt is a Muslim country and scanty clothing can cause offence. Speedy and efficient laundry services are provided by most hotels. See section on clothing (see page 13).

Confidence tricksters

The most common 'threat' to tourists is found where people are on the move, at ports and railway and bus stations, selling 'antiques', 'gems', offering extremely favourable currency exchange rates and spinning 'hard luck' stories. Confidence tricksters are, by definition, extremely convincing and persuasive. Be warned – if the offer seems too good to be true that is probably what it is.

Courtesy

Politeness is always appreciated. You will notice a great deal of hand shaking, kissing, clapping on backs on arrival and departure from a group. There is no need to follow this to the extreme but handshakes, smiles and thank yous go a long way. Be patient and friendly but firm when bargaining for items and avoid displays of anger. Be very careful never to criticize as officials, waiters and taxi drivers can understand more than you think. See page 18 on how to deal with the bureaucracy. **However** when it comes to getting onto public transport, forget it all – the description 'like a Cairo bus' will need no explanation.

Drugs

Ignore all offers of drugs. It is more than likely that the 'pusher', if successful, will report you to the police. Drug enforcement policies are strict in Egypt. The death penalty may be imposed for those

---

Caveat Emptor – the art of bargaining

Haggling is a normal business practice in Egypt and surrounding countries. Modern economists might feel that bargaining is a way of covering up high-price salesmanship within a commercial system that is designed to exploit the lack of legal protection for the consumer. Even so, haggling over prices is the norm and is run as an art form, with great skills involved. Bargaining can be great fun to watch between a clever buyer and an experienced seller but it is less entertaining when a less than artful buyer such as a foreign traveller considers what he/she has paid later! There is great potential for the tourist to be heavily ripped off. Most dealers recognize the wealth and gullibility of travellers and start their offers at an exorbitant price. The dealer then appears to drop his price by a fair margin but remains at a final level well above the real local price of the goods.

To protect yourself in this situation be relaxed in your approach. Talk at length to the dealer and take as much time as you can afford inspecting the goods and feeling out the last price the seller will accept. Do not belittle or mock the dealer – take the matter very seriously but do not show commitment to any particular item you are bargaining for by being prepared to walk away empty handed. Never feel that you are getting the better of the dealer or feel sorry for him. He will not sell without making a very good profit! Also it is better to try several shops if you are buying an expensive item such as a carpet or jewellery. This will give a sense of the price range. Walking away – regretfully of course – from the dealer normally brings the price down rapidly but not always. Do not change money in the same shop where you make your purchases, since this will be expensive.

---

convicted of smuggling or selling narcotics. Possession of even small quantities may lead to prosecution.

Firearms
Firearms including hunting guns may not be imported without prior permission.

Hours of business
Government offices from 0900-1400 every day except Friday and national holidays; Banks are open 0830-1400 Saturday-Thursday; Shops are open 0900-1230 and 1600-2000 in summer and 0900-1900 in winter. Hours on Friday and Sunday will vary.

Mosques
Visitors to mosques (where permitted) and other religious buildings will normally be expected to remove their shoes and cover-all garments will be available for hire to enable the required standard of dress to be met.

Official time
GMT + 2 hrs.

Photography
Egypt's fine weather, clear skies and varying scenery gives opportunities for spectacular pictures. However, photographs of police, soldiers, docks, bridges, military areas, airports, radio stations and other public utilities are prohibited. Photography is also prohibited in tombs where much damage can be done with a flash bulb. Photography is unrestricted in all open, outdoor historic areas but some sites make an extra charge for cameras. Flashes are not permitted in the museum in Cairo nor for delicate relics such as the icons in St Catherine's Monastery. Taking photographs of any person without permission is unwise, of women is taboo and tourist attractions like water sellers, camels/camel drivers etc will require payment. Even the goat herder will expect a tip for providing the goats.

Most types of film are available. Check the sell by date and purchase from shops that appear to have a rapid turnover of films. Bring specialist films with you and take back home all exposed film for processing. High speed film (ISO400) is recommended for night time photography such as Sound and Light shows, and interiors of buildings where a flash is not permitted. Lower speed film is more suitable for the brighter outdoor conditions. The best time to take photographs is early morning or late afternoon as the amount of reflective light in the middle of the day requires a filter. Protect your camera from the fine invasive desert sand with a sturdy polythene bag.

Video cameras must be declared at the customs on arrival in Egypt. Always check that use of a video camera is permitted at tourist sites and be prepared to pay a heavy fee (E£100+) for permission.

Police

Report any incident which involves you or your possessions. An insurance claim of any size will require the backing of a police report. If involvement with the police is more serious, for instance a driving accident, remain calm, read the section on how to deal with the bureaucracy (see page 18) and contact the nearest consular office without delay.

Safety

The level of petty crime in Egypt is no greater than elsewhere. It is unlikely that you will be robbed but take sensible precautions. Leave your valuables in a hotel deposit box and never leave valuables or money around. Avoid carrying excess money or wearing obviously valuable jewellery when sightseeing. There will be pickpockets in crowded places. It is wise not to walk around at night away from the main thoroughfares. External pockets on bags and clothing should never be used for carrying valuables. Bag snatching and pick pocketing is more common in crowded tourist areas. **NB** It is wise to keep a record of your passport number, TCs number and air ticket number somewhere separate from the actual items.

Egypt is a Muslim country and Friday is the day of rest when offices and many

shops are closed. The Christians celebrate Sunday as their sabbath when many of their shops are closed. As the Islamic year is shorter than the Western year the dates of their religious holidays change (see page 355 in Introduction). The Christian Coptic calendar gives a third set of variable dates. It has 12 months of 30 days with the extra 5 days added every 4th year.

Security The disturbances caused by religious extremists have ceased but the national and local security services are still very much in evidence to offer protection at all major tourist areas. While the region containing Assiut, Minya and Qena ought to be avoided travellers should encounter no problems elsewhere.

Restricted areas Permission must be obtained to visit areas near Egypt's frontiers and off-road areas in Sinai. Contact Ministry of Interior travel permit department corner of Sahria Sheikh Rihan/Nubar in central Cairo.

Shopping

Places to shop Normal opening hours are summer 0900-1230 and 1600-2000, winter 0900-1900, often closed Sunday but shops in tourist areas seem to stay open much longer. The most interesting shopping is in the bazaars. This takes time but bargains can be found. The main bazaar in Cairo, *Khan el-Khalili*, has a wide selection of ethnic items. By contrast the smaller *Aswan bazaar*, parallel to and one block behind the Corniche, has less hassle and more time to ponder on the purchases.

Best buys Jewellery (sold by weight) and precious stones – particularly lapis lazuli, perfumes, spices, carpets, copper and brass ware, inlaid wooden boxes with intricate designs and cotton garments.

Tipping

Tipping is a way of life – everyone except high officials expects a reward for services rendered or supposed. Many people connected with tourism get no or very low wages and rely on tips to survive. Advice here is to be a frequent but small tipper on the principal of 'often and little'. Usually 10% is added to hotel and restaurant bills but an extra tip of about 5% is normal. Taxi drivers expect between 5-10%. In hotels and at monuments tips will be expected for the most minimal service. Rather than make a fuss have some very small coins handy. Tips may be the person's only income.

Voltage

220 volts AC. Sockets take standard continental two round pin plugs. Continental adaptors are useful.

Weights and measures

Egyptians use metric measurements (see page 519).

Women travelling alone

Women face greater difficulties than men or couples. Young Muslim women rarely travel without the protection of a male or older female, hence a single Western woman is regarded as strange and is supposed to be of easy virtue – a view perpetuated by Hollywood. To minimize the pestering that will certainly occur, dress modestly, the less bare flesh the better (see page 13), steadfastly ignore rude and suggestive comments directed at you but aimed at boosting the caller's ego, avoid any behaviour which would aggravate the situation, and keep a sense of humour. Single men often attract greater attention from customs officials and are more liable to receive unwelcome propositions.

Visa extensions

Extensions can be obtained (with difficulty) at the Mogamma, Midan Tahrir, Cairo; Sharia Khaled Ibn el Walid in Luxor; 28 Sharia Talaat Harb in Alexandria and at the port in Sharm el Sheikh. You will need your passport, two new photographs, cash to pay for renewal, and receipts proving you have exchanged US$180 for each extra month you wish to extend. Overstaying by 1 or 2 days does not matter, but after a couple of extra weeks be prepared for a fine.

WHERE TO STAY

Hotels

As tourism is one of Egypt's major industries, accommodation is available at the main sites and in all the major cities. This varies from deluxe international hotels to floor or roof space for a sleeping bag – at prices to suit all pockets. Most top quality hotel chains are represented offering top class facilities in their rooms and business centres. There are also cheap hotels which though often clean are very basic and spartan. There is a pronounced seasonality to demand for accommodation and in the spring, autumn and winter months the main tourist areas can be very busy and the hotels fully booked. Reservations in advance are recommended, especially for luxury hotels. Finding cheap accommodation is easy throughout the area, except in high season. Tax and a service charge will be added to the bill. Always ask to see the room first.

It should be noted, however, that, while price is a reasonable reflection of the type of hotel and service you can expect, some hotels are expensive but very ordinary while there are some wonderful hotels which are real bargains. If you are unsure about whether a cheap hotel is any good, only book in for one night, leave your baggage there and then go and explore the other choices.

Prices for the top class hotels are on a par with prices in Europe while medium range hotels are generally cheaper in comparison. In almost every case, the advertised room price, that charged to the individual traveller, is higher than that paid by the package tourist and it may be worth bargaining. The categories used in this *Handbook* are graded as accurately as possible by cost converted to American dollars. Our hotel price range is based on a double room with bath/shower in high season and includes any relevant taxes and service charges but no meals.

Normally the facilities indicated will be available and are therefore not repeated in the descriptions.

Hotel classifications

AL US$150+ Luxury hotel. All facilities for business and leisure travellers are of the highest international standard.

A US$100-150+ Central heated, a/c rooms with WC, bath/shower, TV, phone, mini-bar, daily clean linen. Choice of restaurants, coffee shop, shops, bank, travel agent, swimming pool, parking, sport and business facilities.

B US$75-100 As **A** but without the luxury, reduced number of restaurants, smaller rooms, limited range of shops and sport.

C US$50-75 Best rooms have a/c, own bath/shower and WC. Usually comfortable, bank, shop, pool.

D US$25-50 Best rooms may have own WC and bath/shower. Depending on management will have room service and choice of cuisine in restaurant.

E US$10-25 Simple provision. Perhaps fan cooler. May not have restaurant. Shared WC and showers with hot water (when available).

F under US$10 Very basic, shared toilet facilities, variable in cleanliness, noise, often in dubious locations.

Abbrevations in the listings: a/c = air conditioning, T = telephone, Tx = Telex, F = Facsimile. Bath denotes bath and/or shower.

Ungraded hotels – too primitive to reach the standard of **F** – but may be cleaner and more interesting than **F**.

Youth hostels

Information from Egyptian Youth Hostels, 7 Sharia Dr Abdel Hamid Said, Marouf, Cairo, T 43799. There are 15 hostels located in Egypt's main historic and tourist towns which are open all year round, closed 1000-1400 and 1300-0700. Minimum age 6 years. Overnight fees range from 350-750 piastres incl breakfast. Visitors may stay more than three consecutive nights if places are available. Although cheap meals are available (breakfast is incl, lunch 250 piastres, dinner served from 2000-2100, 250 piastres), all the big hostels have a member's kitchen where guests can prepare meals for themselves (use of the kitchen is free). Holders of membership cards can obtain significant reductions on train journeys. Those who do not already have cards can obtain them from any of the hostels in Egypt. The rules incl no alcohol or gambling, single sex dormitories, lights out between 2300-0600. Groups must make advance bookings at least 2 weeks before their arrival.

Camping

There are only a few official camp sites with good facilities and guards. Sites of varying quality exist in Aswan, Luxor, Cairo, Giza, Sharm el-Sheikh and Marsa Matruh. Hotels are very cheap and probably a more comfortable option. Assess the security of any site you choose and where possible ask permission to avoid any unpleasantness.

FOOD AND DRINK

Bearing in mind the suggestions in the Health section (see page 508) on food best avoided in uncertain conditions, a wide choice still remains. Forget the stories of sheep's eyes and enjoy the selection of filling, spicy and slightly unusual meals. For the less adventurous, Western style food (other than pork) can be found in most hotels.

Food

Egyptian food is basically a mixture of Mediterranean cusines, containing elements of Lebanese, Turkish, and Greek cooking, with few authentic local dishes.

Breakfast is usually *fuul*, fava beans simmered slowly overnight, the national dish and a cheap meal at most cafés. These are served in a thick spicy sauce, either with an egg on top or in a sandwich. Equally cheap and popular is *taamaya*, deep fried balls of ground fava beans spiced with coriander and garlic, again often served in a sandwich garnished with *tahina* (sesame seed dip) and *torshi* (brightly coloured pickled vegetables such as turnips, carrots, and limes). These constitute Egyptian fastfood with the addition of *shawarma*, sliced lamb kebab sandwiches, and *fitir*. The latter sold in special *fatatri* cafés, where the thin dough pancake is made to order with either sweet or savoury fillings.

Bread is the staple of the Egyptian diet, its Arabic name *aish* meaning life. The local *aish baladi*, a brown flat loaf similar to pitta, tastes good fresh but should be eaten on the day of purchase. The white flour *aish shami* is less common.

Lunch is the main meal of the day, eaten anytime between 1400 and 1700. Carbohydrates, usually rice and bread, form the bulk of the meal accompanied by fresh seasonal vegetables and either meat or fish. *Mezzas*, a selection of small salads, are served at the beginning of the meal and include *tahina*, *babaghanoug* (*tahina* with mashed aubergines), olives, local white fetta-style cheese, *warra einab* or stuffed vine leaves, and *kobeiba*, deep fried bulgar wheat stuffed with meat and nuts. Like most Middle Eastern countries, *kebab*, lamb pieces grilled over charcoal on a skewer, and *kofta*, minced lamb, are common main dishes. Chicken and pigeon are also widely available, the latter considered a local delicacy when stuffed with rice and nuts. All meat should be eaten well-done to avoid stomach upsets. Fish is less commonly eaten but nevertheless good. From either the Red Sea or the Mediterranean, try the Sea Bass or the Red Snapper but watch the bones in the latter. Lobster and shrimp are relatively cheap.

Particular Egyptian main dishes include *molokia*, finely chopped mallow leaves, prepared with garlic, spices and either rabbit or chicken, and a good deal more tasty than its glutinous texture suggests; *fatta*, layers of bread, rice, chunks of lamb or beef, yogurt, raisins and nuts, drenched in a vinegar garlic broth; *koshari*, a mix of macaroni, rice and brown lentils covered with fried onions and a spicy tomato sauce; and *mahshi*, vegetables, typically black or white aubergines, tomatoes, green peppers, and courgettes, stuffed with rice and mincemeat.

Fruits, like vegetables, are seasonal although there is a wide variety available all year round. Winter offers dates of various colours ranging from yellow to black, citrus fruits, small sweet bananas, pears, apples, and even strawberries. Summer brings plums, peaches, figs, pomegranates, guava, mangoes, grapes, melons and a brief season, for a few weeks in May, of apricots.

Traditional Egyptian desserts are sweet, sticky, fattening, and delicious. The best of all is *Om Ali*, or Mother of Ali, a warm pudding of bread or pastry covered with milk, coconut, raisins, and nuts. But try the oriental pastries including *atayef*, deep fried nut-stuffed pancakes; *baklava*, honey-drenched filo pastry layered with nuts; *basbousa*, a syrupy semolina cake often filled with cream and garnished with pistachio nuts; and *konafa*, shredded batter cooked with butter and stuffed with nuts.

Vegetarianism is not a concept with which Egyptians are familiar. While vegetable dishes are plentiful, and the majority of Egyptians eat any quantity of meat only once a week, it is difficult to avoid tiny pieces of meat or meat stock in vegetable courses. Even the wonderful lentil soup, like most Egyptian soups a meal on its own, often has the addition of a chicken stock cube.

Drink

Tea is the essential Egyptian drink, taken strong without milk but with spoonfuls of sugar. A pleasant alternative is tea prepared with mint, *chai bil na'ana*, which is good for the digestion. Instant coffee just called Nescafe, is available but avoid the local Misr Cafe which tastes like sawdust. The thick Turkish coffee, which can be laced with cardamom or cinnamon,

Wines, beers and spirits in Egypt

Egypt is Mediterranean by climate but certainly not affected by the Latin love of the vine and its products despite the colonial activities of the French. A mere 10,000 ha of vines are cultivated and annual output is something over a quarter of a million tons of grapes.

Vines grow well enough in the favourable climate of the northern coast lands, producing modest amounts of table grapes and a minor volume of feedstock for wine making. Some 3.5 million litres of wine are produced annually in the Alexandria area.

A fairly reliable red is the *Omar Khayyam* for those with a good sense of humour about their wines. The white and rosé wines such as *Cru des Ptolemees* are very ordinary and should only be taken well cooled.

Egyptian beers, *Stella* for example, are cheap and light. Imported beers are very expensive in the major hotels and bars.

Local spirits such as brandy, gin and whisky are quite palatable and reasonably cheap. Try *zibeeb*, the Egyptian verion of Ouzo (see also page 442).

Rather than risk uncertain brews, why not have an alcohol-free vacation instead?

should be ordered either *saada*, with no sugar; *arriha*, with a little sugar; *mazbut*, medium; or *ziyada*, with extra sugar. The *mazbut* is the most popular – and one is expected to leave the thick mud of coffee grains in the bottom half of the cup. Coffee grinds, like tea leaves elsewhere, are believed to indicate the future. Other hot drinks include a cinnamon tea, *irfa*, reportedly good for colds; and the less common *sahleb*, a milk drink with powdered arrowroot, coconut, and chopped nuts. Cold drinks include the usual soft drink options of Coca-Cola, Pepsi Cola, 7-Up, and Fanta. Of more interest are the traditional *ersoos*, licorice juice; *karkade*, made from the dried petals of the red hibiscus; and *tamarhindi*, from the tamarind. Freshly squeezed juice stands are located throughout the cities, but these may not be very hygenic. Bottled water, either Baraka or Siwa, is sold widely but check that the seal is intact and that the bottle has not been refilled.

Although Egypt is a Muslim country, alcohol is available in bars and good restaurants. While five-star hotels are beginning to import beer in barrels, the local 'Stella' beer is the most popular sold, with the better-quality 'Stella Export', in half litre bottles. Nonetheless, quality for both brands remains variable. Quality is also a problem with the rather rough Egyptian wines, which are reasonably priced. The white is best drunk very cold and cut with soda or bottled water. The best are the Omar Khayyam and Pharaon reds, the Ptolemee dry white or the Rubis d'Egypte rosé. The local spirits, which are bottled to resemble international brands, and include an ouzo called *zibib*, a rum 'Zattos', and a 'Big Ben' gin, are dangerous and should not be touched – they have been the cause of a number of foreign deaths in recent years.

Water

Be prepared for shortage or restriction of water, never regard tap water safe to drink. Bottled water is cheap and easily available. See Health, page 508.

Where to eat and drink

The better hotel restaurants serve international cuisine of a high standard and often have speciality Egyptian restaurants. From there the price but not necessarily the standard falls down to the street stalls which perhaps are best avoided for hygiene reasons. See entries under separate town sections.

GETTING AROUND

AIR

Domestic airlines link the main towns. The services are reliable and can be recommended where long distances of otherwise hot and dusty land travel are involved such as between Cairo and Abu Simbel.

There are daily flights between Cairo, Alexandria, Luxor, Aswan, Abu Simbel, New Valley and Hurghada and less frequently to Marsa Matruh. Contact Egyptair T 922444. There are regular flights from Cairo to St Catherine, El-Arish and Sharm el-Sheikh. Contact Air Sinai at *Nile Hilton* T 760948.

Flight times: Cairo to Luxor 1 hr; Cairo to Aswan 2 hr; Aswan to Abu Simbel 40 mins; Cairo to Hurgarda 1 hr; Cairo to St Catherine's Monastery 50 mins.

TRAIN

Rail networks are limited, slow and generally more expensive than the alternative – the bus. First class is always more comfortable; offering air-conditioning and sometimes sleeping accommodation. Cheaper carriages can be crowded and none too clean. Train travel offers the advantage of views available only from the track.

The rail network extends west to Sollum on the Libyan border, south along the Nile from Alexandria and Cairo to Luxor, Aswan and Abu Simbel. There are links to Port Said and Suez. There are several luxury a/c trains with restaurants to Luxor and Aswan with sleeping accommodation. Contact International Sleeping Cars, T 761319. Inclusive tickets with reduced hotel charges in Luxor and Aswan can be negotiated. Reductions on train tickets are available for students (see Tourist Office in nearest town) and members of the YHA (see Youth hostels below). Cheaper student and group tickets are available. Contact T 753555.

Approximate journey times from Cairo by train:

Alexandria	2¾ hrs
Aswan	15 hrs
Luxor	12 hrs
Port Said	2½ hrs

ROAD

Conditions vary from excellent dual carriageways to rural roads and unnerving one vehicle wide and farflung roads which are a rough, unsurfaced *piste*. Problems include fierce flash floods and encroaching sand.

Bus

Buses, the main mode and cheapest means of transport, link nearly all the towns. Air-conditioned coaches connect the biggest cities and keep more strictly to the timetable. Smaller private vehicles require greater patience and often work on the 'leave when full' principle. Book in advance wherever possible. Orderly queues become a jostling mass when the bus arrives. Inner city buses are usually dirty and crowded and getting off can be more difficult than getting on. They keep to the timetable within reasonable (Egyptian) limits. Sorting out the routes and the fares makes taking a taxi a better option.

Car hire

Car hire quality varies greatly. Car hire is not cheap and the condition of vehicles can be problematic. Make sure that you are well insured as the road accident rate is high. Some companies place restrictions on areas that can be visited. The problems of driving your own or a hired car are two fold – other drivers and pedestrians.

The main car hire firms are **Avis**, **Hertz** and **Budget**. See entry for each town. An International Driving permit is required but own country driving licence is often accepted. Remember driving on the right is the rule in Egypt. Petrol (super) E£1 per litre.

Approximate journey times from Cairo by road:

Alexandria	3 hrs
Sharm el-Sheikh	6 hrs
Aswan	16 hrs
Luxor	10 hrs
Port Said	3 hrs

OTHER LAND TRANSPORT

Bicycles and motorcycles

Bicycle hire is becoming widely available although the mechanical fitness of the machines is often dubious. Traffic conditions can make cycling a dangerous sport. Motorcycles can also be hired. Comments above regarding cycles apply also to motorcycles – but more so.

Hitchhiking

This is really only a consideration in outlying places not served by the very cheap public transport. Rides are often available on lorries and in small open trucks but payment is always expected. Hitchhiking has a measure of risk attached to it and is not normally recommended, but in out of the way places is often the only way to travel.

Taxi

The larger, long distance taxis with metres are good value, sometimes following routes not covered by service buses and almost always more frequent. They run on the 'leave when full' principle and for more space or a quicker departure the unoccupied seats can be purchased. In general these taxis are 25% more expensive than the bus but it is always possible to negotiate. Inner city taxis are smaller, may have a working meter, and can also be shared.

BOAT

The traditional Nile sailing boats *feluccas*, can be hired by the hour but are not recommended for travelling between towns. The Sudanese railway operate a steamer service from Aswan to Wadi Halfa but this is currently suspended. Regular Nile cruises operate between Luxor and Aswan and sometimes between Cairo and Aswan for 5 days (standard tour), 7 days (extended

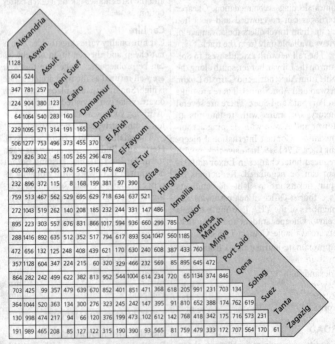

Distances between main towns in Egypt in kilometres

tour) and 15 days (full Nile cruise). The leading Nile cruise companies are Seti, Sheraton, Hilton, Presidential, Sphinx, Pyramid and Eastmar.

Cruises now operates between the Aswan Dam and Abu Simbel – go for the experience and scenery, not for speed.

COMMUNICATIONS

Language

The official language is Arabic, however many Egyptians are proficient in foreign languages, in particular English and French. See Language for Travel, page 512 for a simple vocabulary.

Postal services

Local services: all post offices are open daily except Friday and the Central Post Office in Cairo is open 24 hrs. Airmail letters cost E£0.80 and local letters E£0.10. Postage stamps can be purchased from cigarette kiosks and from hotels where mail can be posted too. Mail services are unreliable so away from the capital do not expect a quick service.

International telegram services are available at the main post offices in Cairo, Alexandria, Luxor and Aswan. **Parcels** for abroad may only be sent from a main post office. Do not seal it until it has been examined. Shops will arrange to send items you purchase. Receiving a parcel may involve import duty.

Telephone services

Country code: 20. **Internal area codes for Governorates** are: Cairo: 02; Alexandria: 03; Aswan: 97; Luxor: 95; Sharm el-Sheikh: 62; Hurghada: 65; put an extra 0 in front of the internal area codes given and add Sadat City 015: 10th of Ramadan 010; Ismailia 064; 6th October 011.

Cheapest time to telephone is between 2000-0800. Local calls can be made from coin operated machines in shops (tip the shop keeper), cigarette kiosks and hotels (which normally add a premium in any case). Long distance and international calls can be made from telephone offices and the better hotels. For International calls dial 00 before country code and subscriber's number. The telephone office has an orange circular dial sign rather than a handset. Most large towns have a 24-hr service. Outside of Cairo the system is overburdened and requires immense patience. International phone calls from Egypt can be paid for with a E£15 phone card which lasts 3 mins. The Egyptian minute is shorter than most but the use of the card saves time. The phone card can be used in all official phone centres. These cards – available from {..........} are generally in short supply – get your full holiday stock when you can.

ENTERTAINMENT

Media

The *Egyptian Gazette* is a daily paper in English. The most influential Egyptian daily is *Al-Ahram*. It publishes an English language *Al Ahram Weekly* on Thursday, 50 piastres. Newspaper-weekly *Middle East Times* for coverage of Egypt and the region E£2 per copy. *Egypt Today*, a monthly publication in English gives up-to-date information.

Ornithology: contact Sherif and Minay Baha el Din, 4 Sharia Ismail el Mazni, Apl 8, Heliopolis, Cairo.

Hollywood on the Nile

The Egyptian State Broadcasting Company are all set to build another Hollywood – on the Nile. They have signed a £190mn contract to build 'Media Production City', a huge studio complex on the outskirts of the capital. The Egyptian film industry is 100-years-old – the oldest in the Middle East – and Egyptian-made productions dominate the viewing. The demand for more material cannot currently be satisfied – hence the planned investment.

Satellite TV

Egyptian satellite TV began broadcasting on 31 May 1998, beaming programmes across the Middle East and Mediterranean. There is scope for 84 channels, however, private broadcasters have been denied the opportunity to use this facility and it is feared that the output will be no more enlightened than previously. Government control of newspapers and magazines also extends to television. The highly conservative influence of Saudi Arabia currently dominates all Arab language broadcasts, Islamic rules being strictly applied. The new satellite transmission will reach every corner of the country but the material will be strictly controlled.

Short wave radio guide

The BBC World Service (London) broadcasts throughout the region. Service wave lengths are given on page 446. Reception quality varies greatly: as a general rule lower frequencies give better results in the morning and late at night and the higher ones in the middle of the day.

Sport

Sport opportunites range from riding horses or camels in the desert to underwater swimming over coral reefs, from floating in balloon over the temples to a leisurely sail in a *felucca* on the River Nile in addition to the more usual golf, tennis, swimming etc. Climatic and geographic features make the Red Sea **the** place to scuba dive and snorkel. An experience not to be missed. Training and equipment are available. See entries under individual towns.

Balloon Flights This is a splendid way to see Egypt – away from the push of people and noise and crush of traffic. Contact *Balloons over Egypt* in Luxor, T 3776515 who also have representatives in Luxor at *Hilton International*, *Sheraton* and *Movenpick Jolie Ville*.

Normally collection is from the hotel, the flight lasts between 45 and 90 mins and takes place on the West Bank over the Valley of the Kings and Valley of the Queens. A post-trip breakfast is often served. These trips are subject to weather conditions over which there is no control. Agility is required to climb into the basket and children under 4'6" are not accepted.

Fishing is becoming a very popular sport, especially on Lake Nasser where there are over 32 species of fish. Specialist operators organize camping/fishing safaris (see page 504). A permit is required both to fish and to visit the lake – costs US$65. All tackle can be hired in Aswan.

HOLIDAYS AND FESTIVALS

1 Jan	New Year's Day
15 Mar	El Fayoum National Day
Sham al-Nessim	(Sniffing of the Breeze, or the first day of Spring) is celebrated 2nd Mon after the Coptic Easter Day with family picnics.
25 Apr	Liberation of Sinai
1 May	Labour Day
18 Jun	Evacuation Day – the day the British left Egypt
23 Jul	Anniversary of 1952 Revolution
26 Jul	Alexandria National Day
6 Oct	Armed Forces' Day – parades and military displays
13 Oct	Suez Day
23 Dec	Victory Day

Approximate dates of Islamic festivals 1998/99:

20 Dec	Beginning of Ramadan
21 Jan	End of Ramadan
31 Mar	Feast of Sacrifice
17 Apr	Islamic New Year 1420
1 Jul	Prophet's Birthday
9 Dec	Beginning of Ramadan

Approximate dates of Coptic celebrations in 1999:

7 Jan	Christmas
19 Jan	Epiphany
13 Mar	Annunciation
2 Apr	Easter
2 Jun	Penticost
19 Aug	Transfiguration

Annual Sporting Events

Jan: Egypt International Marathon – Luxor; National Tennis Championships.

Feb: International Fishing Festival – Hurghada; International Tennis Championships; International Bridge Tournament.

Mar: International Marathon – Cairo-Alexandria.

May: National Fishing Competition – Sharm el-Sheikh; Sharkia Arab Horse Breeding Festival – Sharkia

Jul: National Fishing Festival – Hurghada

Sep: Red Sea International Wind Surfing Competition – Hurghada

Oct: International Competition for Long Distance Swimming – Giza; Port Said National Fishing Competition – Port Said; Pharaoh Rally – Nationwide.

Nov: Duck Shooting; International Yacht Regatta – Alexandria; Zahra'a Arab Horse Breeding Festival – Ain Shams, Cairo; International Fishing Championship – Sharm el-Sheikh.

Dec: Nile International Rowing Regatta – Cairo and Luxor.

Cultural Events

Jan: Cairo International Book Fair – Nasr City, Cairo.

Feb 22: Ramses II Coronation – Abu Simbel.

Mar: Cairo International Fair; Annual Spring Flower Show – Andalucia Gardens, Cairo.

Jul: International Festival of Documentary Films – Ismailia.

Aug: International Song Festival – Cairo; International Folklore Dance festival – Ismailia; (Wafa el Nil) Nile Festival Day – Giza.

Sep: World Alexandria Festival (every 2 years); International Festival for Vanguard Theatre – Cairo; International Movie festival – Alexandria; World Tourism Day; (Wafa el Nil) Nile Festival Day – Cairo.

Oct: International Folk festival – Ismailia; Oct 22 Ramses II Coronation – Abu Simbel; Oct 24 Commemoration of Battle of El-Alamein – El-Alamein.

Nov: Luxor National Day; International Children's Book Fair – Nasr City, Cairo.

Dec: International Film Festival – Cairo; Festival for Arab Theatre – Cairo; Festival for Impressionist Art (every 2 years) – Cairo.

Excursion into Eastern Libya

Benghazi, the Jabal Al-Akhdar, Al-Khalij and the Oases of the South

APPROACHED FROM northern Egypt, the traditional path of conquering armies in the ancient and Islamic periods, Libya presents a great contrast to its eastern neighbour. East Libya, known as Cyrenaica until 1969, is now the back door to a country dominated by the capital, Tripoli, and the densely settled lands around it together with the key oil field zone of the centre around the Gulf of Sirt. Nonetheless, East Libya, with its great number of truly fascinating archaeological sites and rich natural *maquis* forests of the Jabal Al-Akhdar (Green Mountains), is as tempting a destination for travellers as it was in the form of Cyrene and Apollonia in the days of that inveterate wanderer, St Paul, during New Testament times.

The Libya section of the *Handbook* concentrates its attention, first, on the greater Green Mountain area, with its main town in Benghazi making up the Benghazi or Eastern

Province, and, second, on the vast tract of desert connecting the Gulf of Sirt with the Tibesti Mountains in the deep Sahara of the southeast, comprising Al-Khalij Province. The western part of the country as a whole is covered in complete detail in a separate Footprint volume, the *Tunisia Handbook*.

The northern coastal strip of Cyrenaica has been associated throughout history with Mediterranean civilizations such as Rome and Byzantium. The birth of Islam in the 7th century had a delayed impact on Libya but by the 11th century Muslim invasions attached Libya permanently to the Arab world of the E. East Libya retains strong ethnic and emotional roots with the Arab heartlands to this day. Libya fell in the 16th century to the Ottomans whose precarious hold on East Libya persisted until the occupation of the country by the Italians in 1911. There was a protracted resistance to the Italians in East Libya and the colonial power left only a minor legacy to this region in contrast to the major impact of its rule further W.

Cyrenaica took a leading role within the state from Independence in 1951 to the revolution of 1969 after which time it became a political back-water though it was profoundly affected by economic changes as the country's oil wealth grew.

HORIZONS

Official name
Al-Jamahiriyah al-Arabiyah al-Libiyah ash-Shabiyah al-Ishtirakiyah (Socialist People's Libyan Arab Jamahiriyah)

National flag
Green

Official language
Arabic

Official religion
Islam

Libya statistics
Population: 5,648,000 (1997). *Urban*: 86%. *Religion*: Sunni Muslim 97%. *Birth rate*: 44 per 1,000. *Death rate*: 7.7 per 1,000. *Life expectancy*: M 62, F 67. *GNP per capita*: US$6,510.

THE LAND

GEOGRAPHY

Libya, with an area of 1,759,540 sq km, is the fourth largest country in Africa. It has a 1,750 km seaboard with the Mediterranean. Most people live and work in the narrow cultivated strip along the coast. Elsewhere the country fades immediately inland into semi, then full desert South into the deep Sahara. The desert regions are lightly populated.

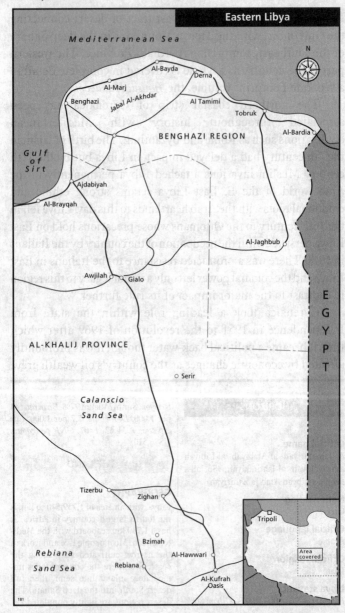

Eastern Libya

Mediterranean Sea

N

Al-Bayda
Derna
Al-Marj
Benghazi   Al Tamimi
Jabal Al-Akhdar   Tobruk
                                Al-Bardia

BENGHAZI REGION

Gulf
of
Sirt

Ajdabiyah

Al-Brayqah

Al-Jaghbub

E
G
Y
P
T

Awjilah   Gialo

AL-KHALIJ PROVINCE

Serir

Calanscio
Sand Sea

Tizerbu
Zighan

Rebiana
Sand Sea

Bzimah

Al-Hawwari
Rebiana

Al-Kufrah
Oasis

Tripoli

Area
covered

Libya and North Africa

Libya is a cultural and geographic bridge between Egypt and the Arabian lands to the east and the territory of the extreme Arab west. Libya acts as a link between the Mediterranean/Europe and Saharan Africa. The Arabic spoken in Libya has a quite separate accent and dialect from the Arabic of the Nile valley.

Libya and Europe

Although Libya was colonized by the Italians for a brief period (1911-1943) as its 'Fourth Shore' and was politically allied to Europe under the Senussi monarchy until 1969, since that time the country has become detached from European values and will seem to be alien to the traveller from the West. Management and administrative systems are generally slow except in the new, small but flourishing private sector. The role of the state is much greater and impinges much further on people's private lives than in Western Europe.

Borders

Libya is bounded to the west by Tunisia and Algeria. In the east, the Libyan frontier with Egypt is for the most part agreed. Libya shares a border with Sudan in the Southeast. The entire southern border was subject to dispute with Chad – now settled.

Relief

A set of geographical districts naturally defined by relief features is recognized in Eastern Libya, the principal natural zones being the densely settled regions of the Gulf of Sirt, the Benghazi Plain, the Jabal Al-Akhdar and Al-Kufrah. In the centre and South very large scale features dominate. The settled zone of the Jabal Al-Akhdar is followed to the south by the Dahar, an extensive area of enormous sand seas, of which Calanscio is possibly the greatest. It is dangerous to travel off the few highways which link the small oases. Water holes are few and population numbers very thin. In the deepest southeast lie the Tibesti Mountains, the land of the Tibu tribes, where security is unreliable and the travel-

ler is advised to enter only when accompanied by an official courier.

Rivers

Libya has only one permanently flowing river, the Wadi Ki'am, in the Western province. Elsewhere the *wadis* run in spate after heavy rains but are dry for the rest of the year. *Wadis* in flood can fill at a dangerous speed. In Cyrenaica the Wadi Derna is a rich area, its stream running for much of the year and providing irrigation water for a fertile oasis adjacent to the port. The generally waterless Wadi Al-Kuf runs through the hills of the Jabal Al-Akhdar in a steep, scenic gorge.

CLIMATE

The Eastern Libyan climate is very varied. The Mediterranean coast has warm winters with an unreliable rainfall, though on average over 200 mm. Extended periods of poor rainfall are experienced even in this coastal zone. Summers are hot and often humid. Relative humidity in July can reach an uncomfortable 80+% for days on end. The mountains of the Jabal Al-Akhdar attract considerably more reliable rainfall in winter and early spring, while in summer the heights are cooler than the surrounding plains. Further south the climate becomes increasingly Saharan. Low temperatures and occasional random rainfall are experienced in winter with a large daily temperature range from 15-20°C during the day to sub-zero at night. Cold nights also occur in early and late summer. Summers are hot and very dry in the South with highs of over 50°C but one can also feel cold in the night when a sweater is welcome.

The *ghibli* wind blows hot air from the Sahara across Northern Libya and carries a large amount of dust which severely reduces visibility. Relative humidity drops immediately at the onset of the *ghibli* to less than 15% and air temperatures rise rapidly. The *ghibli* is often associated with the spring solstice.

FLORA AND FAUNA

Outside the coastal plains and the Jabal Al-Akhdar, the natural vegetation is dominated by tamarind, palm and fig trees. The acacia arabica, alfalfa grass, salt bush and a range of grasses grow thinly except after rain in the semi-desert. Other plants include the asfodel and wild pistachio. The dromedary was the principal animal of the region but is declining rapidly in importance. There is still a residual belief that the region was formerly, perhaps in Roman times, very rich and climatically more favoured than at present. Wall and cave paintings and graffiti of leopards, elephants, wolves and other animals of the Savanna suggest that this was so. There are antelope, gazelle and porcupine. Falcons, eagles, and other birds of prey are present in small numbers. During the period of bird migrations, many small migrant birds get blown into the Sahara and even the occasional exotic species strays into the oases. There are snakes, few dangerous, and scorpions which are to be carefully avoided. See box, page 475.

Agriculture

Agriculture remains the main occupation of the Libyans despite the existence and economic dominance of the oil industry. In good years rainfall turns the countryside green and the semi-desert blooms with a profusion of flowers. Poor rainfall means thin crops from rainfed farming and a reliance on underground water resources lifted by diesel and electric pumps. A series of dry years causes the water table to fall dramatically. Water for both agriculture and human use has become increasingly salty over the years.

The Jabal Al-Akhdar of Cyrenaica has a generally reliable rainfall of more than 300 mm per year but has only limited underground water resources. Here agriculture is rainfed and is mainly concerned with grain production. In the southern areas of the country farming activity is limited to small oases where underground water occurs naturally. The traditional farms have successfully resisted extinction as the economy has been modernized, though many modern reclamation schemes, as at Al-Kufrah, have been abandoned as costs have risen and environmental limitations taken their toll.

In much of the broad zone of Northern Libya, including the semi-arid steppes and the inland *wadi* catchments, various forms of pastoral nomadism were

Mirages – illusions in the desert

A mirage is a most fascinating type of optical illusion. It is caused by the refraction (bending) of rays of light as they pass through air layers of varying temperatures and densities. The most common mirage occurs in the hot desert regions where what appears to be a distant and most welcoming pool of water, perhaps even surrounded by shady palm trees, turns out, to the disappointment of the thirsty traveller, to be only another area of parched sand.

The rays of light that come to the eye directly from the palm trees are interpreted in their correct position. The rays of light that travel through the warmer, less dense air which lies nearer to the hot ground can travel faster as they meet less resistance. They change their direction as they travel bending closer to the ground. However, it is assumed that the rays have come directly to the eye so the brain records the blue sky as a pool of water and the trees as reflections. It is this wide expanse of shimmering 'water' that is the most common and most dramatic illusion and the one favoured by film producers and novelists.

The rays are real, just misinterpreted by the brain, so the mirage can be photographed but that does not, alas, make the so desirable 'water' available to quench the thirst.

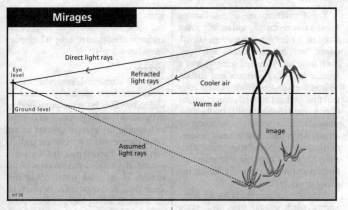

Mirages

Eye level

Direct light rays

Refracted light rays

Cooler air

Ground level

Warm air

Image

Assumed light rays

MT 88

important in the past. Tribal territories spread south from the coast to enable seasonal migrations of the nomads. In the fringes of the Gulf of Sirt and much of the southern slopes of the Jabal Al-Akhdar, forms of full nomadism were practised. Other parts of the North were under types of semi-nomadism (family herding movement) or seasonal transhumance (movements of flocks by shepherds). The coming of the oil era, the imposition of firm boundaries between North African states and other processes of modernization brought much of the nomadic activity to a halt. Some semi-nomadic shepherding of large flocks of sheep and goats still goes on in traditional pasture areas but on a minor scale, involving only small numbers of people.

Agricultural land use in Eastern Libya is concentrated on the coastal strip. In the country as a whole, only 1.2% is cultivated with a further 7.6% as pasture, rough grazing or forest. The only natural woodland, mainly evergreen scrub, occurs on the Jabal Al-Akdar, though this has been much reduced by clearances for agriculture. Total forested land is claimed at 0.4% of the land surface area.

Economic potential

Libyan economic potential is greatly limited by the constraints of a harsh environment. No more than a fragment of the land receives rainfall adequate to support agriculture; underground water reserves are slight and declining. Even the costly movement of water from the South to the North by the Great Manmade River (GMR) projects inaugurated in late 1991 do little to mitigate the problem of water shortage. Other natural resources are scant. Oil, gas and some small chemical deposits occur. There is some potential for the development of the southwest where yellow cake (low grade uranium) is found. Overall, however, the country is poorly endowed and its physical resources inevitably must restrict its future development.

CULTURE

PEOPLE

The **population** of Libya was estimated at 5.65 million in 1995, of which some 1.65 million are in the Benghazi, Jabal Al-Akhdar and Al-Khalij districts. The peoples of Eastern Libya are proud to be mainly Arab. Intermixture through marriage with slaves and other negro origin peoples such as the Tibu from the Tibesti mountains of Southern Libya gives a dimension to the racial variety. The coastal cities contained populations of Jewish, foreign Arab, Maltese, Greek and many others.

Tribal traditions are strong. Eastern Libya was economically and socially structured on *qabila* (tribal) lines with *lahmah* (clans) and extended family sub-clans. Each tribe had a defined territory and a specific history of alliances and friction with adjacent groups. During Italian colonial rule the legal and the economic basis of society was changed, partly through systematic removal but also by the economic upheaval that came with colonial occupation and warfare. Nonetheless, tribal affiliation has social importance in marriage, kinship and status, especially outside the major urban centres.

Some 95% of people are found in the narrow north coastal strip, with more than 86% now crowded into urban areas. Many of those registered as rural in fact commute to work in towns and cities. There is an average of 3.2 persons per sq km, though in the coastal strip the densities are much higher.

It is estimated that 46% of the population is less than 15 years old, 26% between 15 and 29 and a mere 4.1% above 60 years of age, a profoundly youthful population even by third world standards. The balance between males and females is reported as 51% male and 49% female.

Religion

Libya is almost uniformly Sunni Muslim. Practice of Islam is normal for most people though, with some notable exceptions, Islam is kept as a way of life rather than a political force. Within Sunni Islam there is variation in attachment to different schools of jurists. Most Libyans are of the Malekite school.

Literacy

Rates are much improved in Libya from a very poor base level at Independence. By 1995, 88% of males and 63% of females were literate. The educational system has been the subject of constant interference by the authorities, and standards, especially in higher education, have fallen in recent years. Even so there are 73,000 persons each year in higher education with university levels, except in medicine and some other limited areas, approximating in most cases to those of European secondary schools.

Income

As an oil economy Libya generates an apparently high income per head at US$65,100. This figure can be misleading in the sense that the government controls and spends the greatest portion of national income which benefits the population at large. There is poor distribution of income, the isolated rural regions of the country being much worse off in real terms than the coastal cities. Between individuals, however, there is less visible difference in income than in other Arab states. Libyan participation in the workforce is low at 24% of the total population with only 9% of women taking part in paid employment. By far the majority of Libyans work for the government or its agencies, leaving foreign labourers to work in industry and perform other menial tasks.

HISTORY SINCE INDEPENDENCE

British and French military administrations withdrew in 1951 when the state became independent under the first Senussi monarch. King Idris kept close links with the British and Americans, permitting the retention of British land forces and American and British airforce facilities. Libya was economically poor at this period, having one of the lowest standards of living in the world. Foreign aid supported the state until an increasing volume of oil company expenditures in Libya on goods and services for exploration activity gradually improved the economy. Severe strains affected the Libyan nation as Arab nationalist and anti-western ideology generated by Gamal Abdel Nasser in Egypt spread to Libya.

Oil was struck in commercial quantities in 1959 and oil exports began in 1961. Libya rapidly became financially independent and initiated sensible reforms in housing, health and education.

Employment opportunities improved and a development programme for agriculture, industry and infrastructure was set in motion. Young Libyan technocrats were given scope to implement their policies and the country made rapid steps forward from a low economic base level. The king took little part in the management of the country. Politically the nation was concentrated in a United Kingdom of Libya in 1963, with a parliament of limited powers centred in Tripoli. The Palestine question and the spread of Nasserite ideas made Libya politically unstable.

A coup d'état by a group of young army officers took place on September 1, 1969. The leader of the coup was Mu'amar Ghadhafi who was a disciple of Gamal Abdel Nasser, overtly anti-western and deeply convinced of the need to obtain full rights for the Palestinians. He banned alcohol and the use of foreign languages for official purposes. He closed down the remaining foreign military bases on Libyan soil. He abolished most private sector activities in the economy and promised a new Arab socialist society under the banner of the Socialist People's Libyan Jamahiriyah. He elaborated a set of philosophies encapsulated in his **Green Book** which set out his ideas on the nature of an Arab socialist state. He adopted the position of *qa'ed* (guide) and announced that democracy was untenable. Instead he set up people's committees in all administrative districts and work places as best representing the interests of the masses. Perhaps his greatest

The tribes of Libya

Libya remains a tribal society despite an attempt to undermine the system by the Italian colonial authorities, and strong forces for modernization since Independence especially since 1969. Perhaps the growth of an apparently all-powerful state control over the lives of ordinary people gave the tribal system the fillip it needed to survive. Caught up in a political regime many neither understood nor cared for, they turned to their traditional roots, the family, the extended family and the tribe. The genesis of the tribal system and its genealogies are all-important in giving strength to the tribes of the present day.

In North Cyrenaica the tribes are exclusively Arab from the Obeidat of the Ulad Ali in the east to the Al-Magarba of Ajdabiyah and Sirt. All the tribes claim an individual or family as a common origin and it is not unusual for the pure Arab and Berber tribes to be able to establish long family trees. There are formerly saintly clans grouped around a *marabout* as a common ancestor. Some tribes claim their origins in a member of the family of the Prophet Mohammed. Other tribes have genealogies which are suspect but which, nevertheless, serve to unite and bond the tribe. The still-practised custom of marriage between cousins brings a sense of closeness to those families involved.

Each tribe is made up of at least four different levels of organization, the nuclear family, the extended family, the large family group or sub-tribe and the tribe. The family and extended families are represented by the eldest male. The sub-tribe and tribe have a chosen or acknowledged head. Formerly the head or shaikh would act for his group in dealings with tribes or clans of a similar kind and with the outside world. This latter formality is less visible in modern society for, since 1969, the government has not given recognition to the tribal units. An element of social support and economic backing comes from the tribe together with a feeling of a shared territory. A person's identity originates powerfully in his tribal and family name, which declares ethnic origin, historical status and possibly current political strength.

Libya and Islam

The Libyans see themselves as Arabs whose religion is Islam. They are Sunni (Orthodox Muslim) by persuasion and follow the Maliki rite with a small minority of Berbers who embraced Islam according to the Ibadite rite. The religion has never been a source of friction in the country and an absence of different interpretations of Islam has created a simple but strong bond between the people and religion. Although the first Shia (Non-Orthodox) North African state was born in neighbouring Tunisia, with the establishment of the Fatimid State in the town of Mahdia, nothing can be encountered in Libya that is related to the Shia practices of Iran, Lebanon or Iraq.

However, political Islam represented by Islamic movements with political points of view entered the country in the early 1950s, following the purge by Nasser of the Moslem Brotherhood in Egypt. Some of the members of the movement fled to Libya and began to preach there to the Libyan youth. Later came Hizb al-Tahreer which called for the re-establishment of the Caliphate as well as Wahhabism, a puritanical form of Islam from Arabia. Out of the three Islamic movements only Wahhabism is rejected by the Libyan people because of its narrow interpretation of Islam and its belittling of the Libyan's Islamic practices. Wahhabism, through the support of Saudi Arabia, has introduced a new challenge to the Libyans who have a deep rooted belief in their Maliki rite. Using the political vacuum created by the rift between the people and the régime, the Wahhabi succeeded in recruiting some youths to their movement. Hizb al-Tahreer and the Moslem Brothers have not gained a strong enough foothold in Libya to be capable of causing a threat to the régime, and their followers are not advocates of fanaticism or violence.

Fanatic Islam on the scale encountered in neighbouring Egypt and Algeria has not evolved in Libya to become a noticeable phenomena, and this is due, in part, to the nature of the Libyan belief in Islam, the resentment against religious-related violence, and a belief in a separation between politics and religion.

success was in threatening the assets of the foreign oil companies in Libya and in helping to force up oil prices in the early 1970s.

The Libyan role in favour of Arab unity and against western interests was pursued through the creation of a vast and expensive military establishment, political activities abroad designed to frustrate western interests and a solid pro-Palestinian stance. While oil revenues remained very high, Libya's international position gained some notoriety in Lebanon, Uganda and Chad. Military successes were denied the Libyan authorities and, as oil wealth declined first in the mid-1970s and then in the 1980s, Libyan foreign policy ceased to be significant in international affairs.

At home a series of economic plans promised rapid and integrated regional development of the country, but erratic implementation of projects, shortages of money and personnel and distraction abroad diluted the effort. Despite having a small indigenous population, Libya has never quite developed beyond oil as a productive and well-organized state with high personal incomes. In 1989 the socialist system of centralized national and economic management was abandoned piecemeal.

Political power is concentrated in the hands of Colonel Ghadhafi and, to a lesser extent, his close associates. An annual People's Congress permits some ventilation of other ideas and an apparent control system on spending of state revenues. In fact there have been few political changes to compare with the liberalization and privatization of the economy in recent years.

Despite official statements and propaganda images of Libya abroad, most Libyans are gentle and friendly, not least with foreign visitors who are clearly tourists and/or travellers.

MODERN LIBYA

GOVERNMENT

The ideal of government was expressed in the Third Universal Theory, expounded by Colonel Ghadhafi in the early 1970s and enshrined in the **Green Book**, the first sections of which were published in 1976. Ghadhafi attempted to bring together strands of his own beliefs – Islam, freedom from foreign intervention, equality of people and the welfare of the greater Arab nation – within a unified philosophy. He was never taken entirely seriously in this ambition outside the country. Events were also to prove that Libya itself was resistant to his ideas. Despite the single minded expenditure of large sums on imposing socialism at home, including the devolution of bureaucratic powers to the four major regions – Tripoli, Sabha, Al-Khalij and Benghazi – and the removal of all private privileges of ownership of goods, property and even a fully private life, by 1987 the dream had to be abandoned. The structures he established persisted, however. A Basic People's Congress meets to manage the affairs of state, with Colonel Ghadhafi taking the position of 'guide' to the revolution. The congress acts officially through a series of appointed secretariats, which are now, for all practical purposes, ministries in the traditional mode. The revolutionary fervour, which characterized Libya in the 1970s and 1980s, has dimmed considerably and lives on only in the apparatus for security and military matters. Since he has these agents of political control in his hands, Colonel Ghadhafi effectively has the final say in

decision-making in the country. There is no official opposition party and opponents of the régime have generally fled abroad.

The secretariats which look after day-to-day administration are spread out throughout the country as part of a deliberate policy of regionalizing management. Key ministries are in Sirt, though some scattered government offices also exist.

In foreign policy, Libya acted to harass the western powers at whose doors Colonel Ghadhafi laid many of the ills of Libya and the Arab nation. While he could play off the West against the USSR and had access to considerable oil revenues, he successfully worked against the USA and EU states in propaganda and support for their opponents. The demise of the USSR as a world power in 1991, a massive fall-off in oil revenues in the mid-1980s and the rise of the conservative states as leading elements within the Arab world left him vulnerable to foreign pressures to accept international legal norms for state activities. This was signalled in Libyan problems in 1992 with US and British demands over the Lockerbie incident.

ECONOMY

Libya is an oil-based economy. Oil was first exported commercially in 1961 and thereafter output rose rapidly so that at the end of the 1960s Libya was the fifth largest Opec producer of crude oil with more than 3 million barrels per day. This expansion was based geographically on the oilfields in the vast embayment of the Gulf of Sirt where small but prolific oilfields were found in the sedimentary rocks. While some oil was discovered by the major international oil companies such as Esso, Mobil and BP, there were also many small independent oil companies involved, for which Libya was the only source of traded crude oil. By the end of the 1960s a development of oilfields, pipelines and oil terminals had taken place in what had been a barren desert

Colonel Mu'amar Ghadhafi

👣 Colonel Ghadhafi was born in the Gasr Bu Hadi area of Sirt on the coast of the Gulf of Sirte (Sidra) in 1942. His parents were from the Ghadadfha tribe, a mixed Arab-Berber group, which practised semi-nomadic herding of animals with some shifting grain cultivation in the arid steppelands surrounding the traditional tribal territories. He went to secondary school in Misratah before joining the army as an officer cadet. He graduated from the military academy and was eventually posted to Sabha in the Fezzan area. He briefly attended the University of Libya in Benghazi and undertook a short stay in the United Kingdom on a training course.

He rose to fame in September 1969 as the head of a group of revolutionary officers who overthrew the monarchy and set up an Arab republic ruled by a Revolutionary Command Council. The political programme introduced by Ghadhafi was simple and based mainly on the ideas of the Egyptian nationalist leader Gamal Abdel Nasser. Colonel Ghadhafi was anti-western, anti-Israel and in favour of a centrally controlled social and economic system within Libya. British and American military bases in Libya were closed down after the revolution. All public signs had to be written in Arabic and all foreigners, including any remaining Italian residents, were no longer made welcome.

Initially Colonel Ghadhafi was received by the Libyan people with acclaim. His simple creed of Arab nationalism fitted the mood of the day. In the early 1970s Libya became immensely rich in oil revenues as, aided by Libyan actions against the oil companies, the price of oil rose dramatically on the international market. At the same time, Colonel Ghadhafi issued his philosophy to guide the revolution, the so-called **Green Book**, preaching a form of Arab socialism. He also saw for himself a role as messianic leader of all the Arabs and a focus around which the Arab world could be united. At home, he entered into bold programmes for economic development, with expansion of agriculture, provision of state welfare schemes and investments in industry and infrastructure. Power was, at least in theory, devolved down to regional municipal assemblies which reported annually to a General People's Congress.

By the end of the 1970s Colonel Ghadhafi faced increasing difficulties. Abroad, Libya's attempts at Arab unity had failed. Libya had been unable to affect events in the Arab-Israel dispute despite a great deal of fiery rhetoric. Colonel Ghadhafi had also made an unsuccessful attempt to intervene in a war in Uganda to support the unpopular leader Idi Amin. Meanwhile Ghadhafi's political credentials were eroded by the rise of revolutionary Islamic movements in Iran and the Arab world. The collapse of oil prices after 1980 weakened the Libyan economy at a time when Colonel Ghadhafi became deeply embroiled in a territorial dispute with Chad over the Uzu strip, a band of desert lying between the two countries. Despite huge outlays in men and material, the war against Chad was lost and was taken to the International Court for arbitration. Suspicions that there was Libyan involvement in international terrorism came to a head in 1988 when responsibility for the destruction by a bomb of a Pan Am aircraft from UK to the USA at Lockerbie in Scotland was attributed to two Libyan officials. Libya eventually fell under a UN air transport embargo and was isolated from the international community as a pariah state.

In Libya, Colonel Ghadhafi lost some popularity as a result of these adverse changes but remained as the political guide of the country, defended by loyal echelons of the armed forces and without real rivals.

Pan-Arabism

Feelings of pan-Arabism are powerful in Libya. The movement has established very strong roots in the country since the mid-1950s. It was Ghadhafi's adoption of pan-Arabist and Nasserist slogans which consolidated his grip on the country through the support of the people to these slogans. The Libyan people have always identified themselves with Arab issues such as the Algerian struggle for independence and the Palestine cause. These strong convictions of the Libyan people to pan-Arabism and the attitude to Islam as being the religion of the people has created a barrier that stood against the spread of fanaticism or the adoption of political Islam on levels similar to those in other Arab countries. However, it is a misconception to interpret the trend of the return to practising religion in Libya as a resurgence of Islam on the fanatical lines of its neighbours.

area lying between Tripoli and Benghazi. Following the revolution of 1969, economic policies were aligned towards making the country self sufficient.

Traditional agriculture

This was mainly self sufficient with small surpluses going to the many local occasional markets. The coastlands were comparatively rich agriculturally, favoured by adequate rainfall and available underground water for irrigation. Small fragmented farms were the rule on the coast, though many families had access to communal tribal lands for shifting cultivation and grazing animals to the south of the coastal oases.

In Eastern Libya, the Jabal Al-Akdar are used for dryland cereals, some fruit and a large area of fodder. In Al-Khalij oases survive using irrigation for intensive vegetable and fruit production.

Modern farming

Contemporary agriculture other than the private sector activities already noted has until recently been mainly state managed. Underground water resources in the deep Southeast at Al-Kufrah, Tizerbu and Serir were developed for agriculture. Expensive imported technology was employed in these schemes. Labour, too, was brought in from Sudan, Egypt and elsewhere since Libyans were generally not prepared to move to these inhospitable regions. Despite the investment of very large resources, the majority of agricultural schemes in the South were

abandoned or run down when Libya's oil revenues declined during the mid-1980s.

Libya's biggest and most spectacular development, the Great Manmade River (GMR), will carry water in a large diameter pipeline from wellfields in Al-Kufrah, Serir and Tizerbu to the coast and thence to Benghazi in the East and Sirt in the West. The movement of water to the North is at the cost of the closure of most major irrigation schemes in the South. Although the government has promised that the new water will be used in the coastlands for agriculture in addition to supplying industrial and urban areas, high costs of the water delivered there make its use in irrigation questionable. The need for new water illustrates the other great problem for farming in Libya – the falling water tables and intrusion of sea water into aquifers in coastal areas.

Oasis economies

In the oases of the deep South and the small towns at a modest distance from the coast, there is little industry. Here life revolves around earnings from agriculture and remittance income from employment on the coast. Construction of private villas and other housing is the most pronounced area of economic activity in the countryside, though farming is still a way of life for many Libyans outside the major coastal towns and involvement in transportation also absorbs a great deal of energy in these areas.

Petroleum

This provides the government with its principal foreign exchange income, over US$9,500mn in 1996, the main source of general revenues in the annual budget (90%) and the most important single commodity for export (99%). The main area of production is the Gulf of Sirt, with export terminals at Sidrah, Ras Lanuf, Al-Brayqah and Zuwetina. The main oil-fields are linked by pipelines to coastal terminals. Serir oilfield and its associated installations in the extreme southeast are tied in to a terminal at Marsa Hariga near Tobruk (Tubruq). Libyan oil reserves are only moderate, rated at around 26,000 million barrels, which would last some 35 years at present rates of extraction. Libya produces approximately 1.5 million barrels per year and exports some three-quarters of its output, mainly to Western Europe. The National Libyan Oil Co owns refineries in Italy and Germany. Domestic refineries are found at Zaviyah, Al-Brayqah and Ras Lanuf.

Economic plans

The comparatively short life expectancy of Libya as a major oil exporter has given emphasis to the need to develop alternative sources of exports for the future. A set of economic development plans has been adopted by the government, the latest being a programme for 1980-2000. Its aims were to bolster self-sufficiency, create new jobs and lay the foundations for a future non-oil economy. Some successes were won, including an improvement in the country's transport infrastructure. Excellent road systems serve all parts of the country. New hospitals, hotels and schools have been set up so that even the most isolated settlements can offer good housing, health and educational facilities. A North African road link through Libya from Morocco and Algeria to Egypt is

UN Sanctions against Libya

The Libyan government has been in conflict with the USA, the United Kingdom and France over the matter of terrorism. The USA and UK are concerned particularly in the question of the downing of a Pan-Am flight at Lockerbie.

UN sanctions which were imposed against Libya for its alleged involvement in the Lockerbie bombing in 1988 and the shooting down of a French airliner over the Sahara in 1989, began on 15 April 1992 and were renewed in 1993 and 1994. They were in accordance with Security Council Resolution 748, the UN having called in vain for the extradition of the two accused the previous January in Resolution 731.

The UN sanctions against Libya comprise:

- the freezing of Libyan assets in the USA
- the banning of all civil aviation connections with Libya
- an arms embargo
- controls on the transfer to Libya of oil related goods, aerospace equipment and training (Security Council Resolution, December 1993)
- constraints on the international movement of Libyan financial assets, including special arrangements for the treatment of Libyan oil revenues.

Three permanent members of the Security Council are dedicated to the maintenance of UN sanctions until Colonel Ghadhafi hands over for trial two of its nationals indicted for involvement in the Lockerbie bombing and provides further evidence of its involvement in the shooting down of the UTA aircraft over Niger.

In August 1998 the US and UK offered a trial of the Libyan suspects in the Netherlands, opening the way to the withdrawal of US sanctions.

under consideration. Air transport in Libya has been impeded by USA sanctions against Libya which have limited the availability of new aircraft to Libyan Arab Airways, the national carrier.

Industry

Economic development outside transport and other infrastructure has been expensive and limited. In Eastern Libya only petrochemicals, with a large scale complex set up at Ras Lanuf and a smaller operation planned at Sirt, have shown rapid growth, but they depend on the oil sector for raw materials, are highly polluting and employ few Libyans. As from the late 1980s, Libyan entrepreneurs were encouraged to begin work in industry on their own account, a move which saw the opening of many small scale workshops, stores and corner shop businesses.

Economic trends

The poor performance of the oil sector since the mid-1980s has dominated trends since that time. The late 1980s was a poor time for Libya and things have picked up only as better management of limited oil revenues and improved internal economic liberalisation has had an effect. The growth of private enterprise has been the main area of economic growth in the immediate past. The fall in oil revenues in 1997/98 threatened to bring Libya into economic recession.

Jabal Al-Akhdar

ENTERING EAST LIBYA FROM EGYPT

Formalities at the Egyptian border are few but it is busy and can be very hot. There are few reliable facilities at the crossing so travellers from Egypt should be prepared to be self-sufficient between Marsa Matruh in Egypt and arrival in Solum and thence to Derna in Libya. The road from the Egyptian border to Solum and Derna is well served by bus connections. Once in Derna there are frequent buses from Derna to towns all around the country. Buses do not operate to fixed timetables, but coaches in fact leave early in the morning. The General Transport Company has a daily bus to Benghazi. The bus from Benghazi to Derna leaves at the same time.

Derna is an important town on the east side of the Jabal Al-Akhdar. Beautifully situated, surrounded by the last hills of the Jabal with the *wadi* lying in the centre, Derna is a delightful town. The eastern part of the town is mostly new, but the old centre on the west side of the *wadi* is still very pleasing to the eye. From the central square, the covered *souq* goes north with many small streets leading to it. To the west of the *souq* lies the old town with its small streets occasionally leading to tiny squares, still very authentic because still inhabited. The new town has expanded around the old centre and not to the latter's detriment. All the shopping and activity still takes place within the *souqs* and old town. A good time to witness the thriving activity is on a Thursday evening, when the entire population seems to congregate in the centre. This is an occasion to have a coffee in the café in the middle of the central square. Also on the square is the *Jabal Al-Akhdar Hotel*.

History

Derna was founded by the Greeks at the time of the Pentapolis. It was not an important town and never became part of the Pentapolis but did develop during the Ptolemaic period. In 96 BC it became part

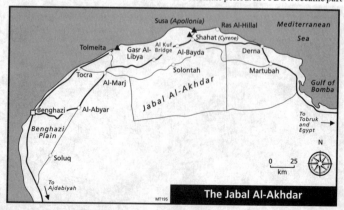

The Jabal Al-Akhdar

Wadi Derna

After S.K. Kezeiri (1982)

Aïn Dabasiyah

Mediterranean Sea

Derna

Lamloudah
Al-Gubah

To Benghazi

Gugab

Wadi Derna

Springs & wells

water pipeline

To Tobruk

0 2
km

N

MT201

of the Roman Empire, and during the Byzantine period was the episcopate for the region. In 693 AD the Greeks attempted to land and take the region but were pushed back by an army led by Abu Shaddad Zuhayr, who was killed in the fighting and subsequently made a town hero.

Under the Arabs, Derna fell into decay. The harbour was less good than others in the region and situated too far north from the main caravan and trade routes that passed about 90 km south. It was only in the 15th century AD that Derna re-emerged with the arrival of Andalusians, mostly migrating from other North African countries where they had already settled. During this period, Derna was involved in rivalries with Benghazi over trade.

During the Turkish occupation, the Dernawis did not like being ruled from Tripoli, and in 1656 an expedition was sent to quell the inhabitants, resulting in large scale destruction of the town and its population. Under the auspices of the Governor Mohammed Ibn Mahmud in the 17th century, the town grew with the building of a Great Mosque and the initiation of irrigation works. In 1805, Derna was the scene of a curious event. The town was bombarded by the American Navy in an attempt to prevent pirate attacks against American ships. The Americans had already tried attacking Tripoli but had failed. An overland expedition left from

Egypt heading for Tripoli, but never got further than Derna, when an agreement was finally made. During the second Turkish occupation, beginning in 1835, Derna was an important base for controlling the hinterland. Finally, during Italian colonization, the town was expanded and cleaned up, attracting many tourists. During WW2, the town changed hands a number of times and suffered from heavy bombing. Today, Derna is an important economic centre with an expanded harbour. It is also at the centre of an important irrigation project. Two dams have been built 2 km and 15 km upstream on the Wadi Derna and water is transported as far as Tobruk.

Places of interest

In the town there is a small organization called *Haila* run by Mohammed Ahneid that concentrates on preserving the cultural heritage of the town. They have an interesting **museum** with rooms recreating the traditional homes which gives a very good insight into the traditional way of life. The organization will also arrange tours of the town and its principal sights as well as the surrounding area. There are a few excellent beaches east of Derna as well as caves in the cliff once inhabited by Christians seeking to escape persecution.

The centre of the town is the most interesting area. Walk around the old town and the *souqs*. The valley of the Wadi Derna is very beautiful. Take the road that follows the river. The road follows an impressive valley, green at the bottom, dry and rocky on the sides. The first of the two dams is at the outskirts of the town, the second about 15 km upstream. About 8 km after the first dam, water can be seen pouring out of the rock from an important spring. Continuing up the valley brings you to the last dam, where the landscape begins to look much less cultivable but the panorama definitely gains in beauty.

WW2 Military cemeteries The intensive fighting in the period 1940-43 in North Africa left large numbers of war dead on all sides. There are two Commonwealth war cemeteries, commemorating 6,124 souls, one 7 km east of Tobruk on the Alexandria/El-Adem road and the other, the Knightsbridge War Cemetery, Acroma, 24 km west of Tobruk on the south of the coast road. German war dead, numbering some 6,026, are interred near Tobruk at El-Adem south of the crossroads in a fort-like structure. The Italian war cemetery of the WW2 period is across the border in Egypt at El-Alamein.

Local information
● Accommodation
D/E *Jabal Al-Akhdar Hotel*, T 08122303, very beautiful entrance with mosaic tiled floor, the rest is awful.

E *Hotel Al-Bahr*, on the seafront, basic, clean, cheap, shared bath, good restaurant.

● Youth hostel
5 km west of centre, 200 beds, meals, kitchen, family rooms, laundry.

● Transport
Air Tobruk to Tripoli Tuesday, Thursday, Friday, Saturday at 1015 and Monday at 1430. Takes 1¼ hrs and costs LD44.

Road Bus: there are frequent buses to towns all around the country. There are few fixed timetables, but most buses leave early in the morning. The General Transport Company has a bus to **Benghazi** at 0800. The bus from Benghazi to Derna leaves at the same time.

TRAVEL IN THE JABAL AL-AKHDAR

Shortly after leaving Derna the road westwards enters the Jabal Al-Akhdar or Green Mountain range running as far as Tocra in the west. The highest point is close to Al-Bayda and reaches 880m. The Jabal is one of the few places where rainfall (about 300 mm per annum) is enough to sustain farming. The beauty of the landscape, the relative coolness in the summer as well as the important Greek and Roman remains make it an important part of any tour within Eastern Libya.

During the Greek Pentapolis period, the Jabal was reputed to be virtually the granary for mainland Greece and ever since has been seen, not entirely correctly, as a very fertile area. Recently, great efforts have been made to develop intensive farming using modern techniques and irrigation. An important underground water supply has made intensive irrigation farming a reality, particularly on the Al-Marj plateau. Production is still low and concentrated on fruits and vegetables, but some progress is being made. There are many new problems, particularly linked with over-pumping and declining water tables, which are limiting development.

The Jabal peoples are historically independently minded and this area is not one that conforms easily with norms set by Tripoli. There was, for many years, difficulty with travel and access to certain areas within the Jabal. Given the ability of the local tribes to feed themselves and to sustain long periods of warfare, the region has been regarded with apprehension by outside groups. The Jabal Al-Akhdar has played a singular role in the history of Libya. It was the stronghold of anti-colonial rule and insurrection, giving great trouble to all would-be colonial rulers. Under the Senussi and Omar Mukhtar, the Cyrenaican tribes sustained many years of modern warfare in a one-sided struggle against the Italians. Today the Jabal is a major trade route to Egypt as well as having significant tourist potential.

THE ROAD FROM DERNA TO SUSA

This is a very beautiful road following the coast, with the Jabal Al-Akhdar to the left. The coast is mostly rocky but the occasional beach provides a good spot to stop for a swim or a picnic.

Ras Al-Hilal (Crescent Headland) is a small but picturesque village by a rocky cape from which it takes its name. The village is mostly modern and of little tourist value apart from its superb location. There are a few small beaches along the coast from the town. In the town right on the beach there is a hotel, currently being refurbished. The hotel is more of a holiday village, with rooms and bungalows to rent.

SUSA (APOLLONIA)

This is a tiny settlement by the coast about 20 km from Shahat. The old town is very beautiful but falling into decay. The real interest of the town is the ruins of Apollonia, Cyrene's harbour. The site is by the sea, but a large part of the town and harbour have been submerged due to landslides. Susa can be reached by a road coming from Shahat, highly recommended because of the fine view over the coast and Susa itself.

Apollonia was founded at the same time as Cyrene and was named after the city's principal god. The harbour was at first a dependency of Cyrene, but later in the 2nd and 3rd centuries it gradually increased in stature, as the mother city declined, and finally became the capital of Upper Libya.

Approaching the site from the west, drive through the town square heading towards Derna and look for the track to the left leading up to the ramparts which leads to parking space on the beach. Entrance 500 dhs. The first important monument encountered is the **Extra-Mural Church** (1). The **City Walls**, from which huge quantities of stone have fallen, continue up the Acropolis hill and turn north to the **Theatre** (2) and the sea. Within the walls the **Cisterns** (3) and the **Chambers** were both used for storage. The **Eastern Church** (4) dating from the 5th century contains green marble columns from an earlier Roman building. The **Baths** (6) to the left of **Main Street** now lie close to the sea, while on the hill top to the south are the extensive remains of the **Byzantine Palace** (5). The **Central Church** (7) and **Western Church** (8) are beyond to the west, the latter built up against the ramparts, making use of the wall in its structure. The

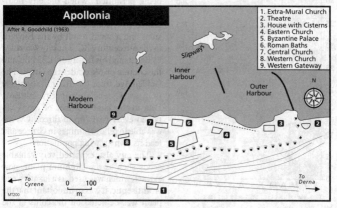

Apollonia

After R. Goodchild (1963)

1. Extra-Mural Church
2. Theatre
3. House with Cisterns
4. Eastern Church
5. Byzantine Palace
6. Roman Baths
7. Central Church
8. Western Church
9. Western Gateway

Modern Harbour

Slipways

Inner Harbour

Outer Harbour

N

To Cyrene

0   100
m

MT200

To Derna

Western Gateway (9), threatened by the encroaching sea, leads nowhere. Further remains lie submerged. The beach at the site is private.

The **Museum** is situated in the centre of the old town. It is small with a collection of mainly Byzantine mosaics and sculpture. There are also a few Roman and Greek exhibits. The collection is not very rich, reflecting the small amount of work put into excavations at the site. Even so, there is an interesting room on traditional clothes, tools and crafts that provides an insight into the traditional way of life in this part of Libya.

CYRENE

Shahat (Cyrene) The modern city of Shahat is of little visual interest but the archaeological remains of Cyrene are very impressive and possibly the most worthwhile site in Libya after Leptis Magna. The situation of Shahat on the upper slopes of the Jabal Al-Akhdar is extremely fine, overlooking a high plateau leading to the sea. The site is as impressive as the actual remains of what must have been a very large city, but the combination of the two make it an absolute must for the traveller along the Cyrenaican shore.

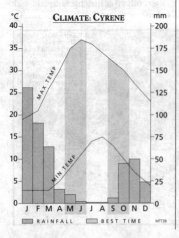

°C | **CLIMATE: CYRENE** | mm
RAINFALL   BEST TIME

MTT38

There is an hourly bus here from Al-Bayda. The last bus returns at 1700. Closed Monday and Friday. There is **no** public transport of any kind around the town so car-less travellers will need to rely on lifts from townspeople to reach the site in bad weather.

History

Cyrene goes back to the first half of the 7th century BC. The first settlers came from the island of Thera (Santorini) and the most plausible explanation is the overpopulation of the island and the necessity of finding an alternative outlet for settlement. The story has it that a young man named Battus went to Delphi to consult the Oracle, who told him to go and settle in Libya. He then left with an expedition, only to land on an offshore island. He later returned to see the Oracle, who told him he had not been to Libya yet. He made another attempt and landed on the mainland, but not yet at the original site of Cyrene. It was only after a 6 year period that the colonists moved to the site of Cyrene and founded what was by the 5th century BC one of the largest cities in Africa.

Relations between the Libyans and the Greeks were friendly, both civilizations gaining from each other, and intermarriage between the two communities being permitted. When the city flourished, large numbers of Greeks came and settled in Cyrene: this gave rise to tensions and a small revolt by the Libyans in the 6th century BC. The city was ruled by Battus and his family until 331 BC and the coming of Alexander the Great. The Golden Age, from 450 BC until about 300 BC, saw Cyrene's prosperity increase. Due to the large number of crops obtained every year (up to three), Cyrene was able to relieve famines in Greece and feed its own growing population.

The city also exported very valuable goods such as the silphium plant, now extinct, which was used as a laxative and an antiseptic. It was so important that the plant was depicted on the coins of the

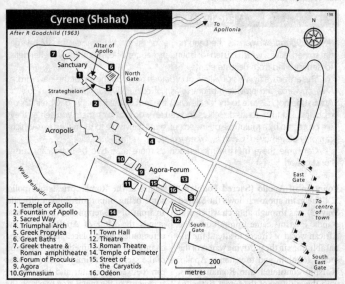

Cyrene (Shahat)

After R Goodchild (1963)

To Apollonia

N

198

Altar of Apollo

7

Sanctuary

6

North Gate

1

5

Strategheion

2

3

Acropolis

4

Wadi Belgadir

10

9 Agora-Forum

East Gate

11

15

13

To centre of town

16

8

14

12

South Gate

South East Gate

1. Temple of Apollo
2. Fountain of Apollo
3. Sacred Way
4. Triumphal Arch
5. Greek Propylea
6. Great Baths
7. Greek theatre & Roman amphitheatre
8. Forum of Proculus
9. Agora
10. Gymnasium
11. Town Hall
12. Theatre
13. Roman Theatre
14. Temple of Demeter
15. Street of the Caryatids
16. Odéon

0   200
metres

country for many centuries. Cyrene became part of the Pentapolis (Cyrene, Barka, Berenice, Tocra, Apollonia), a federation of five cities with agreements on trade, and joint coinage. This type of federation was quite common within Greek colonies until Alexander the Great attempted to unify all the cities.

At Alexander's death, the Greek Empire was split up and Cyrenaica came into the hands of the Ptolemy in Egypt. Cyrenaica passed into Roman hands when the illegitimate son of Ptolemy XI, who had inherited the Pentapolis, gave up his holding. In 75 BC, Cyrenaica was incorporated into the Roman Empire but, due to internal rivalries within the empire, the Pentapolis was neglected. Emperor Augustus restored stability and gave a new span of life and prosperity to Cyrene. Various revolts broke out, the most serious by the Jewish community. In 115 AD Emperor Trajan ruthlessly suppressed the revolts but they brought about the inevitable decline of the city. Emperor Hadrian undertook large reconstruction

works but the city never really recovered. By the 4th century AD the city was largely deserted and falling into decay. It was never again inhabited, except periodically by nomads.

Until the 19th century, very little attention was paid to Cyrene. One of the first expeditions was in 1838 by a British group and a few other outsiders followed in 1861 and 1864, but it was not until the Italian occupation that major excavation work was carried out. No real work on the site has been undertaken since the Italians and their successor under the British Military Administration, Professor Goodchild, left and much work still needs to be done.

Places of interest

The site which is large and complicated to view, as much is obscured by more recent buildings and agricultural land use, can be divided into two main parts, the **Sanctuary of Apollo** and the **Agora-Forum Area**. The sanctuary is situated below the main part of the town, and contains the **Temple of Apollo** (1) and the

Prickly pears or barbary figs

Opuntia Vulgaris is the Latin name for the prickly pear cactus, with large flat spined leaves, which is used for boundary hedges or less commonly shelter belts to deflect wind from delicate plants.

The attractive flowers of yellow or cyclamen occur on the rim of the leaves from May onwards and provide a bright splash of colour. If your visit occurs in July or August do not hesitate to try the delicacy, the fruit of the Barbary fig. Obtain them ready peeled from roadside sellers and certainly **do not** pick them yourself as they are protected by a multitude of fine spines, almost invisible to the naked eye, which can only be removed, painfully, by an expert.

Consume these fruits in moderation as more than two or three can cause constipation.

Fountain of Apollo (Sacred Fountain) (2). The main approach down the **Sacred Way** (3) was through an arch which still stands. Pilgrims came from all over the African world of Greece to attend the ritual ablutions in the purifying waters of the sacred fountain and to venerate Apollo. Worship continued into Roman times, with the addition of the **Great Baths** (6) built by the Emperor Trajan in the 2nd century. Once in the sanctuary, the pilgrims would congregate on the upper terrace and approach the temple through the **Greek Propylea** (5), four lofty pillars. These still stand and are of Doric style dating back to the Hellenistic period. Close by stands the **Strategheion**, built in honour of Apollo to celebrate the victory of three generals in the 4th century BC. It has since been restored and roofed.

The **Temple of Apollo** is certainly one of the oldest buildings in Cyrene, the rest of the sanctuary developing around it. The foundations of the original 7th century BC temple can still be seen, but it was later rebuilt and enlarged in the 4th century BC. Traces of blue paint still exist on the old Greek parts of the temple clearly showing that all buildings were painted, and often in bright colours. As a result of the Jewish revolts, the temple was burnt down and the Romans rebuilt a copy of the original Greek Doric temple. Later, during the Byzantine period, the temple was converted into a Christian chapel. Notice on either side of the entrance the inscriptions with the names of the Roman priests of Apollo, some being important Roman officials. In front of the temple to the southeast stands the **Altar of Apollo** where the ceremonies took place. Traces of the channels which drained away the blood of the sacrificed animals can be seen, as can, between the altar and the temple, fragments of the metal ring to which the animals were tethered.

The **Fountain of Apollo** is situated by the cliff behind the Temple of Apollo. The water was used for purification and was said to have curative properties. Notice the seating inside the tank for people undergoing purification. This is one of the largest buildings in the **Great Baths** complex. The original building by Trajan in 98 AD was destroyed during the Jewish revolt and rebuilt by Hadrian in 119 AD. It is highly decorated, with marbled floors and walls and the baths looking, in their original form, quite superb. Most rooms had vaulted roofs and mosaic decoration. The **Calidarium**, or hot rooms, had raised floors and pipes in the walls for the passage of hot air from the furnace. In the **Great Hall**, a large cold bath is still in very good condition and fed by pipes coming from the Apollo fountain. The baths had more than just a hygienic role and were also highly important as a kind of social club, where all citizens would come and meet. Interestingly, before the reconstruction by Hadrian, mixed bathing was common,

Egypt and Libya build links that will aid the traveller

Egypt is an important political state in the Middle East and North Africa by population size, economic might and because of its historical leadership of the Islamic and Arab nationalist movements. It is no surprise that its immediate Arab neighbours are overshadowed by the Egyptian political presence. Libya in particular has a strong link with Egypt, albeit occasionally mixed with rivalry and suspicion. In recent years there has been construction of transport, oil and political bridges between Cairo and Tripoli – with more to come.

Key to this process is Egypt's need for Libyan financial support and Libya's even greater requirement for Egyptian diplomatic backing in its struggle to get UN and US economic sanctions lifted. The Libyan authorities use Cairo as a centre to promote a pan-Arab response to the renewal of UN sanctions. While Egypt does not actively seek to breach UN/US sanctions, it is not in favour of them and privately supports Libyan demands which hinge about a trial of the two suspects in the 1988 bombing of a Pan Am aircraft at Lockerbie (Scotland) in neutral country. But so far no Arab country has overtly stood out against the USA, UK and France on the issue. For some Arab states – not least Egypt – there are hidden economic gains from sanctions against Libya and politically there is some covert gratification at Colonel Ghadhafi's dilemma in so far as its diminishes unwelcome Libyan interference in the domestic affairs of Egypt.

Encouraged by Egypt, the Arab League at its Cairo meeting announced in September 1997 that it would support a lifting of UN sanctions on Libya. Specifically, the Arab League proposed that flights to and from Libya for humanitarian, religious or hardship purposes should be permitted. Similarly, Libyan funds blocked in Arab Banks should be released. Libyan claims for compensation for the costs to it of the UN embargo also gained Arab League backing. Given that these rulings could be taken up by all 22 League members, comprising significant parts of the Middle East and Africa most of which are also UN voting members, the move in Cairo had serious implications.

In practice, the Arab League resolution on defying UN sanctions will probably prove to be more rhetorical than a guideline for action. The League's decision came at a time when Arab sensibilities were hard driven by the Palestine conflict in which the USA was seen to be no more than a prop for Israeli hard line reneging on the Oslo Accord. The Egyptian government, meanwhile, has both its own policy aims outside the Arab camp and suspicions of Libyan intentions in the Arab world enough to stop it gratuitously offending the USA on this issue.

In 1997 the Egyptian and Libyan ministers of energy met in Cairo to lay the final basis/timetable for the linking of the electric power networks of the two countries between al-Sollum in Egypt and Tobruk in Libya. A 622-km/150,000 b/d crude oil pipeline will also be built to transport Libyan oil to the refinery at Alexandria as part of this programme.

Libyan and Egyptian oil ministers met at Marsa Breqa on the Gulf of Surt in late 1997 when an agreement was signed providing for a joint venture company – the United Investment Company (UIC) – in which Libyan partners will undertake 90% of the investment to provide 46 new service stations on the Cairo-Benghazi international highway by end-1998 in addition to the four already operating under the joint venture. A further 70 units will be set up by the year 2000. This project will make the long journey between the main cities of the two countries much easier and more comfortable than at present and make the border crossing a routine matter – which is good news for the traveller.

but a new law forbade this and two baths had to be built.

The **Theatre**, to the west of the site, is in fact a Roman theatre and not Greek as the building technique would suggest. The Greeks built theatres in hillsides, whereas the Romans generally built them on flat ground. In effect the theatre in the sanctuary is an amphitheatre, that is to say with a circular stage. Due to the sharp fall on one side of the building, seats were provided only on the hill side. Nevertheless, the Roman amphitheatre was probably built on the site of an earlier Greek theatre.

The **Agora-Forum** area is the real centre of the city and had all the conveniences of a metropolis. There were shops, theatres, baths, law courts and temples. The city had as its centre the **Agora**, equivalent to the Roman forum. Most of the main civic buildings were situated here. In the principal square is the **Tomb of Battus**, the founder of the city. This was a very special honour, as generally no tombs were allowed within the city walls. Close by are the remains of the supposed **Gymnasium**, the school for the elite youth where intellectual work was as important as physical exercise. In the square

is the **Naval Monument**, probably erected in the 3rd century BC to commemorate a victory at sea. On the south of the square is the **Prytaneum**, or Town Hall. This building was the administrative centre of the town. The building resembled the plan of a private house, built around a central courtyard, with a sacred fire held in a niche to the east side symbolizing the communal home of the people. The officers of the Town Hall lived and worked within the building and invited privileged citizens and visitors to eat there. The Town Hall dates back to the Hellenistic period with only a few additions during the Roman times. The building was used until the Imperial officials from Rome took over the governing of the city.

On the east side of the Town Hall lies the **Capitolium**. The building dates to the end of the Hellenistic period and was converted by the Romans into the temple where Jupiter, Juno and Minerva were worshipped, symbolizing the empire. The front has four white marble Doric columns and by the entrance are Greek inscriptions commemorating the gratitude of the city for the help Emperor Hadrian gave for the reconstruction of the town after the Jewish revolt.

Getting the measure of Aswan

Eratosthenes was a Libyan. He was born in Cyrene in 276 BC and studied in Athens before taking up residence in Alexandria where he became the director of the famous library. He was noted as a writer of scientific material and also as a writer of poetry. He was an eminent astrologer (making a catalogue of 675 stars), a mathematician and he took an interest in the theatre. But he is famed for being the first man to measure with some accuracy the circumference of the Earth.

It was known that in Aswan the sun at noon on midsummer's day was directly overhead and cast no shadow. Eratosthenes was in Alexandria and using the shadow cast by the sun there measured the angle of the suns's rays on the same day and at the same time. Using information gained from travellers he estimated the distance from Alexandria to Aswan was about 800 km and calculated the circumference of the Earth as 40,000 km, only 75 km out. (His measurements, in stadia, have been converted into units of today for your convenience!) He also worked out the distance from the Earth to the Sun and the Earth to the Moon. His calculation of the angle of tilt of the axis of the Earth at 23°51'15" was an amazing result.

When his sight failed him in old age he is said to have deliberately starved himself to death.

To the east, going from the agora to the **Forum of Proculus** (8), is the **Street of Caryatids** (15). The road was originally lined on the north side with figures standing on pedestals (Caryatids) but they have all fallen over and are very damaged. On the south of the road is one of the most elegant houses in Cyrene, once belonging to Jason Magnus, a priest of Apollo. Built around the 2nd century BC by joining two houses, it is richly decorated, with mosaic floors, some well preserved. The larger of the two houses (on the higher level to the west) held the reception rooms. In the largest of the reception rooms remains of the magnificent marble floor can be seen. On the north, three small temples were incorporated into the house. One of the temples was the owner's private chapel. Both houses were built around a central courtyard. The second smaller house held the family's apartments.

Further east, the remains of a theatre are visible. This was probably built in the 3rd century BC and it is suggested that it was built as a replacement for the theatre in the sanctuary that had been converted into an amphitheatre. To the north of the Street of Caryatids, stands the impressive **Forum of Proculus**, probably built during the Hellenistic period, but later rebuilt by the Romans. The large central courtyard is lined with Doric colonnades, and in the centre lie the remains of an earlier temple, probably dedicated to Dionysius. Various fortifications were added to the forum during the 4th and 5th centuries when Cyrene was in constant fear of Berber attacks. To the northwest of the forum lies a small **Roman Theatre**, which has been renovated and is sometimes used for performances. On the north side of the forum stands a **Basilica** built in the 6th century AD. Such buildings were used as an exchange for merchants or as law courts. The site extends for more than 3 km and this description has tried to give an account of the most interesting monuments, many

of the others being in a poor state or still in need of excavation.

Particularly interesting is the **Necropolis** all around the site, making up an estimated 50 sq km. Tombs were not allowed inside the city walls and all tombs were thus situated on the surrounding lands and in particular in the side of the hill in front of the sanctuary. The tombs were dug out of the rock and formed small caves, often done in conjunction with quarrying, and the bodies placed directly into coffins carved out of the rock. The doorway was then sealed with a large stone. Due to the stones being movable, most of the tombs were broken into and even sometimes inhabited by nomads. It is strange that virtually all the bodies were actually placed within the tomb as, until the Christian period, cremation was commonly practised. Only a few lead urns containing ashes have been found. No clear explanation seems to have been found as to why interment was systematically practised. The shrine tomb was also a widely-used burial chamber. The tombs resembled small mausoleums or temples. These mostly date back to the Hellenistic period. The number of tombs may at first seem impressive, but one must remember that the period of occupation stretched from 700 BC to 400 AD.

Local information
● Youth hostels

Former *Shahat Tourist Hotel*, T (851) 2102, open 0600-1000 and 1400-2400, 200 beds, kitchen, meals, laundry, family rooms, booking rec June-September, charge LD5 per night, bedrooms clean, showers and toilets very dirty, kitchen lacks equipment and also very dirty, meals not rec here.

AL-BAYDA

This is an important administrative regional centre. Once briefly the administrative capital of Libya in 1964, it is now the site of an important Islamic university. This is no coincidence since in 1843 Mohammed Ben Ali Al-Senussi established his radical Islamic movement in Al-Bayda, a movement that was to spread throughout Cyrenaica. In the 19th century the Turks had problems with the Senussi hold on the population and the leaders of the movement had to settle for safety in Jaghbub and Al-Kufrah. The Senussi led the rebellion against the Italians, finally leading Idris Al-Senussi to the throne and Libyan Independence in 1951. Today, Al-Bayda is a good stopover point and is very close to the major archaeological site of Cyrene.

Local information
● Accommodation

There is one good hotel in the main street. The D *Bayda Palace Hotel*, T 084 23455, run down, clean, rooms with bath and a/c, LD17 for double incl breakfast, suites cost LD35; D *Hotel Cairo*, opp *Bayda Palace*, LD15 per night but not so nice.

● Transport

Road Bus: there is a bus station on the main street, by the telecom tower. There are frequent buses to **Shahat** (Cyrene) every hour from 0800-1700. Other main line buses stop here, but there are no fixed timetables, except that the majority of the buses pass here in the morning. Bus to **Benghazi** takes 5 hrs. **Taxi**: shared taxi to Benghazi takes 3 hrs, costs LD5 each.

WADI AL-KUF

On the road between Al-Bayda and Gasr Al-Libya, there is an impressive new bridge crossing a deep gorge at Wadi Al-Kuf (see illustration). The bridge is over 500m above the gorge and the view is breathtaking, definitely worth a stop. It is possible to take the road that goes along the bottom of the gorge. The cliffs in the side of the gorge are filled with small caves and quaint rock formations.

GASR AL-LIBYA

This small town is located on the road from Al-Bayda to Al-Marj. In itself it does not necessitate a visit but a fine old **Byzantine Fort** stands nearby. The site is a few kilometres down a road leading right from the village. The ruins date back to the 6th century and contain a well preserved **Byzantine Church**. The church was most probably fortified. The walls are still in perfect condition but the roof, originally made of wood, has been replaced. In the centre of the nave lies a large mosaic, which is in good condition. There is also a small **museum** that contains a set of mosaics. All the mosaics have been cut out of the floor of another building further down the hill. They are interesting because they give an account of what was clearly an important Christian community at the start of the 6th century. The rest of the ruins are dominated by a small **Turkish Fort** built as a stronghold and lookout over the surrounding countryside: it was later used by the Italians during their attempts to subdue the region. From the top of the fort there is a wonderful view.

TOLMEITA (PTOLEMAIS)

This site is of real interest for the Graeco-Roman ruins of the port of Ptolemais. The village itself is very small, but the situation on the coastal plain is magnificent. The scenery along the road from Al-Marj is very beautiful, particularly when driving down through the mountains towards the sea. The ruins are extensive and cover an area larger than in Cyrene, but remain largely unexcavated. Nevertheless, the site is worth a visit. Tolmeita is literally at the end of the road, for after early morning there are no buses. Transport back to Al-Marj or on to Tocra is by taxi if you can find one.

History

The ancient city of Ptolemais was named after Ptolemy II Philadelphus in the 3rd century BC. The town was actually founded earlier but only became of importance under the Ptolemy's rule as part of the Pentapolis. Ptolemais was originally the harbour for the inland city of Barce (Al-Marj), but later was of importance in its own right. After the Roman occupation the city was altered and buildings constructed, proving its continuing role as an important centre. From the 3rd century, both Apollonia and Ptolemais became the main cities in Cyrenaica. In the 4th century, Ptolemais became the seat of the bishop and the capital of a province and fortifications were increased against raids by Berber tribes, but were insufficient to prevent the Vandals in the 5th century from taking the city. Ptolemais fell into decay with the Arab invasion and its only use was in providing building material for the new village. The site was rediscovered in 1935 by the Italians who started excavations there and set up the museum.

Places of interest

On the site there are several monuments that should not be missed. The **Street of the Monuments** is from the Roman period and was clearly an important place within the city, lined with porticoes, fountains, statues of people and deities, and inscriptions. The **Hellenistic Palace** (Palace of the Columns) is probably the largest and most interesting of excavated monuments dating back to the 1st century BC and altered in the 2nd century. From its size and elaborate decorations, it was clearly the house of a person of note. The house included large reception rooms with mosaic floors and traces of marble-panelled walls. There are two courtyards, one with an ornamental water tank, the other with Corinthian columns and traces of marble and mosaic floors. The house had two storeys, the basement presumably reserved for the servants. To the north of the building, one can see signs of the existence of private baths. On the north side, ie on the street, there is evidence that the front of the house had shops in it, a usual practice for private houses.

Not far from the palace, to the south, lies the **Forum**. This was rebuilt in the 1st century BC on the site of the Hellenistic Agora. The Romans built a large vaulted roof, a technique unknown to the Greeks. The entire structure covers 14 large reservoirs that were almost certainly fed by an aqueduct, traces of which can be seen by the Roman bridge that

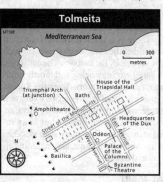

crosses over the *wadi* to the east of the site. The **Headquarters of the Dux** (Caserne d'Anastase) is a massive fortified building which presumably housed the garrison. Excavations of the **House of the Triapsidal Hall** indicate urban life continued here after the Islamic Conquest.

There are other worthwhile monuments to see but the excavations have not yet fully exposed the ruins and are thus not so immediately interesting as those mentioned above. To the west, remains of the walls that protected the city can still be seen. Close to the walls, a fully excavated **Basilica** dating back to the 5th century AD is well preserved. The church is original in that it was not an older converted building, a common practice during this period, and was built with defences. Vaults and arches replace the usual columns, but the nave was still roofed in wood. To the north of the basilica lies the **Amphitheatre**. Built by the Romans in the 1st century BC it was mostly used for gladiator fights and wild animal shows. Unfortunately today there is little to see. The **Odéon** was used both as a theatre and as a council chamber. The **Palace** has a dozen columns standing. To the south, in the hillside, is the **Byzantine Theatre**, probably built in the 2nd century BC. Once again little is visible. Finally, the ancient harbour was at the same place as the modern one. Some traces of buildings and their foundations can still be seen on the east side of the harbour, as can be the location of some of the jetties.

There is a small **museum** located at the end of the road which passes through the village, by the harbour. The collection is small but interesting and mostly holds mosaics and sculptures from the Roman period. Some of the mosaics are very well preserved and are particularly of value, not for their great quality, but as an insight into life in Ptolemais, such as scenes with various wild animals, including lions and tigers.

AL-MARJ

The present Al-Marj is virtually a new city, the old town having been completely destroyed during an earthquake in 1963. The inhabitants were then relocated in the new town with a gigantic modern mosque that dominates the skyline.

● **Accommodation** There is one hotel at Al-Marj which can be used as a good stop-over point. **D** *Al-Marj Hotel*, T (67) 2700, is situated nr the centre of the new town, seems to have known better days, but is nevertheless clean, with a restaurant and cafeteria. **Youth hostels** T (67) 3669, 60 beds, breakfast incl, meals, kitchen, family rooms, bus 600m.

● **Transport Road** The bus and taxi station is about 500m in front of the mosque. There are no fixed times for buses, as they are only passing through, but they stop in Al-Marj in the morning between 0800 and 1000. Best to be there early. Otherwise there are shared taxis leaving throughout the day for destinations east and west.

TOCRA (AL-AQURIYAH)

Tocra is a small town about 60 km from Benghazi. The new town is of little interest but the old part of town and the small central square with its **market** is worth a look around. Tocra has well-researched Roman ruins, though not all the workings are totally uncovered. Nevertheless, they are interesting and the small **Turkish fort** provides a good view over the plain towards the Jabal. A visit to the caves and to the remains of two Byzantine churches has been recommended.

History *Teuchira*, the original Greek name for Tocra, was founded around 510 BC. It became part of the Pentapolis. It changed names more than once and was called Arsinoe after the wife of Ptolemy II, and was briefly known as Cleopatris, the name of the daughter of Cleopatra and Mark Antony. There are still some surrounding walls built by the Byzantine Emperor Justinian in the 6th century and the Turkish fort, most probably built over the site of the Greek acropolis. From the ruins that have been excavated it is possible to deduce that the community at Tocra was poorer than the inhabitants of the other Pentapolis towns.

BENGHAZI

Benghazi is the second largest town in Libya after Tripoli and as such is an important economic and administrative centre. The town acts as the main port for the East of Libya and has a number of food processing and packaging plants as well as other small and medium sized industries.

(*Pop* 804,000 (estimated 1995); *Alt* Sea level; *Maximum recorded temperature* 40.1°C) The city has little to offer to the visitor as many of the older monuments have been destroyed, some during WW2 but most through contemporary 'development' of the city. The present town is therefore relatively modern and charmless, except for areas in the old town and around the *funduq* market. Benghazi is nevertheless a good stopover/terminal point for visits from Egypt and also a jump-off point for journeys south into Al-Khalij province.

The city enjoys a thoroughly Mediterranean climate with hot dry summers and warm winters with some rainfall. The Jabal Al-Akhdar region behind and to the east of Benghazi has a markedly heavier and more reliable winter rainfall of over 300 mm, with the scarp top attracting the larger rainfall total.

Scorpions – the original sting in the tail

Scorpions really deserve a better press. They are fascinating creatures, provided they no not lurk in your shoe or shelter in your clothes.

Scorpions are not insects. They belong to the class Arachnida as do spiders and daddy longlegs. There are about 750 different kinds of scorpions. The average size is a cosy 6 cm but the largest, *Pandinus imperator*, the black Emperor scorpion of West Africa, is a terrifying 20 cm long. The good news is that only a few are really dangerous. The bad news is that some of these are found in North Africa.

They really are remarkable creatures with the ability to endure the hottest desert climates, revive after being frozen in ice, and survive for over a year without food or water. They have a remarkable resistance to nuclear radiation, a characteristic yet to be proved of great use.

Scorpions are nocturnal. They shelter during the heat of the day and to keep cool wave their legs in the air. They feed on insects and spiders, grasping their prey with their large claw-like pincers, tearing it apart and sucking the juices. Larger scorpions can devour lizards and small mammals.

Their shiny appearance is due to an impervious wax coating over their hard outer shell which protects them from any water loss. They have very small eyes and depend on their better developed senses of touch and smell. The sensitive bristles on the legs point in all directions and pick up vibrations of movements of potential prey or enemies. This sensitivity gives them ample warning to avoid being seen by heavy-footed humans.

The oft reported 'courtship dance' before mating is merely repeated instinctive actions. The grasping of claws and the jerky 'dance' movements from side to side are a prelude to copulation during which the male produces spermatozoa in a drop of sticky fluid to which the female is led so that they may enter her body. The male departs speedily after the 'dance' to avoid being attacked and devoured.

Scorpions bear live young. After hatching, the young crawl on to the female's back and are carried there for two or three weeks until their first moult. They gradually drop off after that time and have to fend for themselves.

Most scorpions retreat rather than attack. They sting in self-defence. The sting is a hard spine and the poison is made in the swelling at the base. The sole of the bare foot, not surprisingly, is most often the site of a sting, and the advice in the section on Health (see page 510) is not to be ignored. The African **fat-tailed scorpion** (we do not recommend measuring the size) is described as aggressive and quick-tempered. It is responsible for most of the reported stings to humans and most of the human fatalities in North Africa. The beautifully named *Buthus occitanus*, the small **Mediterranean yellow scorpion** and *Leirus quinquestriatus*, the **African golden scorpion**, also have neurotoxic stings that can be fatal.

History

The town of Benghazi was probably founded around 515 BC, but no real information exists as to the precise date. The first settlers were most probably Greeks from Cyrene who had come down to the coastal plain. It is known that the first settlement was called Euesperides and was situated much further inland than the present city. In 249 BC, Ptolemy III of Egypt subjected Cyrenaica to Egyptian rule and married Berenice, the heiress to the Cyrenaican Kingdom. A new site was found for the town of Euesperides, closer to the sea, probably because the old harbour had silted up, and the town was renamed Berenice. The situation of the ancient city is virtually identical to the present old town of Benghazi. The town then became part of the Roman Empire but once again little is known of its role. In the 6th century AD, the Byzantine Emperor Justinian made a number of repairs to the city after it had suffered an attack by the Vandals.

In 643 AD, the Arabs invaded, led by Omar Ibn el As, but they had little interest in Berenice. The two main cities at the time were Ajdabiyah and Al-Marj, due to their closer proximity to the main trans-African caravan routes. Very little is known of Berenice until the 15th century, when local tradition has it that merchants from Misratah and Zliten once again started using Berenice as a trading place. In 1579 the town was given the name Ibn Ghazi after a holy man of the city at that period. In 1648 the Turks, having previously settled in Tripolitania, advanced on Cyrenaica. By 1650 they held a position of strength in Ibn Ghazi, having built a fort. The town became the main centre for tax collecting. Because of this, few travellers or merchants came near it! In 1711, the Ottoman régime in Libya was interrupted by the Karamanli takeover and this once again plunged Benghazi into a period of stagnation. It was only under the second Ottoman occupation, beginning in 1835, that Benghazi again prospered.

In 1911, Benghazi was subjected to a siege by the Italian Navy, the city only surrendering after bombardment from the sea. The Italians then created a stronghold out of the city, building large walls encircling the centre. It took 20 years for the Italians to gain control of the surrounding areas, and only after 1931 were they in a position to start building up the city. The Italians poured large sums into urbanization projects and virtually managed to recreate an Italian city in North Africa. The real disaster for the town came during WW2 when the city changed hands five times and was incessantly bombed by the Allies or the Axis. When General Montgomery finally liberated the city in November 1942, there was little left. Subsequently, due to the uncertainties as to the future of Libya, no major reconstruction works were carried out by the British Military Administration.

With Independence in 1951, the city gained in importance as the regional capital and as the seat of the Federal Government, but developments were slow, particularly due to the government's lack of funds. In 1959, oil was found in the area around Sirt and the town became an important centre in the

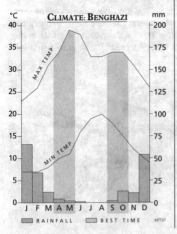

CLIMATE: BENGHAZI

MAX TEMP
MIN TEMP

°C / mm

J F M A M J J A S O N D

RAINFALL   BEST TIME

MTT37

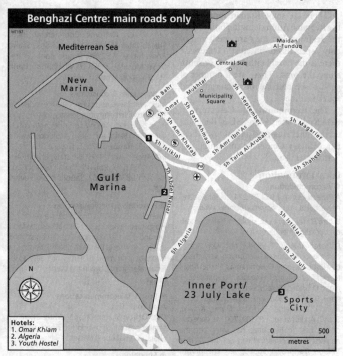

Benghazi Centre: main roads only

MT197

Mediterranean Sea

New Marina

Central Suq

Maidan Al-Funduq

Sh Bahr

Mukhtar

Municipality Square

Sh Omar

Sh Qasr Ahmad

Sh 1 September

Sh Amr Khatab

Sh Istiklal

Sh Amr Ibn'As

Sh Tariq Al-Arubah

Sh Magarief

Sh Shaheda

Gulf Marina

Po

Sh Abdel Nasser

Sh Algeria

Sh Istiklal

Sh 23 July

Inner Port/ 23 July Lake

Sports City

N

0   500
metres

Hotels:
1. *Omar Khiam*
2. *Algeria*
3. *Youth Hostel*

oil trade, particularly with the arrival of a large number of Europeans and Americans working in the oil fields. BP established its main office in Benghazi rather than Tripoli. Throughout the 1960s and 1970s, as oil revenues increased, the town developed rapidly. In the early 1980s the harbour was redeveloped in order to cater for large cargo vessels, new roads were built and small industries started to appear.

SOCIAL INDICATORS Benghazi is similar to Tripoli in per capita income (US$6,600), literacy (M 88%, F 63%) and life expectancy (62/67 years).

ACCESS There are frequent flights from Tripoli and other Libyan cities and, in normal circumstances, ie no UN sanctions, a few international flights. There is a bus service between the airport and central Benghazi (32 km). Taxis run into the town

centre but make sure to agree a price before departure.

Places of interest

Benghazi has few sites of any touristic value, but it is interesting to walk around the old town and see the myriads of small shops selling every imaginable type of merchandise. Particularly interesting is the *funduq*, a large market that mainly sells vegetables and fresh products. The atmosphere is typical of any Middle Eastern market and a worthwhile experience. The surrounding area is filled with stalls, particularly on Friday when traffic comes to a standstill. You will see trucks full of goods from Egypt, especially furniture, as well as a labour market where painters, electricians, carpenters, and so on stand by the side of the road waiting for employment.

There are some **Roman remains** by the Regional Administration building on the seafront, but they are small and of only specialized interest. Otherwise there is the beach, either north or south along the coast. There are a number of good beach clubs, with restaurants and snack facilities.

The **Commonwealth Cemetery** in Benghazi is sited 6 km SSE of Benghazi on the inner ring road and in town there is a **Military Cemetery** containing 311 British war dead.

Local information
● **Accommodation**

A *Tibesti Hotel*, T 97178, 274 rm, largest and newest, luxurious, *hammam*, impersonal.

B *Uzu Hotel*, very clean, modern, half the room overlooking inner harbour.

D *Hotel Al-Anis*, T 93147, rec, very simple, clean, good restaurant, welcoming, very cheap, best in this category; **D** *Hotel Atlas*, Sharah Abdel Nasser, T 92314, not marvellous, acceptable for 1 night; **D** *Ghordabeia Hotel*, Sharah Abdel Nasser, T 97342/5, room with shower, small hotel, friendly proprietor; **D** *Hotel Omar Khiam*, Sharah Abdel Nasser, T 95102, 200 rm, once one of the best in Benghazi, has since become neglected, welcoming, cheap, central; *Tourist Village Garians*, T 96350, very cheap with good recreational facilities, closed in winter.

● **Youth hostel**
Sports City, 1 km southwest of town centre, T 95961, 200 beds, breakfast incl, kitchen, meals, family rooms, laundry, booking rec May-October.

● **Places to eat**
Restaurant Al-Shallal, Sharah Abdel Nasser, by the *Hotel Atlas*, mainly Turkish food; *Restaurant Ali Ayamama* Sharah Abdel Nasser, behind the *Tibesti Hotel*; *Ghordabeia Hotel* restaurant has a Kentucky Fried Chicken licence!! *Restaurant 23 July*, in the gardens by the inner harbour just before reaching the *Uzu Hotel*. Food and snacks are available at the various beach clubs nr the city. Café in *Tibesti Hotel* open all day for snacks around LD5. Good *patisserie* nr car hire Bab Almadena in Sharah Abdel Nasser.

● **Banks & money changers**
Both the *Tibesti* and the *Uzu Hotels* have banking facilities. Otherwise the main banks are as follows: **Central Bank of Libya**, Sharah Abdel Nasser, T 91165; **Jamahiriya Bank**, Sharah Abdel Nasser; **National Commercial Bank**, Sharah Omar Mukhtar; **Sahara Bank**, Sharah Abdel Nasser, T 92766; **Umma Bank**, Sharah Omar Mukhtar, T 93377; **Wahhadah Bank**, Sharah Abdel Nasser, T 94527.

● **Embassies & consulates**
Most embassies and consulates are located in Tripoli to which ultimate reference for assistance must be made. Among countries with consulates in Benghazi are: **Czechoslovakia**, T 92149; **France**, T 27566; **Greece**, Sharah Gamal Abdel Nasser, T 93064; **Italy**, Sharah Amr Ibn'As, T 98077; **Poland**, Sharah Gamal Abdel Nasser, T 98363/92867; **Saudi Arabia**, Fuehat, T 20815.

● **Hospitals & medical services**
Chemists: Sharah Gamal Abdel Nasser.
Hospitals: Benghazi has central hospital facilities and a modern complex on the outskirts of the town. While the air embargo remains in force, bear in mind that it is not easy to be repatriated from Libya in the event of an emergency.

● **Post & telecommunications**
Area code: 061.
Post Office: Sharah Omar Mukhtar. There is a smaller post office behind the *Tibesti Hotel* on Sharah Gamal Abdel Nasser.

● **Shopping**
These are concentrated in the main street and the road leading from the centre west, Sharah Gamal Abdel Nasser, to the so-called Christmas Tree area. Some of the older suburbs have grocery and Arab lock-up shops selling a range of produce.

Markets: the *funduq* offers an abundance of reasonably priced vegetables and other perishable products.

● **Sports**
There are several beach clubs not far from the city centre on the Ghar Yunis road towards the university campus. The bigger hotels, such as the *Tibesti*, have Arab baths. The *Tourist Village Garians*, T 6350, 5 km to the south of the town, has a pool, tennis, bowling, snooker and other sports/recreational activities, facilities can be used by non-residents for a small entrance fee. Only open in summer.

● **Tour companies & travel agents**
Libyan Travel and Tourism Company is located at the start of Sharah Gamal Abdel Nasser,

towards the harbour. This is a new agency specializing in organized tours. It can provide guides and transport. The company also issues tickets for all major airlines, T 93009. *Libyan Arab Airways* have an office on Sharah Gamal Abdel Nasser, behind the *Tibesti Hotel*. Both the *Tibesti* and the *Uzu Hotels* have travel agents that can issue tickets for all major airlines.

● **Transport**

Air Internal: to Tripoli daily at 0800, 1900 and 2000 with extra flights most days at 1500 or 1600. Takes 1 hr, costs LD28; flights per week Ghadames (3), Ghat (3), Hun (4), Al-Kufrah (1), Misratah (5), Sabha (5), Sirt (4), Tobruk (3).

Road Bus: Faltco company. The bus station is after the *funduq* on the right. Be sure to be there well in advance as buses tend to leave earlier rather than later than officially stated. Daily: **Tripoli** (4), **Cairo** (2), **Damascus** Wednesday and Sunday 0800. **General Transport company**. Brand new bus station right next to the Funduq market. Daily: **Tripoli** 0730 (2 buses); **Al-Khums** 0700; **Misratah** 0800; **Al-Kufrah** 0730; **Sabha** Tuesday, Friday and Sunday 0700; **Tobruk** 0730, 1100; **Derna** 0800.

Car hire: Tibesti Car Service is in the foyer of the *Tibesti Hotel*, T 92030, prices for 24 hrs start at LD2; **Bab Almadena** T 99855, PO Box 7268, Sharah Abdel Nasser, nr *Hotel Algeria*. Local taxis are available for short or day-hire at expensive rates. **Taxi**: all the intercity taxis leave from the *funduq* area. They are all grouped by destination and leave when full. Slightly more expensive than the bus. Sample fare to Al-Bayda LD5. Taxis inside Benghazi LD3.

Al-Khalij

AL-KHALIJ WHICH takes its name from the Gulf of Sirt includes the Sirtican coastal embayment together with the routes to and from the entire southeast quadrant of the country down to the borders of Egypt and Sudan. The area of the province is estimated at 730,960 sq km. The province was intended in the period after the coup d'état of 1969 to unite the centre of the country and give a political bloc strong enough to offset the traditional domination of Tripolitania and Cyrenaica. In fact, it has remained as an enormous no man's land around the Gulf of Sirt with a long tail south into the desert, the oases of which retain their individuality from the coastlands to which they were attached.

Entering Al-Khalij

This vast territory contains the oilfield areas along and inland from the Gulf of

Sirt together with the great sand seas of the Sahara. There are several traditional entry points to Libya from Egypt, including the desert routes from Siwa to Jaghbub and Dakhla-Farafra to Al-Kufrah. However, the northern road from Marsa Matruh/Solum into Bardia/ Derna is the easiest and often the only reliable gateway to Al-Khalij from Egypt. Given the attractiveness of the Jabal Al-Akhdar as an access zone, this is not a major impediment to travel in Al-Khalij, though it does mean passing through Benghazi to Ajdabiyah. The latter town is the junction whence roads travel west along the coast or inland to the deep South.

Climate

In this region the climate is Saharan. Extreme temperatures exceed 50°C and lows of well below freezing are experienced, especially at night. Rain is rare but occasional downpours induce flash floods and surface erosion over limited areas. The coast, especially around Sirt, gets a rainfall of more than 100 mm, though this is very erratic and rare wet years are followed by many years of drought.

Land

The Libyan Desert covers the territory between the 18° and 29° parallels north and the 18° and 28° meridians east. Its northern limits are marked by the marginal settlement at Siwa in Egypt and Al-Jaghbub and Gialo in Libya. It comprises a vast sedimentary depression of limestones and clays. The only high relief is in the Jabal Al-Awenat in the extreme southeast with heights of 1,908m at the Libyan-Egyptian-Sudanese border tripoint. The topography of the desert is dominated by sand, in the form of dunes in the Jaghbub sand sea and elsewhere gravel desert such as the Serir Calanscio. Al-Khalij includes two other major sand seas, those of Calanscio, to the west of Serir Calanscio, and Rebiana, in the southwest of Al-Khalij. The coast is also a desert, the Sirt desert made up of a low broken plateau.

The northern coastlands are open to access while southern Al-Khalij still remains difficult to reach from outside. Until the 1980s there was no permanent all-weather highway between the main settlement, Al-Kufrah, and the north coast. Even now a single black top road acts as the link between the two very separate sections of the province, traversing 876 km from Ajdabiyah to Al-Kufrah.

Population

The Libyan population of Al-Khalij is very small, at best 400,000 and possibly as low as 200,000 in 1990 with a further 40,000-45,000 foreign migrant workers. Growth rates have generally fallen according to UN data to about 3% per year, with the exception of the main coastal urban

Climate: Al-Khalij

	Sirt	Ajdabiyah	Gialo	Al-Kufrah
Mean annual minimum °C	8.6	7.3	6.3	4.8
Extreme minimum °C	2.4	0.0	-2.0	-3.3
Mean annual maximum °C	31.0	33.7	37.8	38.9
Extreme maximum °C	46.7	46.7	49.1	46.0
Relative humidity %	51-84	45-82	26-61	11-61
Mean annual rainfall mm	180.8	126.9	9.2	1.9
Maximum monthly rainfall mm	215.7	102.6	26.2	11.2
Maximum annual rainfall mm	429.5	227.6	50.3	11.9
Minimum annual rainfall mm	6.7	3.4	1.0	0.0

Source: *Speerplan*

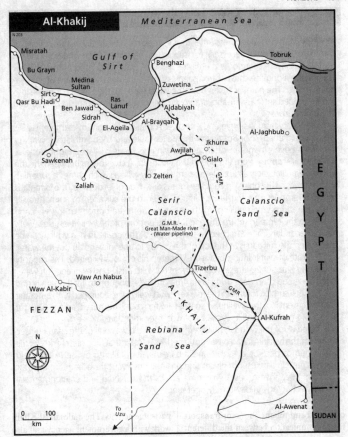

site at Ben Jawad, where 5.5% growth prevails. Overall, it appears that the country and inland areas of Al-Khalij are approximately maintaining their population size while losing many of their younger people to the coast and to the cities outside the region. The populations of the coastal regions are concentrated in the urban settlements. In the south the population is also clustered in small villages for security, except on modern farm estates where, incongruously, farms are laid out geometrically across the desert landscape in the teeth of regional social traditions.

Industry

The main towns of the province are the centres of the oil industry at Al-Brayqah, Ras Lanuf and Zuwetina. The only exceptions are Ajdabiyah and Sirt. The former is a route centre where the road from the south joins the coast. Ajdabiyah district contains approximately half the population of the Al-Khalij region, about 100,000 persons, by far the majority in the town area itself. Inland, the main towns are Al-Kufrah, Gialo-Awjilah and Tizerbu, all very small. The new coastal towns and the modern extensions to the south oases are

The Delu well – traditional well of Libya and North Africa

🐾 Water was always essential to life in North Africa. Given the scarcity of surface water, it was necessary for survival to lift water from underground. In traditional Libya – more or less until the 1960s – water was lifted from a shallow water table along the coast or from depressions in the desert by means of a device called a *delu*. The name is taken from the word for a goatskin, which is made into a bag, dipped into a well and drawn up full of water for both household and irrigation purposes.

The mechanism is simple and effective. A shallow one or 2m diameter well is hand dug to about 2 or 3m below the water table and lined with stone work or cement. Above ground an often ornate gantry is made of two upright stone or wooden pillars rising from the side of the wellhead. A cross beam between the top of the two pillars acts as an axle to a small pulley wheel which carries a rope tied to the mouth of the goatskin bag. The rope is drawn up or let down by the ingenious use of a ramp to ease the task of lifting water to the surface. An animal travels down the ramp when pulling up the goatskin from the bottom of the well and moves up the ramp to return the bag into the bottom of the well. Most *delu* wells have a secondary rope attached to the bottom of the goatskin bag which can be used when the full bag is at the top of the gantry to upend it and tip out the water.

The rate of water lifting by the *delu* method is obviously limited. The capacity of the bag is about 20 litres. Working from dawn to dusk, however, enough water could be raised to irrigate up to 3 or 4 ha of land – enough to feed a family and leave a small surplus for sale in the market. Most wells were equipped with a storage basin adjacent to the wellhead so that water could be raised and stored for household use and to give a reserve of water for irrigation.

The creak of the wooden pulley wheel of the *delu* was one of the characteristic sounds of the North African oases until the 1960s. After that time diesel and electric power pumps became available and the *delu* system fell into disuse. A few *delu* gantries remain as museum pieces and only the observant traveller in the deepest south of the Saharan oases will come across this splendid and environmentally friendly technology in day-to-day operation.

dispersed and reliant on motor transport for communication between the different parts of the town. On the coast, the oil towns are well planned and the residential districts are made up of two areas, first the concentrated bungalow towns set up by foreign oil companies for their employees and second, modern towns built by the Libyan authorities at great expense for civil servants and other services. The oil towns are strung along the coastal highway.

The local economy

In Al-Khalij, approximately 25% of the work force is employed in agricultural pursuits and perhaps 30% in government services. Agriculture is, for Libyans, a part-time activity. The males in Al-Khalij work with a government agency and also labour or manage their own farms in their, often generous, spare time. There are 42,500 ha under cultivation, of which about 11,000 ha is irrigated. Most dryland cultivation and livestock herding is concentrated along the coast, where the rainfall is slightly better and more reliable.

Inland farming is oasis-based in small fields with associated palmeries. Modern sector large settlement projects have been developed at great expense. The units are capital intensive, based on water lifted from deep wells within the Nubian sandstones. The deep wells fed 100 x 100

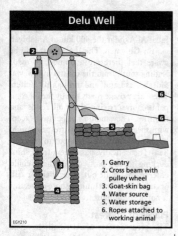

Delu Well

1. Gantry
2. Cross beam with pulley wheel
3. Goat-skin bag
4. Water source
5. Water storage
6. Ropes attached to working animal

EGY210

ha circles of land with water through an automated mobile-rotating arm sprinkler system. They were used first for growing fodder for sheep. The costs were unsupportable and the project was turned over to grain production. Technical and economic problems continued and the units were eventually run down and many abandoned with water switched to supply the Great Manmade River Scheme (GMR).

A settlement scheme was also devised for Al-Kufrah, comprising 5,500 ha of hexagons each made up of 16 farms. The history of the settlement scheme is sad and expensive. Libyans by and large ignored the project and costs ran out of control against a small return in agricultural produce. A similar project was set up further north at Serir. Settlement schemes at Gialo and Tizerbu were also attempted. The residual areas of cultivation can still be seen in these various sites.

Oil and **natural gas** dominate the economy of Al-Khalij. Oil and gas fields are located in the north section of the province, the materials being pumped to the coast where they are exported as crude hydrocarbons or refined. There are many oil-related industries in the region. There is a gas processing plant and oil

refinery at Al-Brayqah and another old small refinery at Zuwetina. New refinery capacity has been added at Ras Lanuf, while petrochemical units have been set up at Al-Brayqah, Ras Lanuf and Marada. Installations associated with the oil industry spread towards Waha, Mejid and Serir oilfields.

Al-Khalij's **water resources** are from three sources, groundwater, surface *wadi* flow and seawater desalination plants. The coastal zone has a limited and much depleted shallow aquifer. In the south there are very large deep aquifers in the Nubian sandstones within the Al-Kufrah basin. The strength of these reserves is uncertain and it is likely that extraction at present rates will be sustained for only 50 years or so. In the early 1980s it was decided to transfer water from the Al-Kufrah Basin to the north coastlands through a large diameter concrete pipeline, the Great Manmade River, costing some US$7bn or more. The GMR runs from the southern water fields to the coast near to Ajdabiyah and from there along the coast towards Benghazi and Sirt. The object of the line is advertised as principally for agriculture but it is thought by many experts that the bulk of water will only be utilized economically in urban water supply and for industrial end use. The GMR has been the largest development project in Libya for the last decade and the future of Libyan agriculture will rest on how the water is put to use.

Zuwetina is a small, formerly agricultural, centre now overwhelmed by the growth of the oil industry in its vicinity and the influx of foreign workers. The old settlement is sited off the highway to the north, where there are still farmed gardens and some fishing.

The **oases of the south** were never heavily populated. They acted as stopover points for the trans-Saharan caravans. Al-Kufrah was in fact a set of scattered palm grove villages in a large low plain in which water seepages occurred. Recent changes have resulted in considerable building activity both for new agricultural estates on the perimeter of the settlements and administrative, military and other buildings, often rather unsympathetic in architecture.

Tizerbu has recently been developed, formerly being no more than a fuelling and water point on the route from the Southern and Western Sahara to Al-Kufrah and Ajdabiyah. It now has most services including garages, fuel and a chemist together with urban services such as telephones, piped water, clinics and electricity. The **Gialo oases** are scattered around water holes some 250 km from Ajdabiyah. Originally very pretty with traditional farms and well laid out palm groves, Gialo-Awjilah has had some development of settlement farms and administrative services. It has fuel, water and limited urban facilities and is well worth a visit.

ACCESS Al-Khalij is reached mainly from adjacent provinces, though there are direct links in from Chad and Sudan, controlled by the military and not recommended both for that reason and because of the problem of finding safe transport overland. **Air** Flights to Al-Khalij are mainly via Tripoli or Benghazi, although lateral entry is possible direct from Algiers or via Sabha or other airports when there are external links open for the entry of foreigners. On internal airlines, Sirt links directly with Tripoli, Benghazi and Sabha, while Al-Kufrah links directly with Benghazi only. **Road** Access is from the north and still principally via the coastal highway coming in from Tripoli to the west and Cyrenaica to the east. Ajdabiyah is then the gateway south to Al-Kufrah. New roads have been built to support the oil industry, some pastureland developments and military/strategic objectives by providing a second land link between the two main parts of the country and reducing reliance of the exposed coast road. The main artery to the west comes in from Bu Grayn via Waddan and Zella through Marada eventually reaching Al-Brayqah and Gialo. A continuation of this road project continues east to Al-Jaghbub, hugging the north edge of the Libyan sand desert and

thence leading north to Tobruk. A second road leads from Tobruk to the south of the Jabal Al-Akhdar the 400 km to Ajdabiyah via Bir Ghiymah. The traveller should be aware that there are a number of roads leading south from the coastal highway at Sidrah, Ras Lanuf and through Bir Zelten. These are private roads run by the oil companies for servicing their oil fields and facilities. They should not be used except with specific permission as trespass might be misinterpreted as a threat to security. **Sea** Theoretically, passengers from ships docking in the ports of Al-Khalij could enter by that route but, other than for sailors taking rare and limited shore leave, this is not open for most travellers.

Places of interest

The great deserts of Al-Khalij have an attraction of their own, though they are at least over large areas heavily visited by commercial activities connected with oil and water developments. Even the extreme south is no longer *terra incognita* in that a major war between Libya and Chad was fought across this region in the period 1980-90. The very light human settlement of the province in past centuries has meant that there is little of human interest by way of monuments to see. Rather, there is a limited number of small oasis sites with a certain charm. Only the dedicated and highly inquisitive traveller can be encouraged to traverse vast distances in Al-Khalij to visit them.

Al-Jaghbub

Local information
● Accommodation
Facilities for travellers and tourists in Al-Khalij are minimal. This, after all, is the country's oil producing area and there are deemed to be few sights that a bona fide tourist would wish to see. Even the official tours run by semi-state agencies steer clear of this area. Provisions are for oil workers, workers in the water industry and for service personnel. Most accommodation, transport and entertainment is dedicated to a specific company workforce. There are some hotels but very few that cater for travellers. Ajdabiyah has a number of rest houses and cheap hotels for migrant Arab workers. They are basic but can be serviceable. The traveller to Al-Khalij must be adaptable and willing to accept hospitality where it can be found or get hospitality from an official agency before entering the region. Prospects for the availability of accommodation are improving but the easiest way for travellers is to ask at the *baladiyah* (local council) offices for a room in the school dormitory or the youth hostel.

● Youth hostel
Sirt, 2 km north of town centre, on Sharah Sawadah, open 0700-2300, 120 beds, kitchen, meals provided, laundry, family groups, bus 1 km, airport 30 mins, T 2867, booking rec.

● Camping
Camping is possible but in the oilfield area this should be done discreetly and preferably with the permission of the owner or the authorities. Elsewhere, camping in the oases can only be undertaken with permission but this is unlikely to be withheld.

● Places to eat
Eating out is difficult except in Ajdabiyah and Sirt where there are local cafeterias or restaurants providing often a limited service in range of meals and opening hours. Elsewhere, the coastal highway has small routestop cafés and cold drink stands where electricity is available. Catering is generally for institutions or households and the eating places are few and far between. Travellers should always have spare food and water, especially on the long inter-centre routes.

SIRT – THE WESTERN ENTRY TO AL-KHALIJ

This small staging post on the coast road was used by the Italians as an administrative centre. It gained new life following the change of régime in 1969 since Colonel Ghadhafi came from the Ghadadfha tribal area close by. Sirt was built up as a military centre and bastion for the government. Developments in communications, industry and agriculture were given priority. The population of the town and its hinterland is estimated at over 150,000. Development of the garrison and administrative centre has meant the emergence of a completely new, if not entirely well-integrated, town with all services but little for the visitor to see. Spreading from the town is a series of valleys and low hills where attempts have been made to develop agriculture, mainly orchards. Sirt has been connected by road to the Al-Jufra oases to the south by a good new 227 km black top road. Sirt has cafeterias, restaurants and hotel accommodation, *Hotel Mahari*, five star, T 60100, in addition to all services such as fuel, workshops, garages, PTT and medical facilities. Travellers should be careful when taking photographs not to include military installations.

Places of interest
Close by Sirt is the unmarked battlefield of **Qasr Bu Hadi** where in WW1 the Italians were beaten by the Libyans in a pitched battle. Along the coast is the site of **Medina Sultan** where the remains of a large mosque and Fatimid city have been discovered and partially excavated. Medina Sultan was set up at the point where a trans-Saharan route met the coast at a sheltered anchorage on the Gulf of Sirt coast. Fragments of pottery and inscriptions can be seen on the site.

Local information
● Transport
Air Air services support the government central administration in the south and there are two daily flights from **Tripoli**. Departures from **Benghazi** to Sirt are Monday, Wednesday, Friday and Saturday. Sirt also advertises direct flights internally to **Sabha** Tuesday, Thursday and Saturday. A direct flight to **Algiers** runs when the embargo is not in force.

Road By shared taxi or bus along the coast road.

AJDABIYAH AND THE ROAD TO GIALO AND AL-KUFRAH

Originally a small Arab town, Ajdabiyah has now been developed to the south of the coastal highway as a residential centre for foreign workers and some Libyan staff associated with the oil industry and government services. It is mainly new but badly maintained with little sense of civic pride. Its utilities including water, telephone, fuel and electricity are good but other services such as hospitals and clinics leave a lot to be desired. The concentration of low paid temporary foreign workers, mainly Sudanese, Egyptian and undenominated central Africans has done nothing to enhance the position of the town and, compared with Ras Lanuf new town and Al Brayqah, it has little to recommend it. Shops, mosques and fuel are all available close to the coastal highway and the road is now dangerous for driving given the unplanned, encroaching shops and housing built close to it.

Places of interest

At Ajdabiyah there are a number of monuments worthy of a visit. A **10th century Fatimid mosque** existed here, highly regarded because of its external staircase and square block base originally carrying an octagonal minaret. The site is now in ruins. The mosque's courtyard is still visible. The sanctuary façade is composed of a series of niches and there is a single arcade surrounding the courtyard. There are small Roman remains in the form of rock-cut inscriptions, indicating that Ajdabiyah was a significant site long before the Arab invasion. Clearly, however, the Fatimid period was the one in which the city flourished.

Local information
● **Accommodation**

The run down *Ajdabiyah Travelling Hotel* is in the town centre. Early buses start from here because the driver sleeps in the hotel.

● **Transport**

Road Bus: there is an excellent de-luxe and a regular bus service from **Tripoli** and **Benghazi** as well as intermediate points on the coast road. Buses start their runs early in the morning covering 161 km from Benghazi and 863 km from Tripoli. **Taxi**: shared taxis run very frequently from Benghazi. Passengers from Tripoli can find their way to Misratah after having visited other Tripolitanian sites before catching the taxi or bus for the long run to Sirt (463 km from Tripoli and 561 km from Benghazi) and Ajdabiyah.

GIALO

History

Gialo is a centre in the Gialo-Awjilah groups of oases with Jkhurra, Leskerre and Bir Buattifel. The site is some 30m above sea level and lies in a shallow 30 km depression in the desert. Water is available from wells and in Awjilah there was formerly an important spring source. Awjilah was the main trading oasis taking advantage of the routes south and to the coast. It had the largest and most productive palmeries with some 50,000 trees. Gialo has in recent times tended to be the main town of the group because of its prominence on the main north-south routeway and its central position within the oasis cluster. Gialo consists of a number of smaller villages, the main ones being Lebba and Al-Areg. Gialo is renowned for the quality of its dates. Its hotel is less memorable.

Places of interest

Outside Gialo itself, the area is thinly populated and consists mainly of palmeries. The rural population of the groups of oases at Gialo is some 20,000, of which about 3,000 are non-Libyans. The Libyan population is almost entirely of Berber origin. There is a unique **mosque** at Awjilah, **Al-Jami Al-Atiq**, built of a series of beehive domes of clay bricks and mud. The building measures approximately 30m x 21m and has been abandoned as an active place of prayer. The minaret has collapsed. On the minaret gallery below there is an inscription in Arabic, 'The witness is here deposited till judgment day, I testify that there are no gods other than God and that Mohammed is His Prophet. May the blessing of God be upon him by Abd Allah Ibn Abdulahmid Al-Qadi 1178 H (1764 AD)'. This is situated about 3 km from the main road through the oasis.

Local information
● Transport
Road Buses and **shared taxi**: services run regularly to Gialo from the main station on the edge of Ajdabiyah or from the junction of the coast road with the south road to Al-Kufrah. The road to Al-Kufrah leaves on a clearly sign-posted road from the coastal highway at Ajdabiyah and cuts across the coastal hills and through a series of *wadis* and internal drainage basins to the settlement at Sahabi to Gialo at Km 250.

AL-KUFRAH

Al-Kufrah is a group of oases long isolated in the Libyan desert by its very distance from the north and lack of wells on the formidable route to it. The site is made up of five major clusters, the main one, Busaimah, in an enormous elliptical desert depression around the Wadi Al-Kufrah. The basin is on a 50 km axis northeast to southwest, and a 20 km axis northwest to southeast. The centre of the oasis is at 475m above sea level. The main oases are Al-Jawf, with 5 km x 3 km of cultivated land in gardens and palmeries. To the east of Al-Jawf is Busaimah made up of two small oases and Ez-Zurgh a former slave settlement.

History
Al-Kufrah was a quiet and rarely visited Tibu settlement until 1840 when it was overwhelmed by the Zuwaya tribe from Awjilah who converted the people to follow the Senussia movement. Al-Kufrah became the centre of the Senussiya when Sayyid Mohammed Ali Al-Senussi moved there in 1894 to escape the influence of the Turkish governor of Cyrenaica. The Senussi thrived at Al-Kufrah and spread their influence deep into the Sahara, developing trade and communications links as they went. Al-Kufrah took on a considerable

prosperity. The site was unvisited by non-Muslims until the Saharan explorer Rohlfs called there in 1879. The period from 1911 when the Italians invaded North Libya to their occupation of Al-Kufrah in 1931 was a difficult one. Al-Kufrah's trading base was cut off and the war in the North depleted the resources of the Senussi.

In the modern period, the Italians made a rough motor road link between the oasis and the North and provided landing strips along its route. Al-Kufrah was a staging post within the Italian colonial system linking with its East African possessions. Modern facilities were set up including an airbase, a garrison, a school, hospital and other facilities. WW2 delivered a severe blow to Al-Kufrah. It was a base in early years for the Italians and then for the British Long Range Desert Group. The colonial subsidy was withdrawn. Trade never recovered and the place relapsed into a backwater until oil exploration began. The oil industry attracted the people of Al-Kufrah to act as guides and drivers in the desert and eventually a promise was made by Occidental Oil to assist in the development of the underground water at Al-Kufrah. Thus started a series of upheavals which entirely changed the oasis into a form of temporary boom town, overwhelmed local agriculture as a way of life and converted the site into a centre for military and civil government offices.

Places of interest
The settlement and production agricultural complexes are still there and can be visited with 4WD vehicles. The water gathering systems for the Great Manmade River are also visible. Otherwise there is nothing of lasting architectural and historical interest to see. Travel around the outlying oases is interesting and some fragments of the original economy remain to be seen. **Al-Jawf** has all services, including guest houses. The *Hotel As Sudan* is superbly clean, a jewel in the desert, central, near

A question of colour

👣 It takes more than a little imagination but the connoisseur can distinguish five quite different colours of camel. By far the most beautiful and the most expensive is the white camel and it is also claimed to be the fastest though that may just be an excuse to charge a higher price; the yellow beast is a very popular second; the red animal is solid, dependable and known as a good baggage animal; the blue is really black but called blue to avoid the evil eye and as such is not high in the popularity stakes, while a camel which is a mixture of white, red and yellow is just another unfortunate beast of burden.

bus station. *Hotel Al-Kufrah* is nearly as good, similar position. *Al Nahr As Sinai* is a guest house in Swedia the newest part of town. Hospitality is best gained from the town council offices if the traveller has not organized a family or official reservation in advance. The cattle and sheep market at the back of Suq al-Arab in Al-Jawf is recommended viewing.

Excursions

Jenzia 7 km south of Al-Kufrah, on the road to Sudan, has an interesting camel market. Taxi LD2. Buses from Jenzia (minibuses) go 3 days a week to Al Fashir in Sudan (more frequently to Benghazi and Ajdabiyah). Service taxis go to Ajdabiyah.

Local information
● Transport

Air The airport is 7 km from Al-Jawf. There are internal flights to Al-Kufrah from Benghazi on Monday and the return the same day connects to Tripoli. There are no buses to/from the airport. A taxi costs LD2.

Road Bus: the road to Al-Kufrah leaves directly south from Gialo as a well maintained black top highway some 625 km in length. Shared taxis and buses run from Ajdabiyah to Gialo regularly. Visits further south can be arranged but there are less frequent departures. For those travelling from Ajdabiyah to Al-Kufrah via the Gialo-Awjilah groups of oases it might be easier to pick up transport in Gialo for Al-Kufrah. An express bus service is promised on the Benghazi-Ajdabiyah-Al-Kufrah route.

OTHER DESERT OASES

In the south **Tizerbu** (see page 484), a palm grove oasis 600 km northwest of

Al-Kufrah is now served by black top road. Tizerbu is an elongated palmery almost 30 km long. It formerly had a tiny Tibu population the remains of whose fort, **Qasr Giranghedi**, can still be seen. Tizerbu has been modernized to manage agricultural development programmes in the oases and some settlement of Sudanese and others has proceeded in recent years.

Al-Awenat lies in the extreme Southeast of Libya, 325 km from Al-Kufrah, to be distinguished from Al-Awenat in the Southwest. The town is small and a security point for the Libyan authorities on the frontier with Sudan and Egypt. The town has basic telephone, health and other services. Visitors to Al-Kufrah by air should ensure that they have return bookings though there is an LAA sales office in the town, T 28701. Flights elsewhere in the south of Al-Khalij are for oil company purposes and are normally available only to company personnel.

AL-JAGHBUB

This is an oasis lying 230 km inland from Tobruk. The 310 km journey from Gialo requires a 4WD vehicle.

History

The oasis was important during the Senussi movement as a centre of resistance to the British and later the Italians. A large *zawia* or religious school was set up there, and the town flourished until the Senussi were forced to go further south to Al-Kufrah in 1895. The town is set in a large basin around Wadi Jaghbub and

The Long Range Desert Group

During WW1 the British army in Egypt developed a light car patrol system using Model T Fords and Rolls Royce armoured cars to penetrate the Libyan desert to protect their western flanks against attacks from Senussi armed groups. This activity was the direct military predecessor of the Long Range Desert Group (LRDG) established in June 1940 as the Long Range Patrols attached to the British army command in Cairo. The organization was the brainchild of R A Bagnold, who gathered an initial team made up of men with great experience of pre-war travel in the desert to harry the Axis forces behind their lines in the Saharan regions of Libya. Early recruits to the team were taken from the New Zealand Command and it was New Zealanders who remained an essential part of the LRDG.

Each patrol was originally made up of two officers and some 30 men supported by 11 trucks, with heavy machine and anti-aircraft guns, though this complement was later halved. The basic skills of the men of the LRDG were in signalling, navigation and intelligence-gathering. Map-making and the determining of routes through the desert were also important activities for the men of the LRDG. The LRDG patrols went out from Siwa in Egypt to Al-Kufrah in Libya, usually in the early days of the war to bring information of enemy movements in Uwainat, Jalu, Agheila and Ain Dua. On 1 March 1941, the Free French General Leclerc captured Al-Kufrah from the Italians and the LRDG thereafter used this oasis as their base for the war in Libya.

During 1942 the LRDG was used in association with Major David Stirling's parachute raiders and other commando groups to attack Axis airfields and aircraft behind enemy lines. Its personnel were important in monitoring General Rommel's troop movements in the period leading up to the battle of El-Alamein in late 1942. After the defeat of the Axis army in Egypt at El-Alamein, the LRGD was engaged in attempts to cut off German forces retreating to Tunisia. Once the North African campaign moved into central Tunisia in 1943, the role of the LRDG came to an end.

parts are below sea level forming closed sub-basins. Three main depressions exist, including the west one which is some 25 km in length, a central basin and an eastern basin. The traditional oasis gardens grow a wide range of irrigated crops such as peppers, tomatoes, potatoes and grain between palm trees. Natural vegetation is sparse with sage bush, and seasonal flora after rain. There is a rich variety of wildlife of the smaller rodents, mammals and gazelle.

Places of interest

The town is small, its traditional, often 2-storey, houses made of natural rock and palm trunks. The main **mosque** which contained the tombs of the Senussi leaders, Mohammed Ben Ali Al-Senussi and Al-Shattabi Al-Hasini Al-Idrisi el-Majia-jhiri and the site of a small **traditional koranic school** have been reduced to heaps of rubble. These were part of the teaching establishment which at one stage in the 19th century made Jaghbub the second most active and famous Islamic religious centre in North Africa. Cars with drivers can be arranged to visit the more distant oases. Lake Malfa to the east is a pleasant spot to visit. The area remains slightly run down but still tranquil.

Local information
● **Accommodation**
Accommodation is difficult though there is provision for travellers at a rest house and the *baladiyah* will be helpful for short-stay guests.

● **Transport**
Road Buses and shared taxis: come from the central public transport stand at Tobruk. Buses seem to run on a twice weekly but irregular basis while fairly cheap, shared taxis are not always

Like a swarm of locusts

The locust, like the more familiar European grasshopper, belongs to the family *Acrididae*. Species found in Egypt and Libya are the desert locust *Schistocerca gregaria*, the migratory *Locusta Migatoria* and the smaller Moroccan locust *Diociostaurus maroccanus*.

All cause problems to the farmer as one locust can eat its own weight in vegetable matter every day. Thus a large swarm containing thousands of millions of locusts will eat all available plant material, destroy whole fields of crops, defoliate trees and cause general devastation and despair. Attempts to control the spread of locusts have been without success. Dusting and spraying from aeroplanes, dropping poisonous bait, digging trenches to prevent the dispersion of hoppers (young, non-flying form) have all been tried.

Nevertheless locusts are fascinating creatures able to fly considerable distances, at speeds of up to 35 km/hr, especially with the help of wind currents. Locusts leap into

the air using their strong back legs so that once airborne they can open their wings and fly. The front pair of wings is strong and tough and folds over the more delicate rear pair when the insect settles back on the ground. Colouring varies from light green to dark orange and black but whatever the colour the jaws chew, chew and chew devouring any vegetation.

available and a private taxi could cost LD60 one way. Bus: Al-Jaghbub to Tobruk, Tuesday and Friday at 1400, Tobruk to Al-Jaghbub, Monday and Thursday at 1300.

WARNING: TRAVEL IN AL-KHALIJ

Other than the detail given above on access and travel facilities in each of the small towns of the region, it must be emphasized that Al-Khalij is generally neutral or hostile to travellers and tourists. The desert is unforgiving to incompetence and bad planning. Very great distances separate the few settlements. The climate is increasingly extreme with travel South. Travellers should at all times stick to the black top roads. Off road travel is only for those with several all-terrain vehicles accompanied by a guide and with radio communication. Plenty of warm clothing, water and food should be carried. Travel in public transport during the cool but light hours of the day.

Al-Khalij is not tourist-friendly in other ways. As an oilfield and water source province of the country, it is run by either large commercial organizations, Libyan administrations or the military. The province is not structured for the normal traveller in either its transport or accommodation systems. To get round this, travellers should make arrangements to have their trip made 'official' by co-opting the help of the oil companies or a Libyan authority before arrival. If Libyan tourist companies offer passages through the area this should be used even by the hardened traveller since it will provide basic services from official sources. Local people can be friendly in this area and hospitality may be expected from the regional or town councils or individuals for a limited time.

There are very limited tourist facilities and guides to the area are few.

Information for travellers

● **General note**

Getting into Libya is not always easy. Visa allocation is carefully controlled and mainly confined to those with bona fide jobs in the country. An invitation from a Libyan official agency or individual will perhaps assist the granting of a visa. Tourism is growing in importance for economic reasons, however, and there is a gradual relaxation of controls on this score. To take maximum advantage of this trend, travellers should take up a package from an officially recognized Libyan travel agency. Private visits to Libya are becoming more common but access at frontier posts, for example, cannot be guaranteed except for residents of the Union of Maghreb States (Algeria, Morocco, Tunisia and Mauritania). Travellers from Europe – Germany, Switzerland, Italy, Austria etc will have no problems. British passport holders must be prepared for a cooler reception. The UN air embargo on international flights to Libya has added to the difficulties of all travellers.

BEFORE TRAVELLING

ENTRY REQUIREMENTS

● **Visas**

Travellers to Libya need a visa, normally issued at the People's Bureau, embassy or consulate overseas. A visa costs around US$50 (£20 for UK nationals), valid for 1 month, must be used within 45 days of issue. Applications with a translation of passport details in Arabic, should be given 10 to 14 days in advance of travel since it is usual for the Libyan authorities overseas to check details with Tripoli before a visa is issued. It is possible to get a visa at the port of entry,

though this carries risks of long delays or capricious acts by border officials. Those with Arab passports normally do not require visas. Non-Arabic passports must be stamped with an official Arabic translation of the personal details of the individual's passport. In the UK the Passport Office 7-78 Petty France, London SW1, T 0171 279 3434 will do this as a matter of routine on presentation of the passport.

Visa extensions For extensions beyond the normal visa period, the immigration police should be informed and the fact noted in the passport. Tourists may extend the visa by 1 month, twice, at LD5 each time.

Registration Immigration and sometimes currency declaration forms are needed on arrival. The forms are in Arabic but English translations are available from the airlines. Only the Arabic question form should be filled in with answers in English or French. Copies of the forms should be carefully retained since they will be requested on exit. Normally hotels register guests on arrival. Insist they do. The fee is LD5. If visitors are not staying in an official hotel, they should register themselves with the police otherwise they can be stopped and delayed. Worse, they can be delayed on departure, even missing flights if officials are convinced that malpractice rather than ignorance is the cause of the problem.

Departure There is no departure tax at land borders. Embarkation cards will be filled in with the help of attendants.

● **Representation overseas**

Belgium, 28 Ave Victoria, 1050 Brussels, T 02 6492113; **France**, Paris, T 45534070; **Germany**, Bonn, T 0228 820090; **Italy**, Rome, T 06 8414518; **Malta**, Dar Jamaharia Notabile Rd,

Balzan, BZN 01, T 010 356 486347; **Spain**, Madrid, T 01 4571368; **Tunisia**, Tunis 48 bis rue du 1 Juin, T 283936; **UK**, London T 0171 486 8250/0171 486 8387, F 0171 224 6349.

● **Tourist information**

Libya is only now awakening to the potential of tourism. Facilities are few and far between. Local tourist offices exist but are generally understaffed and ill-informed. They rarely have useful information, maps or guides. At present the best sources of help and information are the new private travel agencies springing up across the country. They have enterprise and initiative and understand the needs of foreign travellers.

Be warned that while private travel agencies can provide some information and perhaps transport some may imply that without the 'official' guides, which only they can provide, there may be problems with the police. Certainly this is not true.

● **Specialist tour companies**

Arab Tours Ltd, 60 Marylebone Lane, London, WIM 5FF, T 0171 9353273, F 0171 4864237, offer a 9-day tour of Libya's classical cities, via Tunisia, at £897 pp. *Prospect Music and Art Tours*, 454-458, Chiswick High Road, London, W4 5TT, T 0181 9952151, F 0181 7421969.

WHEN TO GO

● **Best time to visit**

The coastal strip of Libya is blessed with a Mediterranean climate which makes it pleasant in most seasons. The outstanding time to visit is in the spring after the rains when the ground is covered with flowers and other vegetation and the almond blossom is out. Autumn, too, can be mild and attractive on the coast after the summer heat.

The ideal time to travel in the South is the period from October to March, when it is cooler. The summer in the South is absolutely to be avoided.

HEALTH

● **Staying healthy**

Certified vaccinations against smallpox are no longer required, but prudence demands that anti-cholera and tetanus injections are received before entry. Travellers expecting to travel into the Libyan South might feel that a voluntary, yellow fever injection is worthwhile. Walkers and cyclists would also be wise to take up any anti-rabies protection that is safely available.

● **Medical facilities**

Libyan hospitals are fairly well equipped but are under-resourced in some critical areas. Travellers must take into account that, with a UN air embargo in place, it is difficult to be airlifted out in case of emergency. There are hospitals and clinics in most towns of over 25,000 population and emergency para-medical services exist to service the main motor traffic routes. In theory treatment is free for all in public hospitals and clinics. In practice it is better to find private assistance if ill.

Most proprietary drugs are available over the counter in Libya and chemist shops are to be found in the main streets of all but the smallest of towns (see Chemist and Hospital sections for each of the regions).

● **Further health information**

See page 505, main health section.

MONEY

● **Credit cards**

Cards can be used only in a small number of big hotels and in some of the larger travel agents. Cash is the normal medium of exchange and most shops are not equipped to handle credit cards of any kind. Credit cards at hotels are best if not of US origin, though generics such as Visa and Mastercard are normally suitable.

● **Cost of living**

Libya is an oil economy and it mainly imports its necessities from abroad. Prices tend to be high reflecting this external reliance, some inefficiency in the distribution system and the high level of mark-up by the merchants. Specialist western foods and commodities like Libyan mutton are very expensive. Eating out is also far from cheap even in the small popular cafés if a full meal is taken. Otherwise fresh vegetables and fruit are moderately priced. Bread is very cheap and tasty. Pharmaceuticals, medical goods and imported high-tech items can be expensive. Personal services from plumbers to dry cleaners are expensive. Travel is comparatively cheap by air (at present not recommended) as well as land but hotels are few and the even fewer good quality hotels are very expensive. In general, assume that most things will be more expensive than in the USA or Western Europe, though this is offset by the generosity of the Libyans in rural areas in finding accommodation for visitors in public buildings.

● **Currency**

The Libyan dinar is the standard currency which is divided into 1,000 dirhams (dhs). Notes in circulation are LD10, 5, 1, 0.50, 0.25; coins LD0.10 and 0.05. Principal banks will exchange TCs and currency notes at the official rate of exchange. There is also a black market in foreign currency in which a very variable rate is available. The black market is however, best avoided.

The Libyan dinar is only convertible at the official rate inside Libya by official institutions. Travellers may have to fill in a currency form on arrival (cash and TCs) and present it together with receipts of monies exchanged on departure. The system is not watertight nor fully implemented but is perhaps best observed. Keep receipts from the banks. A sensible procedure is to make sure that you do not leave the country with either more than a few Libyan dinars or more foreign currency than you arrived with.

For exchange rates at January 1996, see table on page 433.

● **Taxes**

Provided that travellers do not accept official employment in Libya, there are no direct taxes other than the LD3 exit tax payable at the airport before entering the departure gate. Indirect taxes are included in payments as you go.

GETTING THERE

● **Air**

Libyan Arab Airlines is the main carrier. In April 1992, the UN Security Council introduced a ban on air traffic to Libya as part of a campaign to bring to book alleged perpetrators of the Lockerbie air disaster of 1988, hence no flights are available. In mid 1998 first steps were taken to end the UN embargo on air travel.

● **Train**

Libya's railways were gradually dismantled after WW2 and there are no services within Libya. Libya can be approached by train from the Egyptian frontier as far as Marsa Matruh (see Egypt, page 352).

● **Road**

Bus These run from Cairo and Alexandria in Egypt and to the Libyan frontier. Buses from further afield include direct services from Algiers, Casablanca and Amman. Passengers should cross the frontier on foot and then take advantage of Libyan domestic bus services (see Egypt, page 355 for details of arrival at the Libyan border posts). Once in Libya, there are two main bus transport companies, one engaged principally in long-distance international services and the other plying between Libyan cities and towns.

When leaving Libya the traveller can use the Libyan International Bus Company. There are four main destinations, Tripoli, Alexandria, Cairo and Damascus. Fares are low. It costs LD10 to Tripoli, LD37 to Alexandria, LD42 to Cairo and LD68 to Damascus and equivalents in Egyptian or Syrian currency on return. Most services are run on a daily basis except for Damascus which leaves on Tuesday and Saturday only. The coaches used on international runs are of good quality, with a/c and all services provided. Coming into Libya, bookings can be made on Libyan bus lines in Cairo through travel agents. Times of departures can be variable. Otherwise it is as convenient and cheaper, if not so comfortable, to use internal Libyan services once through the international border.

Taxis Both local and international transport is as much in the hands of taxi drivers as the bus companies. They ply for hire normally on a shared basis but can be had for an individual or private group with suitable haggling over the price. On a shared basis they are normally cheaper than the luxury buses and far more frequent in their departures. Driving standards are variable among taxi drivers and good nerves are required of passengers! Travellers entering via land borders are advised that taking a shared taxi is easier and quicker than waiting for the bus. If a bus is preferred, take a shared taxi to the nearest town, Solum, and take the bus from there in conditions of comfort.

● **Customs**

Import-export bans Libya has a stringent ban on the import of alcohol of any kind. It is a pointless risk taking in beer, spirits, or indeed drugs. Severe penalties can be imposed and at the very least passengers can be incarcerated pending deportation. It is rather easier to carry books and newspapers into the country than formerly, though sensitivities remain and it is best not to carry literature which might be misunderstood or thought to be anti-Libyan. Firearms cannot be imported without special permission. Radio transmitters and electronic means of printing will attract official attention and should clearly be for personal use only.

On leaving Libya make sure that you have no antiquities. The Libyan authorities take unkindly to the illegal export of their ancient monuments and penalties for infringement can be ferocious.

ON ARRIVAL

● Clothing

For general guidance, refer to the section on Travelling in Islamic countries on page 13.

There are three imperatives on clothing in Libya:

❏ Do not offend Muslim sentiment by wearing scanty clothing.

❏ Wear clothes which prevent sunstroke and sunburn.

❏ Wear clothes that enable you to keep your key documents on your person.

Libyan traditional workday dress, the *barakan*, is a vestige of the Roman toga made up in woven wool material of 5m length by 2m width which wraps round the head and body. This in a country with the world's highest recorded temperature! Scanty clothing is not regarded as sensible on grounds of either religion or practicality. Women should be careful not to leave arms and legs overly exposed. In a country where women dress well in public in both traditional and modern costume, to wear less could be seen as provocative or indicating moral slackness. In any case, outside the main hotels or private transport the need is to be sheltered from the sun, the sand and the glare. Desiccation problems effecting exposed areas of skin can come on quickly and harshly in the summer months for those who fail to look after themselves.

● Electricity

Libyan electricity services use a standard 240V system for power. Take an international adaptor plug as socket sizes can vary. Electric power is available in all but the most isolated of settlements.

● Hours of business

Working hours vary from summer 0700-1400 to winter 0800-1300 and 1600-1830 in private offices. Official agencies run on a basic day of 0800-1400, though it is always better to start communications with official offices and banks before 0900 since they can become busy and officials can be in meetings at later times. Shops open from approximately 0900-1400 and again from 1630-2030, depending on area and trade.

● Official time

GMT -1.

● Photography

The large sand deserts, arid rock formations and fine ruins of classical antiquity make photography in the excellent light conditions of Libya a great pleasure. Do not photograph military installations, and take care in photographing women: preferably if male do not photograph women at all. The camera still carries the feeling of intrusion and/or the evil eye in some areas. Over zealous local officials make their own rules and can cause some difficulties in this matter. Film is generally available for 35 mm cameras and most other types of film can also be found in Tripoli. Kodak and Fuji brands are readily available in the capital. Check the 'sell by date'. For specialist and video film try to bring reserves from outside. Beyond Tripoli and Benghazi film supplies cannot be guaranteed.

● Safety

This is very good in Libya. Occasional violence causes more noise than damage and walking through the streets is generally safer than in Europe. After dark, and indeed at all times everywhere, in Libya foreign nationals are advised to carry their passports. Libyans are used to foreigners in their midst but their visitors are almost exclusively male. European females need, therefore, to follow a sensible dress code and to act with suitable decorum, especially in Tripoli, to avoid arousing undue interest.

Women A woman travelling alone in Libya must appreciate that this is a totally segregated society, women sit apart and eat apart or after the men. On long distance buses the driver will organize space for the women. As no-one is prepared to speak it can be very lonely. The biggest problem is getting a room in a hotel without a male companion. The bus driver may feel obliged to introduce you to the hotel receptionist thereby giving some respectability, otherwise only the expensive hotels will accept women alone: take this into account when budgeting for a trip. One advantage of a woman being of no significance is the lack of problems at check points and compared with Egypt the lack of hassle. Travel alone in Libya by experienced female travellers can be recommended with the proviso that eventually the sheer masculinity of society and the feeling of isolation caused by the lack of communication makes leaving a welcome relief.

● Shopping

Best buys Libya is more of a consumer society than a producer of goods for export other than petroleum. Craft goods of value are available. Leatherwork, woven palm frond articles and small rugs all have an individual charm. Stamp collectors will find a vast range of interesting stamps available from the main post offices where some small attempt is made to cater for the philatelist.

● **Tipping**

Is not widespread in Libya and is only expected by those giving personal services in hotels, cafés and restaurants. The normal rate is 10%. For small services in hotels use quarter and half dinar notes. At the airport only use porters if you are heavily weighed down with luggage then tip at half a dinar per heavy bag. Taxi drivers should, unless there is actually a working meter and then perhaps in any case, give a price before starting the journey. Tips for Libyan drivers are not the rule but will be accepted. Foreign drivers in Libyan employ tend to be more demanding of tips. Do not get drawn into bribing officials at any level since it is a sure way of bringing increasing difficulties and possibly severe delays.

● **Weights and measures**

Libya uses the metric system. See conversion table on page 519.

WHERE TO STAY

● **Hotels**

Libya is thinly provided with hotels, even in the populated northern coastal area. This is mainly a result of years of state control when tourism was discouraged. The slow re-establishment of the private sector is making for a revival in the hotel trade at the bottom end of the market. Standards are entirely variable and the regional comments on hotels should be read with care.

On the coast there are a number of often well-provisioned beach clubs with residential facilities. They are designed to cater for groups of officially approved visitors but can in certain circumstances be open to all travellers. They are best approached through a Libyan travel agent or a Libyan state organization for sports, youth or scouts.

● **Youth hostels**

Libya has 25 youth hostels. They are basic but often available when hotels are not! The locations, numbers of beds and telephone numbers of Libyan youth hostels are given in all regional sections. Opening hours 0600-1000 and 1400-2300 unless otherwise stated. The minimum age is 14. Overnight fees for members are LD2-3 including sheets, breakfast 500 dhs, lunch LD2 and dinner LD2. Guest cards are available at most hostels. Prices vary! The Libyan Youth Hostel Association is at 69 Amr Ibn Al-As St POB 8886, Tripoli, T 45171. Additionally, it is possible to stay in the dormitories of secondary boarding schools during holiday periods. This is best arranged officially in advance, otherwise through the local *baladiyah* (municipality offices).

Hotel classifications

AL US$150. Luxury hotel. All facilities for business and leisure travellers are of the highest international standard.

A US$100-150. Central heated, a/c rooms with WC, bath/shower, TV, phone, mini-bar, daily clean linen. Choice of restaurants, coffee shop, shops, bank, travel agent, swimming pool, parking, sport and business facilities.

B US$75-100. As **A** but without the luxury, reduced number of restaurants, smaller rooms, limited range of shops and sport.

C US$50-75. Best rooms have a/c, own bath/shower and WC. Usually comfortable, bank, shop, pool.

D US$25-50. Best rooms may have own WC and bath/shower. Depending on management will have room service and choice of cuisine in restaurant.

E US$10-25. Simple provision. Perhaps fan cooler. May not have restaurant. Shared WC and showers with hot water (when available).

F under US$10. Very basic, shared toilet facilities, variable in cleanliness, noise, often in dubious locations.

● **Camping**

Is moderately popular in Libya, though as a mass organized venture through the state. Private camping is less usual except near bathing places on the Mediterranean shore. Here there are picnic sites which double as camping areas. They are crowded on public holidays but otherwise little used. Certain areas near to military camps and oil company installations are closed to all camping and any indications to this end are best complied with. Do not camp close to private farms or housing without an invitation to do so. Whenever possible seek permission from local farmers or land owners before setting up camp.

FOOD AND DRINK

● **Food**

Outside the capital, eating is confined to the main hotel restaurants, their cafés or to popular eating houses which can be found near the centres of most provincial towns. Outside Tripoli, restaurant and popular café opening hours are limited. In the evening eat before 2100 or risk finding them closed. As Libyans prefer to eat at home, restaurants tend to be for foreigners and travellers. The exception is in the use of cafés in the towns where males, mainly younger

Restaurant classifications

Given the variations in price of food on any menu our restaurants are divided where possible into three simple grades:

♦♦♦ expensive, ♦♦ average and ♦ cheap.

males, gather for social purposes. On Friday and holidays, Libyans picnic and buy food from beachside stalls. Libyan cuisine is a Mediterranean mixture with a strong legacy of the Italian period with pastas very popular, particularly macaroni. Local dishes include *couscous*, with a bowl of boiled cereal as a base carrying large pieces of mutton and some potatoes. The best traditional forms of *couscous* in Libya use millet as a cereal though now most meals come with wheat. *Bazin* is a Libyan speciality – hard, paste-like food made of water, salt and barley and is really not recommended except to the gastronomically hardy. '*Aish* is a similar food from the same ingredients but slightly softer and prepared differently. *Sherba* (Libyan soup) is delicious but highly spiced. For the rest, the range of meals is quite sophisticated with Italian influences being greatest in Tripolitania and rather more Arab dishes (less macaroni!) in Cyrenaica. Family life is kept separate from public acquaintances, and invitations to dine in a Libyan home are rarely given. Any foreigner invited to a Libyan home should thus feel very favoured.

The offerings in cafés and restaurants will be very limited and mainly made up of various hot meat, chicken and vegetable stews either with potatoes or macaroni. In the main hotels, cuisine is 'international' and very bland.

Good dates and excellent oranges can be bought cheaply. There are olives of a slightly sour taste, apricots, figs and almonds in season, all of which are good value. The smaller varieties of banana are available at increasingly competitive prices.

● **Drink**

It should be emphasized that alcoholic drinks are banned in Libya. Offers of illegal liquor should be avoided even in private houses unless its provenance is beyond doubt. Local brews or 'flash' can be of questionable quality while traditional brews of *bokha* (a form of arak), or *laghbi* (beer), made from the date palm are illegal and lead to abuse of the date palm. Otherwise, Libyans drink local bottled mineral waters, most of which are not always reliable copies of lemonades, colas and orange drinks available worldwide. Non-alcoholic beer is

widely available in bottles and cans, price LD1.5-2, imported from Egypt, Tunisia, Germany, Switzerland and Netherlands. In season, real orange juice can be bought from stalls on the streets. These drinks are cheap and widely available. Take a bottle opener since most drinks are in glass bottles. The local tap water throughout much of Libya is slightly brackish. For personal use, buy bottled water such as *Ben Ghashir*.

Beverages include Libyan tea, which is heavy boiled thick tea, often with mint or peanuts in a small glass. If ordinary tea is wanted ask for *shay kees* (tea from a teabag) *bil leben* (with milk). Coffees include Nescafé (ask for Nescafé) with or without milk and Turkish (sometimes called Arabic) coffee. With the latter, specify whether you want it *bil sukar* (sweet) or *bedoon sukar* (unsweetened).

GETTING AROUND

● **Air**

There are connecting flights to the main cities. See separate towns for details. Book in advance as all flights are very busy – overbooking is common so arrive early. **NB** the UK Foreign Office has advised travellers to Libya **not** to use internal airlines as a lack of spare parts prevents satisfactory safety standards.

● **Road**

Bus The bus service is excellent including good quality air-conditioned intercity services and more interesting crowded local buses – see individual town entries. On average a bus journey is half the price of the same distance by shared taxi.

Car hire Car hire for self-drive in Libya is not reliable. Vehicles on offer are often old and in only moderate condition. Whilst they are suitable for use in town, they should not be taken on long journeys without thorough pre-travel checks. Among the best hire locations are the main hotels, where agents have desks in the foyer. Hire rates for cars are high and variable. Expect to pay LD20-25 per day, paying 100 dhs per km after the first 100 km.

Cycling Travel by bicycle is unusual. Off the main track, cycling is extremely difficult in stony and sandy, albeit flat terrain. Cyclists are advised to be well marked in brightly coloured clothing. Puncture repair shops exist in the towns alongside the main roads at the point of entry, though they mainly deal with cars and light motorcycles rather than bicycles. In the countryside, repair of cycles will be difficult but the profusion of small pick-up trucks means that it is very easy to get a lift with a cycle into a settlement where repairs can be effected.

Hitchhiking Is used in Libya but not normally for a free ride except in emergencies. There are many shared taxis travelling the road and travellers usually make use of these on a paid basis. Private cars or pick-up trucks will act in the same capacity but will expect a small payment in the normal course. Foreign travellers might find themselves picked up for free for curiosity. In general hitchhiking is not to be encouraged since travellers in the South in particular will not be able to hitch reliably. Carry water and other safety supplies.

Motoring Great effort has gone into creating the road system and very few areas of the country are now inaccessible. Drive on the right of the road. Drivers are supposed to wear seat belts. Driving in Libya is poorly regulated and standards of driver training are very variable. The accident rate is high by international standards. Visitors should drive defensively for their own safety and to ensure that they are not involved in accidents, especially those involving injury to humans, for which they might be deemed culpable. Drivers can be held in jail for long periods and the settlement of law suits against drivers guilty of dangerous driving leading to death or injury of a third party can be protracted and difficult.

Care is needed in **off-road driving** since there are difficult sand dune areas and other regions where soft sand can quickly bog down other than 4WD vehicles. Petrol stations are fairly well distributed but only on the main through roads. Any off road travel should only be undertaken with a full tank and a spare petrol supply. Good practice is never to leave the black top road unless there are two vehicles available to the party. A reliable and generous water supply should also be taken. This is especially important in summer when exhaustion and dehydration can be major problems if vehicles need digging out of sand.

Care is still essential in areas affected by WW2 campaigns. It is estimated that there are more than 5 million **land mines**. The areas are marked and the warning signs observed.

Fuel distribution is a monopoly of a state agency and there are petrol stations in every town and at most key road junctions. But, as noted in the regional sections of this Handbook, motorists should ensure that they fill up regularly rather than rely on stretching their fuel supply, since occasionally a station might be out of use for lack of deliveries or a cut in the electricity supply. Travel in the Saharan regions requires special precautions since running out of fuel can be fatal. There is no equivalent of Automobile Club services in Libya but passing motorists are normally very helpful. Drivers should always be aware of the enormous distances between settlements in Southern Libya and take defensive action to ensure fuel, water, food and clothing reserves at all times (see Surviving in the Desert, page 34). International driving licences are normally required though, in most cases, easily understood (English or Italian) foreign licences might be accepted.

Taxis Individual taxis are more expensive, more flexible and generally more comfortable over the same distance than the local bus. The taxis do have meters but these may not be in use. **Shared taxis** (larger) are a very popular mode of travel, leaving for a particular destination as soon as they are full. Be sure you have settled the price in advance. If in doubt check with the other passengers. These taxis look quite decrepit but generally get to their destination. Prices on shared taxi is about equal to price of air ticket over same route.

● **Walking**
In Libya other than for point to point travel, walking is not normal. Hiking is to be approached, therefore, in the knowledge that it may attract curiosity and possibly disbelief. Maps of good scale for walking eg better than 1:50,000 are very rare and thus travel has to be by sight lines, compass work and common sense. Dogs are not a general problem in Tripolitania except near large farms where they are used for security purposes. Carry a stout stick and have some stones for throwing at approaching aggressive dogs, which is how the Libyans deal with this problem.

● **Boat**
There are no rental facilities for boats and only a limited few individuals own boats for pleasure purposes. There are small boat marinas at Tripoli and Benghazi for sailors bringing their own boats into port. It is occasionally possible to hire small fishing boats with their owners for the hour or day.

COMMUNICATIONS

● **Language**
Arabic is the official language throughout Libya. Given the Arab nationalist leanings of the government under Colonel Ghadhafi, Arabic is regarded with some pride as a cultural emblem.

Immediately after the 1969 revolution, all foreign language signs were removed, including street names, shop names, signposts and indications on official buildings. The result is that it is difficult for non-Arabic speakers to make use of written signs. In normal circumstances Libyans are most helpful to foreigners and will point out routes and other destinations. Unfortunately, however, it is only the older generation who have colloquial English, French or Italian since the educational system is less good than formerly in teaching foreign languages and fewer Libyans travel abroad than previously. The answer to this problem, other than learning the Arabic script and some vocabulary before travelling, is to be very patient asking your way until help is volunteered by a source you can comprehend.

The private commercial sector is likely to be best aware of **English** and **Italian** since companies trade abroad so that calling in offices or agencies can locate assistance in an emergency. English is probably best used in Benghazi, Al-Khalij and the East where there are many oil industry workers who have rubbed shoulders with English speaking personnel. Language difficulties should not put off potential travellers in Libya since the Libyans themselves are helpful and patient. A few words or phrases in Arabic will ease the way considerably. (See Language for Travel, page 512.)

● **Postal services**
Independent Libya inherited a good postal system. Poste restante and post office box facilities are available in the main cities at the central post office. The service to and from Europe, costing LD 350 for a letter, takes about 7 to 10 days in normal circumstances but, bearing in mind the international air embargo, long land transit for mail makes this a much longer (up to 5 weeks has been quoted) and riskier process. Internal mail is cheap, and for in-city letters, fairly fast and efficient. Libya produces a great range of collectors' stamps.

● **Telephone services**
PTT facilities exist in all towns and most villages. Internal calls are straightforward, though there can be some waiting time for a public line at the PTT office. International calls from all points can be more difficult since there are restricted numbers of lines. The PTT offices in Benghazi are still quicker than trying international calls from private telephones. In-coming international calls, by contrast, are comparatively easy to get through. The **international code** for

Libya is 218. Libya internal area codes are **Benghazi** 61, **Benina** 63, **Derna** 81, **Tobruk** 87. Rates for calls are at standard international levels, about LD5-6 for 3 mins.

Fax and telex facilities are available from luxury hotels and the main PTT offices which are advertised as being open 24 hrs a day but suffer from the constraint on telephone lines. Late night automatic fax facilities in private offices are useful if available through friends.

ENTERTAINMENT

● **Media**
Until very recently the Libyan media were powerfully controlled from the centre. This situation is changing only very slowly so that the media reflect the wishes of the régime. This does not make for good entertainment. Other than programmes in Arabic, which technically and in content leave so much to be desired that most Libyans watch videos or foreign stations via satellite especially CNN, not the regular local television, there is a news broadcast in French and English each evening for approximately half an hour each. There is an occasional sports programme, either Arab or international, shown on TV which is culturally neutral. The radio channel carries programmes of western music from time to time. The state produces daily broadsheets in French and English together with Arabic language newspapers. Foreign newspapers can be bought though they are often very out of date even when the air system is working normally. BBC World Service news and programmes can be picked up easily in Libya (see frequency chart, page 446).

● **Sports**
Libya participates in the various Arab League sports tournaments but facilities for individuals are still very limited. Health centres exist for travellers at a few of the main hotels. Swimming is universally available in the Mediterranean or in the pools attached to the beach clubs in the main cities. Libyans themselves play volleyball for which there are plenty of facilities and football. Horse riding and trotting are also generally enjoyed. A Secretariat (ministry) of Sport exists but its activities are not given priority. The beach clubs near Benghazi have first class facilities for tennis, table tennis and canoeing and other sports. In the smaller towns the schools tend to be centres for sports while in industrial towns some of the companies have their own clubs with squash and tennis courts, for example.

HOLIDAYS AND FESTIVALS

Libya, as Muslim country, observes all the main Islamic festivals as holidays (see page 18 for details on Ramadan). Fridays are days of rest. In addition there are several national holidays.

2 Mar: Declaration of thePeople's Authority
11 Jun: Evacuation of foreign military bases
1 Sept: Anniversary of the 1969 Revolution

Approximate dates for 1998/99:

20 Dec: Beginning of Ramadan
21 Jan: End of Ramadan
31 Mar: Feast of Sacrifice
17 Apr: Islamic New Year 1420
1 Jul: Prophet's Birthday
9 Dec: Beginning of Ramadan

FURTHER READING

● **Books and maps**
This section of the *Egypt Handbook* deals only with excursions into Eastern Libya. For coverage of Western Libya, see our *Tunisia Handbook*.

The best available maps are Michelin Carte Routière et Touristique, *Afrique Nord et Ouest* at 1/4,000,000 and Cartographia *Libya* at 1/2,000,000. Cartographia Budapest Hungary produces a 1/2,000,000 sheet. Libyan maps of 1/50,000 are available for the main settled areas but are difficult to find except in the university library and the Secretariat of Planning. There are few contemporary guidebooks to Libya. A very useful book is the Arabic/English language *Atlas of Libya*, available at the Fergiani Book Stores, Sharah 1st September, Tripoli. The *Antiquities of Tripolitania* by DEL Hayes, pub Dept Antiquities, Tripoli 1981; *Cyrene and Apollonia an Historical guide*, by Richard Goodchild, Dept Antiquities, Tripoli 1963.

There are a few books on Libya which are not essentially political. Of these the best are J Davis's (1987) book *Libyan Politics: Tribe & Revolution*. On history J Wright's (1982) *Libya: A Modern History* is a good review while JA Allan's (1981) *Libya: The Experience of Oil* deals with oil and agricultural development.

Rounding up

ACKNOWLEDGEMENTS

We acknowledge the work of Geoff Moss for assistance with illustrations, and thank the following contributors: Elizabeth and Kenneth Longhurst, Marsworth, Bucks; Mrs P Aitken, Buckingham; Martina Heidbüchel, Köln; Dany Marique, Angleur, Belgium; Anne-Marie Scattarreggia and Bruno Marcelo, Basel; Prof. J A Allan, SOAS; Guy Jobbins, Brighton and Sharm el-Sheikh; Fiona Moffit, Cairo; Keith Potter for diving information; Matt Ebiner, California; Dax Driver, West Indies; Eric Linder, e-mail.

FURTHER READING

Books

Buckles, G, *The Dive Sites of The Red Sea*, New Holland, 1997; Durrell, L, *Alexandria Quartet*, Faber & Faber: London; Edwards, IES, *The Pyramids of Egypt*, Pelican Books, 1947/1961; Edwards, A, *A Thousand Miles up the Nile*, Parkway Publishing, 1997 (first published 1877); Emery, WB, *Archaic Egypt*, Pelican Books, 1961; Fakhry, A, *Siwa Oasis*, American University of Cairo Press, 1991; Faulkner, RO, *The Ancient Egyptian Book of the Dead*, British Museum Press; Ghisotti, A, & Carletti, A, *The Red Sea Diving Guide*, incl 100 illustrations of fish and three dimensional diagrams of coral reef dives, E£95; Goodman, SM, & Meininger, PM, *Birds of Egypt*, Oxford Univ Press, 1989; Haag M, *Alexandria*, AUC Press 1993, a full colour guide to Alexandria past and present; Heikal, M, 1975; *Autumn Fury* and *The Road to Ramadan*, London; Hewson, Neil, *The Fayoum*, American University of Cairo; Hirst, D, & Beeson, I, *Sadat*: London, 1981; Hobson, C, *Exploring the World of the Pharaohs – a complete guide to Ancient Egypt*, Thames and Hudson Inc, 500 Fifth Avenue, New York, 1987; Murnane, William J, *A Penguin Guide to Ancient Egypt*, Penguin Books, 1983; Pick, Christopher, *Egypt: A Travellers Anthology*, John Murray Publishers Ltd; Seton, MV, *A Short History of Egypt*, Rubicon Press; Spence, L, *Egypt – Myths and Legends*, Studio Editions, Eastcastle Street, London, 1994; Steindorff, G, & Seele, KC, *When Egypt Ruled the East*, University of Chicago Press; Stephens, R, *Nasser – a Political Biography*: London, 1971; Vatikiotis, PJ, *The History of Modern Egypt: From Mohamed Ali to Mubarak*, Weidenfeld & Nicolson: London; Waterbury, J, *The Egypt of Nasser & Sadat*: Princeton, 1983.

The *Shire Egyptology* series: Shire Publications Ltd, Princes Risborough, Bucks, UK, have a fascinating series £4.99 each incl *Egyptian Coffins*, *Mummies*, *Pyramids* and *Household Animals*, *Temples*, *Tools &*

Weapons. Common Birds of Egypt: American University in Cairo Press, helps to sort out some of the less usual birds. Brown and Rachid, *Egyptian Carpets*, American University in Cairo Press, E£10.

Egypt Focus, a monthly newsletter published by Menas Associates Ltd, PO Box 444, Berkhamsted, Hertfordshire, HP4 3DL, T 01442 872800, F 01442 876800.

MAPS AND TOWN PLANS

Michelin map No 154 covers Egypt. The Oxford Map of Egypt by Oxford University Press is very good. Sinai printed in Switzerland by Kümmerly and Frey gives most of the sites. Look out for three maps produced by SPARE – Society for the Preservation of Architectural Resources of Egypt – with detailed information of The Citadel, Islamic Cairo and Khan al Khalili. Several maps of the whole of Egypt and of the major towns are available from the the Egyptian Tourist Board.

Writing to us

Many people write to us - with corrections, new information, or simply comments. If you want to let us know something, we would be delighted to hear from you. Please give us as precise information as possible, quoting the edition and page number of the Handbook you are using and send as early in the year as you can. Your help will be greatly appreciated, especially by other travellers. In return we will send you details about our special guidebook offer.

For hotels and restaurants, please let us know:

- each establishment's name, address, phone and fax number
- number of rooms, whether a/c or air-cooled, attached (clean?) bathroom
- location - how far from the station or bus stand, or distance (walking time) from a prominent landmark
- if it's not already on one of our maps, can you place it?
- your comments - either good or bad - as to why it is distinctive
- tariff cards
- local transport used

For places of interest:

- location
- entry, camera charge
- access - by whatever means of transport is most appropirate, eg time of main buses or trains to and from the site, journey time, fare
- facilities - nearby drinks stalls, restaurants, for the disabled
- any problems, eg steep climb, wildlife, unofficial guides
- opening hours
- site guides

Useful addresses

EMBASSIES

Australia
1 Darwin Ave, Yarralumla, ACT Canberra, T 062 734437.

Austria
Kreindll Gasse 22, Vienna 1190, T 361134.

Belgium
Ave Leo Errera 44, 1180 Brussels, T 3455015.

Canada
454 Laurier Ave East, Ottawa, Ontario, K1N 6R3, T 613 234 4958.

Denmark
Nyropsgade 47, 3rd Flr, DK-1602 Copenhagen V, T 3312 7641.

France
56 Ave d'Iena, 75116 Paris, T 47209770.

Germany
Kronprinzenstr, Bonn 2, T 228 364000.

Israel
54 Rehov Basel, Tel Aviv, T 5464151.

Libya
Al Fondok Al Kabier, Tripoli, T 45940.

Morocco
31 El Gazaer St, Sawmaat Hassan, Rabat, T 731833.

Netherlands
Borweg 1, 2597 LR The Hague, T 70 354 2000.

Norway
Drammensveien 90A, 0244 Oslo 2, T 200010.

Portugal
Av D Vasco Da Gama No 8, 1400 Lisbon, T 3018374.

Spain
Velazquez 69, Madrid 28006, T 5776308.

Sudan
El Gamaa St, Elmakran, Khartoum, T 72836.

Sweden
Strandvagen 35, Stockholm, T 468 6603145.

Switzerland
61 Elfenauweg, 3006 Berne, T 448012

UK
26 South St, London W1Y 6DD, T 0171 499 2401, F 0171 355 3568

USA
2310 Decatur Palace NW, Washington DC 20008, T 202 234 3903.

CONSULATES

Canada
3154 Côtes-des-Neiges, Montreal H3H 1V6, T 514 937781.

UK
19, Kensington Palace Garden Mews, London W8, T 0171 2298818, open 1000-1200 Monday-Friday for visas.

USA
1110 Second Ave, New York, NY10022, T 212 7597120; 3001 Pacific Ave, San Francisco, CA 94115, T 415 3469700.

Austria
Elisabeth Strasse, 4/Steige 5/1, Opornringhof, 1010 Vienna, T 587 6633.

Canada
Place Bonaventure, 40 Frontenac, PO Box 304, Montreal, T 514 8614420.

France
90 Ave Champs Elysees, Paris, T 00331 45629442.

Germany
64A Kaiser Strasse, Frankfurt am Main 6, T 252319.

Greece
10 Amerikis St, Athens, T 3606906.

Italy
19 Via Bissolati, 00187 Rome, T 00396 4827985.

Japan
19 Akasaka, 2-Chome, Minato-ku, Tokyo, T 5890653.

Kuwait
5 Omar Ibn el-Khatab St, Safat, Kuwait 13133, T 2403104.

Spain
La Toree de Madrid planta 5, Oficina 3, Plaza de Espana, 28008 Madrid, T 5781732.

Sweden
Drottnin 99, Atan 65, 11136 Stockholm, T 102548.

Switzerland
9 rue des Alpes, Geneva, T 022 329132.

UK
170 Piccadilly, London W1V 9DD, T 0171 4935282, F 0171 408 0295.

USA
630 5th Ave, New York 10111, T 212 2466960 and 323 Geary St, Suite 608, San Francisco, Ca 94102, T 415 7817676.

SPECIALIST TOUR OPERATORS

Crusader Travel
57 Church Street, Twickenham, Middlesex, TW1 3NR, T 0181 7440474, F 0181 7440574. The division known as Red Sea Travel Centre is particularly interested in watersports – scuba diving, wind surfing, sailing and snorkelling – they own the Aquasport dive and Watersports centres (at Sharm el Sheikh and Hurghada), offer two-centre and tailor-made visits as well as Nile cruises.

Egyptian Encounter
part of Misr Travel, 51 Brookley Rd, Brockenhurst, Hants, UK, T 015 9022992, F 015 9024025.

Explore Worldwide Ltd
1 Frederick St, Aldershot, Hants, GU11 1LQ, T 01252 319448, F 01252 343170, for hotels/camping in oases of Siwa and Western Desert, also Nile cruises, Abu Simbel, Felucca sail-trek, Red Sea and Sinai.

Goodwood Travel Ltd
Flights of Fancy, Supersonic weekends by Concorde to Cairo, St Andrew's House, Station Road East, Canterbury, Kent CT1 2RB, T 01227 763336, F 01227 762417.

Guerba Safaris and Expeditions
Wessex House, 40 Station Road, Westbury, Wiltshire, BA13 3JN, T 01373 826611.

The Imaginative Traveller
Camping, walking, cycling also first class quality tours.

Oonasdivers
23 Enys Road, Eastbourne, East Sussex, BN21 2DG, T 01323 648924, F 01323 738356, quality liveboard accommodation for divers, also a fascinating Red Sea Diving Safari, camping and diving off the remote southern Red Sea Coast of Egypt.

Regal Diving
22 High Street, Sutton in the Isle, Ely, Cambs, T 01353 778096, F 01353 777897.

Soliman Travel
113 Earls Court Road, London, SW5 9RL, T 0171 2446855, F 0171 8351394, made to measure service, specialist tours to famous battle fields of Western Desert, follow route of Holy Family in Egypt.

Sunbird
PO Box 76 Sandy, Bedfordshire, SG19 1DF, T 01767 682969, F 01767 692481, a variety of locations in Egypt with emphasis on the Red Sea.

Tailor Made Holidays
5 Station Approach, Hinchley Wood, Surrey KT10 0SP, T 0181 3984464, F 0181 3986007, offer **Hooked on the Nile – Fishing on Lake Nasser**, they have six boats fed by a supply boat on Lake Nasser, a civilized safari in a steel hulled boat, with ample opportunities to fish and fish.

The British Museum Traveller
34 Bloomsbury Street, London, WC1B 3QQ, offer a variety of accompanied tours such as Christmas on the Nile, Monasteries in the desert, Egypt at Easter in the footsteps of Howard Carter; Egypt and the Nubian Temples, 10 days in Libya; New Year in Thebes.

Travel Bag Adventures
15 Turk St, Alton, Hampshire, GU34 1AG, F 01420 541022, cheaper end of the market, felucca travel, explore the Western desert by jeep and camel.

Travelscope Worldwide (Gaz Tours)
PO Box 158 Guildford, Surrey GU2 6PU, UK, T/F 01483 69453, an excellent independent travel company, which has been in business since 1972, and which arranges individual and group tours not only to classic sites in Cairo, Luxor and Aswan but also to the oases. Special tours for Christian groups can follow the Holy Family's flight from Egypt, while tours to Sinai cover all the major sites to the Israeli border. The service is excellent because the company specializes in providing a personalized service. Dr Sadek has direct access to the Egyptair computers and can therefore make and confirm flight reservations.

Health

T HE FOLLOWING information has been prepared by Dr David Snashall, Senior Lecturer in Occupational Health, United Medical Schools of Guy's and St Thomas' Hospitals and Chief Medical Officer, Foreign and Commonwealth Office, London.

The traveller to this region is inevitably exposed to health risks not encountered in North America or Western Europe. Despite the countries being part of Africa where one expects to see much tropical disease this is not actually the case, although malaria remains a problem in some areas. Because much of the area is economically under-developed, infectious diseases still predominate in the same way as they did in the West some decades ago. There are obvious health differences between each of the countries and in risks between the business traveller who tends to stay in international class hotels in large cities and the backpacker trekking through the rural areas. There are no hard and fast rules to follow; you will often have to make your own judgements on the healthiness or otherwise of your surroundings.

There are many well qualified doctors in the area, a large proportion of whom speak English or French but the quality and range of medical care is extremely variable from country to country and diminishes very rapidly away from big cities. In some countries, there are systems and traditions of medicine rather different from the Western model and you may be confronted with unusual modes of treatment based on local beliefs. At least you can be reasonably sure that local practitioners have a lot of experience with the particular diseases of their region. If you are in a city it may be worthwhile calling on your Embassy to obtain a list of recommended doctors.

If you are a long way from medical help, a certain amount of self medication may be necessary and you will find that many of the drugs that are available have familiar names. However, always check the date stamping and buy from reputable pharmacists because the shelf life of some items, especially vaccines and antibiotics is markedly reduced in hot conditions. Unfortunately many locally produced drugs are not subjected to quality control procedures and can be unreliable. There have, in addition, been cases of substitution of inert materials for active drugs.

With the following precautions and advice you should keep as healthy as usual. Make local enquiries about health risks if you are apprehensive and take the general advice of European and North American families who have lived or are living in the area.

BEFORE TRAVELLING

Take out medical insurance. You should have a dental check up, obtain a spare glasses prescription and, if you suffer from a longstanding condition such as diabetes, high blood pressure, heart/lung disease or a nervous disorder, arrange for a check up with your doctor who can at the same time provide you with a letter explaining details of your disability (in English and French). Check the current practice for malaria prophylaxis (prevention) for the countries you intend to visit.

For a simple list of 'Health Kit' to take with you, see page 432.

Inoculations

Smallpox vaccination is no longer required. Neither is cholera vaccination. Cholera vaccine is not effective which is the main reason for not recommending it but occasionally travellers from South America, where cholera is presently raging, or from parts of South Asia where the disease is endemic may be asked to provide evidence of vaccination. In Libya, you may be asked for a yellow fever vaccination certificate if you have been in an area (Sub-Saharan Africa for example) affected by yellow fever immediately before travelling to North Africa. The following vaccinations are recommended:

Typhoid (monovalent): one dose followed by a booster in a month's time. Immunity from this course lasts 2-3 years. Other injectable types are now becoming available as are oral preparations marketed in some countries.

Poliomyelitis: this is a live vaccine, generally given orally and the full course consists of three doses with a booster in tropical regions every 3-5 years.

Tetanus: one dose should be given with a booster at 6 weeks and another at 6 months and 10 yearly boosters thereafter are recommended.

Children: should, in addition, be properly protected against diphtheria, whooping cough, mumps and measles. Teenage girls, if they have not yet had the disease, should be given rubella (German measles) vaccination. Consult your doctor for advice on BCG inoculation against tuberculosis. The disease is still common in the region. North Africa lies mainly outside the meningitis belt and the disease is probably no more common than at home so vaccination is not indicated except during an epidemic.

INFECTIOUS HEPATITIS (JAUNDICE)

This is common. It seems to be frequently caught by travellers probably because, coming from countries with higher standards of hygiene, they have not contracted the disease in childhood and are therefore not immune like the majority of adults in developing countries. The main symptoms are stomach pains, lack of appetite, nausea, lassitude and yellowness of the eyes and skin. Medically speaking there are two types: the less serious, but more common, is hepatitis A for which the best protection is careful preparation of food, the avoidance of contaminated drinking water and scrupulous attention to toilet hygiene. Human normal immunoglobulin (gammaglobulin) confers considerable protection

against the disease and is particularly useful in epidemics. It should be obtained from a reputable source and is certainly recommended for travellers who intend to live rough. The injection should be given as close as possible to your departure and, as the dose depends on the likely time you are to spend in potentially infected areas, the manufacturer's instructions should be followed. A new vaccination against hepatitis A is now generally available and probably provides much better immunity for 10 years but is more expensive, being three separate injections.

The other more serious version is hepatitis B which is acquired as a sexually transmitted disease, from a blood transfusion or injection with an unclean needle or possibly by insect bites. The symptoms are the same as hepatitis A but the incubation period is much longer.

You may have had jaundice before or you may have had hepatitis of either type before without becoming jaundiced, in which case it is possible that you could be immune to either hepatitis A or B. This immunity can be tested for before you travel. If you are not immune to hepatitis B already, a vaccine is available (three shots over 6 months) and if you are not immune to hepatitis A already then you should consider vaccination (or gamma globulin if you are not going to be exposed for long).

AIDS

AIDS is probably less common than in most of Europe and North America but is presumably increasing in its incidence, though not as rapidly as in Sub-Saharan Africa, South America or South East Asia. Having said that, the spread of the disease has not been well documented in the North African/Red Sea region so the real picture is unclear. The disease is possibly still mainly confined to the well known high risk sections of the population ie homosexual men, intravenous drug abusers, prostitutes and children of infected mothers. Whether heterosexual transmission outside these groups is common or not, the main risk to travellers is from casual sex, heterosexual or homosexual. The same precautions should be taken as when encountering any sexually transmitted disease. In some of these countries there is widespread female prostitution and a higher proportion of this population is likely to be HIV antibody positive. In other parts, especially high class holiday resorts, intravenous drug abuse is prevalent and in certain cities, homosexual, transsexual and transvestite prostitution is common and again this part of the population is quite likely to harbour the HIV virus in large measure. The AIDS virus (HIV) can be passed via unsterile needles which have been previously used to inject an HIV positive patient but the risk of this is very small indeed. It would, however, be sensible to check that needles have been properly sterilized or disposable needles used. The chance of picking up hepatitis B in this way is much more of a danger. Be wary of carrying disposable needles yourself. Custom officials may find them suspicious. The risk of receiving a blood transfusion with blood infected with the HIV virus is greater than from dirty needles because of the amount of fluid exchanged. Supplies of blood for transfusion are now largely screened for HIV in all reputable hospitals so the risk must be very small indeed. Catching the AIDS virus does not necessarily produce an illness in itself; the only way to be sure if you feel you have been put at risk is to have a blood test for HIV antibodies on your return to a place where there are reliable laboratory facilities. The results may not be ready for many weeks.

COMMON PROBLEMS

ALTITUDE

Mountain sickness is hardly likely to occur. A not-too-rapid ascent is the sure way to prevent it. Other problems experienced at moderate altitude are: sunburn, excessively dry air causing skin cracking, sore eyes (it may be wise to leave your contact lenses out, especially in windy and dusty areas) and stuffy noses. Many travellers, as long as they are physically fit, enjoy travelling in the mountains where it is generally cooler and less humid and there are fewer insects.

HEAT AND COLD

Full acclimatisation to high temperatures takes about 2 weeks and during this period it is normal to feel a degree of apathy, especially if the relative humidity is high. Drink plenty of water (up to 15 litres a day are required when working physically hard in hot, dry conditions), use salt on your food and avoid extreme exertion. Tepid showers are more cooling than hot or cold ones. Large hats do not cool you down but prevent sunburn. Remember that, especially in the mountains, there can be a large and sudden drop in temperature between sun and shade and between night and day so dress accordingly. Clear desert nights can prove astoundingly cold with a rapid drop in temperature as the sun goes down. Loose fitting cotton clothes are still the best for hot weather; warm jackets and woollens are essential after dark in some desert areas, and especially at high altitude.

INSECTS

These can be a great nuisance. Some, of course, are carriers of serious diseases such as malaria and yellow fever. The best way of keeping insects away at night is to sleep off the ground with a mosquito net and to burn mosquito coils containing Pyrethrum. Aerosol sprays or a 'flit' gun may be effective as are insecticidal tablets which are heated on a mat which is plugged into the wall socket (if taking your, own check the voltage of the area you are visiting so that you can take an appliance that will work. Similarly check that your electrical adaptor is suitable for the repellent plug).

You can use personal insect repellent, the best of which contain a high concentration of Diethyltoluamide. Liquid is best for arms and face (take care around eyes and make sure you do not dissolve the plastic of your spectacles). Aerosol spray on clothes and ankles deters mites and ticks. Liquid DET suspended in water can be used to impregnate cotton clothes and mosquito nets. Wide mesh mosquito nets are now available impregnated with an insecticide called Permethrin and are generally more effective, lighter to carry and more comfortable to sleep in. If you are bitten, itching may be relieved by cool baths and anti-histamine tablets (care with alcohol or driving) corticosteroid creams (great care – never use if any hint of sepsis) or by judicious scratching. Calamine lotion and cream have limited effectiveness and anti-histamine creams have a tendency to cause skin allergies and are therefore not generally recommended. Bites which become infected (commonly in dirty and dusty places) should be treated with a local antiseptic or antibiotic cream such as Cetrimide as should infected scratches. Skin infestations with body lice, crabs and scabies are unfortunately easy to pick up. Use Gamma benzene hexachloride for lice and Benzyl benzoate for scabies. Crotamiton cream (Eurax) alleviates itching and also kills a number of skin parasites. Malathion lotion 5% is good for lice but avoid the highly toxic full strength Malathion used as an agricultural insecticide.

INTESTINAL UPSETS

Practically nobody escapes this one so be prepared for it. Some of these countries lead the world in their prevalence of diarrhoea. Most of the time intestinal upsets are due to the insanitary preparation of food. Do not eat uncooked fish or vegetables or meat (especially pork), fruit with the skin on (always peel your fruit yourself) or food that is exposed to flies. Tap water is generally held to be unsafe or at least unreliable throughout North Africa with the exception of large cities in Morocco. Tap water in Israel is also usually safe. Filtered or bottled water is generally available. If your hotel has a central hot water supply this is safe to drink after cooling. Ice for drinks should be made from boiled water but rarely is, so stand your glass on the ice cubes, instead of putting them in the drink. Dirty water should first be strained through a filter bag (available from camping shops) and then boiled or treated. Bringing the water to a rolling boil at sea level is sufficient but at high altitude you have to boil the water for longer to ensure that all the microbes are killed. Various sterilising methods can be used and there are proprietary preparations containing chlorine or iodine compounds. Pasteurized or heat treated milk is now widely available as is ice cream and yoghurt produced by the same methods. Unpasteurized milk products including cheese and yoghurt are sources of tuberculosis, brucellosis, listeria and food poisoning germs. You can render fresh milk safe by heating it to 62°C for 30 mins followed by rapid cooling or by boiling it. Matured or processed cheeses are safer than fresh varieties.

Diarrhoea is usually the result of food poisoning, occasionally from contaminated water (including seawater when swimming near sewage outfalls). There are various causes – viruses, bacteria, protozoa (like amoeba) salmonella and cholera organisms. It may take one of several forms coming on suddenly, or rather slowly. It may be accompanied by vomiting or by severe abdominal pain and the passage of blood or mucus when it is called dysentery. How do you know which type you have and how do you treat it?

All kinds of diarrhoea, whether or not accompanied by vomiting, respond favourably to the replacement of water and salts taken as frequent small sips of some kind of rehydration solution. There are proprietary preparations consisting of sachets of powder which you dissolve in water or you can make your own by adding half a teaspoonful of salt (3.5 grams) and four tablespoonfuls of sugar (40 grams) to a litre of boiled water. If you can time the onset of diarrhoea to the minute, then it is probably viral or bacterial and/or the onset of dysentery. The treatment, in addition to rehydration, is Ciprofloxacin 500 mgs every 12 hrs. The drug is now widely available as are various similar ones.

If the diarrhoea has come on slowly or intermittently, then it is more likely to be protozoal ie caused by amoeba or giardia and antibiotics will have no effect. These cases are best treated by a doctor, as is any outbreak of diarrhoea continuing for more than 3 days. If there are severe stomach cramps, the following drugs may help: Loperamide (Imodium, Arret) and Diphenoxylate with Atropine (Lomotil).

The lynchpins of treatment for diarrhoea are rest, fluid and salt replacement, antibiotics such as Ciprofloxacin for the bacterial types and special diagnostic tests and medical treatment for amoeba and giardia infections. Salmonella infections and cholera can be devastating diseases and it would be wise to get to a hospital as soon as possible if these were suspected. Fasting, peculiar diets and the consumption of large quantities of yoghurt have not been found useful in calming travellers' diarrhoea or in rehabilitating inflamed bowels. Oral rehydration has on the other hand, especially in children, been a lifesaving technique. As there is some evidence that alcohol and milk might prolong diarrhoea, they should probably be avoided during and immediately after an attack. There are ways of preventing travellers' diarrhoea for short periods of time when visiting these countries by taking antibiotics but these are ineffective against viruses and, to some extent, against protozoa, so this technique should not be used other than in exceptional circumstances. Some preventives such as Enterovioform can have serious side effects if taken for long periods.

MALARIA

This disease occurs in all the regions covered by this book but is, however, only common in Libya and bordering the Nile Valley in Egypt. Despite being nowhere near so common as in Sub-Saharan Africa, malaria remains a serious disease and you are advised to protect yourself against mosquito bites as described above and to take prophylactic (preventive) drugs where and when there is a risk. Start taking the tablets a few days before exposure and continue to take them 6 weeks after leaving the malarial zone. Remember to give the drugs to babies and children and pregnant women also.

The subject of malaria prevention is becoming more complex as the malaria parasite becomes immune to some of the older drugs. This phenomenon, at the time of writing, has not occurred in this region so the more traditional drugs can be taken with some confidence. Protection with Proguanil (Paludrine) two tablets per day, or Chloroquine two tablets per week will suffice and at this dose will not cause any side effects. You will have to find out locally the likelihood of malaria and perhaps be prepared to receive conflicting advice on how to prevent yourself from catching it. You can catch malaria even when taking prophylactic drugs, although it is unlikely. If you do develop symptoms (high fever, shivering, severe headache, sometimes diarrhoea) seek medical advice immediately. The risk of the disease is obviously greater the further you move from the cities into rural areas with limited facilities and standing water.

PSYCHOLOGICAL DISORDERS

First time exposure to countries where sections of the population live in extreme poverty or squalor and may even be starving can cause odd psychological reactions in visitors. So can the incessant pestering, especially of women which is unfortunately common in some of these countries. Simply be prepared for this and try not to over react.

SNAKE AND OTHER BITES & STINGS

If you are unlucky enough to be bitten by a venomous snake, spider, scorpion, lizard, centipede or sea creature try (within limits) to catch the animal for identification. The reactions to be expected are fright, swelling, pain and bruising around the bite, soreness of the regional lymph glands, nausea, vomiting and fever. If in addition any of the following symptoms supervene, get the victim to a doctor without delay: numbness, tingling of the face, muscular spasms, convulsions, shortness of breath or haemorrhage. Commercial snake bite or scorpion sting kits may be available but are only useful for the specific type of snake or scorpion for which they are designed. The serum has to be given intravenously, so is not much good unless you have had some practice in making injections into veins. If the bite is on a limb, immobilize it and apply a tight bandage between the bite and body, releasing it for 90 secs every 15 mins. Reassurance of the bitten person is very important because death by snake bite is in fact very rare. Do not slash the bite area and try and suck out the poison because this kind of heroism does more harm than good. Hospitals usually hold stocks of snake bite serum. Best precaution: do not walk in snake territory with bare feet, sandals or shorts.

If swimming in an area where there are poisonous fish such as stone or scorpion fish (also called by a variety of local names) or sea urchins on rocky coasts, tread carefully or wear plimsolls. The sting of such fish is intensely painful and this can be helped by immersing the stung part in water as hot as you can bear for as long as it remains painful. This is not always very practical and, you must take care not to scald yourself but it does work. Avoid spiders and scorpions by keeping your bed away from the wall and look under lavatory seats and inside your shoes in the morning. In the rare event of being bitten, consult a doctor.

SUNBURN AND HEAT STROKE

The burning power of the sun is phenomenal, especially at high altitude. Always wear a wide-brimmed hat and use some form of sun cream or lotion on untanned skin. Normal temperate zone suntan lotions (protection factor up to 7) are not much good. You need to use the types designed specifically for the tropics or for mountaineers or skiers with a protection factor (against UVA) between 7 and 15. Certain creams also protect against UVB and you should use these if you have a skin prone to burning. Glare from the sun can cause conjunctivitis so wear sunglasses, especially on the beach.

There are several varieties of heat stroke. The most common cause is severe dehydration. Avoid this by drinking lots of non-alcoholic fluid and adding some salt if you wish.

OTHER AFFLICTIONS

Athletes foot and other fungal infections are best treated by exposure to sunshine and a proprietary preparation such as Tolnaftate.

Dengue fever is not common in North Africa but there have been cases of this virus transmitted by mosquito bites producing severe headache and body pains. There is no treatment: you must just avoid mosquito bites.

Hydatid disease is quite common in Egypt but can be avoided by keeping well clear of dogs, which is good advice in any case.

Intestinal worms do occur in insanitary areas and the more serious ones, such as hook-worm, can be contracted by walking bare foot on infested earth or beaches.

Leishmaniasis causing a skin ulcer which will not heal is also present in most of the North African countries. It is transmitted by sand flies.

Prickly heat is a common itchy rash avoided by frequent washing and by wearing loose clothing. It can be helped by the regular use of talcum powder to allow the skin to dry thoroughly after washing.

510

Schistosomiasis (bilharzia) occurs particularly in Egypt and can easily be avoided because it is transmitted by snails which live in fresh water lakes so do not swim in such places or in canals.

Rabies is endemic throughout North Africa and the Middle East. If you are bitten by a domestic animal try to have it captured for observation and see a doctor at once. Treatment with human diploid vaccine is now extremely effective and worth seeking out if the likelihood of having contracted rabies is high. A course of anti-rabies vaccine might be a good idea before you go.

RETURNING HOME

Remember to take your anti-malarial tablets for 6 weeks. If you have had attacks of diarrhoea, it is worth having a stool specimen tested in case you have picked up amoebic dysentery. If you have been living rough, a blood test may be worthwhile to detect worms and other parasites.

FURTHER INFORMATION

The following organisations give information regarding well-trained English speaking physicians throughout the world: International Association for Medical Assistance to Travellers, 745 Fifth Ave, New York, 10022; Intermedic, 777 3rd Ave, New York, 10017.

Information regarding country by country malaria risk can be obtained from the World Health Organisation (WHO) or the Ross Institute, The London School of Hygiene and Tropical Medicine, Keppel St, London WC1E 7HT, which publishes a strongly recommended book entitled *The Preservation of Personal Health in Warm Climates*. The organisation MASTA, (Medical Advisory Service to Travellers Abroad), also based at The London School of Hygiene and Tropical Medicine, T 0171 6314408, F 0171 4365389, will provide country by country information on up-to-date health risks.

Further information on medical problems overseas can be obtained from Dawood, Richard (ed), *Travellers Health, How to Stay Healthy Abroad*, Oxford University Press, 1992, costing £7.99. We strongly recommend this revised and updated edition, especially to the intrepid traveller heading for the more out of the way places.

General advice is also available in *Health Advice for Travellers* published jointly by the Department of Health and the Central Office of Information (UK) and available free from your Travel Agent.

Language for travel

I T IS IMPOSSIBLE to indicate in the Latin script how Arabic should be pronounced so we have opted for a very simplified transliteration which will give the user a sporting chance of uttering something that can be understood by an Arab. An accent has been placed to show where the stress falls in each word of more than two syllables.

Numbers

0	sífr	16	sittásh
1	wáhad	17	sabatásh
2	tnéen	18	tmantásh
3	taláata	19	tissatásh
4	árba	20	ishréen
5	khámsa	30	tlaatéen
6	sítta	40	arba'éen
7	sába	50	khamséen
8	tamánia	60	sittéen
9	tíssa	70	saba'éen
10	áshra	80	tmanéen
11	ahdásh	90	tissa'éen
12	itnásh	100	mía
13	talatásh	200	miatéen
14	arbatásh	300	tláata mia
15	khamstásh	1000	alf

Greetings

Hello!	assálamu aláikum	Thank God!	hamdulilláh!
How are you?	keef hálek?	Yes/no	naam, áiwa/la
Well!	kwáyes	Please	min fádlek
Good bye!	bisaláma	Thank you	shukran
Go away!	ímshi, barra	OK	kwáyes
God willing!	inshálláh	Excuse me	ismáh-lee
Never mind	ma'lésh		

Days

Sunday	al-áhad	Thursday	al-khemées
Monday	al-itnéen	Friday	al-júma
Tuesday	at-taláta	Saturday	as-sébt
Wednesday	al-árba		

512

Food

banana	mouz	lemonade	gazóoza
beer	bírra	lunch	ghada
bread	khubz	meat	láhma
breakfast	futóor	menu (fixed price)	ká'ima
butter	zíbda	milk	lában
cheese	jíbna	olive	zeitóon
coffee	qáhwa	restaurant	restaurán
dessert	hélwa	salt	méleh
dinner	ásha	soup	shórba
drink	mashróob	sugar	súkar
egg	baid	tea (tea bag)	shay (shay kees)
fish	sámak	water (bottled)	móyyah (botri)
food	akl	wine	khamr
fruit	fawákih		

Travel

airport	al-matár	papers (documents)	watá'iq
arrival	wusóol	parking	máwkif as-sayyarát
bicycle	bisiclét/darrája	passport	jawáz
birth (date of)	youm al-meelád	petrol	benzéen
bus	autobées	port	méena
bus station	maháttat al-autobées	puncture	tókob
		quickly	sarée'an
car	sayára	railway	as-sikka al-hadeedíya
car hire	sayárat-ujra	road	trik
customs	júmruk/gúmruk	slowly	shwai shwai
departure	khuróoj	station	mahátta
duty (excise)	daréebat	straight on	alatóol
duty free	bidóon daréeba	surname	lákab
engine	motúr	taxi	taxi
fare	ujrat as-safr	taxi rank	maháttat at-taxiyát
ferry (boat)	má'diya	ticket	tázkara
garage	garáge	ticket (return)	tázkara dhaháb wa-eeyáb
here/there	héna/henák		
left/right	yesáar/yeméen	what time is it?	is-sa'a kam?
left luggage	máktab éeda al-afsh	train	tren
map	kharéeta	tyre	itár
oil (engine)	zeit	visa	fisa, ta'shéera

ARABIC NUMERALS

١	1	١٠	10	١٩	19	٨٠	80
٢	2	١١	11	٢٠	20	٩٠	90
٣	3	١٢	12	٢١	21	١٠٠	100
٤	4	١٣	13	٢٢	22	٢٠٠	200
٥	5	١٤	14	٣٠	30	٣٠٠	300
٦	6	١٥	15	٤٠	40	٤٠٠	400
٧	7	١٦	16	٥٠	50	١٠٠٠	1000
٨	8	١٧	17	٦٠	60		
٩	9	١٨	18	٧٠	70		

Common words

after	bá'ad	Libya	Líbiya
afternoon	bá'ad az-zohr	light	nour
Algeria	Aljazáyer	little	sghéer
America	Amréeka	market	sook
and	wa	me	ána
bank	bank	money	flóos
bath	hammám	more/less	áktar/akál
beach	sháti al-bahr	morning	sobh
bed	seréer	Morocco	al-Maghreb
before	qabl	mosque	mesjéed
big	kebéer	near	karéeb
black	áswad	newspaper	jaréeda
blue	ázrag	new	jedéed
camp site	mukháyyam	not	mush
castle	kál'ah	now	al-án
cheap	rakhées	oil (heating)	naft
chemist shop	saidalíya	open	maftooh
church	kenéesa	pharmacy (see chemist)	
closed	múglaq	photography	taswéer
cold/hot	bárid/sukhna	police	bulées/shurta
consulate	consulíya	post office	máktab al-baréed
day/night	youm/lail	price	si'r
desert	sahra	red	áhmar
doctor	tebeeb	river	wádi, wed
Egypt	Masr	roof	sat'h
embassy	sifára	room	górfa
England	Ingiltérra	sea	bahr
enough	bás	shop	dukkán
entrance	dukhóol	shower	doosh
evening	mássa	small	sghéer
exchange (money)	tabdéel	Spain	Espánya
exit	khuróoj	square	maidán
expensive (too)	kteer	stamp	tábi'
film	feelm	street	shári
forbidden	mamnóoh	Sudan	as-Sóodan
France	France/Francia	Switzerland	Esswízi
full	melyán	synagogue	kenées
Germany	Almáni	telephone	teleefóon
good (very good)	táyeb, kwáyes	today	al-yóom
great	ákbar	toilet	tualét
green	khádra	tomorrow	búkra
he/she	húwa/híya	tower	qasr
house	mánzel	Tunisia	Toónis
hospital	mustáshfa	United States	al-wilayát al-muttáhida
hostel	bait ash-shebáb	washbasin	tusht
hotel	fúnduq/hotéel	water(hot)	móyya (sukhna)
how far to..?	kam kilometri...	week/year	usboo'/sána
how much?	bikám	what?	shenu?
I/you	ána/inta	when?	ímta?
information	malumát	where (is)?	wain?
is there/are there?	hinák	white	ábyad
Italy	Itálya	why	laih
key	miftáh	yellow	ásfar
later	ba'déen	yesterday	ams

Glossary

A

Abbasids Muslim Dynasty ruled from Baghdad 750-1258

Affanes Woollen slipper used by nomads

Agora Market/meeting place

Aïd/Eïd Festival

Aïn Spring

Almohads Islamic Empire in North Africa 1130-1269

Amir Mamluk military officer

Amulet Object with magical power of protection

Ankh Symbol of life

Arabesque · Geometric pattern with flowers and foliage used in Islamic designs

B

Bab City gate

Bahri North/ northern

Baladiyah Municipality

Baksheesh Money as alms, tip or bribe

Baraka Blessing

Barakan Woollen wrap 5m by 2m to cover entire body

Barbary Name of North Africa 16th-19th centuries

Basha see Pasha

Basilica Imposing Roman building, with aisles, later used for worship

Bazaar Market

Bedouin Nomadic desert Arab

Beni Sons of (tribe)

Berber Indigenous tribe of North Africa

Bey Governor (Ottoman)

Borj Fort

Burnous Man's cloak with hood – tradional wear

C

Caid Official

Calèche Horse drawn carriage

Calidarium Hot room

Capital Top section of a column

Caravanserai Lodgings for travellers and animals around a courtyard

Cartouche Oval ring containing a king's name in hieroglyphics

Chechia Man's small red felt hat

Chotts Low-lying salt lakes

Colossus Gigantic statue

D

Dar House

Darj w ktaf Carved geometric motif of intersecting arcs with super-imposed rectangles

Deglet Nur High quality translucent date

Delu Water lifting device at head of well

Dey Commander (of janissaries)

Dikka Raised platform in mosque for Koramic readings

Djemma Main or Friday mosque

Djin Spirit

Dólmenes Prehistoric cave

Dour Village settlement

E

Eïd see Aïd

Eïn see Aïn

Erg Sand dune desert

F

Faqirs Muslim who has taken a vow of poverty

Fatimids Muslim dynasty 909-1171 AD claiming descent from Mohammed's daughter Fatimah

Fatwa Islamic district

Fellahin Peasants

Felucca Sailing boat on Nile

Fondouk/Funduq Lodgings for goods and animals around a courtyard

Forum Central open space in Roman town

Ful/Fuul Beans

G

Garrigue Mediterranean scrubland – poor quality

Ghibli Hot dry wind from south

Ginan Small garden or tree embayment

Gymnasium Roman school for mind and body

H

Haikal Altar area

Hallal Meat from animals killed ascending to Islamic law

Hamada Stone desert

Hammam Bath house

Harem Women's quarters

Harira Soup

Hypogeum The part of the building below ground, underground chamber

I

Iconostasis Wooden screen supporting icons

Imam Muslim religious leader

J

Jabal see Jebel

Jallabah Outer garment with sleeves and a hood – often striped

Jami' Mosque

Janissaries Elite Ottoman soldiery

Jarapas Rough cloth made with rags
Jebel Mountain
Jihad Holy war by Muslims against non- believers

K

Ka Spirit
Khedivate The realm of Mohammed Ali and his successors
Kilim Woven carpet
Kif Hashish
Kissaria Covered market
Koubba Dome on tomb of holy man
Kufic Earliest style of Arabic script
Kuttab Korami school for young boys or orphans

L

Lintel Piece of stone over a doorway
Liwan Vaulted arcade
Loculus Small compartment or cell, a recess

M

Mahboub Coins worn as jewellery
Malekite Section of Sunni Islam
Malqaf Wind vent
Maquis Mediterranean scrubland – often aromatic
Marabout Muslim holy man/his tomb
Maristan Hospital
Mashrabiyya Wooden screen
Mastaba Tomb
Mausoleum Large tomb building
Medersa (pl Medressa) School usually attached to a mosque
Medina Old walled town, residential quarter
Mellah Jewish quarter of old town
Menzel House
Mihrab Recess in wall of mosque indicating direction of Mecca
Minaret Slender tower of mosque which the muezzin calls the faithful to prayer
Minbar Pulpit in a mosque
Mosque Muslim place of worship

Moulid/Mouloud Religious festival – Prophet's birthday
Moussem Religious gathering
Muezzin Priest who calls the faithful to prayer
Mullah Muslim religious teacher
Murabtin Dependent tribe

N

Necropolis Cemetery
Nome Province

O

Oasis Watered desert gardens
Obelisk Tapering monolithic shaft of stone with pyramidal apex
Ostraca Inscribed rock flakes and potsherds
Ottoman Major Muslim Empire based in Turkey 13th-20th centuries
Ouled Tribe
Outrepassé Horse-shoe shaped arch

P

Papyrus (papyri) Papers used by Ancient Egyptians
Pasha Governor
Phoenicians Important trading nation based in eastern Mediterranean from 1100 BC
Pilaster Square column partly built into, partly projecting from, the wall
Pisé Sun-baked clay used for building
Piste Unsurfaced road
Pylon Gateway of Egyptian temple

Q

Qarafah Graveyard
Qibla Mosque wall in direction of Mecca

R

Rabbi Head of Jewish community
Ramadan Muslim month of fasting
Reg Rock desert
Ribat Fortified monastery

Riwaq Arcaded aisle

S

Sabil Public water fountain
Sabkha Dry salt lake
Saggia Water canal
Sahel Coast/ coastal plain
Sahn Courtyard
Salat Worship
Saqiya Water wheel
Sarcophagus Decorated stone coffin
Sebkha See Sabkha
Semi-columnar Flat on one side and rounded on other
Serais Lodging for men and animals
Serir Sand desert
Shadoof Water lifting device
Shahada Profession of faith
Shergui Hot, dry desert wind
Sidi Mr/Saint
Souq Traditional market
Stalactite An ornamental arrangement of multi-tiered niches, like a honeycomb, found in domes and portals
Stele Inscribed pillar used as gravestone
Suani Small walled irrigated traditional garden
Sufi Muslim mystic
Sunni Orthodox Muslims

T

Tagine/Tajine Stew
Taifa Sub-tribe
Tariqa Brotherhood/Order
Thòlos Round building, dome, cupola
Triclinium A room with benches on three sides
Troglodyte Underground dweller

U

Uraeus Rearing cobra, sign of kingship

V

Vandals Empire in North Africa 429-534 AD
Visir Governor

W

Wadi Water course – usually dry

Waqf Endowed land
Wikala Merchants' hostel
Wilaya/Wilayat Governorate/district

Z
Zaouia/Zawia/Zawiya Shrine/Sennusi centre

Zellij Geometrical mosaic pattern made from pieces of glazed tiles
Zeriba House of straw/grass

TEMPERATURE CONVERSION TABLE

°C	°F	°C	°F
1	34	26	79
2	36	27	81
3	38	28	82
4	39	29	84
5	41	30	86
6	43	31	88
7	45	32	90
8	46	33	92
9	48	34	93
10	50	35	95
11	52	36	97
12	54	37	99
13	56	38	100
14	57	39	102
15	59	40	104
16	61	41	106
17	63	42	108
18	64	43	109
19	66	44	111
20	68	45	113
21	70	46	115
22	72	47	117
23	74	48	118
24	75	49	120
25	77	50	122

The formula for converting °C to °F is:
$$(°C \times 9 \div 5) + 32 = °F$$
and for converting °F to °C:
$$(°F - 32) \times 5 \div 9 = °C$$

WEIGHTS AND MEASURES

Metric

Weight
1 Kilogram (Kg) = 2.205 pounds
1 metric ton = 1.102 short tons

Length
1 millimetre (mm) = 0.03937 inch
1 metre = 3.281 feet
1 kilometre (km) = 0.621 mile

Area
1 hectare = 2.471 acres
1 square km = 0.386 sq mile

Capacity
1 litre = 0.220 imperial gallon
       = 0.264 US gallon

Volume
1 cubic metre (m^3) = 35.31 cubic feet
                     = 1.31 cubic yards

British and US

Weight
1 pound (lb) = 454 grams
1 short ton (2,000lbs) = 0.907 m ton
1 long ton (2,240lbs) = 1.016 m tons

Length
1 inch = 25.417 millimetres
1 foot (ft) = 0.305 metre
1 mile = 1.609 kilometres

Area
1 acre = 0.405 hectare
1 sq mile = 2.590 sq kilometre

Capacity
1 imperial gallon = 4.546 litres
1 US gallon = 3.785 litres

Volume
1 cubic foot (cu ft) = 0.028 m^3
1 cubic yard (cu yd) = 0.765 m^3

NB 5 imperial gallons are approximately equal to 6 US gallons

Tinted boxes

Diagrams and plans

CHURCHES

HIEROGLYPHS AND CARTOUCHES

MOSQUES AND MEDRESSA

MUSEUMS

PYRAMIDS AND TEMPLES

Index

Maps

Map symbols

Administration

International Border	
State / Province Border	
Disputed Border	
Neighbouring country	
Neighbouring state	
State Capitals	□
Other Towns	○

Roads and travel

Main Roads (National Highways)	R 15
Other Roads	
Jeepable Roads, Tracks	
Railways with station	

Water features

River	River Nile
Lakes, Reservoirs, Tanks	
Seasonal Marshlands	
Salt Lake	
Sand Banks, Beaches	
Ocean	
Ferry	

Topographical features

Contours (approx), Rock Outcrops	
Mountains	
Gorge	
Escarpment	
Palm trees	

Cities and towns

Built Up Areas	
Main through routes	
Main streets	
Minor Streets	
Pedestrianized Streets	
One Way Street	→
National Parks, Gardens, Stadiums	
Fortified Walls	▲ ▲ ▲
Airport	⊗
Banks	Ⓢ
Bus Stations (named in key)	
Hospitals	⊕
Market	Ⓜ
Police station	Pol
Post Office	⊠
Telegraphic Office	
Tourist Office	ⓘ
Key Numbers	1 2 3 4 5
Bridges	
Mosque	
Cathedral, church	✝ ✝
Guided routes	

Other symbols

Pyramid	▲
National Parks and Bird Sanctuaries	◆
Camp site	Λ
Motorable track	
Walking track	
Archaeological Sites	⸫
Places of Interest	○
Viewing point	

Footprint catalogue

Andalucia Handbook

Argentina Handbook

Bolivia Handbook

Brazil Handbook

Cambodia Handbook

Caribbean Islands Handbook 1999

Chile Handbook

Colombia Handbook

Cuba Handbook

East Africa Handbook 1999

Ecuador Handbook

Egypt Handbook

Goa Handbook

India Handbook 1999

Indonesia Handbook

Israel Handbook

Jordan, Syria & Lebanon
  Handbook

Laos Handbook

Malaysia & Singapore Handbook

Mexico & Central America
  Handbook 1999

Morocco Handbook

Myanmar (Burma) Handbook

Namibia Handbook

Nepal Handbook

Pakistan Handbook

Peru Handbook

South Africa Handbook 1999

South American Handbook 1999

Sri Lanka Handbook

Thailand Handbook

Tibet Handbook

Tunisia Handbook

Venezuela Handbook

Vietnam Handbook

New Spring 1999

Singapore Handbook

Web site
Our web site is up and running. Take a look at
http://www.footprint-handbooks.co.uk for the latest
news, to order a book or to join our mailing list.

Mail Order
Footprint Handbooks are available worldwide in good
bookstores. They can also be ordered directly from us
in Bath either via the web site or via the address below.

Footprint Handbooks
6 Riverside Court, Lower Bristol Road, Bath BA2 3DZ,
England   T +44 (0)1225 469141 F +44 (0)1225 469461
Email handbooks@footprint.cix.co.uk